HIDDEN NEW ENGLAND
The Adventurer's Guide
Second Edition

"Really gives the flavor of each place."
—*New Orleans Times-Picayune*

"Comprehensive, well-written and filled with offbeat finds."
—*Oakland Tribune*

"Scores highly as a travel companion. It's sure to show you something new."
—*Car and Driver*

"Fun to read. Caters to those who yearn for something extra."
—*Chevron USA Odyssey*

"Offers a real choice from the more traditional guides."
—*Wilmette Life*

"Helps prove there's still a treasure trove of undiscovered spots."
—*Hartford Courant*

"Fascinating. A 564-page exploration of secluded and more visible locales."
—*San Francisco Examiner and Chronicle*

TEXT

Stacy Ritz

Patricia Mandell

Alberta Eiseman

Ryan Vollmer

Susan Farewell

B. J. Roche

Brenda Fine

ILLUSTRATIONS

Timothy Carroll

EDITED BY

Judith Kahn

Hidden New England

The Adventurer's Guide

Second Edition

Executive Editor   **Ray Riegert**

•

Ulysses Press

Published by: Ulysses Press
3286 Adeline Street   Suite 1
Berkeley, CA 94703

Library of Congress Catalog Card Number 91-68528
ISBN 0-915233-58-4

Printed in the U.S.A. by the George Banta Company

10 9 8 7 6 5 4 3

Production Director: Leslie Henriques
Managing Editor: Claire Chun
Editorial Director: Roger Rapoport

Maps: Phil Gardner, Claire Chun
Cover Designers: Bonnie Smetts, Leslie Henriques
Editorial Associates: Wendy Ann Logsdon, Cathy Chun,
   Laurie Greenleaf, Shelly Smith, Nicole Reader
Indexer: Sayre Van Young

Cover Photography: Front cover photo by Robert Holmes;
   back cover photos by Ron Dahlquist/Superstock,
   Craig Aurness/Westlight, Robert Llewellyn/Superstock

Distributed in the United States by Publishers Group West, in
Canada by Raincoast Books and in Great Britain and Europe by
World Leisure Marketing

Printed on recycled paper

Notes from the Publisher

Throughout the text, hidden locales, remote regions, little-known spots and special attractions are marked with a star (★).

* * *

An alert, adventurous reader is as important as a travel writer in keeping a guidebook up-to-date and accurate. So if you happen upon a great restaurant, discover a hidden locale, or (heaven forbid) find an error in the text, we'd appreciate hearing from you. Just write to:

Ulysses Press
3286 Adeline Street   Suite 1
Berkeley, CA 94703

* * *

It is our desire as publishers to create guidebooks that are responsible as well as informative. The danger of exploring hidden locales is that they will no longer be secluded.

We hope that our guidebooks treat the people, country and land we visit with respect. We ask that our readers do the same. The hiker's motto, "Walk softly on the Earth," applies to travelers everywhere...in the forest, on the beach and in town.

Contents

SPECIAL FEATURES

MAPS

CHAPTER ONE

New England Sojourn

The Why, Where, When and How of Traveling in New England

Why

There is no more instantly recognizable scenery in the American land-scape—or the American mind—than the picture-postcard image of a New England village: the white-steepled church on an emerald green, ringed by white clapboard houses, the whole of it haloed by forests aflame with fall reds and golds.

No wonder people come hoping, wanting, expecting to find this met-aphor for New England life. And this place of centuries past still exists, in many small towns scattered throughout the six states.

But New England is stunningly heterogeneous, possessed of countless rich dimensions. In one state, you find old textile and industrial cities, rivers and lakes, and towering spruce forests whose denizens are moose and black bear. Visitors will discover miles and miles of white sand beaches fringed with dunes and marsh grasses; thriving metropolises like Boston and Prov-idence; mountain ranges with hiking and skiing trails; fishing villages hun-dreds of years old; Indian burial grounds; and coastal resorts where elegant yachts bob in the harbor. Standing fast before time, New England's old wooden saltbox houses have weathered into the colors of the very ground that made them. And with all this variety, no spot in New England is more than a day's drive from any other.

It would be almost impossible to find another place in the United States so densely packed with history. You can barely take a step without stumbling over a colonial battlefield, a historic site or monument, or an 18th-century house. Before your eyes will come to life all that you learned in school about the birth of the United States. And every year or so, another New England town celebrates its 350th anniversary.

Bounded on the north by Canada, on the east by the Atlantic Ocean, on the south by Long Island Sound, and on the west by New York, New England sits squarely in the northeastern corner of the United States. Five

1

states border the ocean, which is never far from anyone's mind. Fishing blessed all who settled here, from the Indians and the Pilgrims to the 19th-century whalers and today's fishermen of Gloucester, New Bedford and Plymouth. New Englanders have always been premier shipbuilders and sailors, and today one of the greatest pleasures is to ride a Maine windjammer, an excursion boat or a tiny sailboat.

The ocean also tempers the weather, making summers cooler and winters less fierce. The seasons pull out all the stops here, parading four kinds of memorable variety every year. In warmer, more monotonous climes, the passing of time recedes to a blur.

New Englanders love and revere their covered bridges, their Revolutionary War-era, federal and Greek revival homes, and their chowder made with milk, not tomato juice, thank you. To a real New Englander, there's nothing quite like the first cider of the fall, real native maple syrup or a clambake on the beach.

To give them credit, many dour old Yankees have expanded their tastes to include the flowers, glass arcades and gourmet restaurants of Quincy Market and whimsical things like balloon festivals.

Still, there is little of glitz about this region. New England simply is what it is, without apology. It's not an invented attraction but a real place, one that stands on the legitimacy and integrity of its origins.

This book was designed to help you explore this wonderful area. Besides leading you to countless popular spots, it will also take you to many off-the-beaten-path locales, places usually known only by locals. The book will tell the story of the region's history, its flora and fauna. Each chapter will suggest places to eat, to stay, to sightsee, to shop and to enjoy the outdoors and nightlife, covering a range of tastes and budgets.

The book sets out in Connecticut, taking visitors in Chapter Two through the rural outlying areas and along its pretty coastline. Chapter Three outlines tiny little Rhode Island's greatly unspoiled topography and gorgeous beaches, as well as elite Newport and historic Providence. Because of its dense population and diversity, Massachusetts is presented in three chapters. Quintessential Boston is explored in Chapter Four, from its Revolutionary War-era sites to Beacon Hill and Back Bay. Chapter Five moves along the Massachusetts Coast, from the North Shore to Cape Cod, Martha's Vineyard and Nantucket, then to Plymouth and New Bedford. In Chapter Six, you'll discover the Pioneer Valley and the Berkshires of central and western Massachusetts.

Chapter Seven covers Vermont, with its Green Mountains and covered bridges. Chapter Eight is dedicated to New Hampshire, land of sparkling lakes, the White Mountains and majestic Mount Washington. Last but by no means least, you'll explore the stately pine forests and rugged coast of Maine in Chapter Nine.

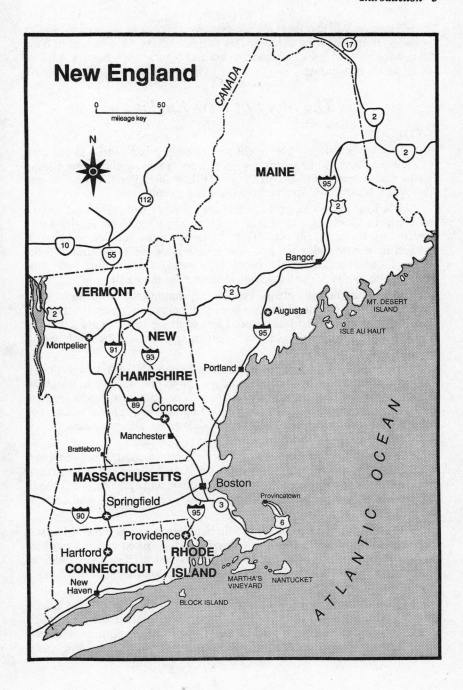

Wherever you choose to go, whatever you choose to see and do, you're bound to find something to like in this infinite variety. Generations of travelers have enjoyed New England's coast and mountains, forests and lakes, in all kinds of weather.

The Story of New England

GEOLOGY

Geology is destiny, you might say. Certainly this is true in the case of New England. Some of the region's most famed symbols, from stone walls, mill towns and rivers, to Bunker Hill, Walden Pond, Cape Cod and the White Mountains, sprang from geologic events.

New England is one of the oldest continuously surviving land masses on earth. In Cambrian times, half a billion years ago, New England was covered by a vast inland sea. When the earth's crust buckled and rose, it pushed up mountainous masses—the ancestors of the Berkshires and the Green Mountains. During the same era, a mass of hot molten rock gave birth to the White Mountains from deep within the earth.

Even while the mountains were rising, running water began to wear away at the land, leveling it and washing sediments down from the uplands. Finally all New England was reduced almost to sea level, like a flat plain. But some of the mountains survived, particularly those in the north, which was less completely leveled.

The earth's crust stirred again, 200 million to 300 million years later, but gently this time. The land rose just enough to give altitude to the slow-moving rivers of the plains, causing them to flow more swiftly, and set them off to carving out valleys. Eventually New Englanders would find these fast-flowing, powerful rivers and build mill wheels on them to run their factories and mills, which you can still see today.

The Ice Age seized the region in a frozen grip about a million years ago, gradually spreading and growing. The mass of ice finally became so vast and heavy that its own weight pushed it down and outward, and it began to move. For thousands of years, the ice cap grew, engulfing all of New England.

As it moved, the ice cap picked up boulders, some as large as houses, and carried them along with it. Fields of boulders, filled with rocks of all sizes, are common in New England. Farmers had to clear their fields of countless rocks before they could plant, and they used them to make stone walls, which still limn the landscape today.

The ice moved in a southerly direction, from Canada to Long Island, paring off hills and ledges as it went. Some of the glacial till was clay, which sticks to itself more readily than to ice. Deposited clay formed into low-lying, oval-shaped hills called drumlins, many a mile or more long and a hundred feet high. Some of the region's most famous drumlins are Bunker Hill and World's End in Hingham, Massachusetts.

The glaciers came and went four times, retreating and advancing for over a million years, finally leaving New England about 10,000 to 12,000 years ago. The last glacial advance formed Cape Cod, Martha's Vineyard, Nantucket, Block Island and the Rhode Island shore. At the front of the advancing ice sheet, released rock debris built up a terminal moraine—a ridge of rubble. These islands and coasts are what remains of the morainal ridges. Watch Hill, Rhode Island, has been called by geologists "one of the finest examples of glacial dumping ground" in the eastern United States.

Large blocks of melting glacial ice formed kettle-hole lakes, deep bodies of water with a rounded shape, of which Walden Pond is a good example. It might also be said that kettle lakes make for fine ice-skating and ice-fishing.

HISTORY

New England is America's scrapbook, the memorabilia of a nation conceived on hardship and perseverance, faith and dreams. It is a riveting story of high adventure and the push for freedom, of ingenuity and despotism, of victory over adverse conditions.

The opening pages tell of Pilgrims who charted a course to Greenland but were blown far southward by violent winds. The year was 1000 A.D., and, according to Norse legend, Norseman Leif Ericsson landed in a strange place, probably along Maine's rocky coast. Discovering friendly Indians and fertile land where grapes and wheat grew wild, he dubbed his find Vinland the Good and returned to Norway with tales of a fascinating world.

More than 450 years would pass before European explorers would again call on the intriguing land. Navigator John Cabot, on assignment from England's King Henry VII and seeking a Northwest Passage to the East, explored the coasts of Maine and Massachusetts in 1497. He found no pass but claimed a considerable chunk of the New World—everything north of Florida and east of the Rockies—for the British crown.

Italian explorer Giovanni da Verrazano staked out the same coast some 27 years later, claiming the territory for his employer nation, France. Just prior to his visit, navigator Miguel Corte Real had been checking out the terrain for Portugal.

Dutch sailor Adriaen Block launched a coastal investigation in 1614, calling a Narragansett Bay island "Roodt Eyland," or Red Island, a likely precursor to Rhode Island. That same year, English captain John Smith mapped the Massachusetts coast and was taken by its beauty. A soldier of fortune, Smith wrote a glowing report of the intriguing land, describing its "sandy cliffes and cliffes of rock" planted with cornfields and gardens.

Though captivated by the new region, none of these adventurers did what seemed the most logical thing: settle the place. Of course, this white man's frontier had been inhabited at least five centuries by Algonquin tribes. A peaceful people who dwelled in wigwams, they were expert growers of corn, tobacco, pumpkins and other crops. They hunted forests plentiful with moose, deer, turkey and goose, and fished the streams and ocean for bass, salmon, lobster and clams, throwing the area's earliest clambakes.

The Algonquins were not populous. Small tribes, sometimes with as few as 200 Indians, were scattered among the forests and along the coast. The Pennacook tribe resided in what would become New Hampshire and Massachusetts; the Abenaki favored the New Hampshire area, too, as well as Maine. The Narrangansetts were natives of today's Rhode Island. All told, New England's Indians numbered about 25,000 when they welcomed the first permanent European settlers in 1620.

Religious asylum, not adventure or fortune, is what those first real settlers were seeking. The Puritans, cut off from Anglican England because of their strict Protestant beliefs, read with interest John Smith's glowing report on the New World. Could it be their Utopia? They were anxious to find out.

In the spring of 1620, the Puritans struck a deal with the Plymouth Company to finance a settlement in the New World. By summer's end, 102 Puritans boarded the *Mayflower* for a rigorous, two-month journey to America. They first sighted land at Cape Cod, then cruised the coast for a month and landed at Plymouth Rock. On December 21, the Plymouth Colony was born.

That first winter proved brutal for the colonists as they fought scurvy, pneumonia and other diseases that killed nearly half their group. But springtime brought relief and the opportunity to plant crops, thanks to help from the Indians who were hospitable to their new neighbors. To celebrate the first anniversary of their friendship, the Pilgrims and Indians feasted together for three days that fall.

As word of the successful colony trickled back to England, more Puritans set out for the New World. In 1630, about 1000 Puritans on 11 ships landed at Salem during the "Great Migration." Drawn by a vast harbor filled with sea life, settlers moved southward and declared Boston their main colony. Fur-trading posts were established in Maine, and small villages sprang up in New Hampshire, Connecticut and Rhode Island.

By 1636, another 12,000 immigrants had arrived. Puritan ministers, sensing the need to train future leaders, founded Harvard College and set up a general court to govern the colonies. Local matters were dealt with by town leaders at regular meetings, the forerunners of today's town council sessions.

Ironically, those same Puritans who sought the New World for religious freedom would not tolerate other beliefs. In 1651, a visitor from the Rhode Island colony was publicly whipped for being a Baptist. Victims of English persecution, Quakers fleeing the Old World were arrested on ships in Boston Harbor before they ever set foot on the new land. And in 1659, two men and a woman were hanged in Massachusetts for espousing Quaker beliefs.

Religious dissidents fled to Rhode Island, which Puritans dubbed "the sewer of New England" and "Rogue's Island." But the tiny colony held fast to religious and social freedoms and by the mid-1660s received New England's first Jews and several hundred French Huguenots and Quakers.

It was Puritan fanaticism that caused the untimely end of several other unfortunate New England souls. Witches, the Puritans said, were lurking about, possessed by demons and casting spells on innocent minds.

The accusations led to witch trials in Charlestown in 1648 and in Boston in 1655, but the most hideous ordeal occurred in Salem in 1692. After hundreds of people were imprisoned in a "Witch House," 19 were executed, including 80-year-old Giles Corey, who was pressed to death when he pled no-contest.

The Puritans were also a nightmare for the Indians. Determined to "save" them from their pagan ways, missionaries translated the Bible into Algonquin and set about converting new Christians. By the 1670s, nearly one-fourth of the Indian population had officially accepted the imposed faith. But it was not enough. The Puritans wanted not just mental converts but a race that would abandon its centuries-old customs, its very mode of existence.

As colonies expanded, the Indians got in the way. Several skirmishes ensued, but it was King Philip's War, from 1675 to 1676, that spelled the beginning of the end for the New England Indians. Pressured by colonists to abandon his land, chief Metacomet (King Philip) led a series of battles against his encroachers. He lost a decisive engagement, the "Great Swamp Fight" near Kingston, Rhode Island, when Massachusetts and Connecticut colonists burned wigwams, killing hundreds of women and children and disorganizing Indian forces.

Betrayed by a fellow Indian, King Philip was captured soon thereafter, his body beheaded and quartered. His head was displayed on a gibbet in Plymouth for 20 years as a reminder of white victory. Just four decades after the Indians had welcomed the first Puritans into their home, the Puritans had decimated them.

Eighteenth-century New England was a place of social, economic and political growth. Life centered around the ocean and rivers, as shipbuilding thrived in towns such as Portsmouth in New Hampshire, Groton in Connecticut, Kittery in Maine and, of course, Boston. Coopers, potters and furniture makers plied their trades along the waterfront, and coastal and international trade boomed.

Colleges and universities that today rank among the nation's best were established: Yale University, New Hampshire's Dartmouth College, and

Rhode Island College, now Brown University. The influx of non-Puritans created a greater cultural and religious mix, and politics flourished as colonists demanded more autonomy from Mother England.

Determined to subdue its wayward child, England in 1764 imposed the Revenue Act, which levied duties on silk, sugar and some wines. Colonists rebelled and promptly boycotted the tariffs.

England didn't flinch. One year later, it slapped colonies with the Stamp Act, taxing commercial and legal papers such as newspapers and licenses. Outraged, colonists denounced the tax and refused to buy European goods. "No taxation without representation," they cried. Every colonial stamp agent resigned, and before the law could take effect November 1, Parliament repealed the act.

But England insisted on political and economic control. Several months later Parliament passed the Townshend Acts, imposing heavy taxes on paper, glass and tea. Colonists again rebelled, and England sent troops to squelch rioting in Boston.

By 1770, hoping to rid the city of "Redcoats"—the colonists' name for the British militia—Bostonians gathered at the Customs House and began taunting the sentry. Troops arrived, and after a series of violent skirmishes, they fired shots into the crowd. When the Boston Massacre was over, five colonials lay dead on King Street, present-day State Street.

England repealed most of the Townshend taxes, leaving duties on imported tea—then the most popular drink in America. New Englanders retaliated by buying smuggled tea. In 1773, when England's Tea Act flooded the market with cheap tea, agents would not accept deliveries—except for Governor Thomas Hutchinson in Boston.

When three tea-filled ships sailed into Boston Harbor, the Committees of Correspondence and Sons of Liberty—prerevolutionary activists— blocked the piers. Governor Hutchinson refused to let the ships return to England, so protestors invited him to a little tea party.

Disguised as Indians, 60 Sons of Liberty boarded the ships on the night of December 16, 1773 and dumped 342 chests of tea into the harbor. It was a defiant move and an ominous portent of what lie ahead: revolution was in the air.

On April 19, 1775, a single musket discharge set off America's first full-scale war. "The shot heard 'round the world" was fired at the Battle of Lexington and Concord, an effort by the Redcoats to crush revolutionary uprisings around Boston.

Forewarned by Paul Revere that "the British are coming," 77 Minutemen crouched in early morning darkness, waiting for the Redcoat attack. The British advanced, killing eight rebels and wounding ten on the present-day Lexington Green before continuing to Concord. There they destroyed a cache of arms and were finally driven out.

The colonies rallied together. Vermont's Green Mountain Boys, led by Ethan Allen and Benedict Arnold, captured Fort Ticonderoga on Lake Champlain, blocking a British invasion from Canada. On June 17, 1775, New Englanders fought the war's first major engagement—known as the Battle of Bunker Hill although it was really fought on nearby Breed's Hill— on the Charlestown peninsula near Boston. After enduring two British attacks, the Americans ran short of ammunition and retreated.

Though a technical victory for England, Bunker Hill cost the crown more than 1000 troops—over twice the colonial losses. More important, it proved that the Minutemen volunteers were a match for the better-trained British army.

On July 4, 1776, the Declaration of Independence was adopted by the Continental Congress. The war raged on in surrounding states for six years, but New England was free.

Economic depression followed the war. Paper money was scarce, loans difficult to obtain and court foreclosures commonplace. When their new state government levied high taxes, Massachusetts farmers rose up in anger. Shays' Rebellion, which lasted from 1786 to 1787 but was unsuccessful at stopping the taxes, proved that democracy was still an elusive concept.

New England heralded the 19th-century with a burgeoning shipping industry, though the War of 1812 temporarily halted matters with stiff trade embargos. With the advent of the cotton mill in Pawtucket, Rhode Island, weavers no longer had to work at home, though their 12-hour workdays and paltry wages led to the nation's first labor strike in 1800. Eli Whitney's cotton gin revolutionized the wool industry, and mills sprang up across New England. By the 1830s, Providence alone produced 20 percent of the country's wool.

Hundreds of other inventions put New England at the forefront of the industrial age. Yale graduate Samuel Morse masterminded the telegraph and his own code, Elias Howe crafted the world's first sewing machine, and Charles Goodyear developed a type of commercial rubber, though he died $200,000 in the red. In Hartford, Samuel Colt opened a munitions factory and Francis Pratt and Amos Whitney manufactured machine tools and interchangeable parts.

As New England grew and the railroad headed west, settlers starting moving into the interior. Wilderness areas of northern Maine, Vermont and New Hampshire were slowly penetrated, and pioneers established small farms. But unforgiving soil and unpredictable weather squelched any hopes of real agriculture, and by 1860 farming as serious business ceased to exist in these states.

The Industrial Revolution sparked a mass immigration of Europeans, with hundreds arriving from England, Scotland, Italy and Portugal. Victims of the 1845 Great Potato Famine, thousands of Irish sailed to Massachusetts with dreams of a new life. By 1850, one of every ten New Englanders was foreign born. Only ten years later, 61 percent of Boston residents had been born abroad.

Not all New Englanders welcomed so many immigrants with open arms. During the 1850s, several political monsters reared their ugly heads. The Know-Nothing Party blatantly opposed all immigrants, particularly the Irish. Together with virulent anti-Roman Catholic factions in Maine, the party burned several Catholic churches. The powerful Know-Nothings managed to control governorships in several states.

At the same time, the abolition movement gripped New England. Connecticut's Harriet Beecher Stowe raised public consciousness in 1852 with *Uncle Tom's Cabin*. A fervent opponent of slavery, William Lloyd Garrison published his *Liberator* newspaper for 34 years in Massachusetts, despite being dragged through streets by angry mobs and threatened constantly.

New England was also experiencing a cultural renaissance. The great "Flowering of New England" was centered in Boston. Now called the "Athens of America," the city saw the founding of such eminent institutions as the Museum of Fine Arts, the Boston Symphony Orchestra and the Boston Pops.

Great minds thrived across the region. Artists, thinkers and literary geniuses would set the dynamic tone in New England for centuries to come. People like Nathaniel Hawthorne and Oliver Wendell Holmes, Henry David Thoreau and Julia Ward Howe, Ralph Waldo Emerson and Robert Frost made New England an intellectual mecca.

By the turn of the century, an ethnic and political metamorphosis had taken place. The long-time bastion of Yankee Protestantism was now being run by Roman Catholics. In 1900, a majority of New England legislators were Catholic.

At the same time came a wave of corruption that would last for several decades. In Rhode Island, Republican "Boss" Charles R. Brayton built his regime by exchanging bought votes for "judgeships and other political jobs," charged journalist Lincoln Steffens. Brayton even paid "yellow dog" Democrats to be loyal to the machine. Iniquity reached its height in Boston's James Michael Curley, elected mayor four times between 1914 and 1950 and state governor from 1935 to 1937. The "Irish Mussolini" perfected ward politics, handing out jobs, favors and money to those who guaranteed his return to office.

The Depression crushed New England. Between 1929 and 1950, more than 149,000 textile workers lost their jobs as the manufacturing industry fell prostrate. Wages were slashed in half for those lucky enough to work, and hundreds of thousands lost their homes.

New England never fully rebounded from those difficult years. During the 1960s and early '70s, foreign imports dealt a blow to most of the manufacturing left in the area. Void of natural resources such as oil and coal, the area was especially hard hit by the 1970s recession.

But today's New England has seen a rebirth of industry and technology. Modern enterprises have flourished, producing such far-reaching wonders as missile and space systems, jet aircraft engines, computers and computer equipment, and biomedical and photographic instruments. The new businesses circle Boston around Route 128 and spill over into Hartford, southern New Hampshire, Rhode Island and even Vermont's Burlington area.

Massachusetts and Connecticut boast one of the nation's largest pools of capital, with Boston claiming more than 50 insurance companies and about 35 percent of U.S. mutual fund holdings. The Greater Boston Metropolitan Area is home to some 21 newspapers, eight television stations, 31 radio stations and many libraries and museums of national stature.

Progressive New Englanders were among the first to push environmental issues to the national front, passing stringent air pollution and zoning laws. As early as the 1960s, rural Vermont banned billboards and nonreturnable bottles. Massachusetts passed the nation's earliest wetlands act.

Higher education is itself a leading "industry" of Massachusetts, the site of some 121 colleges and universities—47 in Boston alone. And New England's immense beauty and rich history make tourism the number two industry, second only to manufacturing.

Today, beyond the high-tech centers and tourist attractions resounds the inescapable presence of New England's colorful past: Revolutionary War monuments, 18th-century covered bridges and statehouses, steepled churches that held this country's first congregations.

One need only explore Paul Revere's House, the Bunker Hill Monument and the Granary Burial Ground in the Boston area to recognize the sites of this country's genesis. For New England's past is America's past. And the region remains a vital part of the nation's present and future.

FLORA

The glorious, flaming reds, oranges and yellows of a New England fall come from changes in its thick stands of hardwood trees, which cover more than three-quarters of the region. The most colorful displays are put on by sugar and red maples, beech, oak, birch, hickory and red oak (see "Fall Foliage: Nature's Kaleidoscope" in this chapter).

Vast and stately pine forests blanket much of the north, creating its characteristic wild and rugged look. Among them are spruce, balsam fir and hemlock. Southern New England, too, has conifers throughout, the most common being white pine. Among the tallest of eastern trees, the sun-loving white pine may live 400 years or more.

New England grows some 2000 species of flowering plants and ferns. Wildflowers bloom in colorful profusion along the roadsides and in parks

(Text continued on page 14.)

Fall Foliage: Nature's Kaleidoscope

Like nature's last fling before a long slumber, the changing hues of New England's fall foliage precede winter with a fantastic display of color gone wild. Meadows are splashed with orange and purple, lakes appear ringed with fire and whole mountains turn from green to gold.

Better than any fireworks show, this phenomenon draws at least 2.8 million visitors to New England each year. Arriving by car, train, bus and bicycle, they pitch tents in forests, settle into cabins and resorts and pack the roadways everywhere. They come not just to marvel at the scenery but to be part of an all-encompassing experience.

The show starts up around mid-September with a few hints of scarlet and gold, as if the mountains were blushing. Then slowly, the blush becomes a sea of reds and orange and purples that melt together like rivers of shimmering watercolors. Each day brings new colors, new perspectives.

What makes it all happen? Prodded by cool nights and shorter autumn days, tree leaves abandon their green veneer to reveal hues ranging from crimson and sunburst to mahogany, violet and bronze.

Of course, each tree has its own brand of color. Maples flash a brilliant red leaf. Shagbark hickory leaves turn yellow and resemble hammered gold, while witch hazel's flaxen leaves camouflage small yellow flowers. The sumac sports purple saw-toothed leaves and fuzzy twigs resembling antlers. Thin and dainty, pin cherry leaves go from bright purple to bright yellow.

Then there's the clever speckled alder, a swamp dweller that doesn't change color at all. Its broad green leaves provide a nice contrast to all those reds and yellows and purples.

The farther north you are, the earlier the show starts. Northern areas of Maine, New Hampshire and Vermont set things off, sending waves of color southward as fall advances. The show usually winds down around mid-October, or after the first few frosts.

Though you can "see the leaves" change almost anywhere in New England, the best leaf-peeping exists in mountain areas. Reputed as one of the best fall-foliage spots in the world, New Hampshire's White Mountain National Forest offers 763,000 acres of uninterrupted timberland that explodes with continuous color.

Next door, Vermont's Green Mountain National Forest has miles of dense woods, gentle mountains and rushing streams that form a spectacular

foliage backdrop. In Maine, head for the area around Machias known as **blueberry barrens** (★). A vast sweep of blueberry fields, the barrens turn flaming red in the fall and stretch as far as the eye can see. Maine's rock-lined coast also provides extraordinary foliage pageantry, with spiraling scarlet trees set against a sea of aquamarine.

Connecticut's foliage beauty lies in its diverse forests that provide the entire spectrum of colors. Travel from the pastel-colored oaks and birches along the coast to the deep red pepperidge trees in the southwest. Then cut up to the yellow and vermilion maple trees in the northwest corner.

Tiny Rhode Island is all ablaze with fall color, though it is most concentrated in the uplands. Located on the north and west corridors, the uplands are a picture of amber rolling hills, thick timbers and nearly 300 lakes and reservoirs rimmed with rainbow hues.

For a special foliage treat, head for Massachusetts' South Shore, where **cranberry bogs** stretch just south of Boston to Bristol. During October harvests, farmers flood the bogs, forcing the berries to the top of the marsh and creating a sea of bright crimson (see "Cranberry Harvesting" in Chapter Five).

If you'd like to take home more than photographs, gather an assortment of your favorite leaves and branches. While they're still supple, press the leaves between layers of cardboard, then secure between heavy boards or books and tie tightly with rope. Store in a warm, dry place for ten days, making sure the rope is always snug.

Branches make beautiful bouquets once preserved. Simply split the stems at the base and cover with a solution of two parts water and one part glycerine. Store in a cool, well-ventilated area until leaves show a slight change in color. Remove and hang upside down until dry.

To get the scoop on leaf-peeping conditions, call the foliage hotlines sponsored by each state: New Hampshire, 603-224-2525; Vermont, 802-828-3239; Maine, 207-289-5710; Connecticut, 203-258-4290; Rhode Island, 401-277-2601; Massachusetts, 617-727-3201. Some states supply foliage guides with tips on picture-taking and leaf identification.

A word of advice: fall-foliage season is *the* most popular vacation time in New England, so it's important to make travel arrangements far in advance—at least six months ahead of time.

and forests. The leader of the wildflowers is the long-stemmed goldenrod, which occurs almost everywhere, as do black-eyed Susans, lupine, purple asters, daisies and Queen Anne's lace. Shady, moist habitats foster several species of orchids, with the pink lady's slipper being the showiest and most common.

Three of the most spectacular wildflower displays are given by the rhododendron, flowering dogwood and mountain laurel, the state flower of Connecticut, which occurs in southern New England. The mountain laurel's lustrous, dark green leaves and six-sided, pink-and-white blossoms form a dense, impenetrable thicket in the forest, sometimes up to 13 feet high.

At the shore grow miles and miles of shrubby wild beach roses with delicate scent and fragile petals of pink, white and fuchsia. Also along the shore grow beach peas, pitch pine, huckleberry, lowbush blueberry, sheep laurel and bayberry, from which the colonists made candles.

Wetlands are prevalent throughout New England, left by glacial action. Swamps, marshes and bogs all have their own little communities of plants, specially adapted to float on the water or emerge from it. Two very characteristic swamp plants are the purplish green skunk cabbage, with a strong odor like a skunk's, and Jack-in-the-Pulpit, which looks like a miniature preacher in a covered pulpit.

In the soft, dark muck and highly organic environs of marshes grow grasses, reeds and sedges such as cattails. Purple loosestrife now covers huge expanses of marsh and wet meadows. Other common marsh plants include duckweed, the smallest flowering plant known; blue flag, a kind of native iris; Joe-pye weed and yellow pond lily.

Sphagnum moss and sedges are partial to bogs, as are knee-high evergreen shrubs, bog laurel, bog rosemary and Labrador Tea, reputedly brewed as a substitute for tea in colonial times. In low-lying, sandy-floored bogs thrive cranberries, a mainstay of the Massachusetts economy.

FAUNA

No single animal is more ubiquitous in New England than the gray squirrel, which flirts its bushy tail as it races along telephone wires, up and down trees in city parks and through backyards. A close second is the dramatically colored eastern chipmunk. Though they are pests to the gardener and the householder, rabbits and woodchucks are numerous, too.

The black bear, New England's only bear, and the moose claim title to being the region's largest land mammals, favoring wilder woodland areas in the north. The homely moose, believe it or not, is a member of the deer family and lives in the deep cover of northern forests in Maine, New Hampshire and Vermont. Another large mammal favored by hunters is the white-tailed deer, which has a bushy white tail, big ears and long legs.

The fallow deer, a native of Asia Minor, was released on Nantucket and Martha's Vineyard. The deer became so numerous that they overran the islands and had to be thinned.

Smaller mammals include beaver, red foxes, raccoons, porcupines, skunks and possums. Pity the poor possum: he is poorly adapted to the cold, and many New England possums lose pieces of their paper-thin ears and bare tails to frostbite.

Off the rocky shores in northern coastal waters, harbor seals cavort, hauling out to sun themselves on islands and rocky shores. The coast is also home to the Atlantic white-sided dolphin and several species of whales, best seen on whale-watching trips.

The arrival of spring in New England is announced vociferously by spring peepers, tiny frogs measuring little more than an inch long that climb trees to sing their lyrical nocturnal chorus.

Other native amphibians include the spotted salamander, green frog and bullfrog, a giant of native frogs, sometimes over eight inches long. Reptiles are represented by snapping turtles, painted turtles, box turtles, garter snakes and black racers. New England also has two poisonous snakes, the timber rattlesnake and the northern copperhead, although you will almost surely never see one, so rare and retiring are they.

Situated as it is right along the Atlantic Flyway, New England is a premier place for birding, especially during spring migration. More than 400 species have been sighted in New England, although more than half are transient migratories, shorebirds that rarely come ashore or accidentals carried in by storm winds. The single most characteristic bird is the gull, found everywhere along the coast.

Canada geese and cormorants have increased their range and numbers, as have ospreys, after being given special nesting platforms on Martha's Vineyard. The handsome loon rules the northern lakes. There are many species of ducks, in both fresh water and salt water.

Endangered species include the piping plover, roseate tern, peregrine falcon, upland sandpiper, short-eared owl and bald eagle, now nesting in the Quabbin Reservoir in central Massachusetts.

The clownlike Atlantic puffin can be seen on the rocky islets of Maine, the only place in the United States where you can spot this bird.

Where to Go

New England is no more all of a piece than is Europe. Deciding what to see and where to go is a tough choice. The good news is, you'll just have to keep coming back to get to know the real New England.

To help you with your decisions, we'll entice you with some brief descriptions of each state. To get the whole story, read the introductions to each chapter, then the more detailed material on the regions that appeal to you.

Connecticut packs several very different regions into its compact space. We first visit the southeastern part of the state, neighbor to New York. Failing in their effort to annex this corner, New Yorkers have nonetheless succeeded in remaking it in their own image: brimming with the fancy gourmet stores and chichi boutiques so vital to Manhattanites. The state's northwest corner offers historic villages and picturesque lakes. The capital city is Hartford, also known as the insurance capital of the world. South along the coast stands the city of New Haven, an urban industrial center whose main claim to fame is Yale University. From New Haven to the Rhode Island border, coastal Connecticut strings together one pretty fishing and sailing village after another: Essex, Old Saybrook, Mystic and Stonington. Connecticut's rural northeastern corner is the least known and developed area.

With two feet in the ocean, **Rhode Island** boasts miles of sandy beaches with rolling surf rivaling those of the Cape. The coastal villages of South County have a quiet, antique charm, while Victorian Block Island is a little island lost in time. Newport's fabled elegance still shines today in the extravagant summer "cottages" built by Gilded Age multimillionaires. Providence, a revitalized urban center, stands tall with one of the nation's finest historic districts, showcasing restored 18th- and 19th-century period houses. Farther north, the Blackstone Valley, stretching from Pawtucket to Woonsocket and west, is known as the "birthplace of American manufacturing."

With its quaint, cobblestoned streets, old-fashioned neighborhoods and big-city charms, **Boston** delights all who visit. Here is where America's most iconographic history lives on, at such sites as Paul Revere's House and the Old North Church in the North End. Much of Boston sparkles with new polish, especially the waterfront. Perennial favorites include Quincy Market, the diminutive brick townhouses and sprightly gardens of Beacon Hill, the imposing brownstones of Back Bay and the soaring architecture of Copley Square. Across the Charles River sits Harvard Square, the thriving nexus of intellectual Cambridge. Rural Lexington and Concord are known for their colonial history.

Wending its way hundreds of miles from Boston's North Shore, around the sandy hook of Cape Cod, to New Bedford in the southeast corner of the state, the **Massachusetts Coast** is studded its entire length with lovely resorts, fine sandy beaches and small fishing villages. Gloucester, Rockport and Salem are the highlights of the exclusive North Shore. The most famous area is Cape Cod, a favored spot for summer vacations. South of the Cape lie the islands of Martha's Vineyard and Nantucket, both prosperous whaling ports in their day and now drenched in the natural beauty of windswept moors, weathered cottages, pine woods and intimate beaches. The Plymouth area is rich in colonial history and lined with attractive fishing and farming villages with neat clapboarded 18th- and 19th-century sea captains' homes. New Bedford and Fall River have troves of whaling and textile history lore, respectively, as well as oodles of discount outlet stores.

Central and western Massachusetts includes a vast part of the state, from the old industrial city of Worcester west of Boston to the resort-oriented Berkshires on the western border. Rural hamlets, wildlife sanctuaries and state parks ring central Massachusetts, where Old Sturbridge Village re-creates the farming life of the 1840s. The Pioneer Valley stretches up the Connecticut River, through another large city with a rich industrial past, Springfield. A summer capital of music, dance and drama, the Berkshires are serene and sylvan settings of mountains, forests and lakes. Here Norman Rockwell made the streetscapes of Stockbridge famous. The Berkshires have produced a lovely commingling of luxurious resorts, charming inns, gourmet restaurants and ski havens.

No single New England state is more rural than **Vermont,** with its miles of open farmland, covered bridges, maple sugarhouses and small towns with classic village greens and general stores. Some of the best skiing in America is here, as is some of the best cheddar cheese you'll ever eat. Lying on Vermont's western border with New York is the magnificent Lake Champlain, named for explorer Samuel de Champlain and popular with boaters, swimmers and ice fishers. The most rugged region is the Northeast Kingdom, three northern counties bordering Canada that make up a realm of tiny townships, mountains, forests and isolated farms.

Though **New Hampshire**'s tiny seacoast measures a mere 18 miles, along it lies Portsmouth, a jewel of a town that is one of the most handsome refurbished antique settlements on the East Coast. Old textile mills and factories sprawl along the Merrimack River, while outlet stores and other commerce thrive in the state's prosperous, booming southern half. The northern half is a wilderness of lakes, mountains and evergreen forests. Large and beautiful bodies of water like Lake Sunapee and Lake Winnepesaukee, and the White Mountains offer sports enthusiasts numerous choices, as well as plentiful resorts. Weathered barns and country towns complete the scenery in the Monadnock Region.

Maine, the land of Downeast, has sent its most famous delicacy, Maine lobster, all over the world. In this state's wilderness and waterways live thick spruce forests, moose, black bear, loons and deer. More developed than the north, the southern coast presents low-key resort towns and outlet stores, as well as the city of Portland, a restored maritime Victorian jewel. North of Portland is the rugged, rockbound coast, the real Downeast, with its independent-minded towns of Damariscotta, Wiscasset, Camden and Castine. Out on Mount Desert Island, the old-money resort of Bar Harbor reigns, alongside the splendid Acadia National Park. Maine is also Andrew Wyeth country, as seen in the turn-of-the-century world of Monhegan Island, just one of hundreds of islands in Casco Bay. To the north, the Maine woods offer an unparalleled wilderness experience, where visitors can travel for a hundred miles without spotting any sign of civilization. The lakes region provides scenic splendors and water sports galore.

When To Go

SEASONS

A constant battle wages here in New England between bristling battalions of cold, dry Canadian arctic air and laid-back, warm, humid air from the tropics. When these two mix it up, which is frequently, you have New England's legendary changeable weather. The morning may dawn fine and sunny, afternoon turn cold and foggy and nightfall bring a raging northeaster.

More than you might think, the weather varies from south to north. Weather in southeastern New England, tempered by ocean winds, is warmer. While mean temperatures for Connecticut range from 27° in January to 73° in July, in Vermont they go from 16° in January to 70° in July. And at the top of New Hampshire's Mount Washington, it may as well be Antarctica.

No matter how you slice it, winters are long and cold here, and the overall effect has been described as "nine months of winter and three of rough sledding." Winters are invariably colder in Vermont and Maine, where temperatures range from minus 10° to 10° and sometimes drop to minus 30. In southern New England, temperatures are more likely to hover in the 20s and 30s in winter.

In the north, snow arrives as early as Thanksgiving and stays on the ground into mid-April, but near the coast in the southeast, it's indecent of snow to put in an appearance until Christmas and subzero weather is almost unheard of. But don't be deterred by the long winter; that's what puts plenty of white stuff on the northern ski slopes.

And, inevitably, there comes the spring thaw, which in the northern country goes by the popular name of "mud season." When the frozen ground starts melting, the result is a muddy morass. Spring is a little less messy in the south, where by mid-March the songbirds are chirping away, followed by greening in another few weeks.

Summer sets in around about mid-June. Days are quite warm, with temperatures ranging from 70° to 90°, turning to slightly cooler evenings, especially along the shore and in the mountains. Despite the tempering ocean breezes, summer can be humid, as well as foggy and rainy. The weather is hottest in central Massachusetts, in the dry valley of the Connecticut River.

Autumn may be the most wonderful season of all to visit, and certainly the most popular one. Fall colors are at their peak, and all the fall harvests of apples, cider, cranberries and pumpkins are in. Sunny days often warm up to "Indian summer" comfort, energized by cool, crisp nights. In the southeast, autumn lasts right into November.

Both autumn and winter are substantially drier than in other locales. Still, it manages to rain, snow or sleet about one day out of three, making for an annual precipitation of 42 inches and an annual snowfall in the mountains of 90 to 100 inches.

Hurricanes periodically strike the region with devastating intensity. This century's worst occurred in 1938 when entire coastal communities were swallowed by the sea. In the fall of 1991 another disastrous hurricane hit New England, damaging, among others, President George Bush's family home in Kennebunkport, Maine.

Tourists flock to New England for fall-foliage season (mid-September through October), when it can be very difficult to get reservations. High summer (July through Labor Day) is also a busy time, especially along the coast. You might want to consider a visit to a seaside resort in the spring or fall, when rates are lower. As well, Christmas, New Year's and ski season (late January through March) are popular with tourists. During the low seasons of April, May and late October through late December, you'll have a much less crowded vacation and a much easier time getting reservations.

CALENDAR OF EVENTS

Each year, New England celebrates its colonial past by reenacting historic events that took place in all six states. Other annual observances celebrate the wonderful largesse of this region: apples, maple sugar, blueberries, scallops, clams. The list of merrymaking goes on, with art, music and dance festivals, and occasions honoring many New England traditions, such as shipbuilding, quiltmaking, sheep shearing and Shaker craftsmanship.

JANUARY

Boston: The **Chinese New Year** is celebrated in January or February, with three weeks of festivities.

Vermont: Sled dog races, parades and downhill and cross-country skiing events comprise the **Stowe Winter Carnival.**

FEBRUARY

Boston: The **Boston Boat Show,** one of the largest on the East Coast, brings out the latest and fanciest in power and sail. Four of the city's biggest hockey-playing colleges (Harvard, Northeastern, Boston University and Boston College) face off in the **Beanpot Hockey Tournament.**

New Hampshire: The **Dartmouth College Winter Carnival** is an exuberant expression of fun during the winter doldrums.

MARCH

Boston: The **New England Spring Flower Show** has been running for more than 100 years, giving a lift to winter-weary Bostonians. The **St. Patrick's Day Parade** thrown by the Irish of South Boston is one of the largest and most festive in America.

Maine: Appropriately, the **Sled Dog Races** take place in frontier town Rangeley. Maple sugarhouses statewide throw open their doors on **Maine Maple Sunday**.

APRIL

Boston: The nation's premier running event, the **Boston Marathon** is only one of several signal events on **Patriot's Day**. Other activities commemorating Revolutionary War events include a parade plus re-enactments of Paul Revere's famous ride and the Battle of Lexington and Concord.

Massachusetts Coast: During Nantucket's **Daffodil Festival**, hundreds of these sprightly blooms decorate shop windows.

Vermont: Quiltmaking is honored at the **Festival of Quilts** in Rutland. At the **Vermont Maple Festival** in St. Albans, sample maple products, watch demonstrations and contests and enjoy the entertainment.

MAY

Connecticut: At the **Dogwood Festival** in Fairfield, 30,000 dogwood trees are abloom. Picnic-style lobster dinners, naturally, are the main event at the **Lobster Festival** at Mystic Seaport.

Rhode Island: **Gaspee Days** in Warwick, which run into June, commemorate the colonists'. burning of Britain's *H.M.S. Gaspee* in 1772—one of the first acts of hostility leading to the Revolution—with historic re-enactments, a parade, arts and crafts, food and entertainment.

Boston: **Lilac Sunday** at the Arnold Arboretum finds 400 varieties of lilacs in bloom.

Central and Western Massachusetts: The **Brimfield antique shows,** also held in July and September, draw hundreds of dealers for week-long events in the small town of Brimfield.

Vermont: **Lilac Sunday** at the Shelburne Museum showcases this museum's stunning lilac collection.

JUNE

Connecticut: Racing shells from Harvard and Yale vie along the Thames River in the **Yale-Harvard Regatta.** One-hundred-and-fifty species of rare, endangered or just plain lovely New England wildflowers are displayed at the **Wildflower Festival** at the University of Connecticut at Storrs.

Rhode Island: Providence's historic east side is on view during the **Festival of Historic Houses.**

Boston: The **Bunker Hill Day Reenactment and Parade** features contemporary patriots dressed in Revolutionary uniforms fighting the famous battle again.

Central and Western Massachusetts: Wine and cheese on the lawn while listening to the Boston Symphony Orchestra is the attraction of the **Tanglewood Music Festival**. One of the Northeast's best-known dance festivals, **Jacob's Pillow**, takes place in the Berkshires. West Springfield's **A.C.C. Craft Fair** is America's largest and most prestigious.

Vermont: Hot-air balloons light up the scenery at the **Balloon Festival and Crafts Fair** in Quechee.

Maine: The **Old Port Festival** brings the historic part of Portland to life with a street fair of arts and crafts, music, jugglers, kids' events, song and ethnic foods. **Windjammer Days** in Boothbay Harbor show off these classic schooners under full sail in a dress parade.

JULY

Connecticut: Soloists of national renown perform **Summer Music** at a scenic seaside setting at Waterford's Harkness Memorial Park.

Boston: The **U.S. Pro Tennis Championship** draws thousands of tennis fans to the Longwood Cricket Club. Every weekend in July and August, **Italian street festivals** honor patron saints with colorful parades and festivities. The multicultural diversity of Cambridge comes alive in the **Cambridge River Festival**, with live performances, crafts and food. The **Boston Harborfest** offers nearly a hundred activities celebrating the harbor at 30 sites, highlighted by a chowderfest.

Massachusetts Coast: The **Yarmouth Clam Festival** dishes up not only clams, but many other seafoods, arts and crafts, music and entertainment.

Vermont: The **Vermont Mozart Festival** presents more than two solid weeks of classical music and a "Mozart Odyssey" of dining and entertainment at the Trapp Family Lodge.

Maine: The **Great Kennebec River Whatever Week and Race** is an apt name for a ten-day event that starts with vaudeville shows and street performers and climaxes with an eight-mile regatta of anything that floats. Lowly spuds, a mainstay of local economy, are paid homage at the **Maine Potato Blossom Festival**.

AUGUST

Connecticut: The **Volvo International Tennis Tournament** showcases top tennis stars in world-class play. The tiny streets of the village of Mystic are lined with artists' canvases during the **Mystic Outdoor Art Festival**.

Rhode Island: Some of the world's best jazz musicians entertain the thousands sprawled out on the green lawns of Fort Adams State Park in Newport at the **JVC Jazz Festival**. B. B. King, Randy Newman and Leon Redbone have all performed at **Ben & Jerry's Newport Folk Festival**.

Massachusetts Coast: **Illumination Night** sets Oak Bluff homes on Martha's Vineyard to glowing with paper lanterns. Also on the Vineyard, the **West Tisbury Agricultural Fair** takes place.

New Hampshire: Some of the state's finest crafts are sold at the **Craftsmen's Fair of the League of New Hampshire Craftsmen Foundation** in Newbury.

Maine: Hundreds of performers from around the world enliven the **Maine Festival of the Arts** with music, dance, crafts, demonstrations and food. An all-you-can-eat blueberry pancake breakfast starts off the week for the **State of Maine Blueberry Festival** in Union.

SEPTEMBER

Connecticut: The South Norwalk **Oyster Festival** has something for everyone: oysters galore, seafood and ethnic foods, nationally known singers and bands, arts and crafts, tall ships and marine skills demonstrations.

Rhode Island: Cajun and bluegrass in New England? Yes, loads, not only music, but food and dance, at the **Cajun & Bluegrass Music & Dance Festival** in Escoheag.

Massachusetts Coast: Tasty crustaceans star at the **Annual Bourne Scallop Festival**. The **Edaville Railroad Cranberry Fair and Festival** celebrates the cranberry harvest.

Central and Western Massachusetts: **The Big E**, or the **Eastern States Exposition**, in West Springfield is the East's largest annual fair, strong on agricultural and animal exhibits, horse shows and rides and food galore. King Kielbasa, "the world's biggest kielbasa," sets the tone for the **World Kielbasa Festival** in Chicopee.

OCTOBER

Boston: More than 3000 oarsmen compete in the **Head of the Charles Regatta**, the largest one-day rowing event in the world.

Massachusetts Coast: Columbus Day is celebrated with parades, floats and arts and crafts at Yarmouth's **Seaside Festival**.

Central and Western Massachusetts: The **Topsfield Fair** is another vintage event, with sheep dog trials, ethnic foods and midway rides.

Maine: More than 135 years old, the **Fryeburg Fair** sticks close to its agricultural roots during week-long festivities.

NOVEMBER

Massachusetts Coast: Have a traditional turkey dinner with all the trimmings in America's hometown, Plymouth, during its annual **Thanksgiving Dinner**.

Central and Western Massachusetts: Cascade mums, standard varieties and new hybrids are shown at the week-long **Chrysanthemum Show** at Smith College.

DECEMBER

Connecticut: Lantern light tours and a **Carol Sing** mark Christmas at the Mystic Seaport Museum.

Boston: The **Cambridge Christmas Revels** celebrate the winter solstice with period song and dance; audience participation is traditional. Hundreds of events mark **First Night**, a New Year's Eve celebration held indoors and out. There's a huge pageant, plus choral groups, ice sculptures, storytellers, acrobats, puppeteers and art and drama presentations. The **Boston Tea Party Reenactment** finds patriots dressed as Indians throwing chests of tea into Boston Harbor one more time.

Massachusetts Coast: The **Nantucket Christmas Stroll** is a festival weekend of holiday cheer and shopping.

New Hampshire: The **Candlelight Stroll** at Strawbery Banke illuminates three centuries of houses.

How to Deal With . . .

VISITOR INFORMATION

New England USA (529 Main Street, Box 36, Boston, MA 02129; 617-241-5441) has a free Travel Planner suggesting itineraries throughout New England.

As well as large cities, many small towns have chambers of commerce or visitor information centers; a number of them are listed in *Hidden New England* under the appropriate state or region.

Travel information on Connecticut is available from the **Tourism Division** (Department of Economic Development, 865 Brook Street, Rocky Hill, CT 06067; 203-258-4290). For Rhode Island, contact the **Tourism Division** (Department of Economic Development, 7 Jackson Walkway, Providence, RI 02903; 401-277-2601 or 800-556-2484).

For Massachusetts information, contact the **Massachusetts Office of Travel and Tourism** (Department of Commerce, 100 Cambridge Street, Boston, MA 02202; 617-727-3201). More detailed information on Boston can be had from the **Greater Boston Convention and Visitors Bureau** (Box 490, Prudential Center, 800 Boylston Street, Boston, MA 02216; 617-536-4100).

For information on vacationing in Vermont, write the **Vermont Travel Division** (134 State Street, Montpelier, VT 05602; 802-828-3236). In New Hampshire, the contact is the **Office of Vacation Travel** (Box 856, Concord, NH 03302; 603-271-2666). In Maine, write the **Maine Publicity Bureau** (P.O. Box 2300, Hallowell, ME 04347; 207-582-9300).

PACKING

Packing for a visit to New England is a little trickier than for other destinations. What you must take is dictated by the fickle Yankee weather, which might change at any minute. A warm, sunny day can turn cool and foggy without so much as a by your leave. The best bet is to bring layers of clothing that can be added or subtracted as needed. Even in the summer, bring some long-sleeved shirts, long pants and lightweight sweaters and jackets, along with your T-shirts, jeans and bathing suit.

Fall and spring call for a full round of warm clothing, from long pants and sweaters to jackets, hats and gloves. While fall days are often sunny and warm, fall nights can turn quite crisp and cool. Bring your heaviest, warmest clothes in winter: thick sweaters, knitted hats, down jackets and ski clothes.

Boston Brahmins notwithstanding, most of New England is a pretty casual place, especially in summer, when everyone has sand in his shoes. No one will look askance if you wear your deck shoes and L.L. Bean pants to dinner at most restaurants, particularly in coastal resort areas like Kennebunkport. New England is less casual, however, than a warm-weather resort, and you can't get into most restaurants or bars without a shirt or shoes, or if you're wearing a bathing suit.

Boston is the most conservatively dressed place you'll visit. Some downtown Boston restaurants have dress codes, requiring men to wear jackets and ties and women to be "appropriately attired."

New Englanders are used to rolling up their car windows every night in summer, knowing it may rain any night. Rain, though not usually heavy, is a big part of every season, so be sure to bring an umbrella and a raincoat, even in the summer.

Some of the streets are almost as old as New England itself. In many areas such as Boston, on these rough, cobblestone ways you need sturdy, comfortable shoes that can take this kind of beating and be kind to your feet. Women should never attempt to navigate cobblestone streets in high heels. Likewise, some New England shores can be rocky. A pair of rubber shoes or old sneakers for swimming is sometimes advisable.

Though New England is not the Caribbean, you can get just as impressive a sunburn here. Bring a good sunscreen, especially to the beach, where sand and water reflect the sun's rays more intensely. Bring insect repellant in the summertime as insurance against the greenhead flies at the shore and blackflies in the mountains.

For the northern woods of Maine and other out-of-the-way places, you'll have far fewer stores to rely on, so come prepared with whatever gear you'll be using. It's wise to consult a backpacking or camping supply store before you leave about what to bring for the weather conditions likely at the time of your travels.

When you come here, you'll need nothing but the best street and road maps. Many roads in New England are winding, poorly marked or not marked at all, following an age-old philosophy that if you live here, you know where you're going, and if you don't, you have no business being here anyway.

You may want to toss in an antique guide along with your other reading; the country's oldest antiques are for sale here. Last but not least, don't forget your camera for capturing quintessential New England vistas of lighthouses and white-steepled villages.

HOTELS

Visiting New England is your opportunity to stay in some of the most historic lodgings this country has to offer. A number of them date to the 18th century, such as Longfellow's Wayside Inn in Sudbury, Massachusetts. Randall's Ordinary in North Stonington, Connecticut, dates to the 17th century.

New England is where the bed-and-breakfast movement gained ground in this country, and the region is thick with historic farmhouses and sea captains' homes turned into bed and breakfasts. These are often rambling, cozy affairs complete with fireplace, bookshelves and resident cat. But bed-and-breakfast booking agencies, especially in urban areas, also list host homes with a spare room, which isn't quite the same thing. Be sure to ask whether a bed and breakfast is a real inn or not.

In addition, accommodations include mom-and-pop motels, chain hotels and rustic seaside cottages where you'll awaken to the sounds of surf and crying gulls. Cities have the most deluxe highrise hotels, but outside urban areas, lodgings are generally casual and lowrise.

Whatever your preference and budget, you can probably find something to suit your taste with the help of the individual chapters in this book. Remember, rooms are scarce and prices rise in the high season, which is summer, fall-foliage time and Christmas throughout New England, and also includes ski season in northern areas.

There are lots of special weekend and holiday packages at the larger hotels, and off-season rates drop significantly, making a week- or month-long stay a real bargain.

Accommodations in this book are organized by state or region and classified according to price. These refer to high-season rates, so if you're looking for low-season bargains, be sure to inquire about them.

Budget lodgings generally cost less than $50 a night for two people and are satisfactory and clean but modest. *Moderate*-priced lodgings run from $50 to $90; what they offer in terms of luxury will depend on their location, but in general they provide larger rooms and more attractive surroundings. At a *deluxe* hotel or resort, you can expect to spend between $90 and $130 for a double; typically you'll find spacious rooms, a fashionable lobby, a restaurant or two and often some shops. *Ultra-deluxe* facilities, priced above $130, are a region's finest, offering all the amenities of a deluxe hotel plus plenty of luxurious extras, such as jacuzzis and exercise rooms, 24-hour room service and gourmet dining.

If you've got your heart set on a room with a water view, be sure to pin that down. Be forewarned that "oceanside" doesn't always mean right on the beach. If you want to save money, try lodgings a block or so away from the water. They almost always offer lower rates than rooms within sight of the surf, and the savings are often worth the short stroll to the beach.

RESTAURANTS

Succulent native seafood stars at legions of New England restaurants, from lobster in the rough and tender bay scallops to codfish, mussels, steamers and milky clam chowder.

Besides seafood and traditional Yankee foods, New England restaurants also serve up ethnic cuisines of every stripe, plus gourmet foods and fast food. No matter what your taste or budget, there's a restaurant for you.

Within each chapter, restaurants are organized geographically. Each entry describes the cuisine and ambience and categorizes the restaurant in one of four price ranges. Dinner entrées at *budget* restaurants usually cost $8 or less. The ambience is informal, service speedy, the crowd often a local one. *Moderate*-priced eateries charge between $8 and $16 for dinner; surroundings are casual but pleasant, the menu offers more variety and the pace is usually slower. *Deluxe* restaurants tab their entrées above $16; cuisines may be simple or sophisticated, but the decor is plusher and the service more personalized. *Ultra-deluxe* establishments, where entrées begin at $24, are often the gourmet gathering places; here cooking is (hopefully) a fine art, and the service should be impeccable.

Some restaurants, particularly those that depend on the summer trade in coastal areas, close for the winter.

Breakfast and lunch menus vary less in price from one restaurant to another. Even deluxe establishments usually offer light breakfasts and luncheons, priced within a few dollars of their budget-minded competitors. These smaller meals can be a good time to test expensive restaurants.

TRAVELING WITH CHILDREN

New England is a wonderful place to bring children. Besides many child-oriented museums, the region also has hundreds of beaches and parks, and many nature sanctuaries sponsor children's activities year-round.

Quite a few New England bed and breakfasts don't accept children, so be sure of the policy when you make reservations. If you need a crib or cot, arrange for it ahead of time.

Travel agents can help with arrangements; they can reserve airline bulkhead seats where there is plenty of room and determine which flights are least crowded. If you are traveling by car, be sure to take along such necessities as water and juices, snacks and toys. Always allow extra time for getting places, especially on rural roads.

A first-aid kit is a must for any trip. Along with adhesive bandages, antiseptic cream and something to stop itching, include any medicines your pediatrician might recommend to treat allergies, colds, diarrhea or any chronic problems your child may have.

At the beach, take extra care with your children's skin the first few days, even though this is not the Caribbean. Children's tender young skin can suffer severe sunburn before you know it. Hats for the kids are a good idea, along with liberal applications of a good sunscreen. Never take your eyes off your children at the shore. If you are traveling in winter, never leave a child alone near a frozen lake.

All-night stores are scarce in rural areas, and stores in small towns often close early. You may go a long distance between stores that can supply you with essentials, so be sure to be well stocked with diapers, baby food and other needs when you are on the go. But all-night stores such as Store 24 and 7-11 are plentiful in urban areas.

To find specific activities for children, consult local newspapers. The *Boston Globe* Thursday Calendar has especially comprehensive listings that cover a good part of New England.

The **Travelers Aid Society of Boston, Inc.** (711 Atlantic Avenue, Boston, MA 02111; 617-542-7286) is a resource for any traveler in need and maintains booths at major transportation terminals. Volunteers can arrange to meet young children traveling alone.

OLDER TRAVELERS

New England is a hospitable place for senior citizens to visit; countless museums, historic sights and even restaurants and hotels offer senior discounts that cut a substantial chunk off vacation costs. And many golden-agers from hotter climes flock to New England for its cool summers.

The **American Association of Retired Persons** (3200 East Carson Street, Lakewood, CA 90712; 213-496-2277) offers membership to anyone over 50. AARP's benefits include travel discounts with a number of firms; escorted tours and cruises are available through AARP Travel Service (400 Pinnacle Way, Suite 450, Norcross, GA 30071; 800-927-0111).

Elderhostel (75 Federal Street, Suite 400, Boston, MA 02110; 617-426-7788) offers many, many educational courses in a variety of New England locations that are all-inclusive packages at colleges and universities.

Be extra careful about health matters. In New England's changeable and sometimes cold weather, seniors are more at risk of suffering hypothermia, especially during prolonged exposure to wind. Older travelers should be very careful when walking to beware of falls. Sidewalks may be poorly paved or buckled in places, and cobblestone streets are easy to lodge an ankle in.

Out-of-state prescriptions are not filled so try to bring extra of whatever medications you use. Or consider carrying a medical record with you, including your history and current medical status as well as your doctor's name, phone number and address. Make sure that your insurance covers you while you are away from home.

The **Travelers Aid Society of Boston, Inc.** (711 Atlantic Avenue, Boston, MA 02111; 617-542-7286) can provide emergency financial assistance and medical and social service referrals, help find low-cost accommodations, give directions and information and assist with banking and check cashing, and train, plane and bus connections. Volunteers can arrange to meet travelers with special needs.

DISABLED TRAVELERS

New England has made real strides toward making its many attractions and services handicapped-accessible. Parking spaces for the handicapped are provided at most services and attractions, although few buses are handicapped-accessible.

Special escorted group tours are offered by **New Horizons Travel for the Handicapped** (P.O. Box 652, Belmont, MA 02178; 617-923-1176, or 800-832-1112 outside Massachusetts), geared to the mentally handicapped and those with cerebral palsy. **The Guided Tour** (613 Cheltenham Avenue, Suite 200, Melrose Park, PA 19126; 215-782-1370) also leads tours for the disabled.

Access Tours (P.O. Box 356, Malverne, NY 11565; 516-887-5798) specializes in travel arrangements for the handicapped with any disability.

Offering general information are the **Society for the Advancement of Travel for the Handicapped** (26 Court Street, Brooklyn, NY 11242; 718-858-5483), **Travel Information Center** (Moss Rehabilitation Hospital, 12th Street and Tabor Road, Philadelphia, PA 19141; 215-329-5715), **Mobility International USA** (P.O. Box 3551, Eugene, OR 97403; 503-343-1284) and **Flying Wheels Travel** (P.O. Box 382, Owatonna, MN 55060; 800-533-0363).

Also providing information for disabled travelers is **Travelin' Talk** (P.O. Box 3534, Clarksville, TN 37043; 615-552-6670), a networking organization.

The **Information Center for Individuals with Disabilities** (27-43 Wormwood Street, Boston, MA 02210; 617-727-5540) provides disabled travelers with information referral and problem-solving concerning the state of Massachusetts. A list of hotels, restaurants and historic sites that are handicapped-accessible is also available.

The **Travelers Aid Society of Boston, Inc.** (711 Atlantic Avenue, Boston, MA 02111; 617-542-7286) can arrange for volunteers to meet handicapped travelers. Travelers Aid also publishes two free booklets, *Cambridge Access* and *Boston Access*, guides to handicapped-accessible sites and services in those areas.

FOREIGN TRAVELERS

PASSPORTS AND VISAS   Most foreign visitors are required to obtain a passport and tourist visa to enter the United States. Contact your nearest United States Embassy or Consulate well in advance to obtain a visa and to check on any other entry requirements.

CUSTOMS REQUIREMENTS   Foreign travelers are allowed to carry in the following: 200 cigarettes (or 100 cigars), $400 worth of duty-free gifts, including one liter of alcohol (you must be 21 years of age to bring in the alcohol). You may bring in any amount of currency, but must fill out a form if you bring in over $10,000 (U.S.). Carry any prescription drugs in clearly marked containers. (You may have to produce a written prescription or doctor's statement for the customs officer.) Meat or meat products, seeds, plants, fruits and narcotics are not allowed to be brought into the United States. Contact the **United States Customs Service** (1301 Constitution Avenue Northwest, Washington, DC 20229; 202-566-8195) for further information.

DRIVING   If you plan to rent a car, an international driver's license should be obtained *before* arriving in New England. Some rental companies require both a foreign license and an international driver's license. Many car rental agencies require a lessee to be 25 years of age; all require a major credit card.

CURRENCY   United States money is based on the dollar. Bills come in six denominations: $1, $5, $10, $20, $50 and $100. Every dollar is divided into 100 cents. Coins are the penny (1 cent), nickel (5 cents), dime (10 cents), quarter (25 cents). Half-dollars and dollar coins are rarely used. You may not use foreign currency to purchase goods and services in the United States. Consider buying traveler's checks in dollar amounts. You may also use credit cards affiliated with an American company such as Interbank, Barclay Card and American Express.

ELECTRICITY   Electric outlets use currents of 117 volts, 60 cycles. For appliances made for other electrical systems you need a transformer or other adapter.

WEIGHTS AND MEASUREMENTS   The United States uses the English system of weights and measures. American units and their metric equivalents are as follows: 1 inch = 2.5 centimeters; 1 foot = 0.3 meter; 1 yard = 0.9 meter; 1 mile = 1.6 kilometers; 1 ounce = 28 grams; 1 pound = 0.45 kilogram; 1 quart (liquid) = 0.9 liter.

Sporting Life

CAMPING

New England offers a rich spectrum of camping experiences, from sites in the deep wilderness of the White Mountains and the Green Mountains and quiet lakeside spots to protected forests and recreational vehicle parks.

For information on camping in the Green Mountain National Forest, contact the **U.S. Forest Service** (RR#1, Box 1940, Manchester Center, VT 05255; 802-362-1251). Brochures on camping in the White Mountains are available from the **White Mountain National Forest** (P.O. Box 638, Laconia, NH 03247; 603-528-8721).

In Connecticut, quite a few state parks and forests are open for camping. The **Bureau of Parks and Forests** (Department of Environmental Protection, 165 Capitol Avenue, room 265, Hartford, CT 06106; 203-566-2304) has information on fees and regulations.

The beautiful Acadia National Park in Maine, as well as about half the state parks, permit camping. For information about Acadia, contact **Acadia National Park** (P.O. Box 177, Bar Harbor, ME 04609; 207-288-3338). To find out about camping in state forests, contact the **Maine Forest Service** (State House Station 22, Augusta, ME 04333; 207-289-2791) or the **Bureau of Parks and Recreation** at the same address (207-289-3821). The **Maine Campground Owners Association** (655 Main Street, Lewiston, ME 04240; 207-782-5874) offers a free camping guide. At privately owned campsites, facilities range from rustic basics in wilderness areas to fairly deluxe cabins and cottages. The **Maine Publicity Bureau** (P.O. Box 2300, Hallowell, ME 04347; 207-582-9300) offers a current listing of trailer parks and campsites.

For information on camping at Massachusetts state forest sites, contact the **State Division of Forests and Parks** (100 Cambridge Street, Boston, MA 02202; 617-727-3180). A free guide, the *Massachusetts Campground Directory*, is published by the **Massachusetts Association of Campground Owners** (RR#1, Box 3040, Kennebunk, ME 04043; 207-985-4864) and is also available from the **Massachusetts Office of Travel and Tourism** (Department of Commerce, 100 Cambridge Street, 13th floor, Boston, MA 02202; 617-727-3201). Camping is also permitted on several of the Boston Harbor Islands (see the "Beaches and Parks" section of the Boston chapter).

New Hampshire Loves Campers, a free guide to New Hampshire campgrounds covering private, state and White Mountain National Forest campsites, is published by the **New Hampshire Campground Owners Association** (P.O. Box 320, Twin Mountain, NH 03595; 603-846-5511).

In Rhode Island, the **Tourism Division** (Department of Economic Development, 7 Jackson Walkway, Providence, RI 02903; 401-277-2601 or 800-556-2484) can provide information on camping facilities and permits,

New England Facts and Foibles

Population: 13.7 million

Square miles: 66,608

Miles of coastline: 6130

States with no coastline: 1 (Vermont)

Square miles of lakes, rivers and streams: 3660

Number of farms: 28,500

Millionaires: 23,900

Income per capita: $18,431

Number of Fortune 500 companies: 49

Percentage of college graduates: 18

Colleges and universities

In New England: 264
In Massachusetts: 121
In Boston: 47

U.S. presidents born here: 7 (including George Bush)

Percentage of native New Englanders in population: 67.8

Inventive inventions—

laughing gas
frozen food
sandpaper
birth control pills
snow-making machines
basketball,
Monopoly
chocolate chip cookies

Gallons of maple syrup produced annually in Vermont: half a million

Covered bridges in Vermont: 109

Pounds of Maine lobster caught annually: 23.5 million

Pounds of Maine blueberries picked annually: 52.3 million

Bushels of New Hampshire apples picked annually: 1.5 million

Miles of stone walls in Connecticut: 50,000

Famous cookie named for a Boston suburb: Fig Newton, for Newton

Highest natural point: Mount Washington in New Hampshire (6288 feet)

Highest manmade point: John Hancock Tower in Boston (790 feet)

Nation's first—

Highway: Route 20, Old Boston Post Road, from Boston to New York City

Synagogue: Touro Synagogue (1759) in Newport

College: Harvard (1639) in Cambridge, Massachusetts

Postage stamp: printed in Brattleboro, Vermont (1846)

Recipient of Social Security: Ida Fuller of Ludlow, Vermont, in 1940 received check #00-000-001 for $22.45

Human Flying Stunt: John Childs (1757), using a half glider/half umbrella, jumped from the steeple of Boston's Old North Church and offers *The Rhode Island Camping Guide*, which lists state, municipal and private campgrounds.

The Vermont Department of Forests, Parks and Recreation (Agency of Natural Resources, 103 South Main Street, Waterbury, VT 05676; 802-244-8711) operates 35 campgrounds with 2200 campsites. The state has about 90 private campgrounds. Write the **Vermont Association of Private Campground Owners and Operators** (c/o Brattleboro North KOA, RD 2, Box 110, Putney, VT 05346) for a free brochure.

WILDERNESS PERMITS

Primitive campsites are provided in certain state parks and recreation areas. While wilderness camping away from designated areas is sometimes not allowed, in other cases it is allowable without a permit.

No permit is needed for wilderness camping in either the Green Mountain National Forest or the White Mountain National Forest. But Acadia National Park does not allow camping away from designated areas.

Connecticut allows backpack camping on state lands; a wilderness permit is needed. Contact the **Department of Environmental Protection** (Eastern District Office, 209 Hebron Road, Marlborough, CT 06447; 203-295-9523) or the DEP's Western District Office (230 Plymouth Road, Harwinton, CT 06791; 203-485-0226).

In Maine and New Hampshire, no permit is required to camp in wilderness areas in state forests.

Rhode Island and Massachusetts do not allow camping outside designated camping areas in state forests.

Groups of more than ten people who wish to camp in wilderness areas in Vermont need a permit; contact the **Vermont Department of Forests, Parks and Recreation** (Agency of Natural Resources, 103 South Main Street, Waterbury, VT 05676; 802-244-8711) for the location of the appropriate local district office. You can also contact the forestry department for a free brochure, the *Vermont Guide to Primitive Camping on State Lands.*

BOATING

Boating is one of the most popular activities in New England. Sailboats, canoes, windjammers, power boats, cruise boats and ferries all ply the coastline and region's large lakes and rivers. You can bring your own boat and get your feet wet doing some New England cruising, or rent or charter a craft here. Each chapter in this book offers suggestions on how to go about finding the vessel of your choice.

Charts for boaters and divers are widely sold at marine shops and bookstores throughout New England.

Boating regulations vary slightly from state to state. In Connecticut, for a list of boating regulations and safety information, contact the **Depart-**

ment of Environmental Protection (Office of Parks and Recreation, Boating Safety Division, P.O. Box 280, Old Lyme, CT 06371; 203-434-8638).

For Rhode Island regulations, contact the **Department of Environmental Management** (Division of Boating Safety, Office of Boat Registration, 22 Hayes Street, Providence, RI 02908-5000; 401-277-6647).

Massachusetts boating information can be obtained from the **Division of Law Enforcement** (Room 910, Ninth Floor, 100 Nashua Street, Boston MA 02114; 617-727-3905).

Vermont boating regulations can be obtained from the **Vermont State Police Headquarters** (103 South Main Street, Waterbury, VT 05671; 802-244-8775).

In New Hampshire, contact the **Department of Safety** (Division of Safety Services, RFD#8, Box 31, Gilford, NH 03246; 603-293-0091).

For Maine regulations, contact the **Department of Inland Fisheries and Wildlife** (284 State Street, Station 41, Augusta ME 04333; 207-289-2766).

Canoeing the region's many rivers is a rewarding experience. The **Connecticut River Watershed Council** (312 First New Hampshire Bank Building, Lebanon, NH 03766; 603-448-2792) can answer questions about canoeing the Connecticut, which winds through most of New England.

Canoe trails in Connecticut are described in two free brochures from the **Bureau of Parks and Forests** (Department of Environmental Protection, 165 Capitol Avenue, Hartford, CT 06106; 203-566-2304)—*Canoe Camping* and *Canoeing in Connecticut.*

The **Vermont Travel Division** (134 State Street, Montpelier, VT 05602; 802-828-3236) also publishes a free canoeing brochure.

WATER SAFETY

Even in winter, you'll find diehard surfers and windsurfers riding the waves in their wetsuits. Swimming, waterskiing, jetboating and floating on inflatable rafts are popular activities in the summer.

People have drowned in New England waters, but drownings are easily avoided when you respect the power of the water, heed appropriate warnings and use good sense.

Wherever you swim, never do it alone. On the ocean or in large lakes like Lake Champlain or Lake Winnipesaukee, always face the incoming waves. They can bring unpleasant surprises even to the initiated. If you go surfing, learn the proper techniques and dangers from an expert before you start out. Respect signs warning of dangerous currents and undertows. If you get caught in a rip current or any tow that makes you feel out of control, don't try to swim against it. Head across it, paralleling the shore. Exercise caution in the use of floats, inner tubes or rafts; unexpected currents can quickly carry you out to sea.

There are some jellyfish that inflict a mild sting, but that is easily treated with an over-the-counter antiseptic. If you go scalloping or musseling, swim in or wade in murky waters where shellfish dwell, wear canvas or rubber shoes to protect your feet.

Remember, you are a guest in the sea. All rights belong to the creatures who dwell there, including sharks. Though they are rarely seen and seldom attack, they should be respected. A wise swimmer who spots a fin simply heads unobtrusively for shore.

Scuba divers should always put out a visible float or flag to warn approaching boats of their presence. On a boat or a canoe, always wear a life jacket; ocean and river currents can be very powerful.

If you're going canoeing or whitewater rafting, always scout the river from land before the first trip, and check the available literature. Rivers have danger areas such as falls, boulder fields, rapids and dams.

FISH AND FISHING

Ever since the Puritans discovered salt cod, New Englanders have been fishing these waters. In the 19th century, men went down to the sea in ships after bigger fish—whales.

Today many people fish just for fun, casting a line into the surf off a rock jetty for flounder, striped bass or bluefish, or perhaps going out to sea for such deep-water game fish as bluefin tuna or shark.

For tamer activities, try harvesting mussels, scallops, littleneck clams or quahogs. And anyone can throw out a lobster pot or two and bring home a deluxe dinner.

Freshwater fishing in streams, lakes and ponds nets rainbow, brook and brown trout, as well as largemouth bass, northern pike, bullhead, perch, sunfish, catfish and pickerel. In cold northern lakes, you can catch lake trout, steelhead, landlocked salmon, smelt, sauger, walleye, largemouth and smallmouth bass, northern pike, muskellunge, yellow perch and channel catfish.

The most common saltwater fish are winter flounder and bluefish. Other saltwater species include striped bass, cod, tautog, mackerel, cod, haddock, pollock, weakfish and smelt.

While all six states require a license for freshwater fishing, no license is needed for saltwater fishing, with a few restrictions.

In Connecticut, freshwater fishing licenses can be bought from town clerks or sporting goods stores. For information on fishing regulations, contact the **Fisheries Division** (Department of Environmental Protection, Room 255, 165 Capitol Avenue, Hartford, CT 06106; 203-566-2287).

In Rhode Island, freshwater fishing licenses can be bought at bait and tackle shops, all town clerks' offices, or from the **Department of Environ-**

mental Management (22 Hayes Street, Providence, RI 02908; 401-277-3576).

For fishing in Massachusetts, contact the **State Division of Fisheries and Wildlife** (100 Cambridge Street, Boston, MA 02202; 617-727-3151) and ask for the Abstracts of the Fish and Wildlife Laws. A saltwater permit is required for tuna or lobster fishing; for this permit, contact the **State Division of Marine Fisheries** (100 Cambridge Street, Boston, MA 02202; 617-727-3193). The Marine Fisheries division also publishes the *Massachusetts Salt Water Fishing Guide*, which includes town-by-town lists of bait shops, boat rentals, jetties and piers, boat-launching sites and party boats.

Fishing licenses in Vermont may be purchased from any town clerk or at many sporting goods stores and state parks. The **Vermont Department of Fish and Wildlife** (Agency of Natural Resources, 103 South Main Street, Building 10 South, Waterbury, VT 05676; 802-244-7331) has details and maps in *The Digest of Fish and Wildlife Laws* and the *Vermont Guide to Fishing*.

For fishing fees and regulations in New Hampshire, contact the **New Hampshire Department of Fish & Game** (2 Hazen Drive, Concord, NH 03301; 603-271-3211).

CHAPTER TWO

Connecticut

Connecticut is the gateway to New England and it offers, despite its diminutive size, a sampling of everything that makes the region famous. Although it takes no more than two and a half hours to drive across the state, these 5000 square miles hold a surprising variety of riches: 250 miles of jagged shoreline; farms, woodland, mountains and rolling hills; villages of white-clapboard houses huddled around classic greens; and cities rich in cultural offerings. Three hundred and fifty years of history are reflected in the varied architecture and in countless sites—vintage houses, museums, historical societies—that celebrate the forceful men and women who made Connecticut their home.

Shaped like a rectangle measuring about 90 miles from west to east and 55 miles north to south, Connecticut is bounded by New York State on its western border, Massachusetts to the north and Rhode Island to the east. The southern edge is traced by Long Island Sound, a sheltered arm of the Atlantic Ocean that was formerly a vital avenue of trade and transportation and is now a prime recreational asset. The state's other major waterway is its namesake: the Connecticut River, longest in New England, which roughly cuts the state in half and was the site of the earliest 17th-century settlements. Before those villages existed, Native Americans knew the area as *Quinnehtukqut*, "long tidal river."

Indian names grace the rivers Housatonic, Quinnipiac and Naugatuck, as well as towns and villages like Cos Cob, Niantic, Saugatuck and Wequetequock. Most towns, however, bear names that have their roots in Great Britain—Windsor, Bristol, New Britain, Greenwich, Norwich—or in the Bible—Bethel, Goshen, Canaan, Bethlehem.

England, their land of birth, and the Puritan faith were crucial influences on the original settlers, who left the fledgling Massachusetts colony in 1633 to found the communities of Hartford, Windsor and Wethersfield on the Connecticut's fertile banks. A few years later, the three settlements joined together as the Hartford Colony—soon to become the Colony of Connecticut—and adopted the Fundamental Orders of 1639. This document, created as a framework for governing the colony, is regarded by many as the world's first written constitution. That's why the words "Constitution State" are heralded on automobile license plates.

Other, less glorious nicknames include "The Nutmeg State," a reference to the days of the itinerant Yankee peddler who went up and down the Atlantic seaboard door to door, selling anything the householder might need, including imported nutmegs, to add flavor to food. Legend has it that wily peddlers would leave the lady of the house holding a "wooden nutmeg"—a fake.

Be that as it may, few of those households could grow much of their own food, since the state's surface is largely glacial soil, too rocky for successful farming. From the beginning, many of the residents had to turn to other endeavors—commerce, shipping, insurance and, in time, manufacturing, which put the state on the map.

Among the products invented, or perfected, by Connecticut Yankees were hats, combs, pins, clocks, seeds, furniture, typewriters, axes, hardware of all kinds, vulcanized rubber, bicycles, textiles—both silk and cotton—silverware and firearms. Samuel Colt developed the Colt 45, "the gun that won the West," at his armory in Hartford. At his firearms factory near New Haven, Eli Whitney, who had previously invented the cotton gin, introduced the concept of interchangeable parts, which led to the flowering of the Industrial Revolution.

Towns and cities grew up around their factories—you'll see handsome brick or stone mills as you drive along the valleys of the Naugatuck, the Quinebaug and other rivers—and each locality became known by the product it manufactured. Waterbury was the brass city; New Britain was the hardware capital of the world; Danbury's fame was hats; Bristol boasted of its clocks.

As mills and factories grew, so did their need for workers. During the late 19th and early 20th centuries great waves of immigrants entered the state from Ireland, Italy, Germany, Poland—every country in Europe. The makeup of the population changed from a homogeneous nucleus of English Protestant descent to the mosaic of nationalities and ethnic groups that characterizes Connecticut's 3.5 million people today.

Industry continues to remain important to some extent: airplane parts are manufactured in East Hartford, helicopters in Stratford; in Groton, Electric Boat builds submarines. But changing patterns and needs across the nation have led to factory closings throughout the state, and to grave problems for older manufacturing cities. At the same time, a number of national corporations have moved their headquarters to Connecticut, creating new sky-

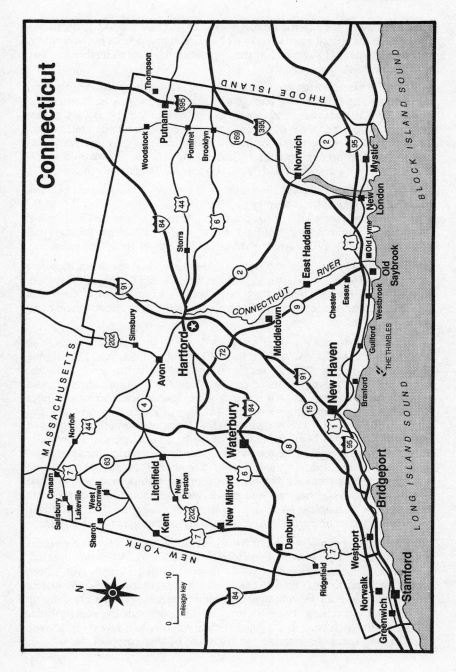

lines and new work in cities like Greenwich, Danbury and Stamford. As a whole, the state continues to be one of the most prosperous in the country, although substantial segments of the population have been unable to share in the wealth.

Despite the importance of manufacturing, a large proportion of the land has remained rural, with vast acreage set aside for recreation and open space in more than 50 state parks and forests, as well as municipal parks and nature preserves. These peaceful oases are scattered throughout the state: along the shoreline, in the pastoral northern corners, even in the more populated valleys near the three largest cities. Bridgeport, with 143,000 people, is followed closely by Hartford and New Haven—all human in scale.

The landscape ranges from a level shoreline dotted with small beaches and coves through rolling country to the green-clad mountains of the northwest corner and gentle hills of the northeast. At the center is the Connecticut River Valley, once fertile farmland whose traditional crops, tobacco and corn, have largely given way to suburban growth in recent decades.

The central section of the state is home to several major universities: Yale in New Haven, Wesleyan in Middletown, Trinity College in Hartford. New London, on the southeastern coast, boasts Connecticut College and the Coast Guard Academy, while the University of Connecticut's main campus is in Storrs.

Though distances are short, the climate varies by several degrees from north to south, with snow and ice lasting longest in Litchfield County, the northwestern region. Winter temperatures can go below zero at times, though seldom for long; summer can be occasionally hot and humid. And yet each season brings its own rewards and calendar of attractions. Winter turns the hilly regions into scenes of skating and ice fishing on lakes and ponds, while downhill skiers rush to half a dozen well-equipped areas and cross-country buffs head for countless trails. In spring, the dogwood's snowy blossoms brighten the roadways, and mountain laurel, the state flower, paints hillsides the very palest pink. Summer is the favorite vacation season, a time of festivals and fairs, swimming, fishing and boating, and crowds of visitors at beaches and parks. Fall, some say, shows the state at its best, with maples, oaks, dogwoods, ferns, even the dreaded poison ivy turning the countryside into a symphony of orange, red and gold.

Connecticut can be explored from several points of entry, but chances are that visitors will be coming in from New York state. With this in mind, the chapter has been organized as one lengthy, S-shaped path, going from southwest to northwest; then to the Hartford area, more or less the state's center; south to New Haven; then east along the shore with a brief jog up the Lower Connecticut River Valley; finishing up with the scenic, little-known northeast corner. It's a journey that could take a few days, a week or a lifetime spent discovering the treasures of this compact state.

Easy Living

Transportation

ARRIVAL

Four major highways thread their way through the state. **Route 95**, the Connecticut Turnpike, runs along the shoreline, all the way from the New York state line to Rhode Island. At New Haven, it connects with **Route 91**, which heads north through Hartford into Massachusetts. **Route 84** enters the state at Danbury and runs northeast through Hartford to join with the Massachusetts Turnpike at Sturbridge. **Route 15**, the celebrated Merritt Parkway, winds its scenic way a few miles north of Route 95, then swings north at New Haven to join with Route 91. The major highways are all linked to each other by north–south roads set at convenient intervals.

Route 1, the old Boston Post Road, goes through the heart of all the coastline communities paralleling Route 95. Unfortunately, most of Route 1 has turned into a commercial strip, with just a few old buildings here and there to recall the historic roadway it once was.

BY AIR

The major airport in the state is **Bradley International Airport** in Windsor Locks, 12 miles north of Hartford. Airlines flying into Bradley include American Airlines, Business Express, Continental Airlines, Delta Airlines, Eastern Airlines, Northwest Airlines, Piedmont Airlines, Trans World Airlines, United Airlines and USAir.

Several bus and shuttle companies provide ground transportation from Bradley Airport. Check with the following for schedules and destinations: **Airport Taxi Limousine** (203-627-3210), **Cotter Executive Sedan** (203-522-2442) and **Peter Pan Bus Lines** (203-627-3210).

Taxi service (203-666-6666) is available 24 hours a day, with uniform flat rates to any destination within Connecticut.

Three smaller airports offer limited service. **Groton–New London Airport**, on the southeastern coast, is serviced by Continental Airlines and USAir.

At Bridgeport's **Igor Sikorsky Memorial Airport**, scheduled flights are offered by Business Express, Continental Express and USAir Express.

Tweed–New Haven Airport is serviced by Continental Express, United Airlines and USAir Express.

Residents of the southwestern section of Connecticut tend to use New York City's two airports, **La Guardia** and **John F. Kennedy**. They are crowded and frantic, but all the airlines fly there; they are less than an hour's drive from the Connecticut line (more at peak traffic time) and connected by frequent limousine service. For information, call **Connecticut Limousine Service** (203-853-3103).

BY BUS

Greyhound/Trailways (800-237-8211) and **Bonanza** (800-556-3815) bus lines provide scheduled interstate service for most points in Connecticut. Greyhound offers service from the following terminals: Bridgeport (203-835-1123), New Haven (203-772-2470), Hartford (203-522-9267), New Milford (203-354-9388) and New London (203-447-3841).

BY TRAIN

Metro North (New Haven Line) (800-638-7646) runs hourly trains (more frequent at commuting time, morning and evening) from New York City's Grand Central Station to New Haven, making stops at all the coastal towns on the way, with connecting service from Stamford to New Canaan, South Norwalk to Danbury and Bridgeport to Waterbury. At New Haven, Metro North connects with **Amtrak's** (800-872-7245) main line to Boston, which stops along the shore at Old Saybrook, New London and Mystic. Also at New Haven, Amtrak links with service to Hartford. Amtrak's conventional service from Washington to Boston makes Connecticut stops at Stamford, Bridgeport and New Haven.

BY FERRY

Two auto ferry lines operate daily, year-round, from points on Long Island in New York state across Long Island Sound, to the Connecticut shore—a pretty ride, indeed. The trip from Port Jefferson, New York to Bridgeport, Connecticut takes approximately an hour and 20 minutes (203-367-3043); Orient Point, New York to New London, Connecticut takes about the same amount of time (203-443-5281). You'll need a reservation if you want to bring your car along.

CAR RENTALS

At Bradley International Airport, you'll find the following car rental agencies represented: **Avis Rent A Car** (203-627-3500), **Budget Rent A Car** (203-627-3660), **Dollar Rent A Car** (203-627-9048), **Hertz Rent A Car** (203-627-3850) and **National Car Rental** (203-627-3470).

PUBLIC TRANSPORTATION

The **Norwalk Transit District** (203-853-3338) has city buses, some of which meet Metro North trains at the railroad station.

Connecticut Transit Company (203-525-9181) operates frequent buses within the city of Hartford and offers service to outlying towns such as Windsor, New Britain, Middletown, Manchester and the Farmington Valley communities of Avon, Canton, Farmington and Simsbury.

Connecticut Transit Company also services the New Haven area (203-624-0151) with city buses as well as buses that go to East Haven, West

Haven, Milford, Cheshire, Waterbury and Wallingford, and frequent commuter buses to the shoreline communities of Guilford, Madison and Clinton. **Dattco Bus Company** (800-382-0023) operates buses that go from downtown New Haven east along Route 1, making stops along the way to Old Saybrook.

The **Southeast Area Transit District** (203-886-2631) runs buses that connect New London, Norwich, Groton, East Lyme, Jewett City, Montville and parts of Mystic.

TOURS

In Hartford, guided walking tours are offered on Sundays from June through October by the **Greater Hartford Architecture Conservancy** (278 Farmington Avenue; 203-525-0279).

In New Haven, visitors can tour the **Yale University campus** (Visitor Information Office, Phelps Gateway, 344 College Street; 203-432-2302) on guided walks that cover much of the downtown area.

Heritage Trails (P.O. Box 138, Farmington, CT 06034; 203-677-8867), a privately owned concern, offers daily scheduled tours of Hartford and vicinity year-round, as well as less frequent visits to other parts of the state.

Hotels

Connecticut accommodations are as diverse as the state itself. You'll find modern hotels and motels close to the highways, resorts and spas, country inns that go back to stagecoach days and a recent flowering of bed and breakfasts in small towns and some cities.

Prices tend to be high. It's seldom easy to find a good budget room—though we've dug up quite a few—and most recommended facilities fall into the moderate to deluxe categories, with some ultra-deluxe thrown in for special occasions. Fortunately, the state abounds in parks and campgrounds, a good solution for outdoor buffs short on cash.

SOUTHWESTERN CONNECTICUT HOTELS

Surrounded by extensive, stately homes in an exclusive part of Greenwich known as Belle Haven, **The Homestead Inn** (420 Field Point Road; 203-869-7500) first saw life in 1799 as a farmhouse. It was converted to an inn 50 years later and eventually acquired a jaunty cupola, a Victorian wraparound porch and two outbuildings that also offer accommodations. A recent million-dollar renovation supervised by designer John Saladino brought everything up-to-date, creating a graceful, sophisticated country inn with 23 guest rooms, ample public spaces and a three-star restaurant, all embellished with carefully chosen antiques. Deluxe to ultra-deluxe.

Set proudly among the tall new office towers of downtown Stamford, the **Stamford Marriott** (2 Stamford Forum; 203-357-9555) boasts more than 500 elegant rooms and such amenities as an indoor-outdoor pool, racquetball courts, a rooftop jogging track and a revolving restaurant with views of Long Island Sound. It may not be everyone's ideal vacation hideaway, but its closeness to Route 95, the railroad station, cultural offerings and a major shopping mall makes it attractive. Ultra-deluxe.

Silvermine Tavern (Silvermine and Perry avenues, Norwalk; 203-847-4558) has a special charm that spells New England, even though it's just a hop from the New York state line. Well-known for its restaurant, this picturesque cluster of rambling, circa-1785 frame buildings offers ten comfortable bedrooms appropriately but not lavishly furnished with country antiques. Overlooking the mill pond and its waterfall, the complex is at the crossroads of a woodsy residential community. Continental breakfast; deluxe in price.

A clutch of motels lines Route 1, the old Boston Post Road and now the area's crowded commercial strip. For one that's clean, quiet and operated by the same family for over 30 years—they live on the premises—try the **Garden Park Motel** (351 Westport Avenue, Norwalk; 203-847-7303). Their 21 units all have air-conditioning, good bathrooms and firm mattresses; there's even a picnic table under a shady tree for the guests' use. Fancy, it's not, but it's budget-priced in an area that tends to be expensive.

The Inn at Longshore (260 Compo Road South, Westport; 203-226-3316) is an unusual place to stay: a 12-room inn with restaurant, lounge and banquet facilities in the midst of a town-owned golf course and park, with lawns that sweep down to Long Island Sound. The rooms (three of them are suites that can sleep six) are almost an afterthought, but they're tastefully done, with up-to-date bathrooms and views of white sails dancing on blue water. Guests may use town facilities on payment of a fee. Deluxe, with continental breakfast.

In serene Ridgefield, set behind a wide lawn and ancient trees, sits **West Lane Inn** (22 West Lane; 203-438-7323), a gracious dowager of a place built as a home in the early 1800s, embellished in the Victorian era and then converted to an inn in the late 1970s. There's a wide porch that wraps around two sides, with colorful hanging baskets and wicker furniture for lazy summer days. A great carved oak staircase leads up to 20 generous-sized rooms. All show restrained elegance, and each is individually designed with plush carpeting, fine upholstered pieces and period-style furniture. Continental breakfast; ultra-deluxe.

The Elms (500 Main Street, Ridgefield; 203-438-2541), operating as an inn since 1799, has been run by only four families in all these years. Today, the famed restaurant occupies most of the main building, with four bedrooms and one suite up a steep, cramped flight of stairs. The annex offers 16 accommodations—three of them suites—which are elegantly carpeted and appointed with four-poster and canopied beds, attractive stenciled wall-papers and period furniture. The rooms over the restaurant are more casual, with rag rugs, hand-stenciled borders on the ceilings and bathrooms sporting a "country" look. Deluxe, breakfast included.

NORTHWEST CORNER HOTELS

Each of the inns studded around Lake Waramaug—a zigzagged, three-mile long body of water that has drawn visitors since the mid-1800s—has a distinct personality, and its own dedicated fans. Here's a selection:

Boulders Inn (Route 45, New Preston; 203-868-0541) offers 17 rooms, six in the picturesque, turn-of-the-century main house and the rest in contemporary cottages set in the hill that rises immediately behind the inn. The rooms are done with flair; those in the stone-and-shingle main house have antique furniture and quilts, while the cottage rooms boast freestanding fireplaces. There's tennis on the premises, hiking on wooded trails and a small private beach with boats for the guests' use. Breakfast and dinner are included in the price of the room. Ultra-deluxe.

The **Hopkins Inn** (New Preston; 203-868-7295) was named for the family who settled the northern shore of the lake in 1847, built a great rambling clapboard home and took in lodgers who came up from the city in the summer. Today, the graceful yellow home is best known for its restaurant, but it does rent nine rooms and an apartment on the second and third floors. The rooms are bright, with colonial-style wallpaper and country antiques—comfortable, not dramatic. Two share a bath, the others have their own, with old-fashioned tub or stall shower. Downstairs, a shaded terrace high over the lake affords spectacular views. The adjoining hillside is owned by Hopkins Vineyards, where visitors can taste and purchase local wines. Moderate in price.

The **Inn on Lake Waramaug** (New Preston; 203-868-0563) boasts 23 guest rooms in three buildings: the main house, circa 1780, and two guest houses of later vintage. It's a little more formal than other lake hostelries, with rooms designed by professional decorators, an imposing dining room and amenities that include an indoor pool and a sauna. There's also tennis and a small sandy beach where refreshments are served, including lunchtime barbecues on summer weekends. The ultra-deluxe rates include breakfast and dinner.

Atha House (Wheaton Road, New Preston; 203-355-7387), a cozy Cape Cod-style inn, is convenient to galleries and antique stores. This bed and breakfast has three rooms looking out on a big yard with evergreen, silver birch and dogwood trees as well as a Connecticut stone fence. There's a fireplace and piano in the living room. Moderate.

More cost-conscious travelers wishing to stay near the lake, yet loathe roughing it at Lake Waramaug State Park, will find four bed-and-breakfast rooms about a mile up the hill at **Constitution Oak Farm** (Beardsley Road,

Kent; 203-354-6495). It's a rambling 1830s farmhouse overlooking ten acres of corn, and its name comes from a majestic oak tree said to descend from the legendary one in which Connecticut's colonial charter was concealed. Two downstairs rooms have baths; those on the second floor share. Breakfast is in the guests' own living room. The owner collects many and sundry things—a boon to some, but irksome to those who dislike clutter. Moderate.

For visitors who prefer to stay in Litchfield, the area's most visited town, there's a choice of two inns, one old, one new but colonial in feeling. The **Litchfield Inn** (Route 202; 203-567-4503), built circa 1980, works hard at being graciously New England even as it highlights facilities for conferences and banquets. Its 31 rooms are spacious and well appointed, with elegant bathrooms. Two units even have a dry bar. A continental breakfast is provided, and there's an elevator—a rare commodity among country inns. Deluxe.

Toll Gate Hill Inn (Route 202, Litchfield; 203-567-4545), built in 1745, is listed on the National Register of Historic Places as The Captain William Bull Tavern. As befits a tavern, you enter through the bar, and you can feel the pride of place in the fine way paneling and fireplaces have been restored. There's a top-rated restaurant. The 20 bedrooms are stylishly decorated with four-poster and canopied beds, authentic wallpapers and antique tables and chests. Breakfast; deluxe to ultra-deluxe.

The **Blackberry River Inn** (Route 44, Norfolk; 203-542-5100), built in 1763, is also listed on the National Register of Historic Places. Set on 17 acres of woodsy Berkshire foothills and complete with its own pool, tennis courts and cross-country ski trails, the inn offers 18 guest rooms, some in the handsome, light grey two-story main building and others in the adjoining carriage house. Most rooms have their own bath, with an occasional clawfoot tub; a few share. The public rooms have an informal, well-used atmosphere. Complimentary breakfast is served in the attractive dining rooms. Moderate to deluxe.

Manor House (Maple Avenue, Norfolk; 203-542-5690) is a sumptuous bed and breakfast, an 1898 Tudor-inspired Victorian mansion with windows designed by Tiffany—he was a family friend. Up the handsome, carved cherry wood staircase, nine guest rooms—all with private bath, some with balcony and fireplace—have been done to a turn in period elegance. There's even vintage clothing hung here and there, for decoration. A classy touch: breakfast—a very hearty one—can be served in the room, even in bed. Moderate to deluxe.

Located on a quiet street, the ten-unit **Milestone Motel** (146 South Pomperaug Avenue, Woodbury; 203-263-2800) is within walking distance of a golf driving range, antique stores and good restaurants. Wood-paneled rooms are comfortably furnished with wall-to-wall carpet and long bureaus. Lake swimming and skiing are nearby. Budget to moderate.

HARTFORD AREA HOTELS

For budget lodgings in the Farmington Valley, the place to go is the **Hillside Motel** (Route 44, Canton; 203-693-4951), 17 miles west of Hartford. It's family owned and operated, and its 14 simple rooms—all with bath, two with cooking facilities—are clean, neat and air-conditioned, though there's nothing fancy. What's more, it's close to that great canoeing and tubing section of the Farmington River known as Satan's Kingdom.

Avon Old Farms Hotel (junction of Routes 10 and 44, Avon; 203-677-1651), once a small motel, has grown gradually into its present role as a major country hotel with 158 rooms. This multiwinged hostelry has a dining room, an outdoor pool, well-landscaped grounds and great views over woods and stream. Rates range from moderate in the older motel— freshly painted and comfortable—to deluxe in the three-story main wing, where the rooms are done in old New England elegance and the carpeted staircase in the lofty lobby just begs for Scarlett O'Hara to sweep down.

If a truly exquisite restoration makes your heart sing, then the **Simsbury 1820 House** (731 Hopmeadow Street, Route 10, Simsbury; 203-658-7658) is a must. Set on a knoll in the center of this historic small town, the three-story, four-chimney brick building was home to generations of distinguished Americans, including Gifford Pinchot, known as the father of the conservation movement. No pains were spared in transforming the graceful grey mansion and the nearby carriage house into a 34-room inn with a fine restaurant. Each room is carpeted and furnished with antiques, with imaginative use made of the nooks, crannies and arched windows. Deluxe to ultra-deluxe.

Behind the ornate 19th-century brick facade of the **J. P. Morgan Hotel at Goodwin Square** (1 Haynes Street, Hartford; 203-246-7500) in the heart of downtown, all is brand new. Once a distinguished apartment house, a local landmark, it was entirely rebuilt inside and appointed in a style that would have pleased the Hartford-born financier the hotel honors. Fine reproductions grace the 125 rooms and suites, service is personal and the ambience is gracious and subdued. Public spaces are adorned with works borrowed from the nearby Wadsworth Atheneum, one of the country's finest museums. Rates are ultra-deluxe but lower on weekends and worth it if a touch of urban elegance fits in your plans.

A luxury downtown hotel that offers moderate, attractive weekend packages is the **Sheraton Hartford** (Trumbull Street at Civic Center Plaza; 203-728-5151), joined by a bridgeway to the Civic Center's many attractions. The Sheraton's rooms, almost 400 and generous in size, tend toward reproductions of antiques and flowered prints—*nouvelle* New England. There's an outdoorsy looking indoor pool, a restaurant and, right next door, the award-winning Hartford Stage Company—food for both the body and the soul.

Budget accommodations can be found on the outskirts of Hartford off Route 91 at exit 27. Of several chain motels, the **Susse Chalet** (185 Brainard Road; 203-525-9306) seemed the most attractive, with an airy lobby, good size outdoor pool and standard motel rooms: clean and small but adequate.

NEW HAVEN AREA HOTELS

New Haven boasts a luxury urban inn, **The Inn at Chapel West** (1201 Chapel Street; 203-777-1201), housed in a restored 19th-century residence. The ten bedrooms, each with its own bath, are elegantly appointed with antique furnishings of different periods; the beds are four-posters, shiny brass or hand-turned wood, covered with colorful quilts or coverlets. Complimentary breakfast is served in the dining room; refreshments, in the late afternoon, are in the parlor. All this comfort and graciousness is just three blocks from Yale's campus and New Haven green. Ultra-deluxe.

The **Colony Inn** (1157 Chapel Street; 203-776-1234) is a modern, five-story hotel with attractive rooms done in contemporary style. Its convenient location makes it popular with Yale visitors as well as those sampling the city's theaters and museums. The Colony has its own indoor garage, a boon in the busy downtown area, as well as a restaurant and lounge with entertainment. Deluxe.

The historic **Hotel Duncan** (1151 Chapel Street; 203-787-1273), a landmark since 1894, has probably seen better days, yet it must be the best buy in town. Behind its handsome Romanesque facade rise five floors of neatly furnished, budget-to-moderate-priced rooms, a bit worn perhaps but clean, with old-fashioned baths. No air-conditioning here, just fans to keep you cool on a hot day, and the pleasure of being part of a tradition.

East of New Haven, the shoreline towns are well stocked with budget- and moderate-price motels close to Route 95. **Host Ways Motor Inn** (30 Frontage Road, East Haven, at exit 51; 203-469-5321), a family-run facility only seven miles from New Haven, has 83 moderate-priced rooms, a pool and complimentary breakfast. It's also near Tweed–New Haven Airport and the popular Trolley Museum.

LOWER CONNECTICUT RIVER VALLEY HOTELS

Westbrook is blessed with that rarest of pearls, a bed-and-breakfast set right on the sea. At **Talcott House** (161 Seaside Avenue; 203-399-5020)— an 1890 dormered, shingled home—guests can cross the quiet street and go swimming, or they can sit in the spacious, informal living room and admire the view. The seven guest rooms range in size and price: four that front on the sea and have private baths are deluxe; the three moderate-priced smaller ones share. All are tastefully done with country antiques.

For accommodations in the budget-to-modertate range, it would be hard to beat the **Maples Motel** (★) (1935 Boston Post Road, Westbrook; 203-399-9345). Forty years of tender loving care by the same family have made it grow into a woodsy, attractive poolside complex of 18 units—some with cooking facilities—and seven "cottagettes" that can be rented by the week. Guests share a picnic area and may use a private sandy beach, minutes away.

For many travelers, the words Connecticut Valley are interchangeable with the **Griswold Inn** (36 Main Street, Essex; 203-767-1812). "The Gris" is a legend; a white, rambling landmark on the picture-postcard main street since 1776. Serving as a meeting place for the town, it's Olde New England to its very bones, with a taproom and restaurant, a gallery of vintage marine art and nightly musical jamborees. Twenty-five guest rooms and suites, moderate to deluxe, are housed in four period buildings. Some are remodeled; in others, the floors list to port or starboard, as if to remind you of the town's maritime past and its nautical present as well.

Copper Beech Inn (46 Main Street, Ivoryton; 203-767-0330) is a classic: a sedate, gracious country inn with an award-winning French restaurant in what was once the home of a wealthy ivory merchant—the trade that put this little town on the map. Four of the 13 rooms are in the main house, meticulously appointed all, with charming old-fashioned baths and antique beds. Set back near the woods, the Carriage House has been remodeled with exquisite taste and a sense of romance, and its nine bedrooms all have french doors leading out to a deck with sylvan vistas. Deluxe to ultra-deluxe.

Antique lovers won't know where to look first at **Riverwind** (209 Main Street, Deep River; 203-526-2014). This bed and breakfast, in the center of one of the valley's quieter towns, is chockablock with country antiques and folk art—some from the owner's own family, others trophies of forays around the country. Rates for the eight attractively furnished, hand-stenciled rooms, all with bath, are deluxe, and include a prodigious breakfast that reflects the innkeeper's southern background. Out in the driveway, a chauffeured 1960 Austin Princess awaits the pleasure of guests.

What could be more pleasant than to waltz across the street to **Bishopsgate Inn** (Goodspeed Landing, East Haddam; 203-873-1677) after enjoying a nostalgic musical at Goodspeed Opera House? Or any time, in fact. The early 19th-century shipbuilder's house stands tall and handsome on a landscaped knoll, and the six moderate-priced guest rooms, all with theatrical names on the door, are done in good taste, with bathrooms carved out of the oddest places. Would you believe a former closet, for one? Breakfast is family-style, served in the spacious country kitchen.

The **Bee and Thistle Inn** (100 Lyme Street, Old Lyme; 203-434-1667) is on every list of all-time favorites. A gambrel-roofed, mid-18th-century house, it's right next door to the Florence Griswold Museum on the town's major street, yet it's set back on extensive landscaped grounds that sweep down to the Lieutenant River, a branch of the Connecticut. Most of the ground floor is devoted to the popular restaurant. Twelve tasteful, uncluttered rooms occupy the second and third floors, each with its own decor, all with bath except for two that share. Also available is the one-bedroom "Innkeepers Cottage" featuring a library with fireplace, kitchen and glass-enclosed sitting room. Rooms in the main house are moderate to deluxe; the cottage is ultra-deluxe.

MYSTIC AREA HOTELS

Don't be lulled by the abundance of accommodations around New London and Mystic; in season, a good room can still be hard to get. There's a big cluster of motels at exit 90 off Route 95, ranging in price from moderate to deluxe (less in winter and spring). Some other options, all within a few miles of the main attractions:

The **Lighthouse Inn** (6 Guthrie Place, New London; 203-443-8411) was the summer home of a steel magnate who decided, in 1902, to build a Spanish-style stucco "cottage" in the meadows overlooking the sea. The meadows have been rezoned residential, but the mansion makes an opulent 50-room inn, with a fine restaurant and individually designed, generous bedrooms with water views, antique furnishings and unusual details. Deluxe to ultra-deluxe, with breakfast.

The cozy **Shore Inne** (★) (54 East Shore Avenue, Groton Long Point; 203-536-1180) is a seven-room bed and breakfast set among small homes right on the water—"like being in grandmother's cottage," the owner says. Grandma should consider new mattresses. Other than that, it's a great place to be: the rates are moderate, or budget if you share a bath, the views are splendid and you can walk to any of three private beaches nearby.

The **Inn at Mystic** (Routes 1 and 27, Mystic; 203-536-9604) is a hilltop potpourri of accommodations: a fine motel and two historic buildings for a total of some 50 deluxe to ultra-deluxe rooms. The exquisitely landscaped complex also includes a restaurant, tennis courts, a pool and a dock with sailboats and canoes. Rooms are individually designed and old-time in feeling, even in the motel. Not so the bathrooms, which are luxuriously up-to-date. Despite the feeling of elegant seclusion, you're only a mile away from Mystic Seaport.

At the **Whaler's Inn** (20 East Main Street, Mystic; 203-536-1506) you'll find a variety of rooms priced moderate through deluxe, housed in the inn itself and two motor courts. You couldn't be more "downtown": the famed bridge is within a few feet. There are two restaurants attached to the inn and a few rooms with fine views of the Mystic River and the Seaport, just a half-mile away. There's also an occasional spot of peeling paint, a few worn rugs, some metal stall showers, as well as a pleasantly informal, unpretentious atmosphere throughout the place.

Two gems lie on the outskirts of Mystic. **Applewood Farms Inn** (★) (528 Colonel Ledyard Highway, Ledyard; 203-536-2022), an early 19th-century farmhouse complete with corn crib and barn, is a few miles north of Route 95 and the visiting crowds. Set on 33 acres and surrounded by farms, this is one bed and breakfast that actually welcomes children, who'll be enchanted by the pony, sheep and goats here and the 50 Arabian show horses next door. The house, a National Historic Register Landmark, is blessed with magnificent fireplaces, and the three common rooms and six guest rooms have distinct personalities, highlighted by an eclectic selection of period pieces. Breakfasts are uniformly bountiful, true country meals. Deluxe.

The **Palmer Inn** (25 Church Street, Noank; 203-572-9000) is southern in inspiration, a columned, porticoed mansion built in this captivating little community in 1907. Here all is graciousness and Victorian elegance—carved mahogany paneling, stained glass, Oriental carpets on polished wood floors—in the main hall, the parlor and the sitting room as well as the six spacious bedrooms up the wide, curving stairs. Rates, as befits the atmosphere, are deluxe and ultra-deluxe; continental breakfast.

NORTHEAST CORNER HOTELS

The **King's Inn** (5 Heritage Road, Putnam; 203-928-7961) makes a handy jumping-off place for exploring the "quiet corner" of the state. In decor, it tries to re-create old-time New England, but what it does best is supply 40 pleasant, moderate-priced motel rooms, adding a pool and two restaurants for your convenience.

The **Ebenezer Stoddard House** (Route 171 and Perrin Road, West Woodstock; 203-974-2552) was built in the early 1800s by a former lieutenant governor of the state, and was later used as an inn. The present owners have lovingly restored it as a bed and breakfast with four moderate to deluxe bedrooms, each with its own' bath and working fireplace and individual touches like queen-sized canopy beds, hand-stenciled floors and collectibles and antiques of all kinds.

In recent years numerous new bed and breakfasts—small, for the most part—have sprouted in this little known area, where accommodations were once hard to find. The **Northeast Connecticut Visitors District** (P.O. Box 598, Putnam, CT 06206; 203-928-1228) will help visitors find one that suits their needs. One with a faithful following is **Altnaveigh Inn** (Route 195, Storrs; 203-429-4490), a 1734 farmhouse less than two miles from the University of Connecticut. The six well cared for rooms are located above a popular restaurant and are simply furnished. Moderate.

Several bed and breakfast reservation services will supply additional suggestions for accommodations throughout the state. Two of them are **Nutmeg Bed and Breakfast Agency** (P.O. Box 1117, West Hartford, CT 06107; 203-236-6698) and **Covered Bridge Bed and Breakfast Reservation Service** (P.O. Box 447, Norfolk, CT 06058; 203-542-5944).

Restaurants

Connecticut is quite sophisticated when it comes to food. You'll find lobster, of course, and other New England favorites, but also fine French cuisine and ethnic offerings from most parts of the world, reflecting the state's eclectic makeup.

SOUTHWESTERN CONNECTICUT RESTAURANTS

For a glimpse of Connecticut dining at its classiest, start with the **Homestead Inn** (420 Field Point Road, Greenwich; 203-869-7500). A 1799 farmhouse turned hostelry and exquisitely restored, the inn stands on a knoll in an exclusive residential area—a treat to the eye as well as the palate. In the restaurant, the ambience is classic French and subdued; the fare is French, sophisticated and up-to-date. Tables sparkle with Wedgwood and fine glass; service is proper. Prices, you might have already guessed, are ultra-deluxe.

Among the myriad Italian restaurants in this part of the state, **Il Falco** (59 Broad Street, Stamford; 203-327-0002) is considered one of the best. Set in the heart of the city, this pleasant spot without glitz or pretension serves regional specialties that don't appear on every menu—gnocchi, *vitello tonnato*, fish in the style of various Italian cities—all cooked with imagination and care. Deluxe.

A Fairfield County grande dame, the **Roger Sherman Inn** (195 Oenoke Road, New Canaan; 203-966-4541) stands in the heart of an attractive residential community. Once a classic country inn and restaurant known for American fare, the Roger Sherman has been totally—and tastefully—renovated and dedicated to French cuisine. The menu leans toward Mediterranean dishes, with game and seafood high on the list of favorites. Deluxe to ultra-deluxe.

South Norwalk, or SoNo, a restored 19th-century neighborhood, is a good place to window-shop for lunch or dinner. On rejuvenated Washington Street and the adjoining still-in-process Main Street, you can read menus in restaurant windows and decide if you're in the mood for Italian, French, Mexican, Chinese, seafood or sandwiches, funky or chic. There's been some turnover among the tenants in this historic district, but **Jeremiah Donovan's** (138 Washington Street, South Norwalk; 203-838-3430) has been a lively meeting place for over a century, a wood-paneled Victorian saloon with unpretentious, budget-priced food—good burgers, salads, sandwiches, their special chowder and hearty bowls of chili—and a prodigious selection of beers. A collection of vintage prizefighter photos adorns the walls, legacy of a regional champ who owned the place many decades ago.

La Provence (96 Washington Street, South Norwalk; 203-855-8958) is a cheerful, small bistro with brick walls and butcher-block tables that offers well-prepared French regional food at deluxe prices. Duck is a specialty, in many guises; crusty French breads, as well as tarts and pies, are made on the spot and are very good.

Silvermine Tavern (Silvermine, Norwalk; 203-847-4558) is a landmark: a country inn, popular for decades, with several antique-filled dining rooms and a romantic terrace for summer dining, overlooking a waterfall and pond. Offerings fit the colonial atmosphere: roast beef, seafood, poultry, the traditional old-time lobster pie, priced deluxe to ultra-deluxe. The daily Innkeeper's Dinner is a bargain, as are Sunday brunch and Thursday-night buffet.

Restaurants come and go in Fairfield County with lightning speed. One that has consistently won awards and led the pack for the past 20 years is **Le Chambord** (1572 Post Road, Westport; 203-255-2654), where classic French cuisine takes precedence over dazzling decor. The setting is dignified and subdued, the price deluxe and ultra-deluxe, except for a special complete dinner (weeknights only) that's moderate and bountiful indeed. Specialties include mussels, daily fish offerings, rack of lamb and, among the desserts, individual chocolate or Grand Marnier soufflés.

Donuts don't often merit hymns of praise, but at the **Coffee An' Donut Shop** (341 North Main Street, Westport; 203-227-3808) they are handmade by the owner, with lots of TLC, each morning before 7 a.m. The resulting confections—glazed, sugared, twirled with cinnamon, rolled in thick chocolate or filled with raspberry jelly—have made addicts for miles around and been dubbed best in the country by food critics of national renown.

Parc 1070 (The Bridgeport Hilton, 1070 Main Street; 203-334-1234) and the hotel that houses it are stepping-stones on the way to the long-awaited renaissance of downtown Bridgeport. The emphasis is on steaks, chops and prime rib roasts—back to the basics! Prices are moderate, for food that is expertly prepared and served in bountiful portions—good reasons for dining in an area not previously known for its cuisine.

For a festive occasion, try **The Elms** (500 Main Street, Ridgefield; 203-438-2541), which has been greeting travelers since 1799. The handsome old white inn has changed a lot since then, needless to say. Its dining rooms are now gracious and serene, all flickering candles, flowered china and snow white linens, and serve impeccably prepared continental fare. Veal is always a specialty, and seasonal game dishes such as pheasant and venison are widely praised. Deluxe to ultra-deluxe.

NORTHWEST CORNER RESTAURANTS

Le Bon Coin (Route 202, New Preston; 203-868-7763) serves deluxe French entrées such as dover sole Riviera, sweetbreads with various garnishes, châteaubriand, game and seasonal specialties. Located in a cottage reminiscent of the south of France, the two small dining rooms are decorated with impressionist paintings á la Toulouse Lautrec.

Each of the several inns around Lake Waramaug has its followers, who proclaim it the best. The **Hopkins Inn** (New Preston; 203-868-7295), a rambling, many-windowed mid-19th-century house, boasts a unique location, high on a hill overlooking sparkling blue water. On a warm day, sitting under the ancient trees on the terrace would be reason enough for deep content, but the eclectic continental menu casts its own spell. Austrian and Swiss traditions are emphasized; wienerschnitzel is a perennial favorite, as is trout, live from the inn's own tank, prepared *à la meunière* or *bleu*, the Swiss way. Deluxe.

Several area places feature both lunch and take-out foods—a pleasant thought on days that call for a picnic. **The Pantry** (Titus Square, Washington Depot; 203-868-0258), which doubles as a cookware shop and small restaurant, serves well-prepared, moderate-priced entrées such as ham-and-leek quiche or stuffed peppers, as well as homemade soups, salads and desserts. The **Litchfield Food Company** (West Street, On-the-Green, Litchfield; 203-567-3113) leans more toward elaborate sandwiches like country pâté or brie cheese and Black Forest ham. There is a bright, pleasant room with tables and a counter for ordering lunch to go. Budget to moderate.

Toll Gate Hill Inn (Route 202, Litchfield; 203-567-4545) is a 1745 tavern restored as an inn in admirably authentic fashion. Two intimate ground-floor dining rooms are most attractive, with dark, wide floor boards and paneling and just a few handsome antiques. Upstairs, the ballroom with its fieldstone fireplace and fiddlers' loft is used for Saturday dinner and Sunday brunch. Deluxe-priced meals feature American cuisine with European touches, including many unusual seafood entrées.

Freshfields (Route 128, West Cornwall; 203-672-6601) stands in a cluster of picturesque old houses built next to the much-photographed covered bridge that spans the Housatonic River. On a summery day, one can dine on a deck overlooking a little stream with emerald banks. The interior is attractive as well, featuring butcher-block tables graced with flowers and lacy curtains. True to the name, the offerings emphasize American country freshness, with seasonal produce and seafood delivered several times a week. Prices range from moderate to deluxe. The grilled fish and roast loin of pork are especially tasty.

Right on Main Street in the historic little town of Salisbury, you'll find the **Ragamont Inn** (10 Main Street; 203-435-2372), where you can dine on a sheltered terrace or in one of two antique-furnished dining rooms. The Swiss-inspired cuisine features veal dishes, with wienerschnitzel gaining the most requests. Homemade pasta is another specialty: black pepper fettucine is one of the chef's creations, served with scallops or shrimp. Prices are moderate to deluxe.

A welcome addition to good eating at the northernmost edge of the state is the **Cannery Café** (★) (85 Main Street, Canaan; 203-824-7333), where canning jars, old and new and in many colors, are part of the attractive, unassuming decor. Here American country cooking is practiced with imagination and skill. The chicken salad, for example, turns out to be grilled chicken breast, still warm when served over mixed greens and vegetables—a novel, fine-tasting dish. Moderate.

HARTFORD AREA RESTAURANTS

"It's not fancy," said our informant, "but everyone likes it." And so it seemed, since **The Pie Plate** (★) (265 West Main Street, Route 44, Avon; 203-674-0087) was crowded with a great variety of people. It offers tasty, homey fare at budget prices and in generous portions—thick soups, New England-style pot pies, a dozen dinner entrées and pies that really taste freshly baked. This Pie Plate, it turns out, has four siblings around the state, in Fairfield, Danbury, Vernon and Waterbury, creations of two Connecticut men devoted to affordable quality food. What an idea!

Apricots (1593 Farmington Avenue, Farmington; 203-673-5405) fronts a lively stretch of the Farmington River. You can sit on a riverbank terrace, drink or sandwich in hand, and almost feel the water as it leaps around shiny rocks. The ground floor of the old building, a former trolley stop, is devoted to a popular pub where the "happy hour" boasts a heaping tableful of complimentary food. Upstairs is the restaurant itself, an oasis of fine American

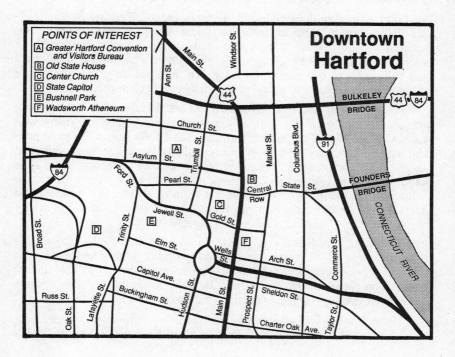

POINTS OF INTEREST
A Greater Hartford Convention and Visitors Bureau
B Old State House
C Center Church
D State Capitol
E Bushnell Park
F Wadsworth Atheneum

Downtown Hartford

cuisine where the ultra-deluxe entrées most in demand are rack of lamb and swordfish. The pub serves a budget-to-moderate-priced menu.

The restaurant at **Simsbury 1820 House** (731 Hopmeadow Street, Route 10, Simsbury; 203-658-7658) is in what was once the cellar of the lovely old mansion. Room dividers give the illusion of intimate dining rooms, enhanced by several distinct styles of decor: exposed brick walls with arches in one area; patterned wallpaper for another; traditional prints of hunting scenes highlighting a third. The atmosphere is elegant and serene, the cuisine continental, the price deluxe. An additional pleasure is a drink on the spacious wicker-furnished veranda overlooking the gardens.

Hartford wears many faces—Old New England as well as corporate glitz and ethnic exuberance; insurance capital as well as capital of the state. A judicious choice of eating places affords a glimpse into some of these worlds. **The Marble Pillar** (★) (22 Central Row; 203-247-4549) has been across the street from the Old State House since 1860, not long after construction of that stately building itself. It only serves breakfast and lunch nowadays, five days a week, plentiful, filling budget meals, German in origin—wursts, sauerbraten, sandwiches thick with meat. A dark wood bar serves as counter, and strangers share plain tables on crowded days. On the walls hang framed photographs of forgotten heroes and politicians. No frills, no polish, but fast service and a touch of the past.

Way up in ultra-deluxe land sits **L'Américain** (2 Hartford Square; 203-522-6500), said by some critics to be the finest restaurant in the state. An inspired version of French and continental cuisine is served impeccably in a series of intimate Queen Anne-style dining rooms carved out of—would you believe?—an old factory building. An herb garden greets the visitor at the door, a prelude to gastronomic delights that are to come.

A few blocks south of downtown, on and around Main Street, is an area that has sprouted some attractive new restaurants in recent years. **Max on Main** (205 Main Street, Hartford; 203-522-2530), one of the most popular with the upscale young crowd, serves eclectic American and continental dishes in an uncluttered, sleek space, contemporary in feeling though the building itself is 19th century. Entrées, ranging in price from moderate to deluxe, emphasize grilled meats and fish with trendy touches: multicolored lentil ragoût, for example, or papaya-tomato-mint sauce. Another specialty is the "stone pie" pizza, filled with a variety of exotic entries.

The **Congress Rotisserie** (7 Maple Avenue; 203-560-1965) does a lively business with a varied menu that highlights poultry and meat done on the spit but offers plentiful options—plentiful portions, too, at moderate prices. The place is open and airy, with wide windows over urban views of fine old houses—a good spot in which to get a feel for the city.

If a visit to the Wadsworth Atheneum is on your itinerary, consider staying for lunch at the **Museum Café** (600 Main Street; 203-728-5989). It's an attractive, restful room off the rotunda on the main floor, enhanced by a changing selection of prints or paintings. Open only for lunch, it offers a dozen entrées that include stir-fry vegetables, fresh fish, chicken and sandwiches with a gourmet touch. Budget to moderate.

When an inexpensive, quick meal is on the schedule, you might consider the food court at Civic Center or the handsomely restored Union Station, where various stands serve up Italian, Greek or Vietnamese food that you can take to a table at the glass-enclosed **Greenhouse Café**. Another option is the **Pavilion at State House Square** (203-241-0100), a stylish new office-and-retail complex whose second floor boasts a dozen eateries. One, **Boonoonoonoos** (Food Court at the Pavilion at State House Square; 203-524-8962)—which means wonderful in Jamaica—features favorites of the city's West Indian population, like curried chicken or goat, puffy cocoa bread and a variety of other ethnic foods.

NEW HAVEN AREA RESTAURANTS

Robert Henry's (1032 Chapel Street, New Haven; 203-789-1010) is for special occasions, as much for the superior French cuisine as for the setting: a tasteful, stately room with arched, stained-glass windows in a building dating to 1902 and once an exclusive club. Food, service and ambience have earned the restaurant numerous awards. Ultra-deluxe.

The Chapel Street area is so rich in theaters, museums and scenic vistas of Yale that it's become a spawning ground for restaurants. **Bruxelles Brasserie** (220 College Street, New Haven; 203-777-7752), in its black-and-white, stylish setting, specializes in roasted meat, fish and fowl, but you can also order pasta or pizza at almost any hour. Moderate.

Gentree Ltd. (194 York Street, New Haven; 203-562-3800) is housed in a wood-paneled, former men's clothing store across from the Yale campus. Now, students and residents crowd the popular restaurant, consuming vast amounts of ribs and other specialties, all well prepared and budget to moderate in price.

You'll find **Scoozzi's** (1104 Chapel Street, New Haven; 203-776-8268) down a flight of stone stairs, between the British Art Center and the Yale Repertory Theater. Location is everything, they say, but here the high-tech setting is attractive as well, and the trendy, Italian-inspired fare pleases the customers. Moderate to deluxe.

Louis Lunch (261 Crown Street, New Haven; 203-562-5507) is one of New Haven's claims to fame—it seems Louis Lassen was the man who first put ground-up beef between two halves of a bun, back in 1903. The small brick building is considered a landmark; in fact, it was moved some years ago to save it from incoming bulldozers. It's old New Haven, where people talk to strangers, and the hamburger—a very fine one—is king.

Pizza on Wooster Street is a must in New Haven—you'll find no disagreement on that. But whether Pepe's is better than Sally's, or vice versa, is cause for arguments in this city that is considered the pizza capital of the state. You'll find **Frank Pepe Pizzeria** at 157 Wooster Street (203-865-5762) and **Sally's Apizza** a few doors down on the same street at number 237 (203-624-5271), as well as many more Italian restaurants alongside these. Prices are budget to moderate at both establishments, and the lines are long but friendly. Maybe you'll try them both, and then decide.

As understated and attractive as the crafts complex that surrounds it, **Indulge** (★) (Branford Craft Village at Bittersweet Farm, Branford; 203-488-9457) is popular not just with those shopping for artwork here but also with residents who appreciate imaginative home cooking, varied daily. The fare is mostly vegetarian at lunch—soups, strudels, quiches—but includes meat, fowl and game on Friday and Saturday nights, when dinner is served. Desserts and breads are a specialty. Moderate.

The **Stony Creek Market** (★) (178 Thimble Island Road, Stony Creek; 203-488-0145) has as many enthusiasts as do the enchanting islands it overlooks. Locals and visitors drop in and order their favorites—three soups each day, unusual salads, breads, scones, muffins and cookies still warm from the oven—then take their choices to a table inside or on the deck. Pizza is available at dinner. Food, views and friendly atmosphere vie for the raves. Prices are moderate.

LOWER CONNECTICUT RIVER VALLEY RESTAURANTS

Seafood lovers think of Westbrook as the home of **Bill's Seafood Restaurant** (Boston Post Road at the Singing Bridge; 203-399-7224). Here at this informal spot, fried-clam aficionados gather inside or on the terrace overlooking the salt marsh. Fish, shrimp and crabmeat have a place on the menu, as do hot dogs and burgers for the landlubber who gets dragged along, but it's the sweet, plump, lightly fried clams that are the attraction. Budget to moderate.

Alongside Old Saybrook's still-operating turn-of-the-century railroad station is **P. F. Murphy** (Old Saybrook Station; 203-388-6611), a budget-to-moderate-priced restaurant offering Italian cuisine. Appointed with nautical decor, the menu features such entrées as pasta "Polo" (chicken with artichokes over linguini), grilled shrimp with lemon sauce and veal picatta.

Historic is a word used lightly around these parts, but surely it applies to the **Griswold Inn** (36 Main Street, Essex; 203-767-1812), established in 1776. Go for lunch, dinner, the famous Sunday "Hunt Breakfast" or a drink, so you can view the warren of wood-paneled, evocative rooms that tumble one into the other. Partake of the New England specialties and other Americana on which the "Gris" has built its reputation, it's an experience one shouldn't miss. Moderate to deluxe.

The **Copper Beech Inn** (46 Main Street, Ivoryton; 203-767-0330) is a landmark, a longtime favorite among followers of fine French cuisine. Set in a tree-shaded, 1890 home, it breathes Old World elegance and charm.

Sterling silver, fresh flowers and fine china grace the tables in the three dining rooms; European antiques and Oriental carpets set the stage. Behind the inn is the greenhouse with wicker tables and chairs for the Saturday-evening cocktail hour; all in all, a most elegant place. Despite ultra-deluxe prices, you'll have to reserve well in advance, at least on weekends.

Fiddlers (4 Water Street, Chester; 203-526-3210) is a pleasantly appointed, unpretentious place residents turn to when they want carefully prepared, really fresh seafood—chicken and meat, too—at prices that range from moderate to deluxe. Fish entrées change according to the market and can be ordered to your taste—sautéed, poached or mesquite-grilled.

The Wheat Market (4 Water Street, Chester; 203-526-9347) creates gourmet sandwiches, as well as changing entrées, salads, soups and a famed deep-dish pizza to eat at tables or take along on a picnic. With Gillette Castle State Park just a five-minute ferry ride away, that might be just the ticket on a nice day.

For years, **The Bee and Thistle Inn** (100 Lyme Street, Old Lyme; 203-434-1667) has been voted the most romantic restaurant in the state by readers of *Connecticut* magazine. It's true, the rambling rooms and porches exude an air of intimacy and warmth appealing to lovers, and other mortals as well. The offerings are elegantly served and very tasty: seafood, game, poultry, meats, each flavored with fresh herbs shipped in or picked from the sunken garden just outside the windows. Deluxe to ultra-deluxe.

MYSTIC AREA RESTAURANTS

Lunching at the **Lighthouse Inn** (6 Guthrie Place, New London; 203-443-8411), you'll glimpse an intriguing view of Long Island Sound between two rows of houses. These good-size 20th-century homes seem to be dollhouses, in contrast to the baronial grandeur of the inn's dining room—dark, heavy overhead beams and dark wainscoting, great fireplaces and heavy, almost grotesque chandeliers. Yet, though the dining rooms seat more than 200, business is brisk. And with good reason: the food is well prepared, heavy on seafood—a favorite around these parts. Moderate to deluxe.

For a meal or snacks at any time of day, the place to go, according to residents of the area, is **G. Williker's!** (156 Kings Highway, Groton, exit 86 on Route 95; 203-446-0660). It has a popular taproom and a friendly staff, the usual faux-Victorian decor and a variety of excellent burgers and all-American favorites such as tacos and pizza. Budget to moderate.

Restaurant Bravo Bravo (in the Whaler's Inn, 20 East Main Street, Mystic; 203-536-3228) features cuisine with Italian and French accents. Entrées include napoleons of veal stuffed with spinach and ricotta then covered with a chanterelle mushroom sauce or garlic shrimp sautéed with pancetta. During the summer, enjoy the outdoor café where you can watch the best show in town: the old drawbridge that opens every hour to let boats go through. The dining room is moderate to deluxe; café, budget to moderate.

If you're spending the day at Mystic Seaport, you'll want to know about **The Seamen's Inne** (65 Greenmanville Avenue; 203-536-9649), located next to the Seaport entrance. It's a large, busy place, built to resemble the New England-style structures nearby, and it specializes in the appropriate fare—basically seafood. Portions are ample, prices moderate to deluxe.

High on a knoll overlooking the harbor sits the **Flood Tide Restaurant** (Routes 1 and 27, Mystic; 203-536-8140), a favorite with visitors to the town. Part of The Inn at Mystic but set apart on the unusually handsome grounds, this bright, airy dining room offers an ambitious continental menu with something for every taste. Moderate to deluxe.

And then there's **Abbott's Lobster in the Rough** (117 Pearl Street, Noank; 203-536-7719), a legend in is own time, a place where dining informally means sitting at waterfront picnic tables or in the simple dining room and truly using your hands for all they're worth. There's chowder, steamed clams, mussels and shrimp, but it's the lobster that has made Abbott's famous for 40 years—caught in local waters, steamed to just the right degree of tenderness. On a summer day, you can expect a wait, maybe a long one. But who minds waiting, when there's a harbor full of boats and a picturesque village to delight? Moderate to deluxe.

In captivating Stonington, the **Harborview Restaurant** (60 Water Street; 203-535-2720) is considered one of the area's best. Classic French dishes rule the menu—bouillabaisse, mussels, veal in many guises. The ambience is elegant and subdued, the price deluxe to ultra-deluxe.

Right behind the Harborview, built on a pier, is **Skipper's Dock** (66 Water Street, Stonington; 203-535-2000), its sister restaurant. In this more casual spot, you can consume your fill of seafood on a terrace overhanging the water or in a glass-enclosed dining room decorated with buoys of all kinds. If you arrive by sea, you can tie up at no extra charge. Moderate to deluxe.

Randall's Ordinary (Route 2, North Stonington; 203-599-4540) is, in fact, unique. Everything on the menu at this inn-with-restaurant—that's what *ordinary* meant in days of yore—is cooked over the fire in authentic Early-American fashion. Guests are invited to stand before the three massive fireplaces and watch dinner cooking; then it's brought to the table by servers in period costumes. The backdrop for this gastronomic journey into the past is a landmark 17th-century country home listed on the National Register of Historic Places. The price is ultra-deluxe, but it does include soup, an entrée of poultry, meat or fish, and dessert.

NORTHEAST CORNER RESTAURANTS

In Thompson, there's an institution called the **Vernon Stiles Inn** (junction Routes 193 and 200; 203-923-9571). Built as a stagecoach tavern in 1814, it has played many roles since then, the current one being that of restaurant. It's a rambling, two-story structure—several dining areas filled with country antiques, old tavern signs and other landmarks of its colorful past. The food is typically American with continental overtones—steak, duckling, filet of sole. Moderate to deluxe.

If you're tooling around the "Quiet Corner" and feel a sudden yen for a real, old-fashioned roadside diner, **Zip's Diner** (Routes 12 and 101, Dayville [Killingly]; 203-774-6335) is the answer to your prayers. It's a legacy from the 1950s with a jukebox at every booth; a true formica-and-stainless-steel classic that serves up pot roast, roast turkey, eggs any way you like, pie and ice cream and lots of hot, strong coffee. All this at budget prices.

The Harvest at Bald Hill (Routes 169 and 171, South Woodstock; 203-974-2240) presents a menu that's as imaginative as its name. Set in a handsome dark red barn complete with cupola, the restaurant is owned by two award-winning chefs who believe in changing the menu with the seasons. It's excellent, intriguing continental cuisine. Moderate to deluxe.

A few miles from the University of Connecticut campus, and a favorite with the "UConn" crowd, is the **Mansfield Depot Restaurant** (57 Middle Turnpike, Route 44, Mansfield; 203-429-3663). The simple 1920s structure has been restored with good taste and restraint, in keeping with its origins as a small country station. The atmosphere is warm and comfortable and the food rates raves from faithful followers. It's regional American cuisine, with an emphasis on fresh fish, along with a choice of vegetarian entrées and specials. Moderate to deluxe.

The Great Outdoors

The Sporting Life

SALTWATER FISHING

Along the coast of Long Island Sound, fishing boats cast off daily with groups of passengers eager to try their luck. Among the party fishing boats that sail on specific schedules and can be boarded on first-come, first-served basis are the following: in New London, at Thamesport Landing, the **Wanderer** (203-443-8502); in Niantic, at Niantic Beach Marina, the **Black Hawk II** (203-443-3662), at Mijoy Dock, the **Mijoy/Mijoy 747** (203-443-0663), at Captain John's Dock, the **Sunbeam Express** (203-443-7259); in Groton, at Hel-Cat Dock, the **Hel-Cat II** (203-535-2066).

Charter fishing boats that can be booked by private groups are more numerous. A sampling follows: in Old Saybrook, at Saybrook Point Marina, the **Provider** (203-663-3099) and the **Sea Sprite** (203-669-9613); in New London, at Thamesport Landing, the **Lady Margaret** (203-433-8502), the **Playing Hookey** (203-433-8502) and the **Wanderer** (203-433-8502; in

Noank, at Noank Village Boatyard, the **Reelin'** (203-449-1980) and the **Trophy Hunter** (203-536-4460).

SAILING AND WINDSURFING

Sailing is a way of life along the Connecticut shoreline. Each harbor, big or small, shelters its own flotilla at the ready, and yet it's hard to find sailboats for rent. Here are a few suggestions: in Westport, you'll find windsurfers and small sailboats at **John Kantor's Longshore Sailing School** (260 Compo Road South; 203-226-4646). Windsurfing equipment can be rented at **Action Sports** (Old Saybrook; 203-388-1291). **Colvin Yachts** (Hammock Dock Road, Westbrook; 203-399-6251) offers a fleet of charter boats 22 to 36 feet in length; the smaller ones can be rented by the day, while the others are available only for a weekend or more. **Mystic Seaport** (203-572-0711) offers a different maritime experience, a sailing education program for young people aged 15 to 19 on the 61-foot schooner **Brilliant**. Youths act as crew for six-day trips, under professional supervision. An adult version of the project involves four-day stints, in spring and fall.

CANOEING AND KAYAKING

The Connecticut River lends itself to a variety of canoeing experiences, from guided overnight trips to rent-your-own. **North American Canoe Tours, Inc.** (65 Black Point Road, Niantic; 203-739-0791) handles both. You can find out about canoe camping at three state parks by writing the **Department of Environmental Protection** (Office of State Parks and Recreation, 165 Capitol Avenue, Hartford, CT 06106; 203-566-2304). For explorations of the Housatonic River by canoe or kayak, contact **Clarke Outdoors** (Route 7, Box 163, West Cornwall, CT 06796; 203-672-6365) or **Riverrunning Expeditions** (Main Street, Falls Village, CT 06031; 203-824-5579). You can paddle the waters of the Farmington River by day or on moonlit nights through the services of the **Main Stream Canoe Corp.** (Route 44, P.O. Box 448, New Hartford, CT 06057; 203-379-6657).

GOLF

Golf courses dot the Connecticut landscape like dandelions on a lawn in spring. Here's a selection of those open to the public: **E. Gaynor Brennan Golf Course** (451 Stillwater Road, Stamford; 203-324-4185) and **Ridgefield Golf Club** (545 Ridgebury Road, Ridgefield; 203-748-7008), both in Fairfield County. In the Northwest Corner you'll find **Stonybrook Golf Club** (263 Milton Road, Litchfield; 203-567-9977) and the **Canaan Country Club** (on Danbury Road off Route 7, Canaan; 203-354-9359). Three of the many in the Hartford area are **Bel Campo Golf Club** (Route 44, Avon; 203-678-1358), **Westwoods Golf Course** (Route 177, Farmington; 203-677-9192) and **Goodwin Park Golf Club** (Maple Avenue, Hartford; 203-525-3601). In New Haven, you can play 18 holes at the **Alling Memorial Golf Course** (35 Eastern Street; 203-787-8013); at Old Saybrook, you can tee off near the sea at **Fenwick Golf Club** (580 Maple Avenue; 203-388-2516); Stonington has the **Pequot Golf Club** (Wheeler Road; 203-535-1898). In scenic Woodstock, you'll want to try the **Harrisville Golf Course** (Harrisville Road; 203-928-6098).

SKIING

The state's ski areas improve on nature with snow-making machines. You'll find the best facilities and downhill trails at **Mohawk Mountain** (Great Hollow Road, off Route 4, Cornwall; 203-672-6100), **Powder Ridge** (99 Powder Hill Road, Middlefield; 203-349-3454) and **Ski Sundown** (off Route 219, New Hartford; 203-379-9851).

TENNIS

There's no dearth of tennis courts in the state—schools, universities, clubs, hotels and municipalities are well supplied—but many are out of bounds to the visitor. Each local parks and recreation department has its own rules; try calling when you come to town or ask your innkeeper or hotel desk person to make arrangements for you if they don't have their own court.

In New Haven, you can play at **Edgewood Park** (Whalley Avenue), **East Shore Park** (Woodward Avenue) and **Cross High School** (Mitchell Drive). For information, call the Recreation Division at 203-787-8538. Courts are open to the public at three of Hartford's parks: **Elizabeth Park West** (Prospect and Asylum streets), **Goodwin Park** (South Street and Maple Avenue) and **Keney Park** (Woodland and Greenfield streets). The city's Parks and Recreation Department can be reached at 203-722-6495. Outside the city, you can play at **Sycamore Hills Park** (West Avon Road, Avon; 203-677-2634) and at **Simsbury Farms Recreation Complex** (Old Farms Road, Simsbury; 203-651-3751).

In the Lower Connecticut River Valley, try **Courthouse 1** (10 Hillside Road, Cromwell; 203-635-5400) or **Old Saybrook Tennis and Swim Club** (Spring Brook Road, Old Saybrook; 203-388-5115). **Lyme Shores Racquet Club** (22 Colton Road, East Lyme; 203-739-6281) has courts available, and farther east you can play at New London's **Toby May Field** (Ocean Avenue; for information call the Recreation Department, 203-447-5230). In Groton, courts are available at **Farquhar Park** (Route 117), **Washington Park** (Mitchell Street) and **Fitch Senior High** (Groton Long Point Road). As you head north, you can test your skills at **Roseland Park** (Woodstock; 203-928-4130), the **Willimantic Recreation Park** (Route 6 and Main Street, Willimantic; 203-456-3593) or on the campus of the **University of Connecticut** (Storrs; 203-486-2837).

BICYCLING

Much of Connecticut is ideal for bicycle touring. The relatively gentle terrain and scenic back roads lend themselves to this unhurried form of exploration—except for the hillier northwest corner, which requires some strenuous pedaling. The **Connecticut Department of Transportation** (P.O. Drawer A, Wethersfield, CT 06109; 203-566-5280) publishes a free bicycle map that indicates touring routes, loop routes and the Connecticut section of the East Coast bicycle trail. It also lists bicycle and repair shops in the state. The suggested routes cover most of the state, avoiding city traffic and high-speed highways.

In addition, two of the state parks provide special bicycle trails. At **Stratton Brook State Park** in Simsbury, not far from Hartford, the old railroad tracks have been replaced by an extensive bike trail traveling along a scenic brook. At **Haley Farms State Park** in Groton, an eight-mile trail winds its way through the picturesque old shoreline farm.

BIKE RENTALS   A few inns and hotels keep a small fleet of bicycles for their guests. Other than that, there are no bikes for rent around Connecticut. Best bring your own, if pedaling is your pleasure.

Beaches and Parks

SOUTHWESTERN CONNECTICUT BEACHES AND PARKS

Sherwood Island State Park—One and a half miles of wide, sandy beach front the calm waters of Long Island Sound, with the coast of Long Island visible on a clear day. Behind the beach are extensive open fields and groves of maples and oaks that shelter picnic tables. Two breakwaters offer fine saltwater fishing.

Facilities: Pavilion with food concession stands, restrooms, bathhouses, lifeguards; information, 203-226-6983. *Fishing:* Good for bluefish, striped bass and blackfish in season. *Swimming:* Excellent.

Getting there: Located in Westport; exit 18 off Route 95.

Putnam Memorial Historic Park—This 183-acre park was the site of the Continental Army's 1779 winter encampment, under the command of General Israel Putnam. Remains of the encampment can be viewed, as well as reconstructed log buildings. Hiking trails fan out into the woods; the pond is suitable for fishing and ice skating.

Facilities: Picnic area, restrooms, historical site; information, 203-938-2285. *Camping:* For youth groups only. *Fishing:* Good in pond.

Getting there: Located three miles south of Bethel on Route 58.

NORTHWEST CORNER BEACHES AND PARKS

Macedonia Brook State Park—Numerous streams course through the forested 2300 acres of this park, and many trails traverse it. One trail reaches the crest of Cobble Mountain, almost 1400 feet, affording splendid views of the Taconic and Catskill Mountains in the adjoining states.

Facilities: Picnic shelter, outhouses; information, 203-927-3238. *Camping:* Permitted in 84 wooded sites. *Fishing:* Good for brook and rainbow trout.

Getting there: Located four miles northwest of Kent off Route 341.

Kent Falls State Park—The foaming waterfall that cascades 250 feet here is at its peak in springtime. It's popular in summer as well, when the welcome spray brings relief from the heat, and in the fall, when the surrounding 275 acres of woods turn red and gold. Then there are those who love the waterfall in winter, when frozen rivulets turn the mountainside to glistening abstract sculpture. You can admire it all from a grassy plain at road level, or you can view it from many different angles as you climb a wide, stepped pathway all the way to the head of the cascade.

Facilities: Picnic grounds, restrooms; information, 203-927-3238.

Getting there: Located four miles north of Kent on Route 7.

Lake Waramaug State Park—Ninety-five wooded acres front this scenic body of water. Visitors can swim or explore countless hidden coves in paddleboats and canoes that can be rented here. Bicycling along the quiet road around the lake is also popular, as is touring the nearby towns by car.

Facilities: Picnic shelter, restrooms, food concession stands, boat and canoe rentals; information, 203-868-0220. *Camping:* Permitted in 88 shady campsites, many with views of the water. *Swimming:* Excellent. *Fishing:* Good for bass, sunfish and perch.

Getting there: Located on Lake Waramaug Road (Route 478).

White Memorial Foundation—This 4000-acre nature sanctuary bordering scenic Bantam Lake is crisscrossed by 35 miles of wooded trails for hiking, birdwatching, horseback riding or cross-country skiing. The legacy of two farsighted residents, this extraordinary preserve is dedicated to conservation education and research as well as recreation. A nature center and museum are open to the public as are the grounds.

Facilities: Picnic areas, restrooms, a trail for the disabled, store, nature center; information, 203-567-0857. *Camping:* Permitted in 68 sites in several locations, including waterfront campsites at popular Point Folly.

Getting there: Located along Route 202, Litchfield.

Haystack Mountain State Park—From the stone tower atop Haystack Mountain (1706 feet above sea level) visitors can see south as far as Long Island Sound and north to the Berkshires' peaks in Massachusetts. You can drive halfway up the mountain, then hike a steep half-mile to the top. Fall foliage is outstanding up there, as is June's show of mountain laurel in bloom.

Facilities: Picnic grounds, outhouses; information, 203-482-1817.

Getting there: Located one mile north of Norfolk on Route 272.

HARTFORD AREA BEACHES AND PARKS

Stratton Brook State Park—An unusual feature of this 148-acre park in the Farmington Valley is a shady bicycle trail built on a former railroad bed. It travels across woodlands and along several scenic brooks, then continues through a town forest. There are also hiking trails and a pleasant pond.

Facilities: Picnic shelter, restrooms, changing rooms. *Fishing:* Good. *Swimming:* Good.

Getting there: Located two miles west of Simsbury on Route 305.

Talcott Mountain State Park—The views from this mountain, of the city of Hartford and the valleys of the Farmington and Connecticut rivers, have been favorites of painters for over 100 years. Atop the mountain stands handsome Heublein Tower, part of a residence deeded to the state by a prominent Hartford family. A one-and-a-half-mile hike leads from the parking lot to the tower, 165 feet high; the ground floor houses a museum of local history, open late April through October (203-677-0662 for information). Along the trail, you might see people hang-gliding: the mountain is considered a good jumping-off place for this sport.

Facilities: Picnic grounds, restrooms, museum, observation tower.

Getting there: Located three miles south of Simsbury, on Route 185.

Dinosaur State Park—This 70-acre park, set midway between Hartford and New Haven, boasts a geodesic dome exhibit center enclosing a celebrated exposure of rock. The ancient rock bears some 500 tracks made by dinosaurs of the Jurassic period—185 million years ago. Visitors may make plaster casts of some tracks May through October. Extensive nature trails wind through the park.

Facilities: Picnic grounds, restrooms, exhibit center; information, 203-529-8423.

Getting there: Located in Rocky Hill, one mile east of exit 23 off Route 91.

NEW HAVEN AREA BEACHES AND PARKS

Hammonasset Beach State Park—Largest of Connecticut's shoreline parks, 919-acre Hammonasset offers a two-mile-long, wide sandy beach that's great for swimming, scuba diving and fishing. You can launch small sailboats at the boat ramp, hike along numerous trails and visit the nature center, which sponsors interpretive programs. Moreover, the park is ideally located for visiting the picturesque shoreline towns.

Facilities: Picnic grounds with shelter, restrooms, food concession stands, pavilion with changing rooms, nature center, boat ramp; information, 203-245-2785. *Camping:* Permitted in 550 campsites, most in open fields, a five to ten minute walk from the beach. *Fishing:* Patient anglers often reel in good-size bluefish, striped bass or blackfish. *Swimming:* Excellent.

Getting there: Located in Madison, it is one mile south of exit 62 on Route 95.

LOWER CONNECTICUT RIVER VALLEY BEACHES AND PARKS

Selden Neck State Park—This one is special, a 528-acre island in the Connecticut River accessible only by water—truly a place to get away from it all. You can hike along woodsy trails that lead to old rock quarries, explore the shore in your kayak or canoe or contemplate the wide, tranquil river.

Facilities: Outhouses, picnic tables, fireplaces. *Camping:* Four primitive tent sites are available for one-night stops.

Getting there: The island is located two miles south of Gillette Castle State Park in East Haddam, which handles information and permits for both parks (call 203-526-2336). Canoes and kayaks can be launched at the ferry slip below the castle.

Gillette Castle State Park—One of the most popular destinations in Connecticut, this mountainside park is topped by the picturesque fieldstone structure built at the start of the century by William Gillette, a well-known actor (see the "Sightseeing" section in this chapter). Views of the Connecticut River are spectacular, and you can hike on shady trails to the water's edge and watch the ferry plying its way between Chester and Hadlyme.

Facilities: Picnic grounds, restrooms, food concession stands, gift shop, canoe rentals; information, 203-526-2336. *Camping:* A few primitive tent sites available for one-night stops for canoers and kayakers only. *Fishing:* Good in Connecticut River.

Getting there: Located four miles south of East Haddam, off Route 82. From the west bank of the river, take the ferry from Chester to Hadlyme and follow the signs up the mountain.

MYSTIC AREA BEACHES AND PARKS

Rocky Neck State Park—The main attraction here is a one-mile sandy beach with excellent swimming and fishing, and a picturesque view of shorefront cottages across the bay. The 700-acre park also encompasses vast salt marshes sheltering a variety of bird life that can be viewed from trails and raised boardwalks.

Facilities: Picnic grounds, restrooms, bathhouses, food concession stands; information, 203-739-5471. *Camping:* Permitted at 169 campsites. *Fishing:* The breakwater is a popular spot. *Swimming:* Excellent.

Getting there: Located three miles west of Niantic on Route 156.

Ocean Beach Park—This city-owned park has a mile-long, crescent-shaped beach of sparkling white sand, backed by an old-fashioned boardwalk for jogging or strolling. Several of the amusement park rides it used to offer are now on hold, but the triple waterslide remains a big draw. There's also miniature golf, shops, snack bars, an arcade and nightly entertainment under the stars.

Facilities: All of the above, plus Olympic-sized pool, picnic pavilion, restrooms, changing rooms, paddleboats for rent; information, 203-447-3031. *Swimming:* Excellent and well guarded.

Getting there: Located in New London; from Route 95, take exit 82A northbound or exit 83 southbound, then follow signs.

NORTHEAST CORNER PARKS

Mashamoquet Brook State Park—Two major hiking trails lead to the park's most famous feature: a wolf den where, in 1742, young Israel Putnam shot a wolf that had terrorized the population. Putnam became a local hero and later gained national fame as a Revolutionary War general. The park also boasts a small, clear pond and a brook. Located at the entrance is Brayton Grist Mill, last in the area, with its traditional machinery intact and a display of blacksmithing tools belonging to three generations of the same family.

Facilities: Picnic grounds, restrooms, concession stand, nature trail; information, 203-928-6121. *Camping:* Permitted at 55 sites. *Fishing:* The brook is stocked with trout. *Swimming:* Good in a small pond.

Getting there: Located five miles southwest of Putnam on Route 44.

Hiking

Although Connecticut is densely populated, a surprising amount of open space has been preserved and provided with trails suitable for hiking. The Connecticut Blue Trails System, established and maintained by the **Connecticut Forest and Park Association** (16 Meriden Road, Rockfall, CT 06481; 203-346-2372), consists of more than 500 miles of cleared and well-marked woodland trails touching on every county. Contact them for a brochure describing the trails. In addition, a portion of the white-blazed Appalachian Trail crosses northwestern Connecticut, and many state parks and forests and nature preserves have created their own hiking routes.

SOUTHWESTERN CONNECTICUT TRAILS

In **Devil's Den Preserve**, 20 miles of interconnecting trails cover a variety of terrain, from wetland, stream and pond through mature forest to rocky knolls with wide-open vistas. Take exit 42 from the Merritt Parkway, go north on Route 57 for five miles, then east on Godfrey Road for one-half mile and turn left on Pent Road.

NORTHWEST CORNER TRAILS

In **Kent Falls State Park** a steep trail (.5 mile) leads up the south side of the falls, across a bridge and down more gradually on the north side, through dense woods and towering hemlock trees. The south side trail hugs the cascade itself, enabling hikers to view the falls from many angles, and to explore the massive rock formations when the flow of water is low enough to allow it.

The blue-blazed **Housatonic Range Trail** (8 miles) follows the general route of an old Indian trail along the hills above the Housatonic River. Along the way are several caves to explore—Tories' Cave is said to have sheltered Loyalists during the Revolutionary War—fine views of Candlewood Lake, the Housatonic and its verdant valley; occasional steep climbing and some areas of rough scrambling over boulders. The trail begins one-and-a-half miles north of New Milford on Route 7.

Macedonia Ridge Trail (6.2 miles) is a loop within Macedonia Brook State Park. The trail, which begins and ends near the parking area at the southern end of the park, crosses bridges and brooks, passes old charcoal mounds and climbs Pine Hill and Cobble Mountain, both with splendid views and demanding ascents.

Bear Mountain Trail (5.6 miles) is a steep, rugged hike to the 2316-foot summit, which reveals a vast panorama of mountains, lakes and forests in three states, as well as of turkey vultures soaring along the edge of the plateau. This hike begins on Route 41, at a small parking lot three-and-two-tenths miles north of its junction with Route 44 in Salisbury.

HARTFORD AREA TRAILS

Heublein Tower Trail (7 miles) is an easy walk along a section of the blue-blazed Metacomet Trail, which circles around a scenic reservoir and climbs steeply up to Heublein Tower in Talcott Mountain State Park. From the tower, you'll see the skyline of nearby Hartford and, on the clearest of days, Long Island Sound and the distant mountains of Massachusetts and New Hampshire. Before setting out, check with a ranger for detailed directions.

Windsor Locks Canal Trail (9 miles round-trip) provides a level hike along the towpath that follows a historic canal built in 1829 to bypass the Enfield rapids on the Connecticut River. The trail begins on Canal Road, off Route 159.

NEW HAVEN AREA TRAILS

Westwoods, a 2000-acre open space in Guilford, is crisscrossed with hiking trails. By taking the white circle trail out and the orange one back, you'll have walked six mostly level miles along marsh boardwalks, stands of hemlock and laurel, rocks, ledges, an abandoned quarry and Lost Lake, a scenic halfway point for a picnic.

Sleeping Giant, two miles north of Hamden, is a series of mountaintops resembling an oversized reclining man. A vast network of trails traverses the titan's anatomy—head, chin, chest—affording distant views of hills and cities. For a strenuous, up-and-down circuit of the major peaks (6 miles round-trip), follow the blue-blazed trail from near the parking lot all the way to the giant's right foot, then back on the white trail, with a detour to the stone tower for the loftiest vista.

LOWER CONNECTICUT RIVER VALLEY TRAILS

Devil's Hopyard Trail (4.5 miles) crisscrosses the state park of the same name, beneath ancient groves of hemlocks, across picturesque foot bridges and along Chapman Falls, which tumbles in a 60-foot cascade. It begins near the parking lot.

MYSTIC AREA TRAILS

Bluff Point Trail (4.5 miles), in Bluff Point Coastal Reserve, leads from the parking area to the bluffs. Wander along the rocky, pristine beach, then wind your way back on a different trail through woods and salt marshes that cover this rare, undeveloped peninsula on Long Island Sound.

NORTHEAST CORNER TRAILS

Wolf Den Trail (5 miles) lies within Mashamoquet Brook State Park and takes you, along up-and-down terrain, into Israel Putnam's celebrated cave. It also loops past a boulder known as Indian Chair and into diverse environments that include swampland and open fields, woods and streams and high ledges that offer fine vistas. The blue-blazed trail starts near the parking lot off Wolf Den Drive.

Mansfield Hollow Trail (8 miles round-trip) is part of the much longer, blue-blazed Nipmuck Trail. Starting in the parking lot of the Mansfield Hollow Dam Recreation Area, it winds along the Fenton River, then veers steeply up a hillside to emerge at a cliff known as 50 Foot, a fine lookout with views of eastern Connecticut.

Travelers' Tracks

Sightseeing

SOUTHWESTERN CONNECTICUT

Guidebooks tend to dismiss southwestern Connecticut, which roughly corresponds to Fairfield County, as merely a bedroom community for New York City, not worthy of a visitor's time. In fact, it's far more complex—a mix of pretty residential towns with roots in the 17th and 18th centuries, once-thriving industrial cities struggling to find new roles for themselves and clusters of tall, sleek corporate headquarters that have transformed the county's way of life. What's more, although the area is far from rural, a surprising amount of open space has been preserved in state parks and nature preserves.

A brief tour to sample this variety should start in **Greenwich**, the first town encountered on crossing into the state from the southwest. Famed as an exclusive residential enclave of affluent New York commuters, this community of 60,000 has acquired an additional role as a business center. A host of corporate office buildings draws some 20,000 workers from other towns, as well as hundreds of foreign executives. The old order changeth, even here!

The beauty of the town remains, as does the atmosphere of quiet privilege. Visitors seeking a glimpse of the **great estates** (★) that give Greenwich its special ambience should wander the "backcountry" roads north and immediately south of the Merritt Parkway, along Lake Avenue, North Street, Round Hill Road and smaller, bucolic lanes and drives—as long as they're not guarded by stone gateposts with "No Admittance" signs! It's a world of white churches and manicured country clubs, ancestral trees and lavishly landscaped grounds, with mansions, neo-Tudor or Colonial Revival, barely visible behind iron gates, stone walls and fences.

One former estate that, happily, is open to the public is the **Bruce Museum** (1 Museum Drive, Greenwich; 203-869-0376; admission), housing American paintings, Indian pottery and textiles, wildlife, minerals and frequent exhibitions that reflect the eclectic nature of the holdings. Other nearby attractions are the **Bush-Holley House** (39 Strickland Road, Cos Cob; 203-869-6899; admission), devoted to the community's long and colorful history, and **Putnam Cottage** (243 East Putnam Avenue, Greenwich; 203-869-9697; admission), a late-17th-century tavern and site of General Israel Putnam's 1779 daring escape against the redcoats—a favorite bit of local lore.

Driving east from Greenwich on Route 95, you'll spot **Stamford's** skyline, which appears as a forest of discordant office towers, huge corporate headquarters built since the 1960s that dwarf the few remaining older structures. An enlightened giant, the Champion International Corporation, houses a branch of New York's prestigious **Whitney Museum of American Art** (1 Champion Plaza, Stamford; 203-358-7652). It's a handsome, sleek gallery space, with enticing exhibits that alternate between traditional and innovative.

A few miles north of downtown you'll find the **Stamford Museum and Nature Center** (39 Scofieldtown Road, Stamford; 203-322-1646; admission), perhaps the most eclectic institution in the state. Set on more than 118 acres, the center offers, in nine widely scattered buildings, galleries devoted to art and history; an auditorium; a planetarium; an observatory; a working dairy farm; and nature trails, picnic grounds and a small lake peopled by all manner of geese, ducks and swans. This one's truly a treat for the whole family. Special seasonal programs are offered.

Next stop along the shoreline is **Norwalk**, a city of 70,000 that was settled in 1645 and thrived on the coastal trade and manufacturing, then went into a slump. After years of neglect, the area closest to the harbor, **South Norwalk,** has been restored, gentrified and listed in the National Register of Historic Places. Its major artery, **Washington Street,** is now a stroller's mecca offering dozens of shops and boutiques, art and craft galleries, restaurants and bars, all set in handsome 19th-century commercial buildings.

Around the corner, on five acres of riverfront, rises a more modern tourist draw, the **Maritime Center at Norwalk** (North Water Street; 203-852-0700; admission). It includes an aquarium with 20 tanks that take you from salt marsh into open sea, sharks and all; a maritime museum displaying classic open boats; video games that teach marine skills such as designing the boat of your dreams; and, in a separate building, a high-tech, 337-seat IMAX theater with a six-story-tall screen that stretches 80 feet. From an adjacent dock you can board **The Seaport Islander** (seasonal; 203-838-9444; admission), an open ferry that goes to the 1868 lighthouse on Sheffield Island, one of 20 that dot the nearby waters. Other vessels take longer jaunts around all the islands.

Information about this and other attractions is available from the **Yankee Heritage Tourism District** (297 West Avenue; 203-854-7825), which occupies the gate house to the **Lockwood-Mathews Mansion Museum** (295 West Avenue, Norwalk; 203-838-1434; admission). This lavish residence, built in the 1860s in French Second Empire style, includes work by some of the finest cabinetmakers and craftsmen of the day. Saved from the bulldozer by local preservationists, it has been gradually restored room by room—frescoed ceilings, inlaid woodwork, glassed-in conservatory—and now serves as a museum of Victorian life.

For a complete change of pace, get on Route 95 and take exit 18. It's called the **Sherwood Island** exit, for the state park that lies just south of the highway. It has a beautiful sandy beach, and if that tempts you, by all means give in, since, unlike this one, most beaches hereabouts are small and owned by municipalities. This means nonresidents are either barred altogether or charged a fee.

Attractive though it is, the state park is not the major destination of this excursion. That would be the enchanting village of **Southport** (★), which showcases as fine a collection of domestic American architecture as you're likely to find. Drive slowly down Pequot Avenue past the parade of homes in the Federal and Greek Revival style and later ones in all the variations we tend to lump together as Victorian.

After you pass a small cluster of stores and antique shops, take a right to the harbor, the original source of the wealth that created the handsome dwellings. The vessels that traded with Boston and New York from this small, sheltered port have given way to sailboats large and small moored at the yacht club, but the homes built by the ship's owners and captains are still lived in and lovingly maintained. Park if you can, and walk up Harbor Road for a fine view of the watery landscape.

Bridgeport, the next city along Route 95, is the largest in the state and no one's dream of a tourist attraction, but **The Barnum Museum** (820 Main Street; 203-331-1104; admission), redesigned and enlarged, will delight both children and adults. For Bridgeport, P. T. Barnum was more than the king of hoax and hokum, more than the creator of the legendary Barnum and Bailey Circus. He was a philanthropist and real estate developer, the city's mayor and its favorite son. The museum established in his will in 1891 is as flamboyant as he was, a gargoyled, towered and domed red building in the heart of the city, a reflection of his eclectic interests. Circus buffs will go straight to the third floor with its mementos of General Tom Thumb, the talented midget who achieved world fame; its big top memorabilia; and especially the 1000-square-foot scale model of "The Greatest Show on Earth," complete with over 3000 miniatures of acrobats, clowns, elephants, trains and tents, every tiny detail hand carved by a craftsman from a nearby town.

Perhaps the most idyllic town in this busy part of the state is **Ridgefield**, a quintessential New England enclave of stately homes, ancient trees and mementos of battles long past. Ridgefield lies about half an hour north of the shoreline, a pleasant drive along Route 33, starting at exit 41 on the Merritt Parkway. Once a way station on the road from New York to Boston, the town provided inns for weary passengers. The tradition continues, with several old but up-to-date hostelries and one that now acts as a museum, the **Keeler Tavern** (132 Main Street; 203-438-5485; admission), whose most famous feature is a cannonball lodged into its wall during the Battle of Ridgefield, April 27, 1777. Benedict Arnold was a hero on that day!

Not far from the tavern, another 18th-century building has been transformed into the **Aldrich Museum of Contemporary Art** (258 Main Street; 203-438-4519; admission). Surrounding the historic main structure and its congenial addition is an outstanding sculpture garden representing the finest artists of the day.

NORTHWEST CORNER

Connecticut's northwest corner is encompassed by Litchfield County, known for the scenic, wooded Litchfield Hills, winding back roads, sparkling lakes and rivers, a dozen state parks and charming small towns, villages and country inns. To get there from Ridgefield take Route 7, which is part highway, part commercial strip, part country road. Bear with the first two stretches.

After New Milford, the road turns into a shunpiker's dream, a gentle rollercoaster with views of fields and streams and vintage houses. Just before Kent, stop at **Bull's Bridge**, one of two covered bridges in the state that cars can drive through—a most picturesque spot. Washington crossed it in March 1781, and it's said that one of his horses fell into the freezing Housatonic River and had to be pulled out.

The town of Kent boasts the **Sloane-Stanley Museum** (Route 7; 203-927-3849; admission), which contains Early American farm and woodworking tools collected by Eric Sloane, artist and writer. The grounds include the ruins of Kent Iron Furnace, one of many used for smelting the iron ore that was the mainstay of the northwest corner from the mid-18th century until the close of the next. A few miles later, on the right of the road, the 250-foot cascade of **Kent Falls** dominates an attractive state park (see the "Beaches and Parks" section in this chapter).

Then the road splits: Route 45 goes south to **Lake Waramaug**, a zigzagged, three-mile long body of water that has drawn visitors since the mid-1800s—by train back then. Drive all around it: the hilly, wooded shores shelter several inns, a state park and—surprise!—**Hopkins Vineyard** (Hopkins Road, New Preston; 203-868-7954), with a winery housed in a restored 19th-century barn, where you can taste and buy both wines and various gourmet items. Since the late 1970s, even as dairy farms have gradually disappeared from the landscape, vineyards have sprung up, half a dozen at least and more to come. From Lake Waramaug it's a short drive to **Washington**, a pristine, white hilltop residential village built around a church. Less than two miles from there, on Route 199, is the **American Indian Archeological Institute** (38 Curtis Road; 203-868-0518; admission), with excellent exhibits, including an Indian long house, a simulated archeological site and an outdoor Indian village—a good way to learn about the region's earliest dwellers.

Litchfield is the most visited spot in the northwest corner, and its spare, graceful **Congregational Church** (junction of Routes 202 and 118), built in 1828, rates among the finest in New England and the most photographed. It is as prosperous a town today as it was as an outpost and trading center for the northwest frontier; and, happily, it still centers on the handsome green that was laid out in the 1770s. The wide, maple-lined streets are edged with homes of unusual distinction, boasting past residents such as Aaron Burr, Ethan Allen and Harriet Beecher Stowe. Burr lived with his brother-in-law, Tapping Reeve (see below); Allen was born on Old South Road, in a small privately owned house; the site on North Street where Mrs. Stowe was born bears a marker—the house itself was moved some years ago.

Two homes that have been turned into museums are the **Tapping Reeve House and Law School** (South Street, Route 63 South; 203-567-4501; seasonal; admission), America's first law school, founded in 1784, and the **Litchfield Historical Society Museum** (Corner of East and South streets, Route 202; 203-567-4501; admission), which owns a fine selection of 18th-century portraits, and houses items of the town's past and present. For a walking tour map and information on events throughout the county, stop at the booth maintained on the green by the **Litchfield Hills Travel Council** (203-868-2214).

Despite its palpable concern for the past, Litchfield is very much alive and offers a variety of attractions, such as **Haight Vineyard and Winery** (Chestnut Hill Road, off Route 118, one mile east of town; 203-567-4045), with winery tours, tastings and vineyard walks; **White Flower Farm** (Route 63, three miles south of town; 203-567-0801), a nationally known nursery with five acres of display gardens and 30 of growing fields; and **White Memorial Foundation** (Route 202; 203-567-0857), the state's largest nature center and wildlife sanctuary—an ideal place for lovers of the outdoors.

In nearby Waterbury, the **Mattatuck Museum** (144 West Main Street, 203-753-0381) exhibits artifacts such as clocks, novelty watches, art deco tableware and some of the buttons locally produced in this former "brass capital of the world." You can also visit a 19th-century boarding house highlighting immigrant memories and a historic brass mill, or peruse the galleries showcasing 18th-century furniture and American masters who have been associated with Connecticut.

After enjoying the museum take the self-guided walking tour of the historic downtown district. Many buildings have been recently renovated thanks to the combined efforts of preservationists and developers. For further information, contact the **Waterbury Convention and Visitors Commission** (83 Bank Street, Waterbury; 203-597-9527).

There's no way to see all the picturesque little towns around these parts, but you should sample the northernmost ones, such as Norfolk, surrounded by mountains and state parks. Along the way, if you go by Route 7, you'll pass the much-photographed covered bridge at **West Cornwall** and the attractive cluster of homes and shops by its side. This section of the Housatonic River is much favored by devotees of kayaks and canoes, which can be rented both here and in **Falls Village,** a few miles to the north. The **falls** (★) in that town's name are channeled to provide electric power part of the year. In spring you have but to cross the bridge in the middle of town and you'll be rewarded by a dramatic rush of water to rival far more celebrated ones.

Alternatively, you could opt to drive north via the picturesque towns of Sharon, Lakeville and Salisbury, passing, along the way, some of the richest, most scenic farmland in the state. Either way, when you get to Canaan, just south of the Massachusetts line, stop by to see the unique **Union Station and Depot** (Route 44, center of town), built in 1872 with two wings at right angles to each other, to service the two railroads that used to come this way. In our near-trainless times, the building houses office space.

Heading east along the swift Blackberry River, Route 44 takes you to tiny, serene **Norfolk.** Affluent families have maintained summer homes in this town since the 1880s, drawn by the cool mountain air and by the much-acclaimed **Chamber Music Festival,** held each year from June to August. From here you can drive to several mountains with stunning views. You have to be on foot to appreciate Norfolk's exquisite green (Route 44), embellished by a fountain designed by Stanford White, eminent architect of the Gilded Age, and surrounded by graceful homes and the Congregational Church, built in 1813.

HARTFORD AREA

Route 44 heads southeast out of Norfolk, leading, some 35 miles later, to Hartford. It's a more scenic road to the state capital than the highways, one that offers the chance to stop at some attractive towns in the **Farmington Valley**. For information about them, stop at the **Farmington Valley Visitors Bureau** (P.O. Box 1550, Avon, CT 06001; 203-674-1035). In fact, if you prefer small towns to city bustle, you could overnight there and take day trips into Hartford.

Take a brief detour south on Route 179 to the village of **Collinsville** (★) for a glimpse of an intact 19th-century mill village—one of hundreds built across the state by the companies that gave them their names. The Collins Company was purveyor of axes and machetes to the world; the **Canton Historical Museum** (11 Front Street; 203-693-2793; admission) will help you trace their fortunes.

Continue on Route 179 into Route 4 as it follows the Farmington River into the residential town of **Farmington**, whose Main Street is a treasure trove of colonial architecture. Just a few blocks away you'll find a little-known gem: the **Hill-Stead Museum** (35 Mountain Road; 203-677-9064; admission). Unique in many ways, Hill-Stead is a turn-of-the-century mansion built for an art-loving industrialist, Alfred A. Pope. It is furnished as if the Popes left yesterday, and on its walls hangs a breathtaking collection of impressionist paintings—works by Monet, Degas, Manet and their American contemporaries, Cassatt and Whistler. The residence was designed by the Popes' daughter, Theodate Pope Riddle, in collaboration with none other than Stanford White, who was a family friend. The personality of this pioneering woman, who went on to become an architect at a time when that profession was unheard of for a female, comes through vividly on a guided tour of the house. And there's a fine, short videotape to enlighten one further. The grounds are noteworthy as well, with hiking trails in the woods and a sunken garden re-created from early 1900s plans.

If you're intrigued by this unusual woman and her work, head north of Farmington by way of Route 10 and take a left onto Avon Farms Road. In a few moments you'll come to the campus of **Avon Old Farms School** (★), a boy's preparatory academy founded during the 1920s by Theodate Pope Riddle and designed by her in what is described as Tudor/Cotswold style—cottage-inspired buildings in reddish sandstone and dark timbers. It's private property, but nobody seemed to mind our driving through the picturesque campus. Avon Old Farms Road winds its way north, emerging in the center of Avon, a busy suburban town that was once an agricultural community.

Not long ago, great **fields of shade tobacco** (★) covered portions of this valley and that of the Connecticut River, a few miles to the west. Suburbanization, highways and, of course, the intense disfavor with which the evil weed is now regarded have cut sharply into this profitable business. Yet there are still some 1800 acres devoted to tobacco in the state. In summer, when the fields are covered by acres of netting, they create a unique, dramatic setting enhanced by the long, narrow red barns used for drying tobacco leaves. Go north on Route 10 through **Simsbury**, noting the many graceful 18th- and 19th-century buildings of this prosperous community. Two miles north of the town center take Hoskins Road, and you'll get a taste of this picturesque, surreal landscape.

From Route 10, as you look to the west, you'll see a ridge of hills topped by a stone tower, the centerpiece of **Talcott Mountain State Park**, which can be reached by Route 185. Hartford lies on the other side.

Truth is, **Hartford** suffers the same image problems that afflict other American cities, and there are many well-traveled residents of the state who've never been there. They're missing a lot. Its long and distinguished history—from newborn settlement in 1635 to shipping center throughout the 18th century, industrial leader in the 19th and capital of the insurance business to this day—is reflected in its varied architecture and active cultural life. For easier sightseeing, the city can be subdivided into three separate parts: downtown; the capitol area, on the opposite side of beautiful Bushnell Park; and Asylum Hill, where Mark Twain built his celebrated mansion.

Start at the dignified **Old State House** (800 Main Street; 203-522-6766), designed in 1796 by Charles Bulfinch and used as the seat of the state's government until 1878, years during which Hartford alternated as capital with New Haven. Parts of the building are now used as museum and part as visitors' center. After touring the House and Senate chambers, ask for the walking tour map of the city prepared by the **Greater Hartford Convention and Visitors Bureau** (1 Civic Center Plaza, Hartford; 203-728-6789). It will guide you to two dozen landmarks, old and new. (As you've no doubt noticed, the former are being squeezed out by the latter; in fact, the venerable Old State House itself was almost bulldozed, until a vocal group of preservationists came to its aid.)

If the printed itinerary seems overwhelming, here's a shortened list: Walk by the **Richardson**, as it is known today, a massive, handsome brownstone building designed in 1876 by Henry Hobson Richardson in his distinctive Romanesque style. It's just north of the Old State House, on Main Street. A few blocks south, and across the street, stands **Center Church** (675 Main Street), built in 1807, whose white portico and ornate white spire contrast with the red brick of the facade. Next to it, the **Ancient Burying Ground** shelters gravestones that date back to 1640.

Across the street is the **Wadsworth Atheneum** (600 Main Street; 203-278-2670; admission), America's oldest free public art museum, opened in 1844 and was later harmoniously enlarged. Walk up the steps of the towered, castlelike original building and turn around before entering. You'll be rewarded with an extensive view of Bushnell Park and the glimmering gold dome of the State Capitol across the park. Inside, you'll find a distinguished collection, strong in paintings of the Hudson River School, colonial American furniture and art and works of our own century. Yet the museum doesn't overwhelm you with size and arrogance; it feels friendly, somehow.

Nestled between the Atheneum and the fine **Municipal Building** of 1915 is **Burr Mall** (★), a small, endearing open space centered on Alexander Calder's giant sculpture *Stegosaurus*. The two classic buildings and the bright red steel abstract sculpture form a wonderful contrast.

On to the **State Capitol,** a monumental Victorian Gothic structure that can be toured, along with the new legislative office building, in groups led by members of the League of Women Voters (Capitol Information Desk and Tour Guide Service; 203-240-0222). The 1878 capitol is a sight to behold: gold-domed, turreted, mansarded, adorned with statues of Connecticut's greats (including Ella Grasso, the late governor, first woman to be elected to that post in her own right). It has undergone a superb, ten-year restoration, outside and in. The soaring, lavishly decorated interior is as exuberant as the facade; clearly Hartford was out to celebrate when it won the designation of sole capital over New Haven in 1875.

The stately building across Capitol Avenue houses the State Library, the Supreme Court and the **Raymond E. Baldwin Museum of Connecticut History** (231 Capitol Avenue; 203-566-3056), with exhibits that include a collection of historic Colt firearms and a trove of documents such as the 1662 Royal Charter.

Asylum Hill is where Mark Twain built his Hartford residence, along with many eminent citizens of the 1870s who fled the downtown area for what was then considered the suburbs. His mansion was part of **Nook Farm** (351 Farmington Avenue; 203-525-9317; admission), an enclave of writers and intellectuals that included Harriet Beecher Stowe. Both the Twain and Stowe homes can be visited on the same tour—hers a discreet Victorian "cottage," his a superornamented extravaganza where he wrote *Huckleberry Finn* and *Tom Sawyer*. A few blocks away is the **Connecticut Historical Society Museum** (1 Elizabeth Street; 203-236-5621; admission), where a variety of lively exhibits will help you place the sights you've seen into historical context.

Hartford's surroundings offer varied attractions that can be visited on day trips. Art buffs won't want to miss the **New Britain Museum of American Art** (56 Lexington Street, New Britain; 203-229-0257), which features a collection spanning 250 years and is strong on Hudson River School painters and artists of the 20th century. North of the capital, the **New England**

Air Museum (Route 75, Bradley International Airport, Windsor Locks; 203-623-3305; admission) exhibits 75 aircraft that trace the history of aviation.

A mere ten miles south of Hartford on Route 91, the town of Wethersfield, one of the original three settlements on the Connecticut River, is famed for its extensive historic district comprising 150 dwellings built before the mid-19th century. Several old Wethersfield homes are open to the public as house museums:

The Webb-Deane-Stevens Museum (211 Main Street; 203-529-0612; admission) consists of three homes built, respectively, for a wealthy merchant, a diplomat and a craftsman, each representing a different style of 18th-century life. The Webb house was the setting for a conference between General George Washington and his French counterpart, Jean de Rochambeau, that led to the British defeat at Yorktown in 1781.

The **Buttolph-Williams House** (249 Broad Street; 203-529-0460; admission) is a late 17th century "mansion house" with a collection of period furnishings. Its overhanging and small casement windows reflect the medieval character of the pilgrim century.

The **Old Academy Museum** (150 Main Street) is a fine 1804 brick building in the federal style housing a library and several offices. Nearby is the **Robert A. Keeney Memorial Cultural Center** (200 Main Street; admission) exhibiting the Wethersfield Historical Society's collection of local history. Also stop by the **Captain James Francis House** (120 Hartford Avenue) which traces a single Wethersfield family through two centuries. For information on all three sites, contact the Wethersfield Historical Society (203-529-7656).

NEW HAVEN AREA

Today's New Haven is a fascinating blend of old and new, urban center and university campus—a must on any tour of the state. Founded as an independent colony in 1638, New Haven soon merged with Hartford and was co-capital with that city from 1784 to 1875. Although it shone as an industrial center in the 19th and early 20th centuries, the special flavor that sets it apart today is due in large part to the presence of Yale University, an institution that has shared the city's fortunes since 1718.

New Haven was planned around a green at its founding, and happily the 17-acre square with its trio of churches in the center has been proudly maintained as open space and still acts as focus of the downtown area. Yale University forms the backdrop to the green's western edge, along College Street and fanning out across a dozen blocks west and north of it. Most of the cultural and architectural landmarks that define this uncommon city can be seen on a walk around the immediate area.

Yale University (Visitor Information Center, Phelps Gateway, 344 College Street; 203-432-2302) offers free guided tours of the campus; the **New Haven Convention and Visitors Bureau** (195 Church Street, 15th floor;

203-777-8550) provides maps and an outline for a walking tour of campus and civic landmarks.

Three hundred years of history and architecture can be traced on these rambles. For the earliest structures, start with the three graceful clapboard homes built by late-18th-century gentry at **149, 155** and **175 Elm Street** (★). They are now private clubs, closed to the public, but the three facades, set among much grander, later buildings, give a glimpse of how the city looked 200 years ago. The only structures on the green itself are the churches—**Trinity, Center** and **United**—erected between 1812 and 1815 in Gothic, Georgian and federal styles.

Yale's oldest remaining building, **Connecticut Hall,** is part of what is known as the old campus, which can be entered through **Phelps Gateway,** the school's massive front door at 344 College Street. It's a bulky, gambrel-roofed brick structure facing a statue of Nathan Hale, who lived there as a student.

Much of the architecture for which Yale is famous is 19th- and early-20th-century Gothic Revival. By crossing the Old Campus onto High Street, the visitor can wander past **Dwight Chapel** (1842), the first Gothic design; **Harkness Tower** (1917), whose turrets and pinnacles are a symbol of Yale itself; and **Sterling Memorial Library** (1927), a modern Gothic. York Street, one block west of High, is also lined with Yale-related buildings, including the legendary **Mory's** (306 York Street), a private club celebrated in "The Whiffenpoof Song."

One of the finest contemporary complexes on campus rises just west of York Street: **Morse and Stiles Colleges,** designed in 1960 by Eero Saarinen, contrasting yet in harmony with the older buildings. Don't miss Claes Oldenburg's powerful sculpture **Lipstick** (★), an anti-Vietnam War statement that dominates the courtyard of Morse College.

Another renowned 1960s structure is Gordon Bunshaft's **Beinecke Rare Book and Manuscript Library** (121 Wall Street; 203-432-2977), a granite and translucent marble landmark that seems to float above a sunken court featuring sculptures by Isamu Noguchi. Step inside to view a Gutenberg bible, original Audubon prints and other exhibits.

Down on Chapel Street, you come upon the **Yale University Art Gallery** (1111 Chapel Street; 203-432-0600) and, across the street, the **Yale Center for British Art** (1080 Chapel Street; 203-432-2800), both designed by architect Louis I. Kahn and exceptional for their use of interior space and light and the quality of their collections. The British Art Center boasts canvases by Turner, Gainsborough and Constable, among other renowned artists. The Yale Art Gallery is known for European, African, Asian and pre-Columbian works, as well as a special gallery devoted to the historical paintings of John Trumbull, the artist-patriot of the American Revolution. One of the Gallery's most appealing features is its idyllic **outdoor sculpture garden** (★).

New Haven has suffered its share of urban ills, and efforts to upgrade its image have sometimes been ill-advised. Two of the more successful projects are the recent creation of an entertainment district on College Street, centering on the renovated **Shubert** and **Palace** theaters (see "Theater in Connecticut" in this chapter). Another area that has been successfully restored is **Wooster Square** (★), between Chapel and Greene streets, six blocks east of the green. This early 19th-century enclave of graceful homes, after years of neglect, is once again a fashionable in-town address.

Among the many cultural and recreational facilities in New Haven are the **Peabody Museum of Natural History** (170 Whitney Avenue; 203-432-5050; admission), with its famed dinosaur collection and a Pulitzer Prize-winning mural entitled *The Age of Reptiles*. Nearby, the **New Haven Colony Historical Society** (114 Whitney; 203-562-4183; admission) contains furniture and decorative arts from early New Haven homes, an art gallery, a maritime collection and industrial displays. Farther out Whitney Avenue you'll find the **Eli Whitney Museum** (915 Whitney Avenue, Hamden; 203-777-1833), dedicated to the New Haven industrialist who invented the cotton gin and then developed the concept of interchangeable parts, which led to modern mass-production methods. Displays trace 200 years of industrial growth on the site.

On a day that calls for outdoor fun, consider trips to **Lighthouse Point Park** (2 Lighthouse Road; 203-787-8005), with facilities for picnicking and swimming and a classic old-time carousel, or the **Shoreline Trolley Museum** (17 River Street, East Haven; 203-467-6927; admission), where you can ride classic, antique trolleys along a scenic three-mile route.

East of New Haven, the shoreline is dotted with a string of attractive residential towns that started life as farming and fishing villages. Just off shore, in the village of Stony Creek, lies a group of enchanting islands called **The Thimbles** (★), some no larger than a rock that disappears at high tide, others topped by a single elaborate Victorian mansion or two. They say Captain Kidd hid stolen treasures on one of these rocky outposts. You'll learn all about that, and other local legends, if you take one of the small **excursion boats** that sail out of Stony Creek and cruise around this miniature archipelago (*Volsunga III*, Town Dock; 203-481-3345; or Thimble Islands Cruise, 34 Sachem Road; 203-481-4841; both seasonal).

Route 146 leads from Stony Creek to **Guilford**, a town that has preserved many pre-Revolutionary War houses, including the **Whitfield House Museum** (Old Whitfield Street; 203-453-2457; admission). This home of the town's first minister, built in 1639, is said to be the oldest stone house in New England. The green is special, generous for a town of this size and evocative of an earlier time. A few miles farther east you might consider a swim at **Hammonasset Beach State Park**. It's Connecticut's largest public beach, over two miles long.

LOWER CONNECTICUT RIVER VALLEY

The Lower Valley of the Connecticut River—stretching north for some 30 miles from Old Saybrook, where the river empties into Long Island Sound, is a favorite destination for visitors from near and far. The area is studded with small scenic towns once known as shipbuilding and sea-going communities. Also blessed with numerous state parks, and sophisticated restaurants and lodgings, the Lower Valley provides a chance to get close to the longest waterway in New England, a river that was central to the development of the young nation.

There's a highway information center on Route 95 (northbound) at **Westbrook**. You'd do well to begin this leg of the trip by stopping there, or contacting the **Connecticut Valley Tourism Commission** (393 Main Street, Middletown, CT 06457; 203-347-6924) for information and detailed maps. In fact, Westbrook, on Long Island Sound, is a good place to begin your exploration of the valley. Take Route 1 east until it joins **Route 154** (★), then ramble with it past salt marshes, causeways and marinas through Old Saybrook, a town with shoreline along both Sound and river and many picturesque watery views. Route 154 (natives call it the Shore Route) leads to **Essex** and points north, as does Route 9, which is speedier and beautiful in its own right, but the older road is best for antiquing and poking; it gives you more of a sense of place. Essex is one of the most visited towns in the state, and with good reason: it's a compact peninsula where the tree-lined streets end at the river and the white houses, set cheek-by-jowl, date back to 18th-century shipbuilding days. Beware of summer weekends, however: Essex's charms have been sung once too often.

At the foot of Main Street, with a river view to make you catch your breath, stands the **Connecticut River Museum** (203-767-8269; admission), housed in a restored 1878 warehouse where steamboats used to stop for freight and passengers on their way to Hartford or New York. Exhibits will help you place the river's role into perspective. And be sure to view the full-size replica of the ill-fated *Turtle* (the earliest submarine), built just before the Revolutionary War by David Bushnell, native son of the region.

The **Valley Railroad** (1 Railroad Avenue; 203-767-0103; admission) is a vintage steam train that winds its nostalgic way through the countryside for about an hour to Deep River, the next town up the line. There, you have a choice of returning by train or riverboat—a good way to spend an hour viewing the peaceful shoreline from the water.

When you head north from Essex, go right at the turnaround at the head of Main Street and take River Road as far as Deep River—just keep bearing right when the road forks. It's a winding, narrow country road with views of quietly flowing waters and the forested banks across the way. Then back on Route 154 and on to **Chester,** a picture-postcard village with a short main street lined with charmingly eclectic buildings—a few shops, galleries and restaurants, all restored to a fare-thee-well. Should you be there in June, you'll want to know about the **Sunday afternoon storytellings (★)** in words and pantomime held on the green, a present to the community by the award-winning **National Theatre of the Deaf** (5 West Main Street, Chester), a company that tours the world and makes its home in this town. (Call 203-526-4971 or 203-526-4974 [TDD] for information.)

Since 1769, Chester has been the site of a ferry to the river's east bank. It's a few minutes' drive east of the town center, on Route 148. By all means, take it. The five-minute crossing operates continuously from 7 a.m. to 6:45 p.m. from April through November, at a minimal charge. Looming above you as you stand on deck you'll see what looks like a medieval fortress atop a steep wooded hill. It's **Gillette Castle,** Connecticut's own castle-on-the-Rhine, the creation of a turn-of-the-century actor/playwright who specialized in playing Sherlock Holmes. It took William Gillette five years to build his eccentric dream house, all to his own designs down to the ingenious locks for all 47 doors and the carved oak trim of the mammoth living room. At his death, it was purchased by the state, which made it the centerpiece of a popular state park with wonderful vistas, **Gillette Castle State Park** (67 River Road, Hadlyme; 203-526-2336; admission, for castle only).

East Haddam, a few miles south on Route 82, holds what many consider the jewel of the valley: the **Goodspeed Opera House** (Route 82, East Haddam; 203-873-8668; admission). Built on the river in the elegant mansard-roofed style of 1876, this petite Victorian beauty was reopened in 1963 and dedicated to reviving American musicals of the past. Tours of the exquisitely restored interior can be taken on Mondays and Saturdays in July, August and September. (For performances, see the "Theater in Connecticut" feature in this chapter.) The little town retains many well-kept buildings, reminders of the days when steamboats made regular stops, and sailing ships before them. High on a knoll is the little red schoolhouse where Nathan Hale taught in 1773–74, two years before he was hanged as a spy by the British.

A brief voyage on the Connecticut River gives new perspectives on the picturesque shores. **Camelot Cruises** (1 Marine Park, Haddam; 203-345-8591) offer lunch, dinner, Sunday brunch and murder mystery outings along the scenic Connecticut River. Also available are all-day trips across Long Island Sound.

Old Lyme lies due south of East Haddam, at the eastern end of the highway bridge that spans the river as it flows to the sea. The town's wealth, reflected in extraordinarily handsome, spacious homes, was born in the days of clipper ships and the China trade, but at the start of this century Old Lyme became a magnet for artists drawn by its beauty and tranquil setting. They called themselves American impressionists: Childe Hassam, Willard

Metcalf, Henry Ranger and others who stayed at "Miss Florence's" boardinghouse. Miss Florence Griswold was a ship captain's daughter and lover of art. Her home, built in 1817, is today the **Florence Griswold Museum** (96 Lyme Street; 203-434-5542; admission), with period furniture and changing exhibitions. Most interesting is the dining room, where the artists painted local scenes on wooden wall and door panels. A long, humorous vignette over the fireplace represents the congenial group at an imaginary fox hunt, each member in a characteristic pose.

The imposing **Congregational Church** that appears frequently in the impressionists' paintings stands at Lyme Street's south end. Admired though it is, it is a 1910 copy, faithful in all details, of the original 1816 structure, destroyed by fire. The **Old Lyme Academy of Fine Arts** (84 Lyme Street; 203-434-5232) continues the town's tradition with a variety of exhibits throughout the summer, as do several galleries on Lyme Street.

MYSTIC AREA

Most people planning a trip to Connecticut think **Mystic**, with its popular aquarium and historic seaport. It's no reflection on these two outstanding attractions to caution travelers to budget their time: the southeastern corner of the state is filled with treasures, well-known and not.

Best to stop at the information center on Route 95 at North Stonington (southbound) or contact the **Southeastern Connecticut Tourism District** (P.O. Box 89, 27 Masonic Street, New London, CT 06320; 800-222-6783) to get the lay of the land—and of the water. New London, Groton, Mystic and Stonington grew prosperous as sea and river ports, and today, the recreational uses of this jagged coastline are central to the communities' appeal. Moreover, New London and Groton are home to water-related military facilities, some of which are open to the public. At the **United States Coast Guard Academy** (Mohegan Avenue/Route 32, New London; 203-444-8270) visitors may tour the grounds, visitors center, museum, the chapel, some of the buildings and, when it's in port, the tall ship *Eagle*, used as a training vessel for the cadets. What a vision, when she sails down the Thames River and out to sea!

Another river scene great to behold is a submarine being towed by a tugboat to or from the United States Naval Submarine base on the Groton side of the Thames—they say "Thaymes" in this area. In Groton, you can tour the *U.S.S. Nautilus* (Route 12; 203-449-3174), the first nuclear-powered submarine, now a National Historic Landmark, permanently berthed and refitted to receive visitors. Alongside is the striking, steel-and-glass **Submarine Force Library and Museum** (Route 12, Groton, 203-449-3174), with hands-on, up-to-date exhibits that trace the history of the submarine from our friend Bushnell's *Turtle* to the sleek, high-tech models of today.

Boat tours of the Groton–New London area offer visitors multiple choices: among them are the hour-long Thames River run called **River**

Queen Cruises (193 Thames Street, Groton; 203-445-9516) and the two-and-one-half-hour educational cruise on the research vessel Enviro-Lab (Avery Point, Groton; 203-445-9007), where passengers learn about marine life firsthand.

Though the glories of whaling days are New London's main claim to fame—be sure to drive past the four magnificent 1832 temple-front mansions, known collectively as **Whale Oil Row (★)** (105-119 Huntington Street)—the city has many strings to its bow: the lively town pier, with charter boats of all kinds; ferries that ply across the Sound to several island destinations; and some fine historic homes and museums.

Visitors of a literary bent will want to stop by **Monte Cristo Cottage** (325 Pequot Avenue; 203-443-0051; admission), boyhood home of playwright Eugene O'Neill and the setting for his two autobiographical plays, *Ah! Wilderness* and *Long Day's Journey Into Night.* The shorefront cottage is part of the **Eugene O'Neill Theater Center** (just a few miles away at 305 Great Neck Road, Waterford; 203-443-5378), an organization devoted to developing new works for the stage. Some of the play readings, performances and rehearsals are open to the public. (See the "Theater in Connecticut" feature in this chapter.) Nearby is New London's **Ocean Beach Park** (Ocean Avenue; 203-447-3031; admission), with a broad expanse of

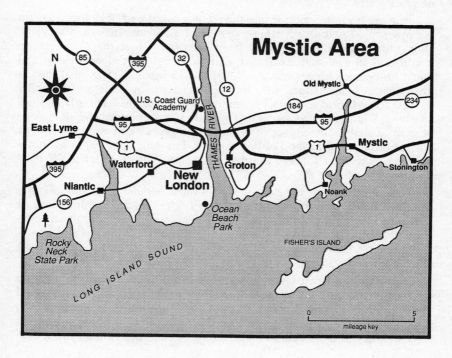

fine sand, a boardwalk and vistas of passing ships, ferries and a handsome lighthouse.

Driving toward Mystic on Route 95, you'll arrive at a scenic overlook where **Mystic Seaport** (50 Greenmanville Avenue; 203-572-0711; admission) comes into view. Just for a moment—as you spot the masts of tall ships in the distance and the smaller craft that ply the Mystic River—you might really believe you're entering a 19th-century New England seaport. When you get there, you and thousands of others, a little of the magic wears off. Yet it's unique, this indoor/outdoor museum on 17 riverfront acres.

Begun in 1929, Mystic Seaport has grown steadily, encompassing a coastal village—church, chapel, schoolhouse, pharmacy, bank, ship's chandlery—several buildings with indoor exhibits of figureheads, marine paintings and ship's models; a lively children's museum; a preservation shipyard where you can watch the craftsmen at work; and a collection of some 300 boats and ships headed by the *Charles W. Morgan* (1841), America's sole surviving wooden whaleship. Crowds or no crowds, you won't want to miss the opportunity to explore its decks, visit the cramped quarters where crews lived for years at a time and watch members of the staff set sails and climb the rigging as they sing traditional chanteys. An ideal time to go is on a drizzly, misty grey day, when visitors are fewer and the atmosphere even more evocative.

Having been transported into the reconstructed past, take time to roam the town of **Mystic** itself, where vessels of all kinds, including whalers, clipper ships and pleasure boats, have been built since the 17th century. You'll find streets, such as Gravel, Clift and High, edged with early- and mid-19th-century homes of ships' owners and captains. The small downtown bustles with visitors, all watching the parade of boats passing under the rare *bascule* bridge (that's French for seesaw) that opens hourly all summer long, while traffic stops dead. There are **windjammers** and all manner of craft available for cruises of an hour or a week. You can help sail, or not, according to the mood of the moment. For details, contact the Southeastern Connecticut Tourism District (27 Masonic Street, P.O. Box 89, New London, CT 06320; 800-222-6783).

Then you'll want to visit the state's most popular attraction, **Mystic Marinelife Aquarium** (Coogan Boulevard; 203-536-3323; admission). It boasts 48 fine indoor exhibits; outdoor habitats for sea lions, seals and penguins; a Marine Theater with hourly demonstrations starring talented whales and dolphins; and in summer, open classroom programs for children, requiring no reservations.

Stonington, the easternmost coastline town in the state, is thought by many to be the most attractive. The densely settled, narrow tongue of land known as Stonington Borough, part of the larger town, is home port to Connecticut's one remaining commercial fishing fleet. Its compact streets are a treasury of architectural styles dating back to the 18th and 19th centuries, when generations of seamen sailed in locally built vessels to trade with China and as far as Antarctica in search of whales and seals. A pleasant walking tour of Main, Water and the short diagonal streets could begin at the **Old Lighthouse Museum** (7 Water Street; 203-535-1440; admission), where the 1823 granite lighthouse displays maritime exhibits and memorabilia of the Oriental trade and whaling and fishing days. Be sure to climb the stone steps to the top of the tower where there is a wonderful view of three states and Long Island Sound.

NORTHEAST CORNER

North of the bustling, sometimes crowded coastline lies the region that has dubbed itself "the quiet corner": Connecticut's little-known, unspoiled Northeast, rich in scenic and historic interest if not in per capita wealth. You'll find no corporate towers here, no hordes of tourists, but interesting small towns, some of them settled in the 18th century, and a wealth of green pastures, rolling hills, rivers and forests. The **Northeast Connecticut Visitors District** (P.O. Box 598, Putnam, CT 06260; 203-928-1228) will supply brochures listing accommodations and points of interest.

To reach the quiet corner from the coast, the fastest route is 395, which branches off from Route 95 west of New London. If you're in Stonington, however, and don't wish to retrace your steps, a pleasant alternative would be Route 2, which winds its way through unspoiled rural areas to Norwich, a historic city at the head of the River Thames. At the junction of Routes 2 and 169, in Norwich, the old **Leffingwell Inn** (348 Washington Street; 203-889-9440; admission), a former colonial "publique house" and now a museum, served as a meeting place for patriots in the Revolutionary War.

From there, Route 169 heads north and passes through the village of Taftville, past an immense, turreted brick construction handsome enough to serve as a king's castle. It's **Ponemah Mill** (★), a former cotton factory thought to have been the largest in the country and the most beautiful, many say. You won't find it on tourist itineraries—it's privately owned and now home to a fine furniture company—but it's an appropriate introduction to an area where the textile industry set the pattern of life from the mid-19th century until recent decades. When the industry moved to the South, it left behind its footprints: imposing riverfront mills, each with its village where the workers lived. Many such complexes—some shuttered and depressed, others used for new purposes—hug the banks of the Quinebaug River, which flows close to Route 169.

The road also passes graceful colonial towns like **Canterbury**, with its neat village green, where the **Prudence Crandall House** (junction of Routes 14 and 169; 203-546-9916; admission) pays tribute to the resolute young teacher who dared to open a school for "young ladies of color" in 1833. The ensuing controversy led to imprisonment—happily, brief—and to the school's closing. Fifty years later, as a restitution of sorts, the state legislature granted Crandall an annuity of $400 per year.

The courthouse where Crandall's trial took place is a few miles north, in **Brooklyn**, where it serves as the current town hall. Near it, on Brooklyn's green, is the first **Unitarian Church** in the state, a simple, elegant white structure built in 1771, with a Paul Revere bell in its lofty belfry. The town is known for its agricultural fair in late August, but it also holds a hidden gem: **Old Trinity Church** (★) (1771), bypassed by time and now open just once a year on All Saints' Day. From the town center, take Route 6 east for one mile, go left on Church Street and you'll find the serene white clapboard structure, with its arched windows and pedimented door, standing next to its ancient graveyard in a leafy grove, surrounded by cornfields.

Pomfret, site of an elite private school, has long been a magnet for affluent city families, who built substantial summer homes and landscaped gardens here. It's still a residential enclave, and its wide, shady streets are great for a brief walking tour. For more information, contact **Northeast Connecticut Visitors District** (P.O. Box 598, Putnam, CT 06260; 203-928-1228).

Woodstock sits high on a hill overlooking a rich agricultural valley. Visitors come from far away to see **Roseland Cottage** (Route 169, 203-928-4074; admission), a bright pink Gothic-inspired mansion built in 1846 by Henry Bowen, a local boy who grew rich in business in New York, then turned his energies toward publishing an antislavery, staunchly Republican weekly called *The Independent*. The lavish house and gardens, which remained in the family for over 100 years, are intact, as is the tradition of festive Fourth of July parties on the grounds.

Across the Quinebaug, and just a few miles from the Rhode Island and Massachusetts lines, the town of **Thompson** boasts a magnificent 19th-century mill fronting the river, as well as a classic residential area on a hilltop—one of the finest. Today, it's as composed and tranquil as any you'll find, with its traditional green—they call it a common here—fine meeting house and white or pale-yellow homes on shady streets. It was a busy crossroads in the past: two major turnpikes intersected there, Boston to Hartford and Providence to Springfield.

The two-story tavern built in 1814, the still-operating **Vernon Stiles Inn** (junction of Routes 193 and 200; 203-923-9571), was a bustling meeting place for important, but weary stagecoach travelers from three states. It also did a brisk wedding business, as young lovers fled the stringent laws of nearby states. The 19th-century innkeeper, Captain Stiles, administered the vows. Today's owners merely provide food and drink in an evocative, charming setting (see the "Restaurants" section in this chapter).

After this spell of old-time tranquility, you'll be ready for the bustle and bounce of an up-to-date university campus. Route 44 will take you west to Storrs, part of the town of Mansfield, location of the main campus of the **University of Connecticut**. (Information Center at 1266 Storrs Road; 203-486-2000.) Now a prestigious university, "UConn" was founded in 1881 as an agricultural school. The sight of emerald pastures dotted with well-fed cows across the street from massive modern buildings makes an intriguing contrast. It also makes for great ice cream, which you can buy at the Dairy Bar, made every day. Refreshed, you'll want to stop at the **William Benton Museum of Art** (245 Glenbrook Road, Storrs; 203-486-4520), where wide-ranging exhibitions are displayed in an attractive, cathedral-ceilinged gallery. The Benton has the honor of being Connecticut's state art museum—a fitting way to finish up a tour.

Shopping

SOUTHWESTERN CONNECTICUT SHOPPING

Fairfield County is a shopper's dream come true. Most of the shoreline towns, as well as several major cities, offer such a variety of consumer experiences that people come from far and wide to browse and buy.

In Stamford, now a mini-metropolis, choices range from such stylish, old-established department stores as **Lord and Taylor** (110 High Ridge Road; 203-327-6600) to the Cadillac of downtown shopping malls, the seven-level **Stamford Town Center** (100 Greyrock Place; 203-356-9700), anchored by **Macy's** (203-964-1500), **Saks Fifth Avenue** (203-323-3100) and **J. C. Penney** (203-964-1115). What more could one wish? Well, there are chic European shops like **Burberry's** (203-325-1450) and **Jaeger** (203-327-0212); prestigious American labels such as **Abercrombie and Fitch** (203-327-4840); **Black, Starr and Frost** (203-356-9660) for your jewelry needs; **F.A.O. Schwartz** (203-324-1643) for the finest in toys; even a branch of **New York's Metropolitan Museum Shop** (203-978-0554)—all connected by high-tech escalators and glass-enclosed elevators and serviced by a mammoth parking garage.

For a totally different mall experience, try **The Factory Outlets at Norwalk** (11 Rowan Street, Norwalk; 203-838-1349), a former hat mill now devoted to 26 stores bursting with designer clothes, shoes and accessories for men, women and children, as well as linens, luggage and gifts. Check out **The Company Store** (203-838-9921) for designer sportswear and leather goods.

Other discount outlets are located up and down nearby West Avenue, including **Loehmann's** (467 West Avenue, Norwalk; 203-866-2548), the grandmother of all off-price designer clothing stores.

Washington Street, the heart of South Norwalk's historic district, is great for browsing through a potpourri of small shops and boutiques devoted to home furnishings, both yesterday's and today's, quirky clothing, jewelry, high-tech lighting fixtures and French ceramics. If stringing beads is something you always wanted to try, **Beadworks** (139 Washington Street, South Norwalk; 203-852-9194) will show you how and sell you all the necessary materials. And if there's always room for one more fine handcrafted piece in your house—a ceramic item, basket, weaving or glass piece—visit the **Brookfield/SoNo Craft Center** (127 Washington Street, South Norwalk; 203-853-6155).

You can't leave Norwalk without a trip to **Stew Leonard's** (100 Westport Avenue; 203-847-7213), say its fans. "The World's Largest Dairy Store" is a near-supermarket with Disneyland overtones, where bigger-than-lifesize animated displays—cows, dogs, giant milk cartons—sing for your children's pleasure, if not yours. Its success is now legendary, largely because dairy products, meat, fish, fruit, vegies, baked goods and ready-cooked foods are superfresh and reasonably priced.

Back to more traditional shopping: a stroll downtown in Greenwich or in Westport provides a mall's worth of attractive shops and boutiques. On Westport's short but lively Main Street you'll find predictable "in" fashion names like **Laura Ashley, Ann Taylor** and **Benetton**, but also several uncommonly well-stocked bookstores, including **Klein's** (44 Main Street; 203-226-4261), a sizable emporium that combines a vast choice of reading material with office supplies and equipment, cameras and stereos, and the aptly named **Remarkable Book Shop** (177 Main Street; 203-227-1000), where the written word reigns but every spare nook and cranny in the charming pink building is filled with imaginative gifts, toys and knickknacks.

Around the corner, **American Hand** (125 Post Road East; 203-226-8883) carries outstanding contemporary craft objects—glass, jewelry, ceramics, wood, fiber, metal—in a wide range of prices. **Artafax** (139 Post Road East; 203-226-9888) calls itself a design shop, and indeed their eclectic—and expensive—furniture pieces and household accessories, old and new, are chosen with a keen eye for form and color.

Greenwich Avenue, the main street of elite Greenwich, and the adjoining blocks on **Putnam Avenue** (Route 1), present a profusion of upscale apparel shops—skiwear to prom gowns, trendy to purest Ivy League. You'll also find fine jewelry, gourmet cookware, furniture, home accessories (check out the exquisite imported ceramics at **Hoagland's of Greenwich**, 175 Greenwich Avenue; 203-869-2127) and such unexpected pleasures as a spacious, well-appointed **Woolworth's** (205 Greenwich Avenue; 203-869-6548), complete with gilt colonial eagles bracketing the store sign, as befits a town proud of its long history.

Antique shops are ubiquitous in Fairfield County, as they are everywhere in Connecticut. (An extensive list of antique dealers around the state is available from the Connecticut Department of Economic Development, 865 Brook Street, Rocky Hill, CT 06067-3405.) One of the most attractive spots for viewing yesterday's treasures is **Cannon Crossing** (23-34 Cannon Road, just off Route 7, Wilton; 203-762-3432), a pre-Civil War farm village.

In the handful of small, picturesque buildings you'll also find dried floral arrangements, fine fireplace tools, quilts, pottery, glassware, a tiny restaurant. Across the way is **St. Benedict Guild** (Cannondale Depot, 22 Cannon Road; 203-762-3633), a cross-cultural shop selling clothing, jewelry and artifacts from around the world.

Another in the state's collection of oversized emporiums is **Danbury Fair Mall** (7 Backus Avenue, Danbury; 203-743-3247). It's huge and glitzy, boasting **Macy's** (203-731-3500), **G. Fox** (203-790-4000), a food court and a wonderful new carousel, in memory of the days when this vast site was the beloved Danbury Fairgrounds.

NORTHWEST CORNER SHOPPING

Every little town in this fashionable rural area hosts a variety of intriguing shops and boutiques, not to mention art galleries, craft studios and antiques of all kinds.

The Silo (Upland Road, New Milford; 203-355-0300) is an uncommon enterprise, a former barn with silo that combines a handsome art gallery with changing exhibitions, a cooking school and a store that stocks everything the home chef might ever need—all in a warren of quaint little rooms.

Historic Litchfield is a paradise for lovers of antiques, who might strike gold right in the center of town, at **Thomas McBride Antiques**, for example (62 West Street, Litchfield; 203-567-5476) or a few blocks west on Route 202 at **Donald Linsley, Inc.** (Harris Plains; 203-567-4245), where English country treasures are the specialty. (For a complete list, contact the **Litchfield Hills Travel Council**, P.O. Box 1776, Marble Dale, CT 06777; 203-868-2214.)

You can window shop for elegant, country-style clothes or home accessories alongside the green, or half a mile west on Route 202 at **Litchfield Common**, an enclave of attractive shops. Flower lovers will want to visit **White Flower Farm** (Route 63, Litchfield; 203-567-0801), a nursery known countrywide for its perennials, garden store and five acres of exquisite display grounds.

Alongside the picturesque covered bridge at West Cornwall, you can stroll into **Cornwall Bridge Pottery Store** (203-672-6545) and purchase attractive pots, lamps and tiles made by Todd Piker. Should you wish to watch this fine craftsman at work, you're welcome to visit **Cornwall Bridge Pottery** on Route 7, one-half mile south of the junction with Route 4 (203-672-6545). **Brass Bugle Antiques** (Route 45, Cornwall Bridge; 203-672-6535) offers furniture, primitives, quilts, china and tools. One of the region's finest antique shops, it's located in an 18th century barn.

If you like fruit and veggies really fresh, stop at **Ellsworth Hill Farm** (Route 4, Sharon; 203-364-0249). During June and July, you can pick as many strawberries as time and your aching back permit. The same applies for raspberries and apples in season. In addition to the apple orchard, cider mill and vegetable farm, you can buy the bountiful produce as well as fresh baked goods.

Salisbury's pretty Main Street is great for gazing at 19th-century homes and window shopping innumerable small, attractive shops that feature clothes, antiques, gifts and books. There are also unusual, exotic teas to buy or sip at tiny tables at **Chaiwalla** (1 Main Street; 203-435-9758).

In Riverton, traditional home of the celebrated Hitchcock chair, you can purchase recently made reproductions at the **Hitchcock Chair Factory Store** (Route 20; 203-379-4826).

HARTFORD AREA SHOPPING

Canton abounds in antique shops, and there's action every Saturday night at 7:30 at **Canton Barn Auctions** (75 Old Canton Road, off Route 44; 203-693-0601).

The **Farmington Valley Arts Center** (25 and 27 Arts Center Lane, Avon Park North, Avon; 203-678-1867) comprises 22 artists' studios, a gallery with changing exhibitions and a shop that sells American contemporary crafts from all over the United States. It's an intriguing complex of handsome brownstone buildings scattered about a landscaped park.

Riverdale Farms (Route 10 North, Avon; 203-677-6437) used to provide fresh milk to Hartford County. Today, it houses 35 varied shops and services in 18 buildings, some old, some new but harmonious. There are fashions, gifts, jewelry, children's toys and clothes, and special stores for people who like to knit and sew.

Downtown Hartford boasts two major, long-established department stores: the original **G. Fox** (960 Main Street; 203-522-1920) and **Sage-Allen** (900 Main Street; 203-278-2570). There are also three extensive shopping malls: **Civic Center Mall** (Hartford Civic Center; 203-275-6100); the **Richardson Mall** (942 Main Street; 203-525-9711), housed in an 1863 landmark building; and the dazzling newcomer, **The Pavilion at State House Square** (30 Main Street; 203-241-0100).

For unusual presents, you might consider the gift shop at the **Wadsworth Atheneum** (600 Main Street; 203-728-5989), which stocks a fine selection of art books, reproductions, prints, cards, elegant wrapping papers as well as games and books for enquiring young minds. The shop at the **Old State House** (800 Main Street; 203-522-6766) leans more toward things historical, as befits this ancient, still lively institution.

NEW HAVEN AREA SHOPPING

When in New Haven, do as the Yalies do—patronize the **Yale Coop** (77 Broadway, New Haven; 203-772-2200), two mammoth floors filled with everything needed by students—and other humans, too. Glance at the striking, geometric facade—a 1960s design by Eero Saarinen—before you succumb to temptation inside. Books are the main attraction here, a most extraordinary selection of titles, but you'll also find men's and women's dress and casual clothes, records and radios, computers and a travel agency.

Among the bountiful bookstores in this learned city is **Atticus Bookstore Café** (1082 Chapel Street; 203-776-4040), a great place to start reading that novel you just bought as you linger over a cappuccino or a sandwich.

The area around Chapel and College streets, home to theaters, museums and numerous restaurants, is great for shopping, too. Some of the stores are multiples—Benetton, Laura Ashley, Brian Alden—while others are New Haven originals. **Endleman Gallery** (1014-A Chapel Street; 203-776-2517) carries one-of-a-kind jewelry by over 100 American designers, while its offspring, **Endleman Two** (1044 Chapel Street; 203-782-2280), presents uncommon accessories and clothes.

Branford Craft Village at Bittersweet Farm (779 East Main Street, near exit 56 on Route 95, Branford; 203-488-4689) is a delight—a cluster of some 30 workshops carved out of buildings that were part of a chicken farm. You can watch craftspeople at their work—woodworker, potter, glass blower, stained-glass artist—and order custom-made pieces or select from their ample stock.

LOWER CONNECTICUT RIVER VALLEY SHOPPING

Antiques are what most shoppers seek in this region, and every little town responds with its own array of specialized offerings. There's even the **Essex Saybrook Antiques Village** (985 Middlesex Turnpike, Old Saybrook; 203-388-0689), where no fewer than 80 dealers hold forth in their own cluster of colonial-looking buildings. The **Connecticut Valley Tourism Commission** (393 Main Street, Middletown; 203-347-6924) has compiled a complete listing of antique shops in the area.

Window shopping along Essex's lovely Main Street is a popular pastime—too popular, you might find, on summer weekends. Many of the stores' names will be familiar; some are originals, like **Honoré** (1 Griswold Square; 203-767-1271), experts in jewelry old and new.

If herbs intrigue you, drive to the **Sundial Herb Garden** in tiny Higganum (Brault Hill Road; 203-345-4290), where you can stroll through an 18th-century-style garden, then browse in the attractive barn-turned-herb-shop stocked with gourmet items, plants, books and a myriad of herbs for sale. Inquire about their afternoon tea (by appointment only) which includes a guided tour of the garden.

MYSTIC AREA SHOPPING

Olde Mistick Village (203-536-4941) is an entire community of colonial-style structures built in the early 1970s to house every kind of shop and boutique known to the traveler—60 businesses on 20 landscaped acres. A bit cutesy, but it's an attractive place for browsing, with winding lanes, a stream, benches, wonderful flowers, even an authentic-looking meeting house with slender steeple and bells that soothe the weary visitor with music.

Within Mystic Seaport itself, the vast **Mystic Seaport Museum Stores** (203-572-8551) emphasize things nautical and traditionally New England: gifts, clothes, foods, books, prints, reproductions from the museum's collection. A separate section houses the prestigious Mystic Maritime Gallery.

Stonington's Water Street offers a wealth of pristine buildings to admire, good antiquing and a clutch of interesting boutiques as well. At **Hungry Palette** (105 Water Street; 203-535-2021) you'll find exclusive, locally designed fabrics and clothes. **Quimper Faïence** (141 Water Street; 203-535-1712) imports its traditional, hand-painted dinnerware and accessories directly from France.

NORTHEAST CORNER SHOPPING

The "quiet corner" offers its own array of antique shops on country roads or quiet main streets. **Northeast Connecticut Visitors District** (P.O. Box 598, Putnam, CT 06260; 203-928-1228) has a complete list available.

Each town has its complement of boutiques and stores, but visitors seeking an unusual buying foray often head for one of the region's scenic vineyards: **Nutmeg Vineyard** (800 Bunker Hill Road, Coventry; 203-742-8402) or the state's oldest farm winery, **St. Hilary's Vineyard** (Route 12, North Grosvenordale; 203-935-5377), which specializes in peach, blueberry and raspberry wines.

Another popular shopping destination is **Caprilands Herb Farm** (534 Silver Street, Coventry; 203-742-7244), most famous of its ilk. On the extensive grounds stand a bookshop, a bouquet and basket shop, a restored 18th-century barn that carries herbs and spices, a greenhouse that sells seeds and plants, and an old farmhouse open for luncheon programs (daily, by reservation only), not to mention 31 different gardens featuring vegetables, herbs and herbal flowers.

Nightlife

There is life after sundown in Connecticut, despite anything you might have heard. Theater-going is a favorite activity. (See "Theater in Connecticut" in this chapter.) The major cities also boast performing centers with varied programs of music and dance, and for those who like to stay up even later there are clubs, bars and taverns with entertainment of all kinds.

SOUTHWESTERN CONNECTICUT NIGHTLIFE

Each season (January through June) the **Stamford Center for the Arts** (The Palace Theater, 61 Atlantic Street, Stamford; 203-325-4466) presents a dazzling potpourri: classical music, jazz, folk, musical theater, dance, all performed by nationally known artists on tour. In the same city, a cozy night spot called **Catch 22** (82 Iroquois Road; 203-323-1787) specializes in New Orleans-style jazz and blues by Hurricane Harry and his trio.

At **Connecticut's Broadway Theater** (65 Tokeneke Road, Darien; 203-655-7667) professional singers perform versions of popular musicals, while patrons dine.

Giggles and Bits (in the Red Bull Motor Inn, Schraffts Drive, Waterbury; 203-597-8000) presents two comedy shows Friday and Saturday performed by three New York comics. Cover.

For music and dancing, follow the crowds to **Shenanigan's** (80 Washington Street, South Norwalk; 203-853-0142). There's live entertainment every night except Monday. This rustic brick and wood dance hall, located in a historic building, offers classic rock-and-roll, rhythm-and-blues and occasional headliners like Bo Diddley and Bonnie Raitt. Cover.

In tiny Georgetown, the **Georgetown Saloon** (8 Main Street; 203-544-8003) saves weekend nights for country music and Thursdays for rock and blues.

The **Charles Ives Center for the Arts** (West Side Campus, Western Connecticut State University, Danbury; 203-797-4002) presents a dramatic outdoor classical music festival during the summer which caters to most preferences: classical, pops, jazz, country, music theater and dance.

Downtown Cabaret Theater (263 Golden Hill Street, Bridgeport; 203-576-1636) varies the formula by encouraging patrons to bring along their own picnic.

NORTHWEST CORNER NIGHTLIFE

Litchfield County attracts devotees of classical music to its two long-established summer festivals: **Music Mountain** (Music Mountain Road, off Route 7, Falls Village; 203-824-7126), presenting chamber music from June to September, and the **Norfolk Chamber Music Festival** (Battell Stoeckel Estate, Route 44, Norfolk; 203-542-5537), from June to August. Both feature musicians of national and international renown.

A classic of a different kind is **Lake Compounce Festival Park** (822 Lake Avenue, Bristol; 203-582-6333), said to be the oldest operating amusement park in the country. It's all spruced up now, and from May to October three concert stages come alive after dark with top acts from around the country.

In stately Litchfield, the **Litchfield Inn** (Route 202; 203-567-4503) is the one place to go for a bit of music after dark. Thursday through Sunday, there's a variety of live bands and dancing.

The **Marblehead Pub** (Route 202, Marblehead; 203-868-1496) is located ten miles north of New Milford, and you'll find it lively every night, summer or winter. Locals, of the young and upscale kind, drop in before

(Text continued on page 98.)

Theater in Connecticut

Over the past two decades, this small state has been gaining a large reputation for excellent theater. Connecticut theater no longer means merely summer stock or road companies of successful Broadway shows. The state has seen a flowering of professional regional theaters, staging their own productions of classics and new plays and sending them forth into the national arena, where they have garnered many top awards.

New Haven, once known as a venue for New York producers testing out Broadway-bound plays, now boasts two prestigious producing companies of its own: **Long Wharf Theater** (222 Sargent Drive; 203-787-4282) and **Yale Repertory Theater** (York and Chapel streets; 203-432-1234). Long Wharf's 448-seat, thrust-style theater is in the heart of the city's wholesale market, adjacent to Route 95—a great location with no parking problems. Its season, from September through May, spans the spectrum of American and European drama and comedy, with an occasional musical or small-cast opera—outstanding productions that have gained recognition around the country.

The prestigious Yale Rep (September through May) is the professional adjunct of Yale University School of Drama, and its artistic director, Stan Wojewodski, Jr., doubles as dean of the drama school. Works such as Lee Blessing's *A Walk in the Woods*, Athol Fugard's *Master Harold . . . and the Boys* and August Wilson's Pulitzer Prize-winning *Fences* made their debut in the attractive church-turned-theater and then gone on to fame and fortune around the land. During the annual, midseason Winterfest three plays by budding dramatists are produced here for the first time.

The state capital is home to the **Hartford Stage Company** (50 Church Street; 203-525-5601), winner of the 1989 Tony Award for Outstanding Achievement in Regional Theater. Housed in a contemporary, 489-seat theater downtown, the company is devoted to innovative, sometimes controversial interpretations of the classics, as well as new works by playwrights of today. (The season is October through June.)

The **Goodspeed Opera House** (Route 82, East Haddam; 203-873-8668) is dedicated to the American musical—to reviving vintage ones and inspiring the new. The legendary *Annie* as well as *Man of La Mancha* were both seen for the first time in this Victorian jewel box on the Connecticut River, as were numerous song-and-dance gems from the past that went on to Broadway. (The season is April to December.) A second stage, the **Norma Terris Theater/ Goodspeed-at-Chester** (North Main Street, Chester; 203-873-8668), opened in 1984 to house workshops of new musicals-in-progress.

The **National Theatre of the Deaf** (5 West Main Street, Chester; 203-526-4971, voice, or 203-526-4974, TDD) makes its home in Connecticut, al-

though it travels during most of the year. A professional ensemble of deaf and hearing actors, NTD combines the spoken word with sign language in unique performances that have touched the hearts of audiences in all 50 states and more than two dozen countries for 25 years. On summer Sundays, they offer free storytellings on the green in Chester.

The **Eugene O'Neill Theater Center** (305 Great Neck Road, Waterford; 203-443-5378) is a nationally known playwrights workshop created on a 90-acre estate overlooking Long Island Sound. Staged readings or run-throughs of works-in-progress are open to the public for a nominal fee during July and August.

These are the big guns on the theater scene, the award winners whose names are recognized by stage buffs around the land. Each year also brings new professional theater groups, such as the **Boston Post Road Stage Company** (25 Powers Court, Westport; 203-227-1072) and **Music Theatre of Connecticut** (246 Post Road East, Westport; 203-454-3883), among others, as well as fine productions by talented campus and community groups. Moreover, there's original dinner theater and cabaret. (See the "Nightlife" section in this chapter.)

Other showplaces present national tours of popular dramas and musicals. Foremost among them is New Haven's historic **Shubert Theater** (247 College Street; 203-562-5666), restored to its stylish 1914 sparkle and offering a varied fall, winter and spring season.

The **American Festival Theater** (P.O. Box 908, Stratford, CT; 203-375-2212) was created in 1955 as the American Shakespeare Festival, and for more than two decades this handsome theater on the banks of the Housatonic River drew enthusiastic audiences to star performances of the Bard. Then fortunes changed, and the building stood empty for a number of years, reopening in summer 1989 with a variety of productions originating on other stages. Now closed for renovations, the theater will reopen in summer, 1993.

Connecticut's straw-hat circuit—how quaint that name seems nowadays—is comprised of numerous theaters, some old, some new, that present generally lightweight fare during the summer. Among them are **Candlewood Playhouse** (junction of Routes 37 and 39, New Fairfield; 203-746-6531); **Ivoryton Playhouse** (Main Street, Ivoryton; 203-767-8348); **Nutmeg Theater** (Jorgensen Auditorium, University of Connecticut, Storrs; 203-486-3969); **Oakdale Theater** (95 South Turnpike Road, Wallingford; 203-265-1501); and the **Westport Country Playhouse** (25 Powers Court, Westport; 203-226-0153), one of the oldest summer theaters in the country.

With such a variety of offerings to choose from, visitors are bound to find their favorite kind of theater in Connecticut.

or after dinner to meet their friends, play a game of darts or pool and try their hand at one of the video games.

HARTFORD AREA NIGHTLIFE

Bushnell Memorial Hall (166 Capitol Avenue; 203-246-6807) has been a major performing arts center for half a century. The vast art deco auditorium is where audiences flock for concerts of the Hartford Symphony and other orchestras, the ballet and the opera, and dramas and musicals on tour.

Hartford Civic Center (1 Civic Center Plaza; 203-727-8080) schedules frequent, star-caliber entertainment.

If you like music of the 1950s and '60s, you'll love **Boppers** (22 Union Place; 203-549-5801), a club that echoes those decades in music and decor. Close by, live jazz and pop bands are featured Wednesday through Saturday at **Bourbon Street North** (70 Union Place; 203-525-1014). Or check out **Picasso's** (50 Union Place; 203-549-5444), a nightclub, bistro and gallery. These clubs bring night owls flocking to this refurbished area around old Union Station.

Among lovers of jazz, one of the favorites is the **880 Club** (880 Maple Avenue; 203-525-2428), where different groups perform each night of the week and Sunday is jam session time.

NEW HAVEN AREA NIGHTLIFE

New Haven is blessed with an outstanding theater scene (see "Theater in Connecticut" in this chapter), frequent concerts by the New Haven Symphony and visiting artists and several late-night spots well worth a visit.

The **Foundry Café** (104 Audubon Street; 203-624-0004) features a variety of jazz performers. **Toad's Place** (300 York Street; 203-777-7431) presents original musical acts, local and national.

Boppers (239 Crown Street; 203-562-1957), like its older Hartford sibling, favors the songs of the 1950s and '60s and is housed in a re-created '50s diner.

The **Elm City Diner** (1228 Chapel Street; 203-776-5050)—an original, restored to its high-style art deco elegance—is a full-service restaurant that offers nightly piano music and weekend jazz.

Performance Studio (986 Chapel Street; 203-562-0777) hosts an eclectic fare: one-act plays, rock concerts and improvisational comedy.

LOWER CONNECTICUT RIVER VALLEY NIGHTLIFE

The elegant **Water's Edge Inn and Resort** (1525 Boston Post Road, Westbrook; 203-399-5901) features top entertainment acts on summer weekends and romantic piano music in the lounge on other nights.

The **Griswold Inn** (36 Main Street, Essex; 203-767-1812) is a favorite meeting place after sundown. A landmark of this exquisite river town ever since 1776, "the Gris" boasts an old taproom as fine as any in the state.

Nightly doings range from Dixieland to sea chanteys to traditional ballads or classic arias, all performed in a warm, friendly atmosphere.

MYSTIC AREA NIGHTLIFE

Ocean Beach Park (New London; 203-447-3031) presents nightly programs with top entertainment acts performing under a spacious tent close to the sea.

The Pony Express Dine and Dance (52–56 Bank Street, New London; 203-443-4637) is a congenial place to head live entertainment weekly. They provide casual dining at its best and come summer, food and drinks are served on their outdoor patio overlooking the Thames.

New London's **Radisson Hotel** (35 Governor Winthrop Boulevard; 203-443-7000) offers visitors a choice of dancing as they dine at **The Winthrop** or listening to live entertainment while relaxing at **Ashley's Lounge**.

It might not be everyone's way to spend an evening, but hundreds travel from far away for **High Stakes Bingo at the Mashantucket Pequot Indian Reservation** (Route 2, Ledyard; 203-572-8946). Nightly games begin at 6:30 in the huge, modern Bingo Hall owned and operated by residents of this Native American reservation, with an average of $16,000 awarded each night.

After a heavy day of sightseeing in Mystic, try the bar at the **Captain Daniel Packer Inn** (32 Water Street; 203-536-3555). The cozy, rustic room with its old fireplace is a favorite gathering place for residents of all ages. It features music Tuesday through Thursday and a relaxing atmosphere seven nights a week.

NORTHEAST CORNER NIGHTLIFE

A welcome addition to the "quiet corner's" nightlife scene is **J. D. Cooper's Fine Food and Spirits** (146 Park Road, Putnam; 203-928-0501). This triple-threat establishment comprises a restaurant, a bar and the Cooper Stadium Sports Bar, where the whole family can enjoy darts, an oversized television screen and several interactive video games.

The **Bidwell Tavern** (1260 Main Street, Coventry; 203-742-6978) dates from the 1800s, but the music that fills this rustic spot is up-to-date, a mix of contemporary Top-40 tunes with jazz and blues performed by local talent or name groups.

The **Jorgensen Auditorium** (University of Connecticut, Storrs; 203-486-4226) is the University of Connecticut's major performing center, presenting a year-round program of music, dance and theater performed by artists of international renown.

CHAPTER THREE

Rhode Island

Rhode Islanders don't think of their state as small; they see it as compact, easy to get around in. They point out with great pride that no place in the state is more than a 45-minute drive away from anywhere else. In fact, one of the quirky traits that sets Rhode Islanders apart from the rest of us is their reluctance to drive "long" distances. (Any commute longer than ten minutes is considered grounds for changing either one's job or one's residence.)

It's not only the locals who benefit from all this cozy proximity. Rhode Island's easy-to-reach destinations make it an ideal state for visitors. In a single day, it's possible to swim in Narragansett Bay, lunch in Newport, tour a mansion or two and still be in Providence in time for dinner.

Rhode Island, as every schoolchild knows, is the smallest state in the union—a mere 1214 square miles to be exact. But crammed into this tiny package is an overload of good things. The state's statistics are impressive: 400 miles of coastline (and this in a state that measures only 48 miles from north to south) with over 100 public beaches, some 18,000 acres of parklands, 12 institutions of higher learning, as well as a statewide storehouse of historically significant spots. ("Little" Rhode Island is home to more than 20 percent of all the Registered Historic Landmarks in the entire country.)

Having mentioned some of the state's obvious attributes, let's peek at some of its hidden virtues. Perhaps the best-kept secret about Rhode Island is the immense diversity within its modest boundaries. Some of its sites are well known throughout the world. Surely everyone has heard of the glittering mansions of Newport, but how many tourists know it is also possible to hike through a natural "cathedral of forest" near the historic village of Hopkinton? And while probably every day sailor on the East Coast has discovered the seaport haven of Block Island, how many have ventured north into Narragansett Bay to set sail for the solitary splendor of Prudence or Patience Islands?

Those travelers who seek an individual path could not have found a more appropriate state than this one founded on an individual search for religious freedom. Back in 1636 Roger Williams settled this territory after he could no longer tolerate the religious constraints of the early Boston Puritans. Migrating south with his wife and daughters, he stopped to settle with the friends he had made among the Narragansett Indian tribe. After years of setbacks and negotiations, in 1663 Williams succeeded in wresting a royal charter from England for his new territory, one that would also allow him to unite Providence with several other settlements nearby.

A truly enlightened clergyman, Williams' religious tolerance was universal; his new state embraced all faiths. Although Williams founded his own Baptist Church in 1639 (the building in Providence can still be toured), Quakers, Jews and any other groups seeking religious freedom were wholeheartedly welcomed. (Touro Synagogue in Newport, built in 1763, stands today as the oldest Jewish house of worship in America.)

This sense of tolerance endured. Although Rhode Island did participate in the infamous "triangle trade" (slaves traded for molasses traded for rum), it was also the first colony to prohibit slavery. Rhode Island was also the first colony to declare independence from Great Britain. And at the end of the Revolutionary War, it was the last of the original 13 colonies to ratify the new Constitution, holding out until the Bill of Rights, guaranteeing individual liberties, was added.

America's industrial revolution began in Rhode Island in 1790, when Samuel Slater started operating the first water-powered cotton mill. That power was provided by the mighty Blackstone River, and the rest is American history. Other successful industrial endeavors in the state have included jewelry and silver manufacturing, both of which have drawn immigrants to Rhode Island from all over the world. The newcomers brought along ethnic riches that can still be found in the state's cuisine, architecture and even the spoken word.

During "La Belle Époque" right before the turn of the century, the seaside town of Newport became the darling of America's newly rich and famous, a status-conscious group who lavished their untaxable millions on opulent "summer cottages." Folks like the Vanderbilts, the Astors and the Belmonts vied to one-up each other architecturally in the designs of these palaces, as well as with the opulent furnishings within. It was truly a gilded age, the spoils of which we can all still marvel over.

But palaces of the past are only part of the splendor of present-day Rhode Island, much of it to be found away from the cities. One glance at a map reveals why Rhode Island is nicknamed the "Ocean State": its flamboyant coastline can only be the handiwork of a creative sea. While its interior boundaries are the work of man (they are pure New England— ruler-straight and right-angled), it's a different story along the coast, where the relentless surf has carved out a wild, exotic profile, etching miles of

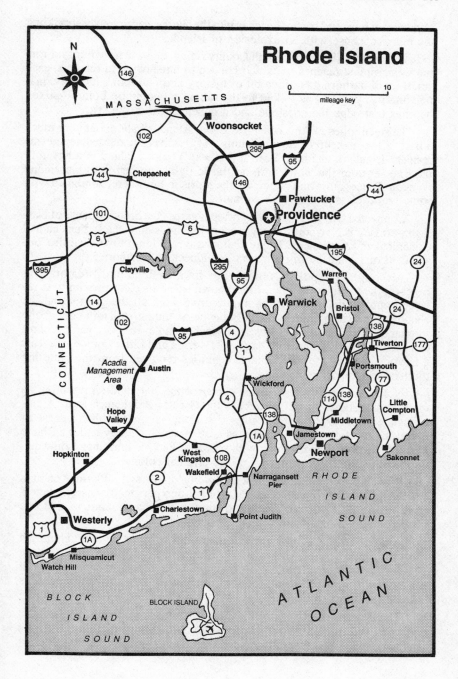

Rhode Island

MASSACHUSETTS

Woonsocket

Chepachet

Pawtucket

Providence

Clayville

Warren

Warwick

Bristol

CONNECTICUT

Tiverton

Acadia Management Area

Austin

Portsmouth

Wickford

Little Compton

Middletown

Hope Valley

Jamestown

Hopkinton

Newport

West Kingston

Sakonnet

Wakefield

Narragansett Pier

RHODE

ISLAND

Charlestown

SOUND

Westerly

Point Judith

Misquamicut

Watch Hill

BLOCK

ATLANTIC

ISLAND

BLOCK ISLAND

OCEAN

SOUND

mileage key

extravagant bays and barrier beaches into the shores, capriciously sprinkling the entire expanse with an explosion of islands.

The coastal villages of South County reflect this watery whimsy. From the westernmost reaches of Watch Hill up to Greenwich in the east, each small town harbors its unique bit of history and maintains its individual personality, yet each is linked to the others by common bonds—silken beaches that edge the coastline and a dependence on the sea.

Thirteen miles off this coast lies Block Island, offshore but very much a part of the makeup of South County. Aggressively underdeveloped (the resident islanders intend to keep it this way!), Block Island is a haven in the true sense of the word, with no traffic lights, no fast-food places and no neon. Peace, quiet and nature are the touristic lures here, combined with some world-class fishing and sailing.

Connected to South County by bridges across the broad expanse of Narragansett Bay is Newport County, occupying the islands the Indians named Conanicut and Aquidneck. Today visitors travel to Jamestown on little Conanicut Island, and the big draw on Aquidneck is Newport.

Although Newport is famous for its mansions and breathtaking beaches, the town has another, little-known side—its close proximity to relaxed country life. A mere ten-minute drive from all the glamor and the clamoring crowds of tourists along Bellevue Avenue stretch miles of bucolic farmlands, wilderness areas, deserted beaches and even a vineyard. A short drive to the postcard-perfect villages of Tiverton and Little Compton reveals a pastoral way of life that remains centuries removed from the glittering tourist passions of Newport.

Northwest of Newport, in the center of the state and representing its metaphysical heart as well, stretches the Greater Providence area. A get-acquainted visit to Providence helps first-time visitors establish a sense of place; the capitol building is here, as are Brown University and the Rhode Island School of Design, along with scores of historic buildings, some dating back two or three centuries to the original colony.

Providence combines the best of big-city/small-town; it's small enough for residents to know each other (Mayor Paolino personally answers letters from residents), yet large enough to support top-rate restaurants and one of the country's outstanding small museums.

Above Providence along the northern tier of the state, throughout the great rectangle of land known as the Blackstone Valley, folks have been gearing up to show off their special blend of treasures to the world. But for the moment, this densely forested river valley is yours to discover, its bounties still largely "hidden."

The Blackstone River itself is the key to this area. Its history includes a starring role in America's industrial revolution, and its future includes landmark status as a federally funded recreation heritage preserve. For the immediate present, the mighty Blackstone awaits your pleasure and your exploration.

Statewide, it is this appealing combination of big-city sophistication and country-style hospitality that makes Rhode Island such an intriguing place to discover. You'll note these qualities in the people you meet; they combine the best of both. Oh yes, and don't overlook their innate sense of independence—that legendary strength of will that surpasses even the rock-bound, generic version attributed to most Yankees. This rugged individuality—one of the principles on which Rhode Island was founded—comes naturally to the people of the Ocean State.

Rhode Island's reputation for championing personal freedoms is once again evidenced in today's newest minority: senior citizens. The state is second only to Florida in its over-65 population. It's especially curious that many of these seniors have moved here from other states, choosing to move to a place far from the Sunbelt's climate. Whatever the reasons for the influx (state statisticians are still puzzling over this one), it becomes fairly obvious that Rhode Island's winters cannot be regarded as a negative factor.

Weatherwise, temperate is the word. Much of the state lies near the ocean or Narragansett Bay, which plunges northward through Rhode Island's center. This watery influence results in light winter snowfalls and temperatures that reach the freezing mark only in January. In summers, the average temperature is around 72°.

Rhode Island has another nickname, "America's First Resort." We're confident you'll enjoy discovering this state for yourself. The only question is whether or not you'll want to share the tales of your adventures in this newfound playground. You may decide you want to keep all these treasures hidden just a while longer, before the word gets out and Rhode Island becomes everyone's favorite place in New England.

Easy Living

Transportation

ARRIVAL

Interstate 95 traverses the state north and south, connecting Rhode Island to Connecticut and to the rest of New England. Along the coast, scenic **1A** hugs the ocean shoreline, a slower but more beautiful drive.

BY AIR

T. E. Green Airport in Warwick is the state's only commercial airport. Regularly scheduled service is provided by American Airlines, American Eagle, Business Express, Continental Express, Delta Airlines, Northwest Airlines, USAir Express and United Airlines.

New England Airlines (401-596-2460) operates daily five-minute commuter flights between Block Island and Westerly.

Several limo and van companies link the airport to cities throughout the state: **Aero Airport Limo Service** (401-737-2868) runs to and from Warwick; **Cozy Cab** (401-846-2500) runs daily shuttles to and from Newport; **Cadillac Cab** (401-232-5731) goes to and from Providence. **RIPTA** buses (401-781-9400) take passengers to the Block Island ferry twice daily.

BY BUS

Scheduled and charter bus services connect all points within the state. They include **Bonanza Bus Lines** (One Bonanza Way, Providence; 401-727-7382), **Pawtuxet Valley Lines** (76 Industrial Lane, West Warwick; 401-828-4100) and **Rhode Island Transit Authority** (RITA) (265 Melrose Street, Providence; 401-781-9400).

BY TRAIN

Amtrak's (800-872-7245) Northeast Corridor service connects Rhode Island with Boston and New York. There is frequent service to and from Providence at Union Station (100 Gaspee Street; 401-727-7382) and less frequent service to Kingston Station (Railroad Avenue, West Kingston; 401-783-2913).

BY BOAT

Ferry service between Block Island and Galilee is provided by **The Interstate Navigation Company** (Galilee; 401-783-4613). Cars and passengers are transported on a year-round basis, although the schedule is abbreviated during off-season. Reservations for cars are essential, even in off-season, and for both passengers and cars during peak summer months.

CAR RENTALS

Major car rental agencies at the Warwick airport include **Hertz Rent A Car** (401-738-7500), **Avis Rent A Car** (401-736-7500) and **Budget Rent A Car** (401-739-8900).

Located across the street from the airport are **Thrifty Car Rental** (2329 Post Road; 401-739-8660), **Dollar Rent A Car** (1989 Post Road; 401-739-8450) and **National Car Rental** (2053 Post Road; 401-737-4800).

PUBLIC TRANSPORTATION

Bus service throughout the state is provided by **Rhode Island Public Transportation Authority** (RIPTA) (401-781-9400). These buses can connect airport passengers with the Block Island ferry in Galilee, as well as direct service from Providence to Newport, Westerly and the South County beaches.

Hotels

Rhode Island's cities and towns are not overloaded with hotels. Providence has only 1000 rooms in total, and Warwick, which leads the state in number of hotels, offers only slightly more than 1400 guest rooms. Smaller inns and bed-and-breakfast homes can be found throughout the state, especially in the South County and Newport areas, and you'll also find a sprinkling of motels and lodges.

SOUTH COUNTY HOTELS

While visitors can always find one or two cookie-cutter chain hotels clustered near the larger towns, it is the rambling Victorians and out-of-the-way inns one remembers, that tend to become a cherished part of the South County experience.

As with most New England resort areas, many lodgings here close for the winter. Rates, too, are seasonal; those indicated below reflect the heady rates of the peak summer season. Because of the crush of visitors, many places will also require two- or three-day minimum stays during high season and holiday weekends.

Personifying the genteel understatement of Watch Hill's old guard is the **Watch Hill Inn** (50 Bay Street; 401-348-8912), an 1890s white clapboard jutting out onto Little Narragansett Bay. The bay breezes cool the inn's 16 non-air-conditioned rooms. Decor is simple—brass beds with puffy quilts, a few period antiques. Some rooms feature modernized baths with stall showers replacing the vintage claw-footed tubs. Guests can rock on the wide porch that overlooks the water and dine in the surprisingly trendy Positano, an upscale Italian restaurant. Deluxe.

Not to be confused with the Watch Hill Inn, the **Inn at Watch Hill** (118 Bay Street; 401-596-0665) is a stretch of modern motel-type suites atop the stores on the town's main drag. While the decor of each unit is utilitarian rather than posh, the views from each open-air deck is pure New England; from your vantage point you can check out everything going on in town, while just beyond the bay, vistas stretch on forever. Specify "Bay View" when reserving; several (designated "Village View") have obstructed views of the water. Each suite has a kitchen area equipped with microwave, refrigerator and sink but without dishes or utensils. Deluxe to ultra-deluxe.

Guests at **Pleasant View House** (65 Atlantic Avenue, Misquamicut; 401-348-8200) get the full ocean treatment. The wide swath of beach unfolds like a carpet just at the edge of the hotel's manicured lawns. The rambling, white wood exterior is accented with sail-blue canvas fronting each private deck. The atmosphere here is vintage seaside; dining rooms, both covered and outdoor, front the ocean, as do many of the guest rooms. Don't look for posh appointments; rooms are decorated in basic motel. But they're clean and comfortable, and the views from the private decks are well worth the price. Deluxe (streetside rooms) to ultra-deluxe (oceanview rooms).

The **Shelter Harbor Inn** (Route 1, Penwagner Road, Westerly; 401-322-8883) looks exactly the way a seaside country inn should look: a spanking white clapboard main building with contrasting window shutters, well-manicured and welcoming. This 1800s farmhouse, its landscaped grounds defined by rustic stone fences, is an inn as well as a popular restaurant. There are ten guest rooms in the main building, each with private bath and some with private sun deck, ten more in the converted barn nearby and four in the coach house. In each room antiques gleam with care, and bedsteads complement the period decor. The public rooms include a cozy library just off the sun porch bar. Deluxe prices include breakfast.

Not all of South County's inns reflect a Yankee heritage. **The Villa** (190 Shore Road, Westerly; 401-596-1054), with its Italianate decor and gaily tiled swimming pool, is decidedly Mediterranean in ambience. Rooms are chock-full, if not cluttered, with knickknacks. Enjoy a continental breakfast or the Italian specialties whipped up as treats for the weekly outdoor barbecues around the pool. Moderate.

Nestled in a wooded inland setting and thoroughly steeped in old New England is the **General Thurston House** (Old Route 3, Hopkinton; 401-377-9049). A 1741 Colonial lovingly restored by owner Doris Silks, this bed and breakfast wraps its guests in cozy country living. Each of the seven guest rooms is different: the "Victorian Room" has two double brass beds; the "Primitive Room" focuses attention on the original stone fireplace and the antique "mammy rocker" bench. Every sitting room comes with a decanter of sherry and fresh-baked sweets. Doris is not only famous for her full country breakfasts, she's also a walking encyclopedia of local history, lore and sights. Moderate.

The **Larchwood Inn** (521 Main Street; 401-783-5454) sits on a hill above the country village of Wakefield, the quintessential manor house. Built in 1831, the three-story house shimmers with family history: portraits of the original owners hang in the front parlor, and one window still bears the signature a daughter etched on the glass pane with her diamond engagement ring. Private baths can be requested, although some of the 12 guest rooms share facilities. There are also six additional units in the annex. Traditional dark wood headboards are brightened by country floral spreads and light streaming in through large windows. Moderate.

Victorian is the word for most of the lodgings on Block Island. Imposing, gingerbread-trimmed structures dominate the island's ocean skyline. A word of caution: some "modernizations" may not please everyone. One such example might be the National Hotel's trendy front-porch scene. Although this place is well-known and located in the middle of the action, its amplified music and noisy camaraderie are not everyone's idea of an idyllic island vacation.

Presiding like a grande dame over all she surveys, the **Hotel Manisses** (Spring Street, Block Island; 401-466-2421) rules with Victorian splendor. Built in 1870 and restored by the Abrams family, innkeepers well-known locally, the Manisses seems to personify Block Island's unique charm and individualism. Afternoon tea is served in the wicker-appointed parlor, where leaded-glass windows rainbow the sunlight. There are a few surprises: several of the 17 guest rooms, like the Princess Augusta, feature jacuzzis rather than Victorian antimacassars; the Antoinette suite opens directly onto the front porch, providing handy access for anyone who dreads climbing stairs; the Pocahontas has its own private deck. Ultra-deluxe.

The **1661 Inn and Guest House** (Spring Street, Block Island; 401-466-2421) combines Victorian charm with sweeping views of Old Harbor. Rooms with water views also sport private decks, and the Samuel Deering room even has its own kitchenette. Rooms are antique-filled and sunny. The inn is also known for its huge breakfast buffet, served overlooking the water. Ultra-deluxe.

NEWPORT AREA HOTELS

In addition to the usual chain hotels, Newport has an abundance of small bed-and-breakfast establishments. As one islander observed, "In this town, almost everyone has an extra room or two to rent." Don't be fooled by that gem of Yankee understatement; we have observed that, in this town where extravagant landmark mansions are almost the norm, the bed and breakfasts tend to follow suit.

The **Wayside** (406 Bellevue Avenue; 401-847-0302) is a trim beige-brick Victorian mansion just across Bellevue Avenue from the famous Elms. Owners Dorothy and Al Posts have restored this sprawling 1896 home, creating a dozen guest rooms blessed with antique furnishings and majestic proportions—and each with its own private bath. There's even a heated pool in the back garden. Deluxe.

The 1855 **Marshall Slocum Guest House** (29 Kay Street; 401-841-5120) sits on a tree-lined, Norman Rockwell kind of street. An American flag flies overhead, and on the spacious front porch rocking chairs await your leisure. Inside, rooms are cheery and graced with antiques. Your gregarious innkeeper, Joan Wilson, who is creative both in the kitchen (fresh-baked quiches and muffins every breakfast) and in decorating, has chosen sunny yellows and marine blues to balance the house's original dark woods. Each of the five upstairs guest rooms has a fireplace, and they share three baths. Breakfast is served on the deck overlooking the sunny back garden in warm weather. Moderate to deluxe.

The **Newport Marriott** (25 America's Cup Avenue; 401-849-1000) is big, modern and close to the water. Most of the 317 rooms and 14 suites command sweeping views of Newport Harbor. Glass-fronted elevators (often exasperatingly slow to arrive) seem to double as kinetic sculpture, providing space-age mobility to the lobby's plant-filled atrium design. Rooms are 1980s-style, featuring a pastel decor and the usual complement of electronic equipment. Among the definite pluses: there's a health club and indoor pool in the hotel; the Gateway Center (Convention and Visitors Bureau) is next door; and shopping and waterfront browsing are within easy walking distance. Ultra-deluxe.

The Viking (1 Bellevue Avenue; 401-847-3300) is Newport's grande dame, a 1920s National Historic Landmark in red brick trimmed in white. The understatement of the tidy four-column entrance is deceptive; inside, the hotel is a sprawl of rooms and levels. (The hotel's full title is: "Hotel Viking and Conference Center.") There are 180 guest rooms, numerous dining rooms and a health club and pool. Rooms are a bit cramped, crammed with heavy antique reproduction four-posters and furniture. In summer, dining at the Garden Patio Café offers a charming alternative to the somewhat overpowering hotel atmosphere inside. Ultra-deluxe.

The Inn at Castle Hill (Ocean Drive; 401-849-3800) sits on 32 acres of secluded peninsula overlooking Narragansett Bay. Built in 1874 for international naturalist Alexander Agassiz, this weathered, shingled inn today retains most of its original Victorian charm. Its rambling structure yields ten guest rooms of unique shapes, bursting with antique decor. Bedrooms are furnished with mahogany four-posters, authentic washstands and upholstered slipper chairs, and are paired with large, modern baths. (Six more guest rooms are found in cliffside harbor houses behind the main building.) Guests like to gather before the unique inlaid-wood fireplace in the downstairs sitting room. Deluxe to ultra-deluxe.

Not everything in Newport is rarified and expensive. The **Comfort Inn** (936 West Main Road; 401-846-7600) offers visitors clean, comfortable and affordable lodgings. The 162 guest rooms are large and creatively decorated with colonial fabrics, contrasting carpeting and wooden spool headboards. Amenities include no-smoking rooms and a heated indoor pool. Moderate.

Because Newport is famous for its colonial houses, it's especially fun to overnight in one, such as the charming **Admiral Farragut Inn** (31 Clarke Street; 401-849-0006). Built in 1702, this trim clapboard house has retained its original 12-over-12 paned windows and authentic colonial cove moldings. The decor in each guest room is different, but all include imported English antiques, handmade Shaker-style four-poster beds, stenciled armoires and a clutch of unusual antiques—like the chair with arms resembling smiling cats. Moderate to deluxe.

PROVIDENCE AREA HOTELS

There are some large, urban hotels in this capital city, with several more under construction.

The **Omni Biltmore Hotel** (Kennedy Plaza, Providence; 401-421-0700), traditionally the area's biggest and best, is newly renovated. The 217 guest rooms reflect a softer decor, with modern pastels in the carpeting and floral spreads. The lobby's grand staircase and glass-cage elevator continue to impress, as does the view from the Grand Ballroom. Ultra-deluxe.

The **Providence Marriott** (Charles and Orms streets, Providence; 401-272-2400), judging from the number of briefcases and power suits, is a favorite site for local business meetings as well as a familiar setting for out-of-town visitors. The all-over design is classic Marriott, although the sprawling layout requires quite a hike to reach the guest room elevators. Rooms are standard issue, modern and clean, with no surprises either good or bad. The lobby bar, Cahoots Lounge, tends to be very popular and noisy at night. The indoor/outdoor pool is also a gathering spot. Moderate.

The **Old Court Bed & Breakfast Inn** (144 Benefit Street, Providence; 401-351-0747) is an antique buff's delight. The building, which began as an Episcopal church rectory in 1863, was restored in 1985. Today each of its ten guest rooms is decorated in authentic treasures: four-poster beds, Victorian coverlets, period washstands. Reserve early; this inn is quite popular. Deluxe.

The **Nathaniel Porter Inn** (★) (125 Water Street, Warren; 401-245-6622) is a combination inn, restaurant and local success story. "Rescued"

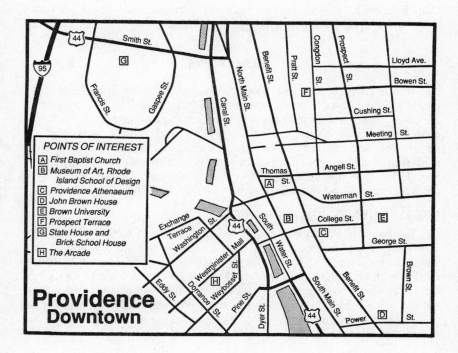

and painstakingly restored by the Lynch family, this red-clapboard colonial house with its jaunty white trim now has three guest rooms and a shared sitting room on the second floor. (Mrs. Lynch will even serve a romantic dinner for two upstairs.) Everything, from the stone fireplaces to the four-poster canopy beds, is authentic and charming. Moderate.

Johnson & Wales Airport Hotel (★) (2081 Post Road, Warwick; 401-739-3000) is the practicum facility for Johnson & Wales University, a hotel, tourism and culinary institute. Opened in 1989, this state-of-the-art hotel offers such wide-ranging facilities and amenities as concierge services, whirlpool and free airport shuttle service. Even better, guests can be sure that the entire staff will be trying extra hard to please; they're students, and they're being graded on their performance. Moderate.

Econo Lodge (2138 Post Road, Warwick; 401-737-7400), a 103-room economy motel, offers excellent value. Guests can look forward to complimentary continental breakfasts and shuttle service to the airport. No-smoking rooms are available. Moderate.

BLACKSTONE VALLEY HOTEL

Surprises await at the **Howard Johnson Hotel** (2 George Street; 401-723-6700) in Pawtucket. There's an "Executive Section" where guest rooms are larger, more fashionably decorated and better appointed than in most chain hotels. This HoJos also has special-function rooms and a staff so courteous and helpful you'll be glad you stayed. Moderate.

Restaurants

Rhode Island is a seafood lover's paradise; favorites from the always-nearby ocean speed directly to your table. Chowder and clam cakes (clams are called "quahogs" in the Ocean State) seems to be every diner's favorite as well as every chef's specialty. Among other local dishes to sample: stuffies, quahogs and stuffing mix served in the large quahog shell; johnnycakes, made from cornmeal ground in a historic mill in South County the old-fashioned way; Indian pudding, an achingly sweet cornmeal dessert; and "family-style chicken," an all-you-can-eat feast that is uniquely Rhode Island.

SOUTH COUNTY RESTAURANTS

Everyone in Watch Hill eats at the **Olympia Tea Room** (Bay Street; 401-348-8211) at one time or another; just sit in the old oak booths and watch the local world go by. Owner Jack Felber stresses a modern American cuisine with an emphasis on fresh seafood. It's a sort of back-to-the-future setting (waitresses wear formal black with white lacy collars and cuffs), but the menu is both homey and eclectic; the Olympia is as famous for its gutsy garlic-laced clam stew as for its dainty dessert pastries shaped like swans. Moderate to deluxe.

The ideal country dining experience is alive and well at the **Shelter Harbor Inn** (Route 1, Westerly; 401-322-8883). Meals are served in several small rooms, each with its stone fireplace, burnished wooden chairs and wildflowers at every table. Selections reflect the local harvest, changing every season. Seafood, as you will have come to expect in this area, is fresh and excellent. Pasta dishes are well seasoned and imaginative. Try the local wine, "America's Cup," from nearby Sakonnet Vineyards. And for dessert, sample the Indian pudding, which arrives warm and fragrant. Moderate.

It looks like an unremarkable storefront from the street, but inside **Main Street Foods & Bakery** (★) (333 Main Street, Wakefield; 401-789-0914) gleams with industrial shelving and bleached wooden shelves loaded with gourmet goodies. Dine there, seated at tables dressed with snowy napery, or take out treats for al fresco feasting. Chef Michael Chapman serves breakfast (oven-baked German apple pancakes, french toast made from challah), lunch (pesto chicken sandwiches, special frittatas, crêpes and quiches) and dinner (risotto of grilled chicken and Italian sausage, grilled duck breast with pecan marmalade). Moderate to deluxe.

Yearn for some Italian food that's good and won't dent the budget? Head for **Terminesi's Narragansett Inn** (135 Boon Street, Narragansett; 401-783-7939). Nothing fancy here, just lots of families, with kids running around. Lots of enjoyment, too, as everyone digs into heaping plates full of seafood marinara, special pastas and veal dishes. Budget to moderate.

Haute cuisine served in rarified surroundings greets visitors to **Basil's** (22 Kingston Road, Narragansett; 401-789-3743). With striped awnings outside and delicate floral wallpaper inside, Basil's is a tiny gem of European-style dining. The service is formal, and guests tend to dress up for the occasion (unusual in a seaside area). The menu includes many usual continental favorites (*vol au vent*, beef Stroganoff, scallops Provençal), but owner and chef Vasilios Kourakis has an inspired hand with herbs and spices, so old favorites tend to become new favorites at first bite. Deluxe to ultra-deluxe in price.

Eating at **George's Galilee** (250 Sand Hill Cove Road, Narragansett; 401-783-2306) has become a Rhode Island tradition. Diners at this casual, wood-paneled spot usually sit before huge windows that offer views of the fishing boat dock. Fare is a traditional mix of clam cakes, lobster, fish and pasta, plus beef and poultry items. Moderate.

Most visitors to Block Island feel they have stepped back in time, into a more gentle era. Among Block Island's bevy of Victorian mansions, the favored lodging is also the preferred dining spot. In summer the **Hotel Manisses** (Spring Street; 401-466-2421) focuses its meal service on the flower-studded outdoor patio; and when chill winds blow in off the Atlantic, the focus shifts indoors, where crackling fires warm the spirits. A vast raw fish bar dominates the entrance and includes a selection of fish smoked over aromatic woods right on the premises. Smoked bluefish is a perennial favorite. Seafood is featured, with some nice variations that include bouillabaisse and several low-calorie selections. Deluxe.

Whether you fancy a sandy beach or a cliff-top ocean view, picnics will become an important part of your Block Island experience. Pick up your favorites at **Humphrey's Sandwich Shop** (★) (Water Street, Old Harbor; 401-466-5411) or the **Old Harbor Take Out** (★) (Water Street, Old Harbor; 401-466-2935), hop on your bike and head for your wilderness pleasure.

Late-fall and early-spring daytrippers who come over to Block Island for a few hours of biking or hiking are often surprised to find the hotels and restaurants closed for the season. No problem. Just join the locals who head for the **Airport Restaurant** (★) (State Airport; 401-466-5468), which serves basic lunch-counter meals all day, every day. They're famous for their lobster rolls. Budget.

NEWPORT AREA RESTAURANTS

As you might expect, the restaurant scene in this posh town can get quite fancy and expensive. For those who prefer a more laid-back approach, there are many waterfront places that specialize in seafood, harbor views and relaxed enjoyment.

Non-guests are welcome to enjoy the legendary Sunday brunch at the **Inn at Castle Hill** (Ocean Drive; 401-849-3800). This three-story, weathered-shingle 1874 Victorian, with its peaked roof and turrets, overlooks the bay from its own peninsula. Inside, the chestnut paneling shines in the glow of Tiffany lamps. Oriental rugs accent hardwood floors. Brunch, served on the lawn or indoors in a gazebo-setting of green and white, combines just the right mix of formal and al fresco eating as you sit peacefully watching the sailboats on Narragansett Bay. The vast spread offers everything from typical breakfast items such as eggs Benedict to tempting entrées such as leg of lamb and whole poached salmon. Moderate to deluxe.

An atmosphere of elegance prevails at the **White Horse Tavern** (Farewell and Marlborough streets; 401-849-3600), a restored 1673 colonial landmark. Although it's America's oldest tavern, don't expect a typical pub scene; this is one of Newport's finest restaurants. The White Horse's interior, too, remains true to its colonial heritage with huge fireplaces, exposed beams and lots of oil portraits of solemn-faced ancestors. While the menu varies with the season, you can count on always finding the house specialties: lobster White Horse Tavern, beef Wellington and wild mushroom ratatouille. Service is formal, lending additional panache to the elegant continental cuisine. Ultra-deluxe.

While not strictly hidden, **Canfield House** (★) (5 Memorial Boulevard; 401-847-0416) is decidedly a find. Relying primarily on satisfied diners to spread its good word, Canfield's maintains a discreet elegance. An unpretentious brick building tucked away in a tiny alley off the main street, Canfield's began as a gambling casino, the joy and toy of Richard Canfield, a colorful figure in the gaming world of the early 1900s. Today's diners enjoy French and continental classics in the main casino, under a vaulted ceiling of intricately carved mahogany. Service is formal and attentive. Visitors and locals (many of whom come to celebrate special occasions) enjoy dressing up to complement the surroundings. Ultra-deluxe.

A Newport classic and the oldest waterfront restaurant in town, **Christie's** (Christie's Landing, off Thames Street; 401-847-5400) is where the young and restless rub elbows with blue bloods just off their yachts. Diners can choose the main dining room, the second-floor Victorian Topside room or a more casual outdoor eating area—all with sea views—or try the indoor or outdoor lounge. Fresh lobster, of course, is the specialty, along with a menu of seafood, steaks, chicken and veal dishes. Prices range from deluxe to ultra-deluxe.

If you've yearned to dine aboard the Orient Express, **The Star Clipper, The Dinner Train** (Newport Depot, 19 America's Cup Avenue; 401-849-7550) provides a handy American version. Two lavishly refurbished railroad cars roll sedately along tracks paralleling Narragansett Bay, making a three-hour journey to nowhere and back, allowing ample time for the four-course meal. Diners choose from entrées of beef, poultry or fish. The mood aboard is festive, with many parties celebrating a birthday or anniversary. (The down side: diners sometimes get very rowdy en route, and noise levels tend to magnify inside a space as small as a railroad car.) Reservations required; ultra-deluxe.

Andrew's at Eastgate (909 East Main Road, Route 138, Middletown; 401-848-5153) is housed in space that was once a new car showroom. Bland and square on the outside, it's spacious and cozy with fireplaces and wood paneling inside. Chef and owner Andrew Gold has created a fresh, innovative menu that often sparks old favorites with a new twist. (One favorite: a cheddar burger with Cajun ketchup. Wonderful.) He also serves salads, grilled meat and sandwiches. Moderate.

Sea Fare Inn (3352 East Main Road, Portsmouth; 401-683-0577) dazzles with festive opulence: chandeliers glitter, and tables are decked in Sunday best, as are the patrons. The cuisine is French, of the unabashedly haute classical variety, the kind that requires (and receives) similarly haute service and attention to detail. Whether you're seated in the large, formal, pillared dining room or in what once was the sun porch of this Victorian mansion, you'll catch the festive spirit of the place. Ultra-deluxe.

The beachside line of people waiting to get into **Flo's Drive-in** (★) (Park Avenue, Portsmouth) is the first clue. A true "clam shack" and the best of the genre, this beachfront haven sells huge, puffy clamcakes, fried steamers and spicy "stuffies" (stuffed clams). Budget.

PROVIDENCE AREA RESTAURANTS

In keeping with its role as state capital, university town and business center, Providence has developed into a sophisticated dining arena. The many local yuppie types demand it, and visitors can enjoy it. Happily, the focus on upscale eateries has not banished the plentitude of casual, ethnic restaurants.

Overlooking a small lake called Spectacle Pond, **Twin Oaks** (100 Sabra Street, Cranston; 401-781-9693) serves seafood, steak and Italian dishes in their classic Rhode Island eatery south of Providence. The restaurant offers two contemporary indoor dining areas with lake views, plus outdoor seating. Moderate.

Fine French cuisine with a creative twist fills the menu at **Rue de l'Espoir** (99 Hope Street, Providence; 401-751-8890). Along with traditional items, the restaurant serves a host of original sauces. Specials change nightly and might include entrées like seafood stir-fry and pasta ratatouille. Their "small plates," served with hot bread from the oven, are popular. The casual French-country decor features hardwoods and tables topped with red tile. Moderate to deluxe.

Al Forno (577 South Main Street, Providence; 401-273-9760) and its siblings, **Lucky's** (577 South Main Street; 401-272-7980) and the hot new **Hot Club** (575 South Water Street; 401-861-9007), were the inspiration of two local innovative foodies, George Germon and Johanne Kileen. Al Forno and Lucky's are renowned for their grilled pizzas (*al forno* means "from the oven"). The style in all three places is casual, but the food is serious, hearty and good. The Hot Club, housed in what was once a factory boiler room, caused the waterfront area of Corliss Landing to become gentrified, elevating it to the status of "in" spot. Several restaurants—including **The Fish Company** (401-421-5796) and the **Wine Bar and Bistro** (401-751-1820)—now share a common outdoor boardwalk along the river. It's a casual, trendy and romantic spot at sundown for predinner drinks on the deck, where you can watch the boats pass. Deluxe to ultra-deluxe.

Adesso (161 Cushing Street, Providence; 401-521-0770) bills itself as a "California Café" and specializes in mesquite grilling. Preferred seating is in the high, skylighted front room. Decor is minimalist, almost hard-edge. The wood-oven pizzas (topped with everything from barbecue chicken to smoked gouda) are popular favorites. Everything on the menu can be ordered to go. Moderate.

In a building that resembles a huge Rubik's Cube, **Hemenway's** (1 Old Stone Square, South Main Street, Providence; 401-351-8570) serves what some consider the area's best seafood. The room's simple black-and-white tiled floor and high-ceilinged decor does not detract from the cuisine, although the spectacular views of the river do tend to vie strongly for one's attention. Moderate to deluxe.

Federal Hill, Providence's "Little Italy," is fairly bursting with wonderful ethnic restaurants; most are family-oriented with menus priced accordingly. A local favorite is **Angelo's Civita Sarnese Restaurant** (141 Atwells Avenue; 401-621-8171), where the decor is strictly luncheonette (and includes a signed photo of George and Barbara Bush), the service is friendly and family-style and the cuisine is traditional, hearty and wholesome. Budget. For a more upscale venue in the same neighborhood, you might sample the fine Italian cuisine at **Camille's Roman Garden** (71 Bradford Street; 401-751-4812). Deluxe.

Across the Providence River in Bristol County is the **Nathaniel Porter Inn** (125 Water Street, Warren; 401-245-6622). Dine indoors in the restored 1750 Colonial's tiny front parlors with their authentic stenciled walls and stone fireplaces or, in summer, out on the garden terrace. Winner of the 1989 Grand Master Chefs of America award, the inn's menu of seafood and game specialties changes seasonally, although two favorites always remain: their award-winning seafood chowder and the "Autumn Harvest" apple pie, voted "best in New England" by the readers of *Yankee* magazine. Prices range from moderate to deluxe.

The tiny town of Warren is the "Clambake Capital of the United States." Local bakemasters take their titles very seriously around here; summer weekend **clambakes** (★) are culinary poetry. Reservations are a must: call Town Hall (401-245-7360) or Chief Perry at the police station (401-245-1311). All-you-can-eat for $15.

Folly's Landing (100 Folly's Landing, Warwick; 401-884-6240) specializes in seafood and Italian dishes served outdoors on its deck overlooking East Greenwich Bay. Moderate to deluxe.

Once inside the cavernous barn of **Rocky Point Shore Dinner Hall** (1 Rocky Point Avenue, Warwick; 401-737-8000), you won't doubt their claim of being the world's largest. The quantities are award-winning, too, with heaps of their famous clam cakes, chowder, baked fish—anything from the sea. All with a view of Narragansett Bay. Budget to moderate.

BLACKSTONE VALLEY RESTAURANTS

Archie's Tavern (47 Mendon Avenue, Pawtucket; 401-727-1700) is a legend in its own time. Owner Freddy Castellucci and his family have created an empire—a wildly popular American-Italian restaurant and an adjacent meat market, bakery and gourmet store, all in one family-oriented location. Locals love Archie's for its prime beef, seafood specialties (including a secret recipe for Boston scrod with cracker stuffing), oven-fresh sticky buns and marinated mushrooms as much as for its megasized portions and fair prices. Cold salads, pastas and quiches offer alternatives to the meat, chicken and fish entrées. Don't be put off by the restaurant's roadhouse exterior; inside, all is warm and cozy, with wood and leather booths, scenic paintings on the walls and often Freddy's mom at the door to greet and make you welcome. Moderate.

In a restored 1911 grain shed, **The Granary** (★) (Sneech Pond Road, Cumberland; 401-334-2036) has been given new life as a gleaming '90s-style food haven. Specialty foods such as nouvelle sandwiches and salads and gourmet cheeses can be taken out or eaten at small wooden tables topped with pots of wildflowers. Best of all: munching your pita pocket out on the Granary's back deck, which cantilevers out over Abbott Run, a post-card-perfect mill stream and waterfall. Budget to moderate.

Wright's Farm Restaurant (84 Inman Road, Harrisville; 401-769-2856) is the undisputed king of the "chicken family-style" dinners that are unique to the Blackstone Valley. This meal must always include soup, mac-aroni, roast chicken, salad, french fries and dessert—served and served until you can't eat another bite. Wright's Farm's dining room can accommodate 1400, so expect busloads of fellow diners, groaning boards and low prices. Moderate.

The Great Outdoors

The Sporting Life

SPORTFISHING

Known as the "Ocean State," Rhode Island is an angler's paradise. The New England Offshore Sportfish Tournament is held here every summer, with weigh-ins at the Ram Point Marina in Port Judith. Local waters teem with tuna, bluefin, albacore, marlin and shark. Charter boats abound, sailing from every port along the coast. In South County, contact the **Snug Harbor Marina Booking Service** (401-783-7766) for charter fishing reservations. On Block Island, contact the **G. Willy Makit** (401-466-5151). **Fishin' Off** (Goat Island Causeway, Newport; 401-849-9642), a 36-foot Trojan sportfish sedan, offers everything including a videotaping of you landing that big one. No license is required for saltwater fishing.

SAILING

While not every Sunday sailor gets to crew during Newport's famed America's Cup races, Rhode Island's bays, sounds and open ocean lure boat-ing fans of all degrees of expertise. In fact, you don't even have to know how to sail at all; there are plenty of vessels that come complete with their own crews. In South County, you can choose from several sail or party char-ters at **Mill Cove Yachts** (1 Phillips Street, Wickford; 401-295-0504).

In Newport, **Island Marine Yacht Charters** (2 Bowen's Landing; 401-849-4820) has bare-boat and crewed charters ranging from 35-foot schooners to an 83-foot ketch, as well as power boats. **Newport Sailing School and Cruises Ltd.** (5 Beaver Road, Barrington; 401-683-2738) offers lessons as well as popular partial or full-day harbor cruises aboard 23-foot and 30-foot sloops.

For boat charters in the Providence area, try the **Bay Queen** (461 Water Street, Warren; 401-245-1350) or **North Star Yachts** (100 Folly Landing, Warwick; 401-884-8909).

WINDSURFING

This sport, which requires both sailing and surfing skills to master, is also pretty to watch. All along Rhode Island's beaches the colorful sails of these water-skimming boards add to the beauty of the ocean views. If you'd like to give it a try, **I. W. Sports** (86 Aquidneck Avenue, Middletown; 401-846-4421) gives group and private lessons and rents and sells boards and gear. The multitalented crew at **Island Moped** (Block Island; 401-466-2700) also offers sailboard rentals and lessons.

GOLF

Throughout the state many public courses welcome visitors. South County clubs open to the public include **Winnapaug Golf Course** (Shore Road, Westerly; 401-596-9164), **Pond View Country Club** (Shore Road, Westerly; 401-322-7870) and **Lindhbrook Country Club** (Woodville-Alton Road, Hope Valley; 401-539-8641).

In the Newport area, try the semi-private **Green Valley Country Club** (371 Union Street, Portsmouth; 401-847-9543) or **Montaup Country Club** (Anthony Road, Portsmouth; 401-683-9882).

In Providence, **Triggs Memorial Gold Course** (1533 Chalkstone Avenue; 401-272-4653) is open to the public.

TENNIS

Courts in Rhode Island range from the modest playground variety to the rarified splendor of the grass courts of Newport's venerable Casino. Regardless of their relative status, most require advance reservations.

On Block Island, courts include **The Atlantic Inn** (401-466-5883), **The Block Island Club** (401-466-5939) and **Champlin's Marine** (401-466-2641).

At the **International Tennis Hall of Fame** (194 Bellevue Avenue; 401-849-3990), you can play on the world-famous Newport grass courts. Lessons are available; reservations required to book one of the 13 courts.

In Providence, **Roger Williams Park** (Elmwood Avenue; 401-785-9450) has ten beautiful clay courts.

HORSEBACK RIDING

Given Rhode Island's wealth of superb wilderness and parklands, one might expect to find a similar abundance of stables offering horseback rentals, but there are relatively few. You can ride English or western style on 107 acres of backcountry trails, seven days a week at the **Richmond Equestrian Center** (124 Kenyon Hill Train, Wyoming; 401-539-2979). Guided rides are offered on the weekends at the **Stepping Stone Ranch** (Escoheag Hill Road, East Greenwich; 401-397-3725) and at the **Sunset Stables** (Twin River Road, off Route 146, Lincoln; 401-722-3033).

BICYCLING

Rhode Island is a cycler's paradise. There are bike lanes everywhere and even a special ten-foot-wide, 15-mile-long "East Bay Bicycle Path" that runs from East Providence to Riverside along scenic shore routes and through several state parks.

For strong cyclists who can handle the hills, Block Island can be biking heaven, with its pristine byways and incredible views.

In Newport, you can cycle the lovely 15-mile Bellevue Avenue and Ocean Drive route that hugs the Atlantic. Across the Sakonnet River, there are 25 to 35 miles of quiet routes that meander through the peaceful villages of Tiverton and Little Compton. As you travel the state's multitude of country lanes, you'll understand why so many Rhode Islanders are avid cyclists.

BIKE RENTALS   Disappointingly few shops rent bikes in the state. The dependables include **FreeWheeler** (Charlestown; 401-364-3851), **Narragansett Bike** (1135 Boston Neck Road, Route 1A, Narragansett; 401-782-4444), **Esta's at Old Harbor** (Water Street, Old Harbor, Block Island; 401-466-2651) and **Ten Speed Spokes** (18 Elm Street, Newport; 401-847-5609). Throughout the state the biking possibilities are superior enough to warrant bringing along your own cycle if you don't want to chance a rental.

Beaches and Parks

SOUTH COUNTY BEACHES AND PARKS

There are 19 government-managed preserves, state parks, beaches and forest areas in South County. The stretch of coastline from Watch Hill to Narragansett is made up almost entirely of sandy beaches.

Napatree Point Barrier Beach (★)—This Watch Hill spit of land evokes a true wilderness feeling; cars are barred from this ecologically fragile, half-mile-long sandy fishhook, allowing the many species of shorebirds and human visitors to enjoy a peaceful coexistence.

Facilities: None. *Swimming:* Good on the south side of the strip.

Getting there: Located at the westernmost end of Watch Hill.

Misquamicut State Beach—One of the largest and most popular beaches in New England, this is a good family beach, with surf that is usually mild and a gradual drop-off. The wide beach is equally good for lazing or walking, and the sand is of fine quality, although August can bring in an excess of seaweed.

Facilities: Picnic tables, restrooms, bathhouse and changing rooms, snack bars; information, 401-596-9097.

Getting there: Located along Atlantic Avenue in Misquamicut.

Ninigret Conservation Area (East Beach)—A four-mile-long swath of broad, sandy barrier beach between Ninigret Pond and Block Island Sound, this is considered by many to be the most beautiful in the state because of its undeveloped expanse of dunes and scrub pines. (The 1938 hurricane blew away all houses, and the state now forbids any development.) The beach is usually not crowded because the state strictly limits parking in the entire conservation area. (Get there early in the morning on weekends for a parking spot.)

Facilities: None. *Camping:* Permitted for four-wheel, camper vehicles only; information, 401-322-0450. *Swimming:* Rocky bottom with a steep drop-off about three feet out. Could be dangerous for small children. Because of drop-off, waves tend to break hard close to shore.

Getting there: Located at the foot of East Beach Road, off Route 1 in Charlestown.

Arcadia Management Area—Thousands of inland wilderness acres have been set aside in the northwest corner of South County and can be enjoyed by outdoor lovers at Rhode Island's largest recreation area. Because it lies along the Appalachian Trail, this park offers some excellent hiking opportunities. There's also boating and swimming from the sandy beaches of Browning Mill Pond during the summer months.

Facilities: Picnic areas, lifeguards; information, 401-539-2356. *Camping:* Permitted at Oak Embers, a private campground in the park open year-round. *Fishing:* Good in freshwater pond.

Getting there: The entrance is off Route 165 at 260 Arcadia Road in Arcadia.

East Matunuck State Beach—A quarter mile of nice shoreline, sand dunes and, on a clear day, a nice view of Block Island, are yours at this popular family beach. A gradual drop-off makes East Matunuck a good place to take the kids.

Facilities: Picnic tables, bathhouse, restrooms, concessions, lifeguards; information, 401-789-8585.

Getting there: Located on Succotash Road off of Route 1 in South Kingston.

Roger Wheeler State Beach—Lying within the protective breakwater of Point Judith Harbor of Refuge, this wave-free spot known locally as Sand Hill Cove is an ideal swimming beach for families. The sand is fine and

(Text continued on page 124.)

Rhode Island's Favorite Island

When describing Block Island, some liken it to Ireland. Many choose to rhapsodize over its bucolic charms, while others see it as a Victorian time warp. Block Island is all these ideals—and more. A modest triangle of land lying 13 miles off the coast of Rhode Island, it measures a scant three miles wide by seven miles long. Yet captured within its 11 square miles are vistas that do indeed recall Ireland at its best: verdant, rolling hills neatly defined by rambling stone fences; grassy meadows strewn with wildflowers; ponds—over 350 of them; and always, the wild Atlantic crashing just off-shore.

As you approach Block Island by ferry, you'll first spot the chalky cliffs that rise 200 feet in a straight vertical from the thundering waves of the sound. It was from these cliffs that the resident Narragansett Indians once dispatched a band of off-islanders who attempted to conquer them; in a now famous battle, they pushed a band of invading Mohegans over the bluffs onto the rocks below.

Although the Mohegans are long gone, Block Island does seem lost in a former time. As the ferry slides into Old Harbor, passengers are greeted by an imposing phalanx of ornate Victorian buildings that stand shoulder-to-shoulder, facing out to sea. These grande dame structures are really most welcoming, offering bed and board to the island's multitudes of summer visitors—the same throngs who swarm the sidewalks of Old Harbor, slurping up mountains of homemade ice cream, purchasing enough "I ♥ Block Island" T-shirts to clothe the entire population of an emerging nation, and generally soaking up the festive salt-air island mood.

Do not misunderstand: Block Islanders are not about to let their idyllic spot fall prey to tourist trappings. There are no fast-food chains and not a glint of neon anywhere. No traffic lights wink on this island; in fact, there is no traffic to speak of. Visitors can get around in local taxis, or they can rent bikes or mopeds. (Mopeds, however, are discreetly discouraged.)

This is an island for travelers who truly want to commune with nature. Just minutes (even by bike) from the bustle of Water Street in Old Harbor, the island's only town, lies a three-mile swath of sand known as **Crescent Beach**. As the island's most popular bathing and sunning beach, Crescent may become too "crowded" for a loner's tastes. No problem: simply pick up your towel and mosey a few yards to the north where an isolated stretch of sand awaits.

Bikers are delighted to find the island's rolling hills offer just the right amount of challenge. The quiet roads wind past a handful of weathered-shingle

cottages and a clapboard Victorian or two. But mostly, it is nature that's on view: brushy bayberry and scrub pines, grassy moors punctuated by ponds.

An astute naturalist will observe that there are very few trees standing on this island. Once there were many. That was back in the mid-1600s, when the first white settlers arrived. They felled the island's forests for lumber for their houses and barns, and for fuel. When that ran out, they burned peat from the marshes. Life has never been easy for islanders anywhere; but these early island dwellers had to cope not only with stern New England winters but also with the resident Indians who took a dim view of the new arrivals.

The white settlers, however, met no fate as harsh as the would-be Mohegan invaders, forced off the high cliffs at the southern end of the island. Today, these **Mohegan Bluffs** are still an awe-inspiring sight, attracting hordes of visitors who peer down at the crashing Atlantic 200 feet below, or who brave the climb down wooden stairs to walk the rock-strewn sands that border the wild ocean.

You might also want to visit the **Southeast Lighthouse,** built in 1873 and currently in peril due to erosion of the cliffs. You can venture inside to tour the minimuseum and perhaps join in the fight to save the lighthouse.

History teaches that several explorers "discovered" Block Island, among them Italian Giovanni Verrazano, who named it "Claudia," in honor of the mother of his patron, Francis I of France. But it was the Dutch navigator Adriaen Block who, in 1614, claimed this bit of land as his own, dubbing it "Adriaen's Eylant."

Today's Block Island is available to visitors on a limited basis. We mainlanders will never really belong; that privilege is only for the handful whose ancestors first settled here. But we are welcome to enjoy the bounties nature has bestowed: the wildlife that inhabits the marshy ponds; the quiet countryside; the pebbly beaches that ring the coastline and the migrating birds that swarm here each spring and fall.

At the entrance to Rodman's Hollow, an ancient glacial crevice that is now a wildlife refuge, locals have posted a hand-carved sign that admonishes all visitors: "This land has been dedicated for preservation in its natural state . . . please respect it so that all human, creature and plant life may share in its peace and beauty." A fitting sentiment that could easily be applied to all of Block Island.

The **Block Island Chamber of Commerce** (Box D, Block Island, RI 02807; 401-466-2982) can fill you in on anything else you want to know about the island.

white, waters are calm and the drop-off is so gradual that it is often necessary to wade great distances just to reach waist-deep water.

Facilities: Picnic tables, restrooms, bathhouse, showers, playground; information, 401-789-3563.

Getting there: Located off Sand Hill Cove Road in Narragansett, near Galilee.

Narragansett Town Beach—Voted the "best swimming beach in the state" by *Rhode Island Monthly* magazine, this swath is visible from every point in town and from every turn along the local stretch of scenic Route 1A. Just south of the elite Dunes Club, it's a quintessential New England beach with miles of fine white sand in a broad sweep from waterline to dune and rollers that can kick up enough to lure surfers in rough weather. The Northeast Surfing Championships are held here every fall. And for wanna-be surfers, free lessons are given by the pros every summer Wednesday at 10 a.m.

Facilities: Bathhouse; snacks available across the street; information, 401-783-3563. *Surfing:* Some of the best in the state.

Getting there: Located on Route 1A, two miles east of Route 1.

NEWPORT AREA BEACHES AND PARKS

Although not quite technically an island, Aquidneck Island has water along almost every inch of its four sides and an enviable selection of ocean, bay and river beaches facing in all directions.

Fort Adams State Park—Built in 1824 to protect the entrance to Newport Harbor, Fort Adams stands now as a National Historic Landmark, its stone fortress off-limits to the public. But its 21 acres of parklands offer a recreational haven for all. The park lies at the toe of Aquidneck Island's boot, facing Narragansett Bay. This vast grassy meadow—home to the Newport Jazz and Folk Festivals and other summer concerts—matches great sounds with spectacular sights such as views of the bay and its active boating scene.

Facilities: Picnic groves with grills, lifeguards; information, 401-847-2400. *Fishing:* From wooden piers. *Swimming:* Good.

Getting there: Located at the end of Fort Adams Road.

Easton's Beach (First Beach)—This swath has a real public beach atmosphere, the only one you're likely to find in the area. A mostly young crowd comes here. This stretch of beach curves, with rougher waves for surfers on the outer edges and a broad inner arc with calmer waters. The sand is fine and very soft, the beach wide.

Facilities: Restrooms, showers, lifeguards. Information, 401-847-2924.

Getting there: Located along Memorial Boulevard, from the northern end of the Cliff Walk southward to Middletown.

Sachuest Beach (Second Beach)—Its two miles of rolling dunes, fine sand and waves for surfing at one end make Sachuest the favorite local beach, and singles tend to congregate here. Beautiful views include St. George's School in the distance. The beach abuts the 21 shoreline acres of the Norman Bird Sanctuary.

Facilities: Picnic tables, restrooms, showers, lifeguards, concession stand; information, 401-849-2822. *Camping:* Permitted in campground with hookups. *Fishing:* Surf fishing from the rocky coast.

Getting there: Located on Sachuest Point in Middletown.

Third Beach—This spot is ideal for families because it fronts the calm waters of the Sakonnet River. Its profile includes high dunes and a beach that's more soil than sand. It's also popular with windsurfers. The view across the river includes Little Compton's sweep of rolling hills.

Facilities: Restrooms, concession stand.

Getting there: Located off Third Beach Road in Middletown.

PROVIDENCE AREA BEACHES AND PARKS

Colt State Park—Formerly the private estate of the Samuel Pomeroy Colt family, this state park in Bristol now provides a 443-acre outdoor haven to all families. A three-mile shore drive traces Narragansett Bay, and a network of bike paths (which links up with the "East Bay Bike Path") crisscrosses the wooded park. In the summer there are plenty of naturalist activities, and the Rhode Island Symphony gives occasional waterside concerts here.

Facilities: Picnic areas; information, 401-253-7482. *Fishing:* Excellent saltwater fishing.

Getting there: Located along Route 114 in Bristol.

Goddard State Park—This beachfront park is beautifully maintained and provides outdoor recreation all year round. The old carousel building on the shore now serves as a performing arts center for band and jazz concerts during the summer. Spread throughout the 500 wooded acres are 18 miles of bridal trails (no horse rentals in the park), a nine-hole golf course and a picnic gazebo. Naturalist hiking programs are available in summer.

Facilities: Picnic areas, lifeguards, bathhouse, concession stands, boat ramp; information, 401-884-2010. *Swimming:* Good, calm water.

Getting there: Located on Ives Road about one mile south of East Greenwich.

BLACKSTONE VALLEY BEACHES AND PARKS

Lincoln Woods State Park—Over 600 acres of woodland make up this popular recreation area north of Providence. Visitors can swim in Olney Pond and hike or ride horses along the oak-bordered trails surrounding it. In the winter, people come here to skate and snowmobile.

Facilities: Picnic areas, restrooms, bathhouse, playing fields, lifeguard, concession stand; information, 401-723-7892. *Swimming:* Excellent, in freshwater lake.

Getting there: Located on Great Road, Route 123, in Lincoln.

Diamond Hill State Park—This woodsy hill is skirted by a mile-long ledge of quartz, thus the park's moniker. The 373-acre spot, crossed by hiking trails, is the site of summer festivals and winter sledding and skating on the small pond.

Facilities: Picnic area, restrooms; information, 401-333-2437 in summer, 401-723-7892 year-round.

Getting there: Off Route 114 on Diamond Hill Road in Cumberland.

Pulaski Memorial State Park—Eighty acres of red pine, white pine and oak woods skirt Peck's Pond, whose beach is a main attraction for visitors here. They can also hike trails through the forest area or get a game going at the ball field.

Facilities: Picnic area, restrooms, changing room, playground, lifeguard; information, 401-568-2013. *Fishing:* Good for bass, perch and trout. *Swimming:* Excellent.

Getting there: On Pulaski Road, off Route 44 six miles west of Chepachet.

Hiking

The entire state of Rhode Island holds wonderful surprises both for serious hikers as well as those who simply enjoy meandering through the great outdoors. In the northern tier of the state, a unique two-state federal project, the Blackstone River Valley National Heritage Corridor, will develop miles of new trails along the banks of the river and the original tow paths along the canal. Even though not fully completed, this linear park offers endless opportunities to those who celebrate wilderness beauty.

SOUTH COUNTY TRAILS

The lowlands of South County are studded with great tracts of protected wilderness areas that are ideal for hiking.

Called "the most beautiful walk in Rhode Island," the **Long Pond–Ell Pond Trail** (4.5 miles) leads to three ponds through what locals call a "cathedral forest" of wild rhododendrons and hemlocks. Located in Hopkinton, this area is listed in the Registry of Natural Landmarks.

Part of the Appalachian Trail, Arcadia Park's **Yellow Dot Trail** (20 miles) can be followed via yellow spots painted on trees. It crosses much of the park's wooded wilderness.

In the 29-acre Kimball Wildlife Refuge near Charlestown, the **Orange Trail** (1.5 miles) leads through postglacial forests of oaks and maples to

Toupoyesett Pond. This trail is one of six maintained by the Audubon Society for hiking, birding and photography.

At Rudman's Hollow on Block Island, venture upon **The Green Way Nature Trail** (2.5 miles), a silent wilderness where you'll encounter the "enchanted forest," rolling hills and open brush. Along the way you'll espy the foundation of an old mill and a cemetery—remnants of an old turnip farm. The only sounds heard are bird calls; this glacial ravine, believed to be the third largest migratory stop along the Atlantic Flyway, provides sanctuary for over 200 species of migratory birds. The trail begins at Beacon Hill. For more information, contact The Block Island Conservancy (P.O. Box 514, Block Island, RI 02807; 401-466-2129).

NEWPORT AREA TRAILS

Newport's famous **Cliff Walk** (3.5 miles) must be counted as unique, if not the ultimate in hikes. Beginning at the Memorial Drive gate and winding its sometimes precarious way along and above the crashing waves, this path provides "hidden" views of the front yards and facades of the great mansions, as well as sweeping views of Rhode Island Sound. Keep to the inside of the path because erosion has weakened outer edges of some sections.

There are a dozen varied trails through the 450 acres of the Norman Bird Sanctuary in Middletown, ranging from the brief **Woodcock Trail** (.5 mile) that leads through level shrublands and a forest of black cherry and black locust, to the 300-million-year-old Paradise Rock formation known as **Hanging Rock Trail** (1 mile), along a 70-foot-high rocky ridge that overlooks the ocean, Gardiner's Pond and the marshlands.

BLACKSTONE VALLEY TRAILS

The "linear park" that will be the **Blackstone River Valley National Heritage Corridor** (★) will preserve both the canal tow paths as well as the river area itself. Although not yet a formal "hiking trail," a three-mile stretch of canal tow path in Lincoln provides a feel of what the finished park will offer. It's a flat walk bordered by dense forest; you'll see great blue heron, woodchucks, rabbits and turtles along the way. (Getting there: Take exit 10 off Route 146 to Route 122 South/Mendon Road. Continue about one-and-one-half miles to Martin Street. Cross two bridges. Park in the pull-off at the second bridge. Skirt the orange guard rail and turn right. After one mile of hiking, you'll see the old Captain Kelly house, the Ashton Mill and the dam. Turn back here.)

Three marked trails crisscross the 77-acre Powder Mill Ledge Refuge in Smithfield. Owned by the Audubon Society of Rhode Island, this refuge is home to many species of birds, spotted turtles, ducks and some snakes in forests of shagbark and pignut hickory, butternut and chestnut trees. The **Orange Trail** (1 mile) and the **Blue Trail** (1.5 miles) are graded as "easy," while the **Yellow Trail** (2 miles) is a bit more difficult. In winter, all three are groomed for cross-country skiing.

Travelers' Tracks

Sightseeing

SOUTH COUNTY

Officially, this southern tier of the state—extending from Connecticut along Block Island Sound and reaching into Narragansett Bay—is called Washington County. But you'll have trouble finding even one resident who calls it that. Rhode Islanders know this area as South County, and so should you if you want to be understood.

South County truly *is* resort country; beach lovers from all over flock here every summer. Even many native Rhode Islanders maintain vacation homes in this coastal area, which provides great seaside escapes from urban pressures.

The sometimes unpronounceable names of many of South County's villages and waterways—Misquamicut, Cocumscussoc, Pettaquamscutt—reflect the region's Indian heritage. Roger Williams befriended the native Indians when he settled Rhode Island and divided his time between Providence and North Kingstown (in South County), where he lived with his wife and two children from 1644 to 1650. The rolling farmlands and white-sand beaches of today's South County—a bucolic landscape mercifully lacking in high-rise condos and fast-food stores—make this history seem ancient indeed.

Among the more high-profile residents of South County's villages are those who live in **Watch Hill**. (This select group strives for seclusion and anonymity, but their lavish dwellings continue to pique the imaginations of outsiders.) Although there's no formal "sightseeing route," many visitors love to drive through Watch Hill's quiet country lanes to ogle the tastefully lavish summer estates of these rich and reclusive folks. It seems that every turn in the road reveals a more lavish, more imposing "summer cottage." Although most were built decades ago, there are one or two new additions to the "Millionaires' Colony." A prime example is "chicken magnate" Frank Perdue's enormous estate, with its acres of manicured lawn, at the corner of Bayberry Street and Ocean View Drive.

In town, at the foot of Bay Street, the country's oldest **merry-go-round** is still spinning its magic. Locals call it the "Flying Horse Carousel" because its gaily painted ponies are hung from chains that spin outward, so the horses "fly." Local custom decrees that as soon as a child's feet can touch the floor, he is too old to ride. Pint-sized riders still grab for the brass ring, squealing in triumph as they store less valuable rings on their horses' pointed ears for safekeeping.

In the nearby town of Westerly, **Wilcox Park** (High Street; 401-348-8362), an 18-acre haven right in the heart of town, has been an oasis for locals and visitors alike since 1898. Designed by Frederick Law Olmsted, the park is listed in the National Register of Historic Places. In addition to biking, strolling and enjoying nature, you can also attend outdoor concerts here every week during the summer.

Inland from South County's coastal areas, along Route 138, lies the century-old **Kenyon Grist Mill** (village of Usquepaugh, West Kingston; 401-783-4054). Run by the same family for years, Kenyon grinds the cornmeal that is the basic ingredient of proper Rhode Island johnnycakes. Although formal tours of the facility—from the original stone grinding wheels to the Queens River behind the mill that once turned its wheels—have been discontinued, Paul Drumm Junior and Senior love to talk about their mill and its history. Drop by for a chat, a look around or for some tips, recipes or cornmeal from the mill's country store.

The history of Native Americans in South County stretches some 12,000 years; this whole area is rich in artifacts and trails. A four-page drive tour through some of the best sightseeing territory—complete with drive guides, detailed maps and historical commentary—has been assembled by the **Museum of Primitive Art and Culture** (1058 Kingstown Road, Peace Dale; 401-783-5711).

Back along the coast, you may want to stop in at the **South County Tourism Council** (4808 Tower Hill Road, Wakefield; 401-789-4422), where the folks can help with maps, brochures and information on the entire county.

From here the coast road starts winding north along Narragansett Bay. When you come to the village of Cocumscussoc north of Wickford, you'll find the building known as **Smith's Castle** (55 Richard Smith Drive; 401-294-3521; admission). Although not a castle by traditional fairy tale standards, this 300-year-old woodframe house does harbor some impressive history. Roger Williams lived here and preached to the Indians in the mid-1630s, when the site was a trading post. Rebuilt in 1678 after a fire, it enjoyed celebrity as Updike Plantation and welcomed such famous guests as Benjamin Franklin and General Lafayette. Today, this grand era is memorialized by the 17th- and 18th-century household furnishings throughout the house.

On a newsworthy note: Experts at Brown University believe that America's oldest mass burial ground may lie beneath Smith's Castle property. In 1675, in the Great Swamp Fight with warring local Indian tribes, many colonists—including women and children—were killed. Archaeologists, who believe some 40 of them were buried here, are conducting a dig at the site.

Also near Wickford stands the **Gilbert Stuart Birthplace and Snuff Mill** (Gilbert Stuart Road, Saunderstown; 401-294-3001; admission). Sounds like an unlikely combination, but the famous "George Washington portraitist" was born here in this 1751 gambrel-roof house, next to where his dad owned and operated America's first snuff mill.

Although Block Island is considered part of South County, this highly independent bit of territory 13 miles offshore marches to its own drummer. From its earliest days, when the native Narragansetts called it "Manisses," meaning "God's Little Island," this spirit has prevailed. (Dutch explorer Adriaen Block, in a 1614 visit, gave it his own name.) Many have compared Block Island's landscape to that of Ireland or Scotland. It's renowned for sightseeing of the natural kind; the island's remote location offers a unique closeness to nature. (See "Rhode Island's Favorite Island" in this chapter.)

NEWPORT AREA

You'll really understand just how much diversity Rhode Island crams within its tiny borders as you leave mellow South County and cross over Narragansett Bay to Newport, with its abundance of high-powered millionaires' yachts and extravagant mansions. These, of course, are the very elements that set Newport apart from other New England resort towns.

Modern-day Newport does retain its fair share of colonial history and landmarks, however. Founded in 1639 by settlers from Providence, the town became an important shipbuilding center and seaport, a landing site for the infamous "triangle trade" in molasses, rum and slaves. By the time of the Revolution, Newport was already prospering.

That prosperity would reach staggering heights during the next century, when wealthy families from New York and Philadelphia started building their summer mansions in this idyllic spot. It is really the lavish excesses of these "gilded age" palaces that everyone flocks here to see; we want an insider's glimpse into the lifestyles of the long-ago rich-and-famous.

The Preservation Society of Newport County (118 Mill Street; 401-847-1000) maintains eight historic house museums, six of them the most dazzling mansions along exclusive Bellevue Avenue. In each, the one-hour tours are well-organized and quite thorough, given by guides who obviously love their work. You'll see examples of mind-boggling wealth and extravagance, holdovers from a pre-income-tax era when vast fortunes could be squandered on palatial "summer cottages" for families with Vanderbilt and Astor-like reputations to uphold. The Preservation Society also offers combination tour tickets. Some of the mansions toured:

Château-Sur-Mer (Bellevue Avenue; admission), built in 1852, remains one of the finest examples of lavish Victorian architecture in America. It was built for William Wetmore, who made his fortune in the China trade—hence, the Chinese "moongate" in the south wall.

Cornelius Vanderbilt commissioned American architect Richard Morris Hunt to build **The Breakers** (Ochre Point Avenue; admission) in 1895. It was designed to replicate the architecture of a massive, four-story Italian palace of the 16th century. After touring the 18th-century reception room, grand state dining room and the rest of the splendid interior, visitors can ramble through extensive grounds that overlook the ocean. If you only have time to tour one mansion, this is the one to see.

Rosecliff (Bellevue Avenue; admission) is architect Stanford White's own version of the Grand Trianon. It was built in 1902 for Mrs. Hermann Oelrichs and was the scene of many extravagant parties.

Marble House (Bellevue Avenue; admission) is most often described as "sumptuous." It was built in 1892 for William K. Vanderbilt, and its interior boasts virtually no surface left ungilded, unmarbled or unembellished. Like The Breakers, it was designed by Richard Morris Hunt, who borrowed features from the Grand and Petit Trianons in Versailles. Out over the ocean end of the vast front lawn sits a charming and authentic Chinese teahouse.

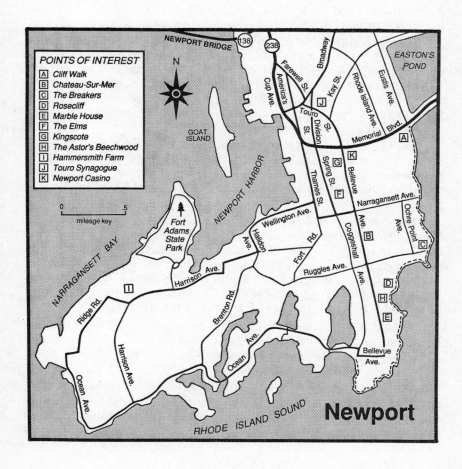

POINTS OF INTEREST
- [A] Cliff Walk
- [B] Chateau-Sur-Mer
- [C] The Breakers
- [D] Rosecliff
- [E] Marble House
- [F] The Elms
- [G] Kingscote
- [H] The Astor's Beechwood
- [I] Hammersmith Farm
- [J] Touro Synagogue
- [K] Newport Casino

The Elms (Bellevue Avenue; admission), as famous for its landscaped grounds as for its lavish, antique-filled interior, was built in 1901 for coal millionaire Edward Berwind to resemble the Château d'Asnières outside Paris.

Kingscote (Bellevue Avenue; admission) is less imposing than its neighboring "palaces." Built in 1839 in a cozy Victorian style, this red-roofed cottage is a charming hodgepodge of dormers, turrets and towers. It's also noted for its Tiffany glass windows and Oriental art.

Unlike the regular mansion tours (whose "gee-whiz" tones often teeter on the edge of sounding reverential), two are refreshing in their unorthodox approach: **The Astor's Beechwood** (580 Bellevue Avenue; 401-846-3772; admission) gives tours with an amusing twist: they are presented as living theater. Costumed actors appear as guides, gossipy servants, eccentric house guests and even as an Astor or two to lead "guests" through both upstairs and downstairs peeks into the life of the privileged in the 1800s. These tours are informative and fun for kids, a nice break from the formula format of the other mansions' tours.

Hammersmith Farm (Ocean Drive; 401-846-0420; admission) offers another kind of unique appeal: a down-to-earth peek into the contemporary old-money lifestyles of the Kennedy-Auchincloss dynasty. Hammersmith was a working farm in 1600s. More recently the farm's cottage and its 50 waterfront acres (landscaped by Frederick Law Olmsted) served as summer home to young Jacqueline Bouvier and as "Summer White House" to her husband, JFK.

The name **Newport Casino** (194 Bellevue Avenue; 401-849-3990; admission) refers not to gambling but to the elegant resort built in 1880 that now houses the International Tennis Hall of Fame and the Tennis Museum, as well as famed grass courts, court tennis (the "sport of kings") and championship courts.

Not *everything* in Newport has to do with gilded monuments to big bucks—the city is one of the oldest in the United States and has an intriguing history stretching back three centuries. One spot that has attracted a horde of historical theories yet remains a mystery is the **Old Stone Mill** (Bellevue Avenue and Mill Street in Pouro Park). Some believe it was erected by Norsemen in the days of Leif Ericsson. Others date it to the 17th century or believe it to be the remains of a 16th-century windmill.

The oldest library building in continuous use in the United States, the **Redwood Library** (50 Bellevue Avenue; 401-847-0292) was erected in 1748–1749 and today boasts an important collection of books and paintings, including several by Gilbert Stuart.

Touro Synagogue (85 Touro Street; 401-847-4794), built in 1763 under the protection of Roger Williams, was the first Jewish house of worship in North America. The Georgian structure is preserved today on the Register of National Historic Sites.

The oldest restored home in Newport, the **Wanton-Lyman-Hazard House** (17 Broadway; 401-846-0813; admission) dates to 1675 and has seen a wealth of history all by itself. Several colonial governors called the place home, but its claim to fame was as the site of a riot following passage of England's infamous Stamp Act of 1765. It seems the stamp master lived in this house, which was nearly destroyed by a distraught Sons of Liberty mob. Today the house features period pieces and a lovely colonial garden.

Nearby stands the **Friends Meeting House** (Marlborough and Farewell streets; 401-846-0813; admission), a Quaker worshipping place since it was built in 1699. The original large English Gothic structure has received two Colonial-style additions, in 1729 and 1807. The Society of Friends still use the site as a meeting house. Currently closed for restoration, the meeting house can be toured by appointment only.

A fine colonial mansion dating to 1748, **Hunter House** (54 Washington Street; 401-847-1000; admission) was owned by Jonathan Nichols, the Deputy Governor of the time. Today it is a restored National Historic Landmark with an excellent collection of 18th-century colonial furnishings, as well as paintings and other decorative objects.

If all of Newport's opulence and history begins to blur together, sort things out with one of **Art's Island Tape Tours** (Gateway Visitors Center, 23 America's Cup Avenue), which provide drive-along narratives for Newport's best loved sights.

Another stress-buster is the **Newport Trolley Transportation** (departs Gateway Visitors Center), which helps you beat Newport's summertime gridlock traffic. Park the car and let the trolley get you to all the attractions.

Newport County Convention & Visitors Bureau (23 America's Cup Avenue; 401-849-8048) is a bustling hub of traveler's information: helpful staff; brochures, maps and guides; multimedia video; and bus, trolley and tourist train terminal.

The towns of Middletown and Portsmouth share Aquidneck Island with Newport. In Middletown, the **Norman Bird Sanctuary** (583 Third Beach Road; 401-846-2577; trail fee) encompasses 531 acres of extraordinarily beautiful wilderness land. Wildlife (pheasant, nesting birds, rabbit and fox) inhabit the 30 acres of hay fields; there are woodlands, salt marshes and craggy ridges. An extremely active program includes guided trail walks, educational workshops, children's programs and themed hikes.

In Portsmouth, **Green Animals** (Cory's Lane; 401-847-1000; admission) is a whimsical garden of more than 80 century-old trees and shrubs sculpted in the European manner to resemble dogs, camels, goats, roosters, bears and even policemen and sailboats. It's a treat for kids, a mecca for horticulture buffs. A Victorian toy museum is housed inside the estate's 19th-century white clapboard house.

To increase the fun of the excursion out to Green Animals, hop aboard the historic **Old Colony & Newport Railway** (America's Cup Avenue and Bridge Street, Newport; 401-624-6951). During the one-hour trip you'll pass a number of the island's maritime sites. There's ample time for viewing the animals before the return train departs.

Across the Sakonnet River from Portsmouth lie the bucolic towns of Tiverton and Little Compton. Comparable to the fashionable bedroom communities found near any urban center, these towns have their fair share of power residents who share the country scene with the gentlemen farmers. Everything is peaceful here; strict zoning laws and sky-high real estate prices conspire to keep things that way.

Sakonnet Vineyards (★) (162 West Main Road, Little Compton; 401-635-8486) is the oldest of the state's three vineyards. Established in 1975, Sakonnet now produces a southeastern New England selection including their popular chardonnay and vidal blanc. There are guided tours and winetastings.

Sakonnet's vineyards and its scenic acres extend down to the banks of the river, an altogether idyllic picnic setting. Stop by the **Provender** at Tiverton Four Corners (3883 Main Road, Tiverton; 401-624-8096), a gourmet food emporium housed in an old mansard-roofed general store, to assemble your dream lunch. You can buy a bottle of wine at Sakonnet's tasting room and ask permission to picnic near the river.

PROVIDENCE AREA

Within the city limits of Providence are enough historical treasures to satisfy even the most insatiable culture buffs—from the architectural beauties of Benefit Street to the marble dome of the State House, which gleams like a beacon above the skyline. The lofty College Hill area is home to Brown University and to a resulting Cambridge-like neighborhood of bookstores, boutiques and trendy restaurants. Revitalized sections—such as Corliss Landing—are springing up like mushrooms almost overnight, bringing new life and lifestyles into forgotten parts of town. There's a vitality, a zingy balance of part and future, to this place that *Newsweek* dubbed a "Hot City" in a late '80s poll of the country's "most livable cities."

This capital city of Rhode Island was also its first, established in 1636 by Roger Williams, founder of the Baptist Church, "in commemoration of God's Providence." Williams' religious bent extended even to the naming of local thoroughfares; visitors today walk along Benefit, Church, Benevolent, Hope and Friendship streets.

Seven hills and the Providence River give the city its geographic complexity. Most fashionable addresses lie on the east side of town (not to be confused with the neighboring town of East Providence). College Hill is a steep incline dotted with many historic sites and crowned by the Brown University complex.

It is fitting to begin at the corner of Main and Waterman streets, site of Williams' **First Baptist Church** (75 North Main Street; 401-751-2266), built in 1775 (although his first congregation was founded in 1638). The 185-foot church steeple, visible from just about anywhere in town, was inspired by designs of Sir Christopher Wren. Actively used by its local congregation, the church opens its vast spaces every spring for the commencement exercises of Brown University.

Nearby is the **Museum of Art—Rhode Island School of Design** (224 Benefit Street; 401-331-3511; admission), which is surely one of America's most underrated treasures. Housed within a deceptively unimposing 1877 six-story, Federal-style brick structure are three floors of artistic masterpieces with dates ranging from the ancient Egyptian period to the present. Throughout the exhibits, you'll encounter clutches of students studying and creating their own artworks; this museum is a treasured storehouse for RISD (pronounced Rizz-dee) students and faculty. Don't miss: the satiny Goddard-Townsend block and shell masterpiece (a 1760s mahogany desk and bookcase, one of only 12 still in existence, whose sibling piece fetched $12 million at a Christie's auction); the Babylonian lion bas-relief (605 B.C.); the impressionists (Manets and Monets); and the Rodin sculptures. Discreet brown-bag lunching is permitted in the museum's interior sculpture garden.

Benefit Street, which traces a path across College Hill's vertical pitch, boasts a "Mile of History," regarded by scholars as the highest concentration of historic buildings anywhere in America. Along this miracle mile are restored colonial, federal and 19th-century buildings, all carefully restored and maintained. They are also homes and businesses, for this is a street of *living* history, as well. Every year, during the first weekend in June, a portion of Benefit Street—along with other historic areas—is open to the public for the "Festival of Historic Houses," a three-day celebration that includes tours, food events and sales. Contact the **Providence Preservation Society** (21 Meeting Street; 401-831-7440) for reservations or details.

One of Benefit Street's historic beauties is the **Providence Athenaeum** (251 Benefit Street; 401-421-6970). Founded in 1753 as one of this country's first libraries, it sits in Grecian splendor looking properly imposing and scholarly. The Greek Doric structure was completed in 1838. A wealth of rare and historic volumes is housed within, along with a bit of famous romantic history. It was here that Edgar Allen Poe met, loved and lost Sarah Helen Whitman, the inspiration for his "Annabelle Lee."

A few blocks south stands the **John Brown House** (52 Power Street; 401-331-8575; admission), built in 1786 for one of the famous Brown brothers (whom locals refer to fondly as Nick, Joe, John and Moe). The name "Brown" is an integral part of Rhode Island history; the Browns were a merchant family who lived in Providence since the city's founding. This three-story brick Georgian, which President John Quincy Adams once called "the most magnificent and elegant mansion I have seen on this continent," also houses an extraordinary collection of 18th century furniture.

Brown University (College Hill, end of College Street; 401-863-2378) is indeed king of the hill, the nation's seventh oldest university, founded in 1764. You'll feel the Ivy League influence throughout the sprawl of Gothic and Beaux-Arts structures and commons areas, dominated by the enormous **John D. Rockefeller, Jr., Library** (corner of Prospect and College streets; 401-863-2167), which houses the university's general collections. **University Hall** (Prospect Street), a National Historic Landmark, served as a barracks and hospital for American troops during the Revolutionary War.

Before leaving College Hill, stop off at **Prospect Terrace** (Congdon Street at Cushing Street), the site of the Roger Williams Memorial, which overlooks downtown Providence. A tiny park is maintained here, making an ideal place for a picnic lunch. Enjoy the panoramic view while you digest all the history you've just seen and prepare to tour the city's other neighborhoods.

Providence's downtown area is dominated by the **State House** (Smith Street; 401-277-2311), considered by some to be the most beautiful capitol building in America. The classic structure's white marble exterior dazzles in the sunlight. Its self-supported marble dome is second in size only to the one at St. Peter's Basilica in Rome. A full-length portrait of George Washington, painted by Rhode Island's own Gilbert Stuart, hangs in the State Reception Room. Free tours of the capitol are given on weekdays.

Several blocks south, you'll find **The Arcade** (65 Weybosset Street), an 1828 Greek Revival-style National Historic Landmark, now a three-story shopping mall.

Many of these sites are covered in the "Walkie Talkies," 90-minute taped audio tours of the College Hill and downtown area with walk-along maps. They're available at the **Providence Preservation Society** (21 Meeting Street; 401-831-7440). For more information on this area contact the **Greater Providence Convention & Visitors Bureau** (30 Exchange Terrace; 401-274-1636).

A short drive away is **Roger Williams Park** (Elmwood Avenue; 401-785-9450), Providence's favorite park since 1871, when Betsy Williams bequeathed her 102-acre farm to the city. Today this spacious parkland combines wilderness areas with such people pleasers as a zoo, complete with a community of penguins (admission), a lake and picturesque boathouse, a lakeside bandstand for concerts, a carousel, an antique train ride and a greenhouse full of exotic plants and flowers. The **Roger Williams Park Museum of Natural History** contains a planetarium, cultural and wildlife exhibits and a model of Narragansett Bay. All this amid landscaped, wooded parklands in the heart of the city.

Across the Providence River, at the toe of the Bristol peninsula, nestles the serene haven of **Blithewold Gardens & Arboretum** (101 Ferry Road, Bristol; 401-253-2707; admission). Jutting spectacularly into Narragansett Bay, Blithewold dazzles with its verdant acres and landscape gardens that border the water. A 17th-century-style manor house, all stone and turrets, plays centerpiece to this bucolic setting. Here lived the Van Wickle family from 1894 until the last heir, Mrs. Marjorie Van Wickle-Lyon, died in 1976 and willed the estate to the Heritage Trust of Rhode Island. Visitors today can tour some of the Van Wickle's private rooms and wander around their gardens. New England's tallest giant sequoia stands here, 82 feet tall, 85 years old and thriving far from its West Coast homeland. Tour the 33 acres of rose gardens, rock gardens and bosquets on your own, or join one of the guided tours. Even winter is special here, with the mansion decked in bows and baubles, its Victorian tree stretching past the balcony to the second-floor ceiling.

A short drive away, across the horseshoe cove of Bristol Harbor, is **Coggeshall Farm Museum** (adjacent to the Colt State Park, Route 114, Bristol; 401-253-9062; admission), a living history museum that brings to life an 18th-century New England salt farm. A costumed guide is on hand to answer questions about the farm or the blacksmith and weaving shop on the premises.

Nowhere in America is July 4th given such notice as in Bristol, where they've been celebrating since 1785, adding a bit more each year. Now, more than 250,000 visitors flood this tiny village each July (regular population: 20,000) to participate in its **Independence Day extravaganza** (★). The country's oldest parade marches along Route 114 (which features a red, white and blue stripe all year), and the festivities continue for days.

For more information about this area, contact the **Bristol County Chamber of Commerce** (645 Metacom Avenue, Warren; 401-245-0750).

Across Narragansett Bay from Bristol lies **Warwick**, the second largest city in Rhode Island. Home to the state's only airport, as well as to the largest concentrations of hotels and retail stores, it bills itself as "Rhode Island's Host City."

There's a bit of big city entertainment in Warwick at the **Rocky Point Amusement Park** (Warwick Neck, Route 117; 401-737-8000; admission), New England's largest. Rocky Point has 76 bayfront acres crammed with over 100 rides and games including the million-dollar Corkscrew Rollercoaster and the two-million-dollar, eight-story Free Fall.

BLACKSTONE VALLEY

To help pinpoint the Blackstone Valley area, visualize the state of Rhode Island as a layer cake: the Blackstone Valley forms the entire top layer. (And the icing, too, its fans would add.) The Blackstone River surges through the eastern portion of this layer with a force powerful enough to have altered the course of our country's history.

America's industrial revolution began in the Blackstone Valley. In 1793, Samuel Slater harnessed the potential of mighty Blackstone River (which subsequently became known as "the hardest working river in America"), creating the first factory in America able to produce cotton yarn by using water power.

Today this entire "top-layer" area is Rhode Island's undiscovered gem, a region dotted with historic industrial towns that lie within huge tracts of rural and forested wilderness areas. You'll drive along scenic country roads that meander past historic sites, charming villages, meticulously restored colonial homes, antique stores and farm stands.

The city of Pawtucket, located at the extreme southeastern edge of the region, is home to Mr. Slater's mill, the place where it all began. Fourth largest city in the state, Pawtucket (an Indian term meaning "falls of water") sits at the upper tidewaters of Narragansett Bay.

Slater Mill Historic Site (Roosevelt Avenue; 401-725-8638; admission) was the site of the 1793 mill and cotton factory. Today, it is a National Historic Landmark. Visitors to this wooden building, resplendent in its original vivid yellow hue, can tour the museum, with its huge looms still intact. Next door is the original rubblestone Wilkinson building that houses the 16,000-pound waterwheel. The gallery upstairs features changing exhibits of textiles and other related topics.

Not far away is the **Children's Museum of Rhode Island** (58 Walcott Street; 401-726-2591; admission), a kiddie wonderland housed in the spectacular 1836 Queen Anne-style Pitcher-Goff House. The kids who swarm noisily all over the museum are oblivious to the house's proud history; they just love the hands-on (and often feet-on, too) exhibits. There's the room-sized floor map of Rhode Island to crawl over, complete with boats to push along Narragansett Bay and trains chugging along the Amtrak rails; all that funny old stuff in Great Grandmother's Kitchen; the messy fun of painting on see-through easels; sitting in the comfy lap of Estrella, the giant chair; and the creative joys of making up and acting in one's own plays. Parents enjoy observing all this activity, too. But they can also explore the many design and architectural gems throughout the house. One such highlight is Colonel Goff's unique solution to a vexing ventilation problem: the ornate design of his library's ceiling conceals dozens of holes drilled to allow his dreaded cigar smoke to escape Mrs. Goff's detection.

Nearby **Slater Memorial Park and Zoo** (Armistus Boulevard; 401-728-0500, ext. 257) is also fun for children and adults. Skip the zoo (its outdated design still keeps the animals penned in tiny enclosures), and head for the carousel. The oldest "stander carousel" in the world, this gem is a genuine Charles Looff creation and one of the few that remain of this master craftsman's handiwork. Built in 1895, it was installed in Slater Park in 1910 and has been thrilling children ever since. The park has ball fields and bike trails, a pond big enough for paddleboats and even a regulation lawn bowling green. Also located within the park is the **Daggett House**, a 1685 farmhouse and the oldest home in Pawtucket.

A few minutes drive north of Pawtucket is **Diamond Hill Vineyards** (3145 Diamond Hill Road, Cumberland; 401-333-2751), which lies nestled in the beautiful Cumberland countryside. After a jostling drive over the private road that runs through fields of vines, you arrive at the trim white two-story home of the owners, the Bernston family, who welcome visitors and invite them to use the spacious porch and rolling front lawn for picnics. Inside is a tasting room and gift shop.

One specialty of Diamond Hill: you can design your own customized labels (complete with photos, personal messages or whatever else) to paste on gift bottles of their fruit wines.

While you're in the area, you might want to stop by the **Blackstone Valley Tourism Council** (Blackstone Valley Electric Office Park, 640 Washington Highway, Lincoln; 401-334-7773) for maps, brochures and information about Blackstone Valley and its activities.

A bit farther north lies Woonsocket, whose residential North End holds an unexpected treasure, the **B'nai Israel Synagogue** (224 Prospect Street; 401-762-3651). This house of worship has a series of spectacular stained-glass windows designed by a disciple of Marc Chagall, as well as Milanese hand-blown glass chandeliers. It's listed in the *Encyclopedia Judaica* as one of America's premiere synagogues.

Shopping

SOUTH COUNTY SHOPPING

The **Sun-Up Gallery** (95 Watch Hill Road, Westerly; 401-596-3430) introduces the wonderful world of dazzling and upscale made-in-America crafts, jewelry and wearable-art fashions to this staid and conservative community.

An old two-story barn filled to the rafters with antiques from the Far East, **The Elegant Dragon** (Thurston-Wells House, Route 3, Hopkinton; 401-377-2006) sounds unusual for this area but somehow fits right in with the colonial ambience of Hopkinton. Although owner Norma Schofield is an importer of these treasures, she will also sell at retail.

The **Hack and Livery General Store** (1006 Main Street, Hope Valley; 401-539-7033) is everything you ever dreamed a country store would be: more than 50 varieties of penny candy temptingly arrayed in glass canisters. Bet you can't walk out with only one of those tiny paper bags full of goodies.

Antique lovers take heart; there are over 25 traditional antique dealers in South County, including such specialists as **The Artists Guild and Gallery** (Post Road, Route 1, Charlestown; 401-322-0506), which features 19th- and 20th-century art, and **The Sign of the Unicorn** (14 Columbia Street, Wakefield; 401-782-1230), with rare and antique books. For a brochure and map pinpointing every shop, contact the **South County Tourism Council** (4808 Tower Hill Road, Wakefield, RI 02879; 401-789-4422).

On the waterfront, **Scarlett Begonia** (Dodge Street, Old Harbor, Block Island; 401-466-7704) is the place to go for quilts, pillows, jewelry, rugs and other handicrafts.

NEWPORT AREA SHOPPING

In Newport even the shopping malls sport a nautical/historical air. **Bowen's Wharf** (just off America's Cup Avenue) is a mix of 18th-century wharf buildings and 19th-century brick warehouses that make up today's complex of open-air seafood restaurants, fashion boutiques and import shops.

Brick Market Place (between Thames Street and America's Cup Avenue) is a three-and-a-half-acre complex of more than 30 shops and restaurants along a—you guessed it—brick road. The original site, a market and granary built in 1762, is now a National Historic Landmark.

Antique lovers might want to slip into **The Nautical Nook** (54 Spring Street; 401-846-6810), where the treasures include lots of those ships in full sail inside glass bottles. There are many other nautically inspired items, as well.

Try **William Vareika Fine Arts** (212 Bellevue Avenue; 401-849-6149) for 300 years worth of American paintings, prints and drawings—many of Newport and Narragansett Bay. It's a delight to shop in this museumlike setting.

If lace is your first love, don't miss **Rue de France** (78 Thames Street; 401-846-2084), where imported laces from France and Belgium shape everything from window-hangings to dainty camisoles. Some laces are sold by the yard as well.

Clustered in a 1750s landmark shingle-sided farm complex called **The Old Almay House** (1016 East Main Road, Portsmouth; 401-683-3737) are several charming country stores that have everything from a "Gentlemen's Emporium" to a year-round Christmas store.

Tiverton Four Corners (Main Road, Tiverton) is a gathering of some very chic merchandise presented in charming old-fashioned surroundings. On one corner, the 1829 **Josiah Wilcox House** (3879 Main Road, Tiverton) is home to Peter's Attic, specializing in antiques, and a candy store. Nearby is the old **Nonquit Grange** (401-624-2142) housing a country home furnishings shop, bookstore, toy store and women's clothing shop; a neighboring old mill and farmhouse sell a selection of country wares. **Provender**

(401-624-8096) purveys gourmet imports as well as fresh-baked goods and fancy take-outs.

PROVIDENCE AREA SHOPPING

Although there are a couple of vertical malls in downtown Providence, the best of the city's shopping is found in independent shops and boutiques all over town.

The Opulent Owl (295 South Main Street; 401-521-6698) is typical of the innovative, trendy stores fronting South Main Street. Here, nifty gift items—unusual frames, fine china, embroidered linens—share space with handsome housewares and accessories for the home.

The Arcade (65 Weybosset Street; 401-456-5403), which occupies three floors of an 1828 majestically columned marble National Historic Landmark building, bills itself as America's first shopping mall. It may be the oldest, but it's far from the nation's finest or most well-stocked. There are lots of small specialty shops to browse but nothing to lure the serious shopper.

The **Museum Gift Shop** (Museum of Art—Rhode Island School of Design, 224 Benefit Street; 401-331-3511) harbors a wealth of reproductions, as well as jewelry, cards, posters and books focusing on the art treasures exhibited throughout the museum.

BLACKSTONE VALLEY SHOPPING

This is *mill country*, birthplace of the mill-end and factory outlet concept. Among the many nearby, we especially like the **Slater Fabric Store** (727 School Street, Pawtucket; 401-725-1730), where printed fabrics from well-known houses sell for $1.25 yard. Store Manager Nancy Lee remembers her goods and can locate a perfect match years after you've bought the original. Contact **Blackstone Valley Tourism Council** (640 Washington Highway, Lincoln; 401-334-7773) for a brochure listing all factory outlets.

There are about a dozen antique stores in the tiny village of Chepachet in the town of Gloucester, but the undisputed star of the group is the **Brown & Hopkins Country Store** (★) (Route 44, Main Street; 401-568-4830). As country stores go, this one is the genuine article; it's also the oldest continuously operated store in America. Opened in 1809, Brown & Hopkins retains much of the old (the roll-top desk near the front door has been there since before the Civil War) while giving today's customers what they want (handmade children's clothes, gourmet foods, hand-dipped candles, even penny candies). The antiques are displayed in room settings on the second floor. Owners Paul and Carol Wilcox have also instituted formal afternoon teas and gourmet evenings in the store's back room, gala reservations-only events that sell out almost as soon as they're announced.

Nightlife

SOUTH COUNTY NIGHTLIFE

The **Windjammer** (321 Atlantic Avenue, Misquamicut Beach; 401-322-0271) brings in big-city lights and stars for the under-30 set (or anyone else who thrives on megadecibel rock). Big-name bands perform in a room that holds about 1800 people.

Colonial Theatre (3 Granite Street, Westerly; 401-596-0810) offers drama, musicals and, in the summer, free Shakespeare performances in nearby Wilcox Park.

What began as a two-story farmhouse in the seaside village of Matunuck back in 1891 is now the home of the famous **Theatre-By-The-Sea** (364 Card's Pond Road; 401-782-8587). In 1931, Alice Tyler converted her farm's barn into a 500-seat theater, and the rest is show-biz history. Several stars, including Marlon Brando, got their start on these boards. Many vacationers plan their schedules according to the theater's productions: *George M!*, *La Cage aux Folles* and *Nunsense* were part of one bill. A handy addition to the farm-theater complex is the **SeaHorse Grill and Cabaret** (401-789-3030) which serves seafood favorites before the show and offers entertainment after the show for those who yearn to stay up a bit later. Theatre-By-The-Sea is part of both the state and the federal Register of Historic Places.

NEWPORT AREA NIGHTLIFE

In summer, Newport's nightlife assumes world-class proportions with its famous festivals: the August Jazz Festival (401-847-3710), the late-July Folk Festival (401-847-3710) and the mid-July Musical Festival (401-846-1133), which features classical concerts at some of the most spectacular mansions of Bellevue Avenue.

Newport Playhouse & Cabaret Restaurant (102104 Connell Highway, near the foot of the Newport Bridge; 401-848-7529) offers dinner theater and cabaret on weekends.

The **Rhode Island Shakespeare Theatre** (in various locations; 401-849-7892) is Newport's resident theater, with productions year-round.

Roger's Roost (Newport Islander Doubletree Hotel, Goat Island; 401-849-2600) has Top-40 live entertainment. On weekends, Saucy Sylvia plays piano with song parodies of favorites since the 1970s.

Ark Restaurant (348 Thames Street; 401-849-3808) has live jazz piano in the upstairs restaurant on Sunday nights.

PROVIDENCE AREA NIGHTLIFE

Two major theater experiences in town offer audiences both local repertory and touring company productions. **Trinity Repertory Company** (201 Washington Street; 401-351-4242) is over 25 years old and going strong. This Tony award-winning repertory company supports a talented group of resident artists and also encourages audience participation.

Providence Performing Arts Center (220 Weybosset Street; 401-421-2997) showcases national touring companies' road shows of Broadway and other hit productions. The PPAC recently moved into the landmark Loew's Theater, a 1920s beauty complete with vintage velvet seats and gilded ceiling.

Challenges (Peck and Pine streets; 401-861-1385), the ultimate sports bar, features wall-to-wall viewing: a theater-sized screen that dominates the room, plus individual sets at each booth and table. There are even videos of highlights and the best games to fill in the dreaded "off-game" times when no sporting event is being broadcast.

Cable Car Cinema and Café (204 South Main Street; 401-272-3970) shows classics and foreign films in at-home comfort; the regular theater seats have been replaced with overstuffed two-seater couches. There's a coffee-house café right in the theater building, with outdoor seating during good weather.

L'Elizabeth's (285 South Main Street; 401-621-9113) looks like a cozy living room in a friend's home: intimate clusters of couches surround coffee tables topped with bowls of flowers. This intimate setting is popular for after-theater coffee and pastries, or for cocktails or drinks.

Providence Civic Center (1 Lasalle Square; 401-331-6700) is the site of family shows, concerts and sporting events.

Warwick Musical Theater (522 Quaker Lane, Warwick; 401-821-7300) is theater-in-the-round with a new twist; here, it's the stage that revolves. Open June through August.

BLACKSTONE VALLEY NIGHTLIFE

City Nights Dinner Theatre (27 Exchange Street, Pawtucket; 401-723-6060) presents a series of dinner shows as well as matinees. A typical season includes mostly musicals and comedies as well as one drama.

Cumberland Company for the Performing Arts (The Monastery, Cumberland; 401-333-9000) presents two seasonal classics on the grounds of a 550-acre 1900s Trappist monastery: "The Summer Repertory Season" which gives audiences 12 summer weekends of swashbuckling excitement. "The Haunted Monastery" is traditionally a comic Halloween thriller. Both productions involve audience participation, as theatergoers must follow the action by walking through the various stage sets.

Chan's (267 Main Street, Woonsocket; 401-765-1900) is, in addition to being a popular Oriental restaurant, renowned throughout New England for its showcasing of international jazz artists. Host John Chan invites only the best to perform.

CHAPTER FOUR

Boston

A stately dominion of brick and brownstone, parks and trees, river and harbor, Boston has stood as the preeminent New England city for more than three and a half centuries. Holding fast to the tip of a tiny peninsula jutting into the Atlantic, the city grew and spread south and west through the centuries, but it's still compact and eminently walkable. Despite its tiny size, Boston has played a mighty role in history, a history etched in the minds of all Americans. For this is the birthplace of our nation, where Paul Revere made his dashing midnight ride, where "the shot heard 'round the world" was fired.

A city of fanatical Puritan roots, Boston has been mocked and scorned by more worldly others as dull, pious and provincial, no match for New York or Los Angeles in sophistication. Rich in artistic and intellectual life, Boston has still been notched down on the big-city scoresheet for its lackluster shopping, dining and hotel accommodations.

But Boston is changing its face. While still revering its history and roots, the city is searching for a new identity as a modern, stylish metropolis. In the 1980s, world-renowned chefs set up shop here, winning over Bostonians and food critics alike. The palatial shopping emporium Copley Place opened, anchored by flashy Dallas retailer Neiman-Marcus, which would never have dared show its face here in the '50s. A building boom pushed up skyscraping, first-class hotels like the Westin, the Boston Harbor Hotel and the Four Seasons, as well as gleaming Financial District office towers. At the same time, old treasures like South Station and the Ritz-Carlton Hotel received much-needed face-lifts.

The push for class continues with a grand ten-year project called the "Big Dig" begun in the late 1980s, which involves carving a giant tunnel to place the ugly, elevated Central Artery expressway underground. The project's completion will bring light and spaciousness to the downtown area. And the city's main eyesore—the burlesque district known as the

145

Combat Zone—is slated to be demolished and replaced with a new cultural district in the 1990s.

The city's Puritan roots were laid back in 1630, when a small band of English Puritans led by Governor John Winthrop arrived and settled on the peninsula. The colonists found Boston waters teeming with cod and, by the 1640s, were shipping dried cod to the West Indies and the Mediterranean. In exchange, they received sugar, gold and molasses. By the 1670s, Boston dominated the West Indian shipping business, and by 1700 it was the third busiest port in the British realm, after London and Bristol.

But Britain resented this young upstart colony and began to impose trade and tax restrictions. The growing city resisted, and soon colonial anger erupted into riots. The British responded by sending troops to occupy the city in 1768. Anti-crown tensions climaxed in the Boston Massacre in 1770, a clash between British soldiers and colonists in which five American men were killed.

More signal events on the road to independence followed in rapid succession. In the 1773 Boston Tea Party, 200 men dressed as Indians tossed three shiploads of tea into Boston Harbor as a protest against the English tea tax. King George closed the port and sent more troops to Boston.

The Revolution began in earnest in and around Boston. The first shots were fired at nearby Lexington and Concord in 1775. In the Battle of Bunker Hill, the British drove off the heavily outnumbered Americans, but only after sustaining severe losses. When George Washington fortified Dorchester Heights in a single night, the British were ousted forever. They evacuated the city on March 17, 1776, and fighting never again touched Boston.

With the ink dry on the Declaration of Independence, thoughts turned to commerce. But lost British markets pushed the city into a depression, and Boston began looking toward the Far East for trade, bringing in silks, spices and porcelain.

The city grew and thrived in the years after the Revolution. Fortunes were made by Boston's more prosperous merchants, a group of influential families who came to be known as the "codfish aristocracy." They dubbed themselves Boston Brahmins, smugly adopting the title of India's priestly caste. This small group counted among them the names of Cabot, Lowell and Hancock. They ruled the city with an unapproachable elitism, letting it be known that "the Lowells speak only to the Cabots, and the Cabots speak only to God."

The Brahmins built brick monuments to their prosperity on Beacon Hill, an elite residential district that defined the social character of Boston throughout the mid-19th century. Beacon Hill was home to such intellectuals as Francis Parkman, William James, Henry Wadsworth Longfellow, James Russell Lowell, Bronson Alcott, Julia Ward Howe and Horace Mann.

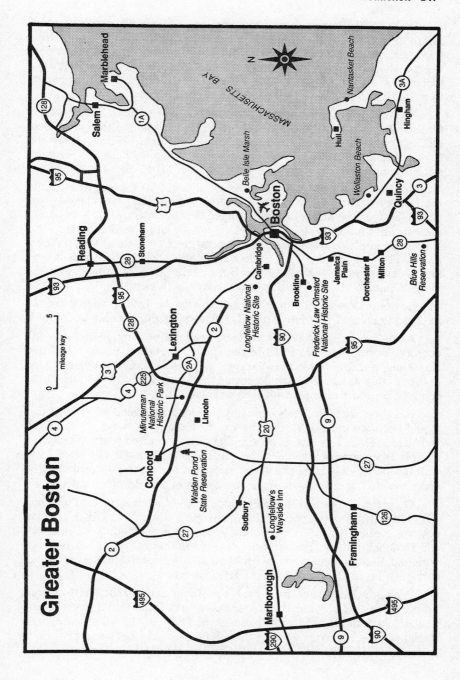

Greater Boston

In the 1850s Boston become the premier builder of clipper ships, sending these graceful craft around the world. To accommodate the growing trade, the city built many wharves along its waterfront. But the clipper era was cut short by the rise of steam-powered ships, which conservative Bostonians did not trust and would not build. Merchants shifted their capital to manufacturing, and the harbor went into a long decline.

The mid-19th century also saw the founding of some of Boston's most famed cultural institutions, among them the Boston Public Library, the Boston Symphony Orchestra, the Massachusetts Institute of Technology and Boston University, the first to admit women on an equal basis. The cultural richness produced a new nickname for the city: "The Athens of America."

Into this bustling urban area swarmed thousands of immigrants, led in the 1840s by the Irish, who had been forced from their homeland by the potato famine. The influx of Irish changed the character of this Yankee city forever. First blatantly discriminated against by old-line Bostonians ("No Irish need apply"), they grew in numbers great enough to win political power. The first Irish mayor was elected in 1885, and the Irish gave us such leaders as former Speakers of the House John W. McCormack and Tip O'Neill, James Michael Curley and the Kennedy clan.

Boston bloomed into an ethnic rainbow in the 1880s, when waves of Italians, Poles and Russians arrived, multiplying the population 30-fold.

At the same time, the city's area was itself multiplying. In the mid-19th century, Boston had begun filling in the bay between Beacon Hill and Brookline, a neighborhood now known as Back Bay. Other swampy land to the south was also filled and became the South End. By the turn of the century, Boston had tripled its size with landfill.

But soon after, Boston's economy suffered a tremendous decline that would last until the 1960s. The city lost its major port status to New York and Baltimore, and its textile, shoe and glass mills moved south in search of cheaper labor and operating costs. Population shrank in the 1940s and '50s, with Boston the only large city to decline in numbers during the postwar baby boom years. The city languished in the throes of this decline for decades.

Good times returned suddenly in the 1960s, as the Protestant elite and Irish Catholics finally cooperated in managing city affairs. Urban renewal projects created the new Government Center and the landmark Prudential and Hancock towers. The technological revolution of the 1970s and '80s enriched Boston's economy, with computer companies and think tanks springing up in Cambridge and Greater Boston.

With prosperity came urban problems. In the early 1970s, court-ordered busing among racially imbalanced schools sparked rioting and protests, particularly in South Boston and Charlestown. The crisis lasted several years. Racial strife eased somewhat in the 1980s as blacks began to gain more power in local and state government and in private business.

Today Boston has a Democrat-controlled legislature and a reputation for liberalism, spearheaded by the reigning scion of the Kennedy clan, Senator Ted Kennedy. The city's low-key mayor, Raymond Flynn, carries the standard for the Irish.

Boston the city is home to a scant 575,000 souls. Half are under 30; some 250,000 students flood the city each September, injecting it with vitality and youthfulness.

The weather is infinitely changeable, varying from warm, humid summers, when temperatures range from the 60s to the low 80s, to dry, crisp falls hovering in the high 40s (and the low 70s during Indian summer), to very cold winters, when temperatures dip to the 20s and 30s, occasionally falling below zero.

The nucleus of Boston proper is a pear-shaped peninsula. At its northernmost tip stands the North End, a small, Italian enclave clustered with shops, cafés and restaurants. The downtown area takes up most of the peninsula, winding between the waterfront and Boston Common from north to south and encompassing a Chinatown that is tiny yet rich in tradition.

High above Boston Common in regal splendor sits Beacon Hill, crowned by the State House and graced with Victorian bowfront brick homes, window boxes and hidden gardens. To the west of Beacon Hill lies its cousin, stately Back Bay, a place of wide boulevards and imposing brownstones. Farther west is the Fenway, sprawling around its marshy gardens and home to baseball's famous Fenway Park.

Just south of Back Bay is Midtown, which encompasses the architectural jewels of Copley Square: the Public Library, Trinity Church and the Hancock Tower. A bit farther south lies the city's largest neighborhood, the South End, another 19th-century brick residential area in the process of gentrification. Cut off from eastern downtown by the Fort Point Channel, South Boston (not to be confused with the South End) is a primarily commercial area, home to the city's fish piers.

The residential neighborhoods, harking back to English architecture, have led to Boston's being characterized "America's most European city." But since Boston has added new space-age layers to the urban quiltwork of centuries, the city wears a more American and international face. Though the city took its time, it has come a long way from its Puritan roots and the days when books by male and female authors were separated on different shelves.

Somehow we know the Puritan roots will never die; today their remnants exist in Sunday blue laws. And Boston will never be mistaken for wilder cities like New York or Los Angeles. It will always remain small, and never a province of punk hairdos. But nowadays, Boston has a lot less to apologize for on the big-city scoresheet and is becoming a first-class city in a class by itself.

Easy Living
Transportation

ARRIVAL

If you arrive in Boston by car, you'll have to watch closely for road markings; routes change numbers and names frequently. Also, roads will be tied up well into the mid-1990s by a major project designed to construct a third harbor tunnel and to depress the Central Artery underground. No one in his right mind would want to bring a car to downtown Boston, where narrow, confusing streets are ruled by legendarily homicidal drivers. Save the car for touring the suburbs of Greater Boston or outlying areas.

From the north, **Route 95** follows a curving, southwesterly path to Boston, changing to **Route 128** as it forms a beltway around the city. **Route 93** runs directly north-south through Boston; its downtown portion is called the Central Artery, and it's known as the John Fitzgerald Expressway and the Southeast Expressway between Boston and Route 128 in Braintree. **Route 90**, the Massachusetts Turnpike, heads into and through Boston from the west. From the south, you can reach Boston by **Route 95, Route 24** or **Route 3**.

BY AIR

Logan International Airport (617-561-1800), the busy and crowded main airport serving Boston, is located two miles north of the city in East Boston. Numerous domestic and international carriers fly in and out of Logan, including Aer Lingus, Air Atlantic, Ltd., Air Canada, Air France, Alitalia Airlines, American Airlines, British Airways, Continental, Delta Air Lines, El Al Israel Airlines, Lufthansa German Airlines, Midway Airlines, Northwest Airlines, Sabena Belgian World Airlines, Swissair, TAP Air Portugal, Trans World Airlines, Trump Shuttle, United Airlines, USAir and Virgin Atlantic.

Limousines and buses take visitors to numerous downtown locations, including **Airways Transportation** (617-267-2981), **Hudson Limousine** (617-395-8080), **Carey Limousine** (617-623-8700), **Commonwealth Limousine Service** (617-787-5575), **Greyhound/Trailways** (617-423-5810) and **Peter Pan Bus Lines** (617-426-7838). You can also take the subway from the airport, by taking a free Massport bus to the Blue Line stop. The slickest way to get downtown is to hop the **Airport Water Shuttle** (617-439-3131), bypassing traffic altogether for a scenic ten-minute ride across Boston Harbor.

BY BUS

Greyhound/Trailways has bus service to Boston from all over the country. The main downtown terminal is at 10 St. James Avenue (617-423-5810). Other bus lines servicing Boston include **Bonanza Bus Lines** (145

Dartmouth Street at Back Bay Station; 617-720-4110) from Cape Cod, **Peter Pan Bus Lines** (555 Atlantic Avenue; 617-426-7838), from New York, New Hampshire and Cape Cod, and **Concord Trailways** (555 Atlantic Avenue; 617-426-8080), from points in New Hampshire only.

BY TRAIN

Amtrak (Summer Street at Atlantic Avenue; 617-482-3660) will bring you from San Francisco to Chicago on board its "California Zephyr" then from Chicago to Boston on the "Lakeshore Limited." Amtrak trains leaving New York City for Boston include the "Night Owl," "New England Express," "Minuteman," "Yankee Clipper," "Mount Vernon," "Ben Franklin" and "Merchants Limited."

CAR RENTALS

Parking grows scarcer and ever more expensive, and you can easily see Boston on foot, but if you must rent a car, you can do so in the airport terminal at **Budget Rent A Car** (617-787-8201), **Hertz Rent A Car** (617-569-7272) and **USA Rent A Car** (617-561-6500).

Companies offering free airport pickup are **Alamo Rent A Car** (617-561-4100), **American International Rent A Car** (617-569-3550), **Avis Rent A Car** (617-561-3500), **Dollar Rent A Car** (617-569-5300) and **Payless Car Rental** (617-286-8788).

Among the used-car rentals in the Boston area are **Rent A Wreck** (617-720-1136) and **Advantage Rent A Car** (617-783-3825).

PUBLIC TRANSPORTATION

Boston's subway system is operated by the **Massachusetts Bay Transportation Authority**, MBTA (617-722-3200), popularly called the "T." In the 1980s, the MBTA spent $2.5 billion to improve and expand the system, and there are sparkling new stations on both the Red and Orange Lines. The T has four lines, the Red, Blue, Green and Orange, which will get you almost anywhere you want to go quite handily. The basic fare is 85 cents. Special seven-day discount passes can be bought at many T stations and the visitor booths throughout the city.

The MBTA also operates a fleet of buses providing extensive coverage of Boston and Cambridge. Exact change is required for the 60-cent fare.

A great boon to getting around Boston is the **Walking Distance Locator** (617-439-9299), a computerized service housed in granite, phone-booth-sized obelisks. A push-button control board points to historic sights, restaurants, hotels, cultural attractions, stores and services in more than 90 categories and prints out the information requested with the address and phone number. Kiosks are at the corner of Washington and School streets, Prudential Center in Back Bay, 60 State Street and several other locations.

TAXIS

Several cab companies serve Logan Airport, including **Boston Cab** (617-536-5010), **Checker Cab** (617-497-1500), **Red and White Cab** (617-742-9090), **Town Taxi** (617-536-5000) and **Cambridge Taxi Company** (617-876-5000).

WALKING TOURS

Uncommon Boston (437 Boylston Street; 617-731-5854) customizes coach and walking tours for any group. Among its specialties are tours for ice cream and chocolate lovers, a literary tour of Beacon Hill, a Halloween tour of graveyards and a Victorian Christmas tour.

Hotels

Glitzy, contemporary skyscraper hotels have joined the city's old grande dames, moving into the downtown and waterfront areas in a 1980s building boom. Several are first-rate hotels, but, unfortunately, most of these new palaces are priced for the traveler on an expense account.

The city's older, vintage hotels, such as the Parker House, the Ritz-Carlton and the Lenox, have risen to the challenge by giving their properties much-needed face-lifts. The older hotels sometimes cost less than their towering competitors and edge them out when it comes to charm.

You will need to be as good as a detective to find truly budget accommodations in downtown Boston, beyond the YMCA or a youth hostel. Not so long ago, there were hardly any bed-and-breakfast digs in the city. But these days, there are legions of them, particularly in the Back Bay, the South End and Brookline, often in lovely old Victorian brownstones. So if you're willing to go a little way from the center of town, you can find accommodations for considerably less than the downtown business-class rates.

You must plan far ahead to book a room during the May college graduation festivities and fall foliage season, when leaf peepers from across the nation hit Boston in force.

DOWNTOWN HOTELS

One of New England's top-rated hotels, the 288-room **Four Seasons Hotel** (200 Boylston Street; 617-338-4400) overlooks the Public Garden. Interiors reflect the Victorian residential character of Beacon Hill, with a grand staircase leading up from the lobby and, in the rooms, leather-topped writing desks, fresh flowers in the bathroom and marble-topped vanities. Duvets are handed out in winter, and there's a spa, whirlpool, exercise room, masseur and lap pool with a view of Beacon Hill. Ultra-deluxe.

Owned by a Swiss company, the 500-room **Lafayette Hotel** (1 Avenue de Lafayette; 617-451-2600) is run with legendary Swiss efficiency and hospitality. Its location is convenient to everything, and the hotel has every luxury you could ask for: 24-hour room service, bathroom telephones, spa, Olympic-size pool with outdoor terrace, sauna, an exercise room, one restaurant and a lounge, where tea and pastries are served in the afternoon. The decor mixes colonial and European styles, with impressive antique furniture and paintings, Waterford crystal chandeliers and imported marble. Rooms are smartly finished in green, mocha or rose. Ultra-deluxe.

The **Hotel Méridien** (250 Franklin Street; 617-451-1900) is one of the country's most highly acclaimed hotels. It opened in 1981 in the former Federal Reserve Bank, built in 1922, a Renaissance Revival granite and limestone structure modeled after a Roman palazzo. Many original interior architectural details remain, including elaborate repoussé bronze doors, gilded, coffered ceilings and sculpted bronze torchières. The Julien Lounge is dominated by two massive N. C. Wyeth murals depicting Abraham Lincoln and George Washington. The hotel has 326 rooms, two restaurants, two bars, an indoor lap pool and health club facilities with whirlpool and sauna. The generous-sized guest rooms are elegantly cozy, with varied color schemes. A matching two-toned silver embroidered sofa and club chair contrast a black lacquer writing desk. Ultra-deluxe.

Omni Parker House (60 School Street; 617-227-8600) is a fabled Boston institution. Many celebrities have stayed here, from Charles Dickens and John Wilkes Booth to Hopalong Cassidy. Its lobby is decorated in the grand old style, with carved wood paneling and gilt moldings, a carved wooden ceiling, bronze repoussé elevator doors and candlelight chandeliers. In the heart of downtown, it's just steps away from Quincy Market. Rooms have writing desks and wing chairs, beige carpeting, pink floral spreads and marble baths. Ultra-deluxe.

The **Boston Harbor Hotel** (70 Rowes Wharf; 617-439-7000) is simply the most visually stunning hotel to be built in Boston in many years. Set right on the harbor and designed in grand classical style, the brick structure is pierced with an 80-foot archway. The waterfront side is lined with Venetian-style piers and crowned with a copper-domed rotunda observatory. A cobblestone courtyard reaches toward the ornate marble-floored and crystal lobby. Many of the 230 rooms have magnificent water views and feature dark wood furniture in a green decor, marble-topped nightstands and paintings of birds. The hotel has a health club and spa, sauna and lap pool, and an award-winning restaurant and bar. Ultra-deluxe.

A small luxury hotel with 152 rooms, the **Bostonian** (Faneuil Hall; 617-523-3600) stands right next to Faneuil Hall and Quincy Market. In its lobby are two exhibits on early Boston firefighting. Besides one of the city's top-rated restaurants, the Bostonian has a multiple-story terraced atrium. A typical room might have a rose carpet and contemporary furnishings like glass-topped tables and white love seats. The bathroom is spacious, with double sinks and a large oval tub. Six rooms even have hot tubs and fireplaces. Complimentary use of a nearby health club is offered. Ultra-deluxe.

There are at least half a dozen bed-and-breakfast agencies in Boston, offering accommodations in host homes from downtown to Cambridge and the suburbs.

Bed & Breakfast Associates Bay Colony (617-449-5302) has rooms in 150 homes, often with full breakfast and private bath, many offering Waterfront, Midtown, Back Bay or Beacon Hill locations. Accommodations range from a bow-windowed room with pine floors, antique brass bed and fireplace in a South End Victorian townhouse, to Beacon Hill and Back Bay homes close to the Public Garden. One of the best deals for the money; moderate to deluxe.

Breakfast is always included in rooms booked through **Greater Boston Hospitality** (617-277-5430), which offers dozens of listings, with many in Back Bay and Beacon Hill. Host homes include a brick Federal house in Beacon Hill with fireplaces, four-poster beds, greenhouse and a lovely hidden garden, and a classic 1890 Back Bay brownstone appointed with 18th-century mahogany furniture and floors and Oriental rugs. Budget to deluxe.

BEACON HILL HOTELS

The only hotel in Beacon Hill is a real find, far less pricey than downtown hotels. The **John Jeffries House** (14 Embankment Road; 617-367-1866) offers 46 spacious studio apartments and suites, all with kitchenettes, in a renovated turn-of-the-century house overlooking Charles Street. Guest quarters are furnished in tasteful pastels, with dark reproduction furniture, large windows and contemporary bathrooms. There is also a large and comfortable lobby. Moderate.

BACK BAY HOTELS

The vintage 1927 **Ritz-Carlton** (15 Arlington Street; 617-536-5700) sparkles after an extensive restoration. A standard room is spacious and airy, with a high ceiling, brown floral drapes and spread and French provincial furnishings. On the walls are prints of antique engravings of Boston and Bunker Hill. The bathroom has polished white marble floors and antique fixtures. Besides an in-house health and fitness facility with sauna and massage, the 278-room Ritz offers complimentary use of a full-service health club nearby. The hotel has two restaurants, an afternoon tea lounge and a bar. Ultra-deluxe.

Beacon Inn Guest Houses (248 Newbury Street; 617-262-1771) has 20 less-than-lovely rooms with twin beds; in the summer 30 units are available. Still, these are moderately priced rooms in the heart of Back Bay, with kitchenettes, air conditioning and private baths.

A pretty streetside patio and stately brownstone facade greet guests of the **Newbury Guest House** (261 Newbury Street; 617-437-7666). Besides its superb location on fashionable Newbury Street, the restored 1882 inn offers 15 guest rooms with pine plank floors, high ceilings and reproduction

Victorian furnishings. Some have bay windows, and all have televisions and telephones—rarities in a small inn. Even better, moderate and deluxe rates include continental breakfast with homemade breads.

Popular with gays, **463 Beacon Street Guest House** (463 Beacon Street; 617-536-1302) also draws a mixed clientele. Twenty rooms, all with stove or microwave and refrigerator, make this turn-of-the-century brownstone an excellent value. The six-story walk-up also offers business services and a laundry. Moderate.

One of the city's smallest, most charming hotels, the **Eliot Hotel** (★) (370 Commonwealth Avenue; 617-267-1607) was built in 1925 by the family of Charles Eliot, a Harvard president. The hotel has a warm, welcoming feeling, and underwent major renovations in early 1990. Its soft green-colored lobby is set with wing chairs, sofas and crystal wall sconces. Rooms are furnished with dark, antique-style furniture. Some have kitchenettes. Moderate to deluxe.

The circa 1860 **Oasis** (22 Edgerly Road; 617-267-2262) caters to a gay crowd but draws a mixed clientele. Fifteen rooms feature antiques, queen-sized beds and, in some cases, decks. Located on a quiet street, the inn serves continental breakfast in the living room. Moderate.

One way around the high cost of Boston hotels is to rent a furnished room. **Comma Realty, Inc.** (371 Commonwealth Avenue; 617-437-9200) has 45 studio rooms and apartments with kitchens that can be rented nightly from November to March, weekly from April to October. The rooms are plain but clean, with serviceable brown carpeting; twin beds and funky blue bathroom fixtures. Budget to moderate.

FENWAY HOTELS

The best deal for budget-minded travelers in Boston just has to be **Florence Frances'** (★) (458 Park Drive; 617-267-2458) 125-year-old brownstone with four guest rooms that share baths and priced on the low side of moderate. Mrs. Frances has traveled around the world and decorated each room individually with an international flair. The Spanish Room, done in red, black and white, has a display of Spanish fans on the wall. The living and sitting rooms are beautifully furnished with antiques and a collection of Royal Doulton figurines. There is also a community kitchen.

The **Boston International American Youth Hostel** (12 Hemenway Street; 617-536-1027) represents the rock bottom of Boston accommodations, both in terms of price and amenities. Dormitory-style rooms hold six beds, with males and females kept separate. You must provide your own sheets, and no alcoholic beverages are allowed. Non-AYH members can stay here by paying a small extra charge for an introductory membership. The hostel can accommodate 220 people in summer and 125 during the academic year. There are laundry and kitchen facilities and a lounge with piano and juice machine.

Unlike the YWCA, the **YMCA** (316 Huntington Avenue; 617-536-7800) allows both male and female guests. More generously appointed than the YWCA, it has a spacious and comfortable wood-paneled lobby, an indoor pool, laundry facilities and cafeteria. But rooms are cell-like and furnished with Salvation Army-type furniture. Budget.

MIDTOWN HOTELS

The grande dame of Boston hotels is the **Copley Plaza** (138 St. James Avenue; 617-267-5300), built in 1912. The hotel was famed for throwing such sumptuous affairs as an "Evening in Venice," with gondolas floating on the parquet floor, converted to the Grand Canal. Every president since Taft has stayed here, as well as royalty from eight countries. JFK was a regular visitor. The Copley Plaza's elegant lobby is appointed with coffered gold ceilings decorated with trompe l'oeil paintings of the sky, marble columns and floors, crystal chandeliers and French provincial furniture. The hotel has two restaurants and a lively piano bar. Bedrooms are decorated with dark period furniture and warm floral patterns, while bathrooms feature vintage marble and chrome fixtures. Ultra-deluxe.

The first independent luxury hotel built in Boston in 40 years, the **Colonnade** (120 Huntington Avenue; 617-424-7000), opened in 1971, sparked the citywide hotel building boom a decade later. Recognized for its bold, Bauhaus architecture, the Colonnade has renovated its 288 rooms in such classy colors as mauve walls with navy-and-pink print spreads. The hotel has a restaurant. Ultra-deluxe.

Built in 1891, the vintage stone **Copley Square Hotel** (47 Huntington Avenue; 617-536-9000) draws lots of families and Europeans to its cozy, friendly 141 rooms. Though the rooms are on the smallish side, they're comfortably appointed with modern furniture and fabrics in blues, greens and mauves. This is a real buy for the Copley Square area. Deluxe.

Real working fireplaces add to the considerable vintage charms of the **Lenox Hotel** (710 Boylston Street; 617-536-5300). Opening at the turn of the century, the 220-room Lenox was popular with such entertainers as Enrico Caruso, who pulled his private streetcar up to the door. The lobby wears its original Gilded Age elegance of soaring white columns, gold-leaf moldings, marble fireplace and handsome royal-blue-and-white decor. A standard room has a colonial-style chandelier, a rocking chair, high ceilings and a colonial or Oriental ambience. Ultra-deluxe.

SOUTH END HOTELS

Although it has only three guest rooms, the **Terrace Townhouse** (★) (60 Chandler Street; 617-350-6520) is a hidden jewel. This 1870 townhouse has been richly redecorated, from its glowing salmon-painted hallway hung with 17th- and 18th-century French and English engravings, to individually themed rooms. The French Dining Room (formerly the house dining room, now a guest bedroom) is done entirely in French antiques, including an armoire, crystal chandelier and canopied bed. Breakfast is served in bed on antique china, and tea and sherry in the library at 4. Deluxe to ultra-deluxe.

Although not everything matches, the tub may be chipped and hallways are narrow and dark, the **Chandler Inn** (26 Chandler Street; 617-482-3450) offers 56 rooms priced closer to moderate than deluxe. Rooms are clean and appointed decently enough, in blues and greens and new oak furniture, with all the basic amenities. The hotel has a restaurant and a bar, which is a gay hangout.

The **Berkeley Residence/YWCA** (40 Berkeley Street; 617-482-8850) offers the most basic budget accommodations for women in the city. No men are allowed outside the public areas. Rooms have twin beds with chenille spreads and battered blond furniture, and bathrooms are down the hall. There are laundry facilities and a cafeteria.

OUTSIDE BOSTON HOTELS

CAMBRIDGE HOTELS

Set in an office tower and shopping complex, the 296-room **Charles Hotel** (1 Bennett Street at Eliot Street; 617-864-1200) is just steps away from Harvard Square. Rooms are styled in grays and blues, with a Windsor bed, upholstered loveseat and armchair, and new oak armoire. The gray-tiled bath has a second phone and television and pink-and-gray marble counters. There are two restaurants and one of the city's best jazz bars, as well as a health spa with steam room, sauna and whirlpool. Ultra-deluxe.

The stepped, pyramidal walls of the **Hyatt Regency Cambridge** (575 Memorial Drive; 617-492-1234) sit right on the banks of the Charles River, offering splendid views of the Boston skyline from many rooms. A 14-story atrium lobby has a semitropical feeling, from the Australian finches in a glass cage to a large fountain and towering potted plants and trees. Lighted glass elevators whoosh you up through the atrium, past a trompe l'oeil mural of an Italian villa and a 100-foot-high glass wall. The 469-room hotel has two restaurants, a lap pool and a health club with sauna, whirlpool and steam bath. The fair-sized rooms have natural woods, contemporary furnishings and carpeting, plus marble vanities in the bathroom. Ultra-deluxe.

A relatively inexpensive but still convenient place to stay in Cambridge is the **Harvard Manor House** (110 Mount Auburn Street; 617-864-5200). Although some rooms are on the smallish side, this 72-room private hotel offers nicely appointed digs with contemporary furniture and floral spreads. Deluxe.

Some of the least expensive, albeit plainest, accommodations are to be had at the **Irving House** (24 Irving Street; 617-354-8249) near Harvard Square. This woodframe walk-up offers 44 plain but clean rooms at moderate prices. Your best bets are the top floor units featuring skylights, private baths and wall-to-wall carpets.

Although it's quite a way from Harvard Square, **A Cambridge House** (★) (2218 Massachusetts Avenue; 617-491-6300) is a special place to stay. A private home built in 1892 with a wide pillared porch, it's listed on the National Historic Register. Beautifully restored and richly furnished with floral print fabrics, patterned wallpapers, period antiques and Oriental rugs, the living room, den and dining room offer guests luxurious spaces. Each of the 26 guest rooms is individually decorated with antiques. The room we saw had a canopied bed with a white lace duvet and a working fireplace. A full breakfast is complimentary; deluxe to ultra-deluxe.

OUTLYING AREAS HOTELS

There's a great deal of historic ambience to **Longfellow's Wayside Inn** (Wayside Inn Road, Sudbury; 508-443-8846), which the poet made famous in his *Tales of a Wayside Inn*. The innkeepers have kept a number of the original rooms furnished with period items, including the bed chamber where Longfellow stayed in 1862. You are welcome to tour all these rooms, as well as several historic buildings on the grounds, including a grist mill and the little red schoolhouse of "Mary Had a Little Lamb" fame. Of the inn's ten rooms, only two are in the older part of the inn. Eight are in a modern addition and feature colonial reproduction furniture, traditional colors of cranberry and green, and new oak floors. The two rooms in the original inn have wide-planked floors and hand-hewn ceiling beams. But they have tiny bathrooms with cramped showers. The inn has a wonderful restaurant that serves traditional country fare. Moderate.

LEXINGTON AND CONCORD HOTELS

Built at the turn of the century, the **John David House** (★) (1963 Massachusetts Avenue, Lexington; 617-861-7376) is now a beautifully restored bed and breakfast inn. The foyer is a visual feast of twin white-balustered staircases, set off by rich, jewel-like wallpaper in red tones. Common areas, spacious and furnished with antiques, include a sitting room and formal dining and living rooms. Four guest rooms all have private baths and are furnished with four-poster brass-and-mahogany feather beds and pillow shams. Bathrooms are gorgeously new with Italian tile, pedestal sinks and pastel colors. Rooms, several of which overlook the Lexington Battle Green, include afternoon tea and continental breakfast. Moderate to deluxe.

If you're looking for an inexpensive place to stay right in the middle of Lexington, you might stop at the **Battle Green Motor Inn** (1720 Massachusetts Avenue; 617-862-6100). The 96 rooms at this L-shaped motel surround two courtyards graced with tropical plants and a heated swimming pool. Inside, guest rooms sport blond furniture and a colonial decor. Moderate.

Concord is greener and more rural than Lexington, making it a more restful place to stay. You can't stay there without stumbling over history.

The **Hawthorne Inn** (462 Lexington Road, Concord; 508-369-5610), built around 1870, is situated on land that once belonged to Emerson, the

Alcotts and Hawthorne, and stands right across the street from the Hawthorne and Alcott houses. The homey inn has seven rooms, three furnished with canopied, antique four-poster beds covered with handmade quilts, as well as colonial-patterned wallpapers and Oriental rugs. The private baths are large and nicely redone. Moderate to ultra-deluxe.

Right on the town green, the **Colonial Inn** (48 Monument Square, Concord; 508-369-9200) dates to 1716. The original part of the house was owned by Thoreau's grandfather. Although the inn has 54 rooms, few are in the historic old inn. Thirty-two rooms are in a newer wing added in 1961 and are comfortable but bland. Fifteen similar rooms are in a nearby annex. The 15 rooms in the original part of the house are larger and have a more historic ambience, with wide-planked floors, hand-hewn beams and four-poster beds. The inn has a restaurant with five dining rooms, and two taverns. Deluxe to ultra-deluxe.

Restaurants

NORTH END RESTAURANTS

In the Italian North End, you can feast on pasta and regional dishes from one end to the other, stopping at little neighborhood "red-sauce" cafés, plush formal dining rooms or late-night espresso bars. Some of the best deals in Boston dining are here, with many restaurants offering moderate prices.

Neighborhood regulars favor **Pat's Pushcart Restaurant** (★) (61 Endicott Street; 617-523-9616), which specializes in northern Italian dishes and also serves up a lot of red sauce. In its casual, speakeasy ambience, the sole homage paid to decor is red tablecloths. But who cares when you can get such wonderful dishes as beef *braciolettini sorrento* and spaghetti marinara at budget-to-moderate prices? Dinner only.

Mamma Maria's Ristorante (3 North Square; 617-523-0077) is the queen of North End gourmet. Highly regarded, it's set in a ritzy townhouse bedecked with brass chandeliers, mirrors and peach-and-gray walls. An upstairs atrium overlooks Paul Revere's little house. Mamma Maria's menu is refreshingly free of red sauce, featuring the lighter, reduced-sauce dishes of Tuscany and Piedmont, which might include grilled swordfish on a bed of pesto garnished with lobster and baby vegetables. Moderate to deluxe.

Café Vittoria (296 Hanover Street; 617-227-7606) is the most colorful of the espresso bistros. It might have been shipped here straight from Italy, so Old World is it. A massive and ancient espresso machine stands in the window, and latticework, marble floors and a mural of the Italian coast add to the feeling. Here's the place to indulge in a late-night espresso, cappuccino or Italian liqueur, accompanied by *gelato* or *cannoli*, all for budget prices.

If you can't visit the Sistine Chapel, you can still see its transcendent frescoes covering the ceiling at **Lucia's** (415 Hanover Street; 617-367-

2353). Art critics come to rave and art students to stare in awe. More magnificent ceiling frescoes show Marco Polo's visit to China, the 12 Apostles and the Last Supper. Lucia's chef hails from Abruzzi and prepares specialties from all over Italy, robust to light dishes, something for everyone. Try the *pollo all'Arrabbiata* or *maccheroni all'Arrabbiata* (angry chicken or angry macaroni). Moderate to deluxe.

At **La Famiglia** (122 Salem Street; 617-367-6711), the portions are so big and the prices so small, you can't believe it. Locals do believe, and they pack the uproarious place nightly to feast on gargantuan helpings of spaghetti and meatballs, lasagna, linguine with clam sauce and other *delicioso* pasta. As the name suggests, the small, bright low-decor eatery is family-owned. Enjoy budget prices *and* leave with leftovers.

Café Paradiso (255 Hanover Street; 617-742-1768) is a favored haunt of local Italians. Downstairs is an espresso bar decorated with hanging plants, mirrors and colorful Italian cakeboxes. The spumoni is handmade, and the *gelato* and *granite* are freshly churned. Upstairs is a secluded, postage-stamp dining room set with white tablecloths, and a menu that offers Northern, Central and Southern Italian dishes. A house specialty is the Paradiso: veal, chicken or shrimp, baked with mushrooms, wine, butter, prosciutto and mozzarella. Moderate to deluxe.

DOWNTOWN RESTAURANTS

Downtown dining covers a wide spectrum, from traditional Yankee bastions to sprightly outdoor cafés and inexpensive ethnic eateries.

It's hard to say which is more stylish at **Cornucopia** (15 West Street; 617-338-4600), the food or the decor. Once a 19th-century literary salon, the historic building was renovated in 19th-century mission and sleek, postmodern style in a design hip enough to be featured in *Metropolitan Home*. Cornucopia's imaginative and innovative new American menu may include grilled trout in corn husk with roast peppers and corn relish, or roast pork with cranberry chutney and buttermilk biscuits. Moderate to deluxe; budget to moderate prices are available in the first-floor café.

Julien (250 Franklin Street, in the Hotel Méridien; 617-451-1900) manages to be both sprightly and elegant, with its impossibly high rose-colored ceilings and massive crystal chandeliers. Wing chairs and rose banquettes guard your privacy, and softly shaded table lamps cast a romantic glow. When the waiter removes the silver cover from your plate with a "*Voilà!*" you'll find a light but vibrant hand has seen to the sauces. The seasonally changing menu emphasizes regional foods, which might include Long Island duckling with yellow vegetable roots or roasted Maine lobster with a lemon, herb, butter and mushroom soufflé. Ultra-deluxe.

Be sure to ask for a table by the window at **Aujourd'hui** (200 Boylston Street in the Four Seasons Hotel; 617-338-4400) so you will have a view of the Public Garden below. Tables are set with one-of-a-kind antique service plates, complemented by antique paintings and a display of porcelain. The regional American menu features game, poultry and seafood dishes. There's also a low-cholesterol menu. One block from the theater district, this is a great place for *après*-theater. Ultra-deluxe.

A bright red railing leads upstairs to Boston's greatest culinary adventure at **Biba** (272 Boylston Street; 617-426-7878), where chef Lydia Shire is unafraid to create from any palette: Chinese, French, Italian, Indian. Where else would you get lobster satay with green papaya and winter mint or beef short ribs with cumin seeds and cilantro? Her dining room feasts the eyes, too, with rich colors and primitive Mediterranean motifs set off by yellow walls. The menu is seasonal; deluxe to ultra-deluxe.

So, you want it kosher? You can get it at the **Milk Street Café** (50 Milk Street; 617-542-3663), a cozy Financial District cafeteria that dishes up some of the best inexpensive homemade food in the city: soups, sandwiches, salads, muffins, bread and, always, desserts such as strawberry shortcake. Breakfast and lunch; budget.

You'll think you're dining al fresco in Italy at **Bnu** (123 Stuart Street; 617-367-8405), with its grape arbors and trompe l'oeil crumbling walls and starry blue ceiling. Close to the theater district, this eatery is famed for its California-Italian cuisine, featuring pastas, chicken and seafood. Moderate.

The sumptuous surroundings at **Essex Grill** (695 Atlantic Avenue; 617-439-3599) hint at days when the building was an opulent hotel. Ornate columns, stuffed chairs and a gleaming mahogany bar accent the lounge, while the dining room is a feast of contemporary design. The popular grill, now residing in an office complex, specializes in seafood dishes such as sautéed scallops and blackened salmon. Moderate.

Among its American mesquite-grilled dishes, **Dakota's** (34 Summer Street, lobby level; 617-737-1777) numbers crab cakes and Atlantic salmon. Fresh seafood, game and meats round out the menu. Stylish Dakota mahogany granite graces the restaurant throughout. Deluxe to ultra-deluxe.

Haymarket Pizza (★) (106 Blackstone Street; 617-723-8585) fronts right on Haymarket, a weekend open-air food market, and the surrounding crowds make it hard to get in the door. But if you do, you'll find some of the best budget pizza in Boston.

Noisy and chaotic, **Durgin Park** (340 Faneuil Hall; 617-227-2038) is legendary for its rude waitresses and community tables set with red-and-white-checked cloths. A Boston institution founded in 1827, it dispenses such solid and hefty Yankee fare as prime rib, corned beef and cabbage, franks and beans, corn bread and Indian pudding. Moderate to deluxe.

You can't beat the **Union Oyster House** (41 Union Street; 617-227-2750) for historic atmosphere. In 1742 it was a dry goods store and in 1775 became a center for fomenting revolutionary activity. The restaurant opened in 1826, and Daniel Webster was fond of slurping down oysters at its U-shaped oyster bar, still standing today. Little alcoves with wooden booths and bare wood tables wend around the several wood-paneled dining rooms, and there are ship's models, a mahogany bar and antique wooden pushcarts in this casual and roisterous eatery. The menu of chowders, seafood and New England shore dinners spans moderate to deluxe prices.

The **Blue Diner** (178 Kneeland Street; 617-338-4639) is a real diner right in the middle of Boston, awash in blue neon and chrome, plus jukebox. Besides omelettes, flapjacks, New York egg creams and "wets"—homemade french fries swimming in gravy—you can get one of the last "bottomless" cups of coffee in urban America. Budget to moderate.

With its tall oak doors lettered in gold, **Tatsukichi** (189 State Street; 617-720-2468) looks like a foreign consulate. The food is just as impressive: almost 50 kinds of sushi and the famed house specialty, *kushiage*, skewers of battered and fried meats and seafood. Dine Japanese-style in a light wood and beige tatami room, or at a Western-style table. Moderate to deluxe.

A playful parody of rococo style, **Rocco's** (5 Charles Street South; 617-723-6800) has a stagy setting of 25-foot ceilings, mammoth swashes of drapery and frescoes of cherubs. Sculptures of pigs, fish and toucans serve as table decorations (they're for sale, too). An Italian menu includes stewed baby clams, shrimp scampi and roasted chicken cacciatora. Moderate to deluxe.

The **Commonwealth Brewing Co.** (138 Portland Street; 617-523-8383) makes its own beer in the basement, serving ten varieties on tap. A vast hall lined with huge copper vats, beer kegs, copper-covered tables and a brass-railed bar, the dining room is popular with sports fans from nearby Boston Garden. You can watch the beer being made behind glass walls. Chow down on hearty fare like three-alarm chili, steak and fish and chips. Budget to moderate.

Far above the crowded bustle of Quincy Market, you can dine in removed splendor at **Seasons** (9 Blackstone Street North, Faneuil Hall, in the Bostonian Hotel; 617-523-4119), one of Boston's top-rated restaurants. Widely spaced tables, gold-rimmed china, mocha banquettes, crisp white napery and mirrored ceilings add to the mood. A creative New American menu is served, changing seasonally, which might include seared quail with polenta and sausage or roasted monkfish with lobster roe. Deluxe to ultra-deluxe.

Las Brisas (70 East India Row; 617-720-1820), blazing with light, glass and brass, is certainly one of the glitziest Mexican restaurants around. The moderate-to-deluxe menu offers fajitas, nachos, bean soup and such specialties as *pollo à la Oscar*, medallions of veal and mesquite grill.

The dining room at **Rowes Wharf Restaurant** (70 Rowes Wharf, in the Boston Harbor Hotel; 617-439-3995) says quite plainly old money. Dimly lit, it blends mahogany paneling and a midnight blue floral carpet with rose-shaded wall sconces and antique prints of English harbor scenes.

Its wide windows overlook Boston Harbor. Artfully prepared meats and seafood are its specialties. Deluxe to ultra-deluxe.

The **Boston Sail Loft** (80 Atlantic Avenue; 617-227-7280) stretches back and back, out onto the harbor for some wonderful views. Some of the best potato skins in town are to be had here, along with burgers, sandwiches, pastas and fish plates, in a nautical atmosphere. Moderate to deluxe.

The **Chart House** (60 Long Wharf; 617-227-1576) is one of Boston's most historic restaurants. Set on cobblestoned Long Wharf, it was built in 1760 and served as John Hancock's counting house. His black iron safe is embedded in the upstairs dining room wall. The Chart House carries a marine motif all the way, with gilt-framed black-and-white pictures of ships, as well as model ships. Famed for its dense mud pie, Chart House also dishes up hearty steaks and seafood. Dinner only; deluxe to ultra-deluxe.

A thoroughly Chinese lobby greets diners at the **Imperial Teahouse** (70 Beach Street; 617-426-8543) in the heart of Chinatown, with Chinese lanterns and gold dragons. Known for its dim sum, the restaurant also serves Mandarin cuisine to lots of appreciative locals. Budget to moderate.

Five take-out restaurants with open kitchens surround a group of tables at the **Chinatown Eatery** (★) (44 Beach Street, second floor), where the same type of chaos reigns as at a Hong Kong food market. Wall-mounted menus are hand-printed in Chinese and English, and Asians predominate among the diners. Taken together, the restaurants offer some 400 items, covering Szechuan, Hunan, Mandarin and Cantonese cuisines. Open from 11 a.m. til 2 a.m.; budget.

At **Ho Yuen Ting Seafood Restaurant** (13-A Hudson Street, 617-426-2316; and 58 Beach Street, 617-426-2341), no-frills service and decor don't diminish the excellent seafood specialties: dishes of shrimp, lobster, crab, clams, conch and snails. Moderate.

BEACON HILL RESTAURANTS

Two steps from the State House, **The Black Goose** (21 Beacon Street; 617-720-4500) specializes in provincial Italian cuisine. Take care not to load up on the home-baked *focaccia* bread, chewy yet light. Likewise the *caprese* salad, a mound of plum tomatoes, mozzarella and basil. Save room for the tasty entrées—among the menu of pastas and grilled meats and fish are linguine *basilico*, chicken *franco* and veal with fresh lemon and sage. Contemporary dash has been added to the dining room, originally part of a historic hotel. Moderate to deluxe.

Murals of top-hatted gentlemen and begowned ladies bring Paris of the Gay Nineties to life at **Another Season** (97 Mount Vernon Street; 617-367-0880), a romantic basement restaurant. Limited entrées are lovingly chosen: beef bourbon, salmon Dana and chicken *chèvre*. Desserts include apricot cheesecake and flourless swiss chocolate gâteau. Deluxe.

Along with its chic boutiques, Charles Street is lined with restaurants representing many ethnic cuisines.

Beacon Hill is the last place you'd expect to find supreme cuisine with moderate prices. But **Rebecca's Restaurant** (21 Charles Street; 617-742-9747) is such a place, a terrific neighborhood eatery with inventive New American dishes. Its little wood tables and booths are always crowded with locals who come for delights such as grilled salmon with purée of butternut squash or veal scallopine with prosciutto, parmesan cheese and fresh sage. Go casual or dressy: the mood here is super-relaxed.

Il Dolce Momento (30 Charles Street; 617-720-0477) is a great coffee-house where you can linger over an espresso or cappuccino and feel welcome in a European way. Its café chairs are always crowded with young students munching on hearty Italian sandwiches and homemade soups. Specialties are fresh *gelato* made in-house, croissants and flaky pastries like *biscotti di prato*. Budget.

Good and spicy Thai food stars over the decor at **The King and I** (145 Charles Street; 617-227-3320). Start off with *satay* and Thai rolls, then move on to dancing squids, seafood *panang* or any number of chicken, duck, beef, tofu and noodle dishes. Budget to moderate.

Step into a Tuscan village at **Ristorante Toscano** (41 Charles Street; 617-723-4090), whose dining room has exposed brick walls hung with paintings of the Italian countryside. Feast on Florentine cuisine including homemade pastas and game dishes. The Tiramesu is a dessert standout. Deluxe to ultra-deluxe.

Surrounded by whizzing cars in a rotary, **Buzzy's Fabulous Roast Beef** (★) (327 Cambridge Street; 617-523-4896) looks unsavory, to say the least. Still, this take-out stand, open until 5 a.m., has the best steakhouse fries in Boston, as well as cheesesteak sandwiches, chili dogs and short ribs. And it's got art: cartoons of John Wayne, Ben Franklin and Rocky Balboa adorn the hand-printed wall menus. Budget all the way.

BACK BAY RESTAURANTS

The **Ritz-Carlton Dining Room** (15 Arlington Street; 617-536-5700) offers one of the most serene and traditional dining spots in Boston. Overlooking the Public Garden, this sparkling, elegant place features cobalt blue Dutch crystal chandeliers, French provincial-style furniture, blue-and-gold fringed drapes and swan-shaped table vases in honor of the Swan Boats. The continental menu changes daily but might include such wonderful entrées as lobster in bourbon sauce, venison, pheasant or whole dover sole sautéed with pine nuts and lemon butter. There are almost 20 desserts, ranging from *bavorois à l'orange* to *crêpes Suzettes flambées*. Ultra-deluxe.

Though it emulates a Parisian bistro about as successfully as a McDonald's, the **Café de Paris** (19 Arlington Street; 617-247-7121) offers better fare than McD's: croissants, omelettes, crêpes and the best chicken sandwich in Boston, with cafeteria-style service. Budget.

High-end Chinese in a unique setting is the specialty at **Mr. Leung's** (545 Boylston Street; 617-236-4040). Cantonese and Szechuan dishes debut in a tiny formal dining room that looks like a dancefloor with its light-bedecked black ceiling. Deluxe.

Suffused in cream and pink and graced with a cathedral ceiling, the **Back Bay Bistro** (565 Boylston Street; 617-536-4477) exudes a stylish informality. Here, roast chicken with garlic glaze is among the menu's offerings. Conveniently, the café chairs and tables move outdoors in summer. Moderate to deluxe.

Skipjack's Seafood Emporium (199 Clarendon Street; 617-536-3500) boasts one of the biggest and most varied seafood menus in Boston—over two dozen kinds of fresh fish daily, ranging from tuna, trout and salmon to lesser-known moonfish, parrot fish and opakapaka. The decor is far from traditional: glass block and glitzy red and blue neon, and changing exhibits of local artists. Moderate to deluxe.

Beautiful people dine at **Davio's** (269 Newbury Street; 617-262-4810), a stylish Italian restaurant with primo service and real panache. Brick walls, white linens and flickering oil lamps create an intimate milieu for superb creations such as *anatra estiva* (grilled duck, fried sweet potato chips and thyme balsamic vinegar glaze) and *pollo arrosto con arrugola* (roast chicken with homemade sausage, pine nuts, arugula and white wine sauce). Deluxe.

A cozy little basement restaurant, the **Kebab n' Kurry** (30 Massachusetts Avenue; 617-536-9835) smells of the spices of India. The tables are set with pink cloths and silk scarves embroidered with lion hunts and elephants, set under glass. Authentic curries from North India, Bombay and South India include chicken, lamb, fish and shrimp dishes. Moderate.

FENWAY RESTAURANTS

You'll halfway expect the girl from Ipanema to stroll into **Buteco** (130 Jersey Street; 617-247-9508), so Brazilian and laid-back is it. Framed photos of Brazil line its white walls, Brazilian guitar music plays softly and tables are simply set with oilcloth covers and fresh yellow primroses. A standout is the *feijoada*—the Brazilian national dish, a stew of black beans with pork, sausage and dried beef, served with rice. Also try the homemade soups and desserts, among them caramel custard and guava paste. Budget to moderate.

The walls of **Bangkok Cuisine** (177-A Massachusetts Avenue; 617-262-5377) look like a museum, lavishly covered with elaborate framed pictures of Thai motifs in gold leaf: a peacock, villagers with elephants, Buddhist figures. Warm orange lights and crystal-and-brass chandeliers add to the exotic flair. Entrées include deep-fried whole fish, hot and sour dishes, curry dishes and rice and noodles. Budget to moderate.

MIDTOWN RESTAURANTS

Boston's only Hungarian restaurant, the **Café Budapest** (90 Exeter Street; 617-734-3388) has a romantic Old World ambience complete with pianist and violinist, crystal chandeliers, leaded-glass windows and a coat of arms over the fireplace. Try the iced cherry soup or wild mushrooms in paprika sauce for appetizers, followed by an entrée of wienerschnitzel à la Holstein, sauerbraten, beef gulyas or beef stroganoff, and apple and cherry strudel desserts. Deluxe to ultra-deluxe.

The **Café Promenade** (120 Huntington Avenue in the Colonnade Hotel; 617-424-7000) has a light and airy feel to its wide-windowed dining room, with caneback chairs, green, rose and white decor and banks of fresh flowers. A continental cuisine of steaks, seafood and sandwiches is offered. Breakfast, lunch, dinner and Sunday brunch; moderate to deluxe.

SOUTH END RESTAURANTS

Ever since yuppies began moving into the South End in the 1970s and 1980s, restaurants have been springing up left and right, from small inexpensive cafés to upscale eateries.

Don't look for any silverware at **Addis Red Sea Ethiopian Restaurant** (★) (544 Tremont Street; 617-426-8727), the nation's first authentic Ethiopian restaurant. A very African decor features authentic basketweave straw tables in a bright geometric pattern, low, carved wooden chairs, and paintings of African villagers. Platters of food cover the entire table surface. Ethiopian *injera* bread is served with chicken, lamb, beef and vegetarian dishes. Budget to moderate.

A high-tech purple, black and gray decor with a black lattice ceiling dominates the noisy **St. Cloud** (557 Tremont Street; 617-353-0202). Fortunately, a lighter hand is taken with the international menu, which ranges from pheasant and grilled swordfish to pumpkin ravioli and shellfish minestrone. Deluxe to ultra-deluxe, but sandwiches, crostini and antipasti are available for more moderate prices.

Hamersley's Bistro (578 Tremont Street; 617-267-6068) embodies Paris, with its chic red, black and yellow dining room, bistro tables and chairs, and Randy Stevens' drawings. You'll be tempted by the dressed-up versions of country fare like grilled mushroom sandwiches and roast chicken with garlic, lemon and parsley. Dinner only; deluxe.

SOUTH BOSTON RESTAURANTS

As you walk east on Northern Avenue, it becomes the Fish Pier, a crowded place of fish processing plants and wharves. Not surprisingly, the Fish Pier is home to a spate of seafood restaurants, some of them among the city's finest.

Here on the pier, two of Boston's most famous restaurants, **Jimmy's Harborside** (242 Northern Avenue; 617-423-1000) and **Anthony's Pier 4**

(140 Northern Avenue; 617-482-6262), have waged a decades-long battle for supremacy in harborside seafood dining. Both offer a long list of fresh fish, from Boston scrod to steamed, boiled or baked lobster, as well as floor-to-ceiling windows with smashing views of Boston Harbor.

Albanian immigrant Anthony Athanas started life in Boston as a shoe-shine boy and built the reputation of his Pier 4 with backbreaking work. The smiling Anthony has posed with Liz Taylor, Red Skelton, Gregory Peck and Richard Nixon, whose photos gaze down from the walls. Despite its fame, Anthony's has its detractors, who say the seafood doesn't live up to its reputation, the expansive dining halls process guests like a factory and the wait for a table is too long. Still, Anthony's has the largest wine list in Boston, and there is outdoor seaside dining on yellow-awninged terraces. Moderate to ultra-deluxe.

We much prefer Jimmy's, founded in 1924 by Greek immigrant Jimmy Doulos, the "Chowder King," whose first customers were fishermen at a nine-stool cafeteria. Since then, JFK, Bobby Kennedy, Tip O'Neill and Bob Hope have dined here, leaving their autographed photos on the wall. The seafood here is served in a nautical decor where the bar is a boat and waiters wear gold-braided blue jackets. Moderate to deluxe.

The Daily Catch (261 Northern Avenue; 617-338-3093) helped pioneer the open kitchen. Its Sicilian menu offers more than a dozen fresh New England fishes and shellfish, as well as black pastas made with squid ink. Bare wood tables and paper placemats suit the Fish Pier's working-class ambience. The restaurant also has locations in the North End and Somerville. Moderate to deluxe.

Largely undiscovered, the **International Food Pavilion** (★) upstairs at the World Trade Center (164 Northern Avenue; 617-439-5000) is one of the least expensive places to eat with a view in Boston. It serves cafeteria-style Chinese, Italian and American food at white tables overlooking the harbor. Breakfast and lunch; budget.

The **No-Name Restaurant** (15½ Fish Pier; 617-338-7539) not only has no name, it has no decor either. Famed for the freshness of its fish bought right off the boats, the No-Name always has long lines. Budget to moderate.

OUTSIDE BOSTON RESTAURANTS

CHARLESTOWN RESTAURANTS

The **Warren Tavern** (2 Pleasant Street; 617-241-8142) dates to 1780, and the small, clapboarded house with gaslights was patronized by Paul Revere and George Washington. The inside appears dark and colonial, with heavy beamed ceiling, wood planked floors, candelabra wall sconces and punched-tin lights, thick lace tablecloths and a roaring fire. The solid fare includes steaks, seafood and a tavern burger with peddler fries. The Warren Tavern also makes its own brand of Indian pudding for dessert. Moderate to deluxe.

CAMBRIDGE RESTAURANTS

East Cambridge is a treasure chest of colorful and ethnic restaurants, particularly along Cambridge Street.

A retrofit, '50s-style decor of diner stools, neon and a black-and-white-tiled floor enlivens the **East Coast Grill** (1271 Cambridge Street; 617-491-6568). The moderately priced southern grilled ribs, pork and chicken are served with coleslaw, baked beans, corn bread and watermelon, and hot drinks to match: blue, green and gold margaritas. Appetizers are equally muscular, notably the "sausage from hell." Leave room for chocolate mayonnaise cake. Dinner only. Next door, East Coast Grill operates a take-out stand, **Jake & Earl's Dixie Barbecue** (1273 Cambridge Street; 617-491-7427), serving the same menu at budget prices. *People* magazine hailed it as one of America's ten best barbecue joints, and who are we to argue? Presided over by a plastic bust of Elvis, Jake and Earl's hews to such "barbecue rules to live by" as, "If it ain't got smoke, it's a joke!"

What's a Cajun restaurant doing in Yankee land? It's doing the bayou cuisine proud, at the **Cajun Yankee** (1193 Cambridge Street; 617-576-1971), starting with appetizers of seafood gumbo, Cajun popcorn and shrimp rémoulade. The moderate-to-deluxe menu features blackened tuna, pan-fried catfish and sausage jambalaya and desserts of sweet potato pecan pie and praline parfait, all served up in a warm, friendly atmosphere. Dinner only.

It would be hard to find a friendlier place than the **Casa Portugal** (1200 Cambridge Street; 617-491-8880), one of only a handful of Boston Portuguese restaurants. Imbibe the Latin mood set by black iron lanterns, red-vested waiters and folk art murals of bullfights and musicians. *Chourico* arrives in a small, flaming grill, followed by spicy dinners of marinated pork cubes with potatoes or mussels, linguica and onions, and squid stew, all served with thickly cut Portuguese french fries. There's a good selection of Portuguese wines and beers, and espresso and cappuccino to top it all off. Moderate.

The family-owned **La Groceria** (853 Main Street; 617-876-4162) looks like an Italian trattoria, with its striped awning, lattice ceiling and exposed brick wall. Famed for its hot antipasti and homemade pasta, La Groceria does old-style Northern Italian dishes such as lasagna, eggplant parmigiana and a seafood marinara that must be eaten to be believed. Its splendid dessert case offers cannoli, *tartufo* and *zuppa inglese*. Ask for the Godfather Family room, a beaded alcove, if it's available. Moderate to deluxe.

Brick, wood-fired ovens line the wall at **Bertucci's Brick Oven Pizzeria** (799 Main Street; 617-661-8356), where you can watch your pizza lifted out with wooden paddles. Outstanding deep-crust pizzas come with 20 toppings, including artichoke hearts, prosciutto and cream sauce, and there are also hearty soups, calzones and pastas. Budget to moderate.

African folk art hangs on the walls of the red, black and white dining room of **Asmara** (714 Massachusetts Avenue; 617-864-7447), yet another Ethiopian eatery in Greater Boston. Chicken, lamb, beef, fish and vegetarian entrées are to be eaten without silverware, in the Ethiopian manner. Budget.

The owners of **The Harvest** (44 Brattle Street; 617-492-1115) researched European cafés to come up with their decor mixing brightly patterned upholstered banquettes with wooden shutters and tables and a Parisian bar. The clientele is ultra-Cambridge—you'll sit next to architects and psychiatrists. The more formal dining room is quieter than the café, and changes color schemes with the season. The menu features American game and seafood. It changes daily at the moderate-priced café, weekly at the deluxe-to-ultra-deluxe-priced dining room.

Upstairs at the Pudding (10 Holyoke Street; 617-864-1933) is located at the home of a Harvard institution, the Hasty Pudding Club and Theatricals. The stairway and dining room walls are plastered with old theatrical posters from Pudding productions dating to the 1800s. Despite its emerald green walls and pink tablecloths, the dining room has the casual feel of a college dining hall. While the fixed-price menu is tabbed ultra-deluxe, it offers one of the top dining experiences in Greater Boston, mixing Northern Italian cuisine with exotic ingredients from seven continents.

The **Coffee Connection** (The Garage, 36 John F. Kennedy Street; 617-492-4881) serves the best coffee in Greater Boston, and the most varieties of it. There are also teas, cocoas and European pastries. Small and intimate, the Coffee Connection is permeated with the thick aroma of fresh-roasted beans. A breakfast and lunch menu includes muffins, quiches, salads and sandwiches. There's almost always a wait at this popular, budget coffeehouse.

The **Algiers Coffeehouse** (40 Brattle Street; 617-492-1557) is one of Cambridge's most Bohemian eateries. With its 50-foot domed ceiling, white stucco walls and copper embellishments, it feels like a cross between a Moroccan palace and a mosque. The budget-priced menu has a Middle Eastern flavor, with lentil falafel and *baba ganoosh*. There are 16 kinds of coffees and hot drinks, teas, iced drinks and Arabic pastries.

Troyka (★) (1154 Massachusetts Avenue; 617-864-7476) is a real Russian restaurant. Even if its interior has the unfortunate look of a gulag dining hall, its hearty peasant fare includes borscht, piroshki, meat-potato pie and Russian dumplings. Russian cakes and meringues appear on the dessert list. Budget to moderate.

Shades of the Southwest pervade the **Cottonwood Café** (1815 Massachusetts Avenue; 617-661-7440), decorated in green-and-purple neon and spiky cactus plants. A southwestern-style menu includes desert pizza, made with chicken, cheese, olives and jalapeños served on a deep-fried tortilla; enchiladas; rocky mountain lamb; grilled chicken or shrimp in barbecue sauce; and Hill Country mixed grill. Moderate to deluxe.

OUTLYING AREAS RESTAURANTS

Don't be deterred by the strip-mall surroundings of **La Paloma** (195 Newport Avenue, Quincy; 617-773-0512), complete with laundromat, sub shop and package store. La Paloma has won several awards from *Boston* magazine including six "Best Mexican Restaurant" awards. People line up outside the doors on weekends for the first-rate Mexican food, including beef and chicken fajitas, Mexican paella and *gorditos* (fried tortillas topped with homemade sausage and sour cream). The dining room feels as warm and festive as a Mexican village, with peachy-colored walls, dim lantern light, airy latticework, tiled floors and Mexican paintings and folk art. Budget to moderate.

The British Relief (★) (152 North Street, Hingham Square, Hingham; 617-749-7713) is a welcoming spot indeed, housed in a red brick storefront and modeled on a British soup kitchen. Vintage signboards and photographs following the soup kitchen theme hang on the walls. The homey furnishings include a massive carved oak table that seats at least ten, and ancient wooden booths. Cafeteria-style service dishes up hearty homemade soups, salads, sandwiches and desserts. The restaurant also operates a deli counter with gourmet take-out. Breakfast and lunch only; budget.

There's no cozier spot in town than **Ye Olde Mille Grille** (8 North Street, Hingham; 617-749-9846), housed in a 1723 building, with dining rooms upstairs and down. Dark wood tabletops and booths glow lustrously in the warm light of shaded table lamps, and the vintage bar is a favorite watering hole for locals. Robust Yankee seafood and meats fill the menu, from fried clams, scallops and shrimp to a hamburger plate, roast lamb and hot turkey sandwich. Moderate to deluxe.

Visions of Longfellow will come to mind immediately when you enter **Longfellow's Wayside Inn** (Wayside Inn Road, Sudbury; 508-443-8846). Before lunch or dinner, you can tour the period rooms of the original inn and several historic buildings on the grounds. Ask for a table in the small and intimate Tap Room, which has a truly colonial ambience. Small and intimate, the Tap Room has two fireplaces, ladderback chairs and brown-and-white-checked tablecloths. The menu features hearty game and seafood dishes such as an 18th-century wayfarer might have dined on: prime rib, rack of lamb, roast duckling, goose, and sole. For dessert, there are deep-dish apple pie and baked Indian pudding. Moderate to deluxe.

LEXINGTON AND CONCORD RESTAURANTS

For a quick bite and a break from sightseeing, stop for an excellent coffee and pastry at **One Meriam Street** (1 Meriam Street, Lexington; 617-862-3006), a cozy and casual café-style eatery. They also serve pancakes, omelettes, sandwiches, burgers and salads. Dinner's served Friday; breakfast and lunch only the rest of the week. Budget.

For elegant dining in Lexington, try **Le Bellecour** (10 Muzzey Street; 617-861-9400). A Parisian ambience is imparted by pink walls and table-cloths, Breuer chairs, brass torchières and paintings of the French country-side. The French continental menu changes seasonally and features such traditional dishes as veal with roasted apples, at deluxe to ultra-deluxe prices. There are also wonderful desserts and an extensive wine list. Lighter fare— sandwiches, soups and salads—is available in the moderately priced café.

Yangtze River Restaurant (21-25 Depot Square, Lexington; 617-861-6030) specializes in Polynesian cuisine, as well as Szechuan and Cantonese favorites. The dining room is noisy and casual, with a jungle of greenery and exposed brick walls. Budget to moderate.

Not everyone will appreciate **The Willow Pond Kitchen** (745 Lexington Road, Concord; 508-369-6529), but we do. Its ma-and-pa, down-home atmosphere hasn't changed since the 1930s, with decor that features moth-eaten stuffed fish, wildcats and opossum, plus tacky formica tables and battered wooden booths. Paradoxically, good food is served here, on paper plates and at budget to moderate prices, including cheeseburgers, lobster rolls and lobster pie, steamed clams and a fine roster of beer and ale. Budget to moderate.

Located upstairs in an old railroad depot turned shopping arcade, **A Different Drummer** (86 Thoreau Street, Concord; 508-369-8700) offers a little bit of everything in an airy, simple dining room with white café chairs and tables, overlooking the tracks. A second dining room overlooks gift shops. Moderately priced items include lots of seafood, pasta and stir-fried and vegetarian entrées. They have the best Sunday brunch in town.

For some traditional Yankee fare in a historic setting, try the **Colonial Inn** (48 Monument Square, Concord; 508-369-9200). Built in 1716, the original part of the house was owned by Thoreau's grandfather. There are five dining rooms, each with its own colonially inspired decor. The menu includes prime rib, steak, scrod, scallops and lobster. Moderate to deluxe.

The Great Outdoors

The Sporting Life

SAILING

Sailing the blue waters of the Charles on a breezy day with views of both the Boston and Cambridge skylines is a moment to be savored. **Community Boating** (21 Embankment Road; 617-523-1038) rents boats to visitors who pass a test and buy a two-day membership. You can also rent boats, with a captain, at the **Boston Sailing Center** (54 Lewis Wharf; 617-227-4198) and the **Boston Harbor Sailing Club** (72 East India Row; 617-523-2619).

WHALE WATCHING

Boston is within easy reach of Stellwagen Bank, a major feeding ground for whales. You can go whalewatching with the **New England Aquarium** (Central Wharf; 617-973-5277), **Bay State Provincetown Cruises** (66 Long Wharf; 617-723-7800) and **A. C. Cruise Line** (28 Northern Avenue; 617-426-8419).

JOGGING

Jogging is very big in Boston, where half the population seems to be in training for the Boston Marathon. The most popular running paths are along both sides of the green strips paralleling the Charles River, which run more than 17 miles. For information call the **New England Athletic Congress** (617-566-7600). Another safe place to jog is the two- and three-mile trails in the **Breakheart Reservation** (177 Forest Street, Saugus; 617-233-0834).

GOLF

You can tee up at numerous public golf courses, including the **George Wright Golf Course** (420 West Street, Hyde Park; 617-361-8313), the **Presidents Golf Course** (357 West Squantum Street, Quincy; 617-328-3444), **Braintree Municipal Golf Course** (101 Jefferson Street, Braintree; 617-843-9781), **Newton Commonwealth Golf Course** (212 Kenrick Street, Newton; 617-244-4763), **Stow Acres** (58 Randall Road, Stow; 508-568-8690) and the **Colonial Country Club** (Audubon Road, Lynnfield; 617-245-9300).

TENNIS

The **Metropolitan District Commission** (MDC) (20 Somerset Street; 617-727-9547) maintains 45 courts throughout the city and Greater Boston, first-come, first-served. Cambridge, too, has public courts (for information, call 617-349-6231). There are numerous private clubs; one open to the public is the **Sportsmen's Tennis Club** (Franklin Field Tennis Center, 950 Blue Hill Avenue, Dorchester; 617-288-9092).

ICE-SKATING

Skaters have been rounding the curves of the lagoon in the Public Garden and the Boston Common Frog Pond for more than a hundred years. The Charles River is almost never frozen enough for skating, but the MDC (20 Somerset Street; 617-727-9547) maintains 21 public indoor rinks, some with rentals available. The Boston Parks and Recreation Department also has rinks (for information, call 617-725-4505). The **Skating Club of Boston** (1240 Soldier's Field Road, Brighton; 617-782-5900) offers public skating and has rentals available.

CROSS-COUNTRY SKIING

The **Weston Ski Track** (Park Road, Weston; 617-891-6575) has gently sloping trails that run over a golf course; lessons and rentals are available. The **Lincoln Guide Service** (Conservation Trail, Lincoln; 617-259-9204) also offers lessons and rentals. The **Middlesex Fells Reservation** (1 Woodland Road, Stoneham; 617-662-5214) has a free six-mile trail with trail maps, suiting a variety of skill levels. **Wompatuck State Park** (Union Street, Hingham; 617-749-7160) has relatively easy trails, with free trail maps at park headquarters.

BICYCLING

Biking is popular around Boston's scenic waterways, including the Charles River, although we wouldn't recommend it in the narrow, congested downtown streets. The Charles River Esplanade on the Boston side of the Charles River has a well-marked 18-mile route named the **Dr. Paul Dudley White Bike Path**, which goes from Science Park, through Boston, Cambridge and Newton, ending in Watertown. The **Stony Brook Reservation Bike Path** runs four miles through forests and fields in Dedham (Turtle Pond Parkway, West Roxbury, Hyde Park; 617-698-1802). The **Mystic River Reservation** also has a nice short bike path, 3.5 miles long, that runs from the Wellington Bridge in Somerville along the Mystic River to beyond the Wellington Bridge in Everett. Some of the best and least crowded biking in the region is at **Wompatuck State Park** (Union Street, Hingham; 617-749-7160), where there are 12 miles of easy-grade trails through some of the oldest forest groves in eastern New England.

If you're up for a really challenging route, try the 135-mile **Claire Saltonstall Bikeway,** the first segment of which runs from Boston to Bourne at the entrance to Cape Cod. Continuing segments follow the Cape Cod Rail Trail all the way to Provincetown at the tip of the Cape.

For information on area biking, contact the **Boston Area Bicycle Coalition** (P.O. Box 1015, Kendall Square Branch, Cambridge; 617-491-7433) or the **Charles River Wheelmen** (1 Belnap Road, Hyde Park; 617-325-2453).

BIKE RENTALS   To rent a bike in the Boston area, contact the **Community Bike Shop** (490 Tremont Street; 617-542-8623), **Ferris Wheels Bicycle Shop** (64 South Street; Jamaica Plain; 617-522-7082) or **Surf 'n Cycle** (1771 Massachusetts Avenue, Cambridge; 617-661-7659).

Beaches and Parks

Some of the information concerning parks appears in the "Sightseeing" section of this chapter. In addition to parks described below, those covered in "Sightseeing" include Boston Common, the Public Garden, Franklin Park, Arnold Arboretum and Castle Island.

OUTSIDE BOSTON BEACHES AND PARKS

Boston Harbor Islands (★)—Some 30 islands lie in Boston Harbor, scattered along the coast from Boston south to Quincy, Hingham and Hull, with eight of them comprising a state park. The Puritans used these islands for pastureland and firewood, and there are tales of buried pirate treasure and ghosts haunting old Civil War forts. Each island has a unique flavor and character. **Peddocks Island,** a 113-acre preserve of woodlands, salt marsh, rocky beaches and open fields, has a turn-of-the-century fort, a wildlife sanctuary and an old cottage community. Peaceful and primitive **Lovells Island** is characterized by long beaches and diverse wildlife, rocky tidepools and sand dunes. The smaller **Georges Island**, the most developed in the park, is dominated by Fort Warren, a National Historic Landmark built between 1833 and 1869. Construction was overseen by Sylvanus Thayer, the "Father of West Point." Other islands in the park system include Gallop's, Grape, Bumpkin and Great Brewster.

Facilities: Picnic areas, restrooms, park rangers, nature trails, fort tours, historical programs, boat docks, concession stand on Georges Island. Information: Peddocks, Lovells and Georges islands are administered by the regional Metropolitan District Commission; contact the MDC's Harbor Region Office (98 Taylor Street; Dorchester; 617-727-5359). Grape, Bumpkin, Brewster and the other islands are state-owned; contact the **Boston Harbor Islands State Park** (349 Lincoln Street, Hingham; 617-740-1605). *Camping:* Permitted on Peddocks and Lovells islands (MDC permit required) and on Grape, Great Brewster and Bumpkin islands (permit required from Boston Harbor Islands State Park). *Swimming:* Permitted on Lovells Island only. *Fishing:* Good from rocky shores and public piers on all the islands except Peddocks; lots of flounder, cod, haddock, pollack and striped bass.

Getting there: Georges Island serves as the entrance to the park and provides free inter-island water taxis from Memorial Day to Labor Day; for information, call the Department of Environmental Management, 617-740-1605. The islands are also accessible by ferry and cruise lines, including Boston Harbor Cruises (1 Long Wharf; 617-227-4321), Bay State Cruise Company (66 Long Wharf; (617-723-7800) and Massachusetts Bay Lines (60 Rowes Wharf; 617-542-8000). The **Friends of the Boston Harbor Islands** sponsors special boat trips and tours; call 617-523-8386.

Belle Isle Marsh (★)—This preserve holds 241 acres of the largest remaining salt marsh in Boston, typical of the wetlands that once lined the shores of the Massachusetts Bay Colony. It's a special place, where you can see lots of wildlife and salt marsh plants rare in an urban area.

Facilities: Nature trails, observation tower, guided tours; information, 617-727-5350.

Getting there: Located at 146 Bennington Street, East Boston.

OUTLYING AREAS BEACHES AND PARKS

Nantasket Beach—Once a classy mid-19th-century resort with grand hotels rivaling those in Newport, the Nantasket Beach area later declined into a tacky strip of bars, fast-food stands and Skeeball arcades. Still, this three-and-a-half-mile barrier beach is one of the nicest in the area, with clean white sand and a wide open vista of the Atlantic Ocean.

Facilities: Picnic areas, restrooms, lifeguards, shade pavilions, board-walk, restaurants and snack stands; information: 617-727-5215. *Swimming:* It's always good. After a storm there's enough surf to go bodysurfing or windsurfing.

Getting there: Located on Nantasket Avenue, at the terminus of Route 228 in Hull.

Wollaston Beach—Come high tide, the beach virtually disappears, so narrow is this two-mile stretch of sand. The beach is backed by a wide sea-wall and a parking strip along its entire length. Here people like to sunbathe in lawn chairs or draped across the hoods of their cars, and to walk their dogs, giving this beach a distinctly urban feel. The sand is gravelly and often crowded, but the beach does have a splendid view of the Boston skyline.

Facilities: Picnic areas, restrooms, bathhouses, playground; snack bars and restaurants across the street with great fried clams; information, 617-727-5293.

Getting there: Located on Quincy Shore Drive, south on Route 3A from Neponset Circle, Quincy.

Blue Hills Reservation—This 6500-acre park is the largest open space within 35 miles of Boston. Great Blue Hill, the highest point on the coast of Massachusetts south of Maine, is the site of the oldest weather station in North America. The reservation comprises dozens of hills, forested land and several lakes and wetlands, as well as 150 miles of hiking, ski touring and bridle trails. There's a natural history museum—the Trailside Museum (617-333-0690)—with live animals and exhibits, and 16 historic sites, including the 1795 Redman Farmhouse.

Facilities: Picnic areas, restrooms, lifeguards, snack bar, tennis courts, golf course, small downhill ski run with ski rentals, ballfields, nature programs; information, 617-698-1802. *Camping:* The Appalachian Mountain Club operates 20 huts in the reservation on Ponkapoag Pond (617-963-9856). Reserve these well ahead. *Swimming:* Houghton's Pond, with its calm waters and sandy bottom, offers particularly good swimming for children. *Fishing:* Ponds are stocked with trout, bass, bullhead, perch and sunfish.

Getting there: Reservation headquarters are located on Hillside Street next to the police station in Milton, where maps are available.

Middlesex Fells Reservation—"Fells" is a Scottish word meaning wild, hilly country, which aptly describes the 2000-plus-acre terrain of this reservation. These rugged highlands were first explored in 1632 by Governor Winthrop, first governor of the Massachusetts Bay Colony. They were acquired as public parkland in 1893, and a 19th-century trolley line brought in droves of picnickers. The region has been used for logging, granite quarrying, ice harvesting and water power for mills that manufactured the first vulcanized rubber products. Fifty miles of hiking trails and old woods roads run through the Fells.

Facilities: Picnic areas, hiking and horseback riding trails, ski touring trails, skating rink, swimming pool; information, 617-662-5214. *Fishing:* Fellsmere, Doleful, Dark Hollow and Quarter Mile ponds hold sunfish, catfish, perch, pickerel and bass.

Getting there: Located six miles north of Boston, off exits 32, 33 and 34 from Route 93.

Hiking

Scant miles outside the urban clatter of downtown Boston, Massachusetts turns to rolling green hills, river valleys and pine and hardwood forests. A surprising number of parks and wildlife sanctuaries are to be found in these rural country towns, where you can hike scenic trails, short or long.

OUTLYING AREAS TRAILS

The **Quincy Quarries Footpath** (2.5 miles) leads past steep quarry walls, the first commercial railway in America and an 1898 turning mill, used to cut and polish the Quincy granite columns and slabs that went into many famous buildings in America.

The main path at **World's End** (★) (4 miles) winds uphill and down over a little peninsula extending north from Hingham into Massachusetts Bay. Its beautifully landscaped, gently curving roads were laid out by famed landscape architect Frederick Law Olmsted for a housing development that was never built. The wide, grassy path meanders through meadows and marshland, past rocky, glacial drumlins, through avenues of English oaks, pine and red cedars, and up a steep knoll, where your reward is a knockout view of the Boston skyline, one of the best on the South Shore.

The **Ponkapoag Trail** (3.5 miles) in the Blue Hills Reservation circles Ponkapoag Pond, passing through wetlands and a golf course. From it, the Ponkapoag Log Boardwalk crosses a floating bog, filled with highbush blueberries, blue flag iris and Atlantic white cedar.

Little-known and little-used, Stony Brook Reservation allows you to walk in solitude among peaceful woods along the **Bearberry Hill Path** (3 miles). The trail leads into the woods toward Turtle Pond, then returns via the east boundary asphalt bicycle path leading past a swampy thicket and a golf course.

The **Skyline Trail** (6.8 miles) in the Middlesex Fells Reservation is a rugged trail that climbs many rocky knobs running between two observation towers. Scenery varies considerably along the way, from a pond with water lilies and frogs, to volcanic-rock-covered hills, wild hardwood forests, an old soapbox derby track, carpets of Canada mayflower and swampy areas.

Although you will do so with crowds of others, you can walk the shores Thoreau walked at **Walden Pond** in Concord. A 1.7-mile circuit trail winds through woods along the crystal clear waters of the pond. At the cabin site where Thoreau lived for two years, travelers from all corners of the globe have piled up stones in memoriam.

Travelers' Tracks

Sightseeing

NORTH END

The North End is Boston's oldest, most colorful neighborhood. Today it's a tightly knit, homogeneous Italian community, established after a gradual takeover from pockets of Irish, Portuguese and Jewish residents starting in the late 19th century. The North End's mostly one-lane streets are crowded cheek-by-jowl with Italian restaurants and food stores. Many residents still greet each other in the language of the Old Country and hang their wash out between the alleys. All summer long, Italians celebrate their patron saints with picturesque weekend parades and street festivals.

On the roundish peninsula that is Boston, the North End juts north into Boston Harbor and is cut off from downtown by the elevated Southeast Expressway, which helps keep it a place unto itself. It's a spot where Boston history still lives.

Probably no name evokes more romance in American history than Paul Revere. His famous ride warning of the British attack in 1775 has been chronicled the world over. The quiet little expanse of North Square, lined with cobblestones and black anchor chain, is where you come upon **The Paul Revere House** (19 North Square; 617-523-2338; admission). This simple little three-story house with gray clapboards and leaded-glass, diamond-paned windows looks almost out of place in Boston today, and well it might. Built in 1680, it's the only example left in downtown Boston of 17th-century architecture. Revere lived here from 1770 until 1800, although not with all of his 16 children at the same time. Inside are period furnishings, some original Revere family items and works of silver.

Next door to Paul Revere's house and entered through the same courtyard is the **Pierce-Hichborn House** (29 North Square; 617-523-2338; admission). Built about 1711 by glazier Moses Pierce, it's one of the earliest remaining Georgian structures in Boston. It later belonged to Paul Revere's cousin, boatbuilder Nathaniel Hichborn.

Also in North Square are the **Seamen's Bethel** (11 North Square) and the **Mariner's House** (12 North Square). An anchor over the door announces the Mariner's House, a place where, since 1838, a seaman has always been able to get a cheap meal and a bed for the night. Said the sailor-preacher of the Seamen's Bethel, "I set my bethel in North Square because I learned to set my net where the fish ran." Once a place where sailors worshipped, it's now a rectory office.

On a street noted for "gardens and governors" lived John F. "Honey Fitz" Fitzgerald, one of Boston's Irish "governors," a ward boss, congressman and mayor. His daughter **Rose Kennedy** was born in this plain brick building at 4 Garden Court Street.

The **Old North Church** (193 Salem Street; 617-523-6676; admission) is the one from which the sexton hung two lanterns the night of Paul Revere's midnight ride ("one if by land, two if by sea"). This beautiful church has Palladian windows and a white pulpit inspired by London designs. The four trumpeting cherubim atop the choir loft pilasters were taken from a French pirate ship. The church houses the historic lanterns in its steeple.

Directly behind Old North Church in the **Paul Revere Mall** stands a life-sized statue of Revere astride his horse—one of the city's most photographed scenes.

On the other side of the mall is **St. Stephen's Church** (Hanover and Clark streets), a brick federal-style church designed by the man who established that style, Charles Bulfinch, America's first native-born architect. The only Bulfinch-designed church still standing in Boston, St. Stephen's has a bell and copper dome cast by Paul Revere. Inside are wedding-cake-white fluted pillars, balconies and Palladian windows, a pewter chandelier and an 1830s pipe organ.

Copp's Hill Burying Ground (Hull and Snow Hill streets) served as the cemetery for Old North Church in the 17th century. Set high on a little green knoll, it overlooks Boston Harbor and Charlestown, which was bombarded by British guns placed here during the Battle of Bunker Hill. Its simple gray headstones bear pockmarks from British target practice. Buried here are Increase and Cotton Mather, Puritan ministers who wielded considerable political clout.

The widest street in all the North End is Hanover Street, a major center for shops and restaurants. Walking south on Hanover Street leads you straight to the **Haymarket–North End Underpass** (★), which leads under the Southeast Expressway to downtown. The underpass is lined with bright, primitive mosaics done by North End children, a kind of urban folk art.

Boston By Foot (77 North Washington Street; 617-367-2345) gives regular walking tours of the North End, as well as many other neighborhoods.

DOWNTOWN

The downtown area comprises several distinct neighborhoods, sprawling around the peninsula and looping around Beacon Hill and the Boston Common. Although Boston's compactness makes it very easy to sightsee on foot, there is no convenient way to see these neighborhoods, and you'll find yourself doubling back more than once.

For the hit-and-run tourist, there's the **Freedom Trail**, a walking extravaganza created in 1974 that links 16 major historic sights from downtown to Beacon Hill, the North End and Charlestown. A walking trail map is available at the **Boston Common Visitor Information Kiosk** (147 Tremont Street; 617-536-4100) or the **Prudential Visitor Center** (800 Boylston Street, Prudential Plaza; 617-536-4100).

But if you do nothing but walk the Freedom Trail, you will have missed many of Boston's riches. We have chosen to show you a route that covers many more sights than the Freedom Trail: It loops northward from the North End to the old West End, back down through Government Center and Quincy Market, and out to the Waterfront. Then it goes up State Street, down through the Financial District to Chinatown and the Theater District, and finally back up Washington Street to Boston Common. Since all these neighborhoods are so small, there's no need to treat them as separate geographic areas. But when a sight lies within the boundaries of a particular downtown neighborhood, we'll be sure to let you know.

When you come out the North End Underpass, you'll be crossing Blackstone Street. Look down at your feet to see a street sculpture called **Asarotan**—bronze castings of ears of corn, fruit, fish and vegetables, recreating the clutter of market day, worn smooth by the passage of feet. The name means unswept floor, and the concept dates to Roman times, when food was similarly portrayed in mosaic floor tiles of banquet halls.

Asarotan was made in honor of **Haymarket** (covering several blocks of Blackstone Street), the country's oldest market, in operation more than 200 years. On weekends, open-air vendors hawk fruits and vegetables, meats, fresh fish and crabs, crowding over several blocks. Ancient hanging metal scales are used to weigh purchases. Prices are good here, but don't try to touch anything without a vendor's permission—he'll scream.

You'll find the **Boston Stone** (★) (Marshall and Hanover streets) easily enough by looking behind the Boston Stone Gift Shop. A round brown stone embedded in the rear corner of the house and dated 1737, it was brought from England and used as a millstone to grind pigment. A tavern keeper named it after the famous London Stone and used it as an advertisement.

Behind Marshall Street is the **Blackstone Block,** tiny alleyways that are the last remnants of Boston's 17th-century byways, the oldest commercial district. Their names, Marsh Lane, Creek Square and Salt Lane, represent the early topography of Boston's landscape.

The **Union Oyster House** (41 Union Street; 617-227-2750), built in the 18th century, became a restaurant in 1826, making it the oldest continuously working restaurant in America. Here Daniel Webster drank a tall tumbler of brandy and water with each half-dozen oysters, and he rarely had fewer than six plates. Before it was a restaurant, exiled French King Louis Phillipe taught French here to wealthy ladies. Upstairs in 1771, Isaiah Thomas published *The Massachusetts Spy,* one of the first newspapers in the United States.

At the western edge of Boston's peninsula, stretching from the Southeast Expressway to Storrow Drive, is an area that used to be known as the West End. Once rich in many-quilted ethnic groups, it's now a mostly commercialized neighborhood.

A popular spot here is **Boston Garden** (150 Causeway Street; 617-227-3200), where the Celtics twinkle their toes and the Boston Bruins bash heads. In addition to basketball and hockey, it's used for circuses, ice shows and rock concerts.

Not on the peninsula at all, but out in the middle of the Charles River, is the **Museum of Science** (Science Park; 617-723-2500; admission), reached via the Charles River Dam. The star of the museum is the state-of-the-art Omni Theater, whose 76-foot domed screen and surrounding sound systems make you feel as though you're actually whizzing down Olympic slopes on skis or moving underwater through the Great Barrier Reef. The museum also houses live animal exhibits, the Hayden Planetarium and changing displays on foreign cultures.

The **Harrison Gray Otis House** (141 Cambridge Street; 617-227-3956; admission) was the first of three Boston houses Bulfinch designed for his friend Otis, a prominent lawyer and member of Congress. Built in 1796, the three-story brick house is classically symmetrical, with rows of evenly spaced windows and a Palladian window. Inside is one of the most gorgeous interiors in Boston, rich with imported wallpapers, opulent swag curtains and carpeting, gilt-framed mirrors, Adams mantels and neoclassical motifs framing every doorway and window. Surviving abuse as a bathhouse, Chinese laundry and rooming house, the building became the headquarters of the Society for the Preservation of New England Antiquities in 1916.

Right next door is the **Old West Church** (131 Cambridge Street; 617-227-5088), a handsome federal-style brick building with a cupola and pillars on three stories. The British tore down its original steeple to prevent signaling across the river during the siege of 1776. Rebuilt in 1806, it houses a Charles Fisk organ.

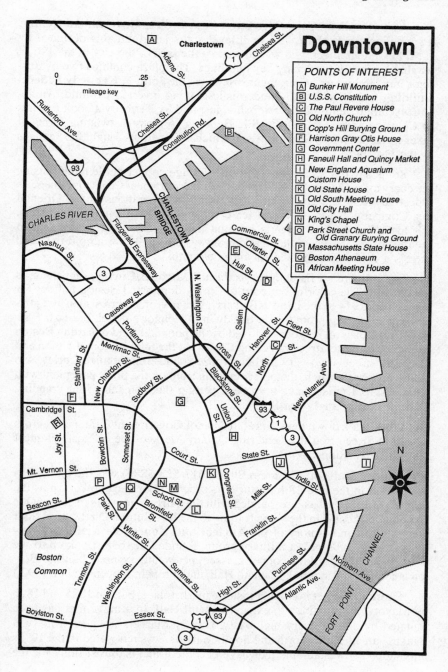

Downtown

POINTS OF INTEREST

A Bunker Hill Monument
B U.S.S. Constitution
C The Paul Revere House
D Old North Church
E Copp's Hill Burying Ground
F Harrison Gray Otis House
G Government Center
H Faneuil Hall and Quincy Market
I New England Aquarium
J Custom House
K Old State House
L Old South Meeting House
M Old City Hall
N King's Chapel
O Park Street Church and
   Old Granary Burying Ground
P Massachusetts State House
Q Boston Athenaeum
R African Meeting House

A short walk up Cambridge Street brings you to **Government Center,** a sprawling brick plaza with multilevel stairs and fountains designed by I. M. Pei, an architect who was to change the face of the city in the 1960s, leaving his imprint on many key buildings. The plaza contains two of Boston's most important government structures, the **John F. Kennedy Federal Building** and **City Hall,** a modernistic-looking inverted pyramid. An abstract sculpture entitled *Thermopylae,* inspired by Kennedy's book *Profiles in Courage,* stands facing the JFK Building. A mass of twisting forms, it takes its name from a Greek battle in which the Spartans fought the Persians to the last man.

Some say the **Steaming Teakettle,** a huge copper kettle hung outside the doorway at 65 Court Street at the edge of Government Center, is America's oldest advertising sign. It once announced the operations of the Oriental Tea Company, Boston's largest tea company. Made by city coppersmiths, it holds 227 gallons, two quarts, one pint and three gills. It gives you a warm feeling to see the teakettle steaming away, especially on a cold day, and there's a coffee shop inside for more warmth.

For a figure so flamboyant as **James Michael Curley,** one statue is not enough. The colorful but corrupt Curley dominated Boston politics for years, from 1914 to the late 1940s, serving as mayor, congressman and governor and figuring prominently in Edwin O'Connor's novel *The Last Hurrah.* This four-term mayor was loved by the poor and fond of calling Boston bankers the "State Street Wrecking Crew." At the intersection of Union and Congress streets, two very lifelike bronze statues immortalize Curley, one sitting on a park bench, the other standing right on the brick pavement with no pedestal. Tourists have been seen patting the stomach of the standing Curley, so temptingly portly is it.

If you walk down the stairs at the rear of Government Center and across Congress Street, you'll be entering Quincy Market, one of Boston's most popular destinations.

Faneuil Hall (off Congress Street; 617-523-3886) was the city's central market in the mid-18th century. Its second floor became known as the "Cradle of Liberty," as it resounded with the patriotic rhetoric of James Otis and Samuel Adams in the years leading to the Revolution. On the third floor is a museum and armory of the **Ancient and Honorable Artillery Company,** the nation's oldest military group, founded in 1638. Look up to see the four-foot-long gilded copper grasshopper weathervane, a familiar Boston landmark and symbol. (Faneuil Hall, under repair, reopens in late 1992.)

Quincy Market is another historic marketplace, built in 1825 and 1826 by Mayor Josiah Quincy to expand Faneuil Hall. In a move that has been imitated by almost every major city, Quincy Market, along with its twin flanking arcades, the North and South Markets, was renovated in the 1970s into shops and restaurants that have become a major tourist draw for the city. The cobblestoned mall is a street festival by day, a lively nightspot in the later hours. It's wonderfully decorated during the holidays.

If you walk out the rear of Quincy Market and under the Southeast Expressway across busy Atlantic Avenue, you'll arrive at the waterfront.

When Atlantic Avenue was built in the 1860s, it sliced right through the center of many of the great old wharves, including **Long Wharf**, the oldest existing one in Boston. Built in 1710, Long Wharf was named for its length—formerly 1800 feet. The British marched up Long Wharf when they occupied the city in 1768, only to retreat back down it when they were evacuated in 1776. Long Wharf also saw the departure of the first missionaries to Hawaii in 1819 and played a role in the 1850s California Gold Rush, when thousands of New Englanders departed for San Francisco.

Buildings imitating Renaissance palazzos and Greek temples were built in the 19th century along Rowes, India, Central, Long, Commercial, Lewis, Sargent's and Union wharves. **Lewis Wharf**, formerly Clarke's Wharf, was once owned by John Hancock. Nathaniel Hawthorne served as a customs inspector at **Long Wharf**. By the mid-19th century, the wharves were a center of clipper trade with China, Europe, Australia and Hawaii.

Some of the old wharf buildings, which once housed ships' chandlers and sail riggers, have been renovated into shops, offices and restaurants, including the **Pilot House, Mercantile Wharf** and **Chart House**, the only surviving late-18th-century building on the waterfront.

Central Wharf is home to the **New England Aquarium** (617-973-5200; admission), signaled by a bright red, 45-foot wind sculpture. Bostonians like to congregate to watch the harbor seals in the outdoor pool. Inside, the Giant Ocean Tank is home to 95 species of exotic reef fish, sea turtles, sharks and moray eels. Sea lions perform next door on board the Discovery, a floating theater.

Waterfront Park (north of Long Wharf on Atlantic Avenue) is a neatly landscaped pocket park with brick walkways and benches that offers a lovely harbor view along with respite.

From the wharves, you can take cruises of Boston Harbor, a great way to while away an afternoon or evening and see the city skyline. Boat lines include **Boston Harbor Cruises** (1 Long Wharf; 617-227-4320) and **Massachusetts Bay Lines** (60 Rowes Wharf; 617-542-8000).

From Long Wharf, walk up State Street. In a couple of blocks, you'll come to the granite Greek Revival **Customs House** (McKinley Square at State and India streets), built between 1837 and 1847, where inspectors once examined all cargoes arriving at the wharves. Incongruously, this building also became Boston's first skyscraper in 1915, when the great clock tower was added. The clock, broken for many years, was restored in the late 1980s, and its bright blue and gold face now glows handsomely at night, visible from great distances.

The **Cunard Building** (126 State Street) was built in 1902 for the Cunard Steamship Line, owners of the ocean liner *Queen Elizabeth II*. Twin brass anchors flank its doors, festooned with dolphins and seashells.

The oldest surviving public building in Boston, the **Old State House** (206 Washington Street, corner of State Street; 617-720-1713; admission) is a pretty little brick building dwarfed by the surrounding skyscrapers. The bronze lion and stone unicorn atop its gables stand as symbols of the English crown. Until the American Revolution, this was the seat of British government. A ring of cobblestones outside marks the site of the Boston Massacre, the signal event launching the Revolution. A museum since 1882, the Old State House features winding galleries of exhibits on the building's history and architecture, early Boston and maritime history, including memorabilia, ship's models, paintings and prints.

Right next door, **National Park Service Visitor Information** (15 State Street; 617-242-5642) has a good selection of maps, tour books and brochures and also sponsors ranger-guided tours to national park sites, including some Freedom Trail stops.

An outdoor flower market fronting the brick, federal-style **Old South Meeting House** (310 Washington Street, corner of Milk Street; 617-482-6439; admission) adds to its charms. Built in 1729, Old South has high-arching Palladian windows, white pulpit and candlelight chandeliers. Many crucial meetings leading to the American Revolution took place here, including the debate that launched the Boston Tea Party. Countless notables spoke here, including Samuel Adams, John Hancock and, later, Oliver Wendell Holmes. Though Old South was repeatedly ravaged—the British turned it into a riding school complete with jumping bar, and it was forced to serve as a temporary post office after a devastating fire in 1872—it has been restored to its 18th-century look. Taped presentations re-create the famous Tea Party debate and others.

Milk Street leads into the heart of the Financial District, a warren of streets stretching south from State Street to High Street and east to Washington Street. Dominated by towering banks and office buildings, the Financial District was considerably built up in the 1980s with bold new buildings, provoking controversy over their design in tradition-minded Boston. One of these—the **Bank of Boston** at 100 Federal Street—is laughingly called Pregnant Alice because of its billowing shape.

In its marching devastation, the **Great Fire of 1872** leveled 60 acres of downtown Boston. The spot where the fire was arrested on its northeastward path is noted on a bronze plaque on the front of the U.S. Post Office at Post Office Square, the corner of Milk and Devonshire streets.

Two bonanzas await in the lobby of the **New England Telephone building** (★) (185 Franklin Street). One, a massive mural called *Telephone Men and Women at Work*, circles the rotunda 360° and depicts decades of telephone workers, from 1880s switchboard operators to later engineers, cable layers and information operators. The other reward is Alexander Graham Bell's Garret, a dark little corner filled with memorabilia surrounding the birth of the telephone in Boston in 1875. The garret looks much as it did when Bell worked in it at its original location at 109 Court Street. (A **bronze plaque** at Government Center in front of the John F. Kennedy Federal Building marks that spot, where sound was first transmitted over wires in the fifth-floor garret.)

At 100 Summer Street stands a mobile that looks like a giant yellow lollipop tree, an ebullient surprise in a city where there is not much outdoor public art. Bostonians call it "the lollipops," but its real name is **Helion** (★), one of a group of pieces called "windflowers" by sculptor Robert Amory.

Walk south down Summer Street, until you come to **South Station** (Summer Street and Atlantic Avenue). South Station was a grand old station house in its day, in fact the largest in the world at the turn of the century. After a thorough restoration completed in 1989, this pink granite beauty stands tall and proud. Ionic columns, a balustrade and clock with eagle decorate the curved Beaux-Arts facade stretching for two blocks. South Station today serves as a transportation hub for subway, rail and bus connections. The interior, designed to resemble a European market square, sparkles with polished marble floors and brass railings and is filled with restaurants, shops and pushcart vendors.

Across the street, you can tour the **Federal Reserve Bank** (600 Atlantic Avenue, corner of Summer Street; 617-973-3451), which processes millions of dollars worth of currency every day. The Fed's unusual design—it looks like a giant white washboard, and there's a gap where the fifth floor should be—is intended to withstand down drafts and wind pressures. The Fed, which boasts a lobby full of sculpture and murals, also hosts jazz and classical concerts and changing art and crafts exhibits.

South Station is just a hop, skip and a jump from **Chinatown**, bounded by Essex and Washington streets and the Southeast Expressway. Compared to Chinatowns in other major cities, Boston's is quite small, just a few blocks long. But this Chinatown was much larger decades earlier, before the Southeast Expressway was built, cutting a wide swath through the district. The Tufts New England Medical Center, too, took a great chunk of Chinatown land when it was built. Now hemmed in by the Expressway and the Combat Zone, Chinatown has little room to grow.

The Chinese were first brought to Boston to break a shoe industry strike in the 1870s, coming by train from the West Coast. They settled close to South Station because of the convenience of the railroad. First living in tents, the Chinese eventually built houses or moved into places previously inhabited by Syrians, Irish and Italians.

Despite its small size, or perhaps because of it, Chinatown is intensely and authentically Chinese. Signs are in Chinese characters, and the area is densely packed with Chinese stores and restaurants. Even the phone booths are covered with Chinese pagodas.

The **Chinatown gates**, a bicentennial gift from Taiwan, stand at the intersection of Beach Street and Surface Road, marking the entrance to Chinatown. White stone with a massive green pagoda on top, they are guarded fore and aft by stone Chinese Foo dogs and sport gold Chinese characters on green marble. The classic characters are not readily translatable in modern Chinese, but they embody such moral principles as propriety, righteousness, modesty and honor.

The **Chinese-Culture Institute** (★) (276 Tremont Street; 617-542-4599) opened in 1980. It houses a gallery where rotating exhibits of Chinese paintings, sculpture, ceramics and folk art are shown. The institute also produces concerts, plays, dance recitals and lectures.

At the corner of Harrison Avenue and Oak Street is the large **Unity/Community Chinatown Mural** (★), painted in 1986, which depicts the history of the Chinese in Boston. Among its pigtailed Chinese figures are construction workers, a launderer and women at sewing machines. Other scenes show the Chinese learning to read, protesting to save their housing and gaining access to professional careers.

Although you may not want to take one home, you can see live chickens squawking in stacks of wire crates at **Eastern Live Poultry** (★) (48 Beach Street), where locals line up to buy them "live or dressed."

Walk two blocks over to Tremont Street, and head south. In short order you'll be in the Theater District, centered on Tremont Street, Warrenton Place and Charles Street South. Boston has a lively and prestigious theater scene, with many tryouts moving on to Broadway. Among the half dozen or so nationally known theaters is the **Colonial** (106 Boylston Street; 617-426-9366), the oldest continuously operated theater in America, built in 1900. At that time the sumptuously decorated Colonial was considered one of the most elegant theaters in the country, with its 70-foot Italian-marble vestibule and foyer rich with ceiling paintings, cupids, plate mirrors, bronze staircases and carved wood. George M. Cohan, Noel Coward, Fred Astaire, Katharine Hepburn and the Marx Brothers have trod its boards.

Formerly the Metropolitan Theatre, the splendid **Wang Center for the Performing Arts** (270 Tremont Street; 617-482-9393) was built in 1925 as a palace for first-run movies in the Roaring Twenties. Restored to its original grandeur, it is opulently decorated with gold leaf, crystal, mirrors and Italian marble, and was designed to be reminiscent of the Paris Opera and Versailles. This 3610-seat theater is one of the largest in the world, and has hosted a variety of artists including the Andrew Sisters, Yo-Yo Ma, Rudolf Nureyev, Luciano Pavarotti, Benny Goodman and the Grateful Dead.

Few people know that **Edgar Allan Poe** (★) had a long history in Boston, so in 1989 a memorial bronze plaque was erected to his memory at the corner of Boylston Street and Edgar Allan Poe Way. Born here, Poe was the son of actors at the Boston Theatre. He published his first book, lectured and enlisted in the army in Boston.

The **Grand Lodge of Masons** (★) (186 Tremont Street, corner of Boylston Street; 617-426-6040) is decorated with blue and gold mosaics of masonic symbols, and its grand lobby houses a small exhibit of masonic memorabilia.

Boston's famed **Combat Zone** on lower Washington Street should be added to the endangered species list. As the pace of development quickened in the late 1970s, its former horde of topless lounges, sleazy bars and adult bookstores and movies shrank to a pathetic few blocks that would be the scorn of any true big-city habitué. These are likely to disappear, too, in the wake of a new cultural district planned for the area for the late 1990s.

Downtown Crossing is the heart of downtown shopping. Lunchtime shoppers crowd the brick pedestrian mall at the corner of Washington and Summer streets, fronting on **Jordan Marsh** and **Filene's**, two of Boston's oldest department stores. Downtown Crossing is street entertainment at its most diverse. Pushcart vendors and street musicians—one day a Peruvian folk band, the next a rock group—vie for space in the crowded mall. A one-man band is a permanent local fixture.

The **Old Corner Bookstore** (1 School Street, corner of Washington Street; 617-523-6658), now called the Globe Corner Bookstore, was a literary hub in the mid-19th century (see "Boston Bookstores" in this chapter). Covered with billboards in the 1950s, it was once threatened by urban renewal but saved by preservationists.

Old City Hall (45 School Street), a grand French Second Empire building, was renovated in the 1970s into offices and a French restaurant. As one of the first 19th-century Boston buildings to be recycled, it helped spark the preservationist movement. In front of Old City Hall stands the **Franklin Statue**, an eight-foot bronze tribute to Benjamin Franklin. Relief tablets at the base illustrate scenes from his career as printer, scientist and signer of the Declaration of Independence.

The **Omni Parker House** (60 School Street) is the oldest continuously operating hotel in America, first opening in 1855. Soon after, it became a hangout of the Saturday Club, a literary group whose members included Nathaniel Hawthorne, Ralph Waldo Emerson, Henry Wadsworth Longfellow, James Russell Lowell, Oliver Wendell Holmes and John Greenleaf Whittier. This little group founded the *Atlantic Monthly*.

King's Chapel (corner of Tremont and School streets; 617-523-1749) looks morosely like a mausoleum. Its steeple was never finished, so its Ionic columns flank a bare, squat granite building. The inside, however, is gorgeous, with carved Corinthian columns and pewter chandeliers. The first Anglican church in New England, King's Chapel eventually became the first Unitarian church in the United States. King's Chapel became famous for its music, since it was the first church in Boston to have an organ—the Puritans didn't believe in music at Sunday services.

Beside the church is **King's Chapel Burying Ground**, the oldest cemetery in Boston. It contains the graves of John Winthrop, the colony's first governor, and William Daws, the minuteman who helped Paul Revere warn the colonists the British were coming.

Park Street Church (corner of Park and Tremont streets; 617-523-3383) is one of Boston's most beautiful churches, with its white Christopher Wren spire and brick exterior. It was known as Brimstone Corner during the War of 1812 because gun powder was stored in its basement. Here William Lloyd Garrison made his first antislavery speech, and the song "America" was sung for the first time. These days, there are evening carillon concerts.

Next door is the **Old Granary Burying Ground**, which took its name from a large grain storehouse the Park Street Church replaced. Buried here are Paul Revere, Boston's Mother Goose (Elizabeth Ver Goose, who became known for her nursery rhymes) and three signers of the Declaration of Independence, including John Hancock. You can't see exactly where each is buried, since the headstones were rearranged for the convenience of lawn mowing. Death's heads, skeletons and hourglasses were popular headstone motifs here.

Times have changed considerably at **Boston Common**, a large tract of forested green, and one of America's oldest public parks. In 1634, its acres served as pasture for cattle, training grounds for the militia and a public stage for hanging adulterers, Quakers, pirates and witches. A few steps from the visitor kiosk is **Brewer Fountain**, brought from Paris by Gardner Brewer in 1868 for his Beacon Hill home and later donated to the city. Notable among the statuary on the Common is the *Soldiers and Sailors Monument* high on a hill, whose figures represent history and peace.

Today, downtown office workers use the crisscrossing paths as shortcuts to work, and it's a popular spot for jogging, Frisbee-tossing and dog walking. You might wander into Park Street Station, the first station built on the nation's oldest subway, which opened in 1897.

Boston Common is the first jewel in Boston's **Emerald Necklace**, a seven-mile tracery of green that loops through and around the city, all the way to Jamaica Plain, Brookline and Fenway. It was designed in the early 1900s by famed landscape architect Frederick Law Olmsted, who believed that parks could provide a psychological antidote to the noise, stress and artificiality of city life. The Emerald Necklace also includes the Public Garden, the Commonwealth Avenue Mall, the Back Bay Fens, Olmsted Park,

Jamaica Pond, Franklin Park and the Arnold Arboretum. The Boston Parks and Recreation Department (617-522-2639 or 617-423-4659) conducts periodic walking and bicycling tours of the entire Emerald Necklace. Other parts of the Necklace will be dealt with under their appropriate neighborhoods.

Leaving the edge of Boston Common, you can walk up Park Street, which brings you to Beacon Hill.

BEACON HILL

Beacon Hill got its name from a beacon that stood atop it in 1634 to warn colonial settlers of danger. "The Hill" used to be much taller; it was leveled by 60 feet to make way for residential building in the 19th century.

After a building boom, Beacon Hill fast became the most elite section of the city, home to doctors, lawyers, writers and intellectuals. Oliver Wendell Holmes called it "the sunny street that holds the sifted few." The first formal residents of the neighborhood were John Singleton Copley and John Hancock. Later residents included Daniel Webster, Louisa May Alcott, William Dean Howells, Henry James and Jenny Lind.

No single section of town is more elegant than Beacon Hill. This charming area still looks like a 19th-century neighborhood with its gas lamps, brick sidewalks and narrow, one-lane streets that wind up and down the hill. Its later brick rowhouses were designed in fine Federal style, with symmetrical windows, fanlight door windows, black shutters and lacy black iron grillwork. Beacon Hill residents love windowboxes and gardens, and many of the houses have beautiful hidden walled gardens. These are opened to the public during the **Hidden Gardens of Beacon Hill** walking tours in the spring, sponsored by the Beacon Hill Garden Club (P.O. Box 302, Charles Street Station, Boston, MA 02114; 617-227-4392).

The crown of Beacon Hill, at its summit, is the **Massachusetts State House** (617-727-3676), a grand replacement for the old State House downtown. After the American Revolution, state leaders wanted a more elegant home for the prosperous new government. Charles Bulfinch designed it for them in 1795 in federal style, with a gold dome, brick facade, Palladian windows and white Corinthian columns and trim. A tour of the interior is well worthwhile. An impressive rotunda, floors made of 24 kinds of marble, unique "black lace" iron grillwork stair railings, stained-glass windows and decorated vaulted ceilings are all part of the appointments. Don't miss the Sacred Cod in the House of Representatives, a wooden fish hung there in 1784 to symbolize the importance of the fishing industry to Massachusetts.

The **Old Court House** (Pemberton Square), now the Suffolk County Courthouse, has a grand rotunda with vaulted ceilings decorated with gilt rosettes and figures of cherubs, urns, scrolls and trumpet-blowing figures. Stone caryatids line the rotunda, representing Justice, Fortitude, Punishment, Guilt, Reward, Wisdom, Religion and Virtue.

Many come to admire **Louisburg Square**—between Mt. Vernon and Pinckney streets—for its sheer beauty. The centerpiece of the square is a serene oval park with a tall black iron fence, ringed with brick bowfront houses. Louisburg Square looks so much like London that a British film company produced *Vanity Fair* here in the 1920s. Louisa May Alcott lived at number 20.

Tiny one-lane **Acorn Street**—just south of Louisburg Square between Cedar and Willow streets—is one of the few old cobblestone streets left on Beacon Hill, and a very picturesque one it is. Coachmen and servants for nearby mansions used to live here.

Although the **Rose Standish Nichols House Museum** (55 Mount Vernon Street; 617-227-6993; admission) was not fashionable for its time, it is a fine example of the late 19th-century row house. Standish Nichols was quite a personage in her day. A noted landscape architect and pacifist, she traveled around the world and was a friend of Woodrow Wilson. Designed by Bulfinch, her home is filled with rare antiques such as Renaissance Flemish tapestries, statuary by noted American sculptor Augustus Saint-Gaudens and unusual imitation leather wallpaper gilded with gold.

Number **85 Mt. Vernon Street** was Harrison Gray Otis's second Bulfinch-designed home, while **45 Beacon Street** was his third, an unheard-of extravagance.

A grander library than the **Boston Athenaeum** (10½ Beacon Street; 617-227-0270) would be hard to find. The interior features high, vaulted ceilings, pillared archways, scores of marble busts, solid wood reading tables and red-leather, brass-studded armchairs. Founded in 1807 by a group including the Reverend William Emerson, father of Ralph Waldo Emerson, it's one of the country's oldest independent libraries. Its picture gallery and sculpture hall served as Boston's first art museum, and the library still maintains an impressive collection of art today, including works by Gilbert Stuart, John Singer Sargent and Chester Harding. The library is also noted for its collections of 19th-century American prints, Confederate state imprints and books from the libraries of George Washington, General Henry Knox and Jean Louis Cardinal Cheverus. Public tours are given by appointment.

The **Appleton-Parker Houses** (39–40 Beacon Street), twin Greek Revival houses alike in every detail, were built for two wealthy merchants. At number 39, Fanny Appleton married Henry Wadsworth Longfellow in 1843. Number 40 is now the home of the Women's City Club.

At 63–64 Beacon Street you can see a few panes of the famous **Beacon Hill purple glass**, with hues caused by a reaction of sunlight. It acquired cachet, along with everything else traditional on "the Hill."

It is intriguing that while most people think of Beacon Hill as a Brahmin bastion, in the 19th century its north slope was the heart of Boston's emerging free black community. Blacks arrived in Boston as slaves in 1638. By

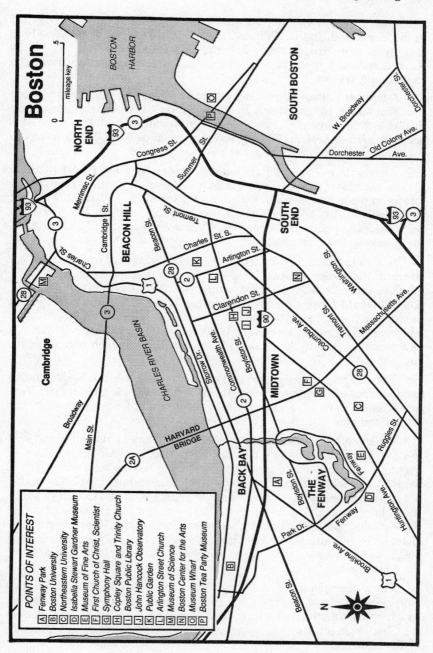

1705, there were more than 400 slaves, and a few free blacks, who settled in the North End. In the 19th century, most blacks lived in the West End, and on Beacon Hill, between Joy and Charles streets. The free blacks worked hard to provide decent housing and education for their own, and to help end slavery.

A number of their houses and public buildings still stand, and you can see them on the 14-stop **Black Heritage Trail** (★). Walking tour maps are available at the Boston Common Visitor Information kiosk and at the **Museum of Afro-American History** (46 Joy Street; 617-742-1854), a stop on the trail.

Among the public buildings are the **African Meeting House** (8 Smith Court), the oldest standing black church in America. Built in 1806, it was known in the abolitionist era as the Black Faneuil Hall. Here, in 1832, the New England Anti-Slavery Society was founded, with black leader Frederick Douglass and abolitionists William Lloyd Garrison and Charles Sumner speaking from the platform.

A stirring tribute to the first black regiment recruited for the Civil War stands at the corner of Beacon and Park streets, and marks the start of the Black Heritage Trail. A bas-relief sculpture by Augustus Saint-Gaudens, the **Robert Gould Shaw and 54th Regiment Memorial** shows the regiment on the march with their young white leader, Bostonian Robert Gould Shaw, and an angel flying overhead. The black military role in the Civil War won new recognition with the release of the film *Glory*, which chronicles the story of the 54th Regiment.

The trail also takes you to one of the first schools for black children and to homes built by free blacks, among them the **Lewis and Harriet Hayden House** (66 Phillips Street), which served as an Underground Railway station and was visited by Harriet Beecher Stowe.

On an entirely different note, television history is also alive and well in Beacon Hill. Like homing pigeons, all tourists head for "Cheers," so we may as well get it out of the way. The setting for the television show is the **Bull and Finch Pub** (downstairs at 84 Beacon Street; 617-227-9605), not to be confused with the impostor, Three Cheers, at 390 Congress Street. Even though the Bull and Finch has made such a big business out of all this—selling "Cheers" T-shirts, mugs and hats in the Hampshire House Hotel lobby upstairs—it's a bar with real atmosphere. Originally an English pub, it was dismantled and shipped here, complete with old leather and walnut paneling.

Yet another point of television trivia can be found in Beacon Hill. Private eye Spenser of "Spenser for Hire" lived above a Boston firehouse, which he entered through a bright red door. The firehouse is right next to the Charles Street Meeting House on Mount Vernon Street, at the corner of River Street.

BACK BAY

Although it started life as a mud flat, Back Bay fast became a fashionable neighborhood. As the city grew, it started running out of room in its original peninsula surrounding Boston Common, so it began filling in the tidal flats of the Back Bay in 1858, the largest land reclamation project of its time. Some 450 acres of marshland were turned into usable land over 20 years.

Given all this room to plan, Back Bay is the only place in town laid out with any perceivable logic. Streets follow an orderly grid, with cross streets named alphabetically for palatial ducal mansions: Arlington, Berkeley, Clarendon, Dartmouth, Exeter, Fairfield, Gloucester and Hereford.

The centerpiece of this grand reclamation project is **Commonwealth Avenue**. Patterned after the Champs Élysées, it's a wide boulevard with a grass strip mall that runs right through the heart of the Back Bay. "Comm Ave," as it's called by natives, is lined with stately brownstones and many historic buildings. Newbury, Beacon and Marlborough streets parallel Comm Ave. Fashionable Newbury Street is lined with chic boutiques, expensive jewelry, fur and clothing stores, art galleries, antique stores and loads of restaurants. Back Bay crosses Massachusetts Avenue, which natives shorten to "Mass Ave," and ends at Kenmore Square.

To the north, the Back Bay ends at the Charles River, where the wide, grassy **Esplanade** is a popular sunning spot in warm weather. Also on the Esplanade is the **Hatch Memorial Shell**, where the Boston Pops Symphony Orchestra and Boston Ballet II perform summer concerts.

If Boston Common is Boston's Central Park, then the **Public Garden** (bordered by Beacon, Charles, Arlington and Boylston streets) is its Tuileries, the first botanical garden in the country. Lavishly landscaped with flowers and trees, it's home to the **Swan Boats**, which circle the weeping-willow-draped lagoon in season. The famous Swan Boats were launched in 1877 by Robert Paget, who was inspired by the swan-boat scene in Wagner's opera *Lohengrin*. The same family continues to operate them. Also in the Public Garden is some notable statuary: **George Washington** on horseback and abolitionist Wendall Phillips.

If you walk straight through the Public Garden gates at the corner of Beacon and Charles streets, you'll come upon **Mrs. Mallard and her brood of eight ducklings** (★) stretched out in a row behind her, all heading for the pond. Placed here in 1987, the bronze, larger-than-life statues represent the ducks made famous in Robert McCloskey's children's story *Make Way for Ducklings*. Each April, the ducklings are feted on Duckling Day with a parade and festival sponsored by the Historic Neighborhoods Foundation (2 Boylston Street; 617-426-1885).

Ever since opening in 1927, the **Ritz-Carlton** (15 Arlington Street; 617-536-5700) has catered to a select clientele. The 17-story brick building overlooking the Public Garden, while not particularly striking on the outside, is the epitome of old elegance inside, where the lobby is graced with a large curving staircase and antique touches such as an exquisite brass railing. The original owner would never permit a reservation without researching the client's reputation in the Social Register or business directories. Many notable people have lived at the Ritz, including Charles Lindbergh and Winston Churchill. Many more have stayed here, among them Rodgers and Hammerstein, Albert Einstein, the Duke and Duchess of Windsor, Tennessee Williams and John F. Kennedy, even Lassie and Rin Tin Tin.

Down the street, the Georgian-style **Arlington Street Church** (Arlington and Boylston streets) features a tall and graceful steeple fashioned in the style of Christopher Wren.

The **New Old South Church** (on the corner of Boylston and Dartmouth streets) is where the congregation of the Old South Meeting House moved in 1875, after they decided their Washington Street neighborhood had become too noisy to hear the sermon. The Gothic facade is dominated by a tower and carved stone rosettes. Inside are Venetian mosaics and 15th-century stained-glass windows depicting the Prophets, the Evangelists, the miracles and the parables.

The **Boston Evening Clinic** (314 Commonwealth Avenue) was created in the 1920s in an 1899 mansion modeled after a Loire Valley château. Its medieval-looking exterior has sculptured stone cherubs and gargoyles looking down from its battlements. Inside the building are spectacular bas-relief mahogany walls, gold-leaf carved ceilings, stained-glass windows and an ornately carved marble staircase.

Nowhere is the opulence of the Back Bay Victorians more amply evidenced than at the **Gibson House** (137 Beacon Street; 617-267-6338; admission), now a museum. Built for the prominent Gibson family in 1859, the Italian Renaissance Revival home is richly furnished with gold-embossed wallpaper and black walnut paneling, imported carpets and most of the Gibson family china and porcelain.

The **Institute of Contemporary Art** (955 Boylston Street; 617-266-5152; admission) has won an international reputation for its wide-ranging artistic events, held here for more than half a century. Housed in an old Boston firehouse, the ICA often shows experimental or controversial works, among them art exhibits, films, videos, music events, lectures and literary readings.

THE FENWAY

The western side of Massachusetts Avenue edges over to the Fenway, the area surrounding the **Back Bay Fens**, another piece of the Emerald Necklace. Fens, from an Old English word meaning low wetlands or marshes, describes the area aptly. Along its sprawling length are several creeks and ponds, a rose garden and private garden plots, remnants of Boston's wartime "Victory Gardens."

No one thinks of the Fenway without **Fenway Park** (24 Yawkey Way; 617-267-8661), the home of the Boston Red Sox and the Green Monster, the famous left-field wall. Fenway Park remains one of the homiest and most old-fashioned ballparks in the country.

The campuses of two well-known Boston colleges are also in the Fenway—**Boston University**, along Commonwealth Avenue, and **Northeastern University**, south of Huntington Avenue.

Visible from Kenmore Square is the brightly lit, red-white-and-blue **Citgo Sign**, a gasoline advertisement and relic of the 1950s. It is the last of six similar signs in the United States.

Housed in a 15th-century-style Venetian palazzo, the **Isabella Stewart Gardner Museum** (280 The Fenway; 617-566-1401; admission) is a little jewel of a museum. It contains the personal collection of Mrs. Isabella Stewart Gardner, amassed over a lifetime of travel to Europe. "Mrs. Jack," as she came to be called, was considered somewhat eccentric and outrageous by proper Bostonians, and she collected what she liked. Her booty includes Italian Renaissance, 17th-century Dutch and 19th-century American paintings, as well as sculpture, textiles, furniture, ceramics, prints and drawings. Built around a beautiful flowered courtyard, the museum also offers weekly chamber music concerts.

Not far from the Gardner Museum is the **Museum of Fine Arts** (465 Huntington Avenue; 617-267-9300; admission), world famous for its exceptional collections of Asian, Greek, Roman, European, Egyptian and American art. The MFA also holds impressionist paintings and works by such American masters as John Singer Sargent, John Singleton Copley and Winslow Homer. The MFA regularly attracts mega-exhibitions, such as traveling shows of Renoir and Monet works. Don't miss the Japanese gardens, and the little first-floor café.

MIDTOWN

Midtown is an area lacking in identity, a bridge between Back Bay and the South End. While some consider it part of the Back Bay, particularly those who would like a better address, it has a distinctly different character, the result of controversial urban renewal in the 1960s that created modernistic buildings alongside 19th-century ones.

The **First Church of Christ, Scientist** (175 Huntington Avenue; 617-450-2000) is the world headquarters of Christian Science, founded in 1879 by Mary Baker Eddy. The mother church is topped by an imposing dome and set in a brick pedestrian plaza with a reflecting pool designed by I. M. Pei. Take a walk through the echoing **Mapparium** in the *Christian Science Monitor* building, a unique 30-foot stained-glass globe with a footbridge through it, for a peek at how the world looked in 1935.

Right across the street from each other at the corner of Huntington Avenue and Massachusetts Avenue are two handsome and famous brick buildings: **Symphony Hall** (301 Massachusetts Avenue; 617-266-1492) and **Horticultural Hall** (300 Massachusetts Avenue; 617-536-9280). Designed in 1900, Symphony Hall is so acoustically perfect it's known worldwide as a "Stradivarius among halls." The Boston Symphony Orchestra celebrated its 100th anniversary here in 1981. Horticultural Hall is the third home of the Massachusetts Horticultural Society, the oldest active incorporated society of its kind in America, founded in 1829. The society maintains the largest and finest horticultural library in the world. This 1901 Beaux-Arts building features limestone and terra cotta cornices and moldings ornately carved with fruits and garlands.

The heart of Midtown is gorgeous **Copley Square** (Boylston Street, between Clarendon and Dartmouth streets), named for artist John Singleton Copley. Boston's religious and intellectual center at the end of the 19th century, the square is dominated by two architecturally imposing structures, Henry Hobson Richardson's Trinity Church and Charles McKim's Boston Public Library.

The French-Romanesque, medieval-style **Trinity Church** (206 Clarendon Street; 617-536-0944), built in 1877, is visually stunning inside and out. One of Richardson's most brilliant creations, Trinity Church has an enormous tower reminiscent of the domes of Venice and Constantinople. Inside, rich colors and exquisite Moorish details cover the vaulted ceiling, rotunda and walls, and there are John LaFarge frescoes and stained-glass windows.

Much more than a library, the **Boston Public Library** (666 Boylston Street; 617-536-5400) houses art and architectural treasures. A wide marble staircase, Corinthian columns and frescoes grace its grand entrance hall (at the side door). Inside are murals by John Singer Sargent, paintings by John Singleton Copley, sculptures by Augustus and Louis Saint-Gaudens and bronze doors by Daniel Chester French. Inspired by Italian Renaissance palaces, it was built in 1895. Take time to sit in the lovely central courtyard, where you'll find a fountain and benches.

The grande dame of Boston's vintage hotels is the **Copley Plaza Hotel** (138 St. James Avenue; 617-267-5300), built in 1912 in high Victorian style. It boasts a wide stone facade, whose curving center echoes the bowfront homes of Back Bay and Beacon Hill. Inside, marble and crystal appointments set off an elegant lobby topped with a trompe l'oeil painting of the sky. The internationally known Copley Plaza has served as a resting place for a dozen presidents and European royalty.

The Beaux-Arts **Berkeley Building** (420 Boylston Street) looks like a wedding cake, so curlicued and beribboned is its frothy white bas-relief terra cotta molding. Tiers of windows are trimmed in sea green, and a black marble entrance sign is flanked with dolphins and sea serpents. Built in

1905, it formerly housed Boston's design center and was beautifully restored in 1989.

There's no better way to view Boston than from the 60-story **John Hancock Observatory** (200 Clarendon Street, Copley Square; 617-572-6429; admission), the tallest building in New England. From 740 feet up, you can see the State House, the White Mountains of New Hampshire and the South Shore. Besides the great view, there are exhibits, a film, photographs and a sound and light show on Boston history. Down on the ground, the Hancock's shimmering glass sides serve as a fantastic mirror, reflecting the surrounding buildings as clearly as a photograph. When the Hancock was built in the late 1960s, architects argued bitterly that the rhomboidal building designed by I. M. Pei would ruin the character of Copley Square. The blue glass windows of this landmark have become collectors' items, ever since they fell out onto the sidewalk in the early 1970s. They were replaced at a cost of more than $8 million.

Like the Hancock, the **Skywalk Observatory** at the Prudential Tower (800 Boylston Street, Prudential Center; 617-236-3318; admission) gives you a bird's-eye view of downtown, this time a 360° one. Commonly called "the Pru," the Prudential Center was built in the early '60s as another piece of urban renewal. It houses shops and offices, and in front of it is a cast bronze statue called *Quest Eternal*, representing man reaching for the heavens.

A major convention hall, the **John B. Hynes Veterans Memorial Convention Center** (900 Boylston Street; 617-954-2000) was extensively renovated and rebuilt in the late 1980s.

SOUTH END

Boston's largest neighborhood is also the least known. Like the Back Bay, it was built on filled land, preceding Back Bay by more than a decade. Victorian brick row houses rose apace as residences for the middle class and well to do. Today, the South End is listed on the National Register of Historic Places as the largest concentration of such houses in the United States.

After the panic of 1873, banks foreclosed on the area, and those who could afford to moved to Back Bay. The area was carved up into rooming houses and factories and became an immigrant ghetto of more than 40 nationalities, notably black, Syrian, Hispanic and Lebanese.

The South End languished for decades, but when Boston's economy rebounded in the 1960s, so did this neighborhood. Since 1965, a new influx of middle-class professionals has renovated old row houses and partly gentrified the area. Not all of the South End has risen again, however, and there are still blighted, unsafe areas. But today the neighborhood is a vital center of artistic activity, and many artists live here. Fashionable shops, restaurants and nightclubs line the main thoroughfares of Columbus Avenue and Tremont Street.

The South End stretches hundreds of blocks, bounded roughly by the Southeast Expressway, Herald Street, the tracks of the MBTA's Orange Line and Huntington Avenue. Although the South End is a massive area to explore on foot, annual house tours are given by the **South End Historical Society** (532 Massachusetts Avenue; 617-536-4445).

If the South End reminds you of Beacon Hill, it's no wonder. The same hidden gardens and black iron grillwork decorate many facades. The oval-shaped **Union Park** resembles Beacon Hill's Louisburg Square. **West Rutland Square**, too, is a lovely little landscaped patch.

The **Boston Center for the Arts** (539 Tremont Street; 617-426-5000) is the center of South End arts activity. Built in 1884 to exhibit a huge circular painting, *The Battle of Gettysburg*, now in Pennsylvania, it's also where Albert Champion developed the spark plug. Its large rotunda hosts art exhibits, plays, festivals and an annual antique show.

Next door to the arts center is the **Mills Gallery** (549 Tremont Street; 617-426-7700), which specializes in exhibits by South End artists. These might include crafts, sculpture, oil paintings and gouache, and are always intriguing.

Once second in size only to the U.S. Capitol, the building that formerly housed the **Chickering Piano Factory** (★) (791 Tremont Street), now a craft guild, has been a Boston landmark since 1853. The pianos made here until 1929 were played not only in Victorian drawing rooms but in the concert halls of Europe and South America. Founder Jonas Chickering was said to be just like his pianos: "upright, grand and square." The building now serves as living, work and exhibition space for artists and musicians.

At the very northeast corner of the South End lies **Bay Village**, which used to be known as South Cove, bordered by Arlington, Tremont and Stuart streets and Charles Street South. This cluster of narrow little streets displays the most charmingly antique character in the area. Gaslights stand on the sidewalks outside these Victorian row houses decorated with black shutters and windowboxes, black iron grilled doorways and hidden, sunken gardens in backyards.

SOUTH BOSTON

Not to be confused with the South End, South Boston lies directly east of it. Despite its name, South Boston juts farther east into the Atlantic than any other point in the city, cut off from Boston by the Southeast Expressway and the Fort Point Channel. Everyone here calls it "Southie," especially the Irish who call it home.

The Irish poured into South Boston in the early 19th century, attracted by the work opportunities of the glass, iron and shipping industries. They stayed, and today this is the most predominantly Irish community in Boston, evidenced by the riotous St. Patrick's Day parade. The Irish are fiercely proud of their L Street Brownies, a local swim club that has won national publicity for swimming every day, even in January.

Ideally positioned for shipping, the peninsula is lined with commercial fishing and shipping piers. The **Fish Piers**, near the World Trade Center and Jimmy's Harborside on Northern Avenue, are a lively scene at dawn, when the fishing boats return to port to unload their catch. The fresh catch is sold at auction right off the boats to retailers.

Three bridges link South Boston with downtown: the Summer Street Bridge, the Northern Avenue Bridge and the Congress Street Bridge, with its Chinese-lantern-style, wrought-iron lamps.

When you cross the Congress Street Bridge, you may not quite believe your eyes, but the first thing you'll see is a giant milk bottle. The 30-foot **Hood Milk Bottle** was a vintage lunch stand from the 1930s and sells snacks again today.

The Hood Milk Bottle signals the beginning of Museum Wharf, a mini-park of several museums. The Children's Museum and the Computer Museum are both housed in the same brick building, a former wool warehouse whose large windows and wool bays lend themselves nicely to exhibit spaces.

You don't have to be a kid to enjoy the **Children's Museum** (300 Congress Street; 617-426-6500; admission), a gigantic toy box filled with four floors of hands-on fun. Make giant bubbles, play instruments in a rock band, learn anatomy from a top-hatted skeleton. The exhibit on multiculturalism was the first of its kind.

As the world's only museum devoted solely to computers, the **Computer Museum** (300 Congress Street; 617-426-2800; admission) aptly dramatizes the swift pace of technology. Forty years of computing history are on display, starting with parts of an early Air Force vacuum-tube computer that occupied a four-story building. There are robots, animated films and a host of microcomputers to play with. To see how computers work, take a stroll through the giant Walk-Through Computer with its 25-foot keyboard and bumper-car-sized mouse.

The last member of Museum Wharf is the **Boston Tea Party Museum** (Congress Street Bridge; 617-338-1773; admission), a floating museum where you can board a two-masted brig and throw your own chest of tea into the harbor (it'll be retrieved by an attached rope for another visitor to heave). Displays here are lively and informative, explaining the events surrounding the 1773 dumping of 340 chests of tea overboard, a tax protest that was one of many spurs to the American Revolution.

A spanking white building with a flag-lined boulevard, the **World Trade Center** (164 Northern Avenue; 617-439-5000) replaced the drab old Commonwealth Exhibition Hall in the 1980s. It hosts many of Boston's biggest trade shows, including the Boston Boat Show.

Four kinds of granite decorate the exterior of the **Boston Design Center** (1 Design Center Place; 617-338-5062), New England's major design center. Architects and designers come here from miles away to search out the latest and chicest in interior designs. Outside the building stands an imposing cast of Auguste Rodin's sculpture *Cybèle*.

Commerce abandoned a good part of the Fort Point Channel area in droves by the 1950s. But today artists have happily moved into its old high-ceilinged, industrial buildings, and more artists live here than anywhere else in the city.

The work of painters, photographers, sculptors and others is on view at the **Fort Point Artists' Community Gallery** (249 A Street; 617-423-4299). You can also visit individual artists' studios by appointment. Look for them along the 200 to 300 blocks on A Street.

Dorchester Heights National Historic Site (456 West 4th Street; 617-242-5642) is where George Washington set up his guns and forced the British to evacuate Boston in 1776, never to return. The British were astounded to see these guns, which had been dragged 300 miles by oxen from Fort Ticonderoga. A 215-foot marble tower marks the spot.

Out at the very tip of South Boston, **Castle Island** (End of Day Boulevard) is a windswept place of green lawns and high granite ramparts, a fine spot for picnicking and exploring. A series of eight forts has stood here since 1634, making it the oldest continuously fortified site in North America. The island was held by the British during the Revolution until Washington forced them out, from his vantage point at Dorchester Heights. The current fort, the star-shaped **Fort Independence**, was built in 1851.

On a peninsula just south of South Boston lies Dorchester, once the home of the country's oldest chocolate manufacturer, the Walter Baker Chocolate Factory, founded in 1780. Today Dorchester is a quiet, residential area known for its characteristic three-story houses called triple deckers.

Don't miss the **John F. Kennedy Library and Museum** (Columbia Point, Dorchester; 617-929-4523; admission), a stirring place to visit both inside and out. In a parklike setting by the ocean that JFK loved so well, the striking, glass-walled building was designed by I. M. Pei. The museum houses JFK's papers, photographs, letters and speeches, and personal memorabilia such as his desk and rocking chair.

The **Franklin Park Zoo** (Franklin Park, Blue Hill Avenue, Roxbury; 617-442-0991; admission), once rated one of the country's ten worst zoos by *Parade* magazine, has made some dramatic improvements. The most impressive is an African Tropical Forest that opened in 1989. Inside the 75-foot-high bubble live tropical birds, antelopes, a pygmy hippo and gorillas, among other tropical denizens.

OUTSIDE BOSTON

CHARLESTOWN

Charlestown is even older than Boston. It was founded by a small band of Puritans in 1630, who later abandoned it for Boston. Charlestown was almost destroyed by the British in the Battle of Bunker Hill, so few 18th-century houses survive.

A walk over the river on the Charlestown Bridge brings you to the Charlestown Navy Yard, the berth of the **U.S.S. Constitution** (617-242-5670; admission), the oldest commissioned vessel in the world. It won its nickname of Old Ironsides when British cannon fire bounced off its sturdy oak hull in the War of 1812. A handsome black-and-white frigate, the *Constitution* once required 400 sailors to hoist its sails. While you can tour the decks and down below, lines are always long; try at lunchtime.

Across the yard from Old Ironsides is the **Constitution Museum** (617-426-1812; admission), which houses exhibits on Old Ironsides' many voyages and victories, memorabilia and paintings. Nearby is the **Commandant's House,** a handsome brick Federal-style mansion where Navy officers lived.

The **Bunker Hill Monument** (43 Monument Square; 617-242-5641) actually stands atop Breed's Hill, where the Battle of Bunker Hill was in fact fought. This encounter became legend with the words of Colonel William Prescott to his ammunition-short troops: "Don't fire until you see the whites of their eyes." The cornerstone of the 220-foot Egyptian Revival granite obelisk was laid in 1825 by General Lafayette, with Daniel Webster orating. There are 294 steps to the observatory, which affords a magnificent view of the city and the harbor.

Companion exhibits at the **Bunker Hill Pavilion** (55 Constitution Road; 617-241-7575; admission) include a multimedia slide show with 14 screens re-enacting the battle.

CAMBRIDGE

Everyone thinks of Cambridge and Boston together, as if they were two sides of the same coin. While Cambridge is actually a separate city, it lies directly across the Charles River from Boston, and the lives of the two cities are very much entwined, linked by a series of foot and vehicular bridges.

Cambridge was founded in 1630, originally named New Towne, and was the colony's first capital. In 1638, two years after the founding of **Harvard,** the nation's oldest university, the city was renamed after the English university town where many Boston settlers had been educated.

Today Cambridge is still very much an intellectual center, home to Nobel Prize winners, ground-breaking scientists and famous writers, among them John Kenneth Galbraith, David Mamet and Anne Bernays. Cambridge became the heart of what came to be nicknamed "Silicon Valley East" when high-tech companies blossomed here during the 1960s and 1970s, as well as in outlying towns scattered along the Route 128 beltway. These think tanks and computer companies fueled a boom in the Massachusetts economy and its population.

Not all of Cambridge is serious or intellectual. It's given life and vitality by throngs of young students, ragtag protesters handing out leaflets, cult followers and street musicians.

The heartbeat of Cambridge is **Harvard Square**, where life revolves around the many bookstores, coffeeshops, boutiques and newsstands. In the very center stands the **Out of Town News and Ticket Agency** (617-354-7777) kiosk, a Harvard Square landmark for many years, famous for its thousands of national and foreign periodicals. Right next to it you'll find the **Cambridge Discovery Information Booth** (617-497-1630), which dispenses tourist information and walking maps.

No one would come to Cambridge without taking a walk through **Harvard Yard**. A stroll of the yard's winding paths, stately trees, grassy quadrangles and handsome brick buildings is a walk through a long history of higher education. Six U.S. presidents have graduated from Harvard.

Enter the main gate by crossing Massachusetts Avenue. On the right, you'll see **Massachusetts Hall**, built in 1718, the college's oldest remaining hall. In the quadrangle of the historic Old Yard, on the left, tucked between Hollis and Stoughton Halls, is a little jewel of a chapel. **Holden Chapel**, built in 1742, has blue gables decorated with scrolled white baroque cornices, ahead of its time in its ornateness.

Along the diagonal path that cuts across Old Yard is the **Statue of John Harvard** by Daniel Chester French, called the statue of the "three lies." Besides giving the wrong date for Harvard's founding, the statue is actually not of John Harvard at all, but of a student model instead; and John Harvard is not the college's founder but its first great benefactor.

Harvard's famed **Widener Library** stands in the New Yard, a massive building with a wide staircase and a pillared portico. With nearly three million books, Widener ranks as the third largest library in the United States, second only to the Library of Congress and the New York Public Library.

Straight across from it is the **Memorial Chapel**, built in 1931 with a Bulfinch-style steeple in memory of the young men of Harvard who died in World War I. Their names are listed in brass on the walls.

Harvard is also home to a spate of museums known the world over for their esoteric collections, including three art museums (all reachable at 617-495-9400). The **Busch-Reisinger Museum** (32 Quincy Street; admission) is noted for central and northern European works of art from the Middle Ages to the present. The **Fogg Art Museum** (32 Quincy Street; admission) holds European and American art, with a notable impressionist collection.

Ancient, Asian and Islamic art are the specialties at the Sackler Museum (485 Broadway at Quincy; admission).

A group of four natural history museums in one is called the **University Museum** (24 Oxford Street; 617-495-3045; admission). The **Botanical Museum** holds the internationally famed handmade Glass Flowers, showcasing more than 700 species. At the **Museum of Comparative Zoology**, the development of animal life is traced from fossils to modern man. The **Mineralogical and Geological Museum** has a collection of rocks and minerals, including a 3040-carat topaz. The **Peabody Museum of Archaeology** displays artifacts from the world over, including Mayan and American Indian relics.

Under the spreading chestnut tree/ The village smithy stands;/ The smith a mighty man is he/ With large and sinewy hands. These words from Longfellow's famous poem "The Village Blacksmith" were written about a real blacksmith, who lived in a house at 56 Brattle Street built in 1811. It's now the **Blacksmith House Bakery** (617-354-3036) and an outdoor café in warm weather. Old World pastries and cakes are made here the same way they have been for decades.

Harvard Lampoon Castle (57 Mt. Auburn Street at Bow Street), a funny-looking building with a round brick turret and a door painted bright red, yellow and purple, befits its occupants: the publishers of Harvard's longstanding satirical magazine, the *Harvard Lampoon.*

Christ Church Episcopal (Zero Garden Street; 617-876-0200), a simple gray-and-white structure with a squat steeple, is Cambridge's oldest church. George and Martha Washington worshipped here on New Year's Eve 1775.

Under an elm tree on the grassy **Cambridge Common** (Massachusetts Avenue and Garden Street), General Washington took command of the Continental Army in 1775. A plaque and monument to Washington mark this spot. Nearby it are three old black cannons, abandoned by the British at Fort Independence when they evacuated in 1776.

The **Longfellow National Historic Site** (105 Brattle Street; 617-876-4491; admission) is where poet Henry Wadsworth Longfellow lived for 45 years and wrote most of his famous works. Painted a cheery yellow and accented with black shutters, the house was built in 1759 for a well-to-do Tory and years later was used by Washington as his headquarters during the siege of Boston. The house has many fine Victorian furnishings, among them Longfellow's desk, quill pen and inkstand.

A handsome, slate-blue Georgian house with black shutters, the **Hooper-Lee-Nichols House** (159 Brattle Street; 617-547-4252; admission) was built by a physician named Richard Hooper. Later it was the home of Joseph Lee, a founder of Christ Church, and then the home of George Nichols.

The western end of Brattle Street is called **Tory Row** because of the lovely homes built there by wealthy Tories in the 18th century. A fine example is at Number 175, the **Ruggles Fayerweather House**, first the home of Tory George Ruggles, later of patriot Thomas Fayerweather. The house served as an American hospital after the Battle of Bunker Hill.

Just down the street sits **Radcliffe College**, once a women's branch of Harvard but now fully integrated into the university. The gates to **Radcliffe Yard** are entered off Brattle Street, between James Street and Appian Way. As you walk the path, the four graceful brick main buildings of the campus will be in a semicircle to your right. First is **Fay House**, a mansion built in 1807, the administrative center. Next you'll find **Hemenway Gymnasium**, which houses a research society that studies women in society. Third is **Agassiz House**, fronted by white classical pillars, which holds a theater, ballroom and arts office. Last is the college's renowned **Schlesinger Library**, which contains an outstanding collection of books and manuscripts on the history of women in America, including papers of Susan B. Anthony, Julia Ward Howe and Elizabeth Cady Stanton.

Who says taking the subway has to be grim? The newest Red Line stations, opened in the 1980s, showcase major works of art in the country's first and largest program of its kind, **Arts on the Line**. Artworks range from stained-glass walls and bronze sculptures to a bright red windmill sculpture, a shimmering mobile and a whimsical mural of black-and-white cows. A favored piece is *Lost Gloves*, immortalized in bronze along an escalator railing. People inevitably reach out to touch these gloves as they ride. Look for some 20 artworks at Harvard, Porter, Davis and Alewife stations.

A few miles east of Harvard Square lies Cambridge's other famous college, the **Massachusetts Institute of Technology** (M.I.T.). Offering a premier education in engineering and technology since 1865, M.I.T. draws students from all over the world, including China, Japan and Vietnam. In distinct contrast to the hallowed ways of Harvard, M.I.T. students are famed for their witty irreverence and stage contests to outdo each other in intellectual pranks. One of their episodes involved placing a car on top of a campus building. Fittingly, the campus looks modern and high tech, with geometrical buildings designed by Eero Saarinen.

OUTLYING AREAS

Although many tourists never leave the bounds of Boston and Cambridge, there is much of interest in the surrounding towns, many of which serve as bedroom communities for Boston workers and have rich colonial histories, too.

Due east of the city and bordering the Fenway, Brookline is one of the more prestigious and wealthy residential surrounding towns. The architect of Boston's Emerald Necklace lived and worked in a little house in a quiet Brookline neighborhood, where he often took his work outside to a landscaped hollow. At the **Frederick Law Olmsted National Historic Site** (★) (99 Warren Street; 617-566-1689), you can tour the house and grounds and see many of his landscape plans, memorabilia and photographs.

President John F. Kennedy was born in Brookline in 1917, in a little house now restored to its period appearance as the **John F. Kennedy National Historic Site** (83 Beals Street; 617-566-7937; admission). The house holds much JFK memorabilia, including his crib and some of his toys.

South of Brookline lies Jamaica Plain, which is technically part of Boston. The star of Jamaica Plain is the **Arnold Arboretum of Harvard University** (125 Arborway; 617-524-1718), one of the more remarkable green strands in Boston's Emerald Necklace. The 265-acre preserve was established in 1872, and growing here are more than 7000 kinds of trees and plants from around the world. The arboretum has one of the oldest and largest lilac collections in North America, 200-year-old bonsai trees and rare specimens from China. A two-mile walk along a nature trail takes visitors through meadows and over valleys and hills, offering serene and secluded vistas of these special collections.

South of Dorchester, the working-class city of Quincy may look uninteresting, but it happens to be the "City of the Presidents"—birthplace of John Adams and his son John Quincy Adams, the second and sixth U.S. presidents. There are several sights surrounding the Adams family history.

At the **Adams National Historic Site** (135 Adams Street, in Quincy Center; 617-773-1177; admission) stands an elegant gray colonial house built in 1731, home to four generations of Adamses. The house is set on several acres strikingly set off with formal gardens that create a beautiful profusion of color in spring and summer. Inside the house are many original furnishings, including portraits of George and Martha Washington, Waterford candelabra and Louis XV furniture. There is also a cathedral-ceilinged library with 14,000 original volumes. As the Adams family prospered, John and his wife, Abigail, who moved into the house in 1787, enlarged it from 7 to 20 rooms. The National Park Service gives excellent tours.

Nearby and part of the same site are the **John Adams** and **John Quincy Adams Birthplaces** (133 and 141 Franklin Street; 617-773-1177; admission), a pair of simple salt box houses where the two presidents were born, built in 1663 and 1681.

East of the Adams National Historic Site lies the **Quincy Homestead** (1010 Hancock Street; 617-472-5117; admission), home to four generations of Edmund Quincys, the family of Abigail Adams. The fourth Edmund Quincy's daughter Dorothy married John Hancock, who was born in Quincy. A colonial-style herb garden and authentic period furnishings embellish the 1686 house, and one of Hancock's coaches is displayed.

The 1872 Gothic Revival **Adams Academy** (8 Adams Street; 617-773-1144) was founded by John Adams and is home to the **Quincy Historical Society**. Exhibits show the city's industrial history.

Dominating downtown Quincy Square is a beautiful granite church, **United First Parish Church** (1306 Hancock Street), designed by Alexander Parris and built in 1828. The church crypt holds the remains of John Adams, John Quincy Adams and their wives.

Across the street is **City Hall**, designed in 1844 in Greek Revival style by Bunker Hill architect Solomon Willard. And near City Hall is the **Hancock Cemetery**, dating to about 1640, where John Hancock's father is buried, as are Quincy and Adams ancestors.

A few miles south of Quincy lies one of the South Shore's most attractive coastal communities, **Hingham**, settled in 1635. Sailing yachts bob in its picturesque harbor, and Hingham's downtown retains the characteristics of a small village, with mom-and-pop shops, restaurants and a vintage movie theater surrounding Hingham Square. A drive along Hingham's long and wide **Main Street** rewards you with views of stately 18th- and 19th-century homes painted pastel colors and sporting neat black shutters. A number of them are on the National Register of Historic Places. These houses are private, but many are open to the public during the **Hingham Historical Society's** (617-749-0013) annual house tour in June, reputed to be the oldest historical house tour in the country, held since 1924.

Two private houses worth a drive by are the **Hersey House** (104 Summer Street), a handsome gray mansion in Italianate style, with a flat-roofed, pillared porch, which dates to about 1857, and the **Joshua Wilder House** (605 Main Street), a beautifully restored house that probably dates to 1760.

The Old Ordinary (21 Lincoln Street; 617-749-0013; admission), a house dating to 1680, numbered among its many owners tavern keepers who provided an "ordinary" meal of the day at fixed prices. Halfway on the day-long stagecoach ride from Plymouth to Boston, the Old Ordinary did a brisk business, and counted Daniel Webster among its patrons. Additions were made to the house in the mid-18th century. Now a museum of Hingham history, the house has an 18th-century taproom, complete with wooden grill, pewter plates and rum kegs. There's also an 18th-century kitchen outfitted with large hearth and butter churn, and a library, dining room and front parlor. Upstairs are four bedrooms furnished in period style. There are a number of rare objects among the collection, including "mourning" samplers, made to honor the dead; a 17th-century Bible box; an 18th-century Queen Anne mirror; chinoiserie; and paintings of Hingham ships that sailed to China.

The Puritan congregation of the **Old Ship Church** (90 Main Street; 617-749-1679) gathered in 1635. Built in 1681, it is the oldest building in continuous ecclesiastical service in the United States. Unlike later New England churches with white spires and sides, Old Ship is built of somber gray, wooden clapboards in Elizabethan Gothic style, as its Puritan worshippers saw fit. Crafted by ships' carpenters, the church has curved oak roof frames like the knees of a ship, and the unusual roof structure resembles an inverted ship's hull.

Surrounding the Route 128 beltway are several more towns of interest to the traveler. A large and urbanized town about 20 miles west of Boston, Framingham offers a lovely respite within the **Garden in the Woods** (★) (Hemenway Road; 508-877-7630; admission), the largest collection of native plants in the Northeast. You can meander 45 acres of woodland trails, planted with some 1500 varieties of flora. Specially designed garden habitats include woodland groves, a lily pond, bog, limestone garden, pine barrens and meadows.

A few miles north of Framingham lie the endearing green colonial towns of Sudbury and Lincoln, still quite rural in character. Just off the historic Old Post Road, **Longfellow's Wayside Inn** (Route 20, Sudbury; 508-443-8846) is a wonderful place to visit, or stay. Built about 1700, the inn was made famous by Longfellow's cycle of poems, *Tales of a Wayside Inn*, which includes "Paul Revere's Ride." Historic structures include an 18th century grist mill and a little red schoolhouse. Restored in 1923, it's a fully functioning inn and restaurant.

Walter Gropius, founder of the Bauhaus school of art and architecture in Germany, had his family home in the rolling green hills of Lincoln. The first house he designed upon his arrival in the United States in 1937, **Gropius House** (68 Baker Bridge Road, Lincoln; 617-259-8843; admission) embodies those principles of function and simplicity that are hallmarks of the Bauhaus style. The house has works of art and Bauhaus furnishings.

Set in a wooded green 30-acre park, the **DeCordova and Dana Museum** (Sandy Pond Road, Lincoln; 617-259-8355; admission) has a collection of 20th-century American art, including paintings, sculpture, graphics and photography. Outdoor summer concerts of jazz, chamber music, ballet, modern dance, rock and folk music are given on the grassy lawn at the amphitheater.

LEXINGTON AND CONCORD

The green and wooded towns of Lexington and Concord, sites of the first battle of the Revolutionary War, are forever historically linked by the events of April 19, 1775. The British planned to advance on Concord from Boston to seize the colonials' military supplies. Warned by Paul Revere the night before, farmer/soldier Minutemen had mustered early before dawn on the Lexington Green.

About 77 men at Lexington Green, and hundreds more at Concord, fought off 700 highly trained British regulars. With heavy casualties, the British retreated back to Boston. "The shot heard 'round the world" had been fired, launching the American Revolution.

When you arrive in Lexington, a few miles north of Lincoln off Route 128, stop first at the **Lexington Visitors' Center** (Lexington Green, 1875 Massachusetts Avenue; 617-862-1450) for maps and brochures, and to see a diorama of the battle.

Across from Lexington Green, in the center of town, stands the **Minuteman Statue** (Battle Green, intersection of Massachusetts Avenue, Harrington Road and Hancocks and Bedford streets), a simple bareheaded farmer holding a musket. The statue's rough, fieldstone base was made of stone taken from the walls the American militia stood behind as they shot at the British. This statue has become symbolic of Lexington history.

On the green next to the Visitors' Center is the yellow, woodframe **Buckman Tavern** (617-862-5598; admission), built in 1709. This is where the Minutemen gathered to await the British after Revere's warning. Smiling elderly ladies wearing mobcaps and long skirts guide you through the house, with its wide-planked floors and 18th-century furniture and musket displays.

About a quarter mile north of the green is the **Hancock-Clarke House** (36 Hancock Street; 617-861-0928; admission), where Samuel Adams and John Hancock were staying that fateful night. Revere stopped here to warn them. John Hancock's father built this pretty little woodframe house with 12-over-16 windows around 1700.

The little red **Munroe Tavern** (1332 Massachusetts Avenue; 617-862-1703; admission), built in 1695, served as British headquarters, and housed wounded British soldiers after the battle. The tavern has been maintained as it was, and there are mementos of a 1789 visit by George Washington.

The **Jonathan Harrington House** (Harrington Road; private) was the home of Minuteman fifer Jonathan Harrington, who died in his wife's arms after being fatally wounded in the battle.

The **Museum of Our National Heritage** (Route 2A and Massachusetts Avenue; 617-861-6560) has changing exhibits on American history in four galleries. Past programs have included retrospectives on Ben Franklin, Paul Revere and the *U.S.S. Constitution*, plus exhibits of clocks, furniture and swords from different periods.

Within the 750-acre **Minuteman National Historic Park** (Route 2A, Concord; 508-369-6993) are several more sites involved in the Battle of Lexington and Concord. In this peaceful, sylvan spot, it's hard to picture the bloody carnage of the historic battle. A wide, pine-scented path leads to the site of the **Old North Bridge** spanning the Concord River, a 1956 replica of the bridge where Concord Minutemen held off the British. Another **Minuteman Memorial** stands across the river, made of melted 1776 cannon, designed by Daniel Chester French. This one shows a farmer with gun and plow in hand. At the **Visitor Center** (174 Liberty Street) are a film and exhibits.

Concord is also famed as the home of four great literary figures of the 19th century: Nathaniel Hawthorne, Ralph Waldo Emerson, Henry David Thoreau and Louisa May Alcott.

The **Old Manse** (Monument Road near North Bridge; 508-369-3909; admission) was home not only to Emerson but also to Hawthorne, who lived there with his wife for two years, while writing *Mosses from an Old Manse*. The restored house is filled with Emerson and Hawthorne memorabilia.

The Alcott family lived at **Orchard House** (399 Lexington Road; 508-369-4118; admission) for almost 20 years. Here Louisa May Alcott wrote her most famous novels, *Little Women* and *Little Men*.

The Alcotts and Hawthorne also lived at **The Wayside** (455 Lexington Road; 508-369-6975; admission). The Alcotts lived here for several years while Louisa May was a girl. Hawthorne bought the house in 1852 and wrote his biography of Franklin Pierce here.

Ralph Waldo Emerson House (28 Cambridge Turnpike; 508-369-2236; admission) is where Emerson lived for almost 50 years, with Thoreau, Hawthorne and the Alcotts as his frequent guests. Almost all furnishings are original.

The **Concord Museum** (200 Lexington Road; 508-369-9609; admission) contains Revolutionary War artifacts, literary relics and other historic items associated with Concord. Emerson's study was reconstructed and moved here, and the Thoreau Room holds the simple furniture Thoreau made for his cabin at Walden Pond.

At the **Thoreau Lyceum** (156 Belknap Street; 508-369-5912; admission) is a replica of the cabin Thoreau built on Walden Pond. Headquarters of the Thoreau Society, the lyceum has a research library and sponsors lectures about the writer.

Few places have been more indelibly stamped by the presence of one individual than **Walden Pond State Reservation** (Route 126 off Route 2; 508-369-3254; admission). "I went to the woods because I wished to live deliberately, to front the essential facts of life, and see if I could not learn what it had to teach, and not, when I came to die, discover that I had not lived," wrote Thoreau in his famous account of his two years spent in a little cabin in these woods, beginning in 1845. Thoreau occupied himself studying nature, fishing and hoeing his bean crop. Today, Walden Pond offers less solitude—it's almost always crowded. But you can swim or fish in the pond, or perhaps try a little boating. Nature trails wind around the pond, and there are picnic tables. You can also visit the little cairn of stones that marks the cabin site.

Concord is also known for **Concord grapes**, developed and cultivated here by Ephraim Wales Bull.

Shopping

NORTH END SHOPPING

The North End is a food lover's shopping dream, chock full of wine and cheese shops and bakeries.

For a pungent whiff of Old World ambience, head for **Polcari's Coffee Shop** (105 Salem Street; 617-227-0786), a tiny shop brimming with open bags of cornmeal and flour, wooden bins of nuts and jars of coffee beans.

At **A & J Distributors** (236 Hanover Street; 617-523-8490), you can pick up almost any Italian cookware you want: pasta racks, painted pasta bowls, pizzaiole and waffle makers.

Overwhelming, tantalizing smells hit the nose in the **Modern Pastry Shop** (257 Hanover Street; 617-523-3783), which dates to 1931. It's hard to choose among the pizzaiole, *zuppa inglese*, amaretto biscotti and macaroons.

DOWNTOWN SHOPPING

Downtown Crossing is the heart of downtown shopping. A brick pedestrian mall at the intersection of Washington and Summer streets, it fronts on **Jordan Marsh** (450 Washington Street; 617-357-3000) and **Filene's** (426 Washington Street; 617-357-2100), two of Boston's oldest department stores and rivals since the mid-19th century. No shopping tour would be complete without a visit to **Filene's Basement** (617-542-2011), the country's oldest bargain store, founded in 1908, which has made a legend out of off-price shopping. In the 1940s, 15,000 women once stormed the doors to get the last dresses to leave Paris before the German occupation.

Detractors say merchandise slipped during the 1980s, when the Basement opened 22 stores in six states. But the Basement is always crowded with women, who used to try on clothes in the aisles until dressing rooms were installed in 1989, and who don't mind the flaking paint and exposed piping when they can pick up designer dresses for less than ten percent of retail price after three markdowns. Or, on occasion, an $80,000 sable coat for $5000.

The biggest tourist shopping mecca in Boston continues to be **Quincy Market**, just a few steps from Faneuil Hall. A Boston marketplace since 1826, Quincy Market is the centerpiece of three shopping arcades filled with more than 160 shops and two dozen food stands and restaurants. Outside the market are a profusion of cheery flower and balloon stands, and under its glass-canopied sides are pushcart vendors selling novelty products. Flanking Quincy Market are two more arcades, the North Market and the South Market. Among the more intriguing shops are **Purple Panache** (617-742-6500), where everything is purple—T-shirts, stuffed animals and novelties—and **Hog Wild** (617-523-7447), where you can buy such piggy products as stuffed pigs, pig jewelry, pig T-shirts and pig mugs. And, who could resist **Tales with Tails** (617-227-8772), a toy store with wild and wonderful stuffed animals, or **Puzzle People** (617-523-9629), a "maze" of puzzle jewelry, puzzle boxes, jigsaw puzzles and other brain teasers? Also browse **Banana Republic** (617-439-0016), purveyors of travel and safari clothing, and **Folklorica** (617-367-1201), which has a fine selection of antique and contemporary gold and silver jewelry. **The Nature Company** (617-227-5005) sells animal videos, telescopes, sundials and a wide selection of nature books.

If there is such a thing as a vintage joke shop, **Jack's Joke Shop** (197 Tremont Street; 617-426-9640) is it. Open since 1922, the narrow shop is festooned with dozens of elaborate Halloween masks and wigs, inflatable skeletons and glasses with noses and mustaches.

Many years ago, the waterfront had legions of marine supply companies. One shop that holds true to the past is **Boxell's Chandlery** (★) (28 Constitution Plaza; 617-523-5678), in operation for more than 50 years. Boxell's sells worldwide navigational charts, foul weather gear and a staggering array of books on navigation, knot tying and racing.

For such a small area, Chinatown has more shops than you might imagine. If you've never experienced Chinese pastries, your mouth will water for them at **Hing Shing Pastry** (★) (67 Beach Street; 617-451-1162), where you can see the bakers at work.

Professional-quality Chinese cooking equipment is sold at **Chin Enterprises, Inc.** (33 Harrison Avenue; 617-423-1725), including two-foot-diameter woks and brass strainers.

BEACON HILL SHOPPING

At the foot of Beacon Hill, little Charles Street is thickly lined with antique shops, art galleries and specialty stores.

Quirky bargains lie in store at the **Beacon Hill Thrift Shop** (15 Charles Street; 617-742-2323), where Beacon Hill matrons bring their best silver along with bric-a-brac.

If you stop by **Rouvalis Flowers** (70 Charles Street; 617-720-5635) you can take home an exotic plant or flower. The shop has a wonderful selection of topiary trees and orchids as well as unusual ginger and heliconia. Shipping is available.

Fanciful handcrafted wood items abound at the **Charles Street Woodshop** (102 Charles Street; 617-523-0797), from yo-yos and birdhouses to breadboards and garden benches.

An amazing selection of beautifully colored and embroidered western-style leather boots awaits at **Helen's Leather** (110 Charles Street; 617-742-2077), along with leather coats and jackets, briefcases and belts.

(Text continued on page 214.)

Boston Bookstores

Boston is a book lover's delight, brimming with bookstores full of quirky personality, charm and the imprint of history. These shops display a colorful, individual stamp, with second-hand shelving, hand-lettered signs and perhaps a beat-up leather chair or two or a resident dog.

Boston's most famous literary emporium is the **Globe Corner Bookstore** (One School Street; 617-523-6658). In the mid-19th century, it was called the Old Corner Bookstore and was a literary haunt of Hawthorne, Longfellow, Lowell, Emerson and Holmes, as well as Dickens and Thackeray when they were in the United States. Today the store's two floors burst with books about world travel and New England.

The **Brattle Book Shop** (9 West Street; 617-542-0210) claims the title of being the successor to America's oldest continuous antiquarian bookshop, dating from the 18th century. Used books sit on battered gray steel shelving and range from fiction, humor and poetry to history, genealogy and heraldry. Old *Life* magazines dating to 1936 march up the stairway and through history, covered with the faces of Tallulah Bankhead, Betty Grable and Hedy Lamar.

Established in 1898, **Goodspeed's Book Shop** (2 Milk Street; 617-523-5970) has been selling used and rare books ever since. Despite the exposed pipes and peeling paint, this little basement shop holds many treasures, and a staff of experts can help you unearth them. The collection is especially strong in marine, genealogical and American history books. A second location at 7 Beacon Street has a stunning selection of antique European and American engravings, first editions, genealogical books and rare autographs, Winston Churchill's and Ulysses S. Grant's among them.

Good food and good books go hand in hand, and never more so than at Boston's two bookstore cafés, **Trident Booksellers & Café** (338 Newbury Street; 617-267-8688) and the **Harvard Bookstore Café** (190 Newbury Street; 617-536-0097). Trident claims the prize for being the funkiest: the province of young hippies dressed in black, a plethora of Third World, gay and alternative publications, and a menu of homemade soups and sandwiches tailored to a struggling writer's budget. It also sells bonsai trees, incense and myrrh, self-improvement videos and campy black-and-white postcards. The store stages Sunday readings of new poetry and fiction. The Harvard Bookstore is comfortably middle-class, and its dining room is middle-class sophisticated. Gleaming new mainstream books emphasize fiction, cooking, art, architecture, travel and home design.

An astonishing 25 bookshops surround Harvard Square. Established in 1856, **Schoenhof's Foreign Books, Inc.** (76-A Mt. Auburn Street, Cambridge; 617-547-8855) is America's oldest comprehensive foreign-language bookstore. It carries reference books in over 130 languages, among them Swahili, Urdu, Tibetan, Navajo and classical Greek and Latin, whatever you need to complete a master's or Ph.D. Still, the shop is not too pedantic to sell children's favorites like *Le Petit Prince* and *Babar*.

Where else but Cambridge could a poetry-only bookshop exist? The **Grolier Book Shop** (6 Plympton Street; 617-547-4648), founded in 1927, is America's oldest continuously operating poetry bookshop, carrying over 10,000 titles from all periods and cultures. Supported by friends of Conrad Aiken, who lived next door in 1929, the shop grew into a meeting place for such poets as Ezra Pound, Marianne Moore and A. E. Housman. The shop sponsors an annual poetry prize and reading.

Many Harvard Square bookshops specialize in rare and out-of-print books, among them the **Pangloss Bookshop** (65 Mt. Auburn Street, Cambridge; 617-354-4003) and **Starr Bookshop, Inc.** (29 Plympton Street, Cambridge; 617-547-6864).

Seven Stars (58 John F. Kennedy Street, Cambridge; 617-547-1317) breathes New Age culture. Besides such titles as *Everyday Zen, Spiritual Emergency* and *The Dynamics of the Unconscious,* the shop sells Tarot cards, incense and gorgeous chunks of amethyst and other crystals, which some believe have healing powers. The shop sponsors lectures and workshops in Kundalini yoga, channeling and the meaning of myths and dreams.

A couple of miles out from Harvard Square, **Kate's Mystery Books** (2211 Massachusetts Avenue, Cambridge; 617-491-2660) is a mecca for mystery lovers and writers. Opening on Friday the 13th in 1983, the store has a black cat logo and walls lined with several hundred black cat figurines. About 10,000 new and used titles range from Dashiell Hammett and Agatha Christie to Tony Hillerman and Robert Parker. A special section focuses on mysteries set in New England. Mystery Writers of America meets here, as does the Spenser Fan Club.

This is just a sampling of Boston's bookstores, large and small. In this area of scholars and writers, there's a bookstore for everyone, with almost 300 listed in the Yellow Pages. That's one for every 2500 inhabitants.

One of Charles Street's oldest and most respected antique shops is **George Gravert Antiques** (122 Charles Street; 617-227-1593), which carries fine antiques.

You ought to be able to find the perfect brass drawer pull at **Period Furniture Hardware** (123 Charles Street; 617-227-0758), which carries a full line of reproduction hardware.

BACK BAY SHOPPING

Back Bay is another of the city's densest shopping districts, concentrated on fashionable Newbury Street, lined from end to end with chic boutiques.

Shreve, Crump & Lowe (330 Boylston Street; 617-267-9100), a Boston jeweler since 1800, has always been the place to go for fine gold and silver jewelry.

A gold swan sculpture over the door signals the **Women's Educational and Industrial Union** (356 Boylston Street; 617-536-5651), founded in 1877 by a group of socially concerned women, the same year the Swan Boats set sail. Its shop sells Italian pottery, jewelry, women's accessories, stationery, cards, children's clothing, even antiques.

Waterstone's (26 Exeter Street; 617-859-7300) is in the former Exeter Theater, once Boston's oldest continuously operating theater. The largest bookstore in Boston, Waterstone's is a book lover's dream come true.

If you like the Italian flair for fashion, consider **Settebello** (8 Newbury Street; 617-262-5280), selling imported women's clothing and fine leather boots and shoes in a salon-style setting of loveseats and Oriental rugs.

Shoes with a cluster of plastic bananas à la Carmen Miranda? You'll find them at **Alan Bilzerian** (34 Newbury Street; 617-536-1001), a chic shop filled with avant-garde clothing for men and women.

Only in Boston would you find chocolates shaped like fax machines and cellular phones. **Chocolate by Design** (134 Newbury Street; 617-424-1115) carries these yuppie chocolates and other unusual, hand-sculpted yummies.

London Lace (167 Newbury Street; 617-267-3506) specializes in reproduction Victorian lace patterns made on the only Victorian machinery left in Scotland. Items include lace curtain panels, table runners, tablecloths and antique linens.

Who would mind buying used men's and women's clothing when it's as fashionable and "gently worn" as that at **The Closet** (175 Newbury Street, downstairs; 617-536-1919)? Only the latest clothes in the finest condition are accepted.

The **Society of Arts and Crafts** (175 Newbury Street; 617-266-1810) is the oldest nonprofit craft organization in the United States, founded in 1897. In its salesroom you can buy whimsical animal sculptures, papier-mâché masks and furniture with real personality, as well as pottery and jewelry. There's a second gallery at 101 Arch Street (617-345-0033).

With its outrageous cards and T-shirts, screaming toy axes and pounding pop music, **In Touch** (192 Newbury Street; 617-262-7676) puts you in touch with strange gifts.

Prem-la (221 Newbury Street; 617-266-8961) sells Himalayan imports, from brightly patterned sweaters and fiber wallhangings to brass figures, beaded necklaces and carved masks.

Step into **Selletto** (★) (244 Newbury Street; 617-424-0656) for handmade products, always enhanced by piñon and cedar incense, where wares come from a worldwide network of artists. There are wreaths, dried flower arrangements and even hand-carved marble peaches from Tuscany.

Vintage clothing, funky jewelry and antique housewares are some of the treasures you'll find at **Odeon Too** (285 Newbury Street; 617-536-1515).

The **Tower Record Building** (360 Newbury Street; 617-247-5900) is a bold, winged stone creation by revolutionary architect Frank O. Gehry. The largest Tower store in the United States, it holds three floors of all the music anyone could want: classical, country, folk, rock, soul, reggae and gospel.

FENWAY SHOPPING

The music of psychedelic '60s groups, '50s jazzmen and other performers of yesteryear rules at **Looney Tunes** (★) (1106 Boylston Street; 617-247-2238), where you can buy used records on the cheap.

MIDTOWN SHOPPING

The jewel of Midtown shopping is brass- and marble-bedecked **Copley Place** on upper Huntington Avenue, resplendent with indoor waterfalls and trees. The Copley Place complex also includes the Westin and Marriott hotels, and the shopping mall is in between the two, connected to both hotel lobbies. A glass pedestrian bridge carries shoppers over Huntington Avenue to the Prudential Center.

Opened in the mid-1980s, Copley Place holds 100 upscale stores, anchored by classy Dallas import **Neiman-Marcus** (617-536-3660). Copley Place also houses outlets of **Polo–Ralph Lauren** (617-266-4121), **Gucci** (617-247-3000), **Enrico Celli** (617-247-4881), **Bally of Switzerland** (617-437-1910) and **Louis Vuitton** (617-437-6519).

Copley Place's much older cousin is the **Prudential Center**, anchored by **Saks Fifth Avenue** (800 Boylston Street; 617-262-8500) and **Lord & Taylor** (660 Boylston Street; 617-262-6000). The "Pru" is currently undergoing a massive renovation which will include a network of glass-roofed pedestrian streets lined with shops.

Bonwit Teller (500 Boylston Street; 617-267-1200) moved to palatial new headquarters in 1989, fronted by a columned courtyard.

SOUTH END SHOPPING

Some of the city's most fanciful and free-spirited boutiques lie on Tremont Street and Columbus Avenue.

Take, for instance, **Divine Decadence** (★) (535 Columbus Avenue; 617-266-1477), which boasts funky, fun household items from the past like vintage jukeboxes and art deco torchières, as well as contemporary neon paintings and sculptures.

Jesse Jackson's **Sticks and Stems** (585 Columbus Avenue; 617-247-2274) features delightful warm-weather greenery such as bromeliads and birds of paradise. Jackson grows the beauties on his Palm Beach, Florida property, and personally updates his shop selections every two weeks.

Open since 1961, **Skippy White's Records** (★) (410 Massachusetts Avenue; 617-266-1002) offers an impressive collection of gospel records, as well as reggae and rap.

OUTSIDE BOSTON SHOPPING

CAMBRIDGE SHOPPING

The **Out of Town Newspapers** (0 Harvard Square; 617-354-7777) kiosk has been declared a National Historic Landmark. Set right in the middle of Harvard Square and surrounded by traffic, the kiosk carries more than 3000 newspapers and magazines from all over the world.

Harvard Square offers a wealth of shopping, from eclectic boutiques to upscale chain stores. Most notable in this intellectual bastion are the many bookshops surrounding the square. (See "Boston Bookstores" in this chapter.)

Yet another Harvard institution is the **Harvard Coop** (1400 Massachusetts Avenue; 617-499-2000), formed in 1882 by several Harvard students as a cost-saving measure. The Coop holds three floors of men's and women's clothing, housewares, gifts, computers and calculators, games and toys, and an astonishing selection of records, art prints, posters and books.

Colonial Drug (49 Brattle Street; 617-864-2222) is like a European perfume shop, with more than 500 kinds of fragrances.

The creativity of Cambridge-area artists is for sale at the **Cambridge Artists Cooperative** (★) (59-A Church Street; 617-868-4434), a treasure trove of whimsical and beautiful things: handmade paper face masks, fiber animals, Raku bowls, handmade quilts and hand-painted silk scarves.

A throwback to the '60s, **Urban Outfitters** (11 John F. Kennedy Street; 617-864-0070) features two floors of mod home furnishings, clothing and jewelry from that ultra-cool era. Downstairs, there's a great bargain basement.

Little Russia (★) (99 Mt. Auburn Street; 617-661-4928) sells authentic Russian lacquered boxes and nesting dolls, jewelry, illustrated Russian fairy tales and pins of Lenin, Stalin and Trotsky.

Nightlife

Boston's arts scene has rich centuries of history behind it and is expanding all the time. The **Bostix Booth** at Faneuil Hall (617-723-5181) offers half-price tickets for many performance events on the day of the show, cash only, first-come, first-served. The **Boston Jazzline** (617-787-9700) offers 24-hour recorded information on local jazz events.

DOWNTOWN NIGHTLIFE

THE BEST BARS

There's a Boston bar for everyone: young singles, bricklayers and stevedores, the State House crowd, Financial District workers, Cambridge academics, sports fans, the Irish.

The **Bell in Hand Tavern** (45 Union Street; 617-227-2098) is Boston's oldest tavern, opened in 1795, and retains a cozy, colonial feeling.

Irish brogues roll so thickly at the **Black Rose** (160 State Street; 617-742-2286) that it sounds like Dublin. Irish beers, Irish folk music and a rollicking good time are house specialties. Cover on weekends.

Duck Soup (617-426-6639) is not only the largest comedy club in New England, it's one of the best. At its splendid location inside Faneuil Hall, the 450-seat theater hosts many of the nation's top comedians as well as big-name Boston acts.

The **Last Hurrah** (60 School Street, in the Omni Parker House; 617-227-8600), imbued with turn-of-the-century tradition, swings with jazz and the music of the '40s.

NIGHTCLUBS AND CABARETS

The **Roxy** (279 Tremont Street, in the Tremont House; 617-227-7699) is a beautiful and elegant art deco-style club where people like to really dress up. It has its own 14-piece orchestra, dance troupe and deejay. Dress code. Cover.

A view of the city from the 33rd floor is offered the prosperous at the **Bay Tower Room** (60 State Street; 617-723-1666), where a four-piece orchestra plays.

Surfboard tables and Hawaiian-shirt-clad deejays add up to California fun with live rock-and-roll or canned music at the **Boston Beach Club** (Landmark Inn, Faneuil Hall, 300 North Market Building; 617-227-9660). Cover on weekends.

A tropical paradise complete with 20-foot royal palms awaits guests of **Zanzibar** (1 Boylston Place; 617-451-1955), which offers rock and Top-40 music. Cover.

Beneath the Wilbur Theater the elegant, upscale **Improv Boston** (246 Tremont Street; 617-695-2989) draws a mixed clientele. Nationally known comedians headline seven nights a week. Cover.

The **Orpheum Theater** (Hamilton Place off Tremont Street; 617-482-0650) hosts nationally known rock performers.

THEATER

Boston's theater district is tightly clustered on lower Tremont Street and several blocks west. **The Colonial Theatre** (106 Boylston Street; 617-426-9366) and **The Shubert** (265 Tremont Street; 617-426-4520) host pre-Broadway tryouts and national touring companies. Popular contemporary plays are offered at **The Wilbur** (246 Tremont Street; 617-423-4008).

The opulent **Wang Center for the Performing Arts** (270 Tremont Street; 617-482-9393), formerly a Roaring Twenties movie palace, sponsors extravaganzas in dance, theater, opera, music and film.

Musical comedies are the specialty at **The Charles Playhouse** (76 Warrenton Street; 617-426-6912), while its **Stage II** (617-426-5225) downstairs has been home to the country's longest-running nonmusical play, *Shear Madness*, a comedy whodunit.

OPERA AND DANCE

Artistic director Sarah Caldwell has established the **Opera Company of Boston** (539 Washington Street; 617-426-5300) as one of the world's premier companies. Occasional rock and pop performances are also held here.

The **Boston Ballet** (19 Clarendon Street, Boston; 617-695-6950) performs classics like *The Nutcracker* and contemporary works at the Wang Center. Its sister company, **Boston Ballet II**, gives free summer concerts at the Hatch Shell on the Esplanade.

BEACON HILL NIGHTLIFE

Despite its fame as the "Cheers" bar, **Bull and Finch Pub** (downstairs at 84 Beacon Street; 617-227-9605) is a watering hole with character. The venerable English pub features big brews, burgers and an uproarious crowd.

BACK BAY NIGHTLIFE

If you're rich or over the hill, head for the dark-paneled **Ritz Bar** (15 Arlington Street; 617-536-5700), where tradition and Brahmin propriety rule. Or visit the elegant vintage ballroom which provides a romantic setting for ballroom dancing at the **Ritz-Carlton** (15 Arlington Street; 617-536-5700).

The **Boston Camerata** (140 Clarendon Street; 617-262-2092), formed in 1954, offers medieval, Renaissance and early baroque concerts, both vocal and instrumental.

For deejay-generated disco music gays head to **Chaps** (27 Huntington Avenue; 617-266-7778). Women are also welcome at this high-energy club which includes a separate lounge off the throbbing dancefloor. Cover.

Boston nightlife doesn't get more local than the **Pour House** (907–909 Boylston Street; 617-236-1767), where an uproarious underground bar features blues and psychedelic music.

Middle-class disco pleases the middle-class crowds at **Club Nicole** (40 Dalton Street; 617-236-1100) in the basement of the Back Bay Hilton.

Housed in a renovated police station, **Division 16** (955 Boylston Street; 617-353-0870) features recorded big band and swing music amidst pink neon, pink walls and art deco wall sconces.

During the Boston Marathon, you can't get in the doors of the **Eliot Lounge** (370 Commonwealth Avenue, in the Eliot Hotel; 617-262-1078), which is decorated with sports memorabilia and photos and the flags of marathon winners' countries.

FENWAY NIGHTLIFE

The **Rathskellar** (528 Commonwealth Avenue; 617-536-2750), fondly called the Rat, first showcased The Police and the Talking Heads and is still a loud hole-in-the-wall offering alternative rock bands. Cover for basement shows.

The **Avalon Ballroom** (15 Lansdowne Street; 617-262-2424), one of the city's largest dance clubs, plays progressive and Top-40 sounds for avid dancers, and hosts top names like Eric Clapton and Prince. Next door, one of the trendiest dance clubs is **Axis** (13 Lansdowne Street; 617-262-2437), which features progressive music. Tuesday is gay night, though a real mixed crowd turns out. Cover at both clubs.

Frenzied dance music pulsates throughout **Venus de Milo** (7 Lansdowne Street; 617-421-9595), where the sounds may be alternative, international or acid house. Wednesday is gay night. Cover.

The leather and levis crowd likes to cruise down to **The Boston Ramrod** (1254 Boylston Street; 617-266-2986). There's a special two-stepping night at this gay-only bar which also offers pool.

At **Tattoo** (1270 Boylston Street; 617-267-1270), gays and lesbians dance to deejay music.

CLASSICAL MUSIC AND THEATER

Under the direction of Seiji Ozawa, the prestigious **Boston Symphony Orchestra** (301 Massachusetts Avenue; 617-266-1492) presents more than 250 concerts annually. Its **Boston Pops** performs lighter favorites in spring and free outdoor summer concerts at the Hatch Shell on the Esplanade.

The **Handel and Haydn Society** (300 Massachusetts Avenue; 617-266-3605) is the country's oldest continuously active performing arts group, started in 1815. They perform instrumental and choral music, and Handel's *Messiah* at Christmas.

The **Huntington Theatre Company** (264 Huntington Avenue; 617-266-3913), Boston University's resident company, specializes in classics, comedies and musicals.

MIDTOWN NIGHTLIFE

The **Lyric Stage Company of Boston** (140 Clarendon Street, Copley Square; 617-437-7172), Boston's oldest resident professional theater, performs revivals and premieres, and Dylan Thomas' *A Child's Christmas in Wales* every Christmas.

World-class pianists play in **The Plaza Bar** (Copley Plaza Hotel, 138 St. James Avenue; 617-267-5300), which resembles a British officers' club in the era of the raj.

Diamond Jim's Piano Bar (710 Boylston Street, in the Lenox Hotel; 617-536-5300) is one of Boston's best piano bars, and a place where you're welcome to sing along.

SOUTH END NIGHTLIFE

The glitz of L.A. has come to Boston with the **Hard Rock Café** (131 Clarendon Street; 617-424-7625), a temple to rock history filled with such memorabilia as Elvis' white boots and Jimi Hendrix's jacket, and gold and platinum records from many groups. Elvis, Chuck Berry and Jerry Lee Lewis stare down from stained glass.

Club Café (209 Columbus Avenue; 617-536-0972), an avant-garde club, sponsors nationally known jazz musicians in a sophisticated art deco setting, attracting a gay and straight crowd. Cover for live shows.

Inside the **Napoleon Club** (52 Piedmont Street, Bay Village; 617-338-7547) the gay crowd enjoys show tunes at the downstairs piano bar. Upstairs there's a cover charge for the dance music.

SOUTH BOSTON NIGHTLIFE

Sailing from Commonwealth Pier and Long Wharf during the summer, **Water Music** (12 Arrow Street, Cambridge; 617-876-8742) sponsors cabaret cruises of Boston Harbor—popularly known as "blues cruises." These feature top jazz and blues bands.

OUTSIDE BOSTON NIGHTLIFE

CAMBRIDGE NIGHTLIFE

The **Plough and Stars** (912 Massachusetts Avenue; 617-492-9653) is that rare thing, an uncorrupted working-class bar where habitués are logo-capped, burly types who belly up for live, boisterous entertainment. Black-and-white caricatures of neighborhood regulars line a whole wall.

Native son Pat Metheny occasionally stops in to jam at **Ryle's** (212 Hampshire Street; 617-876-9330), which features nightly jazz, rhythm-and-blues, Latin music and swing in a casual atmosphere. Cover.

One of the best jazz showcases in Greater Boston, the **Regattabar** (1 Bennett Street, in the Charles Hotel; 617-864-1200) offers an intimate jazz experience in a sophisticated club environment. The Regattabar regularly features such headliners as Miles Davis, Wynton Marsalis, Ahmad Jamal and Stephane Grapelli. Cover.

Nightstage (823 Main Street; 617-497-8200), one of the Boston area's best nightclubs, showcases headliners like Wynton Marsalis and Semenya McCord. Concerts range from jazz, blues and rock, to funk and Brazilian dance bands. Cover. Downstairs is **Indigo** (617-497-7200), a lesbian bar drawing a diverse crowd and featuring alternative music on the weekends. Cover.

Cantares (15 Springfield Street; 617-547-6300) offers reggae, African, Latin and blues sounds in a Cambridge-casual setting. You never know what you'll hear on open mike nights at the **Cantab Lounge** (738 Massachusetts Avenue; 617-354-2685), but the rest of the time it's soulful rhythm-and-blues bands in a let-it-all-hang-out playpen. Cover at both places.

At the **Mystery Café** (1667 Massachusetts Avenue; 617-262-1826), the audience participates in solving a murder over a four-course dinner. Cover.

An industrial dance club with a flair for art, **Man Ray** (21 Brookline Street; 617-864-0400) serves up progressive and alternative music. Gay nights are Thursday (men) and Sunday (women). Cover.

Ever since 1969, **Passim** (47 Palmer Street; 617-492-7679) has been going strong as a showcase for acoustic folk performers, including Tracy Chapman, Jimmy Buffett and David Bromberg, in a clean-cut, no-alcohol basement coffeehouse. Cover.

Harvard's professional theater company, **American Repertory Theatre** (64 Brattle Street; 617-547-8300) produces world premieres and classical works, often taking a nontraditional approach. **Catch a Rising Star** (30-B John F. Kennedy Street; 617-661-9887) showcases rising young comics seven nights a week in a dark and cozy basement club. Cover.

OUTLYING AREAS NIGHTLIFE

The Paradise (967 Commonwealth Avenue; 617-254-2052) draws SRO crowds for its national headliners in live rock music and dance. Cover.

The Tam O'Shanter (1648 Beacon Street, Brookline; 617-277-0982) always gets the audience dancing with live blues and rhythm-and-blues in an unpretentious, down-home setting. Cover.

Ballroom dancers from 18 to 80 love **Moseley's on the Charles** (50 Bridge Street, Dedham; 617-326-3075) for its large ballroom and 1940s ambience complete with sparkling ceiling globe. Cover.

CHAPTER FIVE
Massachusetts Coast

Immortalized in the past by Herman Melville in *Moby Dick* and Henry David Thoreau in *Cape Cod*, the Massachusetts coast today remains fertile territory for noted writers like Paul Theroux. And it's not surprising.

This magnificent stretch of windswept coast abounds with historic seaside villages, vintage lighthouses, glorious beaches and history that reads like an adventure story complete with witches and pirates, authors and artists, Pilgrims and American natives, sea captains and Moby Dick.

The 168-mile coast follows a zigzagging course from the New Hampshire border south to Massachusetts Bay, then into Nantucket Sound to form Cape Cod, then west along Buzzards Bay, ending at the Rhode Island border. Martha's Vineyard and Nantucket are islands below Cape Cod.

An ethnic melting pot of Portuguese fishermen, Yankee blue bloods, old salts and the Irish (who seem to be everywhere), coast residents are very proud of where they live. North Shore loyalists wouldn't think of moving to the South Coast, and vice versa. Everyone calls Martha's Vineyard and Nantucket "the Islands"—except the people who live there. They can't stand being lumped together. And don't even *suggest* that the "islanders" are connected to the Cape in any way, unless you want to start a row.

What unifies everyone is the sea. Rich and poor alike have miniweather stations on their roofs to determine wind direction, and everyone reads tide charts. Kids learn how to fish, sail and dig for clams when they're five years old.

That all-encompassing sea is, of course, what lured Europeans to these shores in the first place. One hundred years before the Pilgrims stepped foot on Plymouth Rock, English adventurers fished the waters around the Massachusetts coast. Between 1600 and 1610, explorers Samuel de Champlain and Bartholomew Gosnold sailed to Cape Cod, Gloucester and other areas along the coast.

Aboard the *Mayflower*, 102 Pilgrims landed on Cape Cod on November 11, 1620. But the area lacked an adequate harbor, farmland and fresh water, so the group sailed across the bay to Plymouth, establishing the first permanent settlement in New England.

By 1640, about 2500 of the new settlers lived in eight communities. Although they came to America to seek religious freedom, the Pilgrims persecuted Quakers and anyone else who didn't adhere to their strict Puritan religion.

Their intolerant thinking helped fuel one of the most infamous pieces of American colonial history—the Salem witch trials of 1692. Salem had been founded six years after Plymouth. Here the Puritans tried to impose their religious laws on rowdy fishermen who lived in nearby Marblehead, but adultery and drunkenness won out. The Puritans were more successful in their witch hunt—20 women were executed for practicing "witchcraft" in a single year.

The gruesome trials took place during a time when witchcraft was thought to be the cause for any unexplained event. Similar trials and executions occurred throughout New England and Europe, but Salem had the dubious distinction of executing the most women in the shortest amount of time.

Fortunately by the 1700s the focus was more on commerce than religion. Salem sailing vessels had opened routes to the Orient, thus establishing the famous China trade and Salem's reputation as a major port. When the Revolutionary War broke out in 1775, America didn't have a Navy, so Salem sea captains armed their merchant vessels and fought the British.

For the next 150 years, shipbuilding, the China trade and commercial fishing flourished along the coast, particularly in the towns north of Boston. Concurrently, New Bedford, near Rhode Island, and Nantucket became leading whaling ports.

All this maritime activity brought great prosperity to the coast. Fortune and adventure lay in wait for any man willing to risk his life on a whale boat or ship bound for the Orient to obtain ivory, spice, silver and gold. It was an exciting, swashbuckling time, filled with tall tales and tragedy. The widows' walks on many historic homes in towns such as Newburyport are a sad reminder of the men who never returned from the sea.

Evidence of the wealth gleaned during these years is apparent in the amazing number of 18th- and 19th-century mansions built by sea captains that dot the coast. Impeccably restored by a people in love with the past, these coast homes make up an architectural feast bulging with Greek Revival, Federal, Queen Anne, Victorian Gothic, Colonial and classic saltbox structures. Historic villages and buildings throughout the area enable visitors to see the evolution of America's unique architectural style.

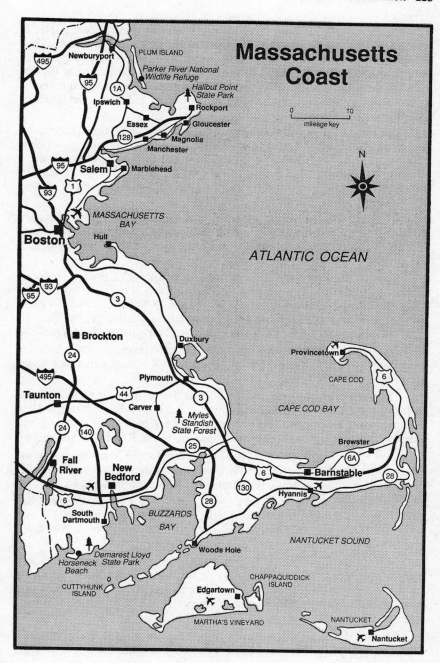

Massachusetts Coast

495
95
Newburyport
PLUM ISLAND
Parker River National Wildlife Refuge
1A
Halibut Point State Park
Ipswich
Rockport
Essex
Gloucester
128
Magnolia
Manchester
95
Salem
Marblehead
93
1

0   10
mileage key

N

MASSACHUSETTS BAY

Boston
Hull

ATLANTIC OCEAN

93
95
3

Brockton
Duxbury
24
Plymouth
Provincetown
CAPE COD
6
495
Taunton
44
3
Carver
Myles Standish State Forest
CAPE COD BAY
24
140
25
Brewster
6A
Fall River
New Bedford
6
Barnstable
28
130
6
28
Hyannis
South Dartmouth
BUZZARDS BAY
NANTUCKET SOUND
Horseneck Beach
Demarest Lloyd State Park
Woods Hole
CUTTYHUNK ISLAND
CHAPPAQUIDDICK ISLAND
Edgartown
NANTUCKET
MARTHA'S VINEYARD
Nantucket

By the mid-1800s everything along the Massachusetts coast started to change. Salem's prominence as a seaport was over. Its harbor was too shallow for the new, faster clipper ships, and railroads provided cheaper and more rapid shipping service. The whaling industry also started to decline as petroleum replaced whale oil and whales became scarce. Eventually the entire industry vanished, plummeting New Bedford and Nantucket into serious depressions.

The Industrial Revolution came along in the nick of time, and manufacturing businesses started to sprout along the coast and throughout New England. In the late 1800s, New Bedford and Fall River became leading textile manufacturers, but this prosperity was short lived. Prior to the Depression, union problems and cheaper labor in the South wiped out the textile industry.

While the coast economy was transforming itself in the mid-1880s, two other developments were evolving that would change the flavor of the coast forever. Tourism began to blossom on Cape Cod, and artists and writers discovered the inspirational charms of the coast.

Rudyard Kipling and Winslow Homer lived north of Boston in Rocky Neck, one of the country's oldest artist colonies. Thoreau settled in Cape Cod. Nathaniel Hawthorne wrote about Salem, which he called home, in *The House of Seven Gables*. Melville immortalized whaling in New Bedford and Nantucket. And Emily Dickinson made her home in Martha's Vineyard.

To this day, creative people are drawn to the Massachusetts coast, now supported by light industry, fishing and a tourist industry that just keeps growing.

The coast can be loosely divided into the five geographic areas explored in this chapter. The North Shore (everything above Boston to the New Hampshire border), Cape Cod, Martha's Vineyard, Nantucket and the South Coast (Plymouth and the area from Cape Cod to the Rhode Island border).

Cape Cod and the Islands have always attracted the lion's share of tourists, but the North Shore and South Coast offer more opportunities to discover hidden villages, inns, restaurants, beaches and more.

The North Shore wears many faces. Immediately north of Boston are the affluent commuter towns of Magnolia, Manchester and Marblehead, where prep schools, yachts and turn-of-the-century seaside mansions are a way of life.

Beyond these towns are Salem, known for architecture, witches and maritime museums; Gloucester, a major fishing port; Rockport, an artist-colony-turned-resort; Essex and Ipswich, pastoral areas with antiques and seafood; and Newburyport, a scenic 19th-century town on the New Hampshire border.

Cape Cod and the Islands are worlds unto themselves. In the summer the Cape is a playground to people from all socioeconomic levels. With over 300 miles of magnificent shoreline, there's just barely enough room for the 3.5 million people who come here from May to October. The Cape offers a lot of everything: historic villages, windswept moors, vast beaches, middle-class neighborhoods, malls, cheap motels and fast-food chains.

The Islands are more exclusive and attract some of Massachusetts' wealthiest families, along with celebrities such as Jackie Onassis and Diana Ross. Both islands have museum-perfect villages, incredibly beautiful scenery and steep prices.

The South Coast is a patchwork of wealthy commuter towns, Portuguese neighborhoods, blue-collar communities and cranberry farms. Its three main towns include Plymouth, "America's Home Town," New Bedford and Fall River. Here you find Pilgrim lore, factory outlets, whaling museums, scenic ports, winding rivers and coastal pastures.

The coast has milder weather than the rest of Massachusetts. Summer temperatures range from the 60s to the 80s. Humidity can be a problem, especially along the North Shore, although ocean breezes keep things from getting too unbearable. In the fall temperatures range from around 45° to 65°. Rain is unpredictable and can happen any time of year.

Traditionally the coast has been a summer destination, but more people are starting to visit in the fall, when prices decline along with the crowds. A bike ride through Nantucket in October when the moors are in bloom is an unforgettable experience.

But no matter when you visit you're bound to be impressed. The scenery is unparalleled, the architecture magnificent, the history fascinating, the seafood plentiful. But there's something else about the coast that can't be explained or labeled—a special kind of chemistry and charisma that draws people back year after year, generation after generation.

Easy Living

Transportation

Special note: For up-to-the-minute information on every conceivable way to get to Martha's Vineyard, Nantucket and Cape Cod short of walking on water, call the **Massachusetts Office of Travel and Tourism** (100 Cambridge Street, Boston; 617-727-3201).

ARRIVAL

On the North Shore, **Route 128** is the main artery connecting Salem, Manchester, Magnolia, Gloucester and Rockport. **Route 95** is the major north–south artery to Essex, Ipswich and Newburyport. **Route 6** cuts through the middle of Cape Cod, ending at Provincetown. **Route 6A** runs along the north side of the Cape, and **Route 28** runs along Nantucket Sound. Both routes connect with Route 6 in Orleans.

On the South Coast, **Route 3** links Boston to Plymouth and ends at the Sagamore Bridge to Cape Cod. **Route 195** is the main east–west artery connecting Fall River and New Bedford.

BY AIR

Seven airports serve the Massachusetts coast: **Logan Airport** in Boston (see Chapter Four), Barnstable Airport and Provincetown Municipal Airport on Cape Cod, Martha's Vineyard Airport, Nantucket Memorial Airport and the New Bedford Airport.

Barnstable Airport in Hyannis is served by Cape Air, Continental Express, Delta, Island Air and Nantucket Airlines.

Cape Air services **Provincetown Municipal Airport**.

Flying into **Martha's Vineyard Airport** are Continental Express, and Edgartown Air.

Nantucket Airport is serviced by Continental Express, Delta, Edgartown Air, Nantucket Airlines and Northwest Express.

Airlines using **New Bedford Airport** are Edgartown Air and Express Air.

For ground transportation from Barnstable Airport to Logan Airport and areas throughout southern Massachusetts, contact **ABC Airport Coach** (508-747-6622), **Brewster Taxi** (508-255-3277) or **Nauset Taxi** (508-255-6965). Taxis and car rentals listed below provide ground transportation to all other airports except Logan.

BY FERRY AND BOAT

Ferries and boats between Boston, Plymouth, New Bedford, Cape Cod, Martha's Vineyard and Nantucket require reservations in the summer. Throughout the year, the **Steamship Authority** (157 Spring Bars Road, Falmouth, Cape Cod; 508-540-2022) transports cars and passengers between Woods Hole, Hyannis, Oak Bluffs, Vineyard Haven and Nantucket.

The following ferries and boats operate seasonally and do not transport cars: **A. C. Cruise Lines** (28 Northern Avenue, Boston; 617-426-8419) goes between Boston and Gloucester. **Cape Cod Cruises** (State Pier, Plymouth; 508-747-2400) goes between Plymouth and Provincetown. **Hy-Line** (Ocean Dock, Hyannis; 508-775-7185) takes passengers to and from Hyannis, Nantucket and Oak Bluffs on Martha's Vineyard. **Cape Island Express** (1494 East Rodney French Boulevard, Billy Woods Wharf, New Bedford; 508-997-1688) operates between New Bedford and Vineyard Haven on Martha's Vineyard. **The Island Queen** (Pier 45, Falmouth; 508-548-4800) goes between Falmouth and Oak Bluffs on Martha's Vineyard. **The On Time** (Edgartown, Martha's Vineyard; 508-627-9794) travels between Edgartown and Chappaquiddick Island. The **MV Alert** (Pier 3, New Bedford; 508-992-1432) connects New Bedford and Cuttyhunk Island.

BY BUS

Greyhound (617-292-4700) offers frequent service to Newburyport and Boston. **Bonanza** (17 Elm Street, Hyannis; 508-548-7588) runs buses to and from Logan Airport, Hyannis, Woods Hole, Falmouth, Bourne, New Bedford, Fall River, Connecticut, Rhode Island and New York. **Plymouth and Brockton Street Railway Company** (17 Elm Street, Hyannis; 508-746-0378) has year-round express service to and from Logan Airport and local service along Route 6 on Cape Cod from Sagamore to Provincetown. **Peter Pan Bus Lines** (17 Elm Street, Hyannis; 508-775-5524) offers service to Hyannis from Mount Holyoke, Springfield, Newton, Worcester and Albany, New York.

BY TRAIN

Amtrak (800-872-7245) runs between Boston and Hyannis with summer bus connections to towns throughout Cape Cod. The Amtrak "Cape Codder" runs between New York and Hyannis from May to September.

CAR RENTALS

Car rental agencies at Barnstable Airport include **Avis Rent a Car** (508-775-2888), **Hertz Rent A Car** (508-775-5825) and **National Car Rental** (508-771-4353).

Budget Rent A Car (508-487-1539) serves Provincetown Municipal Airport.

Martha's Vineyard Airport has **Adventure Rentals** (508-693-1959), **All-Island Rent A Car** (508-693-6868), **Budget Rent A Car** (508-693-1911), **Hertz Rent A Car** (508-627-4127) and **National Car Rental** (508-693-6545).

Nantucket Airport agencies include **Budget Rent A Car** (508-228-5666), **Hertz Rent A Car** (508-228-9421), **Nantucket Windmill Auto Rental** (508-228-1227) and **National Car Rental** (508-228-0300).

Avis Rent A Car (508-999-6900) serves New Bedford Airport.

PUBLIC TRANSPORTATION

Many Boston commuters live on the North Shore; hence **Massachusetts Boston Transit Authority** (617-722-5000) runs numerous buses from Boston's Haymarket Square and trains from North Station to Salem, Beverly, Gloucester and Rockport. **Cape Ann Transportation Authority** (508-283-7916) provides bus service from Gloucester and Rockport.

Cape Cod Regional Transit Authority B-Bus Service (585 Main Street, Dennis; 508-385-8311) offers door-to-door minibus service (reservations required) and regular route service throughout the area. **Cape Cod**

Regional Transit Authority (800-352-7155) makes five daily roundtrips along Route 28.

On Martha's Vineyard, from late May to mid-October, **Island Transport** (508-693-0058) runs shuttle buses between Vineyard Haven, Oak Bluffs and Edgartown. Less frequent service is available up-island; call the above number for schedules. Nantucket doesn't have public transportation. Most people get around with rental cars or bicycles.

Plymouth does not have public transportation. **Southern Eastern Regional Transit Authority** (508-997-6767) provides bus service throughout Fall River and New Bedford.

TAXIS

Taxis serving airports on the coast are as follows: Barnstable Airport, **All Points Taxi** (508-778-1400), **Hyannis Taxi** (508-775-0400) and **Town Taxi of Cape Cod** (508-771-5555); Provincetown Airport, **Martin's Taxi** (508-487-0243) and **Mercedes Cab** (508-487-9434); Martha's Vineyard Airport, **Hathaway's Taxi** (508-627-4462) and **Shaw's Taxi** (508-693-2828); Nantucket Airport, **All Points Taxi** (508-228-5779); New Bedford Airport, **Standard Taxi** (508-997-9404) and **Yellow Taxi** (508-999-5213).

Hotels

The Massachusetts coast is bed and breakfast fantasyland. Cliff-hugging sea captain's mansions, saltbox cottages, 17th-century farmhouses, Victorians—take your pick, it's all here. Hotels and motels are few and far few between except on the Cape and in Plymouth. The best bargains are on the South Coast. However, in the spring and fall rates are reduced substantially in all areas. Many hotels close in the winter, and reservations are mandatory in the summer.

NORTH SHORE HOTELS

Two-thirds of the North Shore's accommodations are in the resort town of Rockport. A sprinkling of motels can be found along Route 127, but they're short on charm and expensive.

A modest-looking green clapboard house, **The Nautilus** (★) (68 Front Street, Marblehead; 617-631-1703) doesn't have a sign outside. "People just know about it," says the owner. Four plain and simple guest rooms with contemporary furnishings occupy the second floor (no private baths). The house stands on a narrow street across from the busy harbor and the Driftwood, a colorful, sea-shanty-style restaurant popular with fishermen and locals. Budget to moderate.

The **Daniels House** (1 Daniels Street, Salem; 508-744-5709) is like a trip back in time. Built in 1667 by a sea captain, it is one of the few bed and breakfasts around here furnished entirely with museum-quality antiques. The five guest rooms have enormous walk-in fireplaces, low beamed ceilings and age-worn pine floors. It's located on a quiet, historic street within walking distance of everything, although the sign outside is small and easy to miss. Deluxe.

If you can't live without a telephone, color television, air-conditioning and room service, stay at **The Hawthorne Hotel** (18 Washington Square West, Salem; 508-744-4080). One of the few real hotels on the North Shore, this impeccably restored Federal-style building is located across from Salem Common. Eighty-nine guest rooms are tastefully decorated with reproduction colonial antiques. Elegant public rooms have wood paneling, brass chandeliers and wing-back chairs. Deluxe and ultra-deluxe.

Tara (★) (13-19 Shore Road, Magnolia; 508-525-3213), a white Tudor mansion, sits high on a bluff overlooking the crashing Atlantic in a residential neighborhood once favored by wealthy Bostonians. The house needs a little paint, but it has a certain kind of faded charm. Tara's owner, Gladys Rundlett, a true Boston Brahmin, is a walking history book. Her home and its three guest rooms (no private baths) are decorated with an eclectic mix of old and contemporary furnishings. Guest rooms are large and light with touches of wicker. A full breakfast is included. In the winter, tea is served in a gracious formal dining room. Moderate.

Beach lovers enjoy the **Blue Shutters Inn** (1 Nautilus Road, Gloucester; 508-281-2706), a lovely old house across the street from Good Harbor Beach, one of the North Shore's most beautiful strips of sand. The inn sits on the outskirts of a secluded, affluent residential area overlooking the ocean and a vast expanse of scenic salt marsh. Blue and white throughout, the inn offers ten rooms and three individual apartments, all with ocean views and sporting furnishings that are homey, simple and sparkling clean. Breakfast included; moderate to deluxe.

Only a ten-minute walk from Gloucester's famed fisherman statue, **Spruce Manor Motel and Guest House** (141 Essex Avenue; 508-283-0614) has economical accommodations to satisfy all tastes. The main guest house, a lovely Victorian built in 1900, has 11 bed-and-breakfast-style guest rooms, some with turret-shaped ceilings and oversized beds. Next to the guest house are one-story motel units overlooking Annisquam River, plus a salt marsh and estuaries. The decor is plain and unobtrusive. Moderate.

A 1791 colonial bed and breakfast, **The Inn on Cove Hill** (37 Mount Pleasant Street, Rockport; 508-546-2701) is a five-minute walk from Bearskin Neck, Rockport's main tourist attraction. Eleven guest rooms have wide pine plank floors, beautiful restored moldings, antiques, country quilts and Laura Ashley-style wallpaper. Some rooms have canopy beds. In summer a continental breakfast is served in the garden; in spring and fall it's served in bed. Moderate.

The **Old Farm Inn** (★) (291 Granite Street, Rockport; 508-546-3237) looks like the original Sunny Brook Farm. Built in 1779, the barn-red inn is shaded by glorious weeping willow trees. Only ten minutes from downtown and within walking distance of Halibut Point State Park, it's a good place for getting away from it all without going to extremes. Four guest rooms in the main house (some featuring sitting rooms) have gun stock beams, wide pine plank floors, fireplaces and antique quilts. Four large guest rooms in a newer building (some with kitchenettes) are decorated with country-style prints, but they lack the charm of the other rooms. Moderate.

JFK and Jackie once slept at the **Yankee Clipper Inn** (96 Granite Street, Rockport; 508-546-3407), one of Rockport's finest hostelries. The main inn, a stately white oceanfront mansion, has magnificent wood-paneled public rooms appointed with model ships, Oriental rugs, paintings and elegant yet comfortable furniture. The Quarterdeck, a separate building built in 1960, has panoramic ocean views and a contemporary look. The Bulfinch House, an 1840 Greek Revival building across the street, has fine period details but limited ocean views. Most of the 27 guest rooms are nondescript, but what they lack in decor is made up for by location. The inn has a good restaurant, saltwater swimming pool and nature paths. Deluxe to ultra-deluxe.

The **Peg Leg Inn** (2 King Street, Rockport; 508-546-2352), a white clapboard colonial, is only steps away from the beach. One of the inn's five buildings is on the ocean and commands the highest rates, but it has spectacular views, a large, sweeping lawn and a granite gazebo. The 32 guest rooms are furnished with chenille bedspreads, braided rugs and reproduction colonial furnishings and wallpaper. Moderate to deluxe.

The **Seaward Inn** (62 Marmion Way, Rockport; 508-546-3471), a rambling brown-shingle building, sits on a beautiful bluff overlooking the ocean. Surrounded by flower gardens, lawns and stone walls, it has a spring-fed swimming pond and bird sanctuary laced with nature paths. Cottages with kitchenettes and fireplaces, located behind the main inn, are ideal for families. Thirty-eight guest rooms, some with ocean views and fireplaces, are simply appointed with homey-looking colonial-style furnishings. The Adirondack-style chairs on a grassy knoll overlooking the windswept shore are perfect for relaxing and reading. Rates include breakfast and dinner. Deluxe to ultra-deluxe.

Morrill Place (★) (209 High Street, Newburyport; 508-462-2808), a three-story, 1806 Federal-style mansion, stands on historic High Street, where wealthy shipbuilders lived in the 19th century. The inn's 12 spacious guest rooms are beautifully decorated. The Henry W. Kinsman room (named for a former owner) is a rich hunter green with an enormous white canopy bed, while the Daniel Webster room has a four-poster antique bed and sleigh dresser. Rooms on the third floor are less formal but charming in their own way, with colonial-style antiques. Some rooms share baths. Moderate.

CAPE COD HOTELS

The Cape has some of the most beautiful inns in the country, plus hundreds of other accommodations in every price range, location and style imaginable. If you plan to stay for at least a week, think about renting a house, apartment or condo; it's usually less expensive than a hotel. Call or write the **Cape Cod Chamber of Commerce** (Junction of Routes 6 and 132, Hyannis, MA 02601; 508-362-3225) for names of realtors handling rentals in a particular area.

NORTH CAPE HOTELS

Located in the heart of Sandwich village, **The Village Inn** (★) (4 Jarves Street; 800-922-9989) is a renovated 1830s Federal-style house. Without sacrificing historic details, the owners have made everything look fresh and new. The eight soothing, uncluttered guest rooms, decorated in shades of raspberry and moss, have lace swag curtains, colonial armoires and pickled four-poster beds. All of the wood furniture is made by the owner and sold in a shop in the inn. A wraparound front porch is a good spot for people watching. Moderate.

The Daniel Webster Inn (149 Main Street, Sandwich; 508-888-3622) is one of the few full-service hotels on historic Route 6A. The Federal-style, 47-room hotel is so much bigger than the other buildings in Sandwich, it looks a little out of whack. But the inside is very warm and cozy. Guest rooms in shades of gold and raspberry or smoke and rose are decorated with reproduction colonial furniture and wing-back chairs; some beds have canopies. Brick paths lead through graceful flower gardens to a gazebo and pool area. The hotel has three restaurants. Rates available with or without breakfast and dinner; deluxe to ultra-deluxe.

The **Beechwood** (2839 Main Street, Barnstable Village; 508-362-6618) is one of the prettiest inns on Route 6A. An ancient weeping beech tree shades a good portion of this buttery yellow, gabled Queen Anne Victorian and its lovely wraparound porch. The entire house is furnished with fine antiques. In the Cottage room you'll find a rare 1860 hand-painted bedroom set, in the Marble room a graceful marble fireplace and 19th-century brass bed. The Garret room on the third floor has steeply angled walls and a half-moon window overlooking Cape Cod Bay. It doesn't matter where you stay—all six guest rooms are wonderful. A full breakfast is served in the wood-paneled dining room and tea on the porch. Deluxe to ultra-deluxe.

A rambling white 1881 Victorian close to the beach, the **Four Chimneys Inn** (946 Main Street, Dennis; 508-385-6317) is the kind of place where you can plop down on the living room couch in front of the fire and settle in for a good read selected from the library. Homey and low-key, the nine guest rooms (two with shared bath) are large, white and airy with high ceilings and chenille bedspreads. A large yard with a garden surrounds the house, which sits well back from the road. Budget to moderate with shared bath; moderate with private bath.

The **Isaiah Clark House** (1187 Main Street, Brewster; 508-896-2223), an 18th-century sea captain's home, is surrounded by five acres of gardens, fruit trees and wild berry patches. Impeccably appointed with Shaker and colonial antiques, many of the guest rooms have stenciled walls, canopy beds, sloping pine floors and fireplaces. Breakfast is served in an appealing room with an enormous fireplace—guests linger here all morning long. Pre-dinner get-togethers and a full breakfast are included. Prices range from moderate to deluxe.

A large turn-of-century gray-and-white house, the **Old Sea Pines Inn** (2553 Main Street, Brewster; 508-896-6114) used to be a girls' school. The spacious public and 21 guest rooms are comfortably furnished with antique brown wicker, slip-covered chairs and sofas. A wraparound porch with rockers, perfect for reading or snoozing, overlooks a yard shaded by pine and oak trees. A full breakfast is served in a bright renovated dining area with many skylights. Budget to moderate.

You get a lot for your money at **The Poore House** (Route 6A, Brewster; 508-896-2094), one of the few bargains on Route 6A. A charming old inn with dark green shutters, the place offers bright and cheery guest rooms with painted floors and some antique furnishings. A full breakfast is served in a cozy living room. Behind the inn stands an attractive garden shop and nursery. Potted flowers and plants arranged along the stone driveway create a profusion of color. (Since you're saving so much money here, consider dining at Chillingsworth [see "North Cape Restaurants"], one of the Cape's most elegant and expensive restaurants. It's within walking distance.) Moderate in price.

OUTER CAPE HOTELS

If you want to capture the essence of Wellfleet, stay at the **Holden Inn** (★) (Wellfleet Bay; 508-349-3450), a long, white farmhouse-style lodging. There's nothing fancy about the place, but like Wellfleet, it has an easy, casual feeling. Located on a shady country lane five minutes from the wharf, the inn offers 27 well-kept guest rooms (some with shared bath) with ruffled white curtains and floral wallpaper or wood paneling. Moderate.

With its dark wood shingles, sky-blue shutters and nursery-rhyme garden, the **Bradford Gardens Inn** (★) (178 Bradford Street, Provincetown; 508-487-1616) looks like an illustration from a Mother Goose book. One of the most inviting cottages in Provincetown, the Bradford has 11 guest rooms and apartments, many with working fireplaces. An apartment on the side of the house with its own entrance has a sitting room, Franklin stove and garden view. A full breakfast is served by the cozy fireplace. Deluxe to ultra-deluxe.

The **Asheton House** (3 Cook Street, Provincetown; 508-487-9966) makes an elegant first impression. A beautiful, curved two-sided stairway leads to the front door of this pristine white 1840 house surrounded by brick paths and an English boxwood garden. The seven guest rooms and one apartment are all decorated differently. The handsome Captains room (shared bath) has a four-poster bed, neutral color scheme and antiques. The Safari room is quite spacious, although its jungle print wallpaper seems more 1966 than 1840. Budget to moderate for room with shared bath; moderate for private bath.

SOUTH CAPE HOTELS

A romantic, dark brown 1807 farmhouse, the **Nauset House Inn** (Beach Road, East Orleans; 508-255-2195) is within walking distance of beautiful beaches. One of the inn's most memorable features is a magnificent 1907 conservatory with white wicker furniture, exotic plants and grapevines. Each of the 14 guest rooms is individually decorated, and may feature tiny floral-print wallpaper, stenciling and antiques such as a hand-painted Victorian cottage bed. Guest rooms in the main house share baths; those in an adjacent carriage house have private baths. Moderate for shared bath; deluxe for private bath.

Chatham Bars Inn (Shore Road, Chatham; 800-527-4884), one of Cape Cod's most luxurious grand resorts, looks like the kind of place where everyone should be wearing white linen and playing croquet. Built in 1914 as a hunting lodge, the horseshoe-shaped gray-shingled inn sits high on a gentle hill overlooking Pleasant Bay. An expansive brick veranda runs the length of the inn. The inviting lobby is aswim with mauves, blues and greys and the adjoining lobby has white wicker chairs with chintz cushions, potted palms and shiny hardwood floors. The 44 guest rooms and 26 cottages are decorated in traditional Cape Cod decor, English pine antiques and wicker. The 80-acre resort has a private beach, heated swimming pool, tennis courts, fishing, sailing, windsurfing, golf and two restaurants. Ultra-deluxe; breakfast and dinner included.

Most of Chatham's hotels are expensive, but not the **Bow Roof House** (59 Queen Anne Road; 508-945-1346), a real bargain. Located in the heart of the high-rent district, five minutes from the beach, this cozy 200-year-old sea captain's house feels comfortable and casual. A patio overlooking a scenic, winding road makes an ideal spot for tea or cocktails in the afternoon. Guest rooms are appointed with colonial bedspreads and nondescript furniture, but they're far apart and private. Budget.

Motels aren't known for beautiful landscaping, but **Pleasant Bay Village Motel** (Route 28, Chatham Port; 508-945-1133) is a welcome exception. Located across from salt marsh, ponds and ocean, Pleasant Bay boasts impeccably maintained rock and flower gardens that are so lush you hardly notice the 58 nondescript guest rooms and apartments. Priced in the deluxe to ultra-deluxe range.

Accommodations in Harwich Port are limited and expensive, but **Harbor Walk** (★) (6 Freeman Street; 508-432-1675) is a refreshing exception. The white 1880 bed and breakfast with gingerbread trim is within walking distance of the town's exclusive beaches. Six guest rooms (two with shared bath) are decorated with a mix of new and antique furnishings. A porch runs the length of this house overlooking the yard. Budget to moderate.

Augustus Snow House (528 Main Street, Harwich Port; 508-430-0528) is one of the most beautiful inns in New England. Every inch of this magnificent Queen Anne Victorian is flawless. It's known for its fabulous wallpapers—some have ceiling borders of antique roses or clusters of fall flowers that look hand painted. Then there are the unbelievable bathrooms—one has an antique Victorian mahogany sink, another a black-and-white diamond tile floor and claw-footed tub. The dazzling public rooms are appointed with thick oak and mahogany paneling, moreen drapes, etched-glass french doors and period antiques. Located in a quiet, affluent town, the inn has five guest rooms and serves a full breakfast. Ultra-deluxe.

Route 28 from Dennis Port to Hyannis is dotted with one indistinguishable motel after another. However, if you head south toward the beach you'll find some nice surprises, like **The Lighthouse Inn** (★) (Lighthouse Road, West Dennis; 508-398-2244). This sprawling, 61-room, Old World resort is remarkably affordable for Cape Cod. Located on the ocean, the inn is formed around a lighthouse that stood at nearby Bass River during the 19th century. The ambience is friendly and unpretentious. Activities include shuffleboard, horseshoes, miniature golf, hiking in nearby woods, swimming in the pool or ocean and nightly entertainment. A children's director provides day and evening babysitting. Guest rooms in the main inn are simply furnished, and separate cottages are also available. Deluxe to ultra-deluxe.

Located in elegant Hyannis Port, the **Simmons Homestead Inn** (288 Scudder Avenue; 508-778-4999) was once a country estate. Built in 1820, this gracious inn is furnished with quality antiques, canopy beds, white wicker and brass. Sweeping porches overlook gardens leading down to Simmons Pond. Unlike those in most old inns, the ten guest rooms here are fairly large. Deluxe to ultra-deluxe.

Tucked away on a tree-lined street in elegant Centerville is **The Inn at Fernbrook** (★) (481 Main Street; 508-775-4334), a large, graceful Victorian with wraparound porches, gables and turrets. The understated decor doesn't compete with the dramatic house. The six guest rooms and cottage are beautiful and unusual. The Spellman Room, named after Cardinal Francis Spellman, a former owner of the house, has a pyramid-shaped ceiling, stained-glass windows, tiled fireplace and enormous Victorian canopy bed. Not surprisingly, it resembles a church. For all its grandeur, there's something serene and unaffected about Fernbrook. It's a good place for collecting one's thoughts. Deluxe to ultra-deluxe.

Horizons Inn (★) (2 Wyoming Avenue, Falmouth Heights; 508-548-3619) is in a magical little neighborhood of turn-of-the-century, dairy-barn-shaped houses with turrets, gables and gingerbread. Hidden from tourists, the inn sits on a bluff overlooking the ocean. Its craftsman-style public rooms have dark oak paneling and bookshelves. Four comfortable guest rooms are simply furnished. Moderate.

The **Village Green Inn** (40 West Main Street, Falmouth; 508-548-5621), a white clapboard house with green shutters and a picket fence, is typical of many of the homes in Falmouth's historic district. Guest rooms are decorated with antiques; four of the five rooms come with fireplaces. One room has impressive wood inlay floors, another a sitting area. Moderate to deluxe.

In 1849 Captain Albert Nye built **Mostly Hall** (27 Main Street, Falmouth; 508-548-3786) for his New Orleans bride, who refused to live in a traditional Cape Cod house. Typical of houses in New Orleans' garden district, this striking, raised Greek Revival mansion has ten-foot windows, louvered shutters, a wraparound veranda, wrought-iron fence and a 35-foot center hall—which is why it's called Mostly Hall. Only steps away from Falmouth's historic village green, this elegant inn is set well back from the road and hidden from view by trees and bushes. The six guest rooms are spacious and airy, furnished with antiques, including four-poster beds. Full breakfast included. Deluxe.

MARTHA'S VINEYARD HOTELS

Upon entering the **Captain Dexter House** (100 Main Street, Vineyard Haven; 508-693-6564), you are greeted by the inviting aroma of cinnamon, cloves and warm bread. This meticulously restored 1843 white clapboard inn has sloping wood floors, Oriental rugs, fireplaces and many antiques. It's luxurious but not pretentious. The eight guest rooms are appointed with contemporary furnishings, colonial antiques and period reproduction wallpaper. Some rooms have fireplaces and four-poster beds with lace canopies. A very warm and friendly place. Deluxe to ultra-deluxe.

A classic 1918 craftsman-style bungalow, **Thorncroft Inn** (★) (278 Main Street, Vineyard Haven; 508-693-3333) is on a quiet, tree-lined residential street. There's nothing very craftsman-like about the decor, which leans towards country Victorian. Some of the 12 guest rooms on the main property have working fireplaces and four-poster lace-canopy beds. One of the best things about Thorncroft is its enormous breakfast of buttermilk pancakes, bacon, french toast, quiche, sausage-cheese pie and more. Priced in the ultra-deluxe range.

The **Oak House Inn** (Circuit and Pesquot avenues, Oak Bluffs; 508-693-4187), an oceanfront Victorian, features oak paneling throughout.

Many of the ten guest rooms are paneled entirely in wainscotting and furnished with brass beds and Oriental rugs. Continental breakfast is served in the dining room while afternoon tea is enjoyed on a sunny porch. Deluxe to ultra-deluxe.

With its elaborate windows and dormers, **The Victorian Inn** (24 South Water Street; 508-627-4784) looks formal from the outside, but it's an easygoing place located one block from Edgartown harbor. Guests enjoy the cool, private garden in the summer. The 14 guest rooms are sweet and tidy with canopy beds, floral wallpaper, antiques and some antique reproductions. Deluxe to ultra-deluxe.

The **Charlotte Inn** (South Summer Street, Edgartown; 508-627-4751) is one of the most elegant and luxurious inns in America. A sparkling white 1860 sea captain's house, it is nestled amid a profusion of flowers, lawns, wisteria and latticework. Guests check in at a gleaming English barrister's desk. Twenty-five meticulous guest rooms are appointed with fine English antiques, hand-painted china and equestrian prints. Suites, located in separate buildings, are quite extravagant—one has its own English cottage garden, another a bedroom balcony and palladium window. A continental breakfast is served in the inn's restaurant, L'Étoile, one of the finest dining establishments in New England and a favorite of Jackie Onassis. Ultra-deluxe.

The **Arbor** (222 Upper Main Street; 508-627-8137) is a quintessential New England cottage, fresh and white with a winsome vine-clad arbor, brick path and English garden. Located a couple of blocks from Edgartown's shopping district, the inn offers guest rooms simply but attractively appointed with antiques and fresh cut flowers. Continental breakfast is served in the old-fashioned formal parlor or in the garden. Moderate to deluxe.

One look at the **Captain R. Flander's House** (North Road, Chilmark; 508-645-3123) and you understand why it was featured in Martha Stewart's *Wedding Book*. The rambling, 18th-century farmhouse sits on a grassy knoll overlooking ancient stone walls, rolling meadows, grazing horses, a sparkling pond, ducks and woodlands. Chilmark is so peaceful and bucolic, it's no wonder the rich and famous have chosen to live here. The inn is simply furnished, but with scenery like this who needs decoration? Guest accommodations (some with shared bath) are comfortable and sparsely appointed with antiques and country-style furnishings. Moderate to deluxe.

Talk about off the beaten path. **Lambert's Cove Country Inn** (★) (Lambert's Cove Road, West Tisbury; 508-693-2298) is down a long country road deep in the woods. Surrounded by vine-covered stone walls, expansive lawns and apple orchards, the white clapboard inn is appointed with Shaker and colonial-style antiques. Some of the 15 guest rooms have private decks, and one has a greenhouse sitting room. Guests have access to Lambert's Cove Beach, one of the Vineyard's most beautiful private beaches. On Sunday an elaborate, festive brunch is served. Deluxe.

NANTUCKET HOTELS

Nantucket has an astonishing number of inns and bed and breakfasts, but perhaps the most well-known is the **Jared Coffin House** (29 Broad Street; 508-228-2400). Built in 1845 by wealthy shipowner Jared Coffin, it features guest and public rooms appointed with antiques, Oriental rugs, crystal chandeliers, period wallpaper, marble fireplaces and canopy beds. A busy, festive establishment, it feels like a big city hotel of the 19th-century. Sixty guest rooms span six different buildings. Deluxe to ultra-deluxe.

Right down the street from the Jared Coffin House is one of the island's few bargain spots, **The Nesbitt Inn** (21 Broad Street; 508-228-0156). The white Victorian was built in 1872 as an inn and has been operated by the Noblit family since 1914. Some of the original furniture still remains. One room has a wood-rimmed bath tub that accommodates two. There are 13 guest rooms, each with a sink and shared bath. The inn's front porch is a great place for people watching. Budget to moderate.

Anchor Inn (66 Centre Street; 508-228-0072), a narrow grey clapboard house with black shutters and window boxes, is typical of Nantucket's many bed and breakfasts. Old and quaint, with narrow halls and sloping wood floors, it offers 11 cozy guest rooms, some hidden under dormers and

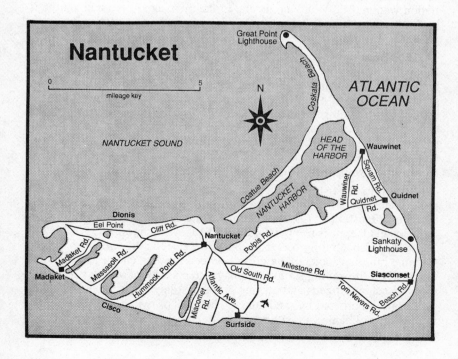

eaves in small irregular spaces. Once the home of the Gilbreth family of Frank Gilbreth's *Cheaper by the Dozen*, the Anchor is furnished with colonial and Shaker-style antiques. A continental breakfast is served in a cheerful blue-and-white breakfast room, and a brick patio in back overlooks scenic Old North Church. Moderate and deluxe.

The **Woodbox Inn** (29 Fair Street; 508-228-0587) is one of Nantucket's oldest and most delightful inns. Built in 1709, it exudes New England charm, with low-beamed ceilings, wood-paneled walls and walk-in fireplaces. The three guest rooms and six suites are furnished entirely in period antiques. Located in a quiet part of town away from all the hoopla, it has an excellent restaurant that can get a little noisy on weekends. Deluxe to ultra-deluxe.

The **Wauwinet** (Wauwinet Road; 508-228-0145), a lavish resort outside of town, is decorated to the hilt with country pine antiques, green wicker, primitive folk art, Victorian carpet runners, white wainscotting and pickled floors. The 35 guest rooms sport gentle sea breeze colors like pale smoke, sage and cream. Guests receive complimentary Crabtree and Evelyn toiletries. White wrought-iron furniture sits prim and proper on a vast lawn overlooking Nantucket Bay, and cushioned wicker furniture line a wrap-around porch. Guests are transported to and from town in a shuttle bus; you can also take a tour around town in an impeccably restored old woody station wagon. The Wauwinet is one of the most expensive inns on the island, attracting a well-heeled young crowd. There is a restaurant on the premises. Ultra-deluxe.

The **Summer House** (South Bluff, Siasconset; 508-257-9976), a rose-covered structure overlooking the ocean, is quintessential Nantucket, the kind of place you dream about but rarely find. Not surprisingly, it once graced the cover of *New York* magazine. Quaint little low-slung, vine-clad cottages surrounding the main house look as though they were designed by and for elves. But they're much bigger and lighter than they seem, and the decor blends just the right mix of rustic country charm. Rooms have features such as a fireplace, jacuzzi, rough-hewn beams, painted wood floor and rosebud wallpaper. There's a lively restaurant. Ultra-deluxe.

If you haven't stayed in a youth hostel since you gave up your backpack, you might want to try it again when you see Nantucket's **Star of the Sea Youth Hostel** (★) (for reservations, write or call American Youth Hostels, Hostel Operators Dept., P.O. Box 37613, Washington, DC 20013; 202-783-6161). Located across from Surfside Beach, this historic wooden A-frame building looks like a cross between a Swiss chalet and a church. Originally a life-saving station, it today attracts a lot of young people, Europeans, senior citizens and cycling groups. Volleyball is played in a large yard in back bordered by sand dunes. The rows of twin beds inside remind most people of camp. As with most youth hostels, Star of the Sea is closed to guests during the day. Budget.

SOUTH COAST HOTELS

Plymouth has an abundance of very ordinary motels that attract families and tour groups. Accommodations are limited throughout the rest of the South Coast, but there is a sprinkling of hidden bed and breakfasts that are quite special.

For a romantic getaway, 15 minutes north of Plymouth, try the **Windsor House Inn** (★) (390 Washington Street, Duxbury; 617-934-0991). This graceful old inn stands on a street lined with houses listed on the National Register of Historic Places, and it's next to a classic white-steepled church. Down the street are a few elegant little shops, a French bakery and small wharf. Windsor House has two tastefully decorated guest rooms and a beautiful suite with pale blue wood-paneled walls and blue-and-white stenciling. All rooms are furnished with Shaker and colonial-style antiques. A dark, cozy restaurant on the ground floor looks like an old seafaring tavern. Moderate to deluxe.

Route 3A in Plymouth is lined with indistinguishable motels, but the **Cold Spring Motel** (188 Court Street; 508-746-2222) is one of the most attractive. The 40-year-old, reasonably priced motel is in pristine condition and beautifully landscaped. In the summer thick yellow marigolds border brick paths leading to the guest rooms. These are spacious and simply appointed with standard-issue motel furniture. Moderate.

The **John Carver Inn** (25 Summer Street, Plymouth; 508-746-7100), a large, imposing, colonial-style hotel, attracts tour groups and gets very crowded in the summer. But it's in the most scenic part of Plymouth, across the street from a row of 17th-century historic homes and a beautiful grist mill. Seventy guest rooms are decorated in soft shades of beige and colonial-style reproduction antiques. A full-service hotel, it has a restaurant, lounge and pool. Moderate to deluxe.

The **Melville House** (★) (100 Madison Street, New Bedford; 508-990-1566) stands on a historic street lined with stately Federal and Victorian mansions built by 19th-century sea captains. The 1855 Italian Empire house was once owned by Herman Melville's sister, and he often stayed here. A spacious inn, it has lofty ceilings, wide halls and sweeping stairways. Tastefully decorated with soft, subtle colors and antiques, the three guest rooms are quite large and some have working marble fireplaces. Two rooms share a bath, but guests often have it to themselves in this little-known place. A full-course breakfast is served in an elegant solarium. Moderate.

If you want solitude and natural beauty, try **The Allen House** (★) (Cuttyhunk; 508-996-9292), the only inn on Cuttyhunk Island. Cuttyhunk—remote, unpretentious, noncommercial—has no shopping, nightlife, tennis or golf, and practically no cars or bicycles. Allen House, a plain Jane sort of place with limited services, reflects the island's no-frills atmosphere. It's perfect if you like long, quiet walks along uncrowded shoreline. The inn serves meals in a glassed-in porch with ocean views. Twelve rooms in the main house share baths, and two cottages are available. Moderate.

A 1760 brown-shingle bed and breakfast, **The Edgewater** (★) (2 Oxford Street, Fairhaven; 508-997-5512) is so close to the water you'd swear you were on a boat when you look out the window. The inn seems miles away from civilization, yet it's only a five-minute drive from New Bedford's historic wharf district. A perfect spot for romance, the handsome house has soft taupe walls and crisp white arched moldings. The blue-and-white Captain's Suite, the best room in the house, has a sitting room and spectacular views. The other four guest rooms are attractive and comfortable. All are appointed with contemporary and antique furnishings. Moderate.

Salt Marsh Farm (★) (322 Smith Neck Road; 508-992-0980), a 200-plus-year-old farmhouse, is in the heart of pastoral South Dartmouth. A perfect retreat for nature buffs, the house is on a 90-acre preserve with trails leading through hay fields, woods and wetlands. Only 15 minutes from New Bedford, Salt Marsh Farm feels like another world and time. The floors are uneven, the doorways low and the rooms small, but it has comfortable, home-spun charm. Sunny guest rooms are furnished with antiques, and breakfast is served in an attractive dining room with a beautiful old fireplace. Moderate.

Restaurants

If you love seafood, you'll be in heaven on the Massachusetts coast. The majority of restaurants serve it fried or butter-drenched, but with a little effort you can find grilled items. Prices depend on location. Nantucket and Martha's Vineyard are as expensive as New York City, but the rest of the coast is fairly reasonable.

NORTH SHORE RESTAURANTS

Rockport has the majority of restaurants on the North Shore, but few are outstanding. Restaurants with a steady local clientele in nearby towns are generally better.

Rockport is a dry town, thanks to Hannah Jumper, a temperance supporter. In 1856 after a raucous Fourth of July celebration, Hannah convinced town fathers to outlaw liquor. Even today you can't buy it in a store or order it in a restaurant. But you can buy liquor in Gloucester, which is only ten minutes away, and bring it to any Rockport restaurant.

King's Rook (★) (12 State Street, Marblehead; 617-631-9838), a romantic café and wine bar, serves many varieties of hot chocolate, coffee, tea, imported beer and ale, wine, sherry, apéritifs and champagne. Also available are light entrées such as pesto turkey sandwiches, pâté, cheese, sausage, soup and salad. The restaurant's low-beamed ceiling, soft peach walls, lace café curtains, candlelight and classical music create an intimate atmosphere favored by couples. Budget.

The **Driftwood Restaurant** (63 Front Street, Marblehead; 617-631-1145) is something of an institution. Homey, friendly and colorful, it attracts fishermen in the wee hours (it opens at 5:30 a.m.) and young professionals late on weekend mornings. The fare is traditional and plentiful: ham and eggs, pancakes, fried dough, clam chowder, burgers, fried seafood. The interior of this modest little establishment is plain and simple with red-and-white checked tablecloths. Tables are jammed close together, and there's a counter. Breakfast and lunch only. Budget.

If you want to do it up right, try **Rosalie's** (18 Sewall Street, Marblehead; 617-631-5353) for imaginative Northern Italian cuisine. Frequently reviewed by *Boston* magazine, this well-known restaurant is housed in a former brick box factory. Elegant and eclectic looking, the three-story restaurant also offers cooking classes. The menu is short and good: lobster ravioli, chowder with fennel and red pepper, swordfish with pesto sauce, veal chop. Deluxe.

A good spot for a casual lunch or dinner, **Tammany Hall** (★) (208 Derby Street, Salem; 508-745-8755) is favored by locals and not as touristy as the restaurants at nearby Pickering Wharf. Complementing the restaurant's political theme, two benches sit in front of the building—one for Republicans and one for Democrats. The cozy wood and brass restaurant serves hamburgers, ribs, sandwiches and entrées with names like Henry Cabot Scrod. Moderate.

The **Rudder** (★) (73 Rocky Neck Avenue, Gloucester; 508-283-7967), an eclectic waterfront restaurant, is so popular Bostonians drive here just for dinner. The decor features a crazy mix of memorabilia collected by owner Evie Parsons, including hundreds of menus from around the world tacked to the low-beamed ceiling. Eyeglasses left here by Judy Garland are displayed in a glass jewelry box. The atmosphere can't be beat, and the food is good too, offering a little bit of everything—pasta, fried clams, steak, escargot. Two of the best dishes are flounder stuffed with spinach soufflé covered with hollandaise sauce and succulent leg of lamb for two. On Saturday nights the place gets jumping to live piano music and after-dinner sing-alongs. Moderate to deluxe.

The North Shore has two first-rate gourmet delis perfect for unforgettable picnics. **Grange Gourmet** (★) (457 Washington Street, Gloucester; 508-283-2639) and **Bruni's** (★) (24 Essex Road, Route 133, Ipswich; 508-356-4877) offer items such as leek soup, cucumber soup, homemade salsa and chips, tortellini primavera salad, chicken salad with green grapes and almonds, big, healthy sandwiches, gourmet desserts and baked goods. You can also pick up different types of coffee and tea, natural sodas and more.

The **Greenery** (15 Dock Square, Rockport; 508-546-9593), located near the entrance to Bearskin Neck, has sandwiches, a salad bar, bakery goods and desserts to go. The back dining room facing the harbor serves all these dishes plus entrées such as pesto pizza, lobster, crab quiche and seafood casserole. The restaurant is appointed with blond wood, brass light fixtures and touches of green throughout. Moderate to deluxe.

Portside Chowder House (14 Bearskin Neck, Rockport) is a good place for a cup of chowder on a cold, blustery day. Cozy and tiny, the dark wood restaurant has low-beamed ceilings, a fireplace and Windsor chairs. Specialties include New England and corn chowder, grilled sausage, crab and chicken. Budget to moderate.

Like many Rockport restaurants, the **Sea Level Café** (14 Bearskin Neck; 508-546-2180) serves classic entrées—baked, stuffed jumbo shrimp, linguine with clam sauce, lobster sauté—but it prepares the food with more care than most of the competition. Sit at the upper-level dining room overlooking the harbor. A roaring fire adds to the romantic atmosphere of this eatery. Moderate.

Downhome and fun, **Woodman's** (Route 133, Essex; 508-768-6451) hasn't changed anything except the prices since it opened in 1914. This roadside institution claims to have created the fried clam. The menu includes steamers, lobster, clam cakes, scallops and corn on the cob. Sit inside at old wooden booths or outside at picnic tables in back. There's a raw bar upstairs and a full liquor bar downstairs. Locals like to come here after a day at nearby Crane's Beach. Budget to moderate.

Tom Shea's (122 Main Street, Route 133, Essex; 508-768-6931) is a fine quality seafood restaurant with large picture windows overlooking Essex River—a great spot for watching the sunset. The wooden interior gives the restaurant an understated, nautical look. The fare is traditional—baked stuffed lobster, fried clams, stuffed sole, grilled teriyaki shrimp, pasta, Cajun dishes plus some beef and chicken dishes. Moderate to deluxe.

Chipper's River Café (★) (Choate Bridge, Ipswich; 508-356-7956) is great for casual fare in an idyllic setting overlooking Choate River. Tucked behind the Choate River Bar, the restaurant has a sign that's small and easy to miss. Chipper's imaginative, health-conscious menu, tile floors, natural wood, art prints and juke box make it look and feel like a California restaurant. In the summer you can sit outside overlooking the river and quaint bridge. Dishes include chargrilled mustard lemon chicken, and changing pasta dishes. Next to the restaurant is Chipper's Bakery, a good source for picnic fare. Budget to moderate.

Chamber music, candlelight, gold gilt mirrors and mismatched antiques give **Scandia** (25 State Street, Newburyport; 508-462-6271) a romantic look. The menu changes with the seasons and the chef's whims. Entrées might include veal and lobster sauté with sweet butter, scallop chowder or seafood sausage—a very popular item. The homemade salad dressings are excellent—fennel herb, maple curry, tomato cheddar and more. Reservations a must. Moderate to deluxe.

Fowle's Restaurant (17 State Street, Newburyport; 508-465-0141) is a nostalgic, 1930s-style soda fountain and tobacco stand. It hasn't changed anything over the years except the menu, which includes everything from granola blueberry pancakes and bagels to homemade stews, chowder, enormous avocado, bacon and sprout sandwiches, malts, sundaes and sodas. Budget.

CAPE COD RESTAURANTS

Restaurants on the Cape fall into three categories: expensive French/nouvelle cuisine, surf and turf and coffee-shop fare. If you crave variety, head for the Outer Cape. Wellfleet has a surprising number of excellent, imaginative restaurants. And Provincetown restaurants serve everything from Italian, French, vegetarian and continental to nouvelle, meat-and-potatoes and bistro-style fare.

THE NORTH CAPE

The **Daniel Webster Inn** (149 Main Street, Sandwich; 508-888-3622) is so colonial looking, you expect it to serve traditional New England fare, but the menu is rather diversified. Lunch includes chicken pot pie, pizza, lobster cakes, sandwiches and salads. Dinner entrées range from veal Oscar, baked scrod and filet mignon to changing specials such as baked swordfish rolled with shrimp and basil stuffing, grilled salmon with rosemary-sherry butter and roast quail over wild rice. Meals are served in a formal dining room with peach walls, mahogany chairs and brass chandeliers or in a greenhouse room overlooking a garden. Breakfast is also available. Moderate to deluxe.

Barnstable Tavern (3176 Main Street, Barnstable; 508-362-2355) serves traditional lunch and dinner fare such as steak au poivre, mussels marinara, shrimp scampi, pasta and spinach salad. Located in a small complex of shops, the restaurant creates a pleasant country-style feeling with Windsor chairs, folk art, brass light fixtures and blond wood floors. The friendly bar is a good place for a drink, and different varieties of wine are served by the glass. Moderate to deluxe.

The food's hearty and predictable, the service fast and friendly at **Marshside Restaurant** (★) (28 Bridge Street, East Dennis; 508-385-4010), a glorified coffee shop popular with locals. Omelettes, bagels, pancakes and french toast are some of the breakfast offerings. Lunch items include lobster salad, quesadillas and fried clams. At dinner it's fried clams, stuffed shrimp, steak, chicken picatta and daily specials. The decor is kitchen-cute with fake Tiffany lamps, bentwood chairs and ruffled curtains. The back room has a spectacular view of a salt marsh meadow. Moderate.

Cozy little **Margarite's Restaurant** (★) (Route 6A, Dennis; 508-385-3279) is a perfect spot for sinfully good desserts and a cappuccino, as well as breakfast, lunch and dinner. Located in a small, colonial-style shopping complex, it resembles a country tea room with ruffled curtains, cranberry tablecloths and an antique wood-burning stove. The traditional menu features quiche, french toast and eggs for breakfast; sandwiches, salads and chowder for lunch; prime rib, stuffed shrimp, veal marsala and pasta for dinner. Desserts change daily. One popular offering is the Hot Fudge Pie. A cross between chocolate fudge and cake, it's very thick, gooey and good. Moderate to deluxe.

Gina's By The Sea (★) (134 Taunton Avenue, Dennis; 508-385-3213), a sweet little white-shingled restaurant within walking distance of Chapin Beach, is far more sophisticated than it looks. The predominately Italian menu changes daily and includes entrées like mussel soup, grilled Muscovy duck and red snapper with champagne sauce. Ruffled curtains, white tablecloths and plain wooden chairs create a casual formality. Moderate to deluxe.

You might find yourself sitting near a well-known actor at the **Playhouse Restaurant** (Route 6A, Dennis; 508-385-8000), located on the grounds of the Cape Playhouse. Banks of windows on three sides of the attractive peach-colored restaurant overlook sweeping lawns and flower gardens. The continental menu includes a host of fish, chicken and steak dishes. Budget to moderate.

Cranberry Moose (Route 6A, Yarmouthport; 508-362-3501) serves new American cuisine in an 18th-century Cape Cod cottage on one of the prettiest stretches of historic Route 6A. A good spot for a special lunch or dinner, the restaurant has an imaginative, seasonally changing menu. Dishes have included seafood terrine, game salad with sage-pine nut vinaigrette and bouillabaisse with fennel, saffron, pernod and orange zest. Cozy yet sophisticated, it has a number of small dining rooms with low ceilings, Windsor chairs and white tablecloths. Deluxe.

With its blond-wood floors, green tablecloths, small library and New Age music, the **Brewster Fish House Restaurant** (★) (Route 6A, Brewster; 508-896-7867) feels more like a café than a fish house. Its small, creative menu features dishes such as chilled grilled scallops with an herb vinaigrette, salmon stuffed with sole mousse and calamari with aioli. Moderate.

Elegant and expensive, **Chillingsworth** (Route 6A, Brewster; 508-896-3640) has been repeatedly praised by the *New York Times* and *Esquire*. The menu changes daily, utilizing seasonal and fresh ingredients. The food is strictly nouvelle, with dishes such as loin of veal with sun-dried tomatoes, risotto and sage, and free-range chicken with greens, chili brown sauce and sweet potato chips. Located in a 300-year-old, tree-shaded colonial house, the restaurant has dining areas combining modern and traditional decorative touches such as contemporary artwork, antique mirrors and white tablecloths. Lunch and brunch are served in the greenhouse and garden. After lunch, browse in the restaurant's antique and pastry shop. The seven-course dinner is served at two seatings, and reservations are mandatory. Ultra-deluxe.

The **Bramble Inn** (Route 6A, Brewster; 508-896-7644) is one of those restaurants people always rave about. Housed in a Greek Revival farmhouse on scenic Route 6A, the place offers a prix-fixe menu that changes daily.

Dinner is served in four small dining rooms complete with Queen Anne chairs, fresh flowers, antiques and china blue walls. Innovative dishes have included grilled seafood in curry sauce, smoked bluefish pâté, and rack of lamb with garlic and rosemary. Ultra-deluxe.

THE OUTER CAPE

The **Bayside Lobster Hutt** (Commercial Street, Wellfleet; 508-349-6333), a noisy, friendly place, is perfect after a day at the beach. Located on a country road leading to Wellfleet's galleries and wharf, it looks like an old white schoolhouse. On the roof, a fisherman statue hauls an enormous red lobster into a boat. Everyone sits at long tables covered with red-and-white-checked oil tablecloths. Buoys and fish nets decorate the walls. The menu features lobster, flounder, steamed clams, scallops and shrimp. There's a raw bar and a take-out window where you can order clambake picnics. Moderate to deluxe.

A combination art gallery and restaurant, **Cielo** (East Main Street, Wellfleet; 508-349-2108) has all the warmth and charm of a European café, plus a five-course, fixed-price dinner. It's located in a 100-year-old saltbox overlooking salt marsh and ponds. The menu combines French and ethnic cooking and includes daily specials such as plum soup, cold Szechuan soy noodles with shrimp, salmon mousse and pork with sausage stuffing. The candle-lit dinner is served in the living room and gallery, appointed with antiques and contemporary art. Reservations a must. Ultra-deluxe.

The **Lighthouse** (Main Street; 508-349-3681) is a Wellfleet institution. If you want to mingle with the locals, come here in the morning for breakfast. The ambience is strictly coffee shop, as is the food, which includes french toast, bacon and eggs, fried seafood, sandwiches, hamburgers and the like. Located in the center of town, it has a kitschy miniature lighthouse on its roof that is impossible to miss. Moderate.

Sweet Seasons (The Inn at Ducke Creeke, Main Street, Wellfleet; 508-349-6535) is an exceptionally pretty restaurant overlooking an idyllic duck pond surrounded by rushes, flagstone paths, locust trees and woods. The pale gray and apricot restaurant serves dishes such as grilled swordfish, shrimp with feta cheese, tomatoes and ouzo, loin lamb chops with mint pesto and roast duckling. Deluxe.

The **Red Inn** (15 Commercial Street, Provincetown; 508-487-0050) is so close to the water, you can't see any land below the large picture windows that run the length of the restaurant. Built in 1805, the red-and-white inn serves traditional American fare, with a sprinkling of newer dishes—roast duckling, filet mignon, balsamic grilled chicken on a warm bed of spinach and lobster sautéed then vodka flambéed and served over fettucine. The bouillabaisse is a favorite. The beautiful bar has a magnificent old fireplace, antique chairs and large-paned windows with expansive views of the ocean. Moderate to deluxe.

Ciro & Sal's (4 Kiley Court; 508-487-0049) is one of Provincetown's most legendary restaurants. Established in 1951 as a coffeehouse for artists, it grew into a full-fledged restaurant serving classic Italian food. In 1959 Sal left and opened his own restaurant (described below). Dripping with atmosphere, the basement dining room resembles an Italian wine cellar with a low ceiling, slate floor and candle-lit tables. An upstairs dining room overlooks a garden. Popular dishes include linguine with seafood in a plum tomato sauce, poached bass with clams and veal tenderloin with mozzarella and prosciutto. Tasty Italian bread is baked on the premises. Moderate to deluxe.

Sal's Place (99 Commercial Street, Provincetown; 508-487-1279) is cozy, dark, intimate and arty. In this seaside cottage with Italian ambience, Chianti bottles hang from the low-beamed ceiling, bay windows are draped with lace curtains and a Modigliani poster adorns a wall. The menu includes 12 kinds of pasta, veal dishes and inventive seafood entrées such as squid stuffed with pine nuts, flounder and shellfish. Moderate.

With its maroon, lavender and blue swirl cloths, peach walls and casablanca ceiling fans, **Gallerani's Café** (133 Commercial Street, Provincetown; 508-487-4433) attracts locals and out-of-towners alike. The prices are a bargain, the food is down to earth and so is the crowd. The room is bright and airy, and the long bar in back is a pleasant place for a drink. Open for breakfast, lunch and dinner, Gallerani's serves dishes such as fruit- and sausage-filled pancakes, homemade granola, chicken pot pie and marinated grilled shrimp. Moderate.

Café Heaven (199 Commercial Street, Provincetown; 508-487-9639) is located on a part of Commercial Street away from the touristy hoopla. Housed in an old storefront with large picture windows, the restaurant is bright and uncluttered, with white wooden tables and pale grey carpeting. A colorful mural by nationally known artist John Grillo adorns one wall. The food is hearty and all American—bacon and eggs, Portuguese french toast, omelettes, tasty scones, lusty sandwiches on thick slabs of bread and salads such as chicken tarragon. This popular hangout for gays and lesbians is open for breakfast, lunch and dinner. Budget.

THE SOUTH CAPE

The Mad Hatter might have enjoyed **The Arbor** (Route 28 and 6A, Orleans; 508-255-4847). Fanciful and eclectic, it has a front yard filled with goofy junk—a bear riding a bicycle, a big wagon wheel. The inside is a hodgepodge of antique clutter—old bottles, vintage photos, tinware, colored pitchers. Tables are set with mismatched china. Somehow it all comes together in a magical way. The menu is as varied as the decor. Many dishes are elaborate and rich—saltimbocca, veal marsala, sweetbread with ham and mushroom caps. Behind the restaurant, the Binnacle Tavern (508-255-7901) is a cozy spot for a drink and light entrées. Moderate to deluxe.

Kadee's Lobster and Clam Bar (Beach Road, Orleans; 508-255-6184) is a colorful, inexpensive sea shanty draped with lobster traps and buoys. The menu includes steamers, lobster, corn-on-the-cob, kale soup and chowder. An outdoor patio shaded by umbrellas is the perfect spot for beer and fried clams after a day at the beach. Budget to moderate.

On their days off, chefs from the Cape's most noted restaurants often dine at **Nauset Beach Club** (★) (222 Main Street, East Orleans; 508-255-8547), on the road to beautiful Nauset Beach. The small grey-shingled restaurant, with indoor and outdoor dining, offers consistently good, reasonably priced Northern Italian fare such as saltimbocca, caesar salad, veal scallopine, a wide range of seafood dishes such as gnocchi and scallops, grilled shrimp scampi and a host of creative pasta dishes. Moderate.

The **Impudent Oyster** (15 Chatham Bars Avenue, Chatham; 508-945-3545) is the place to go for traditional or exotic seafood in an informal setting next to a park. The lunch and dinner menus change with the seasons. Many of the dishes have Chinese, Mexican or Vietnamese ingredients—mussels with sake, ginger and Szechuan peppers; or shrimp, Chinese noodles and vegetables in a Hunan sauce. There are also excellent non-seafood items, such as the grilled duck breast, sun-dried tomato tortellini and wild mushrooms tossed with an orange cognac butter sauce. The cheerful restaurant has skylights, a cathedral ceiling and stained-glass panels. Moderate to deluxe.

In historic Chatham village, **Christian's** (443 Main Street; 508-945-3362) draws an attractive tennis and yachting crowd. The bar does as much business as the two restaurants. A formal dining room on the ground floor, appointed with Oriental rugs, dark wood floors and lace tablecloths, serves dishes such as codfish with champagne hollandaise sauce, seafood sauté, veal chops, and boneless split duck. An informal, wood-paneled restaurant and bar on the second floor serve pasta, quiche, hamburgers and sandwiches. Deluxe downstairs; budget to moderate upstairs.

Very pretty and very French, **Café Elizabeth** (31 Sea Street, Harwich Port; 508-432-1147) bills itself as a French classic restaurant, but the sophisticated food, flawless service, hushed atmosphere and prices feel more big-city than country quaint. Housed in a former sea captain's home, the restaurant has small, intimate dining rooms with lace curtains and linen tablecloths in soft shades of blue and cream. Specialties of the house include lobster, veal, lamb and beef medallions with different sauces, chicken curry and shrimp sautéed in cognac. The desserts are truly memorable. Try the chocolate truffles laced with Grand Marnier, whipped cream and chocolate sauce. Deluxe to ultra-deluxe.

The **Cape Half House** (★) (Route 28, West Harwich; 508-432-1964) looks like just another surf-and-turf restaurant, but the food is surprisingly inventive and reasonably priced. Dishes range from grilled salmon with balsamic vinaigrette and filet mignon with green peppercorn sauce to fisherman's stew and crab cakes. Diners sit in captains chairs at wood tables, and the rough wood walls are adorned with antique tools. Moderate.

It looks like something out of a Popeye cartoon. Half of **The Lobster Boat** (681 Main Street, West Yarmouth; 508-775-0486) is a grey-shingled Cape Cod cottage with cheerful red window boxes, and the other half is an enormous red, white and blue lobster boat that seems to have grown out of the restaurant's side. The dining room overlooks a small harbor, and the decor is very yo-ho-ho with captains chairs, dark wood and rope. The atmosphere is free and easy, with lobster prices to match, plus a traditional menu featuring a variety of fried, sautéed and broiled seafood. Moderate to deluxe.

Penguins Go Pasta (331 Main Street, Hyannis; 508-775-2023) sounds casual, but it's a formal restaurant serving traditional and nouvelle Italian cuisine such as roasted peppers and eggplant, tricolored pasta, braised rabbit with polenta and osso bucco. Exposed brick walls, potted palms, burgundy tablecloths and waiters in black tie contribute to the sophisticated ambience. Moderate to deluxe.

An attractive, reasonably priced nouvelle Italian restaurant, **The Hot Tomato** (Route 28, Mashpee; 508-477-8100) is in Mashpee Commons, an upscale outdoor mall that resembles an old-fashioned Cape Cod village. The clapboard restaurant has lofty ceilings, cream-colored walls, honey-warm wood and terra cotta floors. Fare includes thin-crusted focaccia pizza, pasta, grilled swordfish with basil butter, and veal chop with marsala and rosemary. A take-out counter sells desserts, pasta, salads, sandwiches and espresso. Moderate.

Set in an 18th-century, red-and-white inn on the edge of a duck pond, the **Coonamesset Inn** (Jones Road and Gifford Street, Falmouth; 508-548-2300) serves seafood Newburg, oysters on the half shell, quahog chowder, Indian pudding and other classic New England dishes. The Cahoon Room, one of three dining rooms serving breakfast, lunch and dinner, features primitive paintings by artist Ralph Cahoon depicting life on Cape Cod. The inn and restaurant are tastefully decorated with Shaker and colonial furnishings. Moderate to deluxe.

Located on a winding country road, **Peach Tree Circle** (★) (Old Palmer Avenue, Falmouth; 508-548-2354) is the perfect place for lunch on a lazy summer day. A combination restaurant, farm stand, gourmet health food store and bakery, it is shaded by large graceful trees. Fresh flowers and vegetables are sold in front of the small grey building with nasturtiums climbing its walls. Lunch offerings include big, healthy sandwiches, quiche, chowder, chef salad, fruit and cheese. Budget.

Locals come to **Fishmonger's Café** (56 Water Street; 508-548-9148) because it isn't as touristy as some other Woods Hole restaurants. The café serves California food—avocado tostada, tabouli, garden vegetable salad—

and Cape Cod classics like fried clams, grilled fish and chowder. The atmosphere is casual, the decor salty dog. Paned windows overlook the harbor, and there's a counter where you can have lunch or a beer while you're waiting for the ferry. Budget to moderate.

MARTHA'S VINEYARD RESTAURANTS

Only Edgartown and Oak Bluffs serve liquor, but you can bring your own when you dine in other towns.

A grey-shingled saltbox overlooking the harbor, rustic **Black Dog Tavern** (Beach Street Extension, Vineyard Haven; 508-693-9223) is a Vineyard institution popular with the yachting crowd. The best place to sit in the summer is an enclosed porch with beautiful ocean views. The fare is traditional—clams casino, codfish, roast duckling—with an emphasis on fresh seafood. Deluxe.

Café at the Tisbury Inn (Main Street, Vineyard Haven; 508-693-3416), a trendy establishment with cream-colored walls, deco light fixtures, Southwestern mountainscape mural and grey industrial carpeting, attracts a young, stylish crowd. The menu includes grilled meat, poultry and seafood with different sauces such as Creole or rémoulade. Other dishes include lime chicken pasta pesto, seafood enchiladas and pastas. An awning-covered outdoor patio in front is a good spot for people watching in the summer. Moderate to deluxe.

Popular with locals, **Linden Tree Café** (★) (Main Street, Vineyard Haven; 508-693-4480) looks like a coffee shop with old wooden booths and a long counter, but it serves one of the best budget dinners on the Vineyard. The changing traditional menu includes dishes such as stuffed sole, seafood lasagna, roast beef and more. Budget to moderate.

Papa's Pizza (158 Circuit Avenue, Oak Bluffs; 508-693-1400) isn't your average pizza parlor. This place has class. Located in a bright red, white and green storefront, it has an enormous dining room with a tin ceiling and walls, antique brass light fixtures and long wooden tables. The counter in back is solid granite—an elegant touch. Papa's serves lasagna, pizza, pasta and subs. The portions are healthy and hearty. Budget.

A high-profile watering hole and restaurant that resembles a French bistro, **The Oyster Bar** (162 Circuit Avenue, Oak Bluffs; 508-693-3300) attracts a chic, festive crowd. The green-and-yellow facade has rows of french doors that open to a cavernous dining room with tin ceilings, marbleized columns and an impressive 35-foot mahogany bar. People come here for oysters and champagne or a full meal. The menu includes dishes such as seafood pizza, wild smoked Scottish salmon appetizer and many grilled, sautéed and baked seafood and non-seafood dishes such as veal loin. Deluxe to ultra-deluxe.

With its salmon-colored walls, chintz banquettes and flower-bordered wallpaper, **Martha's Restaurant** (71 Main Street, Edgartown; 508-627-

8316) is bright and feminine. Across the street from Edgartown's town hall, it serves seafood pasta, lamb, duck, chicken and steak dishes. There's even a sushi bar. At lunch, the restaurant attracts hordes of tourists; it's better to come for dinner. Moderate to deluxe.

L'Étoile (27 South Summer Street, Edgartown; 508-627-5187), in the Charlotte Inn, is perfect for a special occasion. An incredibly beautiful restaurant, it's in a 19th-century conservatory with skylights, bowed windows, a brick floor and lush plants adorned with twinkling Italian lights. In this romantic, fantasylike environment, contemporary French cuisine is served. The prix-fixe menu offers fresh game and seafood entrées. Sauces are light and aromatic, flavored with fresh herbs, exotic fruit, shiitake mushrooms and shallots. Ultra-deluxe.

Even if you're not knocked out the by the surf-and-turf menu (steak, salad, lobster, etc.) at **Home Port** (Basin Road, Chilmark; 508-645-2679), come here for the mesmerizing view. The rustic, brown-shingled restaurant overlooks sand dunes, rolling green pastures and idyllic Menemsha harbor. An outdoor patio is available for summer dining. Deluxe.

Small, exclusive **Beach Plum Inn** (North Road, Menemsha; 508-645-9454) is easy to miss. A tiny sign points the way down a dirt road to a building without a sign that looks like a private home with a terraced rock and flower garden. Once you've figured out where to go, you'll be glad you came. The intimate dining room has large picture windows overlooking Menemsha Harbor, a white grand piano and subtle mauve and green decorative touches. Diners have a choice of five prix-fixe dinner entrées that must be ordered in advance when making reservations. The cuisine features items such as steamed lobster, duck with honey-curry sauce and rack of lamb. Ultra-deluxe.

NANTUCKET RESTAURANTS

Among Nantucket's astonishing number of sophisticated restaurants, one of the best is **Le Languedoc** (24 Broad Street; 508-228-2552). Elegant and hushed, it has taupe walls, contemporary art and dark carpeting that are strictly big-city, yet its navy-and-white checked tablecloths and Windsor chairs add a touch of French country. The menu includes poached halibut, black peppered salmon and rack of lamb with a honey-mustard sauce. A lot of care goes into the presentation. Deluxe.

American Seasons (★) (80 Centre Street; 508-228-0397) serves American country specialties such as pan-fried sweetbreads with ragoût of wild mushrooms, pan-fried tuna with alligator fritters and red chili sauce, steak with bourbon gravy and straw potatoes. The restaurant is in a white cottage with window boxes spilling lush pink impatiens. The green-and-white interior is romantically lit with hurricane lamps, and New Age music plays softly in the background. The crowd is young, happy and casual. Moderate to deluxe.

People stand in line for **The Brotherhood** (23 Broad Street) because it serves reasonably priced basics—burgers, sandwiches and fried fish—in an 1840 whaling bar with a low ceiling, brick walls and weathered wooden tables. The Brotherhood is one of the few restaurants that serves until 12:30 a.m. Budget.

The Atlantic Café (South Water Street; 508-228-0570) is on a street that should be called Hamburger Row. Every restaurant on this block serves the same thing—burgers, beer and rock-and-roll. You can smell the fried food before you get here. In the day, the restaurant attracts families with small children, but at night it gets the college crowd. The Atlantic is a clean-looking establishment with white walls, wood beams and a bar in the middle surrounded by wooden chairs and tables. Moderate.

Espresso Café (40 Main Street; 508-228-6930) is good for a cappuccino and a designer brownie, picnic fixings or a casual lunch or dinner. It looks like an old-fashioned ice cream parlor with paddle fans, black-and-white tile floor, tin ceiling and a tree-shaded brick patio is out in back. The food is trendy and hearty—cassoulet, soup, chili, pasta, thick pizza piled high with "yuppie" ingredients such as sun-dried tomatoes and goat cheese. Moderate.

One of Nantucket's most beautiful and versatile restaurants, the **Boarding House** (Federal and India streets; 508-228-9622) has a shady brick patio that's perfect for people watching and a lovely bar and café with floor-to-ceiling windows. (A woman could come to the bar alone and feel totally at ease.) A formal dinner is served in the cellar, a grottolike, candle-lit room with cream-colored arched walls. Dishes change with the seasons. Popular offerings, many served in both the café and dining room, include sautéed duck breast with apples, sage and maple sauce, ravioli and wild mushrooms, free-range chicken and oysters with balsamic vinegar. Moderate to deluxe.

Le Chanticleer (9 New Street, Siasconset; 508-257-6231) is one of New England's most romantic restaurants. In spring, the many-windowed, grey-shingled house is covered with climbing roses, and the garden is a riot of pink, white and lavender flowers. The menu features traditional French cuisine—foie gras, lobster soufflé, fresh figs in sweet white wine and herbs, trout with salmon mousse and lobster ginger sauce. Many locals prefer the restaurant for lunch; the prix-fixe dinner is a major production. Ultra-deluxe.

SOUTH COAST RESTAURANTS

The **Inn for All Seasons** (97 Warren Avenue, Plymouth; 508-746-8823) is a Victorian mansion set in a forested hilltop setting. Choose from one of four carpeted dining rooms brought up-to-date with contemporary furniture. Entrées include filet neptune, veal Oscar, fruits de la mer and chicken parmigiana. You may also want to sample the popular scallops wrapped in bacon or oysters Rockefeller. Chocoholics will definitely want to try the mousse cake. Moderate to deluxe.

Station One (51 Main Street, Plymouth; 508-746-1200) embodies 19th-century elegance. Located in a former fire station, the restaurant has a lovely brick sidewalk café and a cavernous, honey-colored, wood-paneled dining room with crystal, brass and handsome arched windows. The menu has something for everyone—lobster, prime rib, veal parmesan and grilled salmon. Moderate to deluxe.

A ramshackle brown-shingle restaurant a few miles north of Plymouth, **Persy's Place** (★) (117 Main Street, Route 3A, Kingston; 617-585-5464) claims to have "New England's largest breakfast menu," and that's no joke. The menu takes about an hour to read, but some of its offerings include fish cakes, buttermilk pancakes, chipped beef on toast, catfish and eggs, hickory-smoked bacon, raisin, corn, wheat and pumpernickel bread, finnan haddie, no-cholesterol eggs, waffles and much, much more. The restaurant looks like a cross between a coffee shop and a country general store. Breakfast and lunch only; budget.

Hidden and lovely **Crane Brook Tea Room** (★) (Tremont Street, South Carver; 508-866-3235) is a must if you're touring cranberry country. Located in a former iron foundry, the cozy, antiques-filled restaurant overlooks a pretty pond and is surrounded by woods, pastures and cranberry bogs. The restaurant started out serving only tea and pastries, but now it also offers lunch and dinner. A perfect place for a long, leisurely lunch, the Crane Brook has a changing menu of dishes such as grilled duck breast sandwich and imaginative salads for lunch; rack of lamb and spicy pork loin roast for dinner. Deluxe.

Candleworks (72 North Water Street, New Bedford; 508-992-1635) is housed in an 1810 granite candle factory half a block from New Bedford's major sights. During the week it attracts the town's white-collar lunch crowd. A pink, atriumlike room in front is appointed with wooden tables and Windsor chairs. The main dining room has a low-beamed ceiling and rich wood. The menu is continental with an emphasis on seafood and includes such specialties as fish filet stuffed with oysters in a béarnaise sauce. Moderate to deluxe.

There are many Portuguese restaurants in New Bedford, but one of the best is **Café Portugal** (★) (1280 Acushnet Avenue; 508-992-8216). A large, festive restaurant popular with Portuguese families, it features house specialties such as an enormous platter of succulent shrimp and marinated steak served with eggs on top. With its acoustical tile ceiling and plastic flower arrangements, Café Portugal looks a little bit like a banquet hall. Moderate.

A white clapboard building with bright blue awnings, **La Rivage** (★) (7 Water Street; 508-999-4505) overlooks the water in Padanaram, a chic yachting village within South Dartmouth. An outdoor deck with red umbrellas is a good spot for lunch in the summer. The elegant yet understated interior has large picture windows and white tablecloths. Lunch features dishes such as brochette of shrimp, scallops with fresh herbs, salmon with orange sauce and caesar salad. Dinner ranges from veal in madeira sauce to lamb chops with fresh thyme and endive and watercress salad. Deluxe.

Bridge Street Café (10-A Bridge Street, South Dartmouth; 508-994-7200) in the heart of Padanaram, attracts a young, well-dressed crowd. Clean and crisp, with slate floors and skylights, the café has an outdoor deck overlooking the town and harbor. Daily specials range from Creole-grilled swordfish, scallops and pesto pasta, to tuna and shrimp brochette and grilled sirloin. Specialties of the house are smoked brook trout and smoked eastern salmon served with capers and mustard sauce. Deluxe.

It may look like a coffee shop, but **Bayside** (★) (1253 Horseneck Road, Westport; 508-636-5882) serves classic clam-bar fare and other dishes such as chicken burrito and eggplant parmigiana. More "in" than it seems, the restaurant has a clientele ranging from construction workers, senior citizens and families to yuppies and arty types dressed entirely in black. Bayside overlooks rolling pastures, salt marsh, stone walls and the ocean. Budget to moderate.

Lizzie's (★) (122 Third Street; 508-672-7688) is in an 1894 brick office building in the heart of Fall River. Architectural buffs appreciate the authentic, impeccably restored interior, with dark green tin ceiling, paddle fans, brass light fixtures and wood paneling. Warm and inviting, Lizzie's serves hamburgers, pizza, quiche, sandwiches, salads and entrées such as broiled scrod, shrimp and steak dinners. The attractive bar is a good spot for a beer. Budget.

The Great Outdoors

The Sporting Life

Cape Cod, Martha's Vineyard and Nantucket offer a staggering number of opportunities for fishing, boating and other water sports, as well as cycling, golf, tennis and more. The North Shore and South Coast don't attract such vast numbers of sports-oriented tourists as the other areas; hence activities are limited and most golf and tennis clubs are private.

SPORTFISHING

Blue fish, striped bass, tuna, cod and flounder are abundant on the Massachusetts coast. No license is required to fish, and tackle shops are everywhere. For detailed information on what to catch when, where and how, call the Massachusetts Division of Marine Fisheries (100 Cambridge Street, Room 1901, Boston, MA 02202; 617-727-3193).

The North Shore has **Captain Bill's Deep Sea Fishing** (Roses Wharf, Gloucester; 508-283-6995) and **Hilton's Fishing Dock** (54-R Merrimac Street, Newburyport; 508-465-9885).

Among the hundreds of charter and party boat outfits on Cape Cod, some of the most reputable include **The Albatross** (Sesuit Harbor, East Dennis; 508-385-3244), **Naviator** (Wellfleet town pier; 508-349-6003) and **Teacher's Pet** (Hyannis Harbor; 508-362-4925).

Martha's Vineyard has **Larry's Tackle Shop** (25 Dock Street, Edgartown; 508-627-5088), and in Nantucket there's **Albacore** (Straight Wharf; 508-228-1439) and **Moonshadow Sportfishing** (Straight Wharf; 508-228-1512).

On the South Coast, try **Captain John Boats** (Town Wharf, Plymouth; 508-746-2643) for fishing and whale watching, and **Captain Leroy Inc.** (Route 6, on the Fairhaven Bridge, New Bedford; 508-992-8907) for charter and party boat excursions.

SAILING, SURFING AND WINDSURFING

Marblehead on the North Shore is sailboat country. **Coastal Sail School** (617-639-0553), the only rental outfit, has 24- to 30-foot boats and gives lessons.

Cape Cod abounds with marinas and harbors where you can rent sailboats, windsurfing equipment, canoes and more. Try these establishments: **Cape Water Sports** (Route 28, Harwich Port; 508-432-8407), **Cape Cod Boat Rentals** (Route 28, West Dennis; 508-394-9268), **Jack's Boat Rental** (Route 6, Wellfleet, 508-349-9808; Gull Pond, Wellfleet, 508-349-7553; and Nickerson State Park, Brewster, 508-896-8556) and **Flyer's Boat Rental** (131-A Commercial Street, Provincetown; 508-487-0898).

For sailboat rentals and lessons on Martha's Vineyard, there's **Wind's Up** (Beach Road, Vineyard Haven, 508-693-4252). **Laissez Faire** (Owen Park, Vineyard Haven; 508-693-1646) and **Ayuthia Charters** (Coastwise Wharf, Vineyard Haven; 508-693-7245) offer half-day and evening harbor sunset sails on beautiful wooden yachts. **Harborside Inn** (South Water and Main streets, Edgartown; 508-627-4321) rents small sailboats such as Boston Whalers.

In Nantucket, **Indian Summer Sports** (6 Steamboat Wharf; 508-228-3632) rents surfboards, windsurfing equipment, kayaks and body boards.

GOLF

Public golf courses are rare on the North Shore, but there is one beautiful municipal course surrounded by deep woods, the **Beverly Golf and Tennis Club** (134 McKay Street, Beverly; 508-927-5200).

Three of Cape Cod's most scenic public courses, among many, include **Ocean Edge** (Brewster; 508-896-5911), **Highland Golf Club** (Highland Road, Truro; 508-487-9201), right near the Cape Cod National Seashore, and **Harwich Port Golf Club** (Harwich Port; 508-432-0250).

On Martha's Vineyard **Mink Meadows Golf Course** (Franklin Street, Vineyard Haven; 508-693-0600) and **Farm Neck Golf Course** (County Road, Oak Bluffs; 508-693-2504) offer beautiful scenery.

Nantucket has **Maicomet Golf Club** (West Somerset Road; 508-228-9764) and **Siasconset Golf Club** (Milestone Road, Siasconset; 508-257-6596).

Golfing opportunities on the South Coast are limited. There aren't any public golf courses close to Plymouth, but about 30 minutes out of town are **Pembroke Country Club** (West Elm Street, Pembroke; 617-826-4994) and **Bay Point Country Club** (Onset Avenue, Onset; 508-759-8802).

Hilly **New Bedford Municipal Golf Course** (581 Hathaway Road, New Bedford; 508-996-9393) offers golfers a challenging course.

TENNIS

The best spot for tennis in the North Shore is the **Beverly Golf and Tennis Club** (134 McKay Street, Beverly; 508-927-5200). It has ten clay courts open to the public. A limited number of municipal courts are available throughout the North Shore towns.

Most Cape Cod towns have a number of municipal courts. For names and addresses in specific towns, call the **Cape Cod Chamber of Commerce** (508-362-3225). Two privately owned public courts include **Mid-Cape Racquet Club** (193 White's Path, South Yarmouth; 508-394-3511) and **Bissell Tennis Courts** (Bradford Street, Provincetown; 508-487-9512).

Tennis is very popular on Martha's Vineyard. Most courts are private, but one exception is the **Mattakesett Tennis Club** (270 Katama Road, Edgartown; 508-627-9506). Municipal courts are at Church Street in Vineyard Haven, Niantic Park in Oak Bluffs, Robinson Road in Edgartown, Old Country Road in West Tisbury and the Chilmark Community Center on South Road.

Nantucket's **Sea Cliff Tennis Club** (North Beach Street; 508-228-0030) has nine clay courts, and **Jetties Beach Public Tennis Courts** (North Beach Street; 508-325-5334) is right near town.

On the South Coast, municipal courts can be found in New Bedford's woodsy **Buttonwood Park** (Rockdale and Hawthorne avenues) and at **Hazelwood Park** (Brock Avenue), a city park with playgrounds. For park information, call the **City of New Bedford Parks Department** (508-991-6175).

WHALE WATCHING

The Massachusetts coast offers an enormous number of whale-watch excursions, some conducted by naturalists. On the North Shore, Gloucester is the gateway to whale watching. **Yankee Fleet** (75 Essex Avenue; 508-283-0313) is the oldest and largest whale-watch outfit, plus it offers charter and fishing party excursions. Also try **Cape Ann Whale Watch** (415 Main Street; 508-283-5110).

In Newburyport, there's **New England Whale Watch** (Hilton's Dock, Merrimac Street; 508-465-7165) and **Hilton's Fishing Dock** (54 Merrimac Street; 508-465-9885).

Among the many excursions departing from Cape Cod, try **Hyannis Whale Watcher Cruises** (Millway Marina, Barnstable Harbor, Hyannis; 508-775-1622) and **Dolphin Whale Watch** (MacMillan Wharf, Province-town; 508-255-3857).

On the South Coast, excursions depart from Plymouth harbor. Try **Captain John Boats** (Town Wharf; 508-746-2643) or **Cape Cod Cruises** (State Pier; 508-747-2400), which also goes to Provincetown.

CANOEING AND SEA KAYAKING

One of the most beautiful canoe trips in New England is along the North Shore's Ipswich River through the 3000-acre **Ipswich River Wildlife Sanctuary** (★) (Perkins Row, Topsfield; 508-887-9264). For canoe rentals contact **Foote Brothers Canoes** (356 Topsfield Road, Ipswich; 508-356-9771).

According to the folks at **Atlantic Sea Kayak Company** (1025 Main Street, 6A, West Barnstable; 508-362-6896), Cape Cod resident, author and kayak enthusiast Paul Theroux has been largely responsible for the growing popularity of this sport. Atlantic will direct you to the best spots such as Great Marsh Harbor.

South of New Bedford in Dartmouth are many rivers ideal for canoeing. The **Lloyd Center for Environmental Studies** (430 Potomska Road, South Dartmouth; 508-990-0505) organizes day-long canoe trips along beautiful nearby rivers, and **Bibeau's Boat Mart** (Route 6, North Dartmouth; 508-993-6120) rents canoes.

SKINDIVING

In Danvers, the brave and the bold bare the chilly waters with **Northeast Scuba** (125 Liberty Street; 508-777-3483), an outfit that teaches scuba diving, rents equipment and runs trips off the coast.

In Cape Cod rentals and instructions are available at **Cape Cod Diver's** (815 Main Street, Harwich Port; 508-432-9035) and **East Coast Divers** (237 Falmouth Street, Hyannis; 508-775-1185).

HORSEBACK RIDING

Liability insurance has gotten so high, most stables won't rent horses, but a few still do. On the Cape there's **Deer Meadow Riding Stable** (Route 137, East Harwich; 508-432-6580). Eastover Farm (West Tisbury–Edgartown Road, Martha's Vineyard; 508-693-3770) has trails along the beach and through the forest.

Chipaway Stables (600 Quanapoag Road, North Dartmouth; 508-763-5158), a mile north of New Bedford, has guided trail rides and hayrides through local woodlands.

ICE SAILING

Ice sailing is a tradition on Watuppa Pond in Fall River. This graceful sport takes tremendous skill and specially designed sailboats. Rentals aren't available, but it's fun to watch these lighter-than-air boats glide along the icy pond.

BICYCLING

Cape Cod, Martha's Vineyard and Nantucket are a cyclist's paradise. The flat landscape is laced with miles of smooth, paved bicycle paths that meander past sand dunes, salt marsh, woods and pastures. What follows is a modest sampling of some of the best rides. The North Shore and South Coast have limited bike riding areas, but a few choice spots are described below.

Short Bike Rides, by Edwin Mullen and Jane Griffith (Globe Pequot Press) is a handy little book that describes 31 bike rides on Cape Cod, Nantucket and Martha's Vineyard.

Cyclists in the North Shore area recommend riding along scenic **Route 127** between Beverly, Manchester and Magnolia. The tree-lined road dips and turns past seaside mansions and historic homes. It's cool and peaceful in the summer.

The **Cape Cod Rail Trail**, an eight-foot-wide bicycle path, runs along the old Penn Central Railroad tracks from Route 134 in South Dennis to Locust Road in Eastham past classic Cape Cod scenery—ponds, forest, saltwater and freshwater marsh, cranberry bogs and harbors.

Head of the Meadow, a moderately hilly bicycle path in the Cape Cod National Seashore in Truro, traverses some of the Cape's most dramatic scenery including The Highlands—vast expanses of grassy knolls. The 3.3-mile path starts at Head of the Meadow Road off Route 6 and ends at High Head Road.

Talk about dramatic scenery. The **Province Lands Trail** dips and turns past towering sand dunes, silvery mounds of wavy beach grass, two magnificent beaches and the Province Lands Visitors Center. The path starts at Herring Cove Beach parking lot at the end of Route 6 and includes many places where you can stop and picnic.

The **Shining Sea** bicycle path between Falmouth and Woods Hole is popular with experienced cyclists because it's hilly in some areas and very scenic. The 3.3-mile path runs along Palmer Avenue in Falmouth, then down a hill past deep woods and historic homes, and it ends at Woods Hole harbor.

The **Oak Bluffs–Edgartown–Katama Beach** bike path on Martha's Vineyard is smooth and easy, even though it's ten miles long. Departing from Oak Bluffs, the flat path runs along the shore past lovely old homes, beaches, ponds and salt marsh to historic Edgartown, then through heathland dotted with occasional houses to magnificent Katama Beach.

From Vineyard Haven, the hale and hearty bicycle to **Menemsha** and **Gay Head** via State Road to West Tisbury, then Middle Road to the end. The ride is hilly in parts, but the scenery is breathtaking. The beaches in this area have residents-only parking lots, so bicycling is the only way a nonresident can enjoy them.

Bicycling on Nantucket is a snap. Smooth, flat bike paths parallel the island's two main roads. The five-mile **Madaket** bicycle path is the most scenic, dipping and winding past moors and ending at Madaket Beach, the western tip of the island. The seven-mile **Siasconset** path is a straight, flat line that goes past barren scrub pine and sandy scenery, ending at the village of Siasconset on the eastern end of the island.

The **Westport** and **Dartmouth** area on the South Coast doesn't have many cars, and the flat country roads wind past elegant horse farms, pastures and ocean. From Route 195, take exit 12 and head south to Chase or Tucker Road. At this point it doesn't matter which road you take; they're all lovely, and as long as you head south you'll wind up at the beach.

BIKE RENTALS   On the North Shore you can rent bikes at **Seaside Cycle** (23 Elm Street, Manchester; 508-526-1200).

Practically every town on Cape Cod has a couple of bicycle rental shops; try **The Little Capistrano Bike Shop** (Route 6, Eastham; 508-255-6515), **Arnold's** (329 Commercial Street, Provincetown; 508-487-0844), **The Outdoor Shop** (50 Long Pond Drive, South Yarmouth; 508-394-3819) or **Holiday Cycles** (465 Grand Avenue, Falmouth Heights; 508-540-3549).

Rentals in Martha's Vineyard include: **Anderson's Bike Rentals** (14 Saco Avenue, Oak Bluffs; 508-693-9346) and **R. W. Cutler Bike** (Edgartown; 508-627-4052).

Nantucket's wharf has many bicycle rental shops; one of the biggest outfits is **Young's Bicycle Shop** (6 Broad Street, Steamboat Wharf; 508-228-1151).

On the South Coast, try **Sumner R. Crosby** (484 Russell Mills Road, South Dartmouth; 508-992-2176) and **Yesteryear Cyclery** (330 Hathaway Road, New Bedford; 508-993-2525).

Beaches and Parks

The water may be a little brisk even in summer, but nothing stops people from flocking to Massachusetts' spectacular beaches. Shore fishing for blue fish and striped bass is excellent and permitted without a license on all beaches.

The coast is laced with fields of salt marsh, forest and sand dunes. Many of these natural areas are state parks and wildlife sanctuaries that offer a quiet escape from summer crowds.

NORTH SHORE BEACHES AND PARKS

Devereux Beach—On the causeway leading to scenic Marblehead Neck, Devereux is a small, clean beach. There's a lot to see here. The affluent town lies immediately behind the beach on a hill, while across the street lies a windsurfing cove and busy Marblehead harbor. Devereux is popular with families and teens, yet, unlike most North Shore beaches, it isn't always packed on summer weekends.

Facilities: Picnic areas, restrooms, playground, lifeguard, bike rack, snack bar; groceries five minutes away in Marblehead. *Fishing:* Excellent. *Swimming:* Good, but it can get rough.

Getting there: Located on Ocean Avenue, to the south of Marblehead harbor.

Salem Willows (★)—Don't be thrown off by the tawdry-looking Chinese take-out joints and arcade you see when you enter the parking lot. Salem Willows holds some pleasant surprises, including a nostalgic old park overlooking Salem Sound that is shaded with graceful willow trees planted in 1801 to provide a protected area for smallpox victims. Next to the park is a small beach. People come here to stroll in the park, admire the view, fish and rent rowboats. Locals swear by the popcorn and chop suey sandwiches sold in the parking lot.

Facilities: Picnic areas, restrooms, lifeguards, snack bar, rowboat rentals; groceries ten minutes away in downtown Salem. *Fishing:* Excellent from shore and a short pier. *Swimming:* A little rough.

Getting there: Located at the end of Derby Street in Salem.

Singing Beach—This jewel of a beach, only a quarter mile long, has pristine sand that literally squeaks underfoot. Hidden away in a lovely affluent neighborhood, the beach is surrounded by steep cliffs and spectacular mansions. The crowd matches the conservative neighborhood—blond and preppy. The changing rooms and parking lot are for residents only, and parking in the immediate area is impossible. But that doesn't keep out-of-towners away. Bostonians like this beach so much, they take the commuter train to Manchester, then walk one long, sweaty mile to the shore.

Facilities: Restrooms, lifeguard, snack bar; groceries a mile away in town. *Fishing:* Excellent. *Swimming:* Good.

Getting there: Located at the end of Beach Street in Manchester.

Good Harbor Beach—Located in a spectacular natural setting outside of Gloucester, this sweeping, half-mile beach is all ocean, sand dunes, marsh grass and big sky. A small shrub-covered island, positioned between two rocky headlands and accessible at low tide, is fun to explore. The beach is raked clean every day in the summer.

Facilities: Restrooms, showers, lifeguard, snack bar; groceries ten minutes away in Gloucester. *Fishing:* Excellent. *Swimming:* Good but a little rough.

Getting there: Located on Thatcher Road in East Gloucester.

Wingaersheek Beach (★)—This gentle, sloping, fine sand beach on Ipswich Bay is surrounded by rocks, tall marsh grass and homey summer cottages hidden in the woods. There are also tidepools to explore. The beach is quite close to downtown Gloucester and Rockport, but it feels as though it's far out in the country. Families with young children frequent this beach because it has good climbing rocks that aren't too slippery.

Facilities: Restrooms, showers, lifeguards, snack bar; groceries 15 miles away in Gloucester. *Swimming:* Calm.

Getting there: Located on Atlantic Street in West Gloucester.

Rockport Beaches—Rockport has two small beaches right in the heart of town. **Front Beach**, a favorite with small children, is sandwiched between Bearskin Neck, Rockport's main tourist area, and a grassy bluff. A parallel sidewalk gives everyone in town a perfect view of the beach. **Back Beach**, on the other side of the small bluff, is much more private. Bordered by Beach Road and houses, it's popular with a 15-and-up crowd.

Facilities: Restrooms, lifeguards on Front Beach, snack bar. *Swimming:* Calm.

Getting there: Both beaches are located on Beach Street immediately northwest of downtown Rockport.

Halibut Point State Park (★)—This wild and rugged 54-acre ocean-front park, formerly the site of a granite quarry, has one of the most spectacular views on the North Shore. A path goes past the old quarry down a gentle incline to a vast, treeless plain of scrub thicket and wildflowers overlooking the ocean. The stark, rugged shoreline has tidepools and smooth granite rocks large enough for a group of people to picnic on.

Facilities: Restrooms, walking trails, guided tours; groceries nearby in Rockport; information, 508-546-2997. *Fishing:* Excellent. *Swimming:* Permitted, but not recommended because the shore is covered with big, slippery rocks.

Getting there: Located three miles north of Rockport on Route 127.

The Cox Reservation (★)—Formerly the home of famed muralist Allyn Cox, this 31-acre salt marsh farmland is now headquarters for the Essex County Greenbelt Association. Peaceful and pastoral, it has paths leading through gardens of perennials and roses, salt marsh, woods, orchards and open farmland down to winding Essex River. Artists come here in the late afternoon when the river and graceful marsh grass are bathed in a soft golden light, creating a dreamlike environment. It's easy to see why a muralist lived in this romantic and private place.

Facilities: None; groceries nearby in Essex; for information, call 508-768-7241.

Getting there: Located off Route 133 in Essex.

Crane's Beach Memorial Reservation—This massive, four-mile, dune-backed beach is surrounded by over 1000 acres of salt marsh farmland, shrub thicket and woods. In the off-season, the wide beach seems to go on forever. In the summer it's wall-to-wall people. Nature and beachgoers coexist peacefully, however. At certain times of the year, sections of the beach are fenced off to protect nesting birds. A boardwalk leading to the beach protects sand dunes and marsh grass.

Facilities: Restrooms, showers, lifeguards, snack bar; groceries nearby in Ipswich; information, 508-356-4354. *Fishing:* Excellent. *Swimming:* Good.

Getting there: Located on Argilla Road in Ipswich.

Parker River National Wildlife Refuge—This magnificent oceanfront wildlife refuge on Plum Island is only about ten minutes from downtown Newburyport, but it feels very far away from civilization. One-third of Plum Island is covered with ramshackle summer beach houses; the rest is the refuge—4662 acres of bogs, tidal marshes, sand dunes and beach. A boardwalk leads to the beach, and a trail meanders throughout the refuge. The abundant wildlife includes seals, geese, ducks, deer, rabbits and over 300 species of birds. Parker River is dearly loved by Newburyport residents. On a sunny day in the dead of winter, they can be seen strolling with their dogs along the shore looking for snowy owls.

Facilities: Restrooms; information, 508-465-5753. *Fishing:* Excellent winter smelt fishing. *Swimming:* Strong undertow.

Getting there: Located on Plum Island in Newburyport.

CAPE COD BEACHES AND PARKS

Formed 12,000 years ago from an enormous glacier that left in its wake a unique and magical landscape of sand dunes, moors, salt marsh and 300 miles of shoreline, the Cape has a staggering number of utterly beautiful beaches and natural parks from which to choose. What follows are some of the best. Shore fishing is popular all along the coast, but according to locals it's best at Nauset, South Cape and Provincetown beaches.

NORTH CAPE BEACHES AND PARKS

North Cape beaches are on protected Cape Cod Bay. They tend to be quiet and calm, with gentle surf and scenic vistas of soft sand dunes and salt marsh.

Sandy Neck Beach and the **Great Marshes**—This area has all the ecological treasures for which the Cape is known. Very straight and long, beautiful Sandy Neck Beach offers a 360° view of the ocean and rippling sand dunes bordered by the Great Marshes, 3000 acres of protected land harboring many species of marine life and birds. The sand is ideal for beach-combing, and trails meander through the dunes and marsh.

Facilities: Restrooms, snack bar; groceries a short drive away in Sandwich. *Swimming:* Calm.

Getting there: Take Sandy Neck Road off Route 6A in Sandwich.

Grey's Beach—This small, quiet beach is perfect for children. But the main reason people come here is to stroll along the long, elevated walkway stretching across the marsh that skirts the beach. The walkway permits a close-up view of marsh flora and fauna, and from a distance it appears to be floating in grassy water. There's not much to do here, but this area is quite beautiful, especially at sunset.

Facilities: Picnic tables, playground, restrooms, lifeguards; groceries nearby in Yarmouth. *Swimming:* Calm.

Getting there: Located off Route 6A on Centre Street in Yarmouth.

Chapin Beach—The sand-strewn road leading to Chapin Beach passes gentle sand dunes and small, unpretentious, summer cottages. A pleasant spot for walks along the shore, the thin, slightly curved, dune-backed beach has soft, white sand ideal for clean, comfortable sunbathing.

Facilities: Restrooms; groceries are found nearby in Dennis. *Swimming:* Calm.

Getting there: Off Route 6A on Chapin Beach Road in Dennis.

Paine's Creek Beach (★)—There are better beaches nearby for sun-ning and swimming, but Paine's Creek is ideal for quiet walks through time-less scenery bathed in golden light. Weatherbeaten skiffs are moored along the shore, and Paine's Creek, a gentle slip of a stream, winds through a salt marsh meadow down to a narrow strip of soft beach surrounded by tiny coves and inlets.

Facilities: None; groceries nearby in West Brewster. *Swimming:* Calm.

Getting there: Located off Route 6A on Paine's Creek Road in West Brewster.

Nickerson State Park—This 2000-acre park looks more like the Berk-shires than Cape Cod. Dense pine groves, meadows and jewel-like fresh-water ponds with beaches are home to abundant wildlife including red foxes and white-tailed deer. There is so much to do here—hiking, biking, motor boating, canoeing—it gets very crowded in the summer. Quiet beaches and hiking trails can be found around Little Cliff and Flax ponds. In winter there's cross-country skiing and ice-skating on the ponds.

Facilities: Picnic areas, restrooms, showers, ranger station, interpre-tive programs; groceries a short drive away in Brewster; information: 508-896-3491. *Camping:* Permitted in 420 sites on a first come, first served basis. *Fishing:* Excellent at Higgins Pond, which is stocked annually with trout. *Swimming:* In freshwater ponds.

Getting there: Located off Route 6A in Brewster.

OUTER CAPE BEACHES AND PARKS

First Encounter Beach—This is where the Pilgrims first encountered the Wampanoag Indians, who were not exactly happy to see them. Six years earlier an English slave dealer had kidnapped some of them to sell in Spain. When the Pilgrims arrived a mild skirmish broke out, but no one was hurt and the Pilgrims made a hasty retreat. Sandy paths lead through dense green grass to this striking beach bordered by a vast marsh meadow and brilliant sky. The long, wide beach attracts a relatively quiet crowd in the summer.

Facilities: Restrooms, groceries a short drive away in Eastham. *Swimming:* Calm.

Getting there: Take Samoset Road off Route 6 in Eastham.

The Cape Cod National Seashore—This 27,000-acre ecological wonderland includes endless stretches of unbelievably beautiful beaches, 60-foot sand dunes, steep cliffs, wind-bitten moors, salt marsh, freshwater ponds and woodlands. Undisturbed and undeveloped, the area runs from Chatham to Provincetown and is laced with some of the Cape's finest hiking and bicycle trails (see the "Bicycling" and "Hiking" sections in this chapter).

What follows are some of the National Seashore's most renowned beaches and ponds. For more information visit the **Salt Pond Visitor Center** (Route 6, Eastham; 508-255-3421) or the **Cape Cod National Seashore Headquarters** (Route 6, South Wellfleet; 508-349-3785).

Coast Guard Beach—"On its solitary dune my house faced the four walls of the world," wrote Henry Beston of the place he built in 1927 on this extraordinary beach. In 1972 the house washed away in a storm, but Beston's experiences are chronicled in a wonderful book, *The Outermost House*, available at most Cape Cod bookstores. Rugged and wild Coast Guard Beach goes on for as far as the eye can see. Bordered by cliffs, marsh grass and tributaries, a red-and-white coast guard station sits on a bluff overlooking the beach. The beach is ideal for long walks, sunbathing, swimming and surfing.

Facilities: Restrooms, lifeguards; groceries nearby in Eastham. *Swimming:* Good, but can be rough at times. *Surfing:* Good; waves break at high tide.

Getting there: Take Doane Road off Route 6 near Eastham.

Nauset Light Beach and **Marconi Beach**—These impressive beaches —bordered by towering, shrub-covered cliffs—are right next to each other. Long, steep wooden stairways descend to the clean, white sand beaches. The imposing cliffs and expansive vistas make you feel very small and in awe of it all. Walk north along the shore for a quiet spot in the summer, when the beaches get crowded. On the road to Nauset Beach is **Nauset Light,** a classic red-and-white lighthouse, one of the most photographed sights on Cape Cod.

Facilities: Restrooms, showers (at Marconi only), lifeguards; groceries in Eastham or Wellfleet. *Swimming:* Excellent, but watch undertow.

Getting there: Nauset Light is located off Route 6 at the end of Cable Road and along Nauset Light Beach Road in Eastham. Marconi is located off Route 6 on Marconi Beach Road in Wellfleet.

Great Pond and **Long Pond** (★)—Wellfleet has some of the most idyllic freshwater ponds on the Cape. Less than a mile from wild-looking shoreline, these two offer a completely different nature experience. Densely wooded and pine-scented, they look like mountain ponds. The sparkling water is fresh and invigorating. Long Pond has a lovely shaded grassy area with picnic tables, a small sand beach and a float in the water. Great Pond is approached via wooden steps leading down from the parking lot overlooking the pond. It has a pretty sandy beach. Half-hidden houses lie along some of the shoreline.

Facilities: Picnic tables; groceries are found nearby in Wellfleet. *Swimming:* Calm.

Getting there: To reach Great Pond, take Calhoon Hollow Road off Route 6 in Wellfleet; for Long Pond, take Long Pond Road off East Main Street in Wellfleet.

Race Point Beach and **Herring Cove Beach**—"Here a man may stand, and put all America behind him," wrote Thoreau in his book *Cape Cod.* Located at the end of the Cape, both beaches have magnificent 360° views of brilliant sky, ocean, dunes and a silver sea of beach grass. On cloudy days, the winds shift, the colors change and a minimalist environment unfolds. When the sun shines, everything shimmers. Both beaches offer long stretches of clean white sand surrounded by acres of untouched land. Bicycle paths and hiking trails are everywhere.

Facilities: Restrooms, showers, lifeguards, snack bar (Herring Cove only); groceries nearby in Provincetown. *Swimming:* Good.

Getting there: To reach Race Point, take Race Point Road off Route 6 in Provincetown; for Herring Cove, take Province Land Road in Provincetown.

SOUTH CAPE BEACHES AND PARKS

South Cape beaches are usually big and wide with huge parking lots and ample facilities. Located in residential neighborhoods, they're popular with college students and families. Because this is the ocean side of the Cape, the water tends to be rougher than on the North Cape.

Hardings Beach—Big, straight and long, this popular beach attracts a gregarious crowd of kids. Expensive houses on a hill overlook Hardings, a spot good for swimming, sunning and hanging out with the neighbors.

Modest little sand dunes with paths running through them lead down to the beach.

Facilities: Restrooms, showers, lifeguards, snack bar; groceries nearby in Chatham. *Swimming:* Good.

Getting there: Take Barn Hill Road off Route 28 to Hardings Beach Road in Chatham.

West Dennis Beach—The view at the end of this sprawling beach, where the Bass River empties into the Atlantic, is of old summer houses with green lawns spilling down toward docks dotted with boats. There's even a windmill. West Dennis Beach attracts big summer crowds; its parking lot can accommodate 1600 cars. Popular with surfers, families and teens, the beach is bordered by flat salt marsh laced with tributaries from the river.

Facilities: Restrooms, showers, lifeguards, swings, snack bar; groceries nearby in Dennis. *Swimming:* Good.

Getting there: Take School Street off Route 28 to Lighthouse Road in West Dennis.

Ashumet Holly Reservation and Wildlife Sanctuary (★)—A treat for birdwatchers and botany enthusiasts, this 45-acre reserve abounds with many varieties of holly grown by the late Wilfred Wheeler, who donated the land to the Audubon Society. You're definitely out in the wilds here, and nothing looks manicured or fussed over. An easy-to-maneuver trail goes past a pond, forest, dogwoods, rhododendrons and a grove of Franklinia, an unusual, fall flowering shrub discovered in Georgia in 1790. Wildlife includes catbirds, so named because they make a meowing sound, belted kingfishers and pond critters such as ribbon snakes, catfish and turtles with bright yellow heads and dark shells. Since 1935, a barn on the property has been a nesting site for swallows. Every spring up to 44 pairs arrive to nest, then depart in late summer.

Facilities: None; groceries are found nearby in Mashpee; information, 508-563-6390.

Getting there: Located at 286 Ashumet Road in East Falmouth.

Old Silver Beach—This spot, popular with a college-aged crowd and locals, doesn't look like a typical Cape Cod beach. A large, modern resort is on the north end, and most of the beach houses in the immediate area are fairly new. A lovely cove to the south is protected by wooded cliffs jutting down to the shore. The beach itself is somewhat rocky.

Facilities: Restrooms, showers, lifeguards, snack bar; groceries nearby in Falmouth. *Swimming:* Calm; lessons are available.

Getting there: Located off Route 28A on Quaker Road in Falmouth.

MARTHA'S VINEYARD BEACHES AND PARKS

Beaches in rural West Tisbury, Chilmark and Gay Head are dramatic, untamed and less crowded than beaches near the Vineyard's three towns.

But the parking lots are for residents only, and in the summer guards check to see if cars have resident stickers. Nonresidents ride bikes to these beaches. Shore fishing is excellent from all south shore beaches.

Nantucket Sound Beaches—Strung together along protected Nantucket Sound are Oak Bluffs Town Beach, Joseph A. Sylvia State Beach, Bend-in-the-Road Beach and Lighthouse Beach. This is where the movie *Jaws* was filmed, but don't panic, this isn't shark country. The narrow, gently curved shoreline has clean sand and calm water. Swimming lessons are offered at some of the beaches, and bicycle paths run alongside the shore, which is bordered by ponds, salt marsh and summer homes. A stately lighthouse overlooks Lighthouse Beach.

Facilities: Lifeguards; groceries in Oak Bluffs or Edgartown. *Swimming:* Calm.

Getting there: Located along Beach Road between Oak Bluffs and Edgartown.

Cape Pogue Wildlife Refuge and **Wasque Reservation** (★)—If you want to get away from it all, take the two-minute car and passenger ferry from Edgartown to these wilderness areas on Chappaquiddick Island, an undeveloped peninsula of vast, empty beaches and moors. The refuge and reservation are adjacent to each other and form the northeastern tip of the Vineyard. Both offer an assortment of low dunes, ponds, tidal flats and cedar thickets. Wildlife abounds, including noisy least terns, piping plovers, common terns and American oystercatchers. East Beach, part of the Cape Pogue Wildlife Refuge, is the best spot for swimming.

Facilities: None; closest groceries in Edgartown; information, 508-693-3453. *Fishing:* East Beach is great for blue fish. *Swimming:* Good at East Beach, but sometimes rough.

Getting there: Cape Pogue is located at the end of Chappaquiddick Road on the other side of Dyke Bridge. The bridge is closed now and access to Cape Pogue is limited to four-wheel drive vehicles with permits. Wasque Point is located at the end of Wasque Road.

South Beach—Also called Katama Beach, this popular, three-mile-long, Atlantic-facing beach is ideal for swimming and body surfing. Wide, expansive and flat, it is surrounded by heath dotted with 20th-century homes —a rare sight in Martha's Vineyard. In the summer the air is soft and warm from southeasterly winds.

Facilities: Lifeguards; groceries two miles away in Edgartown. *Fishing:* Excellent. *Swimming:* Excellent, but watch undertow.

Getting there: Located off Katama Road, south of Edgartown.

Manuel Correleus State Forest—Right in the center of the Vineyard lie 3900 acres of towering evergreens, scrubland, ponds and streams. Laced with bicycle paths, as well as hiking trails carpeted with soft, thick pine needles, the cool, hushed forest offers a peaceful respite from the Vineyard's wind-bitten moors and wide-open beaches.

Facilities: None; groceries in Edgartown or West Tisbury.

Getting there: Located between West Tisbury and Edgartown off Airport Road.

Long Point Wildlife Refuge (★)—A never-ending, loosen-your-teeth dirt road is the only way to get to this mystical, magical wildlife refuge. The road forks here and there; just stay on the widest part and eventually you come to a small parking lot (seasonal parking with a fee). Shortly beyond lies an endless grass and huckleberry-covered heath that looks like a prairie with two enormous ponds. Tisbury Great Pond and Long Cove are home to black ducks, bluebills, ospreys, canvasbacks and swans. Beyond the ponds you'll discover a sea of silver beach grass and a white sand beach.

Facilities: None; groceries 15 minutes away in West Tisbury. *Fishing:* Excellent. *Swimming:* Good, but can get rough.

Getting there: This place is very difficult to find. It's one mile west of Martha's Vineyard Airport off Edgartown-West Tisbury Road on Deep Bottom Road, a deeply rutted dirt road without a sign. It's best to ask locals for directions.

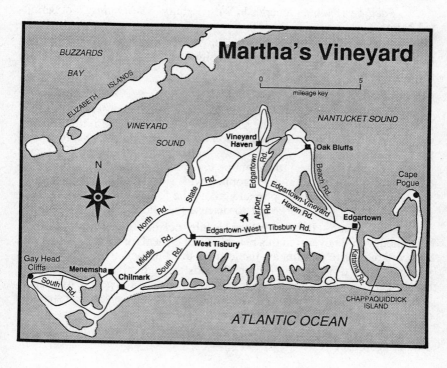

Moshup Beach—Adjacent to the multi-colored Gay Head Clay Cliffs, a national landmark off-limits to the public, this 7.4-acre, flat, sandy beach is extremely popular during the summer. Moshup is great for sunning, swimming and beachcombing, but be cautious of the surf. Although it is illegal, nude swimming is popular here. It costs $10 to park at the lot behind the dunes. You may be better off taking the Up Island Shuttle Bus that runs in the summer.

Facilities: Restrooms, snack bars, groceries at top of cliffs. *Fishing:* Excellent. *Swimming:* Good, but can be a little rough.

Getting there: Located at the western tip of the Vineyard at the end of State Road, which is also called South Road in Gay Head.

Cedar Tree Neck Sanctuary (★)—The raucous chirping of king fishers, song sparrows and Carolina wrens is the first thing to greet you at this 300-acre preserve. This is their kingdom, and what a spectacular place it is. Follow one of two well-marked paths through hilly woods of beech, sassafras, red maple, hickory oak and bettlebung. Soon the sky opens up, and, out of nowhere, extraordinary vistas appear of deep ponds, rolling sand dunes and the ocean beyond. Paths lined with ferns, moss and mushrooms lead down through the woods to an elevated catwalk and the shore. Unfortunately, picnicking is not allowed.

Facilities: None; groceries in West Tisbury. *Swimming:* Not permitted here.

Getting there: From State Road in West Tisbury, take Indian Hill Road to a dirt road with a Cedar Tree Neck sign. The road goes down a hill to the parking lot.

NANTUCKET BEACHES AND PARKS

Bike paths go to Madaket, Dionis, Surfside and Siasconset Beaches, and fishing is great from those on the south shore. Nantucket doesn't have parks, per se, but the **Nantucket Conservation Foundation** (Larsen-Sanford Center, 118 Cliff Road; 508-228-2884) owns and manages more than 7700 acres of undeveloped land open to the public to explore. Foundation land is identified by roadside maroon posts topped with a wave and seagull logo. If you want to know more, stop in and talk to the foundation folks, a friendly group of people who are happy to discuss the island's flora and fauna.

Dionis Beach—If it weren't for a white rock on which the word Dionis is painted, you'd never find this beach, which is ideal for swimming, picnics and cookouts (fire permits available from the Nantucket fire station). Beyond the large dirt parking lot, a path leads through tall sand dunes to the beach. These are dunes protected from natural erosion and people by a fence. The beach has some rocks and seaweed. During low tide, a sand bar stretches out into the water quite a distance.

Facilities: Lifeguards; groceries are found in downtown Nantucket. *Swimming:* Calm.

Getting there: Located three miles west of town off Eel Point Road in Dionis.

Madaket Beach—One of Nantucket's most beautiful bicycle paths ends at this spectacular western-facing beach. Everything about this long, wide beach is just right. The sand is white and clean, the surf fantastic, the sunsets the best on the island.

Facilities: Lifeguards, restaurant; groceries nearby in downtown Nantucket. *Fishing:* One of the best spots on the Vineyard. *Swimming:* Good, but can get rough.

Getting there: Located at the end of Madaket Road in Madaket.

Cisco Beach (★)—The road to this out-of-the-way beach goes past scenic Hummock Pond and rolling heathlands. The wide-open beach is a free and easy place where you can walk for miles on white sand. Popular with seasoned beach rats and young surfer types, it doesn't attract many families because the facilities are limited.

Facilities: Lifeguards; groceries in downtown Nantucket. *Fishing:* Excellent. *Swimming:* Excellent, but watch the undertow. *Surfing:* Good in the summer and fall. *Windsurfing:* Good, but choppy.

Getting there: Located at the end of Hummock Pond Road in Cisco, four miles southwest of town.

Surfside—Narrow sand paths lace the moors leading to this massive beach. Because Surfside is only three miles from town, it gets very crowded in the summer. But it's a great beach—big, long and wide with small rolling dunes to explore and the best surf on the island. Surfside attracts families and college students. To get away from the crowds, walk east along the shore toward Siasconset and soon you'll discover long stretches of blissfully empty beach.

Facilities: Restrooms, showers, lifeguards, snack bar, swings; groceries nearby on Surfside Road. *Fishing:* Excellent. *Swimming:* Good, but watch undertow. *Surfing:* Good. *Windsurfing:* Good but choppy.

Getting there: Located at the end of Surfside Road, three miles south of town.

Siasconset Beach—This lovely eastern-facing beach six miles from town is in the village of Siasconset. People make a day out of bicycling or driving here to explore the beach and the town. Part of the beach is surrounded by grassy cliffs and dunes, then the land dips and becomes flat. To the left of the beach is Sankaty Lighthouse and the summer community of Quidnet. Walk south along the beach for an empty spot. Because of the wind, seaweed can be a problem.

Facilities: Playground, lifeguards; groceries and restaurants a short walk away. *Swimming:* Good, but surf can be heavy.

Getting there: Located seven miles east of town at the end of Milestone Road in Siasconset.

Great Point, Coskata and **Coatue Beaches** (★)—If you really want to leave civilization, consider exploring this narrow stretch of uninhabited land that wraps around Nantucket Harbor. It's like one giant sand dune surrounded by water. Driving through this desertlike landscape is an adventure, and those who make the trek can swim in calm waters lapping a deserted white sand beach and view a nesting ground for eagles, clam and oyster ponds, the remains of a shipwreck and the Great Point Lighthouse. Driving in this area requires an expensive ($50) permit and a four-wheel-drive vehicle equipped with everything you need to dig yourself out of a deep sand rut. Permits are available at the Wauwinet Gate House (Wauwinet Road; 508-228-0006). Beach Excursions Ltd. (Jeff Irion; 508-228-3728) offers a three-hour Jeep ride and picnic in the area. (Other tours and fishing excursions are advertised in the local paper.)

Facilities: None. *Fishing:* Fantastic shore fishing at Great Point, the northernmost point of land. *Swimming:* Calm on Nantucket Sound; not recommended on the Atlantic side, where the current and undertow are rough.

Getting there: Located at the northeast end of the island at the end of Wauwinet Road off Polpis Road.

Sanford Farm (★)—Owned by the Nantucket Conservation Foundation, this former dairy farm consists of 767 acres of classic Nantucket countryside. A magical place for quiet walks and private picnics, it has 15 miles of trails meandering through rare maritime heathlands that look like Scotland. Follow the trail past long and winding Hummock Pond down to the empty beach. In spring and summer Sanford Farm is lush with wildflowers, but its most beautiful time is fall, when the land is a tapestry of burgundy, sage, rose, gold and ivory. Deer can be spotted early in the morning and at dusk. Rare short-eared owls nest on the ground in the grass, and turtles live in the pond.

Facilities: None; groceries are 15 minutes away in downtown Nantucket. *Swimming:* Good, but undertow can be dangerous.

Getting there: Located west of town off Madaket Road near the intersection of Cliff Road and Madaket.

SOUTH COAST BEACHES AND PARKS

Duxbury Beach—This five-mile stretch of clean white sand is one of the finest barrier beaches on the Massachusetts coast. The beach juts out into the ocean and is bordered by a little harbor on one side and the Atlantic on the other. Stretches are dotted with salt marsh, and parts are accessible only by four-wheel-drive vehicles. Located in an affluent residential neighborhood, it attracts a well-heeled crowd.

Facilities: Restrooms, showers, changing room, lifeguards, snack bar, restaurant; groceries in Duxbury. *Swimming:* Good.

Getting there: Located off Route 3 on Route 139 in Duxbury, north of Plymouth.

Myles Standish State Forest—Locals joke that once you're in this 14,635-acre park, you'll never find your way out again. The park is enormous, and the roads winding through the forest and meadows seem to go on forever. Because of its size, it feels remote and peaceful even in the summer. Beautiful and clean, the park has 15 ponds with two beaches. Motorcycle, bicycle, bridle and hiking paths wind through the forest.

Facilities: Picnic areas, restrooms, interpretive programs; groceries and restaurants in Plymouth and Carver; information, 508-866-2526. *Camping:* Permitted in 467 sites with restrooms, hot showers, fireplaces and picnic tables, available on a first come, first served basis. *Fishing:* Good in most ponds. *Swimming:* At College and Fearings beaches.

Getting there: Located off Route 3 on Long Road in Plymouth.

Plymouth Beach—Located in a half rural, half residential area, this straight, three-mile beach dotted with beach grass and clear stretches of sand serves as a nesting ground for migratory shore birds such as terns and sandpipers. The nesting area is fenced off for protection, but the birds can be easily observed. In the summer this busy beach attracts families and local kids.

Facilities: Restrooms, showers, lifeguards, snack bar; restaurant within walking distance. *Fishing:* Excellent. *Swimming:* Good.

Getting there: Located off Route 3A, three miles south of Plymouth.

Horseneck Beach State Reservation—This vast, breezy beach is one of the state's most spectacular and least known. Bordered by fragile dunes that create a barrier between the enormous parking lot and the beach, it has crunchy white sand and fine waves. **Gooseberry Neck (★)** is a narrow, mile-long stretch of sandy, grassy land jutting out into the ocean and laced with paths. There's an abandoned World War II lookout tower at the end that you can climb. Right before Gooseberry Neck is a clam bar, a small parking lot and a tiny beach popular with windsurfers. The road to Gooseberry Neck was destroyed in the 1991 hurricane but the area is still accessible on foot.

Facilities: Restrooms, showers, lifeguards, snack bar; groceries nearby in Westport; information, 508-636-3298. *Swimming:* Good, but can be rough.

Getting there: Located at the end of Route 88 in Westport Point.

Demarest Lloyd State Park (★)—This little-known state park has everything: natural grassy areas for picnics, rambling hills of beach grass, winding rivers, abundant wildlife—deer, hawks, egrets—and a fairly isolated beach. At low tide a long sand bar juts out into the calm, warm waters. Located in the bucolic Dartmouth area, Demarest is a real find.

Facilities: Picnic areas, restrooms, showers, lifeguards; information, 508-636-8816; groceries nearby in South Dartmouth. *Camping:* Permitted in 100 sites on a first come, first served basis. *Swimming:* Calm.

Getting there: Located at the end of Route 88, east of Horseneck Beach in South Dartmouth.

Hiking

The North Shore and the Cape offer excellent opportunities to hike through salt marsh, forest, sand dunes and moors bordering freshwater ponds and the ocean. Many of the hikes are short and easy. The rest of the coast has a limited number of marked trails. For more information on hikes throughout the state, contact the **Massachusetts Department of Environmental Management Trails Program** (100 Cambridge Street, Boston; 617-727-3160).

NORTH SHORE TRAILS

Art's Trail (1 mile), in Dogtown Common, a 3000-acre park near Gloucester, winds through red oak forest past a highland of scrub oak, grey birch, blueberries and huckleberries. Several low areas flood in late winter and spring, forming frog-breeding ponds. Of moderate difficulty, the trail is rocky in parts and requires careful walking.

Whale's Jaw Trail (4.5 miles), a rugged, rocky, hilly hike, starts at Blackburn Industrial Park off Route 128. The trail meanders through former grazing land and past Babson Reservoir, birch groves and cattail marsh. It ends at the top of a hill, where you'll see an enormous split granite boulder that looks like a whale's jaw.

You need a rowboat to get to get to **Hog Island Trail** (1.5 miles), but it's worth it. Located near Crane's Beach, the easy trail leads through vast expanses of salt marsh, beside pastures and along the shore, past a 1725 house and barn, to a hill where you can see Maine on a clear day. The Crane Refuge Visitor Center at the beginning of the hike has bathrooms, picnic areas, a museum and trail maps.

CAPE COD TRAILS

Talbot's Point Salt Marsh Trail (1.5 miles), off Old Country Road in Sandwich, offers excellent views of the Great Marsh. The trail winds through red pine forest, along the fern-filled marsh and past cranberry bogs and the state game farm, where thousands of quail and pheasant are raised.

Nauset Marsh Trail (1 mile) offers some of the Cape's lushest scenery. The trail starts at the Salt Pond Visitor's Center in North Eastham and goes past the shoreline of Salt Pond and Nauset Marsh, then rises through pastoral farmland filled with beach plums, bayberries and cedars.

A mesmerizing view of salt marsh and the ocean beyond greets you at **Goose Ponds Trail** (1.5 miles) in the Wellfleet Bay Wildlife Sanctuary. The path leads through forest down a slight grade past Spring Brook to marshlands covered with wild lupine. A wooden boardwalk leads to a secluded beach. Among the many species of bird life are white-bottomed tree swallows nesting in bird houses located throughout the sanctuary.

Great Island Trail (8.4 miles), a wind-bitten wilderness, is best in the morning when the sun isn't too intense. Located at the end of Kendrick Road in Wellfleet, the trail borders tidal flats, grassy dunes, pitch pine forest, the ocean and meadows where purple marsh peas and fiddler crabs flourish. Great for solitary beachcombing, the trail offers a number of spectacular views.

Beech Forest Trail (1 mile) winds to the Cape's most monumental sand dunes. Most of the trail wanders through cool beech forests and past freshwater ponds, and at one point it opens up to reveal the desertlike sand dunes. It starts on Race Point Road in Provincetown.

MARTHA'S VINEYARD TRAILS

Felix Tree Neck Wildlife Sanctuary Trail (1.5 miles), off the Edgartown–West Tisbury Road, offers many opportunities to view ducks, swans, otters, muskrats, egrets, harrier hawks and other wildlife. The trail winds past waterfowl ponds, salt marsh, the end of a peninsula, wetland vegetation and oak forest. It ends at the sanctuary's exhibit building, which has aquariums, wildlife displays, a library and a naturalist gift shop.

NANTUCKET TRAILS

Nantucket's only marked hiking trail is the **Sanford Farm-Ram Pasture Walking Trail**, offering 15 miles of wilderness to explore. In addition, the Nantucket Conservation Foundation also owns parcels of wilderness the public can explore. For more on this, see the "Beaches and Parks" section in this chapter. Following are two of the most scenic areas in which to hike:

Tupancy Links, off Cliff Road immediately west of town, is laced with paths that overlook Nantucket Sound. A former golf course, today it is a big open grassy field offering dramatic views.

Alter Rock off Polpis Road in the central moors is crisscrossed with unmarked paths and rutted dirt roads. Dotted with kettle hole ponds, rocks and scrub oak thicket, the scenery is classic heathland.

SOUTH COAST TRAILS

East Head Reservoir Trail (3.5 miles) starts behind the Myles Standish State Forest headquarters building in Plymouth. The best thing about this hike is that it covers the full spectrum of habitats in the 14,635-acre park. The relatively flat trail winds past deep forest, marsh, hard and soft wood groves and a pristine pond. A pamphlet available at the start of the hike explains the flora and fauna of each environment. A couple of benches are located along the way.

The **Flora B. Pierce Nature Trail** (2 miles) at Acushnet Cedar Swamp State Reservation in New Bedford follows along a river spanned by several large wooden bridges and travels through deeply wooded inland wetlands.

The **Massasoit State Park Trail** (2.5 miles) in East Taunton meanders through white pine forest and hardwoods and past swamps and brooks. It edges Lake Rico and arrives at a large, secluded sandy beach. Along the way, you'll spot wildlife such as deer, fox and owls.

Travelers' Tracks

Sightseeing

NORTH SHORE

The North Shore is a real sleeper. Unspoiled and relatively uncommercial, it's a place where you can still discover hidden inns, restaurants, beaches and parks. An explorer's destination, it's perfect for people who like to go it on their own.

From Marblehead immediately north of Boston to Newburyport on the New Hampshire border, this craggy stretch of coast offers tremendous diversity. Marblehead has magnificent yachts; Salem means witches and maritime history; gritty Gloucester is filled with old salts; Rockport, the only resort town, has art and beautiful inns; Essex offers antiques; Ipswich has the best seafood; and Newburyport displays 19th-century elegance.

The North Shore is a vacation area and bedroom community to Boston populated by investment bankers, Yankee blue bloods, fishermen, artists and history buffs. In the 18th and 19th centuries, the country's most magnificent ships were built in North Shore towns, bringing great wealth to the area. Hence, the coast is dotted with majestic sea captains' homes, many of them now inns.

To explore this area from Boston, take the Callahan tunnel to Routes 1A and 129 north to **Marblehead**, a small village of clapboard houses, hollyhocks and cobblestone streets. Marblehead is sailboat country. All summer long the harbor is alive with some of the most sophisticated racing vessels in America.

A good place to picnic and enjoy the harbor view is at **Crocker Park** at the western end of Front Street, high on a hill. Marblehead's **Old Town**, which surrounds the harbor, dates back to before the Revolution and is a very pleasant place to stroll. It has many interesting shops and casual restaurants. Locals tend to ignore out-of-towners (unless, of course, they're first-rate sailors).

The **Marblehead Chamber of Commerce** (62 Pleasant Street; 617-631-2868) maintains a visitor information booth at the corner of Pleasant and Spring streets.

Historic sights in Old Town include **Abbot Hall** (★) (Washington Square; 617-631-0528), the Victorian town hall that houses the famous historic painting *The Spirit of '76* by Archibald Willard. Visitors are free to wander in and view this dramatic work of art.

Right down the street is the **Jeremiah Lee Mansion** (161 Washington Street; 617-631-1069; admission), a Georgian home built in 1768 for Colonel Lee, a Revolutionary War patriot. The guided tour is packed with entertaining anecdotes: we learn, for example, that the extrawide stairway in the entrance hall was designed by Mrs. Lee so women could swoop down the stairs in their enormous hoop skirts without knocking over their escorts.

Salem, the largest North Shore town, is only ten minutes away from Marblehead on Route 114. People come here for architecture, maritime museums, Nathaniel Hawthorne and, of course, witches. This beautiful historic town is so civilized and proper looking, it's hard to believe the 1692 witchcraft trials ever took place here.

This macabre piece of American history began in a very innocent way. A group of teenage girls, who had learned black magic from a West Indian woman named Tituba, were diagnosed as bewitched. All hell broke loose, and everyone started accusing everyone else of being a witch. In the nine months to follow, 20 women were hung and 150 imprisoned. The hysteria came to an end when the wives of prominent men were accused of being witches.

Salem's three witch exhibits are somewhat commercial, but kids love them. Every day in the summer, children wearing pointed black hats and capes purchased at nearby witch boutiques stand in long lines waiting to get in. The saving grace of the exhibits is that they are in historic buildings—not re-creations of haunted houses.

Salem Witch Museum (19½ Washington Square North; 508-744-1692; admission) is a computerized sound-and-light show. **Witch House** (310 Essex Street; 508-744-0180; admission) is the restored 1642 home of witch trial judge Jonathan Corwin. **Witch Dungeon Museum** (16 Lynde Street; 508-744-9812; admission) re-enacts the witch trials.

Tourist information booths are at **Riley Plaza** (Washington and Margin streets) and the **Essex Street Mall**. For more information stop at the **Chamber of Commerce** (Old Town Hall, 32 Derby Square; 508-744-0004). An easy way to see historic sights is to follow **Salem's Heritage Trail**, a self-guided walking tour indicated by a red line painted on the street.

To understand the real story of Salem, which was a major port in the 18th and 19th centuries, visit the Peabody Museum and Essex Institute. The first-rate **Peabody Museum** (161 Essex Street; 508-745-9500; admission) houses a treasure trove of objects acquired during Salem's active China trade days, such as an elaborate, moon-shaped, hand-carved wooden Chinese bed.

Essex Institute Museum Neighborhood (132 Essex Street; 508-744-3390; admission) consists of a history and decorative arts museum and three impeccably restored homes and gardens dating from 1684 to 1818. The museum isn't as grand as the Peabody, but the houses are fascinating, especially if toured in chronological order. The architecture and craftsmanship is superb. Anyone who has ever renovated an old house will appreciate a special exhibit about the painstaking efforts that go into museum restoration work. Since bright colors were a sign of wealth in the 19th century, the 1804 Gardner-Pingree House, a fine neoclassical building, holds a few surprises. The kitchen is deep salmon and green; one bedroom wears a vivid peacock blue hue, while another sports canary yellow.

Chestnut Street, one of the most architecturally significant avenues in America, is near Essex Institute. Many of its 17th-century mansions were designed by Salem's famed Federal-period architect and woodcarver, Samuel McIntire. These brick and wood houses are simple in their design, yet the overall effect is graceful and elegant.

Pickering Wharf, a short walk from Chestnut Street, is a new but made-to-look-old commercial development of tourist shops and chain restaurants. About a block east stands **Derby Wharf**—a good area for strolling along the harbor.

Even though it's often crowded with tourists, there's something romantic and compelling about the **House of Seven Gables** (54 Turner Street; 508-744-0991; admission), located down the street from Derby Wharf. Built in 1668, the dark, almost black house is framed by ocean and sky. The tall, imposing gables look a bit like witch hats (although this thought probably wouldn't come to mind in another town). Inside, a labyrinth of cozy rooms with low ceilings, narrow passageways and secret stairs add to the ancient feeling of the place. The guided tour includes a good short film about how the house inspired Nathaniel Hawthorne to write his famous novel.

Northeast of Salem on scenic Route 127, which hugs the coast, are the residential towns of Manchester and Magnolia, known for their old money, private schools and magnificent mansions.

Right off Route 127 is **Hammond Castle Museum** (★) (80 Hesperus Avenue, Magnolia; 508-283-2080). Perched on the edge of a steep, windswept cliff, this seaside castle looks like something out of a Gothic novel. Built by John Hays Hammond, Jr., creator of the radio remote control, the house features an eccentric collection of medieval artifacts, armor and tapestries. Guided tours are available.

Three miles from Hammond Castle on Route 127 is **Gloucester**, the oldest seaport in the United States. Home port to approximately 200 fishermen, it has a salty dog ambience that brings you back to the real world after Hammond Castle. Overlooking the harbor stands the town's famed **Gloucester Fisherman** statue, *Man at the Wheel*, commemorating "They that go down to the sea in ships."

There's not much to see and do in Gloucester, but the **Cape Ann Chamber of Commerce** (33 Commercial Street; 508-283-1601) in the center of town deserves a visit. The largest tourist information center on the North Shore, it has a hotel hotline for last-minute accommodations.

A short hop from Gloucester, off Route 127, is **Rocky Neck Art Colony,** one of the country's oldest artist colonies, dating back to the 18th century. Winslow Homer and Rudyard Kipling lived here. Today it is a quainter than quaint seaside village with tiny houses, restaurants and galleries.

Down the road from Rocky Neck is **Beauport Museum** (★) (75 Eastern Point Boulevard, East Gloucester; 508-283-0800), a sprawling ocean-front English manor formerly owned by noted decorator Henry Davis Sleeper. From 1907 to 1934 Sleeper spent a fortune decorating all 40 rooms with a vast collection of American and European antiques, tapestries, wood paneling from abandoned old homes and much more. An informal pale green dining room has a worn brick floor and two long wooden tables set with a beautiful collection of colored glassware that reflects the light coming in from a bank of ocean-facing windows. Surprisingly, the overall effect is of an intimate English cottage.

Ten minutes from Gloucester on Route 127 is **Rockport,** the quintessential New England seaside village and the North Shore's only resort town. Until the mid-19th century, Rockport was a quiet fishing village. Then artists discovered its scenic charm, and the proverbial seascape was born. Today tourists flock to Rockport in the summer. The town is rather commercial, but the beautiful harbor and windswept cliffs that originally attracted artists are still here to enjoy.

Bearskin Neck, a narrow peninsula jutting out into the ocean, is Rockport's main tourist attraction. It's lined with Lilliputian-sized wooden fishermen's cottages transformed into restaurants and galleries selling everything from T-shirts and seascapes in every style imaginable to model ships made of cut up beer cans. At the end of the peninsula is Motif #1, a red lobster shack, so named because it has been painted by so many artists.

About two miles south of downtown Rockport is the **Rockport Chamber of Commerce** (3 Main Street; 508-546-6575). The folks here can point out local sights like the eccentric **Paper House** (Pigeon Hill Street; 508-546-2629). At first it looks like a normal cottage, but it's made entirely out of newspaper. Even the furniture and fireplace are papier-mâché. Elis F. Stedman, its creator, started the house in 1920; it took 20 years to complete.

About 30 minutes north of Rockport are the rural villages of **Essex** and **Ipswich.** Essex is famous for its antique stores (see the "Shopping" section in this chapter), Ipswich for its clams. A pleasant day can be spent antiquing and enjoying fresh, affordable seafood at one of the many roadside eateries in this area.

This route takes you right past **Whipple House** (53 South Main Street, Ipswich), a steepled, pitched-roofed house built in 1640 and occupied by the Whipple family for over 200 years. As did many colonists, the Whipples built their home in the Elizabethan style popular in England at the time. It has a lovely herb garden and is located in a semirural area close to other historic buildings.

Thirty minutes north of Ipswich, just before the New Hampshire border, lies the handsome 19th-century town of **Newburyport**. When the fog rolls in and the smell of brine and fish fills the air, you can walk along narrow streets bearing names like Neptune and imagine what it was like 100 years ago when this was a major shipbuilding center.

In the late 1970s the downtown area overlooking the harbor was renovated from top to bottom. Today, Newburyport's 19th-century brick buildings are so spit-and-polish clean, the town literally sparkles. As in many European towns, there's a central plaza overlooking the harbor where you can sit and watch the world go by. The shops and restaurants are quite tasteful; T-shirt and souvenir shops are the exception. **Greater Newburyport Chamber of Commerce** (29 State Street; 508-465-0704) is in the heart of the downtown area.

For a healthy dose of the good life circa 1850, walk along **High Street** (Route 1A), which is lined with immaculate 19th-century Federal-style mansions built by sea captains. For a peek inside, visit **Cushing House** (98 High Street; 508-462-2681; admission), home of the Historical Society of Old Newbury. It has 19th-century antiques, plus a genealogical library, French garden and carriage house.

CAPE COD

Every year starting in June, close to 3.5 million people invade this foot-shaped peninsula, grappling with horrendous traffic and crowded beaches just to be on their beloved Cape Cod. It's easy to understand why.

The Cape has it all: silver grey saltbox cottages, historic villages, sports, seafood, art, first-rate theater and more. But those attributes aren't the real reason people come here. It's the land itself. With its ethereal light, comforting woodlands and 300 miles of majestic, untamed shoreline, Cape Cod reaches deep into the soul.

The Cape's first visitors were the Pilgrims, who landed near Provincetown just long enough to write the Mayflower Compact before heading off to Plymouth. In the late 1800s, artists and writers such as Henry David Thoreau discovered the Cape. Tourists were soon to follow, and this once-isolated fishing community was never the same again.

Tourism has taken its toll. The Cape has a commercial side, complete with tired-looking shopping malls, pizza parlors, video arcades, tract houses and ugly motels. But it's easy to avoid all that if you know where to go.

The 70-mile-long Cape juts out into the ocean in an east-west direction for about 35 miles, then becomes narrower and turns northward. Practically everything worth seeing here lies along the shore, so an ideal way to explore is to follow the northern coast along Cape Cod Bay to the tip in Province-town, then go back down along Nantucket Sound to Falmouth and Woods Hole. This is the route we will take.

We have labeled the first segment the North Cape, which follows scenic Route 6A along the north shore past some of the Cape's most charming historic villages. Route 6A eventually joins with busy, Route 6 and soon arrives at Eastham. Here begins the Outer Cape, the region known for sand dunes, rolling moors, impressive beaches and the bohemian and tourist en-clave of Provincetown. Route 28 runs back along the South Cape past a couple of attractive villages and some of the region's less-scenic commercial areas.

There are numerous information booths located throughout the Cape if you have any queries.

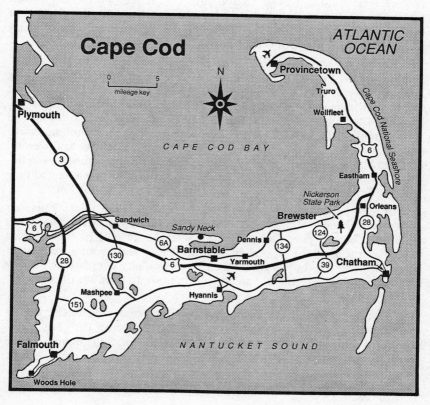

THE NORTH CAPE

Hugging Cape Cod Bay along Route 6A are the beautiful historic villages of Sandwich, Barnstable, Yarmouth, Dennis and Brewster. Once known as Olde Kings Highway, Route 6A is a tree-lined road that dips and turns past lovely old homes, sweeping lawns, stone walls, duck ponds, museums, elegant restaurants and antique stores.

Sandwich, the first town we reach, is very green, woodsy and English looking. It dates back to 1639 and has a 17th-century grist mill. Sandwich has more sights than any town on the Cape except Brewster. Maps are available at the **Cape Cod Chamber of Commerce** (90 Main Street, Bourne; 508-759-3122).

Near the heart of the village stands **Hoxie House** (Water Street, Route 130; 508-888-1173; admission), the oldest house in Sandwich. Built around 1637, this modest saltbox structure has furnishings that are impressive in their simplicity and ingenuity. A 1701 chest is decorated with soot and herb dye to give it a grained look; chairs turn into tables and benches into beds.

A few doors down is the **Thornton W. Burgess Museum,** (4 Water Street, 508-888-4668; admission), the former home of the author of *Old Mother West Wind* and *Peter Cotton Tail*. This homey little cottage overlooking an idyllic, willow-lined duck pond contains a large collection of books by Burgess, beautiful old book illustrations and a gift shop with children's books. The floor of the museum is painted with tiny rabbit footprints.

Heritage Plantation (Pine and Grove streets, 508-888-3300; admission) has a 1912 carousel, an antique car collection (including a stunning Dusenburg once owned by Gary Cooper), a military museum and an art museum. If cars, folk art or military history interest you, you'll be impressed. The military museum has 2000 hand-painted miniatures and all sorts of replica flags and firearms. The art museum includes an impressive collection of antique weathervanes, early American primitive and western art including many Currier and Ives lithographs, and cigar-store carved figures. The plantation's 76 acres of gardens are so perfectly manicured they look artificial.

In the heart of Sandwich village is the **Sandwich Glass Museum** (Town Hall Square; 508-888-0251; admission). In 1825 Deming Jarves, a Bostonian, built a glass factory in Sandwich because of its many ponds (water is crucial to the process of blowing glass) and because he thought his employees wouldn't squander their money on city temptations, as they had in Boston. His formula worked, and in no time Sandwich became renowned for its glass.

The museum's collection includes everything from jars, nursing bottles and tableware to saucers, vases and candlesticks. A lot of the glass is displayed on shelves in front of large picture windows. Sun illuminates the glass, and it lights up the museum in a kaleidoscope of sparkling colors.

A few steps away from the Glass Museum you'll find **Yesteryears Doll Museum** (Main and River streets; 508-888-1711; admission), two floors packed with every antique doll and accessory imaginable—princesses, nurses, Indians, doll furniture, houses, paper dolls, baby buggies, parasols and much more.

The **Green Briar Jam Kitchen** and the **Old Briar Patch Conservation Area** (6 Discovery Hill Road; 508-888-6870) are east of the center of town. "'Tis a wonderful thing to sweeten the world which is in a jam and needs preserving," wrote Thornton W. Burgess to Ida Putnam. As a boy Burgess roamed the woods around Ida's jam kitchen. Today, the Burgess Society produces natural jams, pickles and jellies from Ida's recipes. Nestled deep in the woods next to a pond, the old-fashioned kitchen looks like an illustration from one of Burgess' books. Peter Cotton Tail and his animal friends would have loved it here.

East of Sandwich lies the popular resort town of **Barnstable**, where some of the Cape's most beautiful inns and tempting restaurants and shops are located. Here, too, you'll find the **Donald Trayser Memorial Museum** (Route 6A; 508-362-2092), a brick structure built in 1856, which was once a custom house, then a post office. Named after a local patriot and historian, the museum includes a potpourri of artifacts related to Cape Cod life and history, such as Indian tools and ships in bottles. Next to the museum stands an old jail whose wooden walls are covered with graffiti written by seamen.

Farther along Route 6A, Yarmouthport is the site of two historic homes with impressive antiques. A white Greek Revival home with black shutters, **Captain Bangs Hallet House** (★) (11 Strawberry Lane; 508-362-3021) is furnished with elegant settees, tables and chairs, and many classic old toys such as a rocking horse with real animal hide and hair.

The 1780 **Winslow Crocker House** (Route 6A, Yarmouthport; 508-227-3956), a shingled Georgian with handsome wood paneling and an impressive walk-in fireplace, has a rare 17th-century wooden cradle and blanket chest, a Windsor writing chair and many more valuable antiques.

Brewster has a number of sights for children and history buffs. **Cape Cod Aquarium** (Main Street, Route 6A; 508-385-9252; admission) offers a dolphin pool, touch tanks, an aquarium, tours plus seal and sea lion demonstrations. The **New England Fire and History Museum** (Main Street, Route 6A; 508-896-5711; admission) displays hand- and horse-drawn fire equipment that makes you wonder how they ever put out fires. Kids like all the bells and fire alarms that are constantly sounding off here. The **Cape Cod Museum of Natural History** (Main Street, Route 6A; 508-896-3867; admission) has a working beehive and a weather station, and a curator gives occasional guided walks through salt marsh.

Through the use of enormous oil paintings, special effects and life-sized mannequins, the **Drummer Boy Museum** (787 Main Street, Route

6A, Brewster; 508-896-3823; admission) depicts 21 scenes and events from American history including the Boston Tea Party and Washington crossing the Delaware.

THE OUTER CAPE

Route 6A ends at Orleans, where it intersects with Route 6 and leads to Eastham. At this point the character of the landscape changes dramatically. The woods disappear and the sky opens up to reveal towering sand dunes, miles of silver marsh grass and windswept moors. At the very tip is Provincetown, one of the Cape's largest communities.

About 50 percent of the Outer Cape is under the jurisdiction of the Cape Cod National Seashore, a natural playground with miles of bicycle paths, hikes and the Cape's most dramatic beaches (see the "Beaches and Parks" and "Hiking" sections in this chapter).

Fort Hill (★) off Route 6 in Eastham offers a mesmerizing view overlooking Nauset Marsh that's so beautiful it doesn't seem real. Once productive farmland, the marsh today is laced with wavy ribbons of water that wind through downy, soft green-gold marsh grass past old farmhouses, stone walls and ponds complete with adorable ducks. Trails meander through this area, which is a resting place for blue herons. Near the Fort Hill parking lot is the **Edward Penniman House** (★) (not open to the public), a fairy-tale-like, red-and-yellow French Empire house with an enormous archway of whale jaw bones at its gate. Built by an eccentric whaler in the 19th century, the whimsical structure contrasts dramatically with the Cape's simple saltbox homes.

After Eastham is **Wellfleet**, an unpretentious, wiggle-your-toes-in-the-sand kind of place with a surprising number of good art galleries and gourmet restaurants. On Saturday nights in the summer, many galleries have openings that feel like neighborhood block parties. Wellfleet has many year-round residents, and they all seem to know each other.

Before heading into town, stop at the **Wellfleet Chamber of Commerce** (Route 6; 508-349-2510) for a gallery guide. On the way to Wellfleet is **Uncle Tim's Bridge** (★), a low wooden boardwalk that goes over a field of silvery marsh grass to a small wooded hill. A dreamy sort of place shrouded in delicate mist in the morning and soft mellow light in the afternoon, it's perfect for a picnic or quiet walk.

North of Wellfleet lies magnificent **Truro**, a vast treeless plain of rolling moors surrounded by water and some of the state's most impressive sand dunes. Named after an area of Cornwall, England that's similar in appearance, Truro is a wonderful area for picture taking.

Provincetown, at the Cape's outer tip, is nestled on a hill overlooking the bay. Everything good and bad about Cape Cod can be found here: elegant sea captains' mansions, a honky-tonk wharf, dazzling beaches, first-rate museums, schlocky galleries, hamburger joints and gourmet restaurants.

The people are equally diverse. Provincetown has a large gay population, as well as artists and writers, Portuguese fishermen, aristocrats, beer-guzzling rabble-rousers and plenty of tourists. Of all the towns on the Cape, Provincetown has the most interesting history. The Pilgrims landed here in 1620 before going to Plymouth, and in the 18th and 19th centuries it was a prominent whaling and fishing port, attracting many Portuguese settlers who still fish the waters today.

Around the turn of the century, artists and writers, such as Eugene O'Neill, started moving to Provincetown, and it became one of America's most renowned artists colonies. A renaissance period flourished until about 1945, when tourism evolved and many artists scattered for quieter parts of the world.

To immerse yourself in Provincetown's artistic past, get a copy of *Walking Tours No. 2 and 3* from the Provincetown Heritage Museum, or contact the **Provincetown Chamber of Commerce** (307 Commercial Street, MacMillan Wharf; 508-487-3424). These pamphlets list the name and address of every famous writer and artist who ever lived here. Their former homes aren't open to the public, but it's fun to walk by 577 Commercial Street and imagine what it was like when O'Neill rented a room there.

Provincetown Heritage Museum (Center and Commercial streets; 508-487-0666; admission) provides an overview of the town's historic and artistic past. The *Rose Dorothea*, the world's largest indoor model of a fishing schooner, fills up the entire second floor of the museum. Other exhibits include hand-painted furniture featuring seascapes, photographs of artists at the turn of the century and many paintings.

Walk east on Commercial Street, the main drag, to the **Provincetown Art Association and Museum** (460 Commercial Street; 508-487-1750; admission) for the best art on the Cape. The museum exhibits work by noted Provincetown artists such as impressionist painter Charles W. Hawthorne, who founded the Cape's first art school in 1899. Much of the work is figurative, depicting everyday Provincetown scenes such as a plumber at work, a schooner in Cape Cod Bay, a young girl sewing.

For a picture-postcard view of Provincetown and the surrounding seashore and sand dunes, visit the **Pilgrim Monument** and **Provincetown Museum** (High Pole Hill; 508-487-1310; admission). The 252-foot granite tower, with 30-foot arches and turrets, was copied from the Torre del Mangia tower in Siena, Italy. The museum houses an eclectic collection that includes everything from a model of a Thai temple, antique dolls, Wedgwood china, primitive portraits and scrimshaw to figureheads, a captain's cabin from a whaling ship and Provincetown's oldest fire engine.

THE SOUTH CAPE

This part of the Cape is a hodgepodge of scenic villages, inexpensive motels, mini-malls and gas stations. To explore it from Provincetown, head back on Route 6 to Route 28 in Orleans, a pleasant yet unassuming residential area. At Chatham, Route 28 swings around to the west and runs along the south shore of the Cape along Nantucket Sound.

Chatham, one of the most stylish towns on the Cape, has exquisite inns, good restaurants and beautiful shops. It's a very Ralph Lauren kind of place where everyone looks as though they play tennis.

Chatham's **Information Booth** (533 Main Street; 508-945-0342) is in the middle of town. At the end of Main Street, you run into **Shore Road,** lined with graceful oceanfront homes and a classic lighthouse across from the Coast Guard station.

Nearby is the **Old Atwood House Museums and Murals Barn (★)** (347 Stage Harbor Road; 508-945-2493), an unassuming-looking 1752 brown-shingle house exhibiting antiques, sea shells and Sandwich glass. Next to the house, a barn displays compelling murals by realist painter Alice Stallknecht. The murals depict Chatham townspeople of the 1930s in religious settings, such as Christ preaching from a dory below the Chatham lighthouse.

Monomoy National Wildlife Refuge, a sandy, nine-mile-long island immediately off the coast of Chatham, is home to over 300 species of birds, many on the endangered species list. The island is accessible only by private boat, and parts of it are off limits to the public. **The Cape Cod Museum of Natural History** (Main Street, Route 6A, Brewster; 508-896-3867) and the **Wellfleet Bay Audubon Society** (Route 6; 508-349-2615) offer excellent naturalist-guided day and weekend tours of the island. Overnight accommodations are in a restored 1825 lighthouse—the only structure on the island.

West of Chatham is Harwich Port, a lovely residential area, followed by Dennis Port, West Dennis, West Yarmouth and Hyannis, considerably less attractive spots. This stretch of Route 28 is mostly gas stations, coffee shops and cheap motels. But if you've had it up to here with history and quaint villages, this area is great for slumming. There are 11 miniature golf courses in the region, and one of the best is **Pirates Cove** (728 Main Street, South Yarmouth; 508-394-6200). The Trump Tower of miniature golf, it has an elaborate pirate ship in a fake pond surrounded by terraced rock cliffs and gushing waterfalls.

Because the Kennedys live in **Hyannis,** people usually expect it to be glamorous and beautiful, but most of the town is very commercial. The Kennedys live in the one nice area. People come to Hyannis for three reasons: the airport, ferries to the Islands, and spying on the Kennedys. Even though the Kennedy compound (near Ocean Street) is surrounded by tall hedges, all day long tour buses prowl this area, hoping to catch a glimpse of one of the clan. Their efforts are almost always in vain.

Southwest of Hyannis is the **New Alchemy Institute** (★) (237 Hatchville Road, East Falmouth; 508-564-6301), a nonprofit center that explores new and ancient methods of organic farming, landscape design, greenhouse horticulture and composting. If you're the least bit interested in gardening, this place is a great find. Visitors can wander around the grounds on their own or take a guided tour. There's a compost greenhouse, a geodesic greenhouse dome, vegetable gardens utilizing natural pesticides and striking flower gardens such as an all white one that looks like an enormous wedding bouquet.

At the western end of the South Cape is **Falmouth**, a large and bustling town with a beautiful village green surrounded by some of the Cape's loveliest historic homes. One of these, which houses the **Falmouth Historical Society** (Village Green, Palmer Street), is a creamy yellow, hip-roofed 1790 colonial building with a widow's walk. Six miles north of town, **Ashumet Holly Reservation and Wildlife Sanctuary** (off Ashumet Road; 508-563-6390; admission) offers tours as well as nature trail walks.

The rest of downtown Falmouth isn't as scenic, but it does have a number of beautiful, high-quality clothing and home furnishing stores. The **Falmouth Chamber of Commerce** (Academy Lane; 508-548-8500) is right off Main Street.

Immediately south of Falmouth is **Woods Hole**, a small, deeply wooded, hilly village that's home to the **Woods Hole Oceanographic Institute**. The Institute isn't open to the public; it's strictly a research facility ranked in stature alongside Scripps Institute of Oceanography in California. However, the nearby **National Marine Fisheries Service Aquarium** (Water Street; 508-548-7684) is open to the public in the summer. Its sole function is to preserve regional species, hence everything in its 16 major display tanks is native to the area: cod, lobster, flounder. The aquarium also has a seal tank.

Woods Hole is a scientific community, and it looks and feels like a small university town, with a good bookstore, craft galleries and cafés. This is also where you can catch a ferry for the Islands—Martha's Vineyard and Nantucket.

MARTHA'S VINEYARD

With its museum-perfect villages, Gothic Victorians and scenery that mimics the coast of Ireland, it isn't any wonder this enchanting island swells from around 14,000 year-round residents to 80,000 in the summer.

Discovered in 1602 by the English explorer Bartholomew Gosnold, it was named by him for its proliferation of wild grapes. Who Martha was is anybody's guess, but legend has it she may have been Gosnold's daughter or his mother.

An active whaling port in the 19th century, "the Vineyard," as it's often called, became a popular summer resort in the 20th century. Today it is a summer home to an impressive number of celebrities fiercely protected from ogling tourists by proud locals. Jackie Onassis, Carly Simon, James Taylor, Diana Ross, Beverly Sills, Walter Cronkite, Mike Wallace, William Styron and Art Buchwald have homes here.

One way not to impress the natives is to rent a moped. In the summer these noisy (but fun to drive) motorized bicycles sound like swarms of angry bees. They're considered a menace on the road, and bumperstickers that read "Outlaw Mopeds" are everywhere.

Only 20 miles long and 10 miles wide, the Vineyard can easily be toured in a day. Ferries dock at Oak Bluffs or Vineyard Haven, or you can fly in (see the "Transportation" section in this chapter). The Vineyard's three towns—Vineyard Haven, Oak Bluffs and Edgartown—are on the northeast side of the Island. The western end, known as "up-island," is comprised of bucolic farmland, moors and magnificent beaches.

In the '30s, Lillian Hellman and Dashiell Hammett spent their summers in **Vineyard Haven,** and ever since writers have been coming to this friendly, unpretentious town. Vineyard Haven has never attracted tourists like Edgartown, the island's main resort town, and therein lies its charm. It has the best bookstore, (Bunch of Grapes), attractive shops, restaurants and a handful of wonderful inns. It's also home to the **Martha's Vineyard Chamber of Commerce** (Beach Road; 508-693-0085).

One historical sights of note here is the **Seaman's Bethel Museum and Chapel** (Union Street; 508-693-9317), built in 1893 to provide spiritual guidance to seamen and a refuge to shipwreck victims. Today it is part of a larger organization that still offers social services and ministry to seafarers. The bethel is open to the public, and the small museum houses a collection of seafaring artifacts.

Nearby stand the **Old Schoolhouse and Liberty Pole Museum** (110 Main Street). The schoolhouse, a sweet-looking, one-room, white-clapboard building with artifacts related to early island life, is right in the heart of town. The museum takes its name from an American Revolutionary War incident: British sailors tried to steal the Liberty Pole to replace a broken mast on their ship, but three young girls blew up the pole before the sailors could get their hands on it.

Oak Bluffs is only a couple of miles away. A must-see here is the **Martha's Vineyard Camp Meeting Association** (also known as Cottage City), right off Circuit Avenue, the main drag through town. In 1835, Methodist church groups started holding annual summer meetings in Oak Bluffs, with hundreds of families living in tents for the occasion. Over time the tents were replaced by tiny whimsical cottages with Gothic windows, turrets, gables and eaves dripping with gingerbread and painted in a riot of colors—pink, green and white; peach, yellow and blue. Called "campground Gothic Revival," this is the only architecture native to the Vineyard. In mid-August, on Illumination Night, a custom dating back to 1870, hundreds of colorful glowing Oriental lanterns are strung up all over the cottages, creating a dazzling display of light.

With the exception of Cottage City and Ocean Park—a genteel neighborhood of Queen Anne Victorians overlooking the water on the road to Edgartown—most of Oak Bluffs is hamburger restaurants and T-shirt and souvenir shops. It has a funky, saltwater-taffy kind of charm. In the center of town is the **Flying Horses Carousel** (Circuit and Lake streets; 508-693-9481), an antique, hand-carved wooden carousel still in operation. In the glass eye of each horse is a replica of a small animal.

Not far from Oak Bluffs is elegant **Edgartown**. With its narrow streets, brick sidewalks, graceful yachts and pristine Greek Revival and Federal-style architecture, it looks like a living museum. Prim, proper and perfect, Edgartown is a bit oppressive.

Edgartown has always been a town of considerable wealth and power. Prosperous whaling captains retired here, building magnificent homes along **North Water Street** that can still be seen today. Today's residents include many Boston Brahmin families. Life revolves around the formidable yacht club, where expert sailor Walter Cronkite reigns supreme.

The main thing to do in Edgartown is walk along its tree-lined streets window shopping and admiring the homes. The **Dukes County Historical Society** (Cooke and School streets; 508-627-4441; admission), tucked away on a beautiful side street, maintains a museum exhibiting scrimshaw, ship models, period costumes and whaling gear such as harpoons.

Right off the coast of Edgartown is **Chappaquiddick Island**. Called "Chappy" by locals, it is accessible by ferry (see the "Transportation" section in this chapter). There's not much to do here except go to the beach and take long walks. The island, of course, is noted for the tragic auto accident involving Senator Edward Kennedy that resulted in the death of a young woman. Chappaquiddick Road ends at Dyke Bridge, site of the mishap, which has now fallen apart and is off limits to cars and people. The island's only other road, Wasque Road, leads to Wasque Point, a beautiful natural area.

The up-island section of the Vineyard includes West Tisbury, Chilmark and Gay Head, bucolic rural areas with lush green farms, meadows and scenic harbors. To explore this area from Edgartown, take the Edgartown–West Tisbury Road. It cuts through the middle of the island.

About the only thing in West Tisbury is **Alley's General Store** (★), where locals sit on the front porch drinking coffee and glaring at tourists. On Saturday mornings, the big social event is the outdoor produce market at **Agricultural Hall** (★), down the road from Alley's. Don't be fooled by the casual way the locals are dressed. Look closely and you'll see Rolex watches, $600 cowboy boots and maybe, if you're lucky, James Taylor. This area of the island is where many accomplished writers, musicians and artists make their homes.

From West Tisbury, follow the road to **Chilmark**. There's nothing to do here except admire the scenery and try to guess which unmarked dirt road leads to Jackie Onassis' guarded mansion.

The road ends at **Gay Head Cliffs**, towering ocean cliffs formed by glaciers over 10,000 years ago. Laced with multicolored bands of rust, lavender, wheat and charcoal, constant erosion over the milleniums has actually washed away most of the vibrant hues. This popular tourist attraction is approached by a path lined with chowder and gift shops owned by the native Wampanoag Indians.

Leave Gay Head via Lighthouse Road and stop in peaceful **Menemsha**, a tiny fishing community that looks like a village on the coast of Ireland. Menemsha has a couple of restaurants, some good craft galleries and a scenic little **harbor** (★) that time forgot. From Menemsha head back to Vineyard Haven via North Road and State Road, which goes by **Chicama Vineyards** (★) (Stoney Hill Road, West Tisbury; 508-693-0309). Massachusetts' first and only winery, it offers guided tours and winetastings in an appealing shop that sells wine, homemade jam, mustard and herb vinegar.

NANTUCKET

Located 30 miles out to sea from Cape Cod, this magical, fog-shrouded island is a study in contrasts. With its historic homes and cobblestone streets, it looks like storybook land, circa 1800. Yet it has sophisticated New York City/San Francisco-style restaurants and Madison Avenue shops. Outside of town, Nantucket is a bittersweet world of rolling moors, wild roses and windswept saltbox cottages that appear to have sprouted from the earth itself.

Nantucket was first sighted in 1602 by Captain Bartholomew Gosnold on his way to Martha's Vineyard. English settlers and Quakers farmed the land until the 1830s, when it was one of the busiest whaling ports in the world, a fact noted by Herman Melville in *Moby Dick*. In the 1870s, when kerosene started to replace whale oil as a fuel source and whales were becoming scarce, the industry started to decline and Nantucket lost 60 percent of its population. A depression followed, but around the turn of the century tourism blossomed and the island prospered once again.

Nantucket is so small and flat you can zip across it on a bicycle in about two hours or by car in 30 minutes. There are almost as many bicycle paths as roads, and bicycle rental shops abound on the wharf where the ferries dock. Like Martha's Vineyard, the only way to get here is by ferry or plane (see the "Transportation" section in this chapter).

There is only one town, Nantucket, but it can occupy you for hours or days if you enjoy historic homes, museums, fine restaurants, shopping and gallery hopping.

At the foot of Main Street and the wharf is the **Nantucket Chamber of Commerce** (Main Street; 508-228-1700). Benches are everywhere, so you can sit down and map out an itinerary or just people watch. Nantucket is a busy, colorful town inhabited by George and Barbara Bush types, yuppies and camera-toting tourists. Tail-wagging labradors wander about, and the local gentry stand on corners sipping coffee and chatting.

Nantucket has many historic homes, landmarks and museums. Not to be missed is the **Thomas Macy Warehouse** (Straight Wharf; 508-228-1894; admission), on the wharf where the ferries dock. In 1846 Thomas Macy (of Macy's Department store fame) built the two-story brick warehouse after a fire destroyed most of the town. Today it is a small, attractive brick and wood museum with historical, geological and art exhibits, including a 13-foot diorama of the waterfront before the great fire and a candlemaking demonstration. A recorded voice tells the story of the fire.

The **Whaling Museum** (Broad Street; 508-228-1736; admission) is a couple of blocks north of the Chamber of Commerce. A former candleworks with enormous cross beams, this rustic old building is as fascinating as its exhibits, which include a whale skeleton, a lighthouse lens and a whaleboat.

The **Jethro Coffin House** (Sunset Hill and West Chester streets) is Nantucket's oldest house. Built in 1686, this classic saltbox is characteristic of late-17th-century Massachusetts Bay Colony homes.

If you walk up Main Street past the shops, you'll find many elegant mansions built during the heyday of whaling. Nearby stands the **Maria Mitchell Science Center** (Vestal and Milk streets; 508-228-9198). Mitchell, a Nantucket native, was the first person to discover a comet with a telescope, and the first female member of the American Academy of Arts and Sciences. The center, named in her honor, includes a natural science museum with an impressive insect collection, a library, aquarium, observatory and the house in which Mitchell was born. The center conducts summer field trips.

About a five-minute walk from here on Prospect Street stands the **Old Mill**, a classic red-and-grey shingled windmill that's one of Nantucket's most photographed sights. In the summer when the mill is operating you can see the intricate wooden gears that used to grind corn.

For a heady dose of Nantucket country life, visit **Siasconset**, a doll-sized hamlet of 17th-century pitched-roofed cod fisher shanties transformed into beguiling summer homes. In spring and early summer this endearing village looks as though it's been attacked by roses. Everywhere you look wild pink roses are climbing over fences, up sides of houses and over roofs, creating a dusty pink, grey and sage landscape.

Called "Sconset" by nearly everyone, the village lies seven and a half miles from Nantucket town on Milestone Road, which is bordered by a smooth, flat bicycle path. There isn't much to do here except enjoy the scenery and go to the beach. Sconset has a couple of restaurants, including renowned Chanticleer, and Summer House, one of Nantucket's prettiest inns.

On the way back to town, take scenic Polpis Road. It goes past **Sankaty Lighthouse** and **The Moors**, magnificent, wind-bitten low-lying land that resembles a Persian carpet in the fall. The road also passes the **windswept cranberry bogs (★)**, where you can watch cranberries being harvested in the fall (also see "Exploring Cranberry Country" in this chapter for information about cranberry growing on the South Coast).

The rest of Nantucket is all huckleberry covered-heath dotted with houses surrounded by spectacular beaches (see the "Beaches and Parks" section in this chapter).

SOUTH COAST

The South Coast is a mix of cranberries and Pilgrims, historic whaling ports, Portuguese bakeries, factory outlets, blue-collar workers and blue bloods. It is comprised of small scenic villages, pastoral farmland and three main towns—Plymouth, about 50 minutes south of Boston, and New Bedford and Fall River, next to each other and close to the Rhode Island border.

Each town has a different personality and history. Plymouth, of course, is where the Pilgrims landed. New Bedford, an active fishing port, was once the whaling capital of the world. Fall River, a factory outlet mecca, was a leading textile manufacturer at the turn of the century.

Sights, accommodations and restaurants are limited in Fall River and New Bedford. People usually visit these towns on their way to and from Cape Cod or Boston. Plymouth is much larger and draws over one million tourists annually. It has enough historic sights to occupy an entire weekend, although most people can't take more than a day of Pilgrim lore.

To reach Plymouth from Boston, go south on Route 3 or take scenic Route 3A. It winds along the coast past beautiful, affluent commuter villages with lovely coves and harbors, old lighthouses, stately mansions and winding streets.

Right before Plymouth is wealthy **Duxbury**, an aristocratic residential area of elegant homes. Stop by **The King Caesar House (★)** (King Caesar Road; admission), one of the state's most beautiful historic homes, located off Route 3A on a winding coastal road. A fresh yellow-and-white, Federal-era mansion with green shutters, a sweeping lawn and climbing roses, the house stands across from a massive stone wharf where ships were once rigged. The house has finely crafted wood cornices, moldings, fanlights and balustrades, plus original hand-painted French wallpaper and fine antiques.

From Duxbury head south for **Plymouth**. "America's Home Town" can't seem to make up its mind whether to be a tourist trap or a scenic, historic village. The town is a jarring mix of historic homes, cobblestone streets, '50s-style motels, souvenir shops, a tacky waterfront and tour buses everywhere you look. It's not particularly scenic in parts, yet the town is rich with historic sights.

Plymouth is small, and without trying you bump into everything there is to see. The **Plymouth Information Booth** (508-746-4779 summers or 508-746-3377 year-round) has walking-tour maps.

The first thing everyone heads for is **Plymouth Rock** on Water Street on the harbor. Believed to be the landing place of the Pilgrims, it is housed inside a Greek canopy with stately columns. Don't expect to see a big impressive rock; it's only large enough to hold two very small Pilgrims.

Right next to the rock is the **Mayflower II** (State Pier; 508-746-1622; admission), a brightly painted reproduction of the real *Mayflower* that looks like the pirate ship at Disneyland. The summer-only tour conducted by guides in period costume is worthwhile, even though there's occasionally a line to get in. The *Mayflower* is shockingly small. It's hard to imagine how 102 people ever survived 66 days at sea in such cramped quarters.

For more Pilgrim lore, head for **Pilgrim Hall Museum** (75 Court Street; 508-746-1620; admission), on the main drag. Continuously operating since 1824, the museum houses the nation's largest collection of Pilgrim possessions, including richly styled Jacobean furniture and the relic of a ship that brought colonists to America. Its hull is made out of naturally curved tree trunks and branches, a crude but effective design.

Three miles south of Plymouth is **Plimoth Plantation** (Route 3A, Warren Avenue, Plymouth; 508-746-1622; admission), a "living museum" where men and women in period costumes portray the residents of a 1627 Pilgrim village. This sounds contrived, but it's authentic and well-done. The re-created village, on a dusty, straw-strewn road overlooking the ocean, is comprised of many ramshackle wooden dwellings with deeply thatched roofs. There's not a modern detail in sight—just the village, the ocean and settlers going about the daily tasks of the time, tending the vegetable garden or building a house with 17th-century tools. The villagers speak in Old English, and you can ask them questions about anything—including the politics of the 17th century. There's also a Wampanoag Indian site that re-creates a typical native encampment with woven dome-shaped dwellings.

From Plymouth go west on Route 44, then south on Route 58 to rural **Carver** (★), cranberry capital of the world. In the fall the harvesting process, a breathtaking sight, can be witnessed from the road. There's also an antique train visitors can ride and a cranberry winery. (See "Exploring Cranberry Country" in this chapter.)

About half an hour's drive southeast of Carver lies the former whaling town of **New Bedford**, which gained immortality in Herman Melville's *Moby Dick*. It still looks and feels a lot like a 19th-century whaling city, with a bustling waterfront and large Portuguese population.

(Text continued on page 296.)

Exploring Cranberry Country

Hidden away in Carver, a scenic rural area ten minutes east of Plymouth, you'll find one of Massachusetts' most spectacular and least-known autumn attractions—cranberry harvesting (★). If you think fall foliage is a beautiful sight, wait until you see this dazzling display of color.

Cranberries are the state's number one agricultural product, valued at $100 million annually. Around 458 growers work more than 12,000 acres of cranberry bogs. Little Carver alone produces half the nation's crop, while Cape Cod and Nantucket also have cranberry farms.

One of the few fruits native to North America, cranberries were known to Indians as *sassamenesh*. They ate the tart red berries raw and mixed them with venison and fat to make small cakes called pemmicans. The cranberry's slender, cone-shaped flower reminded early European settlers of the beak of a crane—hence the present name.

Harvest time starts shortly after Labor Day and continues through October. During this time, restaurants and bakeries in southern Massachusetts use the berry in a number of creative dishes, ranging from cranberry horseradish and salsa to cranberry soup, bread, muffins, sorbet and tarts.

To explore the cranberry bogs, from Plymouth take Route 44 east to Route 58 south. Bogs line both routes, and the harvest process is very easy to see from the road. Many farmers don't mind if you observe from the elevated dirt paths bordering the bogs, just as long as you stay well out of their way.

The short, scruffy, dark green cranberry vines are grown in shallow bogs surrounded by deep woods. When the cranberries are ripe, they are picked by either dry or wet harvesting. Dry-picked berries are often sold fresh, while wet-picked fruit usually becomes canned or frozen cranberry sauce.

Dry-harvested berries are combed off the vine with a machine. But it's wet harvesting that's the real treat to watch. First the bogs are flooded with about 18 inches of water. Then farmers in bright yellow slickers cut the fruit off the vine with large water reels that look like giant egg beaters stirring up a waterfall of crimson berries. The buoyant berries float to the water's surface, creating a scarlet sea surrounded by a fiery ring of woods ablaze with fall colors.

The wind blows the floating berries to one end of the pond, where they are corralled with wooden booms. Giant vacuum cleaners then suck the berries into dechaffing machines. Helicopters and trucks transport the berries to packing houses, where they are graded according to size, color and quality.

It's easy enough to explore the bogs on your own, but if you want more information and an official tour, there are a number of options. Right in Plymouth is the **Cranberry World Visitors Center** (Water Street; 508-747-1000). Operated by Ocean Spray, it has exhibits of harvesting equipment, historic and current photographs, a small working cranberry bog and free cranberry juice. It's educational, but nothing compared to seeing the real thing.

Plymouth Colony Winery (Pinewood Road, Plymouth; 508-747-3334), off Route 44 about five minutes east of Plymouth, is in a former berry-screening house in the middle of a ten-acre cranberry bog. It offers free tastings, plus a tour of the winery and bogs.

The **Edaville Railroad,** a steam-belching, antique wooden train, takes visitors on a five-and-a-half-mile ride through 1800 acres of cranberry fields. The train attracts a lot of children, so it's not always quiet. But it travels through areas inaccessible by car, and the scenery is breathtaking—acres of crimson cranberries, splendid pine forests and fall foliage. This is Mother Nature at her flamboyant best.

Until the early 1980s the waterfront area was in disarray. Then, to attract tourists, the town restored more than 100 buildings. Fortunately New Bedford didn't go overboard with cute, contrived tourist attractions. Today it has a number of fine museums, restaurants, antique shops and galleries alongside the harbor. There's something genuine and tasteful about this miniature city.

The New Bedford Visitors Center (47 North 2nd Street; 508-991-6200) occupies a restored brick building, sharing space with a French bakery and chowder shop.

Rotch-Jones-Duff House and Garden Museum (396 County Street, New Bedford; 508-997-1401; admission) is a 19th-century Greek revival with a picturesque rose garden that becomes a Christmas showplace during the holidays. Named for three families who owned the property, it features many of their fine antiques. This 28-room mansion is one of the region's best.

Three sights that shouldn't be missed include **The New Bedford Whaling Museum** (18 Johnny Cake Hill; 508-997-0046; admission), **Seaman's Bethel**, a church across from the whaling museum, and **County Street** (★), where wealthy sea captains built homes in the 19th century.

Start with the Whaling Museum, then enter Seamen's Bethel, and New Bedford won't look the same again. The museum depicts whaling's profound impact on this town, telling the story beautifully with large, dramatic paintings of life aboard whaling ships and an enormous mural created in 1848. You can climb aboard a half-scale model of a fully rigged whaling ship housed in a large room with harpoons and figureheads. The museum is spacious, airy and absorbing.

Across the street is Seamen's Bethel, where whalers prayed before setting out to sea. The pulpit of this plain, sturdy church is shaped like a ship's bluff bows. Its walls are covered with memorial tablets to men who died at sea. A visit to this church is a sobering experience.

"Nowhere in America will you find more patrician-like houses," wrote Herman Melville of County Street, located a few of blocks up a slight hill from the whaling museum. The impeccably restored Federal-style mansions and elaborate Victorians along this street illustrate how grand life was in 19th-century New Bedford.

For a unique change of pace, consider visiting **Cuttyhunk** (★), an island 14 miles offshore from New Bedford accessible by ferry (see the "Transportation" section in this chapter). It's part of the Elizabeth Islands, a chain of 16 tiny islands, 14 of them owned by the Boston Brahmin Forbes family. The island is practically all sand and scrub bushes with a rocky beach. It does have a general store, one hotel, two restaurants and about 100 homes. Cuttyhunk is the opposite of busy, crowded Cape Cod—there's nothing to do but walk and fish—and therein lies its charm.

Immediately southwest of New Bedford off Route 6 are the affluent rural communities of Dartmouth and Westport, where you'll find some of the most exquisite coastal farmland in all of Massachusetts. Like Kentucky bluegrass country, this area has miles of ancient stone walls, lovely old houses, shingled dairy barns, rolling pastures and elegant horse farms.

Off Slocums Road in South Dartmouth sits **Padanaram**, a fashionable yachting resort on Apponagansett Bay. It's home to the famous boatyard Concordia, where beautiful old wooden yachts are restored. The village is only two blocks long, but it has a number of fine restaurants and shops.

Not far from Padanaram is **The Lloyd Center for Environmental Studies** (★) (430 Potomska Road, South Dartmouth; 508-990-0505), a non-profit organization that studies coastal and estuarine environments. Open to the public are an aquarium, resource library and changing exhibits featuring such work as naturalist photography. The best thing here is the dazzling view from the observation deck, which overlooks winding Slocums River and miles of wetlands. The center offers weekly walks, canoe trips and a variety of educational programs.

Heading back to New Bedford, you can take Route 195 west to **Fall River** 15 minutes away. Factory outlets (see the "Shopping" section in this chapter) and Battleship Cove are this town's claims to fame.

At the turn of the century Fall River had more than 100 textile mills, but in 1927 the industry sagged and the town went through serious hard times. Today its large granite mills are occupied by electronic and metals firms and factory outlets, but the effects of the depression still linger.

Fall River's downtown has been spruced up, but there are so many "for lease" signs tacked to its grand 19th-century buildings that the town looks a little lost.

Columbia Street (★), the Portuguese section of downtown, is a colorful place to stroll, sample treats from the many good bakeries and discover the beautiful mosaic sidewalks. The **Fall River Office of Tourism** (72 Bank Street; 508-679-0922) is housed in the former Armory, an impressive granite building.

There's also an information center at **Battleship Cove**, a harbor and park area right in town off Route 195 at exit 5. Docked in the water at Battleship Cove are a World War II battleship, destroyer, attack submarine and PT boat that you can tour (508-678-1100; admission). Not surprisingly, these vessels, which are in excellent condition, are filled with children playing war. Hundreds of scout troops make pilgrimages to this John Wayne playground.

Next to the boats is the **Fall River Heritage State Park Visitors Center** (200 Davol Street; 508-675-5759). It has an attractive waterfront park and a building with a number of exhibits about the town's former textile industry. A moving slide show documents the appalling working conditions, accidents and deaths suffered by children and adult immigrants who worked in the mills.

Shopping

NORTH SHORE SHOPPING

Located in a former tavern, **Antique Wear** (★) (82–84 Front Street, Marblehead; 617-631-4659) offers beautiful earrings, stick pins, broaches, pendants and tie pins made out of antique buttons, some dating back to the 17th century.

In Salem, the **Peabody Museum Gift Shop** (161 Essex Street; 508-745-1876) offers a wonderful assortment of prints, shipbuilding kits and maritime souvenirs, as well as posters and regional history books. You'll also find children's books, Indian jewelry and ceramic plates from China.

Across from the House of Seven Gables is **Ye Old Pepper Companie** (122 Derby Street, Salem; 508-745-2744). Established in 1806, it claims to be the oldest candy store in America. Specialties include gibralters, black jacks and other old-fashioned candies made on the premises.

Hanna Wingate House (11 Main Street, Rockport; 508-546-1008) sells antique quilts, American pine antiques, French country furniture and accessories.

New England Goods (32-B Main Street, Rockport; 508-546-9677) specializes in wooden toys, salt-glazed pottery, Maine wind bells and other quality crafts made in New England.

Rockport has almost as many galleries as bed and breakfasts. The majority sell seascapes—some good, many bad. For an excellent selection of Rockport art, visit the **Rockport Art Association** (12 Main Street; 508-546-6604). All the work on view is for sale.

Walker Creek (★) (Route 133, Essex; 508-768-7622), a real find, offers reasonably priced, finely crafted wood drop-leaf tables, hutches, four-poster beds, one-of-a-kind pieces and custom work loosely based on Shaker or colonial designs.

Essex's 25 antique dealers run the gamut from the **White Elephant** (32 Main Street; 508-768-6901), bargain basement heaven, to **A. P. H. Waller & Son** (140 Main Street; 508-768-6269) for quality antiques. **The Scrapbook** (34 Main Street; 508-768-7404) specializes in antique botanical prints, advertising posters and maps. **Main Street Antiques** (44 Main Street; 508-768-7039) has antique wicker. Always ask if a dealer can do better on a price—you're expected to bargain. But don't hope for major savings. Prices are usually reduced by 10 to 15 percent.

Housed in a former movie theater, **Gabriel** (75 Merrimac Street, Newburyport; 508-462-9640), one of the better factory outlets, sells Ralph Lauren, Calvin Klein, Liz Claiborne, Evan Picone and other designer labels at 20 to 30 percent off.

CAPE COD SHOPPING

Some of the Cape's best shopping is along Route 6A, which is lined with antique stores and artists studios selling pottery, weavings, handcrafted furniture and more.

With its sloping wood floors and wainscotting, **The Brown Jug** (155 Main Street, Sandwich; 508-833-1088) looks like an old general store. But it sells fine quality, hand-blown antique glass. Many of the pieces were made in Sandwich in the 19th century.

The Blacks (597 Route 6A, West Barnstable; 508-362-3955) has beautiful handwoven coverlets, throws, place mats, hats, gloves and wall-hangings in lush colors—rich navy and cream, dusty lavender and grey, russet and forest green. The store is in a large barn-shaped room where you can watch owners/designers Bob and Gabrielle Black working at one of the many looms.

Even if you don't intend to buy a weathervane, stop by **Salt and Chestnut** (Route 6A, West Barnstable; 508-362-6085). It's like a weathervane museum. The shop sells new and antique hand-hammered copper weathervanes in a myriad of styles—a witch on a broom, mermaid, lobster, sailboats, dogs, elephants, deer and more.

One of the nicest sights on Route 6A is the vibrant display of fresh produce and flowers at **Tobey Farm Country Store** (Route 6A, Dennis; 508-385-2930). Stop here in the summer for peaches and plums and in the fall for pumpkins and apples. The white clapboard farm also sells reasonably priced dried wreaths made from German statice, rose hips, lavender, yarrow, dried pink rosebuds, baby's breath purple statice and eucalyptus.

Design Works (159 Main Street, Yarmouthport; 508-362-9698) specializes in antique Scandinavian pine armoires, mirrors, chairs, settees and white linen and lace napkins, tablecloths and bed accessories.

Even if you can't afford anything at **Kingsland Manor Manor** (Route 6A, West Brewster; 508-385-9741), stop and browse through its labyrinth of beautiful rooms and gardens filled with exquisite American and European antiques.

Aptly named **Bird Watcher's General Store** (Route 6A, Orleans; 508-255-6974) sells anything having to do with birds—field guides, glasses, 25 kinds of birdbaths, bath heaters, birdfeeders and carving kits. It's also got coffee mugs, T-shirts, stamps, floor mats and pot holders adorned with birds.

Remembrances of Things Past (376 Commercial Street, Provincetown; 508-487-9443) is fun to explore even if you aren't in the mood to buy. It's full of nostalgic memorabilia from the '20s to the '50s—telephones, jewelry, sports memorabilia and vintage photographs of Elvis, Marilyn and Lucy.

Marine Specialties (235 Commercial Street, Provincetown; 508-487-1730) sounds like a straightforward place, but it's not. Housed in a barnlike room, this eclectic shop is jammed with all sorts of reasonably priced odd-ball nautical and military items such as antique brass buttons, old fashioned oars, bells, baskets, antique diving gear, fog horns, vintage shoe carts, Army and Navy clothing, flags, bicycle lights, shells and fishing nets. Even people who hate to shop love this place.

For beautiful hand-painted dishes from all over the world and European kitchen utensils, visit **Chatham Cookware** (524 Main Street, Chatham; 508-945-1550), a white, pink and blue cottage-style store. Fresh and sweet, it also sells excellent bakery and deli goods and coffee.

There are countless stores on Cape Cod selling nautical decorative items, but few are as classy as **The Regatta Shop** (582 Main Street, Chatham; 508-945-4999). Here you find silver dolphin bracelets, sleek hand-carved house signs, colorful fish-shaped magnets and a wide collection of museum-quality maritime posters.

The Spyglass (618 Main Street, Chatham; 508-945-9686) is a wonderful salty dog store filled to its dark brown rafters with antique telescopes, microscopes, opera glasses, barometers, nautical antiques, paintings and tools.

If you want your home to look as if it belongs in a magazine, **Marshmallow** (193 Main Street, Falmouth; 508-548-6505) has everything you need: hand-painted plates, shaker pine boxes, tables and armoires, couches and chairs, reproduction wicker, woven throws and cotton rugs. There's also a kitchen store for the gourmet chef or novice cook.

MARTHA'S VINEYARD SHOPPING

Bunch of Grapes Bookstore (Main Street, Vineyard Haven; 508-693-2291) is a writers hangout. The best bookstore on the island, it has shelves well-stocked with quality fiction and poetry. The store regularly hosts autograph parties.

Linen, antique English pine furniture, knubby hand-knit sweaters and hand-painted coffee mugs can be found at **Bramhall & Dunn** (Main Street, Vineyard Haven; 508-693-6437).

Silver & Gold (64 Main Street, Vineyard Haven; 508-693-0243) is the best place on the island for beautiful jewelry. Many pieces artfully combine modern and antique styles.

Take It Easy Baby (142 Circuit Avenue, Oak Bluffs; 508-693-2864) is a very hip used clothing store selling leather bomber jackets, vintage Hawaiian shirts, designer women's wear and incredibly chic Canadian foul weather gear such as flannel-lined sou'westers. This is a fun store for the terminally cool.

Edgartown Wood Shop (55 Main Street, Edgartown; 508-627-9853), a cavernous red brick room, sells handsome hand-crafted wooden spoons, plates, bread platters, bowls, cutting boards, Christmas ornaments, tables and benches. Prices are reasonable, and the craftsmanship is superb.

NANTUCKET SHOPPING

Hoorn Ashby Gallery (10 Federal Street; 508-228-9314), one of Nantucket's most beautiful galleries, sells American and European contemporary paintings, antique folk art such as a hand-painted blanket chests, blue and white pottery and more in a sun-filled room with wood-paneled walls, tall columns and floor-to-ceiling windows.

Many shops in Nantucket sell handwoven goods, but **Nantucket Looms** (16 Main Street; 508-228-1908) blankets, throws and shawls are a cut above the rest. Popular designs include a voluminous, fluffy white blanket with thin navy stripes, and a pale pink shawl laced with foggy grey threads.

Four Winds Craft Guild (Straight Wharf; 508-228-9623) specializes in the island's two oldest crafts: antique and new lightship baskets and scrimshaw. The former are tightly woven, bowl-shaped baskets used as purses or decorative items; scrimshaw are items decoratively carved from whale bone and teeth. Both crafts were created in the 18th century by lighthouse keepers and sailors with idle time on their hands. Lightship purses are a status symbol among the island's conservative ladies. The older the basket, the better.

19 Petticoat Row (19 Centre Street; 508-228-5900), one of the island's prettiest home furnishing and gift shops, sells French and English antique bed linens, hand towels, pillow shams, scented soap, potpourri, hand-painted dishes and many other temptations. During the whaling days, the street this shop is on was called Petticoat Row because of all the wives who ran stores here while their husbands were at sea.

SOUTH COAST SHOPPING

The South Coast is outlet country. Fall River has over 100 outlets, and New Bedford and Plymouth have quite a few, too. Until the 1980s these were novel, but today there are so many discount shopping places across the country that they don't seem unique. Choices are somewhat limited because the same brands are sold everywhere: Bass, Farberware, American Tourister, Jonathan Logan, Van Heusen and Vanity Fair to name a few.

Cordage Park (Route 3A, Plymouth; 508-746-7707), housed in a former brick cordage rope factory, is the most attractive factory outlet on the South Shore. The lovely old building is surrounded by ponds, fountains, gazebos, rolling lawns and flower gardens. Some retailers include American Tourister, Van Heusen, Cape Cod Stoneware and Maidenform.

Howland Place (651 Orchard Street, New Bedford; 508-999-4100) is the Rodeo Drive of factory outlets. Located in a restored brick building that could pass for a fancy mall, it has retailers including Perry Ellis, Vakko Leather, Adrienne Vittadini and Alexander Julian, to name a few. Discounts range from 20 to 50 percent.

Calvin Klein Outlet (100 North Front Street, New Bedford; 508-999-1300) has great bargains on sportswear (tailored shirts, T-shirts, jeans and cotton sweaters). Discounts on the better quality merchandise (wool skirts, silk blouses and cashmere sweaters) are not that impressive. Housed in an enormous brick building, the outlet displays everything quite neatly so you can see the merchandise. Discounts range from 20 to 70 percent.

Fall River Outlets: Driving the expressway in Fall River, you can't help but notice the mammoth, six-story granite textile mills transformed into factory outlets. To visit them from Route 195, which runs through town, take Route 24 south to the Brayton exit and follow the signs. All the outlets are close together, and each building has between 50 and 100 retailers selling clothes, dishes, sheets, towels, jewelry, handbags and more. Prices are rock bottom, and the merchandise is pretty low-end. Natural fiber clothing is difficult to find.

Nightlife

If you want fast-paced nightlife, go to Boston. When it comes to entertainment, the coast is pretty quiet. However, in the summer many good theatrical and musical performances are offered throughout the area. Unless specified otherwise, musical and theatrical organizations listed here only perform in the summer.

NORTH SHORE NIGHTLIFE

Every Sunday afternoon Le Grand David and his Spectacular Magic Company perform a highly skilled magic show at the **Cabot Street Cinema Theatre** (★) (286 Cabot Street, Beverly; 508-927-3677), featuring levitations, vanishing acts, comedy and song-and-dance routines, complete with outrageous costumes and sets. The rest of the week the theater shows first-rate foreign and domestic films.

Symphony By The Sea (P.O. Box 8034, Salem; 508-745-4955) concerts take place in the Peabody Museum's (161 Essex Street) spectacular East Indian Marine Hall and are concluded by a reception with the musicians.

The **Gloucester Stage Company** (267 East Main Street, Gloucester; 508-281-4099), under the direction of playwright Israel Horovitz, stages first-rate plays in an old brick firehouse during the summer and December.

Rockport Art Association (★) (12 Main Street, Rockport; 508-546-6604) organizes popular social events such as square dancing and summer concerts.

The **Rockport Chamber Music Festival** (508-546-7391) performs in the Hibbard Gallery of the Rockport Art Association (12 Main Street).

Castle Hill Festival (P.O. Box 563, Ipswich; 508-356-4351) presents a wide range of musical concerts (jazz, ragtime, classical) in Castle Hill mansion or on the manicured grounds.

The Grog (13 Middle Street, Newburyport; 508-465-8008) is an attractive restaurant and cabaret with live entertainment ranging from reggae, rock and rhythm-and-blues to oldies and dance bands. Cover.

CAPE COD NIGHTLIFE

Heritage Plantation Concerts (Pine and Grove streets, Sandwich; 508-888-3300) offers a diverse program including jazz, ethnic and folk music, banjo music, Scottish pipe bands, chorale groups and big bands.

Established in 1926 and America's oldest summer theater, **The Cape Playhouse** (Route 6A, Dennis; 508-385-3911) presents well-known plays and musicals such as *The Sound of Music, Ain't Misbehavin'* and *Betrayal,* performed by Hollywood and Broadway stars. Lana Turner, Gregory Peck and Henry Fonda have been on stage here. Nostalgic and romantic-looking, the Playhouse is in an 1810 meetinghouse surrounded by graceful lawns, gardens and a Victorian Gothic ticket booth.

The Cape Museum of Fine Arts' **Cinema Club** (Route 6A, Dennis; 508-385-4477), on the grounds of the Cape Playhouse, shows quality films, both new and old, such as *Henry V* with Laurence Olivier, *Ginger and Fred* and *House of Games.*

Barnstable Comedy Club (Route 6A, Barnstable Village; 508-362-6333), founded in 1922, is the oldest amateur theater group on the Cape. Throughout the year it gives major productions and workshops. Kurt Vonnegut, an alumni of the Club, acted in many of its earlier productions.

Provincetown has first-rate gay and lesbian entertainment—everything from afternoon tea dances, cabaret and ministage productions to piano bars, discos, you name it. Here are some of the most popular hot spots, a few of which draw straights and gays alike:

Tallulah's Bar (429 Commercial Street, Provincetown; 508-487-3178) offers a pianist/vocalist performing period music from the '30s and '40s. This art deco lounge features a marble bar with etched glass; on warm nights you may want to enjoy the music from the harborside deck. The club draws a mixed crowd and is popular with gays.

The Post Office Café Cabaret (303 Commercial Street; 508-487-6400) is the spot for lesbians during the summer, when it presents noted female performers such as Teresa Trull. The café is open year-round and is a good place to hang out.

A popular spot for quality entertainment is the **Town House Restaurant** (291-293 Commercial Street, Provincetown; 508-487-0292). During the summer it offers a variety of acts—piano music, drag shows and comedians. Cover.

Female impersonators bring to life such legends as Judy Garland and Pearl Bailey at the **Crown and Anchor** (247 Commercial Street; 508-487-1430), housed in a historic waterfront building. Reservations are a must. This place attracts gays, lesbians and straights. Cover.

The hottest gay bar and disco in town is the **Atlantic House** (4-6 Masonic Place; 508-487-3821).

The **Pied Piper** (193A Commercial Street; 508-487-1527) was cited by *Time* magazine as "the best women's bar" in the country. Locals say the best time to go is after ten for the dancing.

During the summer a popular activity is the afternoon tea dance at **The Boatslip Beach Club** (161 Commercial Street; 508-487-1669), a full-service resort on the beach.

In the south Cape area, there's live entertainment nightly in the summer (weekends during the winter) at the **Chatham Wayside Inn** (512 Main Street; 508-945-1800). The music is blues and rock-and-roll. Cover.

Musical acts, comedies and plays are presented at the **Academy Playhouse** (120 Main Street, Orleans; 508-255-1963), in a former town hall built in 1837.

Asa Bears (415 Main Street, Hyannis; 508-771-4444), a lounge and restaurant in a Victorian mansion, offers a little bit of everything—jazz, classical guitar and dance music. Entertainment takes place in the attractive library lounge.

Cape Cod Melody Tent (21 West Main Street Rotary, Hyannis; 508-775-9100), an enormous theater-in-the-round, hosts big names such as Willie Nelson, Tony Bennett, Kenny Rogers, Bob Newhart and Ray Charles.

Falmouth Playhouse (Theatre Drive, North Falmouth; 508-563-5922), on the shores of scenic Coonamesset Pond, stages Broadway musicals such as *Evita, Dream Girls* and *42nd Street*. Ranked in excellence alongside the Cape Playhouse, it has its own restaurant and lounge.

MARTHA'S VINEYARD NIGHTLIFE

Throughout the year at the **Vineyard Playhouse** (Church Street, Vineyard Haven; 508-693-6450), local and equity actors star in Broadway plays such as *Noises Off*.

Island Theatre Workshop (P.O. Box 1893, Vineyard Haven; 508-693-4060) is the Vineyard's oldest theater. Year-round it presents a wide range of plays and musicals performed by Vineyard actors. With no permanent home, it stages productions at different locations throughout the island.

Winton Marsalis, James Taylor and other musicians perform **Twilight Concerts** (call WMVY radio station for schedule and location; 508-693-4994) in an open-air theater in scenic Cottage City.

Atlantic Connection (Circuit Avenue, Oak Bluffs; 508-693-7129), a hopping dance and music club, has live bands and entertainment by groups such as Taj Mahal, Leon Redbone and Queen Ida and her Zydeco Band. Cover for live performances.

Old Whaling Church Performing Arts Center (Old Whaling Church, Main Street, Edgartown; 508-627-4440) offers cultural lectures, classic films, concerts and plays throughout the year. Located in an 1843 Greek Revival church, the center has featured stars such as Patricia Neal and Victor Borge.

Popular with the under-30 set, **Hot Tin Roof** (Martha's Vineyard Airport; 508-693-1137), formerly owned by Carly Simon, has live rock-and-roll bands, comedy nights and a jumping dancefloor in the summer.

NANTUCKET NIGHTLIFE

The **Nantucket Arts Council** (Box 554; 508-228-2227) presents classical music concerts in the Methodist church at the corner of Main and Centre streets. **Nantucket Musical Arts Society** (Box 897; 508-228-3735) gives summer classical concerts in the First Congregational Church on Centre Street.

Throughout the year, **The Theatre Workshop of Nantucket** (Bennett Hall, 62 Centre Street; 508-228-4305) stages plays such as *A Midsummer Night's Dream*, *Murder in the Cathedral* and *Alice in Wonderland*.

Actors Theatre of Nantucket (Folger Hotel, 89 Easton Street; 508-228-6325) has something for everyone: serious drama, light comedy (like Neil Simon's *I Ought To Be In Pictures*), musicals, modern dance, comedians and more. A children's matinee series features musicals, magicians and plays.

For cocktails and live entertainment in a comfortable old tavern, try the **Tap Room at Jared Coffin House** (29 Broad Street; 508-228-2400).

Fun, funky and informal, **The Chicken Box** (Daves Street; 508-228-9717), a bar with live entertainment, presents a variety of bands—rock-and-roll, reggae, rhythm-and-blues and others. Open year-round. Cover for bands.

SOUTH COAST NIGHTLIFE

Free concerts at the **Village Landing Gazebo** (Water Street, Plymouth) range from swing bands to Irish balladeers and children's performances.

Live jazz can be heard free on weekends at the **Sheraton Plymouth Pub** (Village Landing, Water Street, Plymouth; 508-747-4900).

Zeiterion Theatre (684 Purchase Street, New Bedford; 508-994-2900) presents a wide range of musical and dramatic performances—everything from Chuck Mangione, *Dreamgirls* and the Mantovani Orchestra to *Carmen* and the stars of the "Lawrence Welk Show." Located in historic downtown New Bedford, the Zeiterion is a masterfully restored 1923 vaudeville theater with gilded Grecian friezes, elaborate crystal light fixtures and a glamorous atmosphere.

CHAPTER SIX

Central and Western Massachusetts

Take a good long breath once you arrive in this region, and prepare for a relaxing mix of the rural and the urbane: rolling hills and acres of cornfields, winding country roads that meander along rivers and streams, small museums, old houses, historic villages and college towns with maple-lined streets.

Don't bother to bring your high heels or tuxedo to central and western Massachusetts, unless you're spending a weekend in a fancy Berkshire resort. The mood here—and the dress code—is casual.

Culturally, economically and socially, this area has always been strongly defined by its landscape. The forests, fields and vistas of the Berkshire hills attracted poets and authors of a naturalist bent in the 19th century, and they in turn attracted the rich and famous, who built the elaborate estates of the so-called "Gilded Age." The majestic Connecticut River provided a transportation route as well as water power to generate the mills and factories in the last century. Those factories, along with the fertile soil along the Connecticut's shores, attracted immigrant mill workers and farmers, who helped make the area the breadbasket of New England for decades.

Europeans who first arrived here found primeval forestland as well as large, treeless stretches that had been settled by the Mohegan Indians, hunters who had journeyed from the Hudson River area, and by the Mohawks farther north.

Development first came to central and western Massachusetts in the early 17th century, as small forts like Deerfield were built and trading posts like Springfield sprang up along the Connecticut River. These settlements were significant to our nation's history, as they marked the first movement of the colonists into the interior of the Northeast and served as models for further exploration west.

In the 1800s, canals and mills were built in the southern end of the Pioneer Valley at South Hadley Falls. Within 30 years of its founding in

307

1850, the city of Holyoke, the first planned city in the country, would become the "Queen of Industrial Cities" and soon after "Paper City of the World."

Thousands of immigrants from Canada and Europe came to central and western Massachusetts in the late 19th century to work in the mills and factories, and to the east, Worcester was experiencing its historical pinnacle as a city where industrial innovation and forward thinking flourished.

As New England's manufacturing economy ebbed in the 20th century, so did the fortunes of the flourishing cities of Holyoke and Worcester, as well as the smaller rural mill towns. Other areas of the state found new economic life in high-technology industries, but for central and western Massachusetts, it's been a struggle. The area continues to rely largely on smaller manufacturing, education, agriculture and the service industries. As a result, there is a different standard of living in this region than in wealthier areas near Boston.

Today, though the three areas in this chapter are not so far apart geographically, each has its own identity. Central Massachusetts, with Worcester and Sturbridge as its hubs, is made up of small rural and mill towns. The Pioneer Valley, stretching up the Connecticut River, is shifting from an agricultural area into a bedroom community for Springfield and Hartford. The Berkshire area takes its influences more from New York City than from Boston, and it, too, is seeing changes as the manufacturing jobs that once served as the mainstay of the local economy have disappeared.

Many residents of eastern Massachusetts are unaware of just how rural this area is, and "westerners" often quip that the state ends at Interstate 495, which makes a large semicircle around Boston. Every once in a while a local politician brings up the idea of secession for central and western Massachusetts, partly because of the claim that the smaller cities and towns of the region don't get their fair share of state funds.

But it's also because people in this part of the state have a different way of thinking. There's a streak of high-mindedness and independence here that was already evident back in 1787 when Daniel Shays, a farmer from Hatfield, started the nation's first tax insurrection. It continues up to this day, with nearly a hundred citizens in the region who refuse to pay their taxes in protest of U.S. military policy.

Over the centuries, the region has drawn many writers: from Nathaniel Hawthorne (a Salem man who didn't like the Berkshires) and Herman Melville (a Pittsfield man who did). Comedian Bill Cosby has a home in the hills surrounding the Pioneer Valley, and Poet Laureate Richard Wilbur resides in Cummington, carrying on the tradition of poets William Cullen Bryant, who lived in the same town, and Emily Dickinson, who wrote in her home in the center of Amherst in the 19th century.

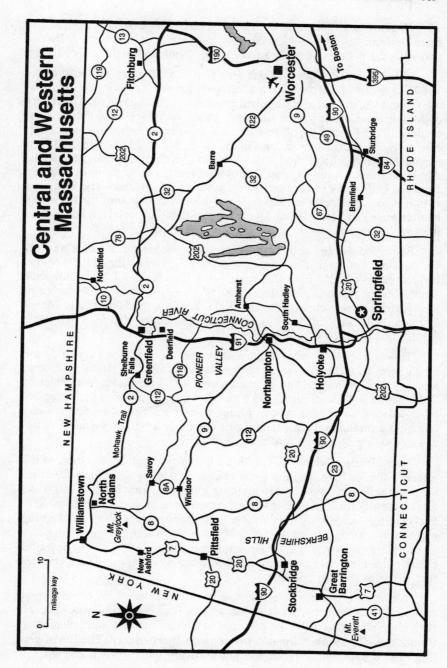

Central and Western Massachusetts

What all these people have found is a place that's close enough to city amenities and resources—New York is less than four hours away, Boston two—but far enough from the urban smog, crime and high cost of living.

Many current residents in this area first came here as students. In the 1960s, western Massachusetts was a haven for the "back to the landers," who found cheap land and stimulating political activities on the University of Massachusetts campus in Amherst. Like everyplace else, the area has mellowed, but for many, political activism remains an important part of life. Most municipal decisions, except in the cities, are made at traditional New England town meetings. And it was here, in Northampton, that '60s radical Abbie Hoffman, Jimmy Carter's daughter, Amy, and a group of students from the University of Massachusetts put the CIA on trial—and won. The region is also rich with craftspeople and artists, drawn here for the area's natural beauty and solitude, and their works fill galleries and studios in even the smallest towns.

Education is big business in these parts: Worcester is home to Holy Cross, Clark University and Assumption College, while the Pioneer Valley boasts the so-called "Five Colleges"—the University of Massachusetts, Smith, Mount Holyoke, Hampshire and Amherst—as well as a number of prestigious private schools like Deerfield Academy and Northfield Mount Hermon. Williams College is located in the Berkshire village of Williamstown.

This is a special place, taken best at a slow pace. Don't try to do too much here; take the time to loll in a sidewalk café in Northampton or to lose yourself in any of the fine museums of Springfield, Worcester or Williamstown. Though summer is the closest thing to paradise in this region, other seasons have their special pleasures as well. Spend an autumn day climbing a mountain to see the foliage colors, or a winter weekend cross-country skiing at a cozy inn in the Berkshires.

Mark Twain's adage "If you don't like New England weather, wait a minute" applies here, and the weather can vary in locations only 20 miles apart in the Berkshires. Expect anything in winter, from brilliant, 50° days after a snowstorm, to stretches when the thermometer doesn't get above 20°. Early spring—maple sugaring season—will bring warmer days and freezing nights, while summer generally offers 70° to 80° days and, oftentimes, thunderstorms in the early evening. Indian summer is truly one of the most beautiful times in this area, with crystal blue skies, stunning foliage and temperatures that range in the 50s and 60s.

You probably won't be eating in gourmet restaurants every evening or mingling with the jet-set, but a visit to this region can put you in touch with simpler things. Like the pleasure of being outdoors and listening to the silence. The exhilaration of a hike down a forested trail. The fun of getting onto a backcountry road and not knowing where you'll end up.

If you're looking for an area that combines the serene pleasures of country life with abundant recreational and cultural opportunities, you will want to return again and again to this scenic refuge.

Easy Living

Transportation

ARRIVAL

This area is easily accessible from **Route 90**, the **Massachusetts Turnpike**, which runs the entire length of the state's southern half and has exits at Worcester, Sturbridge, Springfield and Stockbridge.

From Boston, **Route 2** offers a scenic highway route to the famed Mohawk Trail and the northern portions of central and western Massachusetts.

BY AIR

Many people fly into **Logan International Airport** in Boston (see Chapter Four) to reach central and western Massachusetts. The area is also served by **Bradley International Airport** in Windsor Locks, Connecticut (see Chapter Two), near Hartford, and **Worcester Municipal Airport**, a smaller but increasingly popular alternative to Logan, which is served by Continental Airlines and USAir. Those who are combining a trip to the Berkshires with a visit to Vermont may want to use **Albany County Airport** in Albany, New York.

Peter Pan Bus Lines (800-237-8747) provides regular shuttles between Bradley International and the Springfield Bus Terminal at 1776 Main Street.

There is no public transportation to or from the airport here. **Worcester Airport Limousine** (508-756-4834) provides door-to-door van and minibus shuttle service between the airport and points in Worcester County, including Sturbridge.

Taxi companies serving the Worcester airport include **Yellow Cab** (508-754-3211), **Arrow Cab** (508-756-5184) and **Independent Cab** (508-752-5601).

BY BUS

All long distance bus lines operate from terminals at 75 Madison Street, Worcester, and 1776 Main Street, Springfield.

Greyhound Bus Lines (Worcester, 508-754-3247; Springfield, 413-781-1500) links Worcester and Springfield with the Berkshires, Boston and New York City.

312   Central and Western Massachusetts

Peter Pan Bus Lines (Worcester, 508-754-4600; Springfield, 413-781-3320) provides transportation to Boston; points west, including Springfield, Amherst, Northampton, the Berkshires and Albany; and points south, including Cape Cod, Hartford and New York City.

Bonanza Bus Lines, Inc. (413-781-3320) connects Springfield with the Berkshires, Albany, Sturbridge and Providence, Rhode Island.

Vermont Transit Lines (413-781-1500) connects Springfield with points north: Holyoke, Northampton, Vermont, New Hampshire and Canada.

Englander Coach Lines (617-720-4110) travels through the towns along Route 2 between Boston and Williamstown, and on to Albany and Bennington, Vermont. Buses leave regularly from the Back Bay Train Station at Copley Square in Boston.

BY TRAIN

Amtrak (45 Shrewsbury Street, Worcester; 66 Lyman Street, Springfield; 800-872-7245) serves the Worcester area from New York City and Albany. The "Montrealer" leaves New York City each day with stops in Amherst, and there are several trains daily between Springfield and New York's Pennsylvania Station.

CAR RENTALS

From the Worcester airport, you can rent a car from **Hertz Rent A Car** (508-753-7203) or **Budget Rent A Car** (508-852-0361).

In Springfield, **Orbit Auto Rental** (413-781-0451) offers used car rentals, as well as station wagons and passenger vans.

PUBLIC TRANSPORTATION

In central Massachusetts, **Worcester Regional Transit Authority** (508-791-2389) provides bus service to local destinations within Worcester County.

In the Pioneer Valley, **Pioneer Valley Transit Authority** (413-781-7882) offers frequent service throughout greater Springfield, Holyoke, Northampton and Amherst.

During the school year, the free **Five-College Bus Service** (413-545-0056) links the campuses of the University of Massachusetts, Smith College, Mount Holyoke College, Amherst College and Hampshire College. **Greenfield Montague Transportation Area** (413-773-9478) provides bus service throughout greater Greenfield, South Deerfield, Montague and Turners Falls.

In the Berkshires, **Berkshire Regional Transit Authority** (413-499-2782) links Pittsfield with Williamstown, North Adams, Lenox, Lee, Stockbridge and Great Barrington.

Hotels

Though there are few luxurious, full-service resorts in this region, central and western Massachusetts offers a wide range of accommodations, from the standard chain-motel-by-the-highway to the homey bed and breakfast on a rural hilltop to the quintessential white-columned New England country inn. Peak times are weekends during the summer, and foliage season, mid-September to late October.

Bed and breakfasts are an alternative to hotels in central and western Massachusetts, and while they are often not big on amenities, they do give you a chance to meet fellow travelers, as well as the people who live here. As individual as their owners, bed and breakfasts are often more reasonably priced than hotels. You may spend one night in an 18th-century farmhouse in the Berkshires and the next in a Victorian home on a small-town common.

Several associations of bed and breakfast owners in this region can provide information and reservations with one phone call:

Berkshire and Greater Springfield Bed and Breakfast (P.O. Box 211, Williamsburg, MA 01096; 413-268-7244) is a reservation service that matches travelers with over 90 private homes and small country inns in the Sturbridge, Pioneer Valley and Berkshire areas. Budget to ultra-deluxe.

Hampshire Hills Bed and Breakfast Association (P.O. Box 307, Williamsburg, MA 01096; 413-238-5529) provides a brochure listing 18 bed and breakfasts in the small hill towns of the Hampshire Hills. Moderate to deluxe.

In the Country Bed and Breakfast Association (P.O. Box 5, Buckland, MA 01338; 413-498-2692) offers information on 13 small bed and breakfasts in the farm and hill towns of the Pioneer Valley. Prices range from budget to moderate.

CENTRAL MASSACHUSETTS HOTELS

Worcester has its share of chain motels, but Sturbridge, 18 miles southwest, offers a better variety of accommodations.

Located near the busy University of Massachusetts Medical Center, the **Beechwood Inn** (363 Plantation Street, Worcester; 508-754-5789) is one of the town's newer hotels. The large round building has a lobby decorated with flagstone floors and light oak and lavender trim. The Beechwood offers 58 spacious guest rooms, including some fireplace suites, each decorated in pastels and wall-to-wall carpeting. The restaurant here has earned high praises from local food critics for its classic American cuisine. Deluxe to ultra-deluxe.

The **Old Sturbridge Village Lodges and Oliver Wight House** (Route 20 West, Sturbridge; 508-347-3327), located at the entrance to Old Sturbridge Village, offers a variety of lodging that includes the 200-year-old

Oliver Wight House, the Dennison Cottage suites and Village units. The Oliver Wight House, built in 1789, once served as a tavern providing food and lodging for farmers and travelers. The now-refurbished inn features ten large rooms nicely decorated with Federal-style pieces, including big four-poster beds. Motel-type accommodations are available in the Dennison Cottage, which also offers two luxury suites in a 19th-century country decor with stenciled walls. The Village units are decorated in an early American motif, with colonial reproductions. Though the service is friendly here, the atmosphere is motel-like, without the personal interaction you get at a country inn. Moderate to deluxe.

Offering basic modern motel accommodations, the **Sturbridge Coach Motor Lodge** (408 Main Street, Route 20, Sturbridge; 508-347-7327) has nicely kept grounds and a swimming pool and is convenient to Sturbridge, Worcester and Brimfield. Moderate.

Set on two-and-a-half acres and adjacent to a 100-acre park, **Wildwood Inn** (121 Church Street, Ware; 413-967-7798) is a century-old Victorian. Five budget-to-moderate-priced rooms feature twin, queen and four-poster beds. Antique quilts are supplemented by electric blankets for those cold New England nights. In the warm months you'll gravitate to the wicker furniture on the wraparound porch. The country-casual parlor features antiques such as a spinning wheel and pie safe as well as a fine library. Full breakfast and afternoon tea are delightful.

PIONEER VALLEY HOTELS

The Springfield area offers a large selection of chain motels and luxury hotels, while accommodations in the upper Pioneer Valley include more motels, country inns and bed and breakfasts. Advance reservations are strongly recommended in June, when college graduations and the American Crafts Council Crafts Fair are held, and in September, when the Eastern States Exposition and fall foliage bring a flurry of visitors.

The most elegant hostelry in the Pioneer Valley, the **Sheraton Springfield Monarch Place** (Monarch Place, Springfield; 413-781-1010) has a plush carpeted lobby highlighted by marble, a 12-story atrium and amenities like an indoor pool with a sun deck. The 304 spacious guest rooms are decorated in soft pastels. There are also two restaurants, a lounge and a health club with jacuzzi, weight room and sauna. Ask for a room with a view of the Connecticut River. Moderate to ultra-deluxe.

The **Yankee Pedlar Inn** (1866 Northampton Street; 413-532-9494) has 40 guest rooms in five separate buildings on a busy street in Holyoke. Rooms are individually decorated in early American decor, with period pieces and antiques, canopy and four-poster beds. The Pedlar has a colonial-style tavern, an oyster bar and a restaurant. Although not an isolated country inn, this is a popular place for business travelers, and its location just off Route 91 makes it convenient to all parts of the Pioneer Valley. Moderate.

Standing in the center of Amherst, the **Lord Jeffrey Inn** (30 Boltwood Avenue; 413-253-2576) has been a fixture in this college town for decades. Many of its 50 rooms are decorated with antiques, and some overlook the lovely town common. The inn has the sedate feel of an Ivy League faculty club, with an elegant dining room and tavern, as well as several cozy public sitting rooms, comfortable arm chairs and a fireplace. It's located within walking distance of the shopping area and Amherst College. Moderate to deluxe.

The **Campus Center Hotel** (University of Massachusetts, Amherst; 413-549-6000) offers 116 rooms in standard low-cost hotel decor in a white concrete highrise on the University of Massachusetts campus. The ambience is nothing special, but the hotel is convenient for visitors to the university, and the view of the Holyoke range and the campus is great. Moderate.

Near downtown Northampton and right next to the Smith campus, the **Autumn Inn** (259 Elm Street; 413-584-7660) is a simple, comfortable 30-room hostelry. Rooms here are large, clean and individually decorated with wall-to-wall carpeting, colonial reproductions, brass lamps, Hitchcock rockers and prints from the owner's collection. Extras include a pool and coffee shop with a large fireplace. The place has attracted a regular clientele for its location and attention to detail. Moderate to deluxe.

The **Hotel Northampton** (36 King Street, Northampton; 413-584-3100) has undergone a facelift, converting a once semiseedy, middle-aged downtown hotel into something with a touch of class. There are 69 rooms here, including some with canopy beds and jacuzzis. The lobby is nicely decorated in a colonial motif, and the hotel has become a favorite for Smith College parents for its accommodations and its proximity to the campus. Reservations advised. Deluxe to ultra-deluxe.

One of the few elegant old country inns in the northern Pioneer Valley, the century-old **Deerfield Inn** (Main Street; 413-774-5587) stands along a lovely, tree-lined street in Historic Deerfield. Its 23 rooms are decorated in antiques and Graeff fabric wallpaper. There's a comfortable sitting room with a fireplace to enjoy predinner drinks, and a good restaurant. The regular clientele from Boston and New York enjoy the ambience as well as the services of innkeepers Karl and Jane Sabo, themselves urban refugees. Bed and breakfast or modified American plan available; ultra-deluxe.

THE BERKSHIRES HOTELS

This area offers a larger selection of elegant accommodations and smaller bed and breakfasts. Restrictions are common here, however, and some of the room rate cards are as complicated as life insurance policies. In a nutshell: rates are highest (and they do get high!) on weekends in summer and fall; and most places close to Lenox require a two-night minimum stay on weekends during Tanglewood season, from mid-June through early September.

Budget accommodations are virtually impossible to find in the Berkshires. One budgetary strategy is to make a home base in the towns slightly away from the often-crowded and expensive Lenox-Stockbridge area. To the north, Williamstown offers a wider price range of motels and inns, with fewer restrictions. Just south of Stockbridge, the small towns of South Egremont, Sheffield and Great Barrington offer many historic and pretty inns and bed and breakfasts.

A resort built around a country-inn motif, **The Orchards** (Route 2, Williamstown; 413-458-9611) offers 49 rooms individually decorated in English antiques and fancy bedspreads, some with fireplaces, refrigerators and marble-floored bathrooms. The ambience here is one of quiet elegance, despite the inn's incongruous proximity to the Route 2 commercial strip. Tea is served each afternoon in the graciously appointed lobby, and guests get a chocolate chip cookie with their turned-down beds each evening. Pool, sauna, concierge service and restaurant all on the premises. Ultra-deluxe.

The **Maple Terrace Motel** (555 Main Street, Route 2, Williamstown; 413-458-8101) is a budget-conscious traveler's find. The 16 rooms are clean and renovated with standard motel decor, but the Maple Terrace, set back from the street, is a bit quieter than others along the highway. Behind the motel is an open field, with a spacious swimming pool, picnic tables, swings and several large weeping willow trees. This is a good place for families, within walking distance of the Williamstown Theater Festival, shopping and restaurants. Moderate.

River Bend Farm (★) (643 Simonds Road, Williamstown; 413-458-3121) is a historic bed and breakfast set in a 200-year-old tavern built by Colonel Benjamin Simonds, one of the founders of Williamstown. The place has been meticulously restored by innkeepers Dave and Judy Loomis and has shared baths and five rooms, each individually decorated in colonial-style antiques. Its location makes it convenient to the Williams College campus. Moderate.

The Canyon Ranch in the Berkshires (Bellefontaine, Kemble Street, Lenox; 413-637-4100) is an East Coast version of a famous Tucson fitness resort. It's housed at the 120-acre estate called Bellefontaine, one of the most ornate of the original Berkshire "cottages" and a replica of the French Petit Trianon built by Louis the XV. The 120-room resort is geared for busy city folk looking for a bit of down time away from it all. There's a full fitness program, gourmet "spa cuisine," indoor and outdoor pools, walking trails and gardens. Ultra-deluxe.

A very homey Berkshire cottage, **Garden Gables** (141 Main Street, Lenox; 413-637-0193) is a lovely white clapboard house built in 1908. Though it is located within walking distance of downtown Lenox, the inn is quiet and relaxed, with nice gardens and a swimming pool. The inn's 12 rooms are individually decorated in a mix of styles, and all have private baths; some have jacuzzis, others balconies with a view of the pool. The inn has many regular long-term visitors. "Continental plus" breakfast is offered in a small dining room. Deluxe to ultra-deluxe.

The **Village Inn** (16 Church Street, Lenox; 413-637-0020) is a 200-year-old hostelry with 31 rooms, most offering private baths. All rooms are furnished with country antiques, some with working fireplaces and four-poster beds. This Federal-style building has served as an inn since 1775, and the innkeepers have restored and modernized the building without destroying its integrity. Tea is served here each afternoon, and the low-beamed tavern downstairs offers a full bar. This place has a comfortable, homey feel despite its size and is conveniently located in the center of Lenox. Moderate to ultra-deluxe.

Red Lion Inn (Main Street, Stockbridge; 413-298-5545) is a New England classic. Built originally in 1773 as a stagecoach stop, the inn was destroyed by fire and rebuilt in 1897. Today, the rambling wooden structure is one of the few remaining old wood hotels in the country. An icon of the Berkshires, the Red Lion serves as the centerpiece of Stockbridge Center. The lobby-parlor, with its fireplace, comfortable old couches and rich Oriental rugs, is always full of visitors and diners. And there may be no finer place to enjoy a summer afternoon drink than from a rocking chair on the front porch. The Red Lion has 109 rooms, including some suites with parlors, decorated with antiques and reproductions. Though it offers modern amenities, like an outdoor pool, the Red Lion is an elegant old lady of a place that conjures up images of a bygone era. Deluxe to ultra-deluxe.

Motor Berkshire Inn (372 Main Street, Great Barrington; 413-528-3150) offers proximity to southern Berkshire attractions in a motel setting, with indoor pool and sauna. For those who like to stay in places with televisions and no innkeepers to talk to, this is one of the few motels in the region. Moderate to deluxe.

The Turning Point (Route 23, Great Barrington; 413-528-4777) offers a nonsmoking environment in a handsome, 200-year-old brick inn that served as a stagecoach stop in the 19th century. Innkeepers Irv, Shirley and Jamie Yost emphasize a healthy country ambience and offer vegetarian and whole-grain breakfasts, as well as fruit and herbal teas. The inn has seven rooms and a two-bedroom cottage, with lovely grounds and hiking trails through the surrounding woods and fields. Moderate to deluxe.

The Egremont Inn (Old Sheffield Road, South Egremont; 413-528-2111) is a cozy country inn with 22 rooms decorated in 19th-century furnishings. A feeling of subdued elegance is conveyed by a long white porch where guests enjoy coffee and brunch during summer months. A colonial-era tavern with a low, beamed ceiling adds to the ambience. The Egremont Inn has a full dining room, as well as a pool and tennis courts. Modified American plan offered on weekends, ultra-deluxe; bed and breakfast Sunday through Thursday, moderate.

Located in a 200-year-old New England home, the **Weathervane Inn** (Route 23, South Egremont; 413-528-9580) has ten rooms, all with private baths, plus a swimming pool and a fine dining room. This is a comfortable, informal place with a regular clientele. Deluxe to ultra-deluxe.

Restaurants

CENTRAL MASSACHUSETTS RESTAURANTS

Thai Orchid (144 Commercial Street, Worcester; 508-792-9701) has received good reviews from locals. The Thai cuisine includes pineapple fried rice, chicken or shrimp and vegetables in peanut sauce, crisp fried tofu and other dishes, all served in the restaurant's quiet atmosphere. The decor here is spare and uncluttered, with white furnishings and wood paneling, creating an understated elegance. Moderate.

Serving gourmet fare in the cozy confines of an old house, **The Spoken Menu** (4 Cedar Street, Sturbridge; 508-347-7933) is a treat. There are only about 40 seats, spread out through several rooms, and the food, atmosphere and service are excellent without being pretentious. As the name implies, this restaurant has a spoken menu, with seafood, veal, beef and chicken, including dishes like sea scallops with walnut butter, veal Viennese and roasted stuffed chicken with basil and parmesan. Moderate to deluxe.

The Sunburst (484 Main Street, Sturbridge; 508-347-3097) offers natural foods for breakfast and lunch in a coffee-shop atmosphere. The muffins here are excellent, as is the quiche and granola. Other items include fresh fruit bowls, sandwiches and "nogs," seasonal fruit mixed with milk and eggs. Budget.

A local dining institution, the **Salem Cross Inn** (Route 9, West Brookfield; 508-867-2345) is a restored, 250-year-old New England farmhouse filled with collections of antiques and photographs. The Salem family specializes in some unique eating events that include drinks in the old tavern downstairs, hayrides and sleighrides through their 600-acre farm. In the summer, their Drover's Roasts serve up a large side of beef, slowly cooked as it was in the 1700s, over a fieldstone open pit. In winter, the Hearthside Dinners on the weekends feature prime rib cooked on a 1700s roasting jack in the fieldstone fireplace and apple pie baked in the inn's 1699 brick beehive oven. These meals are worth rearranging your schedule for, and reservations are required. Moderate to ultra-deluxe.

PIONEER VALLEY RESTAURANTS

What the Pioneer Valley lacks in fancy eateries it makes up for with a solid roster of good, moderately priced restaurants, including a number of ethnic and vegetarian spots.

In downtown Springfield, **Tilly's** (1390 Main Street; 413-732-3613) is a good choice for lunch or dinner, with an eclectic assortment of sandwiches, burgers, salads, quiches and pasta. In the old days, this would have been called a "fern bar," with a brick interior and a nice bar. The place used to be an old hotel. Budget to moderate.

The **Quad Café** (on the Quadrangle, Springfield; 413-732-6092) offers lunches—quiche, gourmet salads and sandwiches, herbed pastas and hot dogs for the kids—on the patio next to the Springfield Science Museum. Budget.

The **Yankee Pedlar Inn** (1866 Northampton Street, Holyoke; 413-532-9494) offers breakfast, lunch and dinner. Traditional New England fare is served here, including clam chowder, chicken pot pie, corned beef and cabbage, a large selection of seafood, as well as dishes like seafood alfredo and chicken in a white wine-orange sauce. There's also an oyster bar here, and the dining room is a handsome colonial-style scene, with working fireplaces and wood-planked walls. Moderate to deluxe.

Joe's Café (33 Market Street, Northampton; 413-584-3168) is a quintessential dive, with peeling paint and great Italian food: eggplant parmigiana, spaghetti and a marvelous vegetarian pizza primavera. Mingle with the locals and college students over pitchers of beer, and try to figure out exactly what that mural on the wall means. Joe's is an oasis in an area fast succumbing to culinary gentrification. Budget to moderate.

At the other end of the downtown area and the Italian food spectrum is **Spoleto** (12 Crafts Avenue, Northampton; 413-586-6313), a local favorite. This place is a real find, with imaginative Italian dishes at reasonable prices. Dishes include a sublime chicken rollatini, homemade pasta served with shrimp, scallops, mussels and calamari, vegetarian lasagna and veal scaloppine. Desserts are homemade, and the espresso is strong. Moderate.

Paul and Elizabeth's (Thorne's Market, 150 Main Street, Northampton; 413-584-4832) has a local following for its natural food lunches and dinners. Dishes include salads—hummus, tabouli, spinach and egg—good soups, fish broiled with tamari, a vegetable and seafood tempura, sandwiches and pasta. Decor is light and airy; some nights the place can be bursting with vegetarian baby boomers and their vegetarian babies, but the staff always keeps its cool. Budget to moderate.

French cuisine and excellent service are hallmarks at **Beardsley's** (140 Main Street, Northampton; 413-586-2699). The lunch, dinner and weekend brunch menu includes dishes like beef tenderloin with chanterelle mushrooms, seafood medley, escalloped veal and duck breast. This is a small place, with only 45 seats. The lighting is cool, the walls are wood-paneled and there's a rich ambience to go along with the food. Moderate to deluxe.

For casually intimate Italian dining in an art deco/Victorian setting, why not head for **Café Di Carlo** (71 North Pleasant Street, Amherst; 413-253-9300). The oak floor is framed with black and white tile and the dining room walls are graced with an art show that changes every six weeks. Veg-

etarian lasagna, tomato-basil pasta, veal dishes and roasted garlic are a few
of the popular specialties. Moderate to deluxe.

Classe Café (168 North Pleasant Street, Amherst; 413-253-2291) looks
like your average coffee shop, with big plate windows and cramped tables,
but its menu includes a variety of well-prepared vegetarian dishes, like hummus and homemade soups, in addition to the usual burgers, shakes and salads. Popular with the college crowd, it always has a lively people-watching
scene. Budget.

Judie's (51 North Pleasant Street; 413-253-3491) is an Amherst dining
institution, noted for its sun-room view of the comings and goings of downtown Amherst, its chic clientele and wonderful desserts. The cuisine here
is "nouvelle à la Judie" and includes some unusual dishes like paella and
a chicken breast salad stuffed into an oversized popover. Desserts include
chocolate truffle fudge cake and fried bananas and ice cream. Judie's is also
one of the rare Pioneer Valley spots where you can get a meal until midnight.
Budget to moderate.

The **Riverside Restaurant and Bakery** (★) (4 State Street, Shelburne
Falls; 413-625-2570) serves standard vegetarian dishes and gourmet specials in an old storefront overlooking the Deerfield River. Service here can
be slow, but if you have the time, dishes like New York sirloin with red
wine sauce and stir-fry tofu and vegetables in a tamari-ginger broth are definitely worth the wait. The Riverside is renowned for its desserts, such as
lemon cake and pothole cupcakes, named in honor of the nearby geological
wonders. Budget to moderate.

THE BERKSHIRES RESTAURANTS

There are many restaurants to choose from in the Berkshires, roughly
divided into two classes: the expensive, fancy places that draw weekenders
and visitors, and the places where locals eat, which are generally less expensive, casual and strong on all-American, meat-and-potatoes menus.

Diner fans will adore **Miss Adams Diner** (★) (53 Park Street, Adams;
413-743-5300), a 1949 Worcester lunch car being restored to its original
condition. Here the owners serve traditional diner breakfasts and lunches,
along with some special touches, like hummus salads, cold blueberry soup
and buckwheat flapjacks. Great homemade pies! Budget.

The **Cobble Café** (27 Spring Street, Williamstown; 413-458-5930)
dishes up meals to the locals, including the luminaries who drop by each
summer to work at the Williamstown Theater Festival. The walls are
adorned with artwork from local talent. Fare includes traditional breakfast
and lunch items and more elaborate dinner entrées such as beef tournedos.
Moderate.

Church Street Café (69 Church Street, Lenox; 413-637-2745) offers
an eclectic lunch and dinner menu in a pleasant outdoor café or indoor setting in the heart of Lenox's shopping district. Lunch features sandwiches

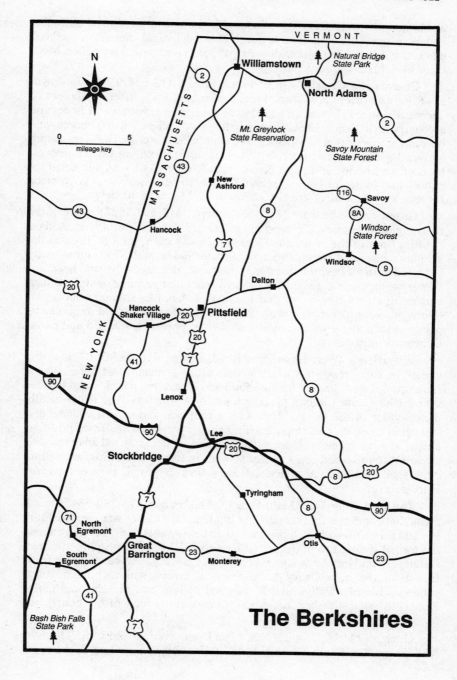

The Berkshires

and burgers, as well as more exotic fare like Louisiana gumbo, tabouli salad and bean quesadillas; dinner features Thai beef salad, Jamaican "jerked" chicken and red chile pasta with corn, peppers, cilantro and jalapeños. Moderate to deluxe.

Cheesecake Charlie's (83 Church Street; 413-637-9779), in downtown Lenox, offers breakfast, lunch, dinner and 45 different flavors of cheesecake in a light and breezy, casual atmosphere, with wood floors and a country-style decor. Lunch features deli sandwiches, salads, burgers and omelettes; dinner includes dishes like clambake cassoulet (lobster, shrimp and scallops baked in a casserole), chicken sautéed with sun-dried tomatoes, broccoli and herbs, and pasta Napoli (fettucine cooked with sun-dried tomatoes and Italian olives and served in an herb pesto sauce). A good place for snacks, too, and of course, cheesecake. Moderate to deluxe.

Gateways Restaurant (71 Walker Street; 413-637-2532) is one of the most highly acclaimed dining spots in Lenox. The restaurant is located on the first floor of the small and elegant Gateways Inn, built in 1912 as the summer mansion of Harley Procter of Procter and Gamble. The entranceway is graced with a sweeping mahogany staircase, rich tapestries and beautiful flower arrangements. Gateways offers continental and classical American cuisine in a prix-fixe menu that includes dishes like salmon continental (Norwegian salmon topped with shrimp and lobster meat and a dill champagne sauce), along with several veal dishes, pheasant, seafood and pasta. Deluxe to ultra-deluxe.

Wheatleigh (West Hawthorne Road, Lenox; 413-637-0610) is a restaurant of some renown, located within walking distance of Tanglewood. It's a special spot, known for fine food and formal service, located in a restored 19th-century Italian palazzo built for a countess. The decor recalls the splendor of the Gilded Age, with a fireplace and crystal chandeliers. Wheatleigh serves contemporary French cuisine in five-course, prix-fixe meals, and the menu includes such imaginative items as red snapper with sauce Genovoise and roast pheasant with fresh white truffles, as well as other fish, beef and game items. Reservations required; jackets for men. Ultra-deluxe.

The **Red Lion Inn** (Main Street, Stockbridge; 413-298-5545) has a menu that combines traditional New England fare like oyster pie, roast turkey and prime rib with such continental dishes as veal Oscar. You can choose the formal dining room, decorated in a colonial style, with pink-and-rose wallpaper and Norman Rockwell prints on the walls, and candles and fresh flowers on the table. Or try the more casual tavern, with its publike atmosphere, wide-plank floorboards, beamed ceiling and red-checked tablecloths. In good weather, lunch and dinner are served in the courtyard. Moderate to ultra-deluxe.

Once an old blacksmith's shop, and yes, even an old mill, **The Old Mill** (Route 23, South Egremont; 413-528-1421) is now one of the nicer restaurants in the southern Berkshires. The menu here includes items like grilled filet of salmon with citrus salsa, broiled sole filet in a hazel nut crust and veal with dijon-shallot butter, in addition to chicken, steaks and chops. The building itself is a handsome one, set on a river, with large beams, rough wood paneling and old tools decorating the walls inside. Deluxe.

The Great Outdoors

The Sporting Life

CANOEING AND KAYAKING

The large number of lakes, ponds and rivers in this region provide ample opportunities for canoers and kayakers. In central Massachusetts, canoe rentals are available at **Fin and Feather Sports** (Route 140, Upton; 508-529-3901). In the Pioneer Valley, **Zoar Outdoors** (Mohawk Trail, Charlemont; 413-339-4010) offers raft trips, canoe rentals and canoe and kayak instruction on the Deerfield River. Canoe rentals are also available at **Barton Cove Nature and Camping Area** (Route 2, Gill; 413-863-9300) and in the Berkshires at **Berkshire Outfitters** (Route 8, Adams; 413-743-5900).

FISHING

A fishing license is required for all freshwater fishing in Massachusetts. Fishing gear is available at **Dave's Sporting Goods** (1164 North Street, Pittsfield; 413-442-2960), **Pittsfield Sporting Goods** (70 North Street, Pittsfield; 413-443-6078) and **Pioneer Sporting Center** (104 Damon Road, Northampton; 413-584-9944). Rod and reel aficionados may also want to visit **Thomas and Thomas Rod Makers** (22 3rd Street, Turners Falls; 413-863-9727).

GOLF

The wide open spaces offer several good golfing spots in central and western Massachusetts. Try **Green Hill Golf Course** (Marsh Avenue, Worcester; 508-852-0913), **Crumpin-Fox Club** (Parmenter Road, Bernardston; 413-648-9101), **Waubeeka Golf Links** (Routes 7 and 43, South Williamstown; 413-458-5869) or the **Skyline Country Club** (405 South Main Street, Route 7, Lanesboro; 413-445-5584).

ALPINE SKIING

The downhill ski areas in this region are tame compared to their sisters to the north, but lift lines are often shorter, the ambience less pretentious and the lift tickets cheaper. These are also good places to take the family. They include **Wachusett Mountain** (Mountain Road, off Route 140,

Princeton; 508-464-5101), **Mount Tom** (Route 5, Holyoke; 413-536-0516), **Berkshire East** (Mohawk Trail, Charlemont; 413-339-6617), **Brodie Mountain Ski Area** (Route 7, New Ashford; 413-443-4752), **Jiminy Peak** (Corey Road, Hancock; 413-738-5500) and **Butternut Ski Area** (Route 23, Great Barrington; 413-528-2000).

CROSS-COUNTRY SKIING

Those who prefer cross-country skiing will find some wonderful spots here, from open farmland to quiet, wooded state parks. For wide, well-groomed trails, try **Northfield Mountain** (Route 63, Northfield; 413-659-3714). For a more rustic ski on narrower trails through the woods, try **Stump Sprouts Ski Touring Center and Guest Lodge** (West Hill Road, Hawley; 413-339-4265). Also try any of the region's state parks, most of which offer good trails, groomed by the ubiquitous (and noisy) skimobile crowd.

BICYCLING

Steep mountains in western Massachusetts make bicycle traveling between regions difficult, but once you're settled in, bicycling is a great way to explore the country backroads.

In the Pioneer Valley, the Amherst-Northampton area offers some fairly flat and easy rides. The **Northampton Bicycle Path** begins at the end of State Street and ends up two-and-three-tenths miles later in Look Park. Several local bicycle groups also offer weekend day-trips, including the **Franklin Hampshire Freewheelers** (413-527-4877). Schedules of the group's trips and events are available in local bike shops.

Country Cycle Tours (140 West 83rd Street, New York, NY 10024; 212-874-5151) offers weekend tours that include inn accommodations in Charlemont, Cummington and the Lenox-Stockbridge area.

BIKE RENTALS   **Valley Bicycles** (319 Main Street, Amherst; 413-256-0880) rents new mountain bikes by the half-week. **The Spoke** (408 Main Street, Williamstown; 413-458-3456) rents one-, three- and ten-speeds by the day, weekend, week and month. **Plaine's Ski and Cycling Center** (55 West Housatonic Street, Pittfield; 413-499-0294) rents all types of bikes by the day, week and month.

Beaches and Parks

CENTRAL MASSACHUSETTS BEACHES AND PARKS

Purgatory Chasm State Reservation—This park offers 187 acres of forestland, including the dramatic and unusual Purgatory Chasm. The chasm itself is a half-mile-long granite fissure, a sharp valley filled with huge boulders that have detached from the walls. Geologists can't seem to agree on exactly how Purgatory Chasm was formed, and its mystery adds to the allure of the place. There are hiking trails, including a difficult one through the chasm.

Facilities: Picnic areas, restrooms; information, 508-278-6486.

Getting there: Located on Purgatory Road, Sutton.

Quinsigamond State Park—This 58-acre preserve is an urban park, offering a grassy, midday break for visitors to the Worcester area. There are several beaches, including Regatta Point and Lake Park. Crew teams from the area's colleges can often be found at Regatta Point, while Lake Park offers tennis courts and a track.

Facilities: There are picnic areas, restrooms; information, 508-755-6880. *Swimming:* Very good.

Getting there: Located off Plantation Street Exit from Route 290.

PIONEER VALLEY BEACHES AND PARKS

Skinner State Park—Located high atop the Holyoke Range, this park offers a view of the Connecticut River that is reminiscent of Thomas Cole's painting *The Oxbow*, depicting an ancient bend in the river. Here the Summit House, a Victorian-style hotel built in 1851, has been restored as a visitor's center. Birdwatchers can view hawk migrations in the park in mid-April and mid-September.

Facilities: Picnic area, restrooms; information, 413-586-0350.

Getting there: Located on Route 47 in Hadley.

Mount Sugarloaf Reservation—Jutting up out of the Connecticut River Valley farmland like a huge monument to nature, Mount Sugarloaf shows a red sandstone face and varied natural life. This forested, 652-acre reservation overlooks the Connecticut River from on high and is a foliage season favorite.

Facilities: Picnic areas, restrooms, lookout tower; information, 413-665-2928.

Getting there: Located off Route 116 in Deerfield.

Mohawk Trail State Forest—One of the state's well-kept secrets, this forest covers over 6000 acres spread along the Deerfield and Cold Rivers. The old Indian Trail used by Mohawks to travel from upstate New York to the Pioneer Valley is etched into the woods here, and open fields and meadows lead down to the river. This park has a regular camping clientele because of its size and the number of activities available here.

Facilities: Picnic areas, restrooms; information, 413-339-5504; groceries nearby in Greenfield, Shelburne Falls and Charlemont. *Camping:* Permitted. *Fishing:* Good trout on the Deerfield River. *Swimming:* Good in a sheltered, sandy pool off the Deerfield River, a little more exciting at the "whirlies," small waterfalls upstream.

Getting there: Located on Route 2 three miles west of Charlemont.

THE BERKSHIRES BEACHES AND PARKS

Savoy Mountain State Forest—Nearly 11,000 acres, this popular retreat bordering on the Berkshire hills is favored by families. North and South ponds offer fishing and swimming, and campsites are located in an old apple orchard. The park has many miles of hiking trails, including a route to Tannery Falls. The dramatic set of cascading waterfalls that once powered small mills there is now one of the prettiest spots in western Massachusetts.

Facilities: Picnic areas, restrooms, nature center; groceries nearby in Adams; information, 413-663-8469. *Camping:* Permitted. *Fishing:* Good trout fishing in North Pond, and trout and bass can be found in Burnett and Bogg ponds. *Swimming:* Good at several beaches on North Pond and South Pond.

Getting there: Located off Routes 2 and 116 in Savoy.

Windsor State Forest—This spot is known for the spectacular Windsor Jambs, a half-mile-long series of waterfalls that travel through sheer granite cliff gorges of up to 100 feet. There are many old roads and trails for hiking and a good 100-foot sandy beach on a dammed-up spot on the Westfield River. This is a popular place for families with small children.

Facilities: Picnic areas, restrooms; groceries nearby in Adams; information, 413-684-0948, summer; 413-442-8928, winter. *Camping:* Permitted. *Fishing:* Good trout fishing in the West Branch of the Westfield River.

Getting there: Located off Route 9 in Windsor.

Mount Greylock State Reservation—If you have time for a visit to only one park on your tour of the area, this is the one to see. This 10,500-acre reserve is located atop the state's highest mountain. Immortalized by Thoreau, Hawthorne and Melville, Mount Greylock is noted for the number of rare species of bird and plant life, and the views in all directions are truly breathtaking. Hiking trails—including a stretch of the Appalachian Trail—and cross-country ski trails are plentiful.

Facilities: Picnic areas, restrooms; Bascom Lodge, has a snack bar and offers evening camp dinners by reservation; information, 413-499-4262. *Camping:* Permitted.

Getting there: Located off Route 7 in Lanesboro or off Route 2 in Williamstown.

Mount Washington State Forest—This 3289-acre expanse stands on the New York–Connecticut–Massachusetts border. The forest spreads out over mountainous, densely wooded land, and there's a feeling of isolation and solitude here. Even during daylight, watch for deer as you drive up into the area; they seem to be everywhere. **Bash Bish Falls State Park**, located within the state forest, is home to Bish Bash Falls, featuring 80-foot drops and cascading pools, along with the serene view of farmland to the west. All this provides a great escape from the sometimes-maddening crowds of Stockbridge and Lenox.

Facilities: Picnic areas, restrooms; groceries nearby in Great Barrington and Egremont; information, 413-528-0330. *Camping:* Permitted. All sites are hike-in, primitive campgrounds. *Fishing:* Good for trout in smaller brooks and streams.

Getting there: Located off Route 41 in Mount Washington.

Hiking

There's no better way to experience the natural beauty of the hills and mountains of this region than on your own two feet, particularly during fall foliage season, when the highways can seem like parking lots. Hiking opportunities abound at any of the region's state parks and conservation areas.

Some private companies offer tours geared to the serious hiker. **New England Hiking Holidays** (P.O. Box 1648, North Conway, NH 03860; 603-356-9696) offers hiking tours of the Berkshires, while nature photographer and tracker **Paul Rezendes** (Bearsden Road, Royalston, MA 01331; 508-249-8810) combines hiking tours with nature photography and animal tracking workshops.

CENTRAL MASSACHUSETTS TRAILS

The **Mid State Trail** (91 miles) travels from Mount Watatic at the New Hampshire border through Worcester County to the Rhode Island border. The trail offers a mixed bag of central Massachusetts scenery, traveling along old cart roads, through forests and across open fields. You can pick up stretches of the trail in several spots in the Worcester area, including Douglas State Forest in Douglas and Rutland State Park in Rutland.

Wachusett Mountain State Reservation (508-464-2987) offers a comprehensive network of 18 trails (total 17 miles) through nearly 2000 acres, with some steep going in parts. Trails take you through hardwood forests of oak and maple, past stands of mountain laurel, spring wildflowers, ponds and meadows. You may catch a view of some wildlife on the mountain, and this area offers some good trails for fall foliage vistas.

PIONEER VALLEY TRAILS

The **Big River Trail** (.5 mile) at Laughing Brook Education Center and Wildlife Sanctuary (Hampden; 413-566-8034) takes you along the Laughing Brook (named by author Thornton Burgess, a one-time resident), across a bridge to the Scantic River and along a boardwalk through a red maple swamp. Burgess' home, the oldest residence in Hampden, may be toured during the summer months.

At Arcadia Wildlife Sanctuary in Easthampton, the **Fern Trail** (1 mile) takes you past many different types of ferns and includes an observation tower for birdwatching. It is one of many self-guided trails that wind through some 650 acres of forests on an ancient oxbow of the Connecticut River.

The **Enfield Lookout Trail** (3 miles) at Quabbin Park leads up to the Enfield Overlook, from which you can spot eagles in the winter months. The trail is part of a 22-mile network that takes you through the largest piece of wilderness land in the state.

Located at Northfield Mountain Recreation and Environmental Center (413-659-3714), the **Hidden Quarry Nature Trail** (1 mile) offers a mini-course in the geology, natural history and wildlife of the upper Pioneer Valley. The trail winds past the ancient beds of Lake Hitchcock, as well as porcupine dens, wooded wildflowers and stands of eastern white pine.

THE BERKSHIRES TRAILS

Pike's Pond Trail (.5 mile) at Pleasant Valley Wildlife Sanctuary in Lenox takes you through fields and forest and ends up near beaver habitats on the pond and nearby Yokun Brook. Other trails at the sanctuary run past meadows, a hemlock gorge and a hummingbird garden.

One of the Berkshires' better-known hiking spots is Bartholomew's Cobble, a rocky-topped hill named after 18th-century farmer George Bartholomew. The **Bailey Trail** (1 mile) at the Cobble is a large loop that leads into the **Sparrow Trail** (1 mile). It's a gentle walk along the flood plain of the Housatonic River, through silver maple groves and rich deciduous woods and past an old oxbow. The Cobble offers wonderful views of the Housatonic Valley and, in late April and early May, a beautiful array of wildflowers.

Travelers' Tracks

Sightseeing

Welcome to the country. Forget the mall-and-monument routine while you're in central and western Massachusetts; here the sightseeing emphasis is on natural beauty, local history and culture. Historic villages and small museums provide a look at western New England's past lives, while the Five College area of Northampton and Amherst offers a full schedule of cultural events all year round. The Berkshires lead a double life; tourism and cultural events crowd its towns in the summer, but it's just as lovely in the off-season, when you might have the place all to yourself.

The cities here—Worcester, Springfield and Pittsfield—are relatively small, and, on the surface, they seem to have little to offer. But even in these places you'll find some exceptional and sometimes offbeat museums. Most people don't come here for the city life, anyway; they come for the quiet, the culture and the small towns, many linked by beautiful country roads. Part of the fun is in the unwinding—relaxing with a picnic by a river, visiting a local agricultural fair, poking through an antique shop or discovering the works of local craftspeople and artists. Don't be afraid to get off the main roads and find your own favorite spot.

CENTRAL MASSACHUSETTS

Worcester (pronounced "Wooster") is the second largest city in the state and has given the world some interesting inventions and people. The Valentine card was invented here, so was the cotton gin and the birth control pill. Abbie Hoffman, father of the Yippies, was born here; so was Clara Barton, mother of the Red Cross. Isaiah Thomas, publisher of the *Massachusetts Spy*, the country's first newspaper, gave the premiere New England reading of the Declaration of Independence here in Worcester, and the American Antiquarian Society he founded was the first national historical society in the country.

Worcester's proximity to Boston hasn't helped its cultural image, and its recent economic history has not been quite as grand. Like its neighbor Springfield to the west, the city's fortunes faded with the manufacturing economy, and it is still struggling to redefine itself. There's not much doing here, but the downtown area is in the process of restoration and revitalization, and there are some interesting museums and sights spread throughout the city.

The **Worcester Historical Museum** (30 Elm Street; 508-753-8278; admission) is housed in a Georgian Revival-style building and features a collection that details the settlement of the Worcester-Boston area. The library here has materials and books on local history for use by researchers.

Founded in 1812 by Isaiah Thomas, the **American Antiquarian Society** (185 Salisbury Street; 508-755-5221) was this country's first national historical society. Its remarkable collection of printed material includes books, manuscripts, newspapers and ephemera produced in the United States before 1877. It also houses Thomas' printing press. Access to the library is limited, but changing exhibits are open to the public, and tours of the collection and its conservation lab are offered on Wednesdays.

The **Worcester Art Museum** (55 Salisbury Street; 508-799-4406; admission) has a fine reputation as one of the best art museums in New England and features a fine collection of European, Middle Eastern, Asian and early American works.

On the outside, the **Higgins Armory Museum** (100 Barber Avenue; 508-853-6015; admission) is a steel-and-glass art deco building, but inside it's a castle filled with dozens of sets of armor collected over the years by John Woodman Higgins, a local steel company owner. The museum details the history of armor from the year 2000 B.C. to the present and even features a set of armor made for "Hell-Mutt" the hunting dog. There's a children's room where kids can try on helmets and medieval costumes.

To the north of Worcester, the landscape opens up into the broad Nash-oba Valley. It's worth the drive 20 miles north to visit the **Fruitlands Museums** (★) (102 Prospect Hill Road, Harvard; 508-456-3924; admission). Fruitlands is an overlooked gem, with four small museums spread out on a hillside offering an expansive view of the valley. It was once the home of Bronson Alcott, father of Louisa May and founder of the transcendental movement of the 1840s, which espoused individualism and self-reliance, among other things, and included in its disciples Ralph Waldo Emerson and Henry David Thoreau. The **Fruitlands Farmhouse** has exhibits detailing the movement, while the **Shaker House** provides a look at Shaker life during the 19th century. The **Picture Gallery**, built by the museums' founder, Boston Brahmin Clara Endicott Sears, houses her collection of landscapes by several Hudson River School painters. The **American Indian Museum** has dioramas and artifacts relating to New England's Indians, including Thoreau's collection of arrowheads. The grounds here are quite spectacular, so bring a picnic lunch and spend the day if you can.

West of Worcester, the land becomes less developed. You've now arrived in the real country. A good introduction to the history of this area comes in **Old Sturbridge Village** (1 Old Sturbridge Village Road; 508-347-3362; admission). Imagine a small New England village where time just stopped somewhere in the 1830s, and you'd probably conjure up a place like Old Sturbridge Village. It is a fascinating living history museum that re-creates New England life of that period, from the shoes on the feet of the costumed interpretive guides to the rooftops of the 40-odd restored buildings.

Traveling the paths that wind through some 200 acres of the small village, gardens, farms and fields, you can learn how 19th-century potters, blacksmiths, basketmakers and other craftspeople created their wares. Every activity here is designed to bring the visitor back 150 years. They host a variety of special events, some of which are based on the seasons and include cider making, vegetable harvesting, preparation and eating of special Thanksgiving dinners, and craft and antique conferences. A good place for families, this is a must stop on any tour of the region.

Just up the road from the entrance to Old Sturbridge Village is **Bethlehem at Sturbridge** (★) (Stallion Hill, Sturbridge; 508-347-3013; admission). Over the past 30 years, J. George Duquette has built a rambling diorama of the birth of Christ that includes more than 800 tiny figurines in 40 different animated areas, complete with smoking campfires and sand and soil that really came from the Holy Land. The 90-seat theater is set up like a chapel, and Duquette has even lit the place with "stars" overhead.

Driving west from Sturbridge on Route 20, you're on the open highway, traveling past forests and ponds to the small town of Brimfield, home of the famous **Brimfield Outdoor Antique Show**, a week-long flea market extravaganza held three times a year, in May, July and September. Spread out along a mile-long stretch in the center of town, over 4000 dealers come here to sell their wares, from old postcards to fine European antiques. *The Brimfielder* is a guide to the different exhibitors, available at any local coffee shop or newsstand. For a schedule and detailed listing of exhibitors, send $3 to Quaboag Valley Chamber of Commerce (P.O. Box 269, Palmer, MA 01069; 413-283-6149).

For more information about the Worcester and Sturbridge area, contact the **Worcester County Convention and Visitors Bureau** (33 Waldo Street, Worcester, MA 01608; 508-753-2920).

PIONEER VALLEY

The Pioneer Valley, actually a section of the Connecticut River Valley, stretches from the city of Springfield in the south to Brattleboro, Vermont, and beyond. Here you'll find an eclectic mix of old mill cities, semichic college towns and country villages, with tobacco, hay and cornfields in between. The farther north you travel from Springfield, the more country you'll find. Northampton and Amherst offer good restaurants and shops, while the towns in the surrounding hills are much more rural and relaxed, some with town commons and white-steepled churches, others with old iron bridges and brick factories along the rivers, remnants of the days when cutlery and other mills fueled the region's economy.

Today, housing developments are starting to encroach on farmland, but the area is still remarkably rural in some parts. This area is often nicknamed the "Happy Valley" for its unique mix of Yankee stubbornness, ethnic influences and a '60s political outlook that remains even today. It's also noted for its craftspeople, who continue traditions started by 17th- and 18th-century furniture makers, architects and others who made the Connecticut River Valley famous for its fine design.

THE LOWER VALLEY

Founded by fur trader William Pynchon in 1636, **Springfield** is the oldest settlement and the largest city in western Massachusetts, as well as the commercial hub of the region. Though it is a city that tries hard, Springfield's glory days seem to lie in the past. It does have a good collection of museums, however, that make it worth spending a rainy day here.

Overlooking the Connecticut River is the **Naismith Memorial Basketball Hall of Fame** (1150 West Columbus Avenue; 413-781-6500; admission). Basketball was invented here in Springfield in 1891, and this place is enjoyable even if you're not a sports fan. There are videos and plenty of interactive displays, including the Spalding Shoot Out, where visitors can shoot at baskets of varying heights while standing on a moving sidewalk.

Court Square (Main Street, between Court and Elm streets) is a pleasant green space in the heart of Springfield bordered by the **Hampden**

County Courthouse, the **Old First Church** and **Symphony Hall**. From here it's a short hike up the hill to **The Quadrangle** (Springfield Library and Museums Association, 220 State Street; 413-739-3871), which features four museums (one admission charge admits you to all four) and the Springfield Library. The **George Walter Vincent Smith Museum** (on the Quadrangle; 413-733-4214) houses a collection of Oriental art, as well as 19th-century European and American paintings.

Across the Quadrangle is the **Museum of Fine Arts** (413-732-6092), which features a diverse collection of Chinese art and works from the early Renaissance to the 18th and 19th centuries. One gallery is devoted to impressionist, expressionist and early modern European works. Of special interest are the works of local 19th-century portrait artist Erastus Salisbury Field, whose gigantic *Rise of the American Republic* is a mind-boggler.

The **Springfield Science Museum** (413-733-1194) offers exhibits in the natural and physical sciences, including a new hands-on Exploration Center for children and the Seymour Planetarium. The **Connecticut Valley Historical Museum** (413-732-3080) offers a glimpse of the social and economic history of the Connecticut River Valley.

Up the hill from the Quadrangle, on the campus of Springfield Technical Community College, is the **Springfield Armory National Historic Site** (1 Armory Square; 413-734-8551), established at a spot chosen by George Washington in 1794. The Springfield Armory produced the first U.S. military small arms—the Springfield rifle—bringing skilled workers to the area and setting the scene for the valley's industrial growth.

More information about Springfield is available from the **Greater Springfield Convention and Visitors Bureau** (34 Boland Way, Springfield, MA 01103; 413-787-1548).

Just north of Springfield are two great amusement parks. **Mt. Tom** (Route 5, Holyoke; 413-536-0416; admission) is a ski area that serves double duty in the summertime with a water park and two hair-raising, 4000-foot drop alpine slides. The park offers activities for children of all ages, including an 8500-square-foot wave pool and two water slides. **Riverside Park** (1623 Main Street, Route 159, Agawam; 413-786-9300; admission) is the largest amusement park in New England, an old-time place that features the Cyclone, one of the largest roller coasters in the country.

Traveling north from Holyoke, you start to get into farm-and-college country. Gradually, the mills and tenements fade away and the land becomes more open. The small town of South Hadley is the home of **Mount Holyoke College** (413-586-3100). Established by Mary Lyon in 1837, Mount Holyoke is one of the oldest women's college in the country. The campus was designed by Frederick Law Olmstead, designer of Central Park, who used a variety of rare trees to provide form, beauty and consistency. A maple-lined road leads the traveler through the 800-acre campus, between two campus ponds and up to the wooded Prospect Hill, which has bridle paths and a lawn for picnicking.

On the Granby town line on Route 116 farther north, you'll come to a funky and fascinating spot, **Nash Dinosaur Land** (★) (Route 116, South Hadley; 413-467-9566; admission), where 200-million-year-old dinosaur tracks were discovered in 1933. Geologist Carleton Nash and his son Cornell have built up a business over the past 50 years, excavating the tracks and building a small museum and shop to display the prints, some as tiny as chicken feet. The Nashes boast the largest footprint quarry in the world, as well as the largest footprints from the Triassic period, and many pieces are for sale. Kids will love this place.

THE UPPER VALLEY

Northampton counts among its past residents Calvinist minister Jonathan Edwards and President Calvin Coolidge, who also served as mayor. Sylvester Graham invented the graham cracker here, and in the early 1800s the place was a thriving industrial center for wool, buttons, paper, and later, cutlery.

Today, it is perhaps the most cosmopolitan town in western Massachusetts (some locals say too much so), with its mix of restored old buildings, galleries, restaurants and trendy Main Street boutiques. The home of Smith College, the town is a pleasant and lively place year-round but especially nice in summer, when the students have gone home.

Smith College is located just outside of the town's center. One of the so-called "Seven Sisters" (as is Mount Holyoke), Smith's campus is quintessentially old-money New England, with old Gothic buildings and beautifully tended gardens. Among its attractions is the **Lyman Plant House**, a rambling, old-fashioned greenhouse filled with hundreds of different flowers, plants and trees and open to the public. The annual bulb show in early spring is a favorite visitor destination. Another idyllic spot is **Paradise Pond**, framed by weeping willows and elm trees and ideal for an afternoon picnic. The **Smith College Museum of Art** (76 Elm Street at Bedford Terrace; 413-584-2700) houses works by Picasso, Degas, Monet and Winslow Homer, as well as local sculptor Leonard Baskin and 19th-century local portrait artist Romanzo Elmer.

Calvin Coolidge, the nation's 30th president, attended Amherst College and settled in Northampton, where he practiced law and began his political career. Coolidge lived with his wife at 21 Massasoit Street, and after his presidency the couple retired to The Beeches, a stately home located on Hampton Terrace. Both homes are private.

Other fine old Gothic buildings around town include **The Forbes Library** (West Street; 413-586-0489), which houses many of Coolidge's papers, and **The Academy of Music** (274 Main Street; 413-584-8435), a former opera house built in 1891 that now serves as a movie theater with occasional live performances.

Historic Northampton operates three homes that highlight local history and daily life in Northampton over the past three centuries. The **Isaac Damon House** (46 Bridge Street; 413-584-6011; admission) was built circa 1813 by Damon, a prominent New England architect of the day. The house includes an 1820 parlor display and a museum gift shop. The **Shepherd House** (66 Bridge Street; 413-584-6011) is furnished to depict the turn-of-the-century lifestyle. Built in the early 1700s, the **Parsons House** (58 Bridge Street; 413-584-6011) features changing exhibitions from its collection, including furniture, textiles and clothing, decorative arts, archaeological artifacts and photographs. Guided tours are offered Tuesdays through Sundays, March through December.

For more information on the Northampton area, contact the **Greater Northampton Chamber of Commerce** (62 State Street, Northampton; 413-584-1900).

Follow Route 9 east across the Coolidge Bridge and you'll reach Hadley, a farming town once noted for its asparagus and tobacco but now fast becoming a suburb. The **Hadley Farm Museum** (Route 9; admission) is housed in a 200-year-old barn moved to the spot in 1929. The museum features a wonderful collection of farm tools, an 18th-century stagecoach, wagons and home utensils used during the 18th and 19th centuries.

Amherst is a pretty college town with shops and restaurants spread out along a maple-lined town common. Though it has been influenced by the gentrifier's wrecking ball, there's still a spark of politics in its downtown area, with tie-dye clad students petitioning against U.S. military policy or in favor of animal rights.

The **Emily Dickinson Homestead** (280 Main Street; 413-542-8161; admission) was the family home of "The Belle of Amherst," reclusive poet Emily Dickinson. The large brick house built by Emily's grandfather in 1813 is now owned by Amherst College, and it has become a mecca for poetry lovers. Part of the home is open to the public.

Founded in 1821, **Amherst College** (Converse Hall; 413-542-2000) gracefully borders the southern side of the Amherst common. With about 1600 students, Amherst is one of the smaller Ivy League colleges, and its campus architecture includes a rich mix of old ivy-covered halls and newer buildings such as the **Robert Frost Library**, named for one of the college's better-known faculty members. The **Pratt Museum** (413-542-2165) houses a collection of local geological specimens, as well as the world's largest mastodon skeleton. The **Mead Art Museum** (413-542-2335) displays an outstanding collection of American art, with an emphasis on 19th- and early-20th-century works.

The **University of Massachusetts** (413-545-0111) is located at the other end of Amherst, and, with an enrollment of 23,000 students, is one of the largest universities in New England. "UMass" has come a long way from its beginnings as an agricultural land-grant college in 1863, and its campus buildings reflect that stretch, from the classic-style **Old Chapel** to the 26-story **Tower Library** that stands beside it. The library, as well as the **Top of the Campus** restaurant at the **Murray D. Lincoln Campus Center**, offer fine views of the Holyoke range. The Campus Pond is the center of fair-weather activities, and the **Fine Arts Center** (413-545-2511) presents varied performances and includes an art gallery.

For more information on the Amherst area, contact the **Amherst Chamber of Commerce** (33 Pray Street, Amherst; 413-549-7555).

Travel north on Route 116, and you'll leave the college towns behind. Here the landscape is punctuated by the long, faded red tobacco barns and cornfields whose crop will feed the area's dairy cows. Just off Routes 5 and 10 is **Historic Deerfield** (Deerfield; 413-774-5581). It's almost jarring to turn off the busy highway and onto the tree-lined main street of Deerfield, because you have, in a sense, left the modern world behind. The mile-long main street of this 300-year-old village (it's just called "The Street") is flanked by a dozen restored Colonial and Federal-style houses, all painted in the muted reds, blues and greys of bygone days. Here you can get a sense of the emerging Connecticut Valley architecture, which was different from the styles in England as well as the coastal New England towns. And the interiors at Historic Deerfield are just as faithful to the past as the exteriors; the village's collection of decorative arts and architecture has been compared to that of historic Williamsburg and the Winterthur Museum in Delaware.

Surrounded by farmland and meadows, Deerfield began in the 17th century as a tiny frontier outpost. The town was massacred by French and Indian attackers in 1675 in the Bloody Brook Massacre and virtually destroyed by a later attack in 1704. Testimony to that fateful day still stands: there's a door with a hatchet hole in it at the **Memorial Hall Museum** (413-774-7476; admission), one of the oldest local historical museums in the country. The town recovered, and Deerfield went on to prosper as a center for commerce and agriculture, as well as an exchange post for travelers between Boston and points west. In 1952, Mr. and Mrs. Henry Flynt established Historic Deerfield, Inc. to carry out the restoration of the town, the first such undertaking in the country.

The **Sheldon-Hawks House** is the best-preserved Deerfield building from the 18th century, and the dark-stained, clapboard structure is one of the oldest houses in town, dating back to 1740. The woodwork is intact, and many of the furnishings are original Deerfield pieces. The Sheldon-Hawks displays New England furniture, European brass and English ceramics, while the **Wells-Thorn House** features a series of period rooms that illustrate the influence of the local economy and changing styles in home life in Deerfield from 1725 to 1850. There is no admission fee to Historic Deerfield, but one admission fee is charged to tour all the individual houses.

The Connecticut River is the backbone of this region, and from June to mid-October, the **Quinnetukut II Riverboat** (Northfield Mountain Recreation and Environmental Center, Route 63, Northfield; 413-659-3714; admission) cruises a 12-mile section of the river, giving you a look at the geology and natural beauty of the area.

If you're lucky enough to be in the area in the late summer or early fall, check out one of the region's many agricultural fairs. The **Heath Fair** (★) is one of the oldest and possibly its funkiest, with games, livestock and agricultural exhibits, tractor pulls and fireworks. It's held at the Heath Fairgrounds, high atop a hill in the small town of Heath, off Route 2, the third week in August. The **Cummington Fair** is another small-town beauty, held in the last week of August. The **Three County Fair** is held during the first week in September at the Tri-County Fairground on Bridge Street in Northampton. The **Franklin County Fair** is held the second week in September, at the Franklin County Fairgrounds on Wisdom Way in Greenfield.

For a complete listing of agricultural fairs around the state, write to the **Massachusetts Department of Food and Agriculture** (100 Cambridge Street, Boston, MA 02202; 617-727-3018).

Route 5 north is a busy two-lane highway that will bring you to Greenfield and the beginning of a section of Route 2 known as **The Mohawk Trail**. The Trail is one of New England's oldest and finest touring roads, winding for some 60 miles past farm towns, forests and some of the best scenic views in western New England. The Trail is dotted with remnants of the 1950s heyday of automobile touring: cabins and old Indian souvenir shops, and two spots with lookouts boasting multistate views.

The Trail is particularly popular in fall, when its hills offer spectacular foliage viewing. If you're traveling in early spring, however, **Gould's Sugar House** (★) (Mohawk Trail, Shelburne; 413-625-6170) is a tasty stop. You're likely to find Edgar Gould out in the back boiling sap to make maple syrup, while his wife and grandchildren are in the restaurant serving it on waffles and pancakes. (Dill pickles are served on the side to cut the sweetness of the syrup!)

There are many opportunities for picnicking here along the Deerfield River, and you may want to stop in Shelburne Falls for supplies. **McCusker's Market** has a good deli and a full supply of health foods, as well as Bart's ice cream, a local favorite.

Take some time here to explore the lovely **Bridge of Flowers**, a former trolley bridge across the Deerfield River that has been converted into an incredible flower garden in bloom three seasons out of the year. Across the bridge and down a side street, you'll find the **Glacial Potholes** (★), formed millions of years ago by "plunge pools" of waterfalls. For more information on local geology, pick up a copy of *Exploring Franklin County, A Geology Guide* at a local bookstore.

As you travel farther on the Mohawk Trail, the curves deepen in the road, and the mountains get steeper. At the crest of the hills, you'll reach Florida and **Whitcomb Summit**. The lookout tower here once appeared as an illustration on the cover of the *New Yorker*. Once one of the hottest tourist spots on the Mohawk Trail, the summit area has become a little honky-tonky, but the view remains spectacular. You can gaze back at the mountains you've just crossed. To the east you can see the huge reservoir that serves the Bear Swamp Hydroelectric Station in Rowe, and to the west, that's Mount Greylock rising up above the Berkshires.

For more information, contact **The Mohawk Trail Association** (P.O. Box J, Charlemont, MA 01339).

THE BERKSHIRES

The lay of the land is different in the Berkshires. It's more rural than the Pioneer Valley and central Massachusetts, with more broad, open valleys and stretches of farmland and forest. There are three kinds of towns here: the old mill towns like Dalton and Great Barrington, which have their own red-brick, utilitarian beauty; small country towns like New Ashford and Monterey, with tree-lined greens, a general store or two and a white church; and the tourist towns like Lenox and Stockbridge, whose identities are closely tied to a plethora of cultural activities. Despite the tourism and second-home building boom of the 1980s, the area is still remarkably rural, and you can find yourself in a Lenox traffic jam one minute, and a few minutes later on the open road with nothing but lush green scenery around you.

The Berkshires have a noteworthy cultural heritage as well. For years, the hills drew authors, poets and artists for their natural beauty and remoteness. The rich followed. At the turn of the century, the area was nicknamed the "inland Newport" for the large number of wealthy families who built their ornate "cottages" (actually, they were 20-odd-room mansions!) here as summer retreats.

The gateway to the northern Berkshires, the city of **North Adams** was once a thriving manufacturing center of textiles and electrical components. Today, the old mills lie idle, and North Adams is a bit down-at-the-heels. The city may be on the comeback trail, however, thanks to plans for the construction of a major museum. A hard hat tour of the under-construction **Massachusetts Museum of Contemporary Art** (87 Marshall Street, North Adams; 413-664-4481) includes a look at the work of Italian sculptor Mario Marz. This 28-building abandoned mill complex will become the world's largest contemporary art museum. Call first to confirm visiting hours.

(Text continued on page 340.)

The Sounds of Music in Rural Massachusetts

It's said that New England has only two seasons, July and winter. That's not exactly true, of course, but folks here do try to pack as much as possible into the fleeting times of good weather. Case in point: the large number of concerts and music festivals held in this area during summer and autumn, many spreading out under the warm, open skies. In central and western Massachusetts, visitors have some rich choices when it comes to music, from Cuban jazz under the stars to chamber music in a church.

The undisputed king of the music festivals in this region, and perhaps in the whole country, takes place at **Tanglewood**, the 210-acre Lenox summer home of the Boston Symphony Orchestra. (Before mid-June, contact at Symphony Hall, Boston, MA 02115; 617-266-1492. After mid-June, contact at West Street, Lenox, MA 01240; 413-637-1940.)

Tanglewood takes its name from a story by Nathaniel Hawthorne, and, with its tall and stately pine trees, rolling lawns and nearby mountains, the place is renowned for its physical beauty as well as the quality of the musicians and composers who perform there. These have included Leonard Bernstein, John Williams, Yo-Yo Ma, Itzhak Perlman and jazz performers like Ella Fitzgerald and Ray Charles.

Weekend symphony concerts are held Friday through Sunday in July and August, and chamber music concerts take place most Thursdays and other selected weeknights. Saturday morning rehearsals are often open to the public, providing an opportunity to see music-making in a more relaxed setting. Seating is available in the Shed, an open-air theater, or, more reasonably, on the lawn. The tradition on the lawn is to bring a blanket or lawn chairs and an elaborate picnic lunch or dinner, complete with candelabra and champagne.

Tanglewood is just one of many music series and festivals in this region, offering all types of music in some spectacular settings. A sampling of some others:

South Mountain Concerts (Box 23, Pittsfield; 413-442-2106), a chamber music series running from August to October, takes place in the acoustically superb, 400-seat South Mountain Concert Hall, built in 1918 and listed in the National Historic Register.

Stockbridge Summer Music Series (The DeSisto Estate, Route 183, Stockbridge; 413-443-1138) includes light opera, popular music, cabaret and jazz concerts performed in a turn-of-the-century mansion. A dinner buffet is served on the estate's rolling lawn before the performance.

Mohawk Trail Concerts (Box 75, Shelburne Falls, MA 01370; 413-774-3690) offers summer and fall chamber music and jazz concerts in the intimate setting of a charming old white clapboard Congregational church on the Mohawk Trail in Charlemont.

Bright Moments Jazz Festival (University of Massachusetts; 413-545-2511) is one of Amherst's biggest summer assets, featuring Caribbean, Afro-pop and jazz concerts on the lawn by the campus pond on Thursday nights in July.

Music in Deerfield (P.O. Box 264, Deerfield, MA 01342; 413-772-0157) offers chamber and contemporary music in a 19th-century brick church located in Old Deerfield.

Although it's always a good idea to reserve tickets ahead of time for most of these events, last-minute seats are generally available. Check local newspapers for concert dates and times, and bring a sweater for those summer evenings that can turn cool once the sun goes down.

Natural Bridge State Park (Route 8, North Adams; 413-663-6392; admission) is the site of the only natural marble bridge in North America, formed by the raging waters of melting glaciers millions of years ago. Also interesting to look at are the many carvings done by quarrymen and visitors, many dating back to the 1800s.

Traveling into downtown North Adams, you'll pass huge mills—monuments to bygone days. **Western Gateway Heritage State Park** (9 Furnace Street Bypass; 413-663-8059) has a fascinating exhibit on the construction of the four-and-three-fourths-mile Hoosac Tunnel between North Adams and Rowe. The tunnel opened up rail traffic between Boston and Albany, and, at the time of its construction in the mid-19th century, was considered to be an engineering wonder.

West on Route 2 is the college and culture town of Williamstown. Established as the town of "West Hoosuck" by Ephraim Williams in 1750, Williamstown is the home of **Williams College**. The college has a rambling, classical campus with many fine buildings.

The **Williams College Museum of Art** (Route 2; 413-597-2429) is housed in an octagonal building inspired by Monticello and a new wing designed by Charles Moore. The museum is one of the best college art museums in the country, with changing exhibitions as well as a strong collection of older and contemporary watercolors, oils, photographs, fabric art and sculpture. A group of watercolors by Charles and Maurice Prendergast provide a look at 19th-century seaside New England.

In the summer, the **Williamstown Theatre Festival** (P.O. Box 517, Williamstown; 413-597-3399) draws crowds from around the country. One of the nation's finest summer theater offerings, the festival showcases productions that are weightier than the average summer stock, such as *The Legend of Oedipus* and works by Anton Chekhov and Tennessee Williams. Regulars include Joanne Woodward and Paul Newman, Christopher Reeve, Dianne Wiest and Olympia Dukakis. The schedule is usually announced in mid-May, and it's a good idea to order tickets as early as possible.

Just west of the center of town, you'll find another fine art museum. The **Sterling and Francine Clark Art Institute** (225 South Street; 413-458-9545), housed in a classical white marble building, has an extensive collection of 19th-century impressionist paintings, including ones by Renoir, Monet, Degas, Pisarro and Sisley, as well as older masters and 17th-century sculptures, prints and drawings.

For a cool dip in some naturally therapeutic waters, turn north onto Route 7 and take a right onto Sand Springs Road to **Sand Springs Pool and Spa** (★) (413-458-5205; admission). This place has a casual, family feel to it. People have been coming here since 1762 to take the natural, 74° waters. There are also two whirlpools and a sauna. The spa is open May through September.

From Williamstown center heading south, Route 43 to Hancock is a pleasant country drive with open countryside and rolling hills dotted with tumbledown barns. **Caretaker Farm** (Route 43, Williamstown; 413-458-4309) is one of the area's most successful community-supported organic farms, and owners Sam and Elizabeth Smith invite visitors to walk through their fields and admire their diverse crops. Call ahead before visiting.

Stay on Route 43 long enough and you'll end up in Stephentown, New York. But just before the state line, you'll come to a sign that reads "Hancock Village." Turn right, and about a mile up on the right is the **Babcock Barn Home** (★) (413-738-5051), home of Richard W. Babcock. He's known around the country as "Mr. Barn" for his work restoring what he calls "roots barns," built by first-generation immigrants to America. The museum is an informal place, with three old barns, the centerpiece of which is a giant, 200-year-old cider press, set up in a 300-year-old Dutch barn. Babcock is a talkative New England resource, a man who is passionate about preserving part of the region's heritage. Call ahead to make sure he's there.

If you love the furniture and crafts of the Shakers, you may also enjoy learning more about how they lived, with a visit to **Hancock Shaker Village** (Route 20, five miles west of Pittsfield; 413-443-0188; admission). Restored in the 1960s, the Shaker settlement at Hancock was the third of 18 communities to be established by the followers of Mother Ann Lee in the early 19th century. At its height in the 1840s, the population in Hancock reached 250 members, divided into six groups called "families." The Shaker economy was built on agriculture, including the growing, processing and selling of medicinal herbs and seeds, as well as the crafting of furniture for which they have become so well known. The guides stationed in each building here are an excellent source of information on the Shaker way of life. Crafts demonstrations take place on a regular basis in many buildings, and the village's round stone barn, originally built in 1826, is a real sight to behold. For gardening and herb enthusiasts, there are workshops and special dinners, which are scheduled year-round. Open April through November. (Note: Visitors coming from the north on Route 7 should be aware that Shaker Hancock Village cannot be reached through the town of Hancock. Keep heading south toward Pittsfield and take Route 20 west.)

With a population of about 50,000, **Pittsfield** is the largest city in Berkshire County, but it's not the most attractive. One exception to Pittsfield's otherwise dull demeanor is the **Berkshire Museum** (Route 7, Pittsfield; 413-443-7171; admission). Established in 1903 by Zenas Crane, a member of the Crane paper family, the museum has 18 galleries of permanent and changing exhibitions, including works by a number of Hudson River School painters and early American portraits by Bierstadt, Copley and Peale.

"The **Lenox and Stockbridge** region is Berkshire in its best dress suit and evening gown," wrote the authors of a Federal Writers Project book on the Berkshires in 1939. The writers were no doubt assessing the remnants of the so-called "Gilded Age" in the days before income taxes, when the Vanderbilts, Carnegies, Roosevelts and others frolicked at their famous "Berkshire Cottages."

These estates, with their ornate architecture, elaborate furnishings and lovely gardens hold an allure even for the staunchest of socialists. **Berkshire Cottages Tour** (The Mount, Plunkett Street, Lenox; reservations, 413-637-1899; admission) offers tours of 20 to 25 summer mansions from the time when Lenox was known as the "Inland Newport." Among these estates are:

The Mount (Plunkett Street, Lenox; 413-637-1899; admission) was built in 1902 as the summer estate of Pulitzer Prize-winning author Edith Wharton. The white Georgian Revival mansion has marble floors and fireplaces, elaborate molding and plaster ceilings, and beautiful grounds; it is even rumored that the ghost of Edith Wharton haunts the place.

Chesterwood (off of Route 183, Stockbridge; 413-298-3579; admission) is a Colonial Revival mansion that served as the summer estate of Daniel Chester French, sculptor of *The Minuteman* and the Lincoln Memorial. French traveled widely, and his home is decorated with a remarkable collection of European and American furnishings, antiques and sculptures gathered in his travels. The grounds feature Italianate gardens and woodland walks, and his studio houses special exhibits, as well as the small-gauge railroad track that French used to move his sculptures into the natural light for viewing. The plaster casts of the Lincoln statue were made here and still dominate his studio.

Naumkeag (Prospect Hill Road, Stockbridge; 413-298-3239; admission), designed by Stanford White, was built in 1886 for Joseph Choate, the ambassador to England. The stately home remains an excellent example of turn-of-the-century design, in its architecture as well as its landscaping and furnishings. Though it is not the largest of the mansions, Naumkeag's collection of antiques and porcelain from the Far East make it worth a visit. And, like those of the other cottages, the gardens and grounds are magnificent.

Route 7 south of Lenox takes you through another piece of lovely farmland, where you'll get a sense of just how rural this area actually is. Before too long you'll come to the town of **Stockbridge**, a pretty, if increasingly glossy small town whose tree-lined main street is dominated by small shops and the rambling wooden Red Lion Inn. Stockbridge has been immortalized in popular culture in two very different ways: as the setting for Arlo Guthrie's song "Alice's Restaurant" (now La Fête Chez Vous) and as the subject of works by its most famous former resident, artist Norman Rockwell. Though there are "Norman Rockwell museums" in other places around New England, the **Norman Rockwell Museum** (Main Street, Stockbridge; 413-298-3822; admission) is the only collection authorized by the Rockwell family. The museum houses the only original collection of Rockwell art in existence, including selections from his *Saturday Evening Post* covers, early drawings for *St. Nicholas* magazine, portraits and advertising works and the famous *Four Freedoms* and *Main Street at Christmas.*

Stockbridge center is worth a stroll, with many shops and small galleries. One of the more interesting ones is the **Image Gallery** (Main Street), owned and run by photojournalist Clemens Kalischer.

The home of poet William Cullen Bryant, **Great Barrington** is a departure from the country-style villages of Stockbridge and Lenox. Its funky downtown looks as though it came straight out of an old Jimmy Stewart movie.

For a pretty country drive, take Route 23 east from Great Barrington to Monterey, and head north to the town of Tyringham.

The **Tyringham Gallery** (Tyringham Road; 413-243-3260) is located in a fairytale-like cottage built in the 1930s by sculptor Sir Henry Kitson. The place could only be described as magical, with an undulating, thatched roof, large, jutting stones built into its walls and a sculpture garden with a lily pond and nature trail.

For further information on the Berkshires, contact the **Berkshire Visitors' Bureau** (Berkshire Common, West Street, Pittsfield; 413-443-9186).

Shopping

CENTRAL MASSACHUSETTS SHOPPING

The Galleria (101 Front Street, Worcester; 508-755-4381) is the largest mall in Worcester County, with over 60 shops, including one of New England's major department stores, **Filene's** (508-752-7551), as well as three restaurants.

Spag's (Route 9, Shrewsbury) is a Worcester institution, with three large buildings and an assortment of tents filled with, well, stuff, of all kinds: from small appliances to clothing to groceries. It's a warehouse-type operation where customers actually line up to get in the place. Leave your plastice behind: cash and carry only.

Museum Gift Shop and **New England Bookstore at Old Sturbridge Village** (1 Sturbridge Village Road, Sturbridge; 508-347-3362) are two outstanding shops that feature crafts made at Sturbridge Village, as well as reproductions of early American items for the home. The bookstore features a wide selection of books about New England history, life and lore, including gardening and the home arts.

For a selection of reproductions of Shaker furniture, baskets and boxes, visit the **Shaker Shop** (454 Main Street, Sturbridge; 508-347-7564).

Sturbridge Yankee Workshop (Route 20, Sturbridge; 508-347-9500) features reproductions of early American furniture as well as decorative accessories.

PIONEER VALLEY SHOPPING

The **Shops at Baystate West** (1500 Main Street, Springfield; 413-733-2171) include more than 60 department and specialty food, gift and clothing stores.

Holyoke Mall at Ingleside (Exit 15, Interstate 91, Holyoke; 413-536-1440) has over 150 specialty and department stores, including **J. C. Penney** (413-536-3963), **Filene's Basement** (413-536-2777) and **Steiger's** (413-538-7370).

Thorne's Market (150 Main Street, Northampton) is an old department store renovated into five floors of shops and boutiques, including a New Age bookstore, a record store, and crafts, clothing and toy shops.

A favorite Sunday excursion for locals, **Yankee Candle** (Routes 5 and 10, South Deerfield; 413-665-8306), with its assortment of hundreds of hand-dipped candles, gifts and a remarkable Christmas shop with ornaments and toys from around the world. A bakery and café offer light lunches, and tours of the candlemaking plant are available.

The Pioneer Valley is especially noted for the large number of craftspeople who make their home here, and their presence is reflected in several fine shops in Northampton and beyond. A few worth looking into include: **Pinch Pottery and the Ferrin Gallery** (179 Main Street, Northampton; 413-586-4509), **Salmon Falls Artisans Showroom** (Ashfield Street, Shelburne Falls; 413-625-9833) and **Leverett Crafts Center** (Montague Road, Leverett; 413-548-9070).

THE BERKSHIRES SHOPPING

Antique lovers will have much to choose from in the Berkshires. Route 7 in Lanesboro offers several antique shops. Two of the better ones are **Victorian Lady** (413-499-1891), which features a large selection of glassware, including Fiesta and Harlequin dishes, as well as furniture, and the **Nostalgia Shop** (413-442-6672), which features glassware, refinished trunks and furniture. Both are located across from the Lanesboro Police Station. On Route 2 in Williamstown the **Country Pedlar** offers three floors of antiques.

Serious antique hunters, however, head to the southern Berkshires and the towns of Egremont, South Egremont and Sheffield. There are dozens of shops in this corner of the state, featuring pieces from early American to European to deco to plain old junk. A few of the better shops include **Bird Cage Antiques** (Route 23, in the South Egremont Post Office building;

413-528-3556) for American painted country furniture, folk art and collectibles; **Darr Antiques and Interiors** (Main Street, Sheffield; 413-229-7773) for 18th and 19th century formal antique furniture and decorative accessories; and **Centuryhurst Berkshire Antique Gallery** (Main Street, Sheffield; 413-229-8131) for old American clocks, Wedgwood and a large collection of Wallace Nutting photographs. Forget the bargains here, however; the area's proximity to New York City money has raised the antique ante substantially.

Nightlife

CENTRAL MASSACHUSETTS NIGHTLIFE

The Centrum (50 Foster Street, Worcester; 508-798-8888) is a 13,500-seat arena, offering rock and pop music concerts, as well as hockey and basketball games and conference events.

Mechanics Hall (321 Main Street, Worcester; 508-752-5608), one of the finest pre-Civil War concert halls in the country, is especially noted for its fine acoustics. The hall draws folk, jazz and classical performers and has even been used for recording of compact discs and records.

Bahama Bob's (21 Foster Street, Worcester; 508-754-7742) offers beachfront ambiance, complete with thatched huts. Dance to rock-and-roll played by a disk jockey or live bands. Open Wednesday through Sunday. Cover.

Sh'boom's (215 Main Street, Worcester; 508-752-4214) is a nightclub with a 1950s style, with disc jockeys and dancing six nights a week. Cover on weekends.

The **Spencer Country Inn** (500 Main Street, Spencer; 508-885-9036) draws locals in their 20s and 30s for its live Top-40 bands on the weekends. The place has a pub-type atmosphere, with cozy booths and lots of antiques, including a horse-drawn carriage, and there's a large dancefloor and a big-screen television for sports fans. Cover.

Legends All-American Sports Bar (Sturbridge Host Hotel, Route 20, Sturbridge; 508-347-7393) offers live Top-40 music and dancing Friday and Saturday.

Those in search of more low-key nightlife should try the popular **Ugly Duckling Lounge**, the loft of the Whistling Swan (502 Main Street, Sturbridge; 508-347-2321). The place has a warm and relaxed atmosphere amid a brass and wood decor, with piano music during the week and a singing acoustic guitarist on weekends.

PIONEER VALLEY NIGHTLIFE

Concerts, arts and entertainment events are held regularly at the **Springfield Civic Center** and **Symphony Hall** (1277 Main Street, Springfield; 413-787-6610).

Stagewest (1 Columbus Center; 413-781-2340), Springfield's resident theater company, presents comedies, dramas and Broadway musicals during its season from October to April.

The Paramount Performing Arts Center (1700 Main Street, Springfield; 413-734-5706) is an old theater restored to its 1929 grandeur. From September to late May, a variety of popular artists and comedians perform here.

In addition to showing the works of area artists, the **Zone Art Center** (395 Dwight Street, Springfield; 413-732-1995) also offers poetry readings and music, film and theatrical events.

The Fine Arts Center at the University of Massachusetts (Amherst; 413-545-2511) offers concerts, plays, lectures and dance events throughout the year.

Katina's (Route 9, Hadley; 413-586-4463) features deejays, comedy and live rock music in a dance-concert setting popular with the college crowd. Cover.

Iron Horse Music Hall (20 Center Street, Northampton; 413-584-0610) offers a wide array of folk, blues, African, Caribbean and Celtic music nightly in a coffeehouse setting. There's a good dancefloor and wide selection of imported beers. Cover.

Pearl Street (10 Pearl Street, Northampton; 413-584-7771) features local and nationally known rock, jazz, blues, reggae and funk performers in a deco-style nightclub. Cover.

THE BERKSHIRES NIGHTLIFE

The Orchards (Route 2, Williamstown; 413-458-9611) features soft rock by a piano and guitar duo in its lounge.

The **Berkshire Performing Arts Center** (40 Kemble Street, Lenox; 413-637-4718) is a 1200-seat concert hall featuring jazz, country, rock and folk performers as well as comedy acts.

Jacob's Pillow Dance Festival (George Carter Road, Becket; 413-243-0745) produces summer dance performances as well as occasional jazz and ethnic music shows.

Under the direction of Tina Packer, **Shakespeare and Company** (The Mount, Lenox; 413-637-3353) offers theatrical performances during the summer season.

In Stockbridge the **Lion's Den** (Red Lion's Inn, Main Street; 413-298-5545) offers solo and duo acts featuring guitar and piano. This lounge focuses on easy listening from the '60s, '70s and '80s.

CHAPTER SEVEN

Vermont

Vermont offers a soothing dose of old-fashioned Americana, a carefully tended piece of pastoral utopia that's down-home, uphill and intrinsically genuine. Here, dreams are lived, farms are cultivated and children are raised the traditional ways. Vermonters are at peace with their land—and it shows.

Its candid beauty is unpretentious and beguiling, a patchwork of slumbering red barns, tangled country roads and old covered bridges riveted against a backdrop of emerald mountains that twist through the heart of the state. Forming the backbone of Vermont's terrain, those towering Green Mountains—New England's oldest range—burst forth some five billion years ago when the earth's crust trembled and buckled.

Though only 9528 square miles in size, Vermont explodes with soul-gripping tableaux—alpine ridges and surging rivers, sporadic flatlands and miles of untamed wilderness. Skinny at the bottom and wide on top, this New England wedge spans an easy 151 miles in length and ranges in width from 41 miles at the Massachusetts border to 90 miles at the Canadian line.

But more than just a spot to behold, Vermont is a place to *be*. For its magic persists not only in its glorious scenery but also in its illustrious history and fastidious Yankee ideals and uncomplicated mode of existence.

Vermont may be the only landlocked New England state (a detail many Vermonters remain quite touchy about), but travelers need only scan the shores of vast Lake Champlain to find a coastline whose beauty parallels any Atlantic Ocean vista.

It was, in fact, that extraordinary lake that seduced the state's first European explorers back in 1609. Frenchman Samuel de Champlain, accompanied by native Algonkian Indians, who told great tales of mysterious waters, led an expedition from Canada and instantly claimed the lake (modestly naming it for himself) and surrounding lands for France.

During the next two centuries, the French, British and Dutch grappled to control the waterway, the sixth largest freshwater lake in the United States. The scrap was finally settled during the War of 1812, when an American naval fleet won a battle off Valcour Island.

Vermont found itself entangled in a different kind of tug-of-war during the mid-1700s, when its territory was claimed by both New York and New Hampshire. England eventually ruled in favor of New York, prompting settlers who had come from New Hampshire to organize a Vermont military force known as the Green Mountain Boys. This troupe, led by Ethan Allen, harassed New York landholders and went on to defeat the British in several decisive American Revolution battles, including the Battle of Bennington.

A flamboyant patriot determined to conquer any who attempted to steal his precious state, Allen vowed to preserve the independence of Vermont or "retire with my hardy Green Mountain boys into the caverns of the mountains and make war on all mankind."

The state supposedly earned its moniker from those cavernous Green Mountains when, in 1763, the Reverend Samuel Peters ascended Killington Peak and proclaimed his beautiful surroundings *Verd Mont*, French for Green Mountain.

Though New Hampshire inevitably surrendered its claims to Vermont, New York persisted. In July of 1777, Vermonters called a convention in the town of Windsor, drew up a constitution and declared their independence.

Drafted by 72 delegates who met for seven arduous days in a town tavern, the constitution prohibited slavery and was the first to establish suffrage for all men. According to local lore, the Windsor document was nearly abandoned by the delegates, who were about to dash off to fight advancing British forces at the state's west border when a fierce storm arose and prevented their leaving.

Despite pleas to the Continental Congress for recognition as a state, Vermont was forced to remain an independent republic for 14 years because of boundary disputes with New York. Finally, in 1791, both sides acquiesced and Vermont became the 14th state.

Early 19th-century Vermont was a land of milk and honey, where cows outnumbered people and people took to fashioning grand Victorian estates and lobbying for abolition. But prosperous times turned tumultuous during the Civil War, as half of Vermont's young men headed for the battlefield. When it was all over, Vermont had lost a larger percentage of its men than

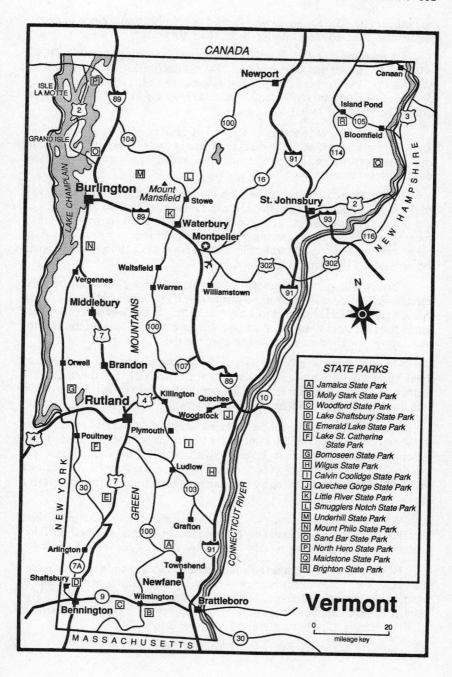

CANADA

Newport

Canaan

ISLE
LA MOTTE

Island Pond

GRAND ISLE

Bloomfield

Burlington

Mount
Mansfield

Stowe

St. Johnsbury

Waterbury

Montpelier

Waitsfield

Warren

Williamstown

Vergennes

Middlebury

Orwell

Brandon

Killington

Quechee

Rutland

Woodstock

Plymouth

Poultney

Ludlow

Grafton

Arlington

Townshend

Shaftsbury

Newfane

Bennington

Wilmington

Brattleboro

STATE PARKS

[A] *Jamaica State Park*
[B] *Molly Stark State Park*
[C] *Woodford State Park*
[D] *Lake Shaftsbury State Park*
[E] *Emerald Lake State Park*
[F] *Lake St. Catherine*
     State Park
[G] *Bomoseen State Park*
[H] *Wilgus State Park*
[I] *Calvin Coolidge State Park*
[J] *Quechee Gorge State Park*
[K] *Little River State Park*
[L] *Smugglers Notch State Park*
[M] *Underhill State Park*
[N] *Mount Philo State Park*
[O] *Sand Bar State Park*
[P] *North Hero State Park*
[Q] *Maidstone State Park*
[R] *Brighton State Park*

LAKE CHAMPLAIN

GREEN   MOUNTAINS

NEW YORK

NEW HAMPSHIRE

CONNECTICUT RIVER

N

Vermont

0   20

mileage key

M A S S A C H U S E T T S

any other state. The four-year war caused population and economic devastation that affected the state for more than 40 years.

Tourism eventually helped set things straight during the early 1900s, when word got out that Vermont was "The Switzerland of North America." Well-to-do New Yorkers set up fancy summer estates, developers threw up dozens of roadside attractions and interstate highways helped fuel the influx. Suddenly, the land boom was on.

By the 1950s, yet another new breed of visitors—the kind with skis—arrived en masse. Much to the dismay of firmly rooted Vermonters, dozens of ski runs were carved in the mountainsides, and resorts were planted where dense forests once thrived.

Today, ski resort areas remain the only real tokens of full-scale development in Vermont, often called the most rural state in the nation. Yankee conservatism has spawned a rigorous array of zoning and antipollution laws meant to stave off mass growth. Vermonters' sentiments toward development were summed up by former Governor Thomas P. Salmon in 1973 when he declared: "Vermont is not for sale."

Forests still cover 75 percent of the state, and a 1960s law banning all roadside billboards has worked wonders for Vermont's highways, which remain pristine and untainted by commercialism. In the 1980s, Vermont became the first state to prohibit automobile air conditioners that use chlorofluorocarbons, chemicals known to damage the ozone layer.

Through the years, Vermont's feisty independence and great beauty have attracted dozens of national and international artists, writers and folk heroes, including Norman Rockwell, Dorothy Canfield Fisher, Robert Frost and Rudyard Kipling, to name a very few.

Today's new artisans follow in the footsteps of those early protagonists of Vermont history, fleeing America's big cities for a simpler existence among the quiet mountains. Together with the die-hard Republicans, patriotic farmers, leftover hippies and well-heeled elite, they form a curious, independent populace, united by their laissez-faire attitudes and unwavering devotion to free living.

With a population just over 500,000, Vermont is the nation's third smallest state, though its exquisite forested mountains and shimmering lakes and rivers pack as much beauty per square mile as any of the other 49.

Best of all, the terrain reveals four distinct faces as the seasons change. Fall brings a sacred occurrence, and nearly half a million people flock to witness the changing foliage. During the season—usually from mid-September to mid-October—the entire state is covered by resplendent colors, and the temperature hovers around a crisp 50 to 60°.

Winter delivers a Currier and Ives backdrop, with carpets of plush white snow that weave through the countryside and temperatures that plunge toward 0°.

Waterfalls thaw and gush forth in spring, and millions of maple trees give up their candied sap for that wonderful Vermont maple syrup. Summer is pure green, a panorama of verdant forests, lucid lakes and blissful, breezy days when the thermometer reads about 75°.

Vermont's enchantment exists not only in its fanciful seasons and scenery but in the 242 small towns that comprise the essence of this state. Sprinkled on hillsides and straddling mountain streams, these quaint villages often cling to the social values of times past and harbor historic legacies and colorful personalities. Their very structures spell tradition: each town will almost certainly have a Main Street, a village square, a general store and a cemetery where you're apt to discover tombstones from the 1700s.

Then, too, each region of the state maintains its own separate, intriguing personality. Southern Vermont is a mingling of forests, ski resorts and small cities that have seen strong influences from neighboring New York, Massachusetts and New Hampshire. In central Vermont, "The Marble City" of Rutland has churned out tons of smooth stone for more than a century, its marble-plated buildings a testament to this vital industry. Nearby Woodstock is the state's center of prosperity, a summer playground of majestic estates, trendy shops and restaurants and total gentility.

Crawling through the upper center of the state, the Northern Mountain Region thrives as an alpine haven of ski centers and maple sugarhouses, obscure mountain hamlets and fields of wildflowers.

Gorgeous Lake Champlain wanders along the western border, edged by New York's Adirondack Mountains and Vermont's fertile Champlain Valley, and supports the state's largest city. Burlington—home to a mere 38,000 people—is a dynamic port and culture center whose well-groomed cityscapes and obvious lack of pollution make it a splendid place to tarry.

The Northeast Kingdom is undoubtedly Vermont's last stand, a 2000-square-mile piece of rural wonderland snuggled against Canada and New Hampshire. Here, craggy peaks hover above dozens of glacier-dug lakes, evergreen spires ache toward the clouds and man and nature exist together simply and peacefully.

But of all Vermont's jewels, perhaps none is so extraordinary as its people. Amiable, generous and always interested, Vermonters know how to make a person feel right at home.

In fact, visiting Vermont is a lot like coming home: Once you're there, you feel like you've always belonged. Once you leave, you'll yearn to go back.

Easy Living

Transportation

ARRIVAL

BY CAR

Automobile travel is quickest (though not very scenic) on **Routes 91** and **89,** Vermont's two interstate highways. Route 91 cuts in from Massachusetts and follows Vermont's eastern border, while Route 89 starts at the New Hampshire line and snakes across the northern center of Vermont to Quebec.

From New York, opt for **Route 7** or **Route 4,** entering on Vermont's western edge. Though not a major highway by any means, **Route 100** is the picturesque thoroughfare slicing north-south through the center of the state.

BY AIR

Burlington International Airport, a small and easily accessible facility in Burlington, is the major air gateway for Vermont. Carriers serving it are Continental Airlines, Delta Airlines, United Airlines and USAir.

Burlington Airport Ground Transportation (802-863-1889) provides service from the airport to anywhere in the state.

BY BUS

Vermont Transit Lines (802-864-6811) provides extensive service throughout New England, with major Vermont stops at Brattleboro (junction of Routes 5 and 91; 802-254-6066), Bennington (126 Washington Avenue; 802-442-4808), White River Junction (Sykes Avenue; 802-295-3011), Rutland (122 Merchants Row; 802-773-2774), Burlington (135 St. Paul Street; 802-864-6811), St. Johnsbury (Railroad Street; 802-748-8306) and Newport (Coventry Street; 802-334-2132).

BY TRAIN

Amtrak (800-872-7245) offers direct service from Washington, D.C., Philadelphia, New York, Connecticut and Montreal. The train stops in Vermont at White River Junction (Railroad Row), Montpelier (Montpelier Junction Road), Waterbury (Park Row) and Essex Junction Station (29 Railroad Avenue, near Burlington).

CAR RENTALS

If you arrive at Burlington International Airport, you'll find the following car rental companies: **Avis Rent A Car** (802-864-0411), **Budget Rent A Car** (802-658-1211), **Hertz Rent A Car** (802-864-7409) and **National Car Rental** (802-864-7441). **Thrifty Car Rental** (802-863-5500) is located near the terminal and provides free airport transfers.

Hotels

Staying in Vermont is a lot like sleeping over at Grandma's house. Chances are, you'll find yourself surrounded by family heirlooms and friendly innkeepers who insist on pampering you to death. Bed-and-breakfast sojourns mean experiencing part of the innkeepers' lives, being greeted by the family dog, picking berries in a backyard patch and waking up to the heavenly smell of bacon frying.

The state possesses more than 250 bed and breakfasts, guest houses and inns, all offering some slice of local ambience and most dispensing a feast for breakfast. There are scattered motels and motor inns and a handful of hotels. Spring and summer are off-season (except in lake areas), offering an abundance of accommodations and low rates. During the spectacular fall foliage season—generally from late September through mid-October—rooms are expensive and scarcer than sandy beaches, so book several months in advance. Winter brings ski season, and though it's fairly easy to find a room, prices are high.

SOUTHERN VERMONT HOTELS

Art deco in Vermont? Just check out **The Latchis Hotel** (50 Main Street, Brattleboro; 802-254-6300), a 1938 deco charmer in the heart of downtown. This four-story find sparkles in bright terrazzo floors and curved chrome designs and boasts 40 guest rooms in soft pastels offset by black lacquer furniture and some restored 1930s pieces. The best part is that many rooms peek a view at the Connecticut River. Budget to moderate.

Something about the **Old Newfane Inn** (Route 30, Newfane; 802-365-4427) makes you instantly feel as though you've come home. Perhaps it's the lazy wraparound porch with creaky rocking chairs, the warm parlors with brick hearths or the wonderful old general store across the street. It could be the eight rooms, decorated without pretension in rich woods and country wallpapers, or the massive pine trees that stand across the front lawn. Whatever the reason, the magic is there—and has been since this venerable country inn opened way back in 1787. Deluxe.

The sophisticated serenity of the **Four Columns Inn** (230 West Street, Newfane; 802-365-7713) has long drawn celebrities (Mick Jagger and Michael Jackson among them) seeking a quiet reprieve from life's fast lane. Set amidst 150 forested acres, the 19th-century Greek Revival inn sports a swimming pool enveloped in flowers and a cobblestone path that wends across brooks and meadows. Its trademark is four majestic columns that stand astride the loggia—a marvelous place to mellow out and listen to birds chirp. The 15 guest rooms offer wide plank floors, lace curtains and a mix of canopy and four-poster beds. Two suites are also available. Deluxe.

The Old Tavern (Routes 35 and 121; 802-843-2231) is possibly the most renowned spot in Grafton, and rightly so, since guest rooms are scattered in ten different historic buildings across town. The main house is an 1801 colonial design brimming with lovely antiques, original pine floors and pewter and brass. Formerly a popular stagecoach stop, the tavern boasts a not-so-shabby guest list that included Ulysses S. Grant and Ralph Waldo Emerson. Rooms and cottages might feature braided rugs, Victorian furnishings and full kitchen. Deluxe to ultra-deluxe.

If you want to escape from absolutely everything, consider **The Hermitage** (★) (Coldbrook Road, Wilmington; 802-464-3511). This 18th-century farmhouse is a hidden treasure tucked down a piece of dirt road and nestled against a rushing brook. The owner's love of hunting is evidenced by the English setters that roam the 24 acres, as well as hundreds of antique decoys found throughout the inn. Fifteen guest rooms—many with working fireplaces—are adorned in hunting motif and feature four-poster beds. Deluxe prices include breakfast and dinner at the inn's exceptional gourmet restaurant.

Skiers seeking close proximity to the slopes should check out **The Mount Snow Resort Center** (89 Mountain Road; 802-464-7788), a cluster of lodges and condominium buildings at the base of Mount Snow. There are 240 accommodations, ranging from modern, apartment-style lodging to alpine villas. Many rooms offer slope-to-front-door skiing, as well as use of indoor pools and tennis courts. Moderate.

Twelve miles west of Wilmington, the **Greenwood Lodge American Youth Hostel** (Route 9, adjacent to Prospect Ski Mountain, Woodford; 802-442-2547) lolls peacefully in a picturesque wooded glen. Rustic but tidy, the mountain lodge has 44 beds in two large dorms and five private rooms. There's a fireplace and community kitchen, plus fishing ponds, canoeing and great cross-country skiing. Budget.

A gorgeous Victorian mansion cloaked in a sea of trees, the **South Shire Inn** (124 Elm Street, Bennington; 802-447-3839) is positively dazzling. The first floor is a series of parlors and sitting rooms suffused with mahogany woods, etched-glass doors, high carved ceilings and a knockout spiral staircase. Upstairs, nine guest suites are suited for indulgence, with Queen Anne beds, eyelet quilts, window sofas and jacuzzi tubs. For a bit of nostalgia, read through the century-old guest diary, which contains wonderful anecdotes. Deluxe to ultra-deluxe.

For homey in-town accommodations, consider the **Molly Stark Inn** (1067 East Main Street, Bennington; 802-442-9631), an 1860 Victorian house that's been carefully restored by an enthusiastic and artistic young innkeeper. The six bedrooms are small but charming, featuring hardwood floors, clawfoot bathtubs, lace curtains and wall stencils. There's also a wraparound front porch and nifty antique wood-burning stove in the living room. Moderate.

"Who is there, I wonder, who doesn't want to escape from the speed and rudeness of today's living . . . ?" When Norman Rockwell penned those words, he likely had in mind his secluded farmhouse in West Arlington. Today, the 1792 timber house is **The Inn on Covered Bridge Green** (★) (River Road, four and one-half miles west of Route 7A; 802-375-9489), a beguiling bed and breakfast offering a glimmer of the rural cheer that Rockwell's paintings so cleverly depicted. The scenic Battenkill River runs by the five-acre grounds, smothered in apple orchards and dotted with tranquil horse and dairy farms. There are five bedrooms, set off by broad pine floors and provincial antiques, and a tennis court that Rockwell built. Deluxe.

Ethan Allen and his Green Mountain Boys checked in **The Equinox** (Route 7A, Manchester Village; 802-362-4700) once for a little rest and relaxation. It was the late 1700s, and the hotel was *the* place to stay. Two centuries later, the place still draws history-makers, as well as anyone seeking indulgent surroundings. A main four-story building, fronted by Greek Revival columns, features 174 guest rooms graced with Vermont pine floors and furniture and adorned with Victorian accents. There are indoor and outdoor pools, a country club, 18-hole championship golf course, spa, tennis courts and several restaurants. All set on 350 acres etched with cross-country ski trails. Who could ask for more? Ultra-deluxe.

For close proximity to Manchester's factory outlet stores, consider **Barnstead Innstead** (Route 30; 802-362-1619). Built in 1830, the post-and-beam hay barn has been nicely converted with all its charm intact. Twelve tidy bedrooms are eclectically outfitted with old-time furniture and wall-to-wall carpets, and there's a heated pool out back. Moderate.

CENTRAL VERMONT HOTELS

There's plenty of room in the apartmentlike suites at **Hogge Penny Inn** (Route 4, Rutland; 802-773-3200), a modern hostelry just outside downtown. Set at the foot of the mountains, the medley of two-story frame buildings is accented by generous landscaping and a broad swimming pool. Expect one- and two-bedroom suites with vaulted ceilings, sectional couches, distinctive windows and kitchens with modern appliances. Motel rooms are also available. Deluxe.

Nestled on a bank of rolling hills between Rutland and Killington, **The Vermont Inn** (Route 4; 802-775-0708), is a congenial 1840 farmhouse trimmed in chimneys and red-and-white awnings. The whole place is terribly cozy, a timeless structure of rubbed pine floors, cherrywood furniture and wallpaper with pictures of country flowers. Bedrooms follow suit with homespun accents such as eyelet quilts, lace curtains and four-poster beds. Deluxe and ultra-deluxe rates include breakfast and dinner.

The **Grey Bonnet Inn** (Route 100, North Killington; 802-775-2537) mixes new and old with 40 modern guest rooms decorated in 1800s country motif and accompanied by amenities such as indoor and outdoor pools, tennis courts and an exercise room. Outside the two-story building wood shingles scale the walls and balconies, while inside the lobby is an intimate affair donned in carved wood beams, antique spinning wheels and a stately grand-father clock. Cross-country ski through the lodge's 25 acres, or take on Killington's slopes just two miles away. Moderate.

Daniel Boone would have felt right at home in the **Inn at Long Trail** (Route 4 between Killington and Pico; 802-775-7181), a woodsy resting place with big country throw rugs, mounted deer heads, lamps made of pine cones and chairs formed with twisted tree limbs. Six fireplace suites are heaped with rough-hewn wood furniture, and 16 smaller rooms feature crude antiques and down quilts. But what ole' Dan would have liked best is the "relaxation room" fitted with a huge redwood hot tub. Moderate to deluxe.

Ski zealots will want to plant themselves at the **Mountain Green Ski and Golf Resort** (Killington Road, Killington Village; 802-422-3000), a maze of 216 alpine-style condominiums skirting the foot of Killington Peak. Here, convenience and amenities are stressed: lifts are within walking distance, and so are the heated outdoor pool, hot tub and health club. Accommodations range from studios to four-bedroom suites, all with fireplaces and modern designs such as vaulted ceilings and carpeting. Moderate to ultra-deluxe.

About 16 miles north of Rutland, the lovely town of Brandon is a labyrinth of beautiful historic buildings, shade-giving maple trees and fine-trimmed lawns. Stashed away high in the mountains above Brandon, the **Churchill House Inn** (★) (Route 73 East; 802-247-3078) is a fetching 1871 farmhouse known best to cross-country skiers and hikers. Three stories tall and fashioned in the Federal style, the inn features cozy sitting rooms with early American furniture and potbellied stoves, as well as homey bedrooms adorned with pine plank floors and rocking chairs. Deluxe prices include wonderful homecooked breakfasts and dinners.

Northeast of Brandon is a sleepy town called Rochester, where the historic **School House Youth Hostel** (Route 100; 802-767-9384) has long been a favorite stopover of bicyclists and hikers. Built in 1827 as a church and later converted to a school, the two-story white frame edifice maintains beautiful stained-glass windows, dusty wood floors and a few church pews and wooden desks. Budget-priced accommodations are sparse but clean and include two large dorm rooms with bunk beds and several private rooms.

The quintessence of Old World luxury exists at **The Canterbury House** (43 Pleasant Street; 802-457-3077), an elegant 1880 Victorian townhouse within walking distance of Woodstock's best sights and activities. Seven bedrooms are named after the *Canterbury Tales* (there's a Parson's Tale and Monk's Tale) and decorated with refinement: antique spool and brass beds, pedestal sinks and old-fashioned clawfoot tubs. Deluxe.

Perhaps no other Vermont inn has received so much acclaim as the **Woodstock Inn & Resort** (Route 4, Woodstock; 802-457-1100), partly because of all the luminaries who frequent the place. The other part is that it's just plain wonderful to look at and, of course, *be* at. Nestled against the village green, the grand, colonial-style estate sports a ten-foot stone fireplace in its lobby and a country-style motif of braided rugs, rough-hewn beams and columns and artwork from the Rockefeller collection. Most of the 143 ultra-deluxe-priced rooms are furnished rather simply, but extensive amenities include a huge sports center, a Robert Trent Jones-designed golf course and a ski touring center.

A sprawling 1793 farm that was home to Vermont's first lieutenant governor, **The Quechee Inn** (Clubhouse Road, Quechee; 802-295-3133) radiates a spirit of untamed romanticism. Furry teddy bears cuddle in rocking chairs next to a brick hearth in the living room, while 24 bedrooms are embellished with satin-and-lace comforters and hints of sweet-smelling potpourri. Outside, a rolling green lawn dotted with tulip beds and willow trees surrounds a scenic lake. Ultra-deluxe prices include breakfast and dinner.

The **Abel Barron House** (37 Main Street, Quechee; 802-295-1337) is a delightful in-town bed and breakfast that doubles as an arts and crafts gallery. Built in the early 1800s, the house has five guest rooms with queen-sized brass beds, Victorian antiques and chandeliers and oak armoires. Don't miss afternoon tea, served in an adorable glass greenhouse filled with orchids and morning glories and streams of sunshine. Moderate to deluxe.

NORTHERN MOUNTAIN REGION HOTELS

The closest proximity to downhill skiing can be found at **Sugarbush Village Condominiums** (Mountain Access Road, Sugarbush Village; 802-583-3000), where you can choose from 500 condos (many ski-in and ski-out) sprinkled about the base of Mt. Ellen. Most accommodations are modern apartment-style, though they vary widely from small studios and loft apartments to townhouses and four-bedroom condominiums. Ultra-deluxe.

Set on a lovely hill, enveloped by terraced lawns, cobbled paths and winding streams, **Sugarbush Inn** (Sugarbush Access Road, Warren; 802-583-2301) is the plushest hostelry near the ski slopes. Inside the vanilla clapboard inn is a lobby done in dark, polished woods and rich burgundies, and 46 guest rooms adorned with country wallpapers, handloomed rugs and reproduction antiques. The sun terrace restaurant, with its brick floors, French doors and mountain views, is a marvelous place for breakfast. An extensive health club, a golf course and 11 tennis courts make this the best resort choice in Sugarbush. Deluxe to ultra-deluxe.

You can get a true feel for Vermonters and their lifestyles if you stay at **Lareau Farm** (Route 100, Waitsfield; 802-496-4949), a picturesque 45-acre spread hugging the Mad River. The owners are convivial and genuine, ready to show you their farming methods, local customs and all the town crazies. The 1832 farmhouse is quintessential New England: big gracious rooms with wide-plank floors and fireplaces, a fabulous lattice porch overlooking the mountains and 14 very comfortable bedrooms with antique beds and plush quilts made by the owners. Don't miss the summer hayrides or winter sleigh rides. Deluxe.

Call it pastoral luxury or rural fancy, but **Newton's 1824 House Inn** (Route 100, Waitsfield; 802-496-7555) is the place to indulge while soaking up the country. Set on 52 scenic acres in the Mad River Valley, this two-story gabled farmhouse is awash with beautiful antiques, Oriental rugs, French doors and a distinct air of elegance and precise design. There are six luxurious bedrooms with feather beds done in different themes, plus a gracious dining room where guests get treated to oatmeal soufflés, blueberry cornmeal pancakes and poached pears for breakfast. Deluxe.

The most eloquent place to stay in the state capital is **The Inn at Montpelier** (147 Main Street, Montpelier; 802-223-2727), a pair of stately antebellum buildings that breath history. There are high ceilings and beautiful Victorian furnishings, ten fireplaces and an enormous wraparound porch dotted with hanging plants and fan-back chairs. Lavishly decorated in rich ruby and teal hues, the 19 guest rooms feature mirrored armoires, Queen Anne and teak poster beds and polished pedestal sinks. Well worth the deluxe price tag.

Snatching a bird's-eye view of the capitol building, the **Days Inn** (100 State Street, Montpelier; 802-223-5252) is where you'll find a business and political throng. Built back in 1826, this downtown hostelry is a clubby affair with pine walls and floors and brass lamps and mirrors. The 79 guest rooms are modern but not fancy, all providing plenty of space, two queen beds and wall-to-wall carpets. Moderate, with deluxe foliage-season rates.

Butternut (Mountain Road, Stowe; 802-253-4277) is one of those inns that tries to be homey and elegant at the same time—and pulls it off swimmingly. Wrought with dozens of beautiful country American antiques, the three-story lodge is nearly a museum. There's more refinement outside, where twinkling lights meander through evergreens, and a gazebo overlooks a swimming pool and perennial gardens. But the fireside breakfasts, cozy game room and warmly decorated bedrooms suggest quite a snug lodging experience. Deluxe.

One of the best bargains in the area is **The Siebeness** (Mountain Road, Stowe; 802-253-8942), a straightforward country inn with comfy bedrooms and moderate prices. Count on a homelike setting with two floors of rooms adorned simply but tastefully in heavy wood antiques, downy, hand-stitched quilts and wall stenciling. There's a large pool and a hidden mountain stream out back, plus bountiful breakfasts that are extra special.

Endless waves of mountains and evergreen valleys create a milieu that's nothing short of sensational at the **Trapp Family Lodge** (Luce Hill Road, Stowe; 802-253-8511). This peaceful, 2000-acre slice of nirvana was set up as a 1940s singing camp by Maria Von Trapp. Tyrolean in style, the enchanting buildings have flowerpots that brim with kaleidoscopic colors and 93 guest rooms simply adorned in dark woods and muted colors and featuring modern amenities. You can't miss the scenic pond, two swimming pools edged with lawn, greenhouse and gardens—and many more sightseers than guests. Ultra-deluxe, with breakfast and dinner included.

A serene Georgian mansion obscured down a winding mountain road, **Edson Hill Manor** (Edson Hill Road off Mountain Road, Stowe; 802-253-7371) offers 300 acres of solitude amid majestic surroundings. Featuring brick walls, hewn-wood ceilings and Oriental rugs, the main house offers nine spacious rooms—five with beautiful fireplaces—while a carriage house maintains 16 guest rooms. You'll also find a terraced swimming pool, nature trails and plenty of cross-country skiing possibilities. Ultra-deluxe.

CHAMPLAIN VALLEY HOTELS

Near the southern end of the Champlain Valley lies the vibrant college town of Middlebury. Here, the **Swift House Inn** (Route 7 and Stewart Lane; 802-388-9925) reposes among enormous elm and maple trees and broods with New England history. The 1814 main house, a Federal-style building that was home to former Vermont Governor John W. Stewart, has ten rooms done in peach and plum hues, with poster beds and some marble fireplaces. An 1876 Victorian carriage house offers five cozy rooms with fireplaces and whirlpool tubs. Moderate to deluxe.

Occupying a choice 700 acres along Lake Champlain, the **Basin Harbor Club** (Basin Harbor Road off Route 22A, Vergennes; 802-475-2311) has been a prime waterside getaway since 1886. Sprinkled along the lake banks and peeking across to New York's Adirondack Mountains are 38 rooms and 77 cottages with simple, lodge-style furnishings. This self-contained retreat, open from mid-May through mid-October, boasts an 18-hole golf course, heated pool, tennis courts, top-notch restaurant and airstrip. Ultra-deluxe.

Perhaps the most distinguished lodging address in all the Champlain Valley is the **Shelburne House** (Harbor and Bay Roads, off Route 7, Shelburne; 802-985-8498 late May to mid-October, 802-985-8686 mid-October to late May). Formerly home to Lila Vanderbilt Webb, the 1899 shingled brick manor has all the Vanderbilt trimmings: incredible Lake Champlain and mountain vistas, more than 100 rooms with opulent Queen Anne Revival furnishings and 1000 acres of lovely farmlands sprinkled with 19th-century buildings. Settle in, soak up the history of this fascinating place and pretend you'll never have to leave. Closed mid-October to late May. Deluxe and ultra-deluxe.

Burlington, Vermont's largest city, offers little in the way of homey bed and breakfasts and quaint inns but does have a smattering of motor lodges, motels and hotels.

At the **Sheraton Burlington Inn** (870 Williston Road; 802-862-6576), you will find 309 spacious rooms with contemporary furnishings, marble vanities and mountain views (though in the distance), as well as a health club with a removable glass atrium over the pool. Fashioned around a mid-1800s farmhouse, the original, low-slung building sports lighted cupolas, though newer four- and five-story structures have been added. Deluxe to ultra-deluxe.

Over on the northeast side of town, **The Maple Motel** (23 College Parkway, Burlington; 802-655-0900) is a no-nonsense destination where you can swipe a clean, modern-style room with a moderate price. The three-story design is generic motel, though the decor is a notch above, with cushy couches, designer draperies and cedar siding. Suites are deluxe-priced.

NORTHEAST KINGDOM HOTELS

A genteel Victorian house like **The Looking Glass Inn** (Routes 93 and 18, St. Johnsbury; 802-748-3052) seems so out of place at the junction of two major highways. But step inside and you'll discover an oasis of beautiful high ceilings, French windows, cherrywood banisters and Oriental rugs. A hoppin' stagecoach stop during the early 1800s (there's still a dancefloor above the garage), the Looking Glass bears six moderate-priced rooms with handmade quilts, antique headboards and wash basins and modern carpets.

When it comes to exhilarating views, it's tough to beat **Fox Hall** (★) (off Route 16, Westmore; 802-525-6930), a turn-of-the-century Cape Cod-style mansion that preens along glorious Lake Willoughby. Situated on 68 forested acres, the manor is flanked by two large turrets and a large wraparound porch and boasts seven fireplaces. All nine bedrooms are cozy, but the turret rooms (with four windows each) are the choicest. Moderate to deluxe.

Standing by Lake Willoughby, the **Willough Vale Inn** (Route 5A, Westmore; 802-525-4123) offers spectacular views and a rustic elegance. Though built in 1987, the colonial-style inn harkens to yesteryear with stained-wood floors, antiques and Oriental rugs. Most of the nine rooms snatch a lake view and are enhanced with simple oak furniture and country prints. Moderate.

Just getting to **Heermansmith Farm** (★) (half-a-mile from Coventry Village; 802-754-8866) is a joyous adventure. Truck two miles down a dusty washboard road, past the grazing cows and romping dogs, then navigate a picturesque covered bridge and you'll arrive at the prim whitewashed farmhouse. This country gem, enveloped by strawberry fields and total solitude, has been in the same family since 1807. The innkeepers are marvelous, the atmosphere congenial and the bedrooms very agreeable with antique beds, pitchers and basins and large closets stacked with well-thumbed paperbacks. Rooms with shared baths are budget-priced, with private baths, moderate.

Restaurants

To dine out in Vermont is to initiate a love affair with the foods of our American heritage. Here you'll find sentimental cuisine that tugs at your heartstrings: fluffy pancakes with warm Vermont maple syrup, homegrown apples, berries picked from the patch down the street and partridge and pheasant culled from the state's Green Mountains. Vermont's fare is uncomplicated comfort food, and it can be discovered in cozy bed and breakfasts, quaint roadside diners and elegant cafés tucked along the mountainsides.

SOUTHERN VERMONT RESTAURANTS

The diminutive venue of **T. J. Buckley's** (132 Elliot Street, Brattleboro; 802-257-4922) is the last place you'd expect to find some of the city's finest gourmet fare. But here it is, served in an adorable Worcester diner with eclectic decor and only eight tables. Four entrées are offered nightly on an ever-changing menu. Selections might include breast of chicken with ground corn and pistachio nuts, jumbo shrimp with mozzarella and tomato, or Norwegian salmon. Deluxe.

Climb a battered flight of stairs to the second-floor roost of **The Common Ground** (25 Elliot Street, Brattleboro; 802-257-0855), a venerable mecca of ethnic and organic creations. Formerly a mid-1800s fire station, the eatery has dusty plank and brick floors and a glass solarium overlooking the downtown hubbub. The open kitchen, a jumble of pots and chefs, is where all the vegetarian goodies get whipped up. Try the cashew burger, seaweed salad and homemade ginger ale. Budget.

Things take on a subdued pace at **Peter Havens** (★) (32 Elliot Street, Brattleboro; 802-257-3333), a tiny but sophisticated eatery obscured beneath streetside awnings. Continental fare focuses on fresh seafood, including curried shrimp, sea scallops Provençal and grilled swordfish with geneva butter. Linen tablecloths, original artwork and only ten tables make this a cozy spot for two. Moderate.

A majestic country establishment built in 1787, the **Old Newfane Inn** (Route 30 on the village common, Newfane; 802-365-4427) possesses quite an impressive restaurant. The surroundings are pure Vermont: dark pine floors, high beamed ceilings and brick walls sprinkled with beautiful antiques. The bill of fare includes an array of highbrow delights such as smoked goose pâté and frogs' legs Provençal. Dinner only. Deluxe.

Charm and elegance embrace at the **Four Columns Inn** restaurant (230 West Street, Newfane; 802-365-7713), renowned across the region for its exceptional native cuisine. Built in 1839 of hand-hewn timbers, the colonial-style inn exhibits four grand columns across its loggia. Inside, candlelit tables are arranged cozily around a brick fireplace accented by windows draped in lace sheers. Try the marinated quail with pesto couscous, Vermont veal with Grafton (local) cheddar cheese and the steamy New England bouillabaisse. Deluxe.

The Old Tavern (intersection of Townshend Road and Route 121, Grafton; 802-843-2231) imparts a warm formality that reveals its rich heritage. Indeed, the inn's handsome pine floors and beam ceilings, which date back to the late 1700s, have seen the likes of Oliver Wendell Holmes and Henry David Thoreau. Two lavish dining rooms are decorated with antiques and American portraits, while a sunny greenhouse affords picturesque views of gardens. The menu focuses on local fare such as Green Mountain lamb, smoked pork loin and New England salmon. Moderate to deluxe.

A down-home eatery with spectacular views, the **Skyline Restaurant** (Route 9, Marlboro; 802-464-5535) is a great place to while away the morning. Perched 2000 feet up on Hogback Mountain, the Skyline offers simple decor and a vista that stretches more than 100 miles. Breakfast is the highlight, with goodies like banana and coconut griddlecakes smothered in (what else?) Vermont maple syrup, bountiful omelettes and steamy oatmeal. For dinner, try pan-fried trout or sugar-cured ham. Moderate.

Tucked down a washboard road on the mountainside, **The Hermitage** (★) (Coldbrook Road, Wilmington; 802-464-3511) is a tribute to gracious country dining. Fashioned in cool blue and cream tones, the three dining rooms are graced with picture windows, large hearths and hundreds of antique decoys collected by an owner who loves bird hunting. There's more evidence of his passion on the menu, which often features partridge, quail, pheasant and duck. The owner has also garnered national recognition for his wine collection, which exceeds 40,000 bottles. An exceptional dining choice. Deluxe to ultra-deluxe.

You find plenty of local color at **Poncho's Wreck** (Main Street, Wilmington; 802-464-8668), a pub-style eatery with nautical decor and stained-glass windows. The food is dependably good and ranges from Mexican fare and pizzas to smoked meats and seafood. The mode is casual but festive, particularly during ski season. Moderate.

Deerfield's (Route 100, Wilmington; 802-464-5634) is a bustling, family-style restaurant with fare that runs the gamut from American to Mexican and Oriental entrées. The country decor is plain, with wooden tables, ruffled curtains and rather tattered carpets. But the food is reliable. Try the baby back ribs, Cajun shrimp and scallops or eggplant parmigiana. Moderate in price.

An old timey coffee shop, **Geanneli's** (520 Main Street, Bennington; 802-442-9778) is a downtown tradition. Waitresses in pinafores scurry across faded yellow carpet, doling out hearty breakfasts and solid country cooking. There's also a counter where plenty of local chatting gets done. Budget-priced, this spot features liver and onions, fried chicken, grilled ham steak and voluminous homemade pies.

When it comes to fabulous views, it's tough to surpass the **Publyk House Restaurant** (Route 7A, Bennington; 802-442-8301). This remodeled 1940s barn is the perfect place to gaze upon Bennington's battle monument and beautiful Mount Anthony. Carved wood doors, stained-glass windows and loads of greenery make for aesthetic surroundings. Expect interesting American-style fare including poultry, seafood and steak dishes. Moderate.

During the mid-1940s, Norman Rockwell took a fancy to the **Quality Restaurant** (Route 7, Manchester; 802-362-9839). Chances are you will, too. This downtown tradition, which has long served as the local socializing nest, reeks of character. Polished wood floors saunter up to a worn pine bar where Rockwell used to read the daily paper. Along a wall hangs an inspiring print of *War News*, in which the artist captured the bar's essence during World War II. Breakfast, lunch and dinner are all-American affairs, from blueberry pancakes to burgers to smoked salmon alfredo. Moderate.

CENTRAL VERMONT RESTAURANTS

The surrounding Green Mountains make a perfect setting for the Austrian-style **Countryman's Pleasure** (Off Route 4 East on Town Line Road, Mendon; 802-773-7141). Delicate pine chairs, pink draperies and straw wreaths create a soothing effect, reminiscent of the majestic Alps. The impressive menu boasts roast duck with raspberry sauce, veal medallions with *cepes* and fiddleheads (a Vermont specialty) with Jarlsberg. Moderate.

Just north of Rutland, **Swadi's Steak and Seafood** (Route 7, Pittsford; 802-773-8124) enjoys a longstanding reputation for serving thick, juicy, aged beef and fresh, no-nonsense seafood. The menu also features cajun-style entrées, as well as nightly blackboard specials. Wood tables and chairs, dim lighting and a blazing fire make for a venerable Vermont atmosphere. Moderate.

For a bit of mountain funkiness, drop in **Mother Shapiro's** (Killington Access Road, Killington; 802-422-9933), a joint that promises "Hot Food Till Last Call." Caricatures of local people line the stone walls of this slightly worn eatery. Portions are large and range from kosher breakfasts and meat loaf to seafood salad and yummy chicken soup. Popular with the après-ski set. Budget to moderate.

Beautifully prepared, innovative cuisine has garnered **Hemingway's** (Route 4, Killington; 802-422-3886) quite a reputation around these parts. Everything is fresh and scrupulously served among elegant surroundings of white tablecloths and crystal. There's cream of garlic soup with ham, softshell crab with fresh corn and hand-rolled pasta with wild mushrooms. The desserts are true works of art. Deluxe.

Spooner's (Route 4, Woodstock; 802-457-4022) is a straightforward kind of place that serves porterhouse steak and rocky road cheesecake. Situated in an old barn, the eatery bears a long brass bar, multiple archways and picture windows framing a pretty courtyard. Pickings are basic American, from burgers to sole. Moderate to deluxe.

Rathskellers are always so much fun, and the **Stone House Tavern** (Route 4, Woodstock; 802-457-3609) is no exception. Located in the cellar of an 1834 stone house, the eatery is a maze of cozy brick cubbyholes, beautiful glass and mirrors, and light oak tables. Some of the entrées offered are baked scrod, barbecued pork spare ribs and chicken kabobs, while daily specials may include roasted duck and shrimp scampi. Dinner only; moderate in price.

It began as a modest greenhouse that later took on a soda fountain. Now **Bentley's** (3 Elm Street, Woodstock; 802-457-3232) is the local noshing post, an uptown eatery decked in Oriental rugs, lace curtains and fringed lampshades. You can show up in casual or dressy attire and feast on treats such as scampi pescatore and gourmet chili. The stacked croissants and chicken dishes are tops. Moderate to deluxe.

Simon Pearce Restaurant (Main Street, Quechee; 802-295-1470) affords an unusual blend of sophisticated cuisine and artistic talent. Quechee glassblower Simon Pearce—who's quite well known around New England —has fashioned beautiful stemware and globes that rest on formal tablecloths. His creative continental cuisine menu is a perfect accompaniment, highlighted by roast duck with mango chutney, sole with vermouth and chanterelles and marinated grilled seafood. The brick building—a story in itself—was an 1830s mill that produced the country's largest supply of wool flannel. Deluxe.

NORTHERN MOUNTAIN REGION RESTAURANTS

This is ski country, and most restaurants cater to those tired skiers with hearty appetites. Oftentimes, you'll find a cauldron of soup steaming over a blazing hearth and cushy chairs for snuggling.

The refinement and understated elegance of **The Common Man** (German Flats Road, Warren; 802-583-2800) has earned it a solid culinary reputation across Vermont. Situated in a 19th-century barn, the place is simply romantic. Pretty chandeliers hang from high beam ceilings, while well-spaced tables hug a large stone hearth. The cuisine is *très* gourmet, with an accent on native offerings. There's *faisan rôti* (Vermont pheasant), Vermont veal sweetbreads and *caneton* normandy (roasted duckling with apple glaze). Moderate.

Two miles down an unmarked dirt road rests the **Dinersoar Restaurant** (★) (Airport Road, Warren; 802-496-8831), a splendid spot to observe all the local airplane activity. Nestled on the top of a teeny building called the Warren-Sugarbush Airport, the Dinersoar affords exhilarating views of the surrounding Green Mountains and valleys. A diligent young owner serves budget-priced breakfasts, soups and deli fare, along with delicious baked desserts. A great place to hang loose.

A charming 1850s inn and restaurant, the **Millbrook** (Route 17, Waitsfield; 802-496-2405) truly captures the flavor of Vermont. The decor is warm and inviting, with wide-plank floors, country antiques and paintings of local life. A congenial couple act as manager and chef, serving hand-rolled pastas and very special pies. Entrées include free-range Vermont veal, *badami rogan josh* (lamb) and shrimp curry. Moderate.

Many of Vermont's restaurateurs grow their own produce and herbs, and such is the case at **Tucker Hill Lodge** (Route 17, Waitsfield; 802-496-3983). From sweet baby strawberries to brilliant radicchio and arugula, the menu brims with freshness and imagination. There's partridge and tuna, chicken and tenderloins, all served in a setting of soft music and a crackling fire. Monday nights are special, when locals pack the place for wafer-thin "flatbread" pizza that's grilled over a wood-fired, earthen oven. Deluxe.

In Montpelier, the New England Culinary Institute operates three restaurants where you'll discover very vogue cuisine at moderate prices. The most popular of the trio is **Tubbs** (1820 Elm Street; 802-229-9202), a two-story brick affair with high carved ceilings, impressionist paintings and a small outdoor deck. The menu changes seasonally and offers jewels such as roasted duck with fresh papaya and ginger, lobster and crab with yellow curry sauce and jasmine rice, spicy Oriental shrimp with grilled polenta and rack of lamb with mustard crust, roast garlic and madeira. The desserts are the kind to die for: try the chocolate rum fantasy or lemon-poppy seed brulée with fresh fruit.

For more casual surroundings, visit the Culinary Institute's **Elm Street Café** (38 Elm Street, Montpelier; 802-223-3188), which offers gourmet salads and game, or **La Brioche Bakery and Café** (26 Elm Street; 802-229-0443), where you can pick up puffy croissants, gourmet cookies, napoleons and other baked goodies.

The glistening gold-plated dome of the state capitol peeks through the windows of **The Horn of the Moon Café** (8 Langdon Street, Montpelier; 802-223-2895), a bohemian habitat with bamboo shades and scuffed wooden floors. Politicians like to hobnob over the vegetarian inventory of imaginative soups, salads, pies and couscous. Try the chapati salad with tahini dressing, the fresh fruit yogurt drinks, barley and hazelnut salad or tomato nut curry. Moderate.

For top-notch Mexican fare, check out **Julio's** (★) (44 Main Street, Montpelier; 802-229-9348). This serene downtown niche, stashed up a rickety flight of stairs, offers up basic south-of-the-border entrées plus interesting selections such as Mexican pizzas and egg rolls. There's a shiny oak bar, brick archways and walls covered with south-of-the-border prints and blankets. Moderate.

Jack's Backyard (9 Maple Avenue, Barre; 802-479-9134) is a popular town rendezvous with real flair. The two-story, ranch-style eatery is flanked by wagon wheels and exhibits walls smothered in old license plates and farm tools. Popcorn is divvied up in tin pails for those with "drinking" appetites, but most opt for the potpourri of stacked sandwiches, chili, crêpes and salads. Budget to moderate.

To experience the true flavor of **McCarthy's** (Mountain Road, Stowe; 802-253-8626), get there just after dawn when local farmers arrive dressed in overalls and straw hats. This congenial breakfast and lunch café offers friendly service, huge portions and budget prices. You'll find apple and blueberry pancakes with hot Vermont syrup, country eggs Benedict, sticky buns and pumpkin bread. Surroundings are modern and airy with Irish country touches.

The beautiful **Trapp Family Lodge** (Luce Hill Road, Stowe; 802-253-8511) boasts one of the area's most renowned dining rooms. Situated in a marvelous mountain setting, the restaurant is simple yet elegant, with picture windows, draped hanging plants and light oak tables. The food is gourmet with Swiss touches. Try the *fungfernbraten* (braised pork tenderloin served with sliced pickles) or wienerschnitzel. Ultra-deluxe.

Culinary aficionados won't want to miss **Isle de France** (Mountain Road, Stowe; 802-253-7751), a classic French restaurant with all the trimmings. The decor is terribly Parisian, accented by provincial furniture, impressionist paintings, huge, ornate mirrors and well-spaced tables designed for romance. The deluxe-priced menu is an assortment of fresh seafood, steak, poultry, sweetbreads and frogs' legs, all draped in a variety of heady sauces and beautifully served. But here's the real scoop: dine in the cozy lounge and those same entrées are about half price.

CHAMPLAIN VALLEY RESTAURANTS

Burlington is Vermont's largest city and its restaurant capital, so not surprisingly, you'll find a medley of choice dining establishments. Some of the best can be found on Church Street's four-block Marketplace, a brick-lined pedestrian mall packed with outdoor cafés and college students.

The Queen City Tavern (103 Church Street, Burlington; 802-864-0550) offers casual alfresco dining under a canopy tent. The crowd is a mix of sports fans (there's a sports bar inside) and Europeans who chat over croissants, fancy coffees and hefty burgers. Try the grilled chicken and snow pea salad and crab mushroom ya ya soup. A great place to people-watch. Budget to moderate.

A rare Vermont sushi bar is part of the **Marketplace at Sakura** (2 Church Street, Burlington; 802-863-1988), a simple but cheery restaurant with a *tatami* room and small wooden tables that peek out over the street. The sushi and sashimi are superfresh and cleverly served on wooden trays with pretty designs. If you prefer a hot Japanese meal, opt for *yakitori* (broiled chicken on skewers) or *gyoza* (pork dumplings) or select from the host of teriyaki and tempura entrées. Moderate to deluxe.

The place for fresh New England seafood is the **Ice House** (171 Battery Street, Burlington; 802-864-1800), a restored harborside building with a venerable seafaring aura. There's a wharf and ferry station a stone's throw away. Specialties include grilled swordfish, shrimp scampi, Maine lobster and sea scallops, Nantucket-style. The place is draped in wood and stone and features an oyster bar and outdoor deck.

Waterworks (The Champlain Mill, Winooski; 802-655-2044) is a typical yuppie-style bistro with one very special attraction: water. The outdoor terrace here affords a sweeping view of the Winooski River, where waves of water rush and swirl across huge boulders, creating quite a commotion and a sublime dining environment. The cuisine is reliable and includes an assortment of moderately priced chicken, seafood and steak dishes, as well as sandwiches. Inside, you'll find red brick walls, high ceilings and large windows for good water views.

NORTHEAST KINGDOM RESTAURANTS

Cuisine here reflects the ruggedness of the land, and, though restaurants are far apart, they're certainly worth the scenic drive.

Aime's (Routes 2 and 18, St. Johnsbury; 802-748-3553) is a roadside diner with elevator music and faded brown carpets. But beyond the tacky decor, you'll find a keen stroke of gourmet, inventive game dishes such as smoked Vermont duckling, charbroiled Colorado buffalo, medallions of venison and stuffed quail. Locals also crowd the joint for down-home fixin's like baked ham and roast pork. Moderate to deluxe.

A charming oasis bordering a noisy highway, **Cucci's Bistro** (43 Eastern Avenue, St. Johnsbury; 802-748-4778) is truly romantic. Surroundings are European country, a fusion of stained-wood booths, brass railings and frilly draperies accented by a single tapered candle on each table. Culinary selections lean toward northern Italian. Try the *scarpiello* (chicken in garlic lemon sauce) and veal sautéed with *pormo* ham and mozzarella. Deluxe.

Nestled serenely on a glacier-carved lake, the **Willough Vale Inn and Restaurant** (Route 5A, Westmore; 802-525-4123) affords some of Vermont's most scintillating views. Polished wood tables, Oriental rugs and mauve and cream tones lend a rustic elegance to the dining room, which overlooks captivating Lake Willoughby. The menu features an ample selection of fresh fish, poultry, beef and pasta, all nestled in light sauces and herbs. Moderate to deluxe.

Stuffed deer heads hang haphazardly from the facade of **Buck and Doe Restaurant** (★) (Route 105; 802-723-4712), a local institution in a beautiful nowheresville called Island Pond. This one-room coffee shop is bathed in gaudy red-and-yellow decor but wins customers with its tasty entrées such as roast Wisconsin duckling, leg of lamb, Maine lobster and exceptional prime rib. Moderate to deluxe.

Locals know that to dine at **Heermansmith Farm Inn** (★) (Coventry Village; 802-754-8866), you must make reservations several days in advance. This 1807 farmhouse, concealed two miles down a washboard road, is an absolute find—the kind of place that instantly warms your blood. It's dinner only, served in a living room graciously adorned with antique lanterns, pine bookcases, a stone hearth and picture windows overlooking rolling strawberry fields. The moderate-priced menu exhibits great flair with entrées such as roast duck masked in strawberry and chambord sauce, shrimp dijonaise and pecan chicken. A place worth finding.

Il Piano Scorza (981 East Main Street, Newport; 802-334-1000), Italian for "upper crust," couldn't have a better name: The restaurant is perched atop a bakery. Even better, though, are the gourmet Italian dishes and rich adornments of white linen, china and crystal chandeliers. Try the eggplant parmesan, shrimp scampi or lobster fra diablo. With moderate prices, you can't go wrong.

The **Miss Newport Diner** (East Main Street, Newport; 802-334-7742) is one of those adorable town gossip spots that serves up great breakfasts and homestyle lunches. The 1947 Worcester diner bears five booths and a row of red-and-silver counter stools where all the socializing gets done. The menu features four pages of eggs, omelettes and pancakes—most priced under $2. For lunch, there's budget-priced meat loaf and fried chicken, ham steak and fresh turkey.

The Great Outdoors

The Sporting Life

SKIING

The thrills of downhill and cross-country skiing draw tens of thousands of enthusiasts to Vermont every year. Ski resort villages exist all over the state, offering a variety of challenges and settings that cater to families, singles and the elderly.

Before you go, send for the *Vermont: Skiing in its Finest State* brochure from the Vermont Ski Areas Association (26 State Street, Montpelier, VT 05602; 802-223-2439).

Haystack Mountain (Route 100, Wilmington; 802-464-5321) is Vermont's southernmost ski resort area, with 42 trails and six lifts catering primarily to families with children. Nearby, **Mount Snow** (Route 100; 802-464-3333) climbs 3600 feet up and boasts a large array of alpine villas, condos and restaurants. Here you'll find 74 trails (many quite difficult), 18 lifts and a vertical drop of 1700 feet.

The place to be in central Vermont is **Killington** (off Routes 4 and 100; 802-773-1330), a sprawling, six-mountain network of 107 trails (including 18 black diamond), 18 lifts and a vertical drop that plummets 3175 feet.

Sugarbush (off Route 100, Warren; 802-583-2381), a two-mountain area with 80 trails, maintains a congenial atmosphere with its quaint shops and medley of fine restaurants and accommodations. Nearby **Stowe** (Route 108; 802-253-7311) harbors Vermont's highest peak, 4393-foot Mount Mansfield, and a stunning alpine milieu with 44 trails and nine lifts.

Vermont's best-kept ski secret is **Burke Mountain** (off Route 114, East Burke; 802-626-3305), nestled in the outposts of the Northeast Kingdom. Here you'll find excellent skiing in an uncrowded (yes, no lift lines!) place, along with 30 trails, five lifts and a nice vertical drop of 2000 feet.

The varied terrain of gentle hills and fields, old carriage roads and frozen ponds—combined with an excellent interconnecting gridwork of trails—attract vast numbers of cross-country skiers to Vermont. In fact, tiny Vermont boasts more cross-country ski centers than any western state.

For a list of ski centers, write for the *Destination Directory* from Cross-Country Ski Areas of America (259 Bolton Road, Hinsdale, NH 03451).

Known as the "Longest Cross-Country Ski Trail in North America," the **Catamount Trail** will stretch 280 miles across the length of Vermont when it's completed sometime in the year 2000. Portions of the trail are open now, including a nice trek between the **Mountain Top Inn** in Chittenden and the **Long Run Inn** in Lincoln. For further information on the Catamount Trail call 802-864-5794.

Another scenic route traverses the farmlands and forests between the **Craftsbury Nordic Center** (802-586-7767) in Craftsbury Village and the **Highland Lodge** in Greensboro. Less demanding trails connect inns around **Warren** and **Waitsfield** in the Sugarbush area.

SLEIGHING

Sleigh rides afford wonderful opportunities to meet local folks and take in the beautiful countryside. Trips are offered by **Adam's Farm** (Higley Hill, Wilmington; 802-464-3762), **Santa's Land** (Route 5, Putney; 802-387-5550), **Autumn Crest Inn** (Clark Road, Williamstown; 802-433-6627), **Hawk Inn and Mountain Resort** (Route 100, Plymouth; 802-672-3811), **Pond Hill Ranch** (Pond Hill Road, Castleton; 802-468-2449), **Trapp Family Lodge** (Trapp Hill Road, Stowe; 802-253-8511) and **Smuggler's Notch Riding** (Mountain Road, Jeffersonville; 802-644-5347).

SPORTFISHING

From salmon and trout to shad and walleye, Vermont's extensive network of streams, rivers and lakes teem with a multitude of fine fishing opportunities. Winter ice fishing has become increasingly popular all over the state but particularly in the Northeast Kingdom, where northern pike, smelt and perch can be plucked from frozen lakes.

Fishing charters are available from **Strictly Trout** (off Route 121 just south of Saxton River Village; 802-869-3116), **The Vermont Fly Fishing School** (Clubhouse Road, Quechee; 802-295-7620), **Yankee Charters** (Route 7, Middlebury; 802-388-7365) and **The Fly Rod Shop** (Route 100, Stowe; 802-253-7346).

Outfits that will set you up with rental boats and/or fishing equipment include **Duda's Water Sports** (Creek Road, Hydeville; 802-265-3432), **Sailing Winds** (Route 30, Wells; 802-287-9411), **Charlie's Northland Lodge** (Route 2, North Hero; 802-372-8822) and **South Burlington Rent All** (340 Dorset Street, Burlington; 802-862-5793).

To find out where the fish bite, contact the **Vermont Fish and Wildlife Department** (Information and Education Division, 103 South Main Street, Waterbury, VT 05676; 802-244-7331).

CANOEING

Whether you're in it for sightseeing or for rugged adventure, canoeing through Vermont can be an idyllic experience. Canoe outfitters in the state include **Connecticut River Safari** (Putney Road, Brattleboro; 802-257-5008), **Battenkill Canoe Ltd.** (Route 7A between Arlington and Manchester; 802-362-2800), **Sailing Winds** (Route 30, Wells; 802-287-9411), **The Mustard Seed** (Dam Road, Chittenden; 802-483-6081), **Clearwater Sports** (Route 100, Waitsfield; 802-496-2708), **Charlie's Northland Lodge** (Route 2, North Hero; 802-372-8822) and **The Village Sport Shop** (Route 5, Lyndonville; 802-626-8448).

HORSEBACK RIDING

What could more exciting than tromping on horseback through the unspoiled Vermont countryside? Plenty of ranches will provide horses and directions to the best trails. Check with **Mountain Top Stables** (Mountain Top Road, Chittenden; 802-483-2311), **Kedron Valley Stables** (Route 106, South Woodstock; 802-457-1480), **Pond Hill Ranch** (Pond Hill Road, Castleton; 802-468-2449), **Vermont Icelandic Horse Farm** (Spring Hill Road, Waitsfield; 802-496-7141), **Navajo Farm** (Route 100, Moretown; 802-496-3656) and **Smugglers' Notch Stables** (Mountain Road, Jeffersonville; 802-644-5347).

GOLF

You can tee up at numerous public courses across the state. In southern Vermont, try the **Sitzmark Golf Course** (East Dover Road off Route 100, Wilmington; 802-464-3384) or **Mount Anthony Country Club** (Bank Street, Bennington; 802-464-3384). In central Vermont, there's **Killington Golf Course** (Killington Access Road, Killington; 802-422-4100) and **Neshobe Golf Club** (Country Club Road, Brandon; 802-247-3611). You'll find **Club Sugarbush** (Sugarbush Access Road, Sugarbush Village; 802-583-2722) and **Stowe Country Club** (Cottage Club Road off Cape Cod Road, Stowe; 802-253-4893) in the Northern Mountain Region. **Kwiniaska Golf Club** (Spear Street, Shelburne Village; 802-985-3672), **Burlington Country Club** (568 South Prospect Street, Burlington; 802-864-4683) and **Marble Island Country Club** (150 Marble Island Road, Mallets Bay; 802-864-4546) are top spots in the Champlain Valley. Up in the Northeast Kingdom, head for **St. Johnsbury Country Club** (Route 5, St. Johnsbury; 802-748-9894).

TENNIS

Racquet fans will find both outdoor and indoor courts all across Vermont. Check out **Mount Anthony Country Club** (Bank Street, Bennington; 802-442-2617) or **Manchester Recreation Area** (off Route 30, Manchester; 802-362-1439) in southern Vermont. In central Vermont, try **Summit Lodge** (Killington Access Road, Killington; 802-422-3535) and **Vail Field** (Route 106 behind the Woodstock Inn, Woodstock). In the Northern Mountain Region, **The Bridges Resort and Racquet Club** (Sugarbush Access Road, Sugarbush Village; 802-583-2922) is an excellent indoor/outdoor facility. In the Champlain Valley, **Leddy Park** (North Avenue, Burlington; 802-864-0123) has public courts, and **Prouty Park** (Veterans Avenue, Newport; 802-334-7951) offers fine facilities in the Northeast Kingdom.

BICYCLING

Vermont's mountains and abundance of back roads create a perfect environment for bicycling. To help get you started, **Vermont Bicycle Touring** (Box 711, Bristol, VT 05443; 802-453-4811) offers tours with all levels of difficulty and will assist independent bicyclists. In addition, the book *25 Bicycle Tours in Vermont* (available from The Countryman Press and Backcountry Publications, P.O. Box 175, Woodstock, VT 05091) offers a wealth of information, including where to find emergency repairs.

There's a two-day **Rivers Tour** near the center of Vermont, taking in the posh village of Woodstock, the birthplace of Calvin Coolidge and numerous choice fishing and swimming holes. Main roads here are Routes 4, 12, 107 and 100.

In the **Sugarbush** area there's a 16-mile excursion along Route 100 and East Warren Road, winding through the scenic Mad River Valley and taking in the quaint towns of Warren and Waitsfield.

You can take an easy but lengthy 51-mile trek through the fertile **Champlain Valley,** meandering among apple orchards and cornfields and skirting beautiful Lake Champlain. Stick to Routes 125, 17 and 23, picking up Lake Street along the lake.

BIKE RENTALS   In southern Vermont, try **Brattleboro Bike Shop** (178 Main Street; 802-254-8644).

Bikes can be rented in the central Vermont area at **Vermont Pedal Pushers** (Manchester; 802-362-5200) and **Taylor Rentals** (135 Strongs Avenue, Rutland; 802-775-2021) and in the Northern Mountain Region at **Clearwater Sports** (Route 100, Waitsfield; 802-496-2708).

For touring around the Champlain Valley, check out **Bicycle Holidays** (RD3 Box 2394, Middlebury; 802-388-2453) or **The Ski Rack Bike Shop** (81 Main Street, Burlington; 802-658-3313).

Up in the Northeast Kingdom try **Village Sport Shop** (74 Broad Street, Lyndonville; 802-626-8448).

Beaches and Parks

Nothing else so totally captures the soul of this great state than its parklands. Scattered across the mountains and valleys and skirting quiescent waterways, these generous public areas frequently offer close-up encounters with wildlife and vegetation, numerous adventurous activities and, of course, just plain solitude.

Most parks open on Memorial Day and close either on Labor Day or Columbus Day.

SOUTHERN VERMONT BEACHES AND PARKS

Green Mountain National Forest—This colossal tract of greenery constitutes the spine of Vermont, uniting over 340,000 acres that slice through the center of the state. Technically, it's divvied into two big chunks, starting at the Massachusetts border and climbing to the town of Wallingford, then picking up again in Mendon and heading northward to Bristol. Dense, verdant and pristine, the forest provides asylum for thousands of animals and birds, including black bears, coyotes, moose, white-tailed deer, wild turkeys, raptors and endangered peregrine falcons. You can spot these intriguing inhabitants by exploring miles of nature trails and canoeing the waters.

The trees themselves are no less enthralling, those great sweeps of maple, beech and birch, intermingled with black cherry, white ash, balsam firs and occasional hemlock forests. Rivers gush forth from the mountains, giving rise to imaginative waterfalls and tiny, pebble-studded brooks perfect for wading. To see everything the park has to offer would take several weeks, though there are several choice spots perfect for an afternoon rendezvous.

Facilities: Picnic areas, restrooms, nature trails and ranger stations are dispersed throughout the forest. Before you go, contact the Green Mountain National Forest (151 West Street, Rutland, VT 05702; 802-773-0300) about maps and information on the huge forest network. *Camping:* Several good campsites exist, including primitive camping at Hapgood Pond, on Hapgood Road in Peru, five miles from the intersection of Routes 11 and 30;

and Moosalamoo, a developed campground on Ripton-Goshen Road, 3.2 miles from Route 125 and one mile east of Ripton. *Swimming:* Excellent at several spots, including Hapgood Pond and Grout Pond (★), an undeveloped site in Stratton on Kelley Stand Road, six miles west of Route 100. *Fishing:* Excellent fishing from 440 miles of rivers and tributaries. Anglers ply the Otter Creek for brook trout and the Battenkill, West, White and Deerfield rivers for salmon, rainbow and brown trout.

Getting there: Route 7 scales the west side of the forest, while Route 100 borders the east side. In between, Routes 73, 125, 9, 11 and 30 slice through the middle. Along these roads you'll find all 32 access points for trails, waterfalls, ponds, rivers and campgrounds.

Fort Dummer State Park (★)—Stashed along some sylvan back roads, this 217-acre, heavily forested park is named after the first white settlement in Vermont, established back in 1724. There's a small shaded clearing for picnicking and a mile of nature trails that ramble through evergreens to nice views of the Connecticut River and less scenic peeks at the Vermont Yankee Power Plant.

Facilities: Picnic tables, restrooms, playground; information, 802-254-2610. *Camping:* Permitted at 61 wooded sites, including ten lean-tos, with showers and fireplaces but no hookups; information, 802-254-2610.

Getting there: Ready? From Routes 91 and 5 in Brattleboro, take Route 5 south one-tenth of a mile to Fairground Road, then head east one-half mile to Main Street. Go south on Main Street—which turns into Old Guilford Road—for one mile. The park is near the dead end.

Townshend State Park—Resting amidst a slew of craggy green mountains, this fine park spans 856 acres and borders the scenic West River. For delightful views, take a hardy hike 1680 feet up to the top of Bald Mountain; for sunbathing and swimming, take a two-mile trek down to **Townshend Dam Recreation Area**, where an 1800-foot thread of tawny sand stretches lazily along the river. You'll also find nice nature trails near the dam.

Facilities: There are picnic tables, restrooms; information, 802-365-7500. *Camping:* Permitted at 34 sites with fireplaces and showers but no water or sewer hookups. *Fishing:* Try by the dam for brook trout, walleye and smallmouth bass.

Getting there: On Town Road, three miles south of Route 30 near Townshend.

Living Memorial Park—As municipal parks go, this one is tops. Blanketing 53 acres of gentle hills, this shady sanctuary teems with recreational opportunities, including a swimming pool and ice skating rink, ski hill with T-bar lift, outdoor and indoor tennis courts and an expansive playground with some state-of-the-art equipment. Families love this place, and it's one of the few parks that manages to be packed (or even open) year-round.

Facilities: Picnic pavilions, lifeguards, two snack bars, softball fields; information, 802-254-6700. *Swimming:* Good in pool.

Getting there: Located on Route 9 two miles west of Route 91, near Brattleboro.

Molly Stark State Park—Magnificent stands of maple and birch blanket this pristine area, marked by a babbling brook and lots of beavers, deer and rabbits. There's a broad clearing that affords cool picnicking and a two-hour roundtrip hike to the summit of Mount Olga. Once you're there, climb the abandoned fire tower and be rewarded with a view into New Hampshire.

Facilities: Picnic tables, shelters; stores located two miles west on Route 9 in Wilmington; information, 802-464-5460. *Camping:* Permitted at 34 sites, including nine lean-tos, with showers and fireplaces but no hookups.

Getting there: On Route 9, about four miles east of Wilmington.

Jamaica State Park—The arrow-straight, wide, rocky West River plows right through this beautiful park, creating a cool, 689-acre playground for outdoor lovers. A short cord of gravel forms a semibeach against the river, where you can roll up your pants legs and explore. But the best part is a trail along an old railroad bed that leads to the Ball Mountain Dam, a monstrous structure that's unleashed twice a year for popular canoe and kayak races. There's also a wooded trail leading up to Hamilton Falls, where eons of torrential water flow have formed curious miniature bathtubs among slippery rocks.

Facilities: Restrooms, picnic tables, playground; stores one-half mile south on Route 30 or north on Route 100; information, 802-874-4600. *Camping:* Excellent, with 57 sites, including 15 lean-tos, with showers and fireplaces but no hookups. *Swimming:* Good in river. *Fishing:* Excellent for walleye, brook and brown trout and panfish.

Getting there: Just off Route 30 in Jamaica.

Woodford State Park—Certainly one of the most picturesque parcels in the state, this 400-acre mountain woodland teems with wildflowers and all sorts of wildlife, from moose, deer and bear to very active beavers and otters. Much of the activity centers around Adams Reservoir, dotted with small boats and canoes and rimmed by a small beach with coarse grey sand. At 2400 feet up, the setting is cool and serene.

Facilities: Picnic areas, boat and canoe rentals, nature trail; store one-half mile east on Route 9; information, 802-447-7169. *Camping:* Some of the most extensive in the state, with 103 sites, including 20 lean-tos, with fireplaces and hot showers. *Swimming:* Good, though the water can be murky at times. *Fishing:* When the reservoir is stocked, the trout are biting.

Getting there: Located ten miles east of Bennington on Route 9.

Lake Shaftsbury State Park—Situated along a fine, clear lake, this park possesses 101 acres sprinkled with evergreens and maple trees, nature trails and those industrious beavers. Locals fancy the 600-foot beach of fine, ginger-colored sand that allows great sunbathing.

Facilities: Picnic areas, boat and canoe rentals; stores nearby in Arlington; information, 802-375-9978. *Camping:* Group camping area with bathhouse. *Swimming:* Excellent. *Fishing:* Good for bass and rainbow trout, along parts of shore or from boats.

Getting there: On Route 7A in Shaftsbury.

Emerald Lake State Park—True to its name, this body of water glistens with a green glow and is so clear you can see much of its sandy bottom. A choice thread of tawny sand forms a popular beach, while nature trails crisscross the hillside terrain. Here you'll also find some of the tallest (more than 100-foot) maple trees in Vermont.

Facilities: Playground, restrooms, canoe and boat rentals; information, 802-362-1655. *Camping:* Permitted in 105 sites, including 36 lean-tos, with showers and fireplaces but no hookups. *Swimming:* Excellent. *Fishing:* Good for panfish, smallmouth bass and northern pike.

Getting there: On Route 7 in Dorset.

CENTRAL VERMONT BEACHES AND PARKS

Green Mountain National Forest—See "Southern Vermont Beaches and Parks."

Lake St. Catherine State Park—With a three-mile shoreline, St. Catherine is one of Vermont's largest and most beautiful lakes. The 117-acre park borders only part of the lake, but its 250-foot beach draws large crowds, particularly on weekends. There's also a trail where you're apt to see deer, raccoons and rabbits.

Facilities: Picnic areas, playground, boat rentals and ramp; stores nearby in Poultney; information, 802-287-9158. *Camping:* Permitted in 61 sites with hot showers, fireplaces and ten lean-tos but no hookups. *Swimming:* Exceptional. *Fishing:* Excellent opportunities for rainbow and lake trout, smelt, yellow perch, northern pike, bullhead and smallmouth and largemouth bass.

Getting there: Route 30, three miles south of Poultney.

Bomoseen State Park—This vast area harbors Vermont's largest lake, the 2360-acre Lake Bomoseen, along with an incredible stretch of forest sprinkled with dormant slate quarries. The park itself spans 365 acres and contains yet another large freshwater body called Glen Lake. There's a nice long tawny beach on Bomoseen, plenty of surrounding nature trails, plus a visiting naturalist who conducts bird and wildflower walks and other programs.

Facilities: Picnic areas, snack bar, boat and canoe rentals; information, 802-265-4242. *Camping:* Permitted in 66 sites with hot showers, fireplaces and ten lean-tos but no hookups. *Swimming:* Good only in Lake Bomoseen.

Fishing: Exceptional in both lakes, with possibilities for panfish, yellow perch and bass.

Getting there: Along Route 4 (also West Shore Road) about four miles north of Hydeville.

Calvin Coolidge State Park—The 30th president spent most of his life in this incredibly scenic, remote swath of forest, which spans 16,165 acres and now serves as a nucleus for hiking, fishing, snowmobiling and relaxation. The dusky Black River and gurgling Broad Brook—great for wading and stone collecting—cut through dense, cool pine stands. Trails will lead you to magnificent views atop Shrewsbury and Killington Peaks.

Facilities: Picnic tables, restrooms, hiking and nature trails, extensive snowmobile network; historic Calvin Coolidge Homestead only two miles away; information, 802-672-3612. *Camping:* Permitted in 60 sites including 35 lean-tos, with hot showers and fireplaces but no hookups. *Fishing:* Good for brook, rainbow and brown trout and panfish.

Getting there: In Plymouth on Route 100A, two miles north of intersection with Route 100.

Camp Plymouth State Park—There's gold in them there hills—at least in this park. Believe it or not, this 300-acre wooded spread attracts a sprinkling of gold diggers, who wade ankle-deep and pan the silty bottom of the Buffalo Brook. Of course, no one has struck it rich lately, but who cares? This hilly park's other claim to fame is shimmering Echo Lake, which possesses a very pretty but small slice of cinnamon-colored sand.

Facilities: Picnic tables, playground, restrooms, snack bar, volleyball, nature trails, rental boats; information, 802-228-2025. *Camping:* Group camping with six lean-tos. *Swimming:* Good in Echo Lake. *Fishing:* Excellent in Echo Lake. Try for smelt, trout, bass and yellow perch.

Getting there: Off Route 100 in Ludlow.

Wilgus State Park—This 100-acre park draws life from the very wide, very fertile Connecticut River. Most of the area is heavily wooded, but a small clearing allows for cool picnicking and nice views across the river to New Hampshire. There's no beach, but an opening in the steep river banks makes way for canoes.

Facilities: Picnic areas, restrooms, playground, canoe rentals, nature trails; information, 802-674-5422. *Camping:* Group camping area with lean-tos, including hot showers and fireplaces. *Swimming:* Not good. Currents very strong. *Fishing:* Excellent angling on Connecticut River.

Getting there: On Route 5 south of Ascutney.

Quechee Gorge State Park—This is one of the most visited parks in Vermont, and rightly so, since it provides access to the geological phenomenon called Quechee Gorge. Carved by glaciers during the Ice Age, the 165-foot gorge provides a cool, scenic milieu along the Ottauquechee River.

Quite large, the 612-acre park mostly skirts calmer, flatter parts of the river and provides asylum for plenty of white-tailed deer.

Facilities: Picnic tables, restrooms, top-notch nature trails; plenty of stores nearby, west on Route 4; information, 802-295-2990. *Camping:* Permitted in 54 campsites including six lean-tos with hot showers and fireplaces but no hookups. *Fishing:* This area is trout land.

Getting there: On Route 4 three miles west of the junction of Routes 89 and 91 near White River Junction.

NORTHERN MOUNTAIN REGION BEACHES AND PARKS

Green Mountain National Forest—See "Southern Vermont Beaches and Parks."

Little River State Park—A dense, bushy area lying within Mount Mansfield State Forest, this park spans 12,000 acres of maple, birch and fir forests and a big manmade body of water called the Waterbury Reservoir. There are three beaches—two in a wooded camping area and one in a large picnic clearing—comprised of silver, silty sand. Nature lovers will revel in the excellent gridwork of trails.

Facilities: Picnic tables, restrooms, playground, boat rentals and ramp; information, 802-244-7103. *Camping:* Permitted in 101 sites with hot showers, fireplaces and 20 lean-tos; information, 802-244-7103. *Swimming:* Good all over reservoir. *Fishing:* Excellent for perch, rainbow trout, and small and bigmouth bass.

Getting there: From the junction of Routes 100 and 2, take Route 2 one and one-half miles west to Little River Road and go north for three and one-half miles.

Groton State Forest—This 25,625-acre wonderland nurtures several natural jewels, among them the picturesque **Boulder Beach**, where bulky rocks dot a coarse, cream-tinted sand that edges Lake Groton. Small boats laze across the water, surrounded by mighty stands of evergreen trees. In separate areas, the Groton Nature Center houses interesting displays of plant and animal life, while Osmore Pond offers a scenic clearing for picnicking.

One of the most popular forest activities is the hike to the summit of **Owl's Head Mountain**, where incredible views stretch across Camel's Hump Forest.

Facilities: At Boulder Beach, picnic areas, restrooms, boat rentals, snack bar, pavilion; information, 802-584-3823. At Groton Nature Center, restrooms, nature walks, films; information, 802-584-3827. At Osmore Pond, picnic tables, restrooms, pavilions; stores nearby in Groton; information, 802-584-3820. At Owl's Head Mountain, picnic tables, primitive toilets; information, 802-584-3820. *Camping:* Groton Forest has five camping areas, including primitive, group and developed campgrounds. *Swimming:* Excellent along a calm, shallow shelf at Boulder Beach. *Fishing:* Good at the campgrounds, but the best place in the forest is Seyon Fly Fishing Area (802-584-3829), where you'll find a great trout pond, rental canoes and overnight lodges.

Getting there: To Boulder Beach: From Groton, go two miles west on Route 302, then six miles northwest on Route 232, then two miles east on Boulder Beach Road. To Groton Nature Center: Located one mile west of Boulder Beach on Boulder Beach Road. To Osmore Pond: Located on Route 232, nine and a half miles northwest of Route 302. To Owl's Head Mountain: Located on Route 232, eight and a half miles northwest of Route 302. To Seyon Fly Fishing Area: Off Route 302, three miles west of Groton.

Smugglers Notch State Park—Wedged at the apex of two stony, sheer mountains, Smugglers Notch offers idyllic surroundings of rock ledges and formations, fern grottos and damp caves for exploring. The park itself comprises 25 acres of shady, brookside picnic grounds, but you can walk to many choice sights outside the park grounds, including frigid Big Springs pool and the 6000-ton King Rock that broke from the mountain in 1910. Check out the great elephant head formation just above King Rock.

Facilities: Picnic tables, restrooms, hiking trails; information, 802-253-4014. *Camping:* Small area with hot showers and fireplaces but no hookups.

Getting there: On Route 108 (Mountain Road) in Stowe, about eight miles north of Route 100 junction.

Underhill State Park (★)—Remote and rustic, this pretty park lies in the midst of back country, smothered in maple and birch trees and filled with deer, rabbits and raccoons. It covers 150 acres of mountain terrain and features three popular trails that ascend the western flank of Mount Mansfield. To get here, you'll have to tackle four miles of steep gravel road—but it's well worth it.

Facilities: A picnic shelter, restrooms; information, 802-899-3022. *Camping:* Permitted—small primitive area.

Getting there: From the town of Essex Junction, go nine miles east on Route 15, then four miles east on Pleasant Valley Road, then three miles east on the gravel road (there's a sign at this point).

CHAMPLAIN VALLEY BEACHES AND PARKS

Mount Philo State Park—Resting right on top of Mount Philo, this park rewards those who tackle its very steep but paved road with astonishing panoramas. From here, you can peer across Lake Champlain into New York's Adirondacks and farther. A total of 168 acres, most of the park is vertical and forested. There is a nice picnic area and many splendid hiking trails.

Facilities: Picnic tables; store one mile south on Route 7; information, 802-425-2390. *Camping:* Permitted at 16 sites with hot showers and fireplaces.

Getting there: Off Route 7, six miles north of Route 22A near North Ferrisburg.

Sand Bar State Park—One of the flattest areas in the state, this ever-popular locale borders Lake Champlain and some of its swampy areas. Families and college students crowd the coarse, mocha-colored sand and grassy areas lining the lake, while windsurfers and sailboats whiz along just off-shore. The views across the lake of the Adirondack Mountains are exceptional.

Facilities: Picnic facilities, bathhouse, volleyball courts, sailboat and windsurfing rentals, snack bar; information, 802-372-8240. *Swimming:* Very good; water is waist-deep at least 100 yards out.

Getting there: On Route 2 near Milton, four miles north of Route 89.

North Hero State Park—From its perch on a thickly wooded peninsula, this 400-acre park captures a prominent view of Lake Champlain and glances backward on North Hero Island. Though it actually borders two miles of lake, the only real accessible shore is a small but pretty shale beach at the peninsula's tip, a secluded spot favored by Canadians and local sailboaters.

Facilities: Picnic tables, restrooms, playground, rowboat rentals and boat ramp; store three miles south on Route 2; information, 802-372-8727. *Camping:* Permitted at 117 sites with hot showers and fireplaces but no hookups. *Swimming:* Good, but you must wade out past a rim of slippery rocks. *Fishing:* Immense Lake Champlain provides superb fishing opportunities, from smelt and pike to perch, walleye and pickerel.

Getting there: Off Route 2, six miles southwest of Alburg.

NORTHEAST KINGDOM BEACHES AND PARKS

Prouty Park—This popular municipal park corners the market on local views. Situated along tranquil Lake Memphremagog, Prouty preens across the water to the town of Newport, with its quaint downtown and historic church spires. A 100-foot sliver of tawny sand skirts the lake, protected by a row of weeping willows. And with tennis and basketball courts, miniature golf and soccer fields, who could get bored?

Facilities: Picnic pavilions, restrooms, snack bar; information, 802-334-7951. *Camping:* Immaculate campground with sewer and water hookups, washers, dryers and showers. *Swimming:* Good; water is shallow. *Fishing:* Try from shore or on a boat for trout, salmon, pike and bass.

Getting there: On Veterans Avenue in Newport.

Maidstone State Park (★)—Ringed with majestic mountain peaks and tucked in the middle of nowhere, this gorgeous preserve possesses a very special feature: the crystal clear, shallow Maidstone Lake. It's enough to just sit and gaze at reflections of trees in the water, but the more adventurous might choose to sunbathe on a generous stretch of cream-colored sand. Don't be intimidated by the remoteness of this park. Once you're there, you'll be thankful you made the drive.

Facilities: Picnic tables, hiking trails, boat and canoe rentals; information, 802-676-3930. *Camping:* Permitted at 82 sites; fireplaces and hot showers but no hookups. *Swimming:* Good, though the water is quite chilly, even in summer. *Fishing:* Excellent for lake and rainbow trout as well as salmon.

Getting there: From the town of Bloomfield, go south along the Connecticut River for five miles on Route 102, then turn southwest at the State Forest Highway (it's marked). This is a gravel road that extends six miles to the park.

Brighton State Park (★)—Even with the fiercest of competition, this has to be the prettiest park in all of Vermont. The setting is absolutely magnificent, the mood incredibly serene. Nestled along poignant Spectacle Pond, Brighton claims a sliver of crystalline tawny beach and 152 acres packed with spruce, firs, pines and many other very green, very big trees. There's also a nature museum and plenty of forested trails that scale the billowy terrain.

Facilities: Picnic tables, restrooms, showers, snack bar, fireplaces; information, 802-723-4360. *Camping:* Permitted at 84 sites, including 21 lean-tos, but no water or sewer hookups. *Swimming:* Good. *Fishing:* Excellent for trout on Island Pond, bass on Spectacle Pond.

Getting there: Off Route 105, two miles east of Island Pond.

Hiking

With more than 700 miles of splendid hiking terrain—including 512 miles on state and national forest lands—Vermont is a hiker's nirvana. The best time to go, of course, is early summer to late fall, avoiding the spring "mud season" from mid-April to late May.

Vermont's hiking authority, **The Green Mountain Club** (P.O. Box 889, Montpelier, VT 05602; 802-223-3463), can supply books, brochures and guidance on the subject.

The longest uninterrupted trek exists on **The Long Trail** (265 miles), a primitive footpath that crawls along the crest of the Green Mountains from Massachusetts to Canada. Purists love the abundance of wildlife and foliage on this trek, which ambles through dense evergreen forests and shaded glens and alongside quiescent ponds and rivers. An inspiration for the Appalachian Trail, which links the mountains from Georgia to Maine, the Long Trail includes 175 miles of side trails and climbs as high as 4393 feet.

SOUTHERN VERMONT TRAILS

Bald Mountain Trail (4 miles), off Route 30 in Townshend State Park, makes a loop past an alder swamp and a cascading brook and through a hemlock forest. There are some fine mountain views along the way.

A nice, short hike in southern Vermont can be found along **Harmon Hill Trail** (3.4 miles) off Route 9 east of Bennington. There's a steep then moderate climb to the summit, where views of Bennington and Mt. Antone are fabulous.

A few miles north, **Baker Peak** and **Griffith Lake Trails** (8 miles), off Route 7 near Danby, wind through brooks and streams then scale Baker Mountain for a magnificent look at the Otter Creek Valley and marble quarry on Dorset Peak.

CENTRAL VERMONT TRAILS

A dramatic crevice can be seen along the **Clarendon Gorge and Airport Lookout** trail (1.6 miles), which picks up off Route 103 east of Route 7 near Clarendon. A path crosses a suspension bridge over the Mill River, then ascends steadily to a nice vantage point with views of the Otter Creek Valley and Bird and Herrick mountains.

For a history lesson capped by great scenery, take the **Mt. Independence** trail (7.8 miles) past well-preserved remains of Revolutionary War fortifications built back in 1775. You'll also discover superb views of Lake Champlain, Fort Ticonderoga and surrounding valleys. The trail begins off Route 73A west of Orwell Village.

Abbey Pond Trail (5.8 miles) affords a close look at beautiful wilderness areas teeming with marsh plants, deer, rabbits, bear and other wildlife. Follow the trail from Route 53, near Forest Dale, past a series of cascades to a view of the twin peaks of Robert Frost Mountain.

The **Battell Mountain and Skylight Pond** trail (5 miles) commences at Steam Mill Clearing, a pretty meadow and former logging camp, and meanders easily up Battell Mountain, then continues to picturesque Skylight Pond. Pick up the trailhead off Route 125 seven miles east of East Middlebury.

NORTHERN MOUNTAIN REGION TRAILS

For a 180° view of the Champlain Valley and New York's Adirondack Mountains, opt for the **Sunset Ledge Trail** (2 miles), off Route 100 in the scenic Lincoln Gap.

Mount Mansfield is Vermont's highest peak (4393 feet) and naturally the most hiked. The easiest trek is via the **Long Trail** (4.6 miles), the most ghoulish endures along **Hell Brook Trail** (3.6 miles), a supersteep rocky climb recommended only for experienced hikers. Both trailheads begin off Route 108 in Stowe.

One of the most beautiful, secluded spots on the Long Trail is at **Devil's Gulch Trail** (8.2 miles), an interesting rock defile and fern grotto. You'll find the trailhead along Route 118 five miles west of Eden.

CHAMPLAIN VALLEY TRAILS

Take a hike to Lake Champlain on the **Red Rocks Park Trails** (2.5 miles), a series of short paths through cool pine woods that lead to vantage points on the lakeshore. The park is off Queen City Park Drive west of Route 189 in South Burlington.

Grand Isle State Park Trail (.3 mile) is short on distance but long on views. The path cuts through a lush thicket and makes a loop over a low bluff to an observation tower. You can see Lake Champlain in the distance. The park is on Route 2 one mile south of Grand Isle.

Knight Point State Park Trail (1 mile) follows Lake Champlain's shoreline through a dense hardwood forest. You'll find it on Route 2 in North Hero.

NORTHEAST KINGDOM TRAILS

Mount Pisgah Trail (6.9 miles) crosses this 2751-foot mountain via thick forests and wooden walkways over beaver ponds. There are exceptional views packed into this trek, including a 60-mile panorama from Lake Memphremagog and Jay Peak to beyond Camel's Hump. The trail starts along Route 5A just outside West Burke.

The remote Northeast Kingdom offers some glorious hikes, including the **Wheeler Mountain Trail** (5.4 miles), which creeps through meadows and woods and across open rocks to a 2371-foot summit. Along the way, you'll catch splendid views of Mount Mansfield and Lake Willoughby. The trail picks up off Route 5 east of Barton.

Travelers' Tracks

Sightseeing

No doubt its copious history, relentless, marvelous vistas and peaceful aura combine to make Vermont one of the country's foremost sightseeing regions. Splendid museums, white-steepled churches and vestiges of this nation's heritage are there to be relished, though some of the best scenes abound along rural byroads, where the views can set your heart aflutter.

Don't be afraid to venture down dirt roads. There are many in the Green Mountain State, and nearly every one holds a surprise: a hidden apple orchard or covered bridge, a maple sugarhouse, a mountain stream where you can laze away the afternoon in solitude. You might, perhaps, even happen upon a place where no traveler has ever been before.

Tourist information is readily available everywhere, in stores and restaurants, inns and post offices. Sightseeing winds down in winter, with the majority of places closing from November through April. Many of the 250 towns and cities publish individual sightseeing maps, and, of course, people everywhere are more than happy to assist with your explorations.

SOUTHERN VERMONT

Edged by New York, Massachusetts and New Hampshire, this southerly precinct serves predominately as a gateway for skiers, weekenders and other seekers of pleasure and solace. Here, spun into one fine geographical web, are all the components that typify Vermont—wooded mountain corridors, lazy farmlands, bucolic villages and a cornucopia of history.

Two of Vermont's largest cities, Brattleboro and Bennington, anchor the state corners and bring culture, politics and manufacturing into the region. Nestled nicely between the Connecticut River and a string of western mountain ledges, **Brattleboro** debuted as a sparse colony in 1724, making it Vermont's first permanent settlement. Today, the city owes its industrial image to large factories that churn out paper and furniture products and leather goods.

The **Visitors Information Booth** (Putney Road; 802-257-1112) and **Brattleboro Chamber of Commerce** (180 Main Street; 802-254-4565) stock loads of maps and can help with itineraries.

Every proper 1800s Brattleboro home simply *had* to have a parlor organ, and a few of those relics still remain at the **Brattleboro Museum and Art Center** (Main and Vernon streets; 802-257-0124). Located in a 1915 native stone railroad station, the museum has eight beautiful wood Estey organs, manufactured locally by the thousands until the plant shut down in the 1960s. You'll also encounter dynamic rotating exhibits of visual arts as well as historical programs.

Back in 1892, Rudyard Kipling put down roots just north of Brattleboro in the village of Dummerston. Here, in an odd, ship-shaped house called **Naulakha** (Kipling Road, two miles north of Mountain Road), he lived for four years with his wife, Vermont native Carrie Balestier, and penned *Captains Courageous* and two *Jungle Books*. Now a private residence, the dwelling is set back from the road and cloaked in tall trees.

To experience the rural rhythms of this state, head north on Route 30 to **Newfane**. Settled in 1774, this beguiling village is a paradigm of Vermont culture, showcasing 40 exquisite buildings that harken back to the 1700s. White clapboard houses mingle with graceful maple and elm trees and vast green. The grand **Windham County Courthouse** (802-365-4257), a Greek Revival design with enormous pillars, edges the green and is the village focal point. Across the green rests the **Old Newfane Inn** (802-365-4427),

(Text continued on page 388.)

Vermont Maple Syrup

It begins quite subtly during the first hint of spring: a tiny sprig of green sprouts, a bird chirps gaily and the sap inside a maple tree breaks free from its icy chamber and trickles ever so gently toward the warm ground.

Squirrels, rabbits and other forest dwellers scurry to lap up the sweet elixir, a welcome indulgence after a long, frigid winter. Along comes another mountain inhabitant, a farmer, who pierces the maple trunk with a plastic tap, drawing the sticky sap into a clear plastic tube. He does this hundreds, perhaps thousands of times, tapping trees and connecting them with little tubes until their sap trickles harmoniously down the mountain.

And so it goes. Each spring, millions of Vermont maple trees surrender their gooey, candied essence for the sake of that sought-after substance known as maple syrup. Called "sugarbushes" or "maple orchards," these grand stands of trees blanket the mountains with their stalwart trunks and burgeoning canopies of delicate toothed leaves.

Vermont is the country's largest supplier of maple syrup, producing an annual average of half a million gallons. Though the harvesting processes are fairly simple, they've changed quite a bit since Native Americans cooked sap over an open fire back in the 1500s.

Today, most farmers use the plastic tubes, drawing sap by gravity or with a vacuum system, but some still opt for the time-honored metal bucket system. In this method, sap drips from trees into large buckets, which are carted on sleds down the mountains.

Back at the sugarhouse, sap is boiled all day (and sometimes all night) in huge metal pans until it's reduced to a smooth syrup. It takes an average of 40 gallons of sap to net one gallon of syrup.

All the cooking takes place in hundreds of wooden sugarhouses—characterized by vented roofs to help steam escape—that dot verdant mountains and valleys. You can peek in on all the action by visiting large syrup mills, but for the most rewarding experience, stop in on a family-owned operation.

Here, cordial folks will bring you up to snuff on the sweet stuff as well as share their lifestyles and family histories.

You'll discover small, family-owned farms all over the state, and while many display a small sign that says "Maple Syrup," others have no sign (these you can find out about at the local general store). More than 150 large and small operations are listed in *Maple Sugarhouses*, a dandy, free brochure published by the Vermont Department of Agriculture (116 State Street, Montpelier, VT 05602; 802-828-2416). Listings are by town and provide information on number of taps, size of sugarhouses, methods of operation and tours.

The **New England Maple Museum** (Route 7, Pittsford; 802-483-9414; admission) promises "The Sweetest Story Ever Told" if you visit its displays of maple sugar nostalgia. A great place to bone up on syrup history, the museum stocks old artifacts like wooden buckets and taps and horse-drawn sleds used for toting sap. The best part, though, is the free syrup tasting.

Or, immerse yourself in syrupy activities at the **Vermont Maple Festival** (contact the Vermont Maple Festival Council, Box 255, St. Albans, VT 05478; 802-524-5800), held each April in St. Albans, north of Burlington. Feast on pancakes smothered in syrup, watch a lumberjack at work and savor the honeyed flavor of assorted syrup varieties.

Plan to visit from late February (in southern areas) through mid-April (in northern areas). The choicest syrup, a fancy golden extract, is harvested first. As the season progresses, syrup turns a medium amber, then a dark amber and finally a bitter, murky consistency that's seldom edible.

Of course, the finer things in life always cost more, and such is the case with maple syrup. Usually double and triple the price of blended syrups, the real stuff will cost you about 40 to 60 cents per ounce.

But be forewarned. Those accustomed to blended syrup shall unwittingly be seduced by the pure maple kind, a victim of their own newly enlightened taste buds. Syrupoholics say it's sort of like switching from jug wine to fine wine: once you've tasted the good stuff, it's impossible to go back.

a venerable 1787 colonial building trimmed in white lattice porches and chimneys.

A drive northward on Route 30 and then Route 35 will put you smack in the middle of back country, a piece of terrain laced with mountain brooks and meandering meadows, occasional farms and one-room schoolhouses.

If you're like Ulysses S. Grant and Oliver Wendell Holmes, you'll make a pit stop in Grafton at the **Old Tavern** (Routes 35 and 121; 802-843-2231), an 1801 colonial-style inn that's filled with marvelous antiques and Old World character. Once a popular stagecoach layover, the tavern also hosted the likes of Ralph Waldo Emerson and Rudyard Kipling.

Some say **Grafton** got its name in a bidding contest—won with $5 and a flask of rum—back in 1791, though the village owes its existence to sheep farming (12,000 grazed here during the 1800s). Grafton now boasts two covered bridges, 650 residents and a network of well-preserved white frame buildings.

Exquisite views await back along Route 9, to the west of Brattleboro, where the road climbs 2350 feet to the top of **Hogback Mountain**. This captivating plateau, surrounded with lofty spires of spruce and fir trees, affords a 100-mile panorama across New Hampshire and the Berkshires of Massachusetts.

Tucked in the basement of the Hogback Mountain Gift Shop, the **Luman Nelson Museum of New England Wildlife** (★) (Route 9, Marlboro; 802-464-5494) offers a walk on the wild side. This bizarre grotto, "stuffed" with thousands of familiar and unusual birds and animals, represents the lifetime work of taxidermist and naturalist Luman Nelson. The winged collection alone is staggering: more than 1000 different bird species are there, including a large eagle and owl collection and the extinct passenger pigeon and heath hen. Even stranger, though, are the albino deer and skunks.

Continue through this forested mountain wonderland, traveling west on Route 9, and you'll descend into the town of **Wilmington**. Long a juncture between Brattleboro and western Bennington, this bucolic town of 1800 swells to 12,000 during winter when skiers pack nearby **Haystack Mountain** and **Mount Snow**. Of course, summertime activities abound, too, and you can learn about these and other leisure pursuits at the **Mount Snow/ Haystack Region Chamber of Commerce** (Routes 9 and 100, Wilmington; 802-464-8092).

Heading west toward Bennington, Route 9 cuts through the broad, verdant expanse of the **Green Mountain National Forest**. This sinuous, heady trail explodes with brilliant color during fall foliage season, though the views border on amazing the rest of the year, too. Keep an eye out for bears, coyotes and moose, which roam the area frequently.

You can see it before you get to Bennington, an intimidating limestone obelisk looming over the city like some celestial figure. The 306-foot **Ben-**

nington Battle Monument (15 Monument Circle, Old Bennington; 802-447-0550; admission), the region's geographical frame of reference, pays tribute to the 1777 Battle of Bennington, a decisive conflict during the American Revolution. Though American general John Stark organized his troops and supplies here in Bennington, the battle was actually waged five miles away on a New York hill.

Bennington is Vermont's southwesternmost city and the first town chartered in the state, though residents didn't arrive until 12 years later in 1761 because of fierce raids during the French and Indian War. Suffused with culture and Revolutionary War history, the city is flanked by the Green Mountains and the Taconic range, a setting that's nothing short of spectacular.

The downtown area is pretty but naturally quite commercialized, so you'll want to spend most of your time in **Old Bennington**. Draped across a hill on the city's west quadrant, this pristine borough harbors marvelous expressions of early American history. Here you'll find more than 80 well-preserved 18th- and 19th-century buildings, comprising a sort-of outdoor museum.

Before you start exploring, pick up a walking tour map from the **Bennington Area Chamber of Commerce** (Route 7; 802-447-3311).

American history becomes an enthralling experience at the **Bennington Museum** (West Main Street, Old Bennington; 802-447-1571; admission). This vine-covered, 1855 building—one of New England's finest museums—evokes America's past with Civil War and American Revolution artifacts, 18th- and 19th-century furnishings and paintings, a rare collection of blown glass and a New England genealogical library packed with 3000 volumes.

Housed in a separate wing of the museum is the frame schoolhouse, moved from Eagle Bridge, New York, that **Grandma Moses** attended as a child. This structure displays the largest public collection of her paintings and working utensils in North America. The spirit of this remarkable woman—who began painting at age 76—shines through in her paintings of New England rural cheer, in her portraits and photographs, and in her tilt-top painting table, shawl and apron.

West on Main Street rests Vermont's colonial shrine, the **Old First Church** (1 Monument Avenue, Old Bennington; 802-447-1223), erected in 1806 and now a much-photographed sight. Nestled on the green in Old Bennington, the simple white building has columns formed with single pine trees, arched Romanesque windows and well-preserved pine box pews. In this state of tradition, some of today's church members are descendants of the original founders.

Beside the church on a shady knoll, symmetrical rows of granite comprise the **Old Burying Ground**, where you can stroll peacefully among tombstones dating back to the 1700s. Many epitaphs are intriguing, ruminations of early settlers and soldiers who toiled here under a more difficult life, but perhaps the most reflective endures on the grave of poet Robert Frost: "I had a lover's quarrel with the world."

Head north from Old Bennington on Fairview Street, cross one of three quaint covered bridges, and you'll arrive at **Bennington College** (Route 67A; 802-442-5401). A medley of colonial designs, the campus lazes peacefully across 550 acres on a pretty hill overlooking mountains and valleys.

Since it's founding in 1929, the tiny liberal arts school has initiated some of the country's most progressive teaching styles, employing accomplished (and oftentimes renowned) artists, writers and musicians to act as both teachers and colleagues to students. Among the more famous who have graced these halls are dancer and choreographer Martha Graham and author Bernard De Voto. Rigorous scholastic and artistic exercises students must endure are often referred to as "The Bennington Experience."

Perhaps the most intriguing sight on campus is **Jennings Hall**, a grand three-story structure carved of solid granite. Built in the mid-1800s, the building was home to the Frederic B. Jennings family, who donated their estate to the college.

When you've taken in the city, you can retreat into the heart of the surrounding mountain area with **Back Road Country Tours** (★) (P.O. Box 517, Shaftsbury, VT 05262; 802-442-3876). Vermont native Niles Oesterle transports visitors along roads less traveled in the 200,000-acre Green Mountain National Forest, using a jeep to get close to deer, wild turkeys, grouse, fox and other forest dwellers. One-hour to full-day tours are offered, with pickup service anywhere in Bennington County.

The cozy pastoral spirit and thoughtful personalities of **Arlington**, 16 miles north of Bennington off Route 7A, remain preserved on *Saturday Evening Post* covers, sketched by Norman Rockwell when he lived here during the 1940s and early '50s. Rockwell's farm and studio are now **The Inn on Covered Bridge Green** (★) (River Road, four and a half miles west of Route 7A, West Arlington; 802-375-9489), a scenic resting place nestled among apple orchards and dairy farms.

You can chat with some of the local people Rockwell painted if you stop by the **Norman Rockwell Exhibition** (Route 7A, Arlington; 802-375-6423; admission), a 19th-century church where several hundred *Saturday Evening Post* covers, illustrations and prints are displayed.

Meander north on Route 7A to Sunderland, then head west on **Skyline Drive** toll road for a hair-raising, five-mile trek to the top of **Mount Equinox**. At 3816 feet up, the panorama is inspiring, the air brisk and the feeling serene.

On the way down the mountain, stop off at the **Southern Vermont Art Center** (West Road, Manchester; 802-362-1405; admission) for a tryst with culture and nature. A beautiful late-1800s Georgian mansion holds ten galleries and over 700 artworks, chiefly contemporary paintings, graphic art and photography. Set on 375 acres of forest and pastureland, the center also boasts a performing arts pavilion for outdoor concerts, an extensive botany trail and a sculpture garden sprinkled with wildflowers. Open late May through late October.

Avid fishers—and even nonanglers—will get a kick out of the **Museum of American Fly Fishing** (Route 7A, Manchester Village; 802-362-3300). Peruse more than 30,000 flies and 1000 rods and reels, tracing the history of this intriguing sport. You'll see what Dwight Eisenhower, Daniel Webster and Ernest Hemingway used to snag a fish, along with artifacts from famous rod-makers like Thomas Orvis. A real treat for anyone fishing for fun.

Just a stone's throw northward on Route 7A lies **Manchester**, which made its imprint last century as a thriving summer resort town and this century as a nucleus for designer outlet stores. But its main claim to fame is a former resident, Robert Todd Lincoln, eldest son of Abraham Lincoln, who built a Georgian Revival mansion here in 1905 and called it **Hildene** (Route 7A, Manchester Village; 802-362-1788; admission).

Possibly one of New England's finest historic scenes, Hildene offers a glimmer of the gilded, intriguing life of Robert Lincoln, an attorney, minister to Great Britain and U.S. Cabinet member. Laid against 412 acres of beautiful formal gardens, evergreen trees and nature trails, the 24-room mansion is extremely well-preserved and filled with original furnishings and possessions including a grand 1908 Aeolian pipe organ once played by the Lincoln women.

CENTRAL VERMONT

Sprawled across the lower waist of the state are a diverse lot of mining cities, picturesque mountain hamlets, ski areas and affluent riverside towns. Driving through this fertile area, you'll encounter a variety of lifestyles and people—fifth-generation farmers, descendants of European immigrants, small-time merchants and established aristocrats.

On the region's west side, Rutland and nearby villages are pocked with marble quarries that have churned the wheels of industry for two centuries. Eastward, Woodstock is a meld of tree-lined streets and gracious 19th-century architecture that owes its affluence and elegance to a line of wealthy partisans, including Laurance S. Rockefeller and railroad magnate Frederick Billings. Beyond Woodstock rambles the lazy Connecticut River, a natural divider between Vermont and New Hampshire.

Just south of Rutland and off Route 7 is a mandatory side trip (via a few dirt roads) to **Shrewsbury** (★) (North Shrewsbury Road, about eight miles east of Route 7), a quiescent village of 800 that seems buried at the end of the world.

You can't miss the majestic steepled church that doubles as town hall, but the local fixture is **W. E. Pierce Groceries** (Lincoln Hill Road, Shrewsbury; 802-492-3645), a charming A-frame general store that's been run by the same family since 1835. (The 1918 brass cash register is still the only one.)

Just around the corner, **Meadowsweet Herb Farm** (★) (729 Mount Holly Road; 802-492-3565) is a joyous feast for the senses, a skein of luxuriant gardens and greenhouses radiating brilliant flowers and redolent herbs. You get "free sniffs and pets" of herbs, plus a wonderful shop filled with potpourri, spices and dried-flower arrangements. Pack a lunch and picnic by the pond under the apple trees.

Northward lies **Rutland**, which earned the name "Marble City" during the mid-1800s when local marble mining exploded, though it was also the state's largest railroad junction. This commercial city—Vermont's second largest with 20,000 people—bears a handful of marble-plated buildings, but much of its marble was used for more than 250,000 headstones at Arlington National Cemetery in Virginia as well as the Lincoln Memorial in Washington, D.C., and the U.S. Supreme Court.

The **Rutland Region Chamber of Commerce** (7 Court Square, Rutland; 802-773-2747) will assist with sightseeing in the area.

The marble bridge, sidewalks and high school are a testament to more than a century of serious quarrying in nearby **Proctor**, where you can check out the **Vermont Marble Company Exhibit** (61 Main Street; 802-459-3311; admission), a series of intriguing marble displays with history to boot.

A short (and very worthwhile) trip north on Route 7 will bring you to the town of **Brandon**, where you'll find one of the state's best expressions of 19th-century architecture. This fertile farming town, lined with serene, shady streets, was chartered in 1761 and was the birthplace of Stephen A. Douglas, the famous Illinois debater who lost the 1860 presidential race to Abe Lincoln. Excellent walking-tour maps are available at the **Brandon Area Chamber of Commerce** (Central Square; 802-247-6401).

A sensational drive along Route 73, **Brandon Gap** cuts through precipitous mountains and miles of forest and gurgling brooks. While you're there, why not take an all-day **Llama Trek** (★) (book reservations at the Churchill House Inn, Route 73 East; 802-247-3300)? It's an unusual experience, to say the least, tromping through beautiful mountain trails with these curious, light-footed South American animals, which are cousins of the camel.

East of Rutland, **Killington** and **Pico** constitute the state's largest and perhaps most popular ski area, though the resort scene seems quite contrived when compared to the genuine quaintness of surrounding villages (as most any native Vermonter will quickly point out).

Vermont supposedly acquired its name on top of **Killington Peak**, the state's second largest summit, in 1763 when the Reverend Samuel Peters ascended on horseback and proclaimed the area *Verd Mont*, French for green mountain.

From Killington, go east on Route 4 to Route 100 South, then it's just a few miles to **Plymouth**. This gloriously remote mountain hamlet harbors the **Calvin Coolidge Homestead** (Route 100A; 802-672-3773; admission; closed mid-October through mid-May), where the 30th president was born and spent most of his life. The entire scene is quite striking, a thread of well-preserved white clapboard and stone buildings and gravel lanes set against stalwart trees and mountain peaks. There's a one-room schoolhouse that Coolidge attended, a general store operated by his father and the home where, following President Harding's sudden death, he took his 2:47 a.m. presidential oath. Coolidge and his family are buried nearby on a grassy knoll.

A short drive east on Route 4 transforms you from bucolic byroads to overt affluence and centuries of prosperity in **Woodstock**. Superb red brick and white clapboard buildings skirt the beautiful oval green, fashionable shops and restaurants line side streets and a chalkboard called the **Woodstock Town Crier** (corner Central and Elm streets) provides the scoop on local goings on.

For more detailed information, stop by the **Woodstock Area Chamber of Commerce** (4 Central Street; 802-457-3555).

While some Vermonters bash Woodstock as bombastic, the community's attempts to preserve the natural surroundings shine through any pretentions that may exist. Power lines are hidden from sight, thanks to donations from resident Laurance Rockefeller, and rural beauty has been preserved at **Billings Farm and Museum** (Route 12; 802-457-2355; admission).

A railroad magnate and Rockefeller's father-in-law, Frederick Billings established the farm in 1890, planted 10,000 trees and waged wars for agrarian protection. Today, exhibits take you through those early days of sidehill plows, corn planters and "nooning" (lunching) in the fields, providing an interesting reflection on 19th-century farming. You can even watch the cows being milked every afternoon.

Picturesque and subtly beguiling, neighboring **Quechee** lolls across the banks of the Ottauquechee River and claims a large concentration of resort estates. These grand mansions and sprawling country villas serve as summer homes for members of society's upper echelons and as eye-pleasing spectacles for passersby.

Even more inspiring than the resort estates is **Quechee Gorge** (Route 4, three miles north of Interstates 89 and 91), a mammoth rocky chasm chiseled by the Ottauquechee River. Maple and fir trees skate down the rocky walls of the 165-foot-deep gorge, carved by glaciers during the Ice Age. It's a mile walk to the bottom, but the trek is scenic, cool and rewarding.

NORTHERN MOUNTAIN REGION

Interminable forests of maple trees, or "sugarbushes," have earned this region its image—along with a handsome maple syrup industry. Indeed, the entire region evokes a sense of ultimate Vermont charm, a place crisscrossed with valley farms and corn fields, winding country roads, hidden swimming holes and the whizzing Mad River that inspires virtually every part of local life.

Most of the tranquil villages here can trace their roots to the early 1800s (some even further back), making them a delight to visit and investigate. Tiny, endearing Montpelier, the state capital, was established way back in 1805 after Vermont's legislature roamed for almost 30 years. Austria-like Stowe, its great alpine peaks forming a sea of green, harkens back to 1833 when it was a crossroads for travelers on horseback.

While longtime Vermonters surely appreciate the region's idyllic aura, it's the flatlanders—natives of New York, Massachusetts or any other place that's not Vermont—who have lately sought out the serenity of these vertical reaches. Typically owners of small businesses or bed and breakfasts, these "immigrants" have left the so-called good life in big cities for what they say is a better life among Vermont's Green Mountains.

Though the Sugarbush ski resort area churns up the most activity, the real local beauty lies in **Warren** (off Route 100 east of Lincoln Gap Road) and **Waitsfield** (northward along Route 100), a pair of pastoral towns with covered bridges, general stores and friendly, down-home folks.

The region's alpine setting and excellent thermal currents make it a splendid place for **gliding**. Ride the air currents 5000 feet up and secure a bird's-eye view of farmlands and mountaintop beaver ponds. Flights are offered at the **Warren-Sugarbush Airport** (Airport Road off Route 100; 802-496-2290), where a pilot will take one or two passengers for rides lasting 15 to 30 minutes.

East on Route 89 lies **Montpelier**. With a population of only 8500, Montpelier is the smallest state capital in the nation, though its grand old buildings and manicured cityscapes may well be the country's most charming.

To direct you around town—and the state—the **Vermont Travel Division** (134 State Street; 802-828-3236) provides an impressive array of information on sights as well as history, culture and the economy.

The **State House** (115 State Street; 802-828-2228), with its gold-leaf dome resting dramatically against the evergreens of Hubbard Park, easily takes center stage. Modeled after the Greek temple of Theseus, the 1838 granite granddaddy sports a statue of Ceres, Roman goddess of agriculture. Take a free tour, or wander around and muse over the Civil War murals, Victorian decor and quotations by Theodore Roosevelt, Ethan Allen and other national legends.

Across the street, the **State Agriculture Building** (116 State Street; 802-828-2416) commands a look with its red brick facade, fancy turrets and arched, convex windows.

Don't miss the fine exhibits at **The Vermont Museum** (109 State Street; 802-828-2291), housed in the old red brick Pavilion Hotel, built in 1876. There's an impressive collection of fine and decorative arts, farm and industrial equipment and memorabilia that imaginatively traces the state's history.

Montpelier's sister city is **Barre**, though no two siblings could be less alike. Barre is the rough-and-tumble one of the pair, a working-class town put on the map by the granite industry. During the late 1800s, thousands of European and Canadian immigrant stoneworkers flocked to town, making Barre quite a bustling place and along the way producing frequent labor disputes and strong movements toward socialism.

Today, this self-proclaimed Granite Capital of the World harbors the largest monumental granite quarry in the world, known as **The Rock of Ages** (Main Street, off Route 14; 802-476-3115). This colossal stony pit, which plunges more than 350 feet deep and spans 30 acres, is strewn with mining equipment and boulders.

Some of the granite found its final resting place at the **Hope Cemetery** (Merchant Street, Barre), a fascinating collection of memorial art. The delicate engravings of granite craftsmen (often designed for their deceased brethren) survive on everything from small headstones and ornate monuments to giant mausoleums. There are scrolls, hearts, religious sculptures and even a large soccer ball.

Remember those two crazy guys named Ben and Jerry who hit the big time with an ice cream recipe? Here's where you'll find them, smack in the middle of Vermont rural country, at **Ben & Jerry's Ice Cream Factory Tours** (Route 100, Waterbury; 802-244-5641; admission). The factory—the state's number two tourist attraction—is a lesson in American free enterprise. You'll see the creamy stuff being made, get free samples and learn about two guys who haven't let success stand in the way of having fun. Ben and Jerry are revered around this state, and not surprisingly, since one out of ten Vermont families owns stock in their ice cream corporation.

Another fun stopover is the **Cold Hollow Cider Mill** (Route 100, Waterbury; 802-244-8771), an old barn that houses a small apple cider mill and a vast country gift shop. To view the apple presses at work, arrive from mid-August through mid-October.

Northward along Route 100 lies picturesque, alpine **Stowe**, a country town augmented by a bustling ski resort area and set against a deep green necklace of mountains.

The busy "downtown" area, situated at the crossroads of Route 100 and Mountain Road, is a pleasing meld of 19th-century buildings and contemporary marts and restaurants. All the ski action awaits up Mountain Road, a seven-mile jog lined with hotels and inns, shops, pubs and eateries of every culinary calling.

Vermont's highest peak, **Mount Mansfield**, looms 4393 feet above the town and presents an incredible backdrop, its craggy profile resembling the silhouette of a human face. During the summer, you can take an **auto toll road** or **gondola ride** (Mountain Road; 802-253-7311) to the summit, or navigate a plastic sled down a thrilling **alpine slide** (Mountain Road; 802-253-7311; admission).

Several decades after the film *The Sound of Music* was released, Stowe visitors still keep asking the same question: how do we get to the **Trapp Family Lodge** (Luce Hill Road off Mountain Road; 802-253-8511)? Certainly much of the town's appeal is bound to the history and beauty of this place, built as a singing camp during the 1940s by Maria Von Trapp and her family. The baroness chose the spot because she said it resembled her beloved Swiss Alps. The Tyrolean-style buildings of the lodge sit high on a mountain, surrounded by 2000 acres of forest, ponds and pasture. Alpine ridges extend as far as the eye can see. During the summer, popular Sunday concerts are held in an adjacent meadow. Though Maria died in 1987, her family still runs the lodge.

There's no sign for **Bingham Falls** (★) (off Mountain Road, about 100 yards north of The Lodge resort), but you won't want to miss this pristine look at nature's handiwork. A rocky footpath winds one-quarter mile through the evergreen forest, culminating at a scenic gorge where rushing, gurgling water swirls around large boulders. A great swimming hole, if you don't mind chilly waters.

Perhaps the area's ultimate nature encounter occurs at **Smugglers Notch** (Mountain Road), a slender, sensational pass through the mountains with dramatic sheets of silver rock on either side. Used as a secret passage between Canada and the U.S. during the War of 1812, the notch harbors dozens of intriguing rock formations (check out the singing bird and elephant head) and a rock crevasse where the summer temperature hovers around 49°. Keep an eye out for rock climbers who navigate the cliffs and repel down.

CHAMPLAIN VALLEY

A great big meeting of mountains, water and islands, the Champlain Valley is a prosperous, breathtaking region that ambles leisurely along Vermont's northwestern edge. Lake Champlain, the area's frame of reference, stretches 130 glistening miles and divides Vermont's flat, irregular lakefront border from New York's Adirondack Mountains. Back in 1609, French explorer Samuel de Champlain discovered the lake, named it for himself and laid the groundwork for its flourishing maritime history.

The state's most popular attraction lies in this region. Just south of Burlington, the **Shelburne Museum** (Route 7, Shelburne; 802-985-3346; admission, good for two days) is really a *collection* of buildings—37 to be exact. It takes two days to tackle this amazing 45-acre trek through Vermont and New England history. There's something for everyone here, from the 892-ton sidewheel steamship and toy shop to the round barn, 1890 slate jail and 1786 sawmill. Kids and adults will love the circus museum with its carousel ride and remarkable 500-foot miniature circus parade that took 30 years to complete. A 168-foot covered bridge, built in 1845 and moved to the museum from Cambridge, Vermont, is the state's only remaining two-lane bridge with a footpath. If snipes, loons and yellowlegs are your bag, stop in the wildfowl decoy museum, where an eye-popping 1000 specimens line the walls. A marvelous place to muse, the hat and fragrance house has hat boxes, costumes, perfumes and lace dating back to the early 1800s. You'll also find the state's largest collection of fine art, divided among several buildings.

Board a covered wagon for a tour of **Shelburne Farms** (Bay and Harbor roads, off Route 7, Shelburne; 802-985-8686; admission), a vast land empire that gives new meaning to the term "pastoral aristocracy." Sprawled across 1000 acres along Lake Champlain, the estate was designed back in the 1800s for Dr. William Seward Webb and wife Lila Vanderbilt, whose 100-room Queen Anne Revival farmhouse is still the largest in Vermont. The beautiful grounds—a series of free-flowing perennials, statues and fountains—were designed by Frederick Law Olmstead, architect of New York City's Central Park.

Just north of Shelburne, skirting the lake and reigning over the valley, is Vermont's Queen City, **Burlington**. With a population of over 40,000, it's the state's largest city but one that manages to maintain an intimate milieu. Burlington's remarkable alliance of mountain and water vistas were lauded by none other than Charles Dickens when he landed here back in the mid-1800s. Today, art centers, innovative theater, two universities and four colleges add to the cultural mix of this spirited, youthful metropolis.

In fact, nearly half of Burlington's population is made up of college students, many of whom attend the statuesque hilltop campus of the **University of Vermont** (off University Place and Colchester Avenue; 802-656-3480). The university's **Robert Hull Fleming Museum** (Colchester Avenue; 802-656-0750), a grand Colonial Revival building, houses an excellent collection of European and American paintings, decorative artworks and costumes, and ethnographic objects from around the world.

To help get you started in the area, stop by the **Lake Champlain Regional Chamber of Commerce** (209 Battery Street; 802-863-3489).

The city's best side exists, naturally, on glittering Lake Champlain. Stroll along **Lake and Battery streets** and peer across the water to New York's Adirondack Mountains, then take a two-hour roundtrip **ferry** (King

Street Dock, King and Battery streets; 802-864-9804) over to Port Kent, New York while absorbing all the scintillating views. Keep your eyes peeled for "Champ," Vermont's own Loch Ness Monster, whose bulky outline and distinct humps were first sighted by Samuel de Champlain and recorded in his ship's log.

Most of the day and nighttime activity occurs on **Church Street Marketplace** (Church Street between Main and Pearl streets), a thriving pedestrian mall jammed with outdoor cafés, trendy shops, strolling musicians and magicians and graced with 19th-century architecture. The effect is European, to say the least.

Northward, the **Champlain Islands** comprise Vermont's own "seacoast," a virgin outpost of apple orchards and dairy farms, rustic lakeside retreats and shores lined with fishers casting their nets. Though today there's a causeway linking these isles to Burlington, 19th-century residents had to make do with small skiffs and winter weather, when a frozen lake afforded the best access to the mainland. Route 2 traces a 30-mile path over water and land through this quiescent, largely undeveloped archipelago.

Revolutionary War veteran Jedediah Hyde, Jr., built a log cabin on the largest island, Grand Isle, back in 1783. Today the **Hyde Log Cabin** (Route 2) is thought to be the oldest log cabin in the country, a one-room alcove of rough-hewn beams held together by clay and straw. Amazingly, some of the original furniture and farm tools remain intact.

Up on Isle La Motte, 19th-century stone houses and a meandering rocky coastline form quite a beautiful tableau. The **St. Anne Shrine** (off Route 129) denotes the site of Fort St. Anne—Vermont's earliest settlement—built in 1666 by Captain Pierre La Motte.

NORTHEAST KINGDOM

This vast rural outback could well contain the largest stretch of splendid scenery in all of Vermont. A broad land inhabited by log cutters, cattle drivers and mountain folk, it forms a fine skein of glacier-dug lakes, mellow ponds and rivers, untamed evergreen forests and abrupt alpine ridges. Fall foliage first peeks out its gorgeous head up here, snow falls early and huge bodies of water turn to compact ice.

Beginning in St. Johnsbury and extending northward to the Canadian border, the Northeast Kingdom could well be termed Vermont's last stand. Its thin population and lack of major industry perpetuate considerable unemployment (by Vermont's standards), though firmly rooted residents vow their rugged country living surpasses that in southern ski meccas any day.

St. Johnsbury, the region's largest city, is a blue-collar town located where the Moose and Sleepers rivers flow into the Passumpsic River. The local **Visitors Information Booth** (corner of Eastern Avenue and Main Street; 802-748-3678) will provide walking-tour maps and regional information.

A perfect spot to learn about local history is the **Fairbanks Museum and Planetarium** (Main and Prospect streets; 802-748-2372; admission), where exhibits are imaginative and informative. The extensive wildlife collection includes stuffed condors and owls, pythons and chamois, and monstrous polar bears and Kodiaks. The building itself, with a barrel-vaulted ceiling and Romanesque designs of red sandstone, is marvelous.

Tucked in the back of a beautiful 1871 library, the **St. Johnsbury Athenaeum Art Gallery** (★) (30 Main Street; 802-748-8291) is a step back in time. The place bills itself as "oldest unaltered art gallery in the United States," and indeed, its collection has not changed since the mid-1920s. The 100-plus paintings feature numerous American landscape scenes by Albert Bierstadt and other famed Hudson River School artists. The library, a lovely Victorian-style masterpiece, has seen minimal architectural change over the century.

Travel north of the city on Route 5 to Route 5A and you'll arrive at what may be the state's single most stupendous vista. **Lake Willoughby**, an incredible expanse of water chiseled by glaciers, shimmers peacefully beneath the craggy peaks of Mounts Pisgah and Hor. Rimmed with rocky shoreline, fine carpets of grass and just a few cabins (due to the foresightedness of local leaders), the lake dispenses all the beauty the eye can handle.

Take Route 5A north to Route 105, then backtrack south on a splendid trek revealing yet another flawless meld of mountain and water. Gaze at the hilltop homes that scope out scenic views, at the farmers bailing hay and at old frame homes with laundry draped across their porches.

Soon you'll come to **Island Pond**, where bait shops, log cabins and a gas station form an earthy setting. The town green overlooks the water and was the site of the first international railroad in North America. There's also a Civil War cannon and a World War II monument.

Head toward Canada again, traveling north along Route 111, and you'll quickly feel the French vibes of our northern neighbor. Enormous **Lake Memphremagog** shares its waters (nearly equally) with Vermont and Quebec.

Newport is a special town, resting on a procession of hills that skirt the lake and crowned by the spires of beautiful **St. Mary's Star of the Sea Church** (5 Cleremont Terrace; 802-334-5066). Downtown offers a nice array of shops and restaurants and a helpful **Chamber of Commerce** (The Causeway; 802-334-7782) that will load you up with information.

There are three dirt roads that lead to the valley hamlet of **Brownington**, though the less adventurous will opt for the one that's paved. Here awaits an enchanting museum called **The Old Stone House** (Brownington Village; 802-754-2022; admission), built as a school dormitory in 1836 by the Reverend Alexander Twilight, the country's first black college graduate and legislator. Thirty rooms are filled with inspiring memorabilia that form endearing snapshots of early American life. Nearly everything here was donated by local families, including the 18th-century furniture, Revolutionary War uniforms (worn by Brownington men) and a wonderful collection of 1800s newspapers.

A block from the Old Stone House is **Prospect Hill Observatory** (★) (take dirt road beside Brownington Congregational Church), a wooden tower perched atop a grassy hill. Climb a short flight of stairs and be rewarded with a 180° panorama of rolling mountains and evergreen spires. A splendid way to remember Vermont, for sure.

Shopping

For the most part, Vermont shops are down-home and unpretentious, a smattering of country gift marts, antique nooks and epicure emporiums with locally made cheeses and maple syrup. To assist with shopping excursions, the **Vermont Travel Division** (134 State Street, Montpelier, VT 05602; 802-828-3236) has excellent brochures on where to find antiques, designer outlets, cheese and Christmas trees (in case you brought the car).

SOUTHERN VERMONT SHOPPING

If you're throwing a Vermont-style shindig, **Vermont Gatherings Country Gifts** (183 Main Street, Brattleboro; 802-257-0919) will provide everything from salsa and syrup to yankee tablecloths and candles.

Little people will adore **Jeannie Mac** (119 Main Street, Brattleboro; 802-257-2679) which sells 100% cotton clothes for tots made exclusively in Vermont.

Pick up your designer clothes with discount price tags at **Sam's Army and Navy Department Store** (74 Main Street, Brattleboro; 802-254-2933), a downtown institution housed in a ruddy brick building.

The fun and funky selections at **Bartleby's Books & Music** (North Main Street, Brattleboro; 802-464-5425) reflect the owner's love of fiction, Vermont, cooking and rock-and-roll.

Mountain Jeanery (Route 9, Wilmington; 802-464-5818), an 1800s blacksmith's shop, caters to die-hard '60s fans with an assortment of tie-dyed T-shirts, quilted vests and beaded necklaces.

You can dress like Marilyn Monroe (or Madonna—take your pick) after a visit to **The Next Store** (Route 9, Wilmington; 802-464-5818), a vintage clothing mart with elbow-length lace gloves, rhinestone sunglasses and Indonesian earrings.

Now and Then Books (439 Main Street, Bennington; 802-447-1470) has a top-notch collection of used and out-of-print books.

The outstanding **Bennington Museum Gift Shop** (West Main Street, Bennington; 802-447-1571) features Grandma Moses prints, Danforth pewter, salt-glazed pottery and books on collecting.

A tad futuristic, **Panache** (437 Main Street, Bennington; 802-442-8859) is equipped with mod clothing and accessories like neon sashes, Indonesian and Pacific jewelry and wild art stationery.

CENTRAL VERMONT SHOPPING

Chocolate peppermint, pineapple sage and lemon-scented marigold herbs create some fine smells (and tastes) at **Meadowsweet Herb Farm** (★) (729 Mount Holly Road, Shrewsbury; 802-492-3565), where several greenhouses and gardens make for merry shopping.

Christmas is a year-round affair at **The Christmas Tree Barn** (48-B Cold River Road, North Clarendon; 802-775-4585), a voluminous 1800s barn with every imaginable holiday item, plus potpourri, oils and antiques.

For unusual hand-crafted items, check out **Truly Unique** (Route 4 East, Rutland; 802-773-7742). Also available are various Vermont food products.

Woodstock's wealthy set fosters quite a posh shopping nest, centered downtown where strolling is very pleasurable. **The Vermont Workshop** (73 Central Street, Woodstock; 802-457-1400), in an 1826 brick house, has an impressive cache of quilts, clocks, old-fashioned sundials and farm bells.

Great kitchen treasures await at **F. H. Gillingham & Sons** (16 Elm Street, Woodstock; 802-457-2100), where you can pick up picnic baskets, costly wines and froufrou cooking devices.

Indulge your eyes and nose together at **Primrose Garden** (26 Central Street, Woodstock; 802-457-4049), a venerable assortment of fragrant potpourri and silk flowers, candelabras and blown glass.

Vermont-style paraphernalia, from maple products and cheese to wicker baskets and country cookbooks, are jammed under one big red roof at the vast **Timber Rail Village** (Route 4 West, Quechee; 802-295-1550).

NORTHERN MOUNTAIN REGION SHOPPING

Absolutely don't miss **The Warren Store** (Main Street, Warren; 802-496-3864), a former stagecoach inn that's like Grandpa's general store. The place starts with a jumble of fresh farm produce, jams, homemade honey and baskets, continues with a wonderful bakery, then finishes upstairs with clothing, jewelry and leather goods.

The **Blue Toad** (Route 100, Waitsfield; 802-496-2567) is a florist with a twist: It carries candles, soaps and doll boxes from Russia, Poland and other countries.

Even if you leave empty-handed, don't miss a trip to **The Store** (Route 100, Waitsfield; 802-496-4465), a bi-level, cook's fantasy world of gourmet gadgets galore.

More than 50,000 books crowd **The Yankee Paperback Exchange** (11 Langdon Street, Montpelier; 802-223-3239), where you'll find everything from old classics and out-of-print gems to volumes on religion, cooking and lifestyles.

Candles, incense, hammered jewelry and offbeat reading material are featured in an eclectic bazaar called **The Mystic Trader** (23 Langdon Street, Montpelier; 802-229-9220).

Everything Cows (Main Street, Stowe; 802-253-8779) possesses bovine treasures such as cow ties and T-shirts, moo lights and clocks and "udder" necessities.

Beautiful hammered jewelry, beaded necklaces and hand-fired porcelain await in an underground nook called **The Silver Den** (★) (Main Street, Stowe; 802-253-8787).

Women won't need to vacillate at **Decisions, Decisions** (Mountain Road, Stowe; 802-253-4183), where they can choose among beautiful satin and lace lingerie and sexy swimsuits.

CHAMPLAIN VALLEY SHOPPING

It nearly takes a miracle to find **Authentica African Imports** (★) (Greenbush Road about one mile north of Ferry Road, Charlotte; 802-425-3137), but once you're there, it's worth it. More than just a shop, this place offers a look at African styles and customs, with jewelry from Kenya and Senegal, rugs made of camel hair and goat skin, Mali blankets, Ethiopian rugs, Zulu clay pots, fertility statues from Malawi and much more.

Stroll Burlington's four-block **Church Street Marketplace** (Church Street between Main and Pearl streets) and you'll be rewarded with a bevy of fine, trendy shops. Forests find their ways into clocks, toys, furniture and mirror frames at **Once A Tree** (96 Church Street; 802-658-1441). Funkiness prevails at **Nuevo Wavo** (28 Church Street; 802-863-8655), a mod cache of Slinkies, psychedelic ties, weird cards and hip clothes.

NORTHEAST KINGDOM SHOPPING

Step down into **Annie's Closet** (77 Main Street, Newport; 802-334-8534), a wild and classy emporium with chiffon dresses, crazy sunglasses, funky earrings and hats and even a few housewares.

Going fishing, perhaps? **The Great Outdoors Trading Co.** (73 Main Street, Newport; 802-334-2831) has loads of fishing gear, plus mountain bikes and skis.

Ties 'n Tails (67 Main Street, Newport; 802-334-2953) has not only men's formal attire but jeans and sportswear for both sexes.

Nightlife

Though not known for its flashy nightclubs, Vermont does possess some fine pubs and piano bars, particularly in ski resort areas, along with a wealth of performing arts possibilities. The hottest night scene pulses in Burlington, where 16,000 college students feed a multitude of discos, progressive clubs and bebop joints.

SOUTHERN VERMONT NIGHTLIFE

A profusion of plants and wood make the **Outback Saloon** (142 Elliot Street, Brattleboro; 802-254-3278) look like an Aussie fern bar. The pop music is recorded, and the crowd is over 30.

A marvelous neighborhood bar with a vast draft beer selection including their own brewed on the premises, **Dewey's Ale House** (90 Elliot Street, Brattleboro; 802-254-2553) features recorded jazz and contemporary music.

Locals go underground at **Mole's Eye Café** (Main and High streets, Brattleboro; 802-257-0771), a noisy, crowded nook with booths and occasional blues and rock bands.

Deacon's Den (Route 100, West Dover; 802-464-9361), near Wilmington, is a wood and glass tavern where skiers stop off for a cold brew. There's live rock-and-roll and blues on weekends during winter. Cover.

Smack in the middle of ski action, **The Snow Barn** (South Access Road, Mount Snow; 802-464-3333) draws huge winter crowds with live rock-and-roll. Cover.

One of the most prestigious thespian groups in Vermont, **Oldcastle Theater Company** (Everett Mansion, Southern Vermont College off Monument Avenue, Bennington; 802-447-0564) stages drama, comedy and musicals in an elaborate, historic ballroom.

T. P.'s Pub (135 Depot Drive, Bennington; 802-442-3014), a worn sports bar with dusty wood floors and outdoor volleyball action, has live contemporary tunes on weekends. Cover.

CENTRAL VERMONT NIGHTLIFE

The Other Room (Mother Shapiro's Restaurant, Killington Access Road, Killington; 802-422-9933), a local watering hole with real character, features karaoke singing.

Skiers jam into the **Pickle Barrel** (Killington Access Road, Killington; 802-422-3035), where you'll find late-night rock-and-roll, a huge dancefloor and a barnlike environment.

The heart of trendiness, **Bentley's** (3 Elm Street, Woodstock; 802-457-3232) is (and has been, forever) the town noshing spot, decked in lace curtains, antique lamps, Oriental rugs and one long, polished bar. Tunes are snazzy, leaning toward jazz and classical.

NORTHERN MOUNTAIN REGION NIGHTLIFE

The Blue Tooth (Mountain Access Road, Warren; 802-583-2656) is an after-the-slopes place to hang loose and listen to live contemporary music.

Local theater in Vermont tends to be high quality, and such is the case at **Valley Players Community Theater** (Route 100, Waitsfield; 802-496-3485), which focuses on drama and comedy performed in a 200-seat, two-story, brick building.

The dancefloor is small and tables scarce, but the disco at **Chez Henri** (Sugarbush Village; 802-583-2600) may be the hottest spot around during ski season.

Politicians rub elbows at **The Thrush** (107 State Street, Montpelier; 802-223-2030), a tiny watering hole with framed old photos and occasional live folk music.

Tattered carpets lie before a worn pine bar at **Charlie O's** (Main Street, Montpelier; 802-223-6820), a pool hall with rock music and a sound system that cranks.

For a relaxing time, head to **The Pub at Stowe** (Mountain Road, Stowe; 802-253-8669).

The Matterhorn (Mountain Road, Stowe; 802-253-8198), a voluminous club perched near the base of Mount Mansfield, hosts big-name rock groups during summer and transforms into an après-ski dance club during winter. Cover.

Catch a lineup of comedy, jazz and soul music at the intimate **B. K. Clark's** (Mountain Road, Stowe; 802-253-9300). Cover on weekends.

CHAMPLAIN VALLEY NIGHTLIFE

The Flynn Theater for the Performing Arts (153 Main Street, Burlington; 802-863-5966), a 1400-seat art deco palace and old vaudeville house, offers a terrific lineup of international and Broadway theater and major symphony and dance.

A dark, smokey cubbyhole with a crowd predominantly in their 30s, **Nectar's** (188 Main Street, Burlington; 802-658-4771) serves up top-notch live blues and rock. Upstairs at **Border** (802-864-0107), there's progressive and African music and live funk. Cover.

The place to cut a rug is **Sh-na-na's** (101 North Main Street, Burlington; 802-865-2596), where a sprawling checkered dancefloor is accented by pinups of Elvis and other '50s paraphernalia. With recorded music from the '50s through the '80s, this joint is packed nightly. Cover Wednesday through Saturday.

Sweetwaters (corner of Church and Collins Street, Burlington; 802-864-9800) is undeniably the area's upscale meeting place, where patrons linger around a shiny bar and watch all the street activity through large glass windows.

Late-nighters flock to **The Vermont Pub and Brewery** (144 College Street, Burlington; 802-865-0500), a spacious but cozy brew house with brick walls, archways, mirrors and hanging plants.

The ever-popular **Sneakers Bar & Grill** (36 Main Street, Winooski; 802-655-9081) is a down-and-dirty pub with a lineup of jazz, funk, bluegrass and country-and-western. Cover.

NORTHEAST KINGDOM NIGHTLIFE

Other than a few motel lounges and pool halls, this remote mountain area is short on nightlife.

Have a drink by the lake at **The Eastside** (Lake Street, Newport; 802-334-2340), or catch the comedy acts hosted several times a week.

The Nickelodeon Café (41 Main Street, Newport; 802-334-8055), a smart pub with Irish decor, is a nice spot for a cold brew.

Canada and the United States share the **Haskell Opera House** (Casswell Avenue, Derby Line; 819-876-2471—in Canada), a marvelous, ornate historic building that hosts major comedy, musicals and drama as well as symphony, jazz and ballet. A chalk line divides the building nationally, with the wooden seats in Vermont and stage in Quebec.

CHAPTER EIGHT

New Hampshire

New Hampshire. It's a heart-stopping collage of sculpted mountains, stony profiles, seamless country roads, expansive lakes and broad beaches. A place you yearn to clutch tightly, to safeguard and to proclaim.

That slender fragment of Yankee domain framed by Vermont, Maine and Massachusetts, New Hampshire is all this and much, much more. It is a region that seems not quite real when you first reach the state, yet you're certain you've been there before. New Hampshire's daunting landscape flirts with the imagination; its spirit roams wild around untamed timberland, wilderness expanses and riots of flowers.

Born of molten granite and giant glaciers, the state's geologic surface was but a labyrinth of smoke, dust and ice sheets some 300 million years ago. Hot rock hissed beneath the earth, forced its way up and drove the ground to buckle and split. Advancing ice sheets smoothed the rock, forming it into hills and mountains, then swiftly melted to create rivers and lakes.

Along the way, these icy torrents deposited thousands of granite chunks. All that stone gives today's New Hampshire a rugged veneer, as well as its moniker of "The Granite State." Boulders lie strewn across farmlands, jut out into the sea and loom atop mountains, their mystic profiles often evocative of some familiar face or object.

Human rumblings in this area go back at least 8000 years, when the Abenaki and Pennacook Indians roamed the lands. Members of Algonquin tribes, they fished the swift rivers, hunted forests for game and fruit and culled maple sugar from the trees. Their first European visitor, British captain Martin Pring, sailed up the Piscataqua River in 1603, though it was not until 1623 that the first settlement was founded at Odiorne Point in present-day Rye.

Several towns soon sprang up along the coast and river. Strawbery Banke, now Portsmouth, became the capital and commercial center of New Hampshire life as fishers, coopers and shipbuilders plied their trades there.

In 1643, a greedy Massachusetts annexed the settlements into its Bay Colony, holding them for 36 years until England declared New Hampshire a royal province.

Thick forests, bitter winters and unforgiving earth made life difficult for those who tried to tame New Hampshire's interior. Even worse, previously friendly Indians came to resent white intrusion and exploitation, and a series of violent skirmishes ensued. In one infamous incident, Indians captured a settler named Hannah Dustin, a 39-year-old mother of 12, and took her to River Islet, near present-day Concord. During the night, Dustin killed and scalped her ten sleeping captors, escaping with her life.

During the mid-1700s, settlers struggled to cultivate the rocky soil that became bloodied by French and Indian conflicts. The French and Indian War finally settled the matter in 1763, though the subsequent American Revolution only brought more strife to a battered land.

New Hampshire entered the Revolution with a vengeance. In December 1774, when patriots received word from Paul Revere that British soldiers would soon be at Portsmouth, they stormed Fort William and Mary. Six months later, England's governor was driven from the colony. In January 1776, New Hampshire became the first independent American state.

After the war, people gave up on agriculture and turned to textile manufacturing. But an even more lucrative source of income was about to arrive: the stream of pleasure seekers who, lured by bewitching landscapes and a bevy of natural resources, started coming to New Hampshire in droves. Exclaimed one well-traveled visitor: "There is no doubt but the scenery of New Hampshire is more varied and beautiful than can be found in any other state in the Union."

Thousands of new arrivals, known as "summer people," converged on the land. Those with money built grand estates or lavish hotels, while the majority put up frame houses and white picket fences and settled on their front porches for the summer. All of a sudden, New Hampshire's first tourist industry was raging.

By the late 1800s, a different kind of industry had emerged. Virtually overnight, logging businesses penetrated the White Mountains and cleared thousands of acres of trees to feed a voracious lumber demand. Within 20 years, barren patches scarred the mountainsides and wildlife was dwindling.

It might have been the undoing of New Hampshire's precious mountains had not public outcry prompted Congress to halt the destruction. The Weeks Act of 1911 called for federal purchase of most of the state's forest lands, which today make up the 768,000-acre White Mountain National Forest.

Now forests cloak 84 percent of the state, while some 1300 lakes form pockets of beauty and intrigue. Shaped like a skinny triangle that points toward Canada, New Hampshire spans only 168 miles from top to bottom and 90 miles at its broadest point. Its 9304 square miles cover six geographic

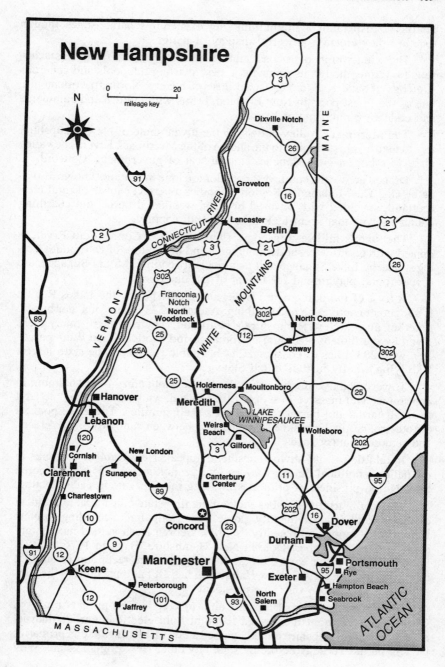

New Hampshire

MAINE

VERMONT

MASSACHUSETTS

ATLANTIC OCEAN

CONNECTICUT RIVER

WHITE MOUNTAINS

LAKE WINNIPESAUKEE

0   20
mileage key

N

Dixville Notch

Groveton

Lancaster

Berlin

Franconia Notch

North Woodstock

North Conway

Conway

Holderness

Moultonboro

Meredith

Weirs Beach

Wolfeboro

Gilford

Hanover

Lebanon

Cornish

New London

Claremont

Sunapee

Charlestown

Canterbury Center

Concord

Keene

Manchester

Dover

Durham

Portsmouth

Rye

Exeter

Peterborough

Jaffrey

North Salem

Hampton Beach

Seabrook

regions so disparate you might think they existed in separate states, though together they create a powerful display of nature.

The wind-whipped seacoast ambles a mere 18 miles from Massachusetts to Maine, though its dramatic jetties, swirling tidepools and generous stretches of sand pack a state-sized dose of beauty. Northern Portsmouth, one of the finest ports in New England, brims with culture and commerce and endearing remnants of history.

The Merrimack Valley crawls up the lower spine of New Hampshire, its old textile mills clinging to the shores of the Merrimack River. The valley claims its largest city, Manchester, and seat of government, Concord.

Draped across the southwest corridor are lone mountains known as monadnocks. The Monadnock Region embodies a perfect canvas of rural New England, speckled with covered bridges, weathered barns and charming country towns that seem locked in the 18th century.

The state's midwestern edge, flanked by the Connecticut River, is graced with cornfields, subtle mountains and the culture of Dartmouth College. Nearby Lake Sunapee and its attendant sentinel, Mount Sunapee, are a year-round playground for lovers of the outdoors.

A tryst of twinkling azure water and gentle peaks, the Lakes Region is altogether captivating and soothing. A total of 273 bodies of water bundle together across New Hampshire's heartland. Their names—many were given by the Indians—conjure up romance and exotica. Lake Winnipesaukee, with 283 miles of coast and 274 habitable islands, is the sixth largest lake lying wholly in the United States.

Towering above the lakes are the White Mountains, overwhelming in appearance and massive in scope. Life slows down up here as people tend to small farms and businesses and raise their families. There are pockets of tourism, particularly ski resorts, nestled between canopies of evergreens and remote country roads.

In addition to its obvious aesthetic appeal, New Hampshire basks in the nation's political limelight every four years. Since 1915, it has secured the edge on presidential primaries, holding the first one in each election.

This claim to firstdom has yielded the tiny state considerable political clout, as candidates frequently gauge their campaigns according to New Hampshire's mood. As recently as 1988, George Bush gained momentum after he trounced Robert Dole in New Hampshire. Back in 1976, a little-known Jimmy Carter earned credibility after a warm reception in the first primary. And since 1952, New Hampshire has all but once chosen the candidate who would go on to be president.

It's certain that New Hampshire aims to keep its first-primary position. Once, when Vermont mentioned it might hold elections earlier than its neighbor, New Hampshire quickly passed a law mandating that its primaries be held on the Tuesday before those of any other New England state. Wily

Massachusetts once made the mistake of scheduling its primary on the same day as New Hampshire's. Indignant, New Hampshire pushed its elections up one week.

Indeed, politics is serious business in New Hampshire. The state legislature has 424 members—making it the third largest governing body in the English-speaking world (behind Great Britain's Parliament and the U.S. Congress). Though the state tends to vote Republican, the pendulum often swings the other way.

"Live Free or Die" is New Hampshire's motto, as every native reminds you. It's emblazoned on state license plates, on not a few homes and across some businesses. But despite this constant assertion of autonomy, the state still sees fit to restrict itself in curious ways.

Nightclubs and bars standing alone are banned; they must be connected to a restaurant, sports club, bowling alley or similar business. You can purchase hard liquor only from state-run stores, many of which dot major highways and interstates. These cobwebbed laws have been in place since Prohibition and don't seem likely to change in the near future.

For the most part, freedom to New Hampshire inhabitants means no sales tax and no personal income tax. Not surprisingly, these particular freedoms have lured throngs of people who now live in New Hampshire but work in nearby states. Miffed at the situation, Maine responded by taxing its workers who live in New Hampshire—as well as their spouses who live *and* work in New Hampshire. Needless to say, the two states continue a classic Yankee feud.

The state's unswerving individualism, coupled with its bucolic settings, have enticed some of the country's most creative minds. Robert Frost, Nathaniel Hawthorne, Ralph Waldo Emerson, Thornton Wilder, sculptor Augustus Saint-Gaudens and many other talents employed New Hampshire's rural reaches as their studios.

Today's New Hampshire is home to a new band of artists, as well as the factory workers and bankers, innkeepers and small business people who run the general stores. Its low unemployment rate, thriving tourism and aesthetic surroundings make the state a desirable place to live for its 1.11 million residents. In fact, it's the fastest-growing state in New England and the seventh fastest-growing in the country.

Despite some apparent modernization, New Hampshire still clings to its founding principles. It is a world focused on clapboard houses and slender steeples, Yankee ingenuity and memories of Pilgrims, town halls and the freedom to worship and vote.

Over the years, New Hampshire changes—yet somehow stays quite the same. Lifestyles and customs are passed on through generations firmly rooted in its granite soil. With a seashore, mountains and lakes that remain poignant and timeless, this state is a glorious place under the sun.

Easy Living

Transportation

ARRIVAL

The fastest means of road travel are New Hampshire's interstate highways. **Route 93** scoots up the north-south center of the state, while **Route 95** cuts in from Massachusetts, follows the seacoast, then heads out into southern Maine. On the west corridor, **Route 91** actually lies in Vermont but is used by many New Hampshire drivers as a major north–south artery.

There's no quick way to reach the state's northern wilderness, but **Route 16** and **Route 3** will take you there while skirting some spectacular scenery.

BY AIR

New Hampshire's air traffic flows through **Manchester Airport,** a small but quite convenient facility in Manchester. Several major carriers provide service, including Continental Airlines, Delta Airlines, United Airlines and USAir.

Boston's **Logan Airport,** located about 30 miles from New Hampshire's seacoast, is also a major air gateway for the state (see Chapter Four). **Hudson Limousine Service** (603-883-4807) transports passengers from Logan to most points in southern New Hampshire, including Nashua, Merrimack and Manchester.

BY BUS

Concord Trailways (603-228-3300) operates a broad network across New Hampshire. Buses start from Boston's Logan Airport and stop in Manchester, Concord and smaller towns as far north as Dixville Notch.

BY TRAIN

Train travel is practically nonexistent here, though **Amtrak** (800-872-7245) does provide service to Vermont's White River Junction and Bellows Falls, along New Hampshire's western border. The trains make direct routes from Washington, D.C., New York and Montreal.

CAR RENTALS

Arriving at Manchester Airport, you'll find the following car rental companies: **National Car Rental** (603-627-2299), **Hertz Rent A Car** (603-669-6320), **Budget Rent A Car** (603-668-3166) and **Avis Rent A Car** (603-624-4000). **Thrifty Car Rental** (603-627-8800) is located near the terminal and offers free airport transfers.

Hotels

New Hampshire's varied terrain has produced a wealth of different lodging prospects, from oceanside villas and mountain chalets to rustic lakefront cabins and 18th-century farmhouses. True to Yankee traditions, they all proffer gracious hospitality and a chance to experience local customs and New England's fascinating past.

Low and peak seasons vary depending on location. In the seacoast and lake regions, rates soar during summer, then plunge the rest of the year. Across the White Mountains, prices remain high during summer, as well as fall foliage and ski seasons. Rates are pretty consistent year-round in the rest of the state, though fall foliage time—generally from mid-September through mid-October—sees a definite increase.

SEACOAST HOTELS

A noisy sub shop is tucked in the bottom of the **Sunrise Guest House** (65 Ocean Boulevard, Hampton Beach; 603-929-0636), but with budget-priced oceanside rooms, who cares? This adorable, two-story shingled beach house sports two pilasters and has three simple but modern apartments, all with small refrigerators and private baths. Ask for the one in the back, which has a skylight and private bath.

Toward the north (and somewhat quieter) end of Hampton Beach, the **Hampton House** (333 Ocean Boulevard; 603-926-1033) offers very comfortable accommodations amid contemporary surroundings. A breezy lobby edges the busy beachfront street and comforts with soothing ocean views from the floor-to-ceiling glass windows. Three floors of spacious rooms feature wall-to-wall carpets, modern wood furnishings and private balconies that yield some fine ocean views and people-watching opportunities. Deluxe.

From the outside, you'd swear it's little more than a generic beach motel. But wander into the **Oceanside Hotel** (365 Ocean Boulevard, Hampton Beach; 603-926-3542) and you'll enter a world of superb 19th-century Victorian designs. Handsome pine floors show off period furniture and braided rugs. Each of ten rooms (including two that face the ocean) is named after Hampton Beach settlers, with decor matching the pioneer period. Moderate to deluxe.

Hampton Motor Inn (815 Lafayette Road, Hampton; 603-926-6771) possesses all the charm and detail of a fancy bed and breakfast. The guest rooms offer such personal touches as mirrored armoires, quilted headboards and dust ruffles, vaulted pine ceilings and scents of jasmine. Among the other niceties of this family-fun inn are an indoor pool and jacuzzi, an exercise room and, of course, a congenial staff. Moderate.

For the charm of a country inn with the luxuries of a large hotel, consider the **Sise Inn** (40 Court Street, Portsmouth; 603-433-1200). Set in an 1881 Queen Anne home within walking distance of most downtown Portsmouth sights, the hostelry features a lobby that soars three stories and is highlighted by pretty teak banisters and Oriental rugs. Oversized guest rooms are suited with bay windows, four-poster beds, showers *and* tubs (some with whirlpools) and nice extras like VCRs. Deluxe to ultra-deluxe.

Resting on a shady knoll adjacent to a busy thoroughfare, the **Martin Hill Inn** (404 Islington Street, Portsmouth; 603-436-2287) will send you back in time. This gracious pair of 19th-century buildings, linked by a flower-lined brick path, lies awash in lovely antiques accented by bouquets of day lilies. Seven bedrooms are decorated in Williamsburg wallpaper, brass and spindle beds and clawfoot tubs. Deluxe.

The **Bow Street Inn** (121 Bow Street, Portsmouth; 603-431-7760) claims an unusual resting place: a second-floor roost above a performing arts center. Not to worry—all ten rooms are nicely soundproofed and come with accoutrements like brass beds, plush carpets and ruffled curtains. A brewery during the 19th century, the ruddy brick building peers across the Piscataqua River (as do half the rooms) and rests only a few blocks from central downtown. Moderate to deluxe.

Around 1800, Christian ship captains—anxious to separate themselves from military captains—settled in modest homes west of downtown Portsmouth. Now the **Inn at Christian Shore** (335 Maplewood Avenue; 603-431-6770) harkens back to those early days with simple, Federal-style design and sunny ambience. Six bedrooms are cheerfully outfitted with floral wallpaper and antique furniture. The dining room, with its low-slung beam ceilings and large fireplace, is quite cozy. Moderate.

Northwest of Portsmouth, the historic mill town of Dover maintains a handful of motels and one very special bed and breakfast called the **Silver Street Inn** (103 Silver Street; 603-743-3000). Built in the 1880s by well-to-do mill owners, the ornate mansion displays such Victorian indulgences as high carved ceilings, marble and slate floors, Spanish mahogany doors and Italian-tile hearths. There's a formal library and dining room and ten bedrooms ranging from simple to lavish. Moderate to deluxe.

MERRIMACK VALLEY HOTELS

Small chain motels are the most frequent accommodations along New Hampshire's industrial combe, though you will find a few very special inns and bed and breakfasts.

One of the nicest chain motels, **Appleton Inn** (4 Amherst Road, Merrimack; 603-424-7500) mingles the new and old with its Federal-style red brick design and its many modern amenities. There's a swimming pool out back and a lobby fashioned with reproductions of Victorian antiques and framed prints of hunting scenes. You'll find more antiques in the 114 guest rooms, along with designer wallpapers and a crisp, manicured feeling. A good value at budget-to-moderate rates.

Think about it this way: with rooms offering Italian marble hot tubs, big-screen televisions and gorgeous four-poster beds, how could you *not* adore **The Bedford Village Inn** (2 Old Bedford Road, Bedford; 603-472-2001)? This vanilla-coated estate, a medley of Colonial-style buildings, barns and grain silos, is a lesson in ultra-indulgence, a place where staying in your room may well be preferred to venturing out. Wet bars, pine chests and huge bay windows are also standard room accessories, or opt for the two-bedroom apartment with a fireplace and six-foot whirlpool. Rates, needless to say, are deluxe to ultra-deluxe.

Accommodation choices in Manchester are generally limited to motel and hotel chains. Nicely situated downtown, the **Center of New Hampshire Holiday Inn** (700 Elm Street; 603-625-1000) caters mostly to business travelers and thus features plenty of extras like an indoor pool, sauna, two restaurants and adjacent mini-mall. Expect upscale motel decor in 250 rooms, including plush carpets and marble countertops. Deluxe to ultra-deluxe.

For exploring the state capital, the **Ramada Inn** (172 North Main Street, Concord; 603-224-9534) provides prime proximity to downtown sights. The layout is classic motel, with a four-story, nondescript exterior and 123 comfortable rooms decorated with wall-to-wall carpets, formica dressers and headboards and standard conveniences. There's also an indoor heated pool and sauna. Deluxe.

Standing amid acres and acres of rambling meadows and gardens and surrounded by mountain peaks, **Wyman Farm** (★) (Wyman Road, Loudon; 603-783-4467) is a place worth finding. Built back in 1783, the lovely farmhouse awaiting down a labyrinth of obscure country roads is the family homestead of one of the innkeepers. There are three bedrooms (one's available only spring through fall) warmly fashioned with old pine floors, sitting rooms or parlors, and Oriental or hook rugs. For a real treat, request the room with the copper tub. Budget to moderate. (To get there, take Route 106 to the Clough Pond Road exit, then turn left on Flagg Road. Go eight-tenths of a mile on Flagg Road to Wyman Road, a dirt road.)

Staying at the **Hitching Post** (Routes 4 and 202, Chichester; 603-798-4951) is like visiting Grandma's house. A gregarious Danish grandma runs the bed and breakfast, a 1787 farmhouse that's rustic yet inviting. Walk through the carriage house, strung with dozens of dusty farm tools, then climb the creaking stairs to four small bedrooms (with shared baths) outfitted in country lace curtains, four-poster beds and early-1900s wallpaper. Wake up in the mornings to homemade Danish pastries, sausages and potato pancakes. Moderate.

MONADNOCK REGION HOTELS

Nestled in a marvelous Currier and Ives setting, **The Birchwood Inn** (Route 45, Temple; 603-878-3285) oozes history and enchantment. Fashioned of deep red brick, the 1775 Federal-style building brandishes twin chimneys and lazes across from a white steepled church and a grassy hill topped with war memorials. Murals of itinerant artist Rufus Porter spread across dining room walls, while seven bedrooms exhibit different themes and eclectic decor. An "editorial room" features newsprint wallpaper, while a "music room" is arranged with musical instruments. Lose yourself in the 18th century at this place. Moderate.

The ultimate New Hampshire hideaway may well be **Woodbound Inn** (★) (east of Route 202 on Woodbound Road, Jaffrey; 603-532-8341), a captivating retreat stashed deep in a mountain forest. Here you have the trying task of choosing between several accommodations: Early American-style bedrooms housed in a 19th-century farmhouse; contemporary rooms with brass beds in the annex; or cozy lakeside cabins with fireplaces. It's easy to kick back in any of the three, or explore the inn's 176 acres thick with pine and fir trees. There's also a nine-hole golf course, numerous cross-country ski trails, clay tennis court and superb restaurant. Deluxe to ultra-deluxe.

For up-to-date motel accommodations, consider **Jack Daniel's Motor Inn** (Route 202, Peterborough; 603-924-7548). A single, two-story building covered with wood shingles, the inn maintains 17 quite modern guest rooms with plush carpets, high-back chairs, large showers and upstairs balconies. Some rooms overlook the pretty Contoocook River. Deluxe.

The **John Hancock Inn** (Routes 123 and 137, Hancock; 603-525-3318) radiates an ancient aura, and rightly so—it's the oldest continuously operating inn in New Hampshire. Braided rugs rest atop the 1789 floor, bouquets of fragrant flowers bask on old tabletops and walls sport early-17th-century Rufus Porter murals and Moses Eaton stencils. Upstairs in ten bedrooms, sunlight streams in through rows of windows framed with ruffled curtains, and antique chests and beds provide a cozy demeanor. Don't miss the library and antique buggy seats in the lounge. Moderate.

Beautifully restored and carefully embellished with handsome furnishings, **Thatcher Hill Inn** (★) (Thatcher Hill Road, west of Route 124, Marlborough; 603-876-3361) is pleasing to the eye and mind. Shiny plank floors adorn the 1790s farmhouse, where spacious bedrooms are stocked with comfy beds, plump quilts and old-fashioned tubs. Outside, stately Mount Monadnock hovers in the distance and a cupola preens atop an enormous barn. Best of all, the innkeepers are warm and personable, pampering guests and sharing local "hidden" sights. Moderate.

LAKE SUNAPEE–DARTMOUTH AREA HOTELS

No signs even hint of **Goddard Mansion** (★) (25 Hillstead Road and Route 12, Claremont; 603-543-0603). Pity those who bypass this camouflaged treasure, a European-style estate that exudes elegance and refinement. The expansive, ornate living rooms and parlors feature high-beamed ceilings, carved mantles and a baby grand piano. A breezy porch overlooks the manicured lawn and croquet court, and bedrooms are designed to gratify. Several rooms command views of mountains all the way to Vermont. Moderate to deluxe.

Lingering in the shadows of Mount Sunapee, **The Backside Inn** (Brook Road off Route 103, Sunapee; 603-863-5161) tenders home-style accommodations in an 1835 farmhouse-cum-inn. Four acres of pines envelop the inn, which has ten comfortable bedrooms featuring wall-to-wall carpets or stenciled wood floors, double and bunk beds, and pretty antiques. You can walk to a 49-acre pond or take the five-minute drive to sprawling Lake Sunapee. Moderate.

Barely 12 miles from Lake Sunapee, **New London Inn** (Main Street, New London; 603-526-2791) is one place that has grown beautiful with time. Built back in 1792, the three-story clapboard inn overlooking the town green and bandstand is surely the prototype of gracious New England sojourns. Spacious porches wrap around the lower floors, wood hallways lead to carpeted rooms, and beams crisscross ceilings. Thirty bedrooms have personality and flair, adorned in brass, wicker or poster beds and lovely antique dressers and chairs. Moderate to deluxe.

Its milieu is rural and unpretentious, but the history and intrigue of **The Chase House** (★) (Route 12A, four miles north of Route 131, Cornish; 603-675-5391) is enough to liven your spirit. Within the walls of this modest 1775 colonial dwelling, Salmon P. Chase (as in Chase Manhattan Bank) was born and spent his early childhood. Chase was also a founder of the Republican Party and treasury secretary to Abraham Lincoln, among other things. Today, stacked firewood rests on the porch, and flower beds brighten the yard. The six bedrooms—all with private baths—are heavy on country decor, including canopy beds and original hardwood floors. Moderate to deluxe in price.

Snuggled nicely against the upper Connecticut River, **The Sunset** (Route 10, West Lebanon; 603-298-8721) tenders simple accommodations at moderate prices. The configuration is standard motel L-shape, with 18 modest but clean rooms. Expect industrial-grade carpets, formica furniture; some rooms have splendid views across the river and mountains.

The place to stay in Hanover is **The Hanover Inn** (Main and Wheelock streets; 603-643-4300). For one, it's right across from (and owned by) Dartmouth College, thereby drawing all sorts of Ivy Leaguers. For another, it's one of those beautiful old buildings that absolutely commands respect. Graced in red brick and crowned by a sloping shingled roof, this granddaddy has been accommodating the rich and prestigious since the late 1700s. Four floors of rooms reflect early colonial designs but throw in amenities like cable television and air-conditioning. Ultra-deluxe.

A former stagecoach stop, **The Lyme Inn** (Route 10, Lyme; 603-795-4404) lounges under the shadows of the White Mountains and harkens back to the early 1800s with an unhurried pace and old-fashioned design. Indeed, the whole place is brimming with gorgeous antiques, from old clocks and handmade quilts to maple hutches and a pretty sleigh. There are no less than ten fireplaces, and 12 rooms and suites accented with stenciled wallpaper, wingback chairs and hooked rugs. Moderate to deluxe rates include breakfast at the inn's excellent restaurant.

LAKES REGION HOTELS

Along placid Newfound Lake rests a grand old summer house and former stagecoach station called the **Pasquaney Inn** (★) (Star Route 1, Bridgewater; 603-744-9111). Here you'll discover great vistas, fabulous sunsets, friendly innkeepers and a completely unhurried pace. The 26 rooms are casually decorated and offer painted wood floors or carpets, some canopy beds and wicker chairs. During summer, there's a sandy lakefront beach across the street; during winter, the lake freezes and makes for splendid ice fishing, skating and skiing. Moderate to deluxe.

The Inn on Golden Pond (Route 3, Holderness; 603-968-7269) took its moniker from the movie (not vice-versa), and its serene ambience does resemble the restful house depicted in the film. Stationed in a 50-acre wooded glen near Squam Lake—not on it—the graceful white clapboard house offers nine comfortable units enhanced by country decor with contemporary touches. Early American dressers and braided rugs contrast nicely with lace curtains and sleek bathrooms. Out back, a breezy lawn provides solace. Deluxe to ultra-deluxe.

Shielded from a busy road by a string of giant rocks, the **Boulders Motel** (Route 3, Holderness; 603-968-3600) fits the standard motor court genre with one exception: every room claims a fabulous view of Squam Lake. There's also a small but pristine sandy beach out back, a great place to gape at passing boats. Accommodations range from 12 clean but sparse rooms to six efficiencies and three rustic cottages. Moderate to deluxe.

Lake views, dreamy colonial architecture, shops and restaurants right outside your door. Sound enticing? Then **The Inn at Mill Falls** (Route 3 in the Mills Falls Marketplace, Meredith; 603-279-7006) is where you want to be. Residing in a restored turn-of-the-century mill, the spiffy resting place has 54 rooms done in rose chintz dust ruffles and draperies and designer shower curtains. A busy road is all that separates guests from Lake Winnipesaukee. Deluxe to ultra-deluxe.

A short distance from the lake you'll happily discover **The Red Hill Inn** (★) (Route 25B and College Road, Center Harbor; 603-279-7001), a sublime country estate ringed with mountain vistas and a lovely herb path. Fashioned in 1904 as a summer retreat, the inn now boasts 21 rooms in the main house, two old farmhouses and an unusual stone cottage. Rich colors and period furniture spell traditional elegance. Moderate to ultra-deluxe.

Greystone Motel (★) (132 Scenic Drive, off Route 11 in Gilford; 603-293-7377) has two very important virtues: It's hidden down a scenic, little-traveled side road, and it's right on gorgeous Lake Winnipesaukee. There are two cottage-type buildings with basic but clean accommodations and a glass solarium, though the name of the game here is boating, fishing and outstanding panoramas. Moderate.

Wolfeboro's premier lodging establishment is undoubtedly **The Wolfeboro Inn** (44 North Main Street; 603-569-3016), a rambling, Cape Cod-like manor resting beside Lake Winnipesaukee. The lobby is a fusion of wood beams, stone floors and velvet high-back chairs, while 43 rooms feature modern touches of sleek oak and pine furniture and pedestal sinks. Deluxe to ultra-deluxe.

Wolfeboro is lucky enough to border three lakes, and you can catch views of two at **The Lake Motel** (Route 28; 603-569-1100). Nestled on the picturesque corner of Lake Wentworth and Crystal Lake, the motor court takes advantage of its surroundings with an enormous lawn stretching to the shorelines. Most rooms offer water views and are aesthetically furnished with textured wall coverings and wall-to-wall carpets. Moderate.

WHITE MOUNTAINS REGION HOTELS

A rustic old-time air fills the **Woodstock Inn** (Route 3, North Woodstock; 603-745-3951), a homey kind of resting place that beckons to the late 1800s. Rosy wallpaper, pine floors and lacy Victorian draperies frame the 17 rooms, many of which face the Pemigewasset River. Moderate.

Wild winds whip through a slender valley, become trapped in a narrow opening and whirl backward to form what's known as a bungay jar. This explains the moniker of **The Bungay Jar** (★) (Route 116, just south of Sugar Hill Road, Franconia; 603-823-7775), a beautifully renovated 18th-century barn positioned at the mouth of just such a "tunnel valley." Set in a wooded mountain nest, this cozy bed and breakfast features six rooms decorated with antiques. Guests enjoy the use of a small library, sauna and living room, formerly the barn's hayloft. Moderate to deluxe.

Perhaps it's the dozens of nostalgic curios, or the cozy feel of the six bedrooms, or even the hardwood floors that glide so smoothly under bare feet. Regardless of the reason, **The Hilltop Inn** (★) (Route 117, Sugar Hill; 603-823-5695) is sure to make you feel at home. Situated along a secluded byroad, the inn is run by an amiable couple who love to work around the house. Moderate to deluxe.

By far one of New England's grandest summer retreats, **The Mount Washington Hotel and Resort** (Route 302, Bretton Woods; 603-278-1000) has been displaying its magical opulence ever since 1902. Set at the foot of the Presidential Range, the imposing, red-roofed mansion rests on 2600 acres and is striking from miles away. Horse-drawn carriages meander through rolling manicured hills sprinkled with flower and rock gardens. Inside, an expansive lobby is heavy with archways, Doric columns and ornate chandeliers, and a rear porch seems to stretch for miles. The staff numbers 350, the rooms 180. Expect room decor ranging from simple to extravagant. Ultra-deluxe.

Accommodations may be minimal, but you'd be hard pressed to find a more scenic spot than the **Crawford Notch Youth Hostel** (Route 302, Carroll; 603-466-2727). Mountains and wide-open valleys surround this bucolic niche, a favorite of hikers and cross-country skiers. Budget-priced lodging takes the form of two dorms lined with bunk beds and two rustic cabins, also with communal sleeping. Kitchen facilities provided.

Logs stay stacked on the stone porch of **The 1785 Inn** (Route 16, North Conway; 603-356-9025), a gracious old house that seems to say "Do drop in." One of the oldest homesteads in Mount Washington Valley, the inn was built as a "publik house" by Revolutionary War veteran Elijah Dinsmore. These days, 17 guest rooms offer simple accommodations featuring country wallpaper, antique bed frames and ample mountain scenery. Deluxe.

The quintessence of New England lodging exists at the **Christmas Farm Inn** (Route 16B, Jackson Village; 603-383-4313), a tranquil place tucked high in the mountains. Resembling a quaint colonial village, the inn includes a main house built in 1786, plus a cozy log cabin, 1777 saltbox and pretty honeymoon cottage. Rooms are carefully accented with canopy beds, vaulted ceilings, whirlpool tubs and beautiful quilts. Congenial innkeepers make Christmastime here special, organizing caroling, eggnog breaks and visits from Santa. Ultra-deluxe.

There's not much besides a restaurant and two general stores in the nowheresville called Jefferson, but you'll also find a cozy little gem called **The Davenport Inn** (★) (Davenport Road, just off Route 2; 603-586-4320). Perched along a gravel road, the 1809 house lazes among apple trees and offers total solitude. The innkeeper, a cordial woman who left Boston's nine-to-five grind, has adroitly enhanced the rooms with plush carpets and quilts, brass mirrors, polished teakwood furnishings and old-fashioned tubs. Breakfast is extra special. Moderate.

The Balsams (Route 26, Dixville Notch; 603-255-3400) is one of those places that makes you wonder how guests can ever bring themselves to leave. This self-contained mini-city sprawls across 15,000 acres of exquisite landscape. This is escapism at its height, a reveling in alpine ridges and thick forests and spectacular lakes and rivers. Stashed way up in New Hampshire's northern boondocks, the rambling, castlelike resort boasts 232 rooms decorated in French provincial style. There's a movie theater, 27 holes of golf, Olympic swimming pool, croquet and tennis courts, and an outstanding restaurant. The ultra-deluxe price tag includes three meals and the use of all facilities.

Restaurants

From oceanside seafood nooks and urbane bistros to cozy mountainside pubs, New Hampshire brims with culinary finds. Though international cuisine can be found throughout the state, it's the locally grown treasures that steal the show: juicy red raspberries, apples and cranberries, wild turkey and duckling, fresh brook trout and salmon, and, of course, that delectable Maine lobster. Best of all, people here take the delightfully slow approach to dining—once you sit down, the table is all yours for the evening.

SEACOAST RESTAURANTS

Back in 1764, a 26-year-old grenadier named Thomas Fletcher reportedly died of fever after drinking a hot beer. Forlorn and eager for companionship, his widow turned their tiny frame home into a tavern. Today, **Widow Fletcher's Tavern** (401 Lafayette Road, Hampton Village; 603-926-8800) remains one of New England's supreme pubs, framed in hand-hewn wood beams and booths and wide plank floors worn to a perfect 200-year-old patina. Fare goes a step beyond standard tavern food, with entrées such as seafood linguine, prime rib stroganoff and broiled haddock, and a slew of excellent salads, sandwiches and appetizers. Moderate.

Count on at least a short line at **The Old Salt** (83 Ocean Boulevard, Hampton Beach; 603-926-8322), a great beachfront cranny with nautical accents and plenty of cheap eats. Breakfast means apple and blueberry waffles, three-cheese omelettes and pancakes, while dinner brings hefty portions of spaghetti, meat loaf and mashed potatoes, baked chicken with cranberry sauce and other home-cooked gems.

For superb seafood amidst some hopping beach action, try **Ashworth by the Sea** (295 Ocean Boulevard, Hampton Beach; 603-926-6762). Lobster fiends will revel in the ten different lobster entrées such as baked stuffed lobster pie, lobster à la newburg and a sinful baked stuffed lobster with extra lobster. For non-seafoodites, there's veal and chicken plus roast Vermont turkey. Decor is generic seafood house: natty brown carpets and draperies, mirrored walls and big windows overlooking the street and beach. Ultra-deluxe.

Possibly the finest seafood restaurant on New Hampshire's 18-mile coast is popular **Ron's Beach House** (965 Ocean Boulevard, Hampton Beach; 603-926-1870). Elegant yet quite relaxed, this breezy white colonial house sits a block from the ocean, yet the Atlantic views are marvelous from its second-floor sun porch. Small tables draped in starched cloth and perfectly folded napkins create intimate nooks for diners. The continental menu features a generous seafood selection plus interesting chicken and beef entrées. Sunday brunch is special. Moderate to deluxe.

The Eatery (★) (behind the Hampton Motor Inn, 815 Lafayette Road, Hampton; 603-926-8639) is a very special place: Here the homecooked delights are served by a local couple and their eight children. The restaurant is warm and inviting, with its oil lamps, skylights and several tables that overlook the woods. For lunch, there are thick chowders and stacked sandwiches; for dinner, chicken divan, cajun steak tips and scallop gratiné. Breakfasts feature homebaked breads and pancakes. Moderate.

Paul's Carriage House (2263 Ocean Boulevard, Rye; 603-964-8251) provides a curious mix of colonial and seaside ambience—and pulls it off swimmingly. The two-story casual nook rests across the street from Jenness Beach but looks like a mountain eatery. Early American wood tables and booths encircle a big hearth downstairs, while upstairs a smaller room promises great views of the beach. The continental-style bill of fare offers gems like steak au poivre, roast Long Island duckling with red raspberry and onion glaze and sole Oscar with lobster and asparagus in a champagne shallot sauce. Moderate to deluxe.

East of Hampton Beach, the town of Exeter is home to Phillips Exeter Academy, one of the country's most renowned and oldest preparatory schools. Here, the student population sustains a happy array of quaint street cafés, one of the best being **The Loaf and the Ladle** (9 Water Street; 603-778-8955). Everything is homemade and super-fresh, served cafeteria-style by friendly young people. There's black bean soup and country pâté, stacked sandwiches on fresh-baked bread, cheesecakes and chocolate mousse. Budget.

Another departure from traditional New England fare is **Guido's** (★) (67 Bow Street, Portsmouth; 603-431-2989). Here, Tuscan cuisine is the order of the day. The menu changes seasonally and might include such indulgences as tortellini stuffed with roasted pumpkin and amaretto cookies, veal scallopine with leeks, artichokes, olives and marjoram and the heady *fettunta* bread that's grilled and rubbed with raw garlic. It's all served in a stylish, second-floor dining room overlooking the river. Deluxe.

The place for sushi is **Sakura** (40 Pleasant Street, Portsmouth; 603-431-2721), a small but airy downtown nook that serves up fresh nori rolls and sashimi, tempura and teriyaki dishes, and interesting appetizers like a gingered raw beef (seared outside but raw inside). The decor borders on plain, with a small sushi bar, wood tables and railings, but it's as neat as a pin. Very popular with the business set. Budget to moderate.

The **Harbor's Edge Restaurant** (250 Market Street, in the Sheraton Portsmouth; 603-431-2300) captures a superb view of the harbor amidst romantic surroundings. Decked in hues of rose and emerald, the eatery conveys an air of refinement with crystal and carnation-topped linen tablecloths. Cuisine falls in the nouvelle category, with items like herb-crusted quail with peach compote, shrimp with curry-thyme butter, loin lamb chops and blackened prime rib. Moderate to deluxe.

Portsmouth's famous old spaghetti house is **Rosa's** (80 State Street; 603-436-9715), a great family-style place that opened back in 1927.

Adorned with dimly lit wood booths and old-time photographs, the restaurant serves up those heart-stopping, traditional Italian favorites like parmigianas and cacciatores, lasagna, ravioli, tortellini and thick-crusted pizza. Moderate to deluxe.

MERRIMACK VALLEY RESTAURANTS

Just south of Manchester, **Hannah Jack Tavern** (Everett Turnpike, Merrimack; 603-424-4171) complements its round of warm dining rooms with marble fireplaces, stained-glass windows and New England wall murals. Locals show up for the homemade breads (the raisin nut brioche is divine), the 100-label wine list and the prime rib, cut daily at the restaurant. Hannah Jack's does something that more restaurants should do—it offers smaller portions of many entrées. Moderate to deluxe.

Downtown Manchester's place to nosh is clearly **Café at the Atrium** (1001 Elm Street; 603-623-7878), a delightful underground post with plenty of breathing space. Small bistro tables are well-spaced and enhanced by mirrors, glass and bright yellow accents. The menu is heavy on seafood and steak, often bathed in light sauces and accompanied by pastas. Nightly specials may include wienerschnitzel, veal Oscar or rack of lamb. Try the Grand Marnier parfait for dessert. Moderate to deluxe.

In a world of Americanized Mexican restaurants, it's rare to strike authentic south-of-the-border cuisine. That, of course, is what makes **Hermanos** (6 Pleasant Street, Concord; 603-224-5669) so very special. Here, surrounded by Aztec murals and paraphernalia, you discover hefty burritos, enchiladas, quesadillas and tostadas, served with verve and panache. The specials are interesting, too—try the *estufada* (spicy stew), Mexican pizza and *taco pastor* (soft-shelled tacos stuffed and wrapped in grilled corn tortillas). Moderate.

Tucked away in the bucolic lull of Shaker Village, **The Creamery (★)** (Shaker Road, in Shaker Museum, Canterbury; 603-783-9511) offers a leap back in time. Indeed, the village and its 22 colonial buildings have changed little since the early 1800s. Dine on heavy wood tables, surrounded by simple country decor. In keeping with Shaker mandates of absolute freshness, menus utilize locally grown foods and might feature roast duckling with crabapple, summer tomatoes with currants and lalencia, freshwater catfish with bacon and horseradish, and peach oatmeal pie. The ultra-deluxe price tag includes a tour of the village or a musical program.

MONADNOCK REGION RESTAURANTS

Huddled beneath the great profile of Monadnock Mountain, the **Monadnock Inn** (Route 124, Jaffrey Center; 603-532-7001) proffers relaxed New England dining in a perfectly provincial setting. Polished oak floors set off a cozy dining room, while plastic tables and chairs are settled around a breezy screened porch that offers plenty of countryside views. For dinner, they offer rack of lamb, grilled salmon and filet mignon; for lunch, they serve bay shrimp and chicken stir fry as well as sandwiches, quiche and pastas. Moderate to deluxe.

For quick, budget-priced Italian pies, try the **Jaffrey Pizza Barn** (Blake Street, Jaffrey; 603-532-8383), a modest downtown cubbyhole with just four rows of orange formica booths. Thick-crusted pizzas come with a good selection of toppings (including steak and eggplant), and there are hot and cold grinders, too.

One of the toniest addresses around, the **Boiler House** (Route 202 South, Peterborough; 603-924-9486) captures an elegant feeling with black lacquer chairs, crisp white linens and a glass wall overlooking the Contoocook River. Formerly a 19th-century boiler room, the place has retained its now-hip exposed steel pipes. The setting is a perfect one for gastronomic encounters with veal in whiskey cream with chanterelles, Chesapeake softshell crab amandine and lamb and shrimp au pernod. Moderate to deluxe.

"Epicurean collage" is how owners of **Latacarta** (6 School Street, Peterborough; 603-924-6878) describe their unusual but successful natural cuisine. Inspiring soups, sandwiches and hot entrées are prepared with imagination and a philosophy of freshness. Housed in a recycled cinema, this very popular eatery is decorated with rotating local artwork, track lighting and cane chairs. Try the pan-grilled tofu sandwich or open-faced fried chicken sandwich with Yankee barbecue sauce. Moderate.

The John Hancock Inn (Main Street, Hancock; 603-525-3318) doles out some of the best Yankee cookin' around, dependable fare like chicken turnovers and fresh Boston scrod, roast beef hash and cranberry shrub. Set in New Hampshire's oldest operating inn (circa 1789), the three dining rooms feature wide-plank pine floors, beamed ceilings and cultured country decor, and face a rambling flower garden. Moderate to deluxe.

Over in the small but bustling city of Keene, **Henry David's** (81 Main Street; 603-352-0608) packs 'em in with moderately priced, dressed-up American fare and greenhouse surroundings. Light streams in through second-floor skylights, giving life to the more than 1300 plants draped across ceilings and walls. Named after *the* Mr. Thoreau, the place features outstanding prime rib and soups and baked stuffed shrimp.

LAKE SUNAPEE–DARTMOUTH RESTAURANTS

For solid American-style fare, the **Claremont Railroad Junction** (Plains Road, Claremont; 603-543-0017) is your destination. The layout is fancy diner, with worn wood booths, brass ceiling fans and a miniature choo-choo that chugs around an overhead track. The bill of fare includes plenty of seafood, pastas, chicken and beef, with specialties like steak tripoli (with crab and béarnaise sauce) and chicken florence. Moderate.

If your tastes run toward the southwest, you simply must dine at **Santa Fe Opera House** (155 Route 11, New London; 603-526-8060). Here the steak and seafood are grilled over a smoking mesquite fire that seals in the juice and spice. Blackened catfish and swordfish, served with a dollop of spiced rice, are musts for entrées. Pastel schemes, painted desert scenes and loads of cacti provide a real change of pace in colonial New Hampshire. Moderate.

Depending on what's in season, the **Millstone** (Newport Road, New London; 603-526-4201) might be serving venison, pheasant, swordfish or even Bavarian schnitzel. Fashioned as a country inn, this congenial restaurant is embellished with bow back chairs, linen tablecloths and local artwork. Freshness is the key word on this varied menu, and it keeps showing up in the seafood, game vegetables and herbs. Moderate.

You'll swear you've reached the outer limits of the universe by the time you arrive at **Home Hill Country Inn** (★) (River Road, off Route 12A, Plainfield; 603-675-6165). Stashed five mountain miles up a wooded sinuous road, the restored mansion conceals a French restaurant with a serious following. The dining room is intimate, with plank floors and blazing hearths. An ultra-deluxe, prix-fixe menu changes daily, offering delights such as scallops and shrimp in a sun-dried tomato sauce and veal in sage and crimini mushroom sauce.

Dartmouth students love to hang loose at **Peter Christian's Tavern** (39 South Main Street, Hanover; 603-643-2345), an underground habitat with great character and soul-warming grub. Zesty beef stew (some of the best anywhere) and fish chowder are definite favorites, but you can't go wrong with the spudley doright (stuffed potato) and Peter's Russian mistress (turkey sandwich with bacon, swiss and spinach). Wood beams criss-cross a low stucco ceiling, oversized mugs hang above the bar and knotty-pine booths are battered to a perfect college pub complexion. Budget to moderate.

It's tough to miss the big bubble windows of **Molly's Balloon** (43 South Main Street, Hanover; 603-643-2570), a chic little nook that has "yuppie" written all over it. There's an expansive oak bar in the middle, enveloped by brass railings and loads of hanging plants and trendy young diners. Moderately priced, the cuisine runs the gamut from stacked deli sandwiches, soups and salads to Mexican fajitas, baby-back ribs and pasta dishes.

LAKES REGION RESTAURANTS

Diminutive, intimate and remote, **The Pasquaney Inn** (★) (Star Route 1, Bridgewater; 603-744-9111) restaurant is a marvelous spot with rough pine floors, tables topped with fresh flowers and windows framing serene Newfound Lake. The key here is the chef, who owns the inn with his family and brings his refreshing French Belgian style into the cuisine. Touches of bacon are added to many dishes (the dandelion salad with sautéed bacon is unusual), or try the smoked salmon with endives and mustard truffle dressing, veal sweetbreads with mushrooms in Madeira cream sauce, or other culinary dreams. Deluxe.

Mismatched formica tables are strewn about, paper menus serve as placemats and crooked photos slouch on the walls, but hey, what do you expect from a place called **Nothin' Fancy** (Lakeside Avenue, Weirs Beach; 603-366-5764)? Despite the strange decor, the place rests right across from Lake Winnipesaukee and serves up exceptional Mexican food, grub like giant quesadillas, tostaditas, burritos and enchiladas, and soothing chili and spanish rice soup. Budget to moderate.

On a fancier note, **The Millworks** (Route 3 in the Mills Falls Marketplace, Meredith; 603-279-4116) offers a chic mall setting where lush ferns dangle from exposed pipes and beams and sunlight streams in through pretty picture windows. Moderately priced, the fare ranges from baked stuffed shrimp and crown rack of lamb to Maine lobster and ratatouille. Steaks are especially good.

The Common Man (Main Street, Ashland; 603-968-7030) enjoys a sterling reputation around the lakes, undoubtedly for its steadfast, uncomplicated cuisine and nostalgic surroundings. Old farm tools and classic *Life* and *Saturday Evening Post* covers are parked on the walls of the two-story brick eatery, formerly an early-1800s home. Go for the steaks (the prime rib is heady stuff) or the fresh fish and seafood. There's also chicken Oscar, pasta primavera and barbecued spareribs. Moderate.

A splendid provincial manor in the grand style, **The Red Hill Inn** (★) (Route 25B and College Road, Center Harbor; 603-279-7001) will make you forget life's worries. Set on the crown of an obscure country hill, the place has an outstanding restaurant adorned in period furniture and offering marvelous mountain views. The cuisine is unequivocally New Hampshire, sophisticated and heart-warming. Try the oven-fried rabbit, roast pheasant, chicken breast stuffed with cranberry sauce and herbed bread, or lemon pepper sea scallops. Moderate to deluxe.

It's not hard to figure out why **West Lake Asian Cuisine** (Route 28, Wolfeboro Center; 603-569-6700) stays perpetually packed. Snuggled in a wooded area along Lake Wentworth, the eatery headlines over 100 different and delicious dishes that make choosing extremely difficult. You'll find seafood, poultry, beef and pork dunked in steamy sauces with garlic, chili or black beans, along with specials like mala lamb, and dragon and phoenix (whole lobster paired with chicken and scorched red peppers). Moderate.

The Chequers Villa (Route 113, Tamworth; 603-323-8686) is synonymous with outstanding Italian fare around the lakes, serving up a bright array of hearty, fresh dishes prepared with imagination. The place is warm and friendly, decorated in a medieval motif with stucco archways and oil lamps. Spaghetti entrées might feature a medley of seafood, tomatoes and herbs, or mounds of parmesan cheese and bacon in egg sauce. There's also lasagna blanca (layered with chicken breast, spinach and cheesey cream sauce) or linguine pollo Don Juan (with artichoke hearts and black olives). Moderate.

Lake residents frequently mob **The Yankee Smokehouse** (junction of Routes 16 and 25, West Ossipee; 603-539-7427), a modest cinderblock joint parked on the corner of a rural intersection. Smoke trundles out the top, and an old air conditioner hums away while diners scarf down massive portions of ribs and chicken that hang off plastic plates. Also known for its sliced beef and pork and killer barbecue sauce, the smokehouse offers summer outdoor dining on picnic tables. Moderate.

WHITE MOUNTAINS REGION RESTAURANTS

Local college students know that **Suzanne's Kitchen** (36 South Main Street, Plymouth; 603-536-3304) is the place to go for budget-priced, wholesome natural foods. Recorded jazz echoes off unfinished pine floors while diners cozy around a freestanding brick fireplace. For breakfast, there are honey whole wheat croissants and veggie omelettes; lunch and dinner bring peanut butter, honey and banana sandwiches, soy burgers, tofu fries and spanakopita. Don't pass up the marvelous bakery on your way out.

A popular town spot that's just plain fun, **Truants Taverne** (Main Street, North Woodstock; 603-745-2239) has pull-down wall atlases, library shelves and a menu that lists "electives," "detention delights" and "prerequisites." The decor is casual wood-lined pub, the food basic continental, with items such as chicken parmigiana, chimichangas and broiled swordfish. Moderate.

Polly's Pancake Parlor (Route 117, Sugar Hill; 603-823-5575) was little more than a backwoods diner before the "Good Morning, America" crew wandered in one day. Ever since, the place has been invaded by tourists who line up outside the 1830 red-shingled carriage shed for home-style breakfast and lunch goodies. Polly's is still out in the boondocks, but views of the countryside are special. Ditto the griddle cakes, made from whole wheat and cornmeal batters and smothered in a choice of maple syrup, maple sugar or maple spread. Budget to moderate.

Stationed along a wooded mountain backroad, **Horse and Hound Inn** (★) (Wells Road off Route 18, Franconia; 603-823-5501) abounds in colonial gentility. Lofty pine beams and large hearths are accented by a hunting motif in the 1832 farmhouse. Deluxe-priced, the menu includes filling fare like veal marsala, lamb chops, roast duckling and a chicken covered with artichoke hearts and mozzarella. On warm summer days, opt for the breezy outdoor terrace overlooking the forest.

Small gas lanterns flicker on linen tablecloths, beautiful valanced draperies hover across walls and a weekend harpist strums beautiful melodies at the **Christmas Farm Inn** (Route 16B, Jackson; 603-383-4313). The romantic mountain hideout purveys "French country" cuisine, exceptional dishes such as grilled lamb kebabs, sauté of trout and medallions of veal with wild mushrooms. For breakfast, there are waffles with bananas in yogurt cream and corned beef hash. Moderate to deluxe.

The **Scottish Lion Restaurant** (Route 16, North Conway; 603-356-6381) provides a nice change of pace with fare from the British Isles. There's a sandwich lineup for lunch, including Scottish bridie (puff pastry turnover), while dinner is strong on roasts and steaks. Hearty appetites should opt for the highland game pie (with venison, beef, hare, pheasant and goose). Surroundings are merry, with red plaid wallpaper, red-and-white tablecloths and dark brick walls. Moderate to deluxe.

The views are superb, the surroundings intimate and the cuisine sublime at **The 1785 Inn** (Route 16, North Conway; 603-356-9025). The restaurant, a pretty glassed-in porch that scans a broad mountain range, resides in a venerable 18th-century home-turned-inn. French dishes are served with flair and understated elegance and include appetizers like cinnamon-spiced shrimp and entrées like raspberry duckling and shrimp capri. Deluxe.

Mount Washington Valley's premier noshing post is **Horsefeathers** (Main Street, North Conway; 603-356-2687), a downtown pub with awnings that command "Get in Here!" The food—mostly burgers and munchies like pouch potatoes and nasty nachos—isn't half bad, but the main reason you go here is to see and be seen. Get there early—lines are known to form at the drop of a "feather." Moderate.

It takes a bit of searching, but you'll eventually find **The Cinnamon Tree** (★) (Pleasant Street Plaza off Pleasant Street, Conway; 603-447-5019). One of those charming country diners with lacy curtains and "Welcome Friends" wallpaper, "The Tree" features swivel stools that wind around a U-shaped counter. Customers belly up for breakfast and lunch eats such as chili omelettes, blueberry pancakes and burgers. Budget to moderate.

The Great Outdoors

The Sporting Life

SKIING

Both downhill and cross-country skiing are pursued with a vengeance in New Hampshire. Ski centers are sprinkled along highways and a few rural roads, while backwoods trails exist everywhere.

For ski information, write to the **New Hampshire Office of Vacation Travel** (Box 856, Concord, NH 03302; 603-271-2666). A report on current ski conditions is available by calling 603-224-2525.

Though the seacoast has no downhill facilities, you can ski through the countryside along New Hampshire's western corridor. Two of the best (and least-known) cross-country spots are **Applecrest Farm Orchards** (★) (Route 88, Hampton Falls; 603-926-3721), where you can ski through hills of apple orchards, and the **University of New Hampshire's College Woods** (★) (Route 4, Durham; 603-862-1234), a 200-acre preserve covered with wooded trails.

Pats Peak (Route 114, Henniker; 603-428-3245), just outside Concord, is the largest downhill ski facility in the Merrimack Valley, offering 19 trails and seven lifts. The valley has several cross-country ski centers, including **Pine Acres Ski Touring Center** (Raymond; 603-895-2519) and **Plausawa Valley Touring Center** (Route 3, Pembroke; 603-224-6267).

In the Monadnock Region **Temple Mountain** (Route 101, Peterborough; 603-924-6949) features 17 trails and a 598-foot plunge. There are plenty of cross-country locales in the region, such as **Inn at East Hill Farm** (off Route 12, Troy; 603-242-6495) and **Tory Pines Ski Resort** (Route 47, Francestown; 603-588-2000), which has more than 33 miles of trails.

For skiing in the Lake Sunapee-Dartmouth area, try **Mount Sunapee** (Route 103, Sunapee; 603-763-2356) which has 32 trails and a 1510-foot drop or **King Ridge** (41 King Ridge, New London; 603-526-6966) which offers 20 runs. For cross-country skiing in these parts, try **Snowhill at Eastman** (intersection of Routes 89 and 10, Grantham; 603-863-4500) or **Norsk Touring Center** (off Route 11, New London; 603-526-4685).

Around the Lakes Region, **Gunstock** (Route 11A, Gilford; 603-293-4341) features 25 trails and a 1400-foot vertical drop. **Highland Mountain Ski Resort** (Highland Drive, Northfield; 603-286-2414) has 20 trails and 800 feet of vertical drops. Wooded lakeside trails exist at **Red Hill Inn** (★) (Route 49, Center Harbor; 603-279-7001) and **Perry Hollow Cross Country** (Middleton Road off Route 28, Wolfeboro; 603-569-3055).

Of course, the White Mountains Region possess an enormous number of ski possibilities, so take your pick. Five of the largest downhill ski centers run along (and just off) the spine of Route 93, including **Tenney Mountain** (Routes 25 and 3A, Plymouth; 603-536-1717), **Waterville Valley** (Route 49, Waterville Valley; 603-236-8311), **Loon Mountain** (Kancamagus Highway, Lincoln; 603-745-8111), **Cannon Mountain** (Route 3 in Franconia Notch State Park; 603-823-7771) and **Bretton Woods** (Route 302, Bretton Woods; 603-278-5000). Cross-country ski centers also exist at Waterville, Loon and Bretton Woods.

Way up in the northern wilderness, the **Balsams** (Route 26, Dixville Notch; 603-255-3951) is a marvelous setting with 12 downhill runs and over 30 miles of cross-country trails.

HORSEBACK RIDING

What better way to take in New Hampshire scenery than on horseback? Take a ride in the seacoast area at **Green Acre Stable** (Drew Road, Dover; 603-742-3377) on 140 acres of trails. In the Merrimack Valley try **Dawn Mar Riding Academy** (Stumpfield Road off Route 202, Hopkinton; 603-746-3884) or **Winged Spur Ranch** (24 Currier Road, Candia; 603-483-5960).

Over in the scenic Monadnock Region, **Honey Lane Farm** (Gold Mine Road, Dublin; 603-563-8078) has winter wonderland and fall foliage rides. **Morning Mist Farm** (15 College Hill Road, Henniker; 603-428-3889) offers trail rides southeast of Lake Sunapee.

Around the Lakes Region you'll find superb riding at **Castle in the Clouds** (Route 171, Moultonboro; 603-476-2352) and **King's Western Trail Rides** (off Route 3A, Hill; 603-934-5740). Up in the White Mountains, check out **Nestlenook Inn and Equestrian Center** (Dinsmore Road, Jackson; 603-383-0845) or **The Riding Place** (off Route 302, Bretton Woods; 603-278-1836).

SPORTFISHING

Aficionados of both saltwater and freshwater fishing will find a bounty of opportunities in New Hampshire. Angle for pollack, cod, mackerel and bluefish off the seacoast, or for trout, salmon, cusk, perch and bass in one of several hundred ponds and lakes.

Deep-sea fishing charters are offered by **Eastman's Fishing Parties** (River Road, Seabrook Beach; 603-474-3461), **Al Gauron Deep Sea Fishing** (Hampton Beach State Pier on Ocean Boulevard, Hampton Beach; 603-926-2469), **Smith & Gilmore Fishing Pier** (3A Ocean Boulevard, Hampton Beach; 603-926-3503) and **Atlantic Fishing Fleet** (Route 1A, Rye Harbor; 603-964-5220).

Freshwater anglers should head for **Landlocked Fishing Guide Service** (Sibley Road, Center Harbor; 603-253-6119), **Squam Lakes Fishing Tours** (Route 3, Holderness; 603-968-7577) or **Gadabout Golder** (Route 16, West Ossipee; 603-539-4138).

You can rent fishing boats around the Lakes Region at **Meredith Marina** (Bay Shore Drive, Meredith; 603-279-7921), **Winni Sailboarders' School** (687 Union Avenue, Laconia; 603-528-4110), **Fay's Boat Yard** (Varney Point Road, Gilford; 603-293-8000) or **Thurston Enterprises** (Route 3, Weirs Beach; 603-366-4811).

WHALE WATCHING

Humpbacks, finbacks, minke and other New England whales are known to put on quite a show. Whale-watching expeditions are offered by **Eastman's Fishing Parties** (River Road, Seabrook Beach; 603-474-3461), **Al Gauron Deep Sea Fishing** (Hampton Beach State Pier on Ocean Boulevard, Hampton Beach; 603-926-2469), **New Hampshire Seacoast Cruises** (Route 1A, Rye Harbor; 603-964-5545), **Oceanic Whale Watch Expeditions** (315 Market Street, Portsmouth; 603-431-5505) and **Bay & Ocean Charters** (Dame Road, Durham; 603-659-3288).

GOLF

Golf enthusiasts will happily find an array of scenic courses in New Hampshire.

Along the seacoast, there's **Sagamore Hampton Golf Club** (101 North Road, North Hampton; 603-964-5341) and **Wentworth By-The-Sea Golf Club** (Route 1B, Rye; 603-433-5010). In the Merrimack Valley, check out **Manchester Country Club** (South River Road, Bedford; 603-624-4096). In the Monadnock Region, try **Bretwood Golf Course** (East Surry Road, Keene; 603-352-7626). **Claremont Country Club** (Maple Avenue, Claremont; 603-542-9550) and **John H. Cain Golf Course** (Unity Road, off Routes 11 and 103, Newport; 603-863-7787) are in the Lake Sunapee–Dartmouth area.

Waukewan Golf Club (Waukewan Road, West Center Harbor; 603-279-6661) is in the Lakes Region. Up in the White Mountains, there are **Waterville Valley Sports Center** (Route 49, Waterville Valley; 603-236-8371) and **Mount Washington Hotel and Resort** (Route 302, Bretton Woods; 603-278-1000).

TENNIS

Tennis anyone? You'll find courts along the seacoast at **Exeter Recreation Park** (Route 101C, Exeter; 603-778-0591). Public tennis courts in Portsmouth are located on the South Mill Pond, Junkins Avenue. In the Merrimack Valley, there's **Memorial Field** (South Fruit Street, Concord; 603-225-8690). **Wheelock Park** (Park Avenue, Keene; 603-357-9829) is in the Monadnock Region, and **Dartmouth College Athletic Complex** (Wheelock and South Park streets, Hanover; 603-646-2109) offers courts in the Lake Sunapee–Dartmouth Region.

In the Lakes Region, try **Prescott Park** (Route 3, Meredith; 603-279-8197) or **Moultonboro Tennis Courts** (Playground Drive, Moultonboro; 603-253-4160). Up in the Green Mountains Region, you'll find **Mountain Club Fitness Center** (Route 112 at Loon Mountain, Lincoln; 603-745-8111, ext. 5280) and **Waterville Valley Sports Center** (Route 49, Waterville Valley; 603-236-8371).

BICYCLING

This state of grand mountains, vast lakes and rocky coastline is truly a bicyclist's nirvana. Before you set out, send for the New Hampshire Bicycle Map, available from the **New Hampshire Department of Resource and Economic Development** (Office of Recreation Services and Vacation Travel, Box 856, Concord, NH 03301; 603-271-2666).

One of the most popular routes in all New Hampshire, the 18-mile **Atlantic Shoreline** wends along the rugged seacoast on Route 1A from Massachusetts to Portsmouth. Caution is advised during summer months, when traffic is extremely heavy.

Seven miles of rolling hills and apple orchards await along Route 88 between **Exeter and Hampton Falls**. In the Merrimack Valley, there's a 34-mile trek from **Milford to Concord** along Route 13, lined with old red barns, rivers and streams and superb vistas.

For a picturesque, less-traveled odyssey, take Route 149 from **South Weare to Hillsboro** (★), in the Monadnock Region. The 12-mile excursion slices through archetypical New England villages and rambling farmlands.

With its gorgeous water and mountain views, the 62-mile loop around **Lake Winnipesaukee** is understandably a favorite of cyclists everywhere. Terrain varies from flat to very hilly, and roads can be congested during summertime. Stick to Routes 28, 109, 25B and 11.

The strong at heart will opt for a very steep ten-mile journey on Hurricane Mountain Road from **North Conway to the Maine Border.** An easier mountain route that's just as scenic, Route 16 and Side Road edge the Androscoggin River for 29 miles from **Errol to Berlin.**

BIKE RENTALS   Because of high liability insurance rates, bike rental centers are scarce across New Hampshire. Here are a few locations to try: **The Ped'ling Fool Bike Shop** (77 West Main Street, Hillsboro; 603-464-5286) in the Merrimack–Monadnock area; **Piche's** (318 Gilford Avenue, Gilford; 603-524-2068) in the Lakes Region; and **Valley Bikes** (Town Square, Waterville Valley; 603-236-4666) and **Loon Mountain Bike Center** (Kancamagus Highway, Lincoln; 603-745-8111) in the White Mountains.

Beaches and Parks

For the most part, New Hampshire's parks are open only for the summer, usually from Memorial Day through Labor Day. During the off-season, contact the New Hampshire Division of Parks and Recreation (Box 856, Concord, NH 03302; 603-271-3254).

SEACOAST BEACHES AND PARKS

Hampton Beach State Park—One of the most popular parks in all New Hampshire, this place boasts a quarter mile of broad pewter-colored beach flecked with smooth stones. A jetty shoots several feet into the ocean, and there's a long row of sand dunes, some of the few remaining in the state. From here, you have tremendous views northward of Great Boars Head.

Facilities: Gazebo with picnic tables, restrooms, bathhouse, snack bar, lifeguards; information, 603-926-3784. *Fishing:* Good from the jetty for striped bass, cod and flounder. *Swimming:* Excellent.

Getting there: Located on Route 1A at the southern tip of Hampton Beach.

Hampton Seashell State Park—This is *the* liveliest sand in New Hampshire. For six months a year, thousands jam a three-mile stretch of fine ashen grains whipped by waves and surrounded by street action. The boardwalk, with its sidewalk vendors, carnival food and trinket shops, follows the beach and creates constant activity. Despite the size of this beach, the crowds do follow a certain order: families cluster around the north end, older folks lay claim to the south tip and the skimpy-suited, let's-party group stakes out the middle near the Beach Patrol Station.

Facilities: Restrooms, playground, lifeguards, pavilion, volleyball courts, amphitheater and band shell; restaurants, stores, nightclubs and motels line the boardwalk; information, 603-926-6705. *Swimming:* Good.

Getting there: Located in Hampton Beach along Ocean Boulevard between M Street and Great Boars Head.

North Beach—A thick seawall hides this beach from the roadway, though rough waves occasionally send salt water over the top and onto passing traffic. The narrow cord of hard-packed sand, stretching only half a mile, is submerged during most high tides, when locals congregate atop the wall for prime wave watching.

Facilities: Restrooms; stores within walking distance; information, 603-926-2862. *Swimming:* Good. *Surfing:* This is the most popular spot in New Hampshire; best around Great Boars Head, a rocky bulkhead on the northern end of the beach.

Getting there: Located in Hampton Beach along Ocean Boulevard between Great Boars Head and 19th Street.

Plaice Cove Beach (★)—Strewn with grey boulders and pebbles, this volcaniclike beach is encased in sand as silver as gunpowder. Small but picturesque, it rests before beautiful homes and appears to be a private beach. Locals know it as one of the quietest spots around and assemble here at low tide when the sand area is widest. Seagulls hang around the north end, scurrying about seaweed patches and constant ocean sprays.

Facilities: None; stores located within walking distance. *Swimming:* Okay at low tide during summer, though water is frequently quite rough. *Surfing:* Good.

Getting there: Take the unmarked footpath that starts on Route 1A, across from Ron's Beach House restaurant just north of the intersection of Route 101C in Hampton Beach. The path leads between two houses down to the beach.

North Hampton Beach State Park—Stretching 1000 feet along the ocean, this fine sliver of mocha sand covers a short lapse between seaside neighborhoods. Families favor the park for its subdued tone and gentle waves. Lovely Little Boars Head, a rocky ocean spur, looms to the north.

Facilities: Restrooms, bathhouse, lifeguards; snack shops across the street; information, 603-436-9404. *Fishing:* Good. *Swimming:* Good.

Getting there: Located along Ocean Boulevard just south of Little Boars Head in North Hampton.

South Rye Beach—This so-called "beach" consists solely of millions of silvery pebbles (bad for the back but pretty to look at) that extend about one-quarter mile. Dedicated sunbathers set up lawn chairs and wear sturdy shoes, but the real action centers around surfing. Board toters call this beach "Rye on the Rocks" and arrive en masse anytime there's a whiff of wind.

Facilities: None; stores less than a mile away in Rye.   *Surfing:* Top-notch waves.

Getting there: Located on Route 1A, south of Causeway Road in Rye.

Rye Harbor State Park—Situated on Ragged Neck Peninsula, this park offers commanding views of Rye Harbor and a 200-foot jetty for prime fishing and sightseeing. There's no beach, but a grassy lawn is flecked with trees and playground equipment. On a clear day, the historic Isles of Shoals hover in the distance.

Facilities: Picnic areas, restrooms; information, 603-436-5294. *Fishing:* Excellent from the jetty. Try for flounder and pollack.   *Swimming:* Good in the calm cove.

Getting there: Located on Route 1A at Rye Harbor Road in Rye.

Wallis Sands State Park—Wild and scenic, Wallis Sands boasts one of the coast's choicest swaths of copper-colored sand punctuated by a dramatic jetty. On windy days, waves slash the rocks, sending sprays as high as 60 feet. Only 18 acres in size, the park features soft patches of grass and a concrete walkway that edges the beach. Get there at low tide, when the beach spans up to 800 feet. When the tide comes in, the sand shrinks back to 150 feet—the only drawback of this beautiful place.

Facilities: Restrooms, bathhouse, showers, lifeguards, snack bar; information, 603-436-9404.   *Fishing:* Good from jetty.   *Swimming:* Good.

Getting there: Located at Route 1A and Marsh Road in Rye.

Odiorne Point State Park—New Hampshire's first settlers landed amid these rocky headlands and marshes back in 1623. Today, the natural sanctuary accounts for 327 acres and two miles of shoreline—the largest undeveloped tract on the coast. You can spend days exploring all the goodies this place offers, including old grave sites and stone walls, three World War II bunkers, remains of a formal garden, five miles of trails, two ponds, dozens of tidal pools and a visitor's center with wildlife exhibits, bookstore and local history displays. Besides historical secrets, the park harbors a secluded beach on **Frost Point** (★), known along the coast as the only spot to swim in your birthday suit. There's no sand here, only grass and pebbles and total seclusion. Just north of the point, sandy shores draw larger crowds.

Facilities: Visitors center, restrooms, bathhouse, pavilions; information, 603-436-7406.   *Fishing:* Best during spring and fall for striped bass and flounder.

Getting there: There are two entrances on Route 1A in Rye. To get to Frost Point, park at the north entrance and take the rocky trail about one-quarter mile through the woods.

Great Island Common—Picturesque and serene, this municipal beach belongs to the tiny island of New Castle, near Portsmouth. Swampy meadows share the shoreline with hard-packed sand and several rocky beaches. There's a spacious grassy area for excellent picnicking and a series of jetties that offer interesting tidepooling. A lighthouse hovers in the distance, occasionally sounding its foghorn.

Facilities: Picnic areas, restrooms, playground; stores nearby in New Castle village; information, 603-431-6710. *Fishing:* Good from the jetties. *Swimming:* Good in sheltered coves.

Getting there: Located off Wentworth Road in New Castle.

MERRIMACK VALLEY BEACHES AND PARKS

Silver Lake State Park—Locals mob this place on summer weekends for one reason: a very special sliver of sand. These toffee-colored granules extend 1000 feet along Silver Lake and churn up a storm of activity. The 34-acre lake itself is also quite stunning, sheltered by a cascade of grassy knolls and gracious pine trees.

Facilities: Picnic area, restrooms, bathhouse, play field, refreshment stand; information, 603-465-2342. *Fishing:* Good. *Swimming:* Good.

Getting there: Located on Route 122 one mile north of Hollis.

Pawtuckaway State Park—Tucked just outside the bustle of several major cities, this 5500-acre park has it all. There's 803-acre Lake Pawtuckaway with its broad mocha beaches and islands, a vast oak and hickory forest and hemlock ravine, 25 acres of wooded picnicking spots and the Pawtuckaway Mountains, surrounded by curious rock formations carved some 275 million years ago. There are extensive trails for hiking, snowmobiling and cross-country skiing. You need to explore all three areas to get a good feel for this diverse park, so plan to spend some time.

Facilities: Picnic area, restrooms, snack bar, playground, rental boats, pavilion; information, 603-895-3031. *Camping:* Horse and Big islands offer 170 tent sites, many right on the lake. *Fishing:* Excellent—lakes are usually well stocked with bass. *Swimming:* Excellent.

Getting there: Located off Route 156, three and a half miles north of Route 101 in Nottingham.

Bear Brook State Park—This mammoth place covers 9600 acres and offers a slew of activities. Of the park's six ponds, Catamount Pond attracts the most activity with its wide beach, ball fields and picnic facilities for 1500 people. Cool, dusky Bear Brook snakes through the park, which is dense with red and white pines. You'll also find more than 30 miles of hiking trails, a physical fitness course, snowmobile museum, nature center with a popular glass beehive, and two archery ranges.

Facilities: Numerous picnic areas and pavilions, snack bars, restrooms and bathhouses, playgrounds, lifeguards; information, 603-485-9874.

Camping: Beaver Pond features 81 tent sites.   *Fishing:* Excellent for trout, perch, bass and pickerel in several lakes and streams. Archery Pond is reserved for fly fishing.   *Swimming:* Excellent in Beaver and Catamount ponds. (Swimming is restricted to campers only at Beaver Pond.)

Getting there: Located off Route 28, five miles northeast of Hookset.

Winslow State Park—After a 1820-foot climb (via auto) up Mount Kearsarge, the park rewards with magnificent panoramas that stretch into Vermont. It was named for Civil War admiral John Winslow and is now popular with hang glider enthusiasts, who hurl themselves from the summit, landing (hopefully) in a parking lot below. A steep, one-mile hike takes you to the peak—2937 feet up.

Facilities: Picnic area, restrooms; stores nearby in Wilmot; information, 603-526-6168.

Getting there: Located off Route 11, three miles south of Wilmot.

MONADNOCK REGION BEACHES AND PARKS

Monadnock State Park—The lonely, imposing peak of Mount Monadnock has long been a fixture of southwestern New Hampshire, inspiring poets and intriguing all those who cast eyes upon it. Frequently called the world's most-climbed mountain, its barren granite pinnacle has been scaled by Mark Twain, Ralph Waldo Emerson, Henry David Thoreau and thousands of others. Today, the 5000-acre park remains a hiker's mecca, crisscrossed with 40 miles of trails enriched by views of every New England state.

Facilities: Picnic area, restrooms, refreshment center, environmental center, guided nature tours; information, 603-532-8862.   *Camping:* 21 tent sites are open year-round.

Getting there: Located off Route 124, four miles west of Jaffrey.

Contoocook Lake Public Beach (★)—It's a rare find indeed, this tiny but choice spot. Edging the shore of beautiful Contoocook Lake, a sliver of beach features glistening white sand as soft as talcum powder. During the summer, the town closes part of the road and spreads sand across it, making it a great spot for small children.

Facilities: Picnic areas, restrooms; information, 603-532-8305; stores nearby in Jaffrey.   *Fishing:* Good.   *Swimming:* Good.

Getting there: From the intersection of Routes 124 and 202 in Jaffrey, take Stratton Road southeast to Squantum Road. Head east on Squantum Road, and you'll soon arrive at the beach.

Miller State Park—New Hampshire's oldest state park was settled back in 1891 and named for General James Miller, a hero of the War of 1812. It rests atop the 2300-foot summit of South Pack Monadnock Mountain, a one-and-a-half-mile semivertical drive with numerous hairpin curves. Incredible vistas extend to the skyscrapers of Boston.

Facilities: There's a picnic area, primitive restrooms; information, 603-924-7433.

Getting there: Located off of Route 101, three miles east of Peterborough.

Rhododendron State Park—No doubt, this place is extra special. Arrive around mid-July and revel in the explosion of rhododendrons that form a pink-and-white canopy across 16 acres. A one-mile trail meanders up Little Mount Monadnock, ensuring a feast for the senses and lovely views of Mount Monadnock. Other jewels bloom here, too, including the jack-in-the-pulpit, trillium, mountain laurel and pink lady's slipper.

Facilities: Picnic area, restrooms; stores nearby in Fitzwilliam; information, 603-239-8153.

Getting there: Located off Route 12, two and one-half miles north of Fitzwilliam.

LAKE SUNAPEE–DARTMOUTH AREA
BEACHES AND PARKS

Pillsbury State Park—A 5000-acre wilderness of forests, ponds and subtle hills, Pillsbury was once a bustling village of sawmills and frame homes. Today there's no hint of that 18th-century activity as ducks, deer and other wildlife roam the moist hammocks and dense thickets. Hiking and picnicking here are superb, and nine ponds provide havens for serious fishers.

Facilities: Numerous picnic areas, pit toilets; stores nearby in Washington; information, 603-863-2860. *Camping:* 20 primitive sites border May Pond.

Getting there: Located off Route 31, four miles north of Washington.

Mount Sunapee State Park—This ever-popular park is more like a resort (minus the accommodations), a year-round recreation haven that caters to swimmers and sunbathers, hikers and skiers, ice fishers and sightseers. Chair lifts cruise up 2720-foot Mount Sunapee for downhill skiing and lovely views of Lake Sunapee and the surrounding alpine mountains. There's a cafeteria up here and another at the mountain's base, where you'll find a sun terrace, auditorium and exhibition trout pool. And there's more: the 2700-acre park claims a ski school and shop, nursery and lineup of events like state craft shows, bike races and outdoor concerts. Across the street, **Sunapee State Beach** is a 900-foot ribbon of crystalline sand edging the lake.

Facilities: Picnic areas, restrooms, bathhouses, lifeguards, cafeterias, snack bars; information, 603-763-2356. *Fishing:* Spring-fed Lake Sunapee is renowned for trout and salmon fishing. *Swimming:* Good.

Getting there: Located on Route 103, three miles west of Newbury.

LAKES REGION BEACHES AND PARKS

Bristol Town Beach (★)—There's something about a really obscure beach that warms your soul, and this pristine sandbox fits the bill. Sheltered by pine and maple trees, it stretches like powdered cinnamon along Newfound Lake and opens onto a broad expanse of very clear water. A local beach, it's packed on summer weekends. If you're not a resident, you'll need a permit to park near the beach.

Facilities: Picnic area, volleyball nets; stores are nearby in Bristol. *Swimming:* Crystal clear water and sloping sandy bottom create perfect swimming conditions.

Getting there: Located on West Shore Road, one-quarter mile west of Route 3A in Bristol.

Wellington State Park and Beach—Secluded pine coves, strings of granite boulders and a brow of chestnut sand amble around Newfound Lake at this ultra-scenic spot. Lying on a peninsula and framed by small peaks and isles of evergreens, Wellington *has* the views. The lake's white sandy bottom and gentle shores make it one of the best swimming holes in New Hampshire.

Facilities: Picnic area, pavilions, bathhouse, restrooms, playground, snack bar; information, 603-744-2197. *Fishing:* Good. *Swimming:* Excellent.

Getting there: Located off Route 3A, four miles north of Bristol.

Endicott Rock Park and Beach—This *is* the beach at Weirs Beach, the paradigm of summertime family vacations. It rests in an elbow of Lake Winnipesaukee and bears a half moon of amber granules bordered by grassy slopes. Though the lake views are pretty spectacular, the beach itself is nothing to write home about. Still, crowds flock here for the carnival mood stirred up by the adjacent boardwalk and amusement centers.

Facilities: Picnic area, restrooms, playground; stores and restaurants across the street; information, 603-524-5046. *Swimming:* Good.

Getting there: Located off Route 3 at Lakeside Avenue in Weirs Beach.

Ellacoya State Park and Beach—The only state park on Lake Winnipesaukee and one of its few parcels of public land, Ellacoya combines a 600-foot beach with birch groves and fabulous sunsets. Mocha-colored sand, flecked with pine needles and cones, weaves about the lake and courts sublime views of the Ossipee and Sandwich mountain ranges.

Facilities: Picnic areas, restrooms, bathhouse, seasonal refreshment stand; information, 603-293-7821. *Swimming:* Good.

Getting there: Located on Route 11 in Gilford.

WHITE MOUNTAINS REGION BEACHES AND PARKS

White Mountain National Forest—A colossal land mass draped across northern New Hampshire, the forest is New England's largest piece of public land and one of the most popular forests in the country. It is so all-encompassing that you soon realize it *is* much of New Hampshire. Its 763,000 acres (45,000 lie in Maine) gobble up several state parks and 1200 miles of hiking trails, 45 lakes and ponds, 650 miles of fishing streams and 20 campgrounds. Most of the Northeast's highest peaks call this forest home, as do whitetail deer, black bear, moose, beavers and a host of other wildlife. The state's most spectacular fall foliage displays occur here, and one of the best places to see the changing colors is along the 34-mile Kancamagus Highway from Route 302 to Route 3A. Hiking trails, including part of the Appalachian Trail, are scattered throughout the forest.

Facilities: Picnic areas; information, 603-528-8721. *Camping:* Permitted in 20 campgrounds, including primitive and trailer camps. *Fishing:* Endless possibilities for trout, salmon, bass, perch and cusk in ponds, lakes and streams. Some of the best are Basin Reservoir and Russell, Sawyer and Long ponds. *Swimming:* Good in numerous brooks and ponds.

Getting there: The forest stretches more or less from Percy southward to Rumney, and from Benton eastward into Maine. Several main routes cut through, including Routes 93, 302, 16 and 2.

Franconia Notch State Park—This is the flagship of New Hampshire parks, the one that everyone raves about. A truly incredible place, Franconia blankets 6500 acres, hosts more than 2 million visitors a year and boasts a dizzying array of natural and manmade wonders that make it seem like the Disney World of parklands. Flanked by rocky peaks and riddled with rivers and lakes, the park encompasses the Cannon Mountain ski area and tramway, an intriguing rock pool called the Basin, a minicanyon known as the Flume, and the famous granite profile of **Old Man of the Mountains**. Then there are sandy beaches, miles of hiking trails, beautiful fern grottos and some of the finest bike paths in New Hampshire. The best advice here? Plan to spend some time. (For more information, see the "Sightseeing" section in this chapter.)

Facilities: Picnic areas, restrooms, bathhouse, cafeterias and snack bars, New England Ski Museum, boat launches; information, 603-823-5563. *Camping:* Lafayette Campground has 97 tent sites and includes showers. *Fishing:* Good in several lakes and streams; particularly popular in Echo Lake. *Swimming:* Good in Echo Lake.

Getting there: Located north of North Woodstock. Access all sights from Franconia Notch Parkway, which is also Route 93 for the eight-mile length of the park.

Crawford Notch State Park—A rugged mountain pass navigates some of the most untamed forest and rocks in New Hampshire. It forms a six-mile shear through the U-shaped Saco River Valley and harbors numerous ponds, trails and cascades, including Arethusa Falls, the highest in the state. Several log cabins commemorate the Willey Family, some of the area's first settlers who were killed in 1826 while fleeing a horrible landslide.

Facilities: Picnic areas, restrooms, gift shop, snack bar; information, 603-374-2272. *Camping:* Dry River Campground features 30 tent sites. *Fishing:* Good in ponds and streams.

Getting there: Located along Route 302, six miles north of Bartlett.

Mount Washington State Park—This 60-acre park wraps around the hood of Mount Washington, the highest peak in the northeastern United States. The summit—some 6288 feet up—tingles the spine as you peer across a cosmos of mountains and forests that seem to fall off the horizon. The mountain itself has long been the subject of curiosity and wonder. Its sometimes freakish weather can change from toasty to blizzardlike (or vice versa) in a matter of minutes, and its plant life is an unusual mix of sparse lichens, shrubs and rare wildflowers. Back in 1934, it endured the highest wind velocity (231 miles per hour) ever recorded on earth. You'll find more on this uncanny butte at the Observatory Museum, parked right on the treeless, rocky crest.

Facilities: Restrooms, snack bar, museum, gift shop, post office; information, 603-466-3347.

Getting there: Located off Route 302 north of Crawford Notch.

Coleman State Park (★)—It's safe to say that this place is virtually at the end of the planet. Purists will find the surroundings heady stuff, a coalition of thick timbers, broad mountains and sparkling lakes. Much of the activity (though there's really not much) centers around Little Diamond Pond, sprinkled with small fishing boats and surrounded by rolling hills.

Facilities: Picnic area, recreation building; stores located 12 miles west in Colebrook; information, 603-237-4520. *Camping:* Permitted in 30 tent sites. *Fishing:* Good trout fishing in Little Diamond Pond and several streams.

Getting there: From Route 26 in Kidderville, take Diamond Pond Road north into the park.

Hiking

New Hampshire's gridwork of vast timberlands and lakes, wide mountains and ravines makes it a hiker's haven. Forests cover 87 percent of the state, and the White Mountain National Forest alone has over 1200 miles of trails. For information on many of these trails, contact the **White Mountain National Forest** (Box 638, Laconia 03246; 603-528-8721).

The Appalachian Mountain Club's **White Mountain Guide**, considered the hiker's bible, is available through the club (Box 298, Pinkham Notch, NH 03581; 603-466-2721). For inn-to-inn hikes, get in touch with **New England Hiking Holidays** (Box 1648, North Conway, NH 03860; 603-356-9696, or 407-778-4499 from December through April 15).

SEACOAST TRAILS

Though you won't scale any broad peaks along the coast, you can explore some very scenic footpaths. One of the best spots to try is **Odiorne Point State Park,** where five miles of trails wander along gently curled shoreline, gray pebble beaches and stands of pines, oaks and wild roses.

A few miles inland, the **University of New Hampshire's College Woods** (★) offers a labyrinth of nature trails that crisscross more than 200 thickly forested acres. There's also the **College Brook Ravine** trail (1 mile), which follows a brook through a 15-acre ravine and offers peeks at 155 species of plants.

MERRIMACK VALLEY TRAILS

In the Merrimack Valley, the **Uncanoonuc Mountain Trail** (.6 mile) cuts through a stone wall and hemlock forest and passes a small cave on the way to the summit, where views of Manchester await. To find the rather obscure trailhead, take Route 114 east from Goffstown to Mountain Road. Go south for a mile, then bear left for a mile and a half.

MONADNOCK REGION TRAILS

Isolated Mount Monadnock, often called "the world's most-hiked mountain," offers more than a dozen trails with all levels of difficulty. For detailed information, stop by the visitors center (off Route 124, four miles west of Jaffrey). **White Arrow Trail** (1 mile), one of the mountain's oldest footpaths, ambles across brooks, ledges and narrow gullies to the summit. It commences at the end of the mountain toll road.

Pumpelly Trail (4.5 miles) zigzags up Monadnock, following a ridge and passing a huge rectangular boulder and several glacial carvings. The trailhead starts on Old Marlboro Road off Route 101, just west of Dublin.

Hikers took the **Marlboro Trail** (2.2 miles) as early as 1850, tackling the steep nose of Monadnock's ridges to open ledges. Start on the dirt road off Route 124, west of Monadnock State Park.

A gentle crossing along Monadnock's south slope, **Parker Trail** (1.6 miles) slices through dense woods. It begins in Monadnock State Park near the outlet brook.

Wapack Trail (23 miles) is a popular skyline trek along the Wapack Range, running from Watatic Mountain in Ashburnham, Massachusetts across the Pack Monadnocks in New Hampshire. Filled with open ledges and beautiful views, it navigates a large spruce forest.

LAKE SUNAPEE–DARTMOUTH AREA TRAILS

The **Monadnock–Sunapee Greenway** (50 miles) crawls across ridgetops between Mounts Monadnock and Sunapee. You can also scale **Mount Sunapee** via its ski slopes (3 miles), which plow through heavy forests to gorgeous, secluded Lake Solitude and then go on to the summit.

LAKES REGION TRAILS

With its marvelous union of mountains and water, the Lakes Region provides some of the most scenic hiking in New Hampshire. On the north end of Squam Lake, a pair of low-lying mountains called the Rattlesnakes feature easy treks with unparalleled views.

Old Bridle Path (1.8 miles), off Route 113 near Center Sandwich, meanders along an old cart road to the summit of West Rattlesnake. **Ridge Trail** (2 miles) connects East and West Rattlesnakes, beginning northeast of the cliffs on the western mountain.

In the Red Hill area of Squam Lake, **Eagle Cliff Trail** (2.3 miles) ambles through a thicket and dense woods, scales the steep cliff and ends at the fire tower for great views from Red Hill. The trailhead is off Bean Road, 5.2 miles from the junction of Routes 25 and 25B in Center Harbor.

For excellent views of Lake Winnipesaukee, try the **Mount Shaw Trail** (3.5 miles), which travels through a hemlock forest and past several streams and brooks to an open knob. It starts at a dirt road on the north side of Route 171 west of Tuftonboro.

East Gilford Trail (2.1 miles), which begins on Bickford Road off Route 11A, climbs Belknap Mountain and affords several fine outlooks over Lake Winnipesaukee.

WHITE MOUNTAINS REGION TRAILS

Spectacular hiking exists everywhere in the White Mountains Region.

Offering splendid scenery, **Welch Mountain Trail** (1.5 miles) follows rock outcroppings and gives the feeling that you're above the timberline. The trailhead is along the Mad River at the entrance to Waterville Valley.

Along the beautiful Kancamagus Highway near Conway you'll find **Boulder Loop Trail** (.5 mile), a gradual climb with panoramas of Mount Chocorua and the Swift River Valley. **Sabbaday Falls Trail** (.4 mile) wanders to a series of cascades in a narrow chasm.

The Franconia Notch area is a maze of trails for all hiking levels. **Falling Waters Trail** (3.2 miles) navigates lovely cascades and brooks, shady glens and narrow gorges, and offers great vistas of the notch. It starts at Lafayette Place.

Whitehouse Trail (.8 mile), which winds along the Pemigewasset River, makes a nice trek through Franconia Notch State Park. Pick up the trail at the Flume Visitor Center.

Bald Mountain–Artists Bluff Trail (.8 mile) makes a panoramic loop in the notch, starting at Peabody Base on Route 18. Nestled up in the mountains, **Lonesome Lake Trail** (1.3 miles) offers commanding views of surrounding peaks. It commences at the Lafayette Campground off Route 93.

Often overlooked, **Kinsman Falls Trail** (5 miles) is a stroll through verdant foliage along Cascade Brook. The trail begins at the White House Bridge in Franconia Notch State Park and ends at the Kingsman Pond Shelter.

One of the state's most popular hikes, **Tuckerman Ravine Trail** (2 miles) is a rugged cirque with bare slopes and sheer cliffs on Mount Washington. A moderately difficult path, it commences at the Appalachian Mountain Club's Pinkham Notch Camp on Route 16.

Thompson Falls Trail (.8 mile) clambers up the south side of Wildcat Brook to several cascades and great views of the Presidential mountain range. The trailhead starts at Wildcat Ski Area on Route 16.

Travelers' Tracks

Sightseeing

Few tiny plots of earth can claim such a generous helping of gratifying scenery as New Hampshire. Indeed, this slim state packs a potent dose of naked beauty, apparent in its daunting mountain canopies, rushing rivers, glistening lakes and smidgen of ocean-swept coast.

Best of all, you can experience all these wonders in the same day. The fertile Lakes Region is less than an hour's drive from the White Mountains or the seacoast or the quaint old towns of the Monadnock Region. No matter where you are in New Hampshire, you can easily journey to another place that's just as scenic yet so very different.

Many spots in New Hampshire are closed during winter months, so if you're vacationing then, remember to call ahead.

SEACOAST

Despite its diminutive size—only 18 miles in length—New Hampshire's seacoast is one of the state's most revered possessions. And rightly so, for its alliance of pounding surf, rocky headlands and tidepools, stately mansions and nature preserves offers a wealth of beauty and continuous intrigue.

Naturally the dramatic seaboard is a driver's paradise, which explains why it remains perpetually clogged with traffic. Warm summer breezes and sunshine draw the most crowds—particularly on weekends—though locals claim witnessing winter snow fall on the sand is truly a sight to behold.

Just north of the Massachusetts line, whiffs of salty marsh air will signify you've reached the town of **Seabrook**. Families favor this small oceanside nook for its amusement centers and pretty beaches, though the main attraction is **Seabrook Greyhound Park** (Route 107; 603-474-3065; admission). More than 1000 agile racing dogs call this fast track home, performing for bettors year-round.

Since 1976, Seabrook has received national attention because of the controversial **Seabrook Station Nuclear Power Plant** (Routes 107 and 1; 603-474-9521). Though citizens groups and the state of Massachusetts waged a long and costly battle to block the opening of the plant, it began operating in March 1990—three years after it was completed. The controversy continues today. For a closer look, the 1150-megawatt, $6.5 billion facility offers bus tours around the outside of its containment building, along with a ten-minute video of what's on the inside.

Traveling northward on Route 1A, you'll notice the scenery changing from marshlands to wide open beaches as you approach the seacoast's most animated stretch of sand, **Hampton Beach**. Mobbed by hundreds of thousands of vacationers every year, this heavily developed tract is one giant pleasure center, its nucleus an oceanside promenade that reels with constant activity.

Start out by walking the promenade, a three-mile human fiesta extending along Ocean Boulevard from Dumas Avenue to Hampton Beach State Park, taking in the well-strolled boardwalk jammed with trinket and T-shirt vendors, low-slung motels and the aroma of carnival food. This is people-watching at its best, a place where a whole spectrum of humanity—drifters, beach bums and the highbrow—converges on one long slab of concrete.

There's a constant hum of cars, joggers, bicyclists and curious sightseers who stop to ponder the **New Hampshire Marine War Memorial** (Ocean Boulevard and Nudd Avenue), a tribute to soldiers lost at sea. The granite statue features a forlorn maiden draped in rolls of stone cloth and clutching a wreath.

Great Boars Head (Ocean Boulevard and Dumas Avenue), a rocky bulkhead in the ocean, projects an imposing silhouette just north of Hampton Beach. Topped with grand old mansions and seaside homes, Boars Head is particularly intriguing at sunrise, when the day's first light and the ocean mist produce a surreal portrait.

To help get you organized with local sightseeing, stop by the **Hampton Beach Area Chamber of Commerce** (180 Ocean Boulevard; 603-926-8717), located a couple miles west of Hampton Beach in Hampton.

A ten-minute drive west will land you in the rural respite of **Applecrest Farm Orchards** (Route 88 west of Interstate 95, Hampton Falls; 603-926-3721), where 20,000 apple trees and two pumpkin patches bask along the hillsides. Show up from Labor Day to mid-October and pick your own, or check out the applemart, an 1812 barn stocked with apple ciders, pies, butter, sauce and other great-smelling goodies. During the summertime, strawberries, raspberries and blueberries come ripe for pickin'.

The best place to snag those plump, radiant raspberries is nearby **Raspberry Farm** (★) (Route 84 [also Kensington Road], three miles west of Route 1, Hampton Falls; 603-926-6604). There's no sign for this 60-acre spread, but it's a honey of a find. Wander through luxuriant patches, pluck your own berries and receive harvesting facts from the caretaker. Don't miss the market filled with raspberry candy, pies, ice creams, teas and breads.

Hop back over onto Route 1A, heading north along this roving high road flanked on one side by a turgid ocean and on the other by regal New England mansions known as "Millionaire's Row" for the old-monied families who live here.

The largest tract of undeveloped coastline exists at **Odiorne State Park** (Route 1A, Rye; 603-436-7406), which wanders along two oceanfront miles and covers 327 acres. Back in 1623, New Hampshire's first white settlers landed here and found thick vegetation and whistling winds. The park includes grave sites, old stone walls, remains of a formal garden and several World War II bunkers. A visitors center, open during summer, will fill you in on local history.

From here you can peer out to sea and spy the stony profile of the **Isles of Shoals**, an archipelago that harbors great mysteries and torrid tales of pirates, treasures and wrecked ships. In 1614, Captain John Smith dubbed the isles "barren piles of rocks with a few scrub cedar," and they've seen minimal change since. Blackbeard and Captain Kidd supposedly stashed their loot among the rocky crevices, the former abandoning his wife there in 1723. Some say her spirit still roams the shores.

The isles later drew many artists and writers, including Nathaniel Hawthorne and Childe Hassam. Today, you can visit the islands via the **New Hampshire Seacoast Cruises** (Rye Harbor State Marina, Route 1A, Rye; 603-964-5545; admission), which offers narrated tours seasoned with history.

Anchoring the northern end of the seacoast, **Portsmouth**, with its rich maritime history, has long played a critical role in the state's prosperity and development. Lying at the mouth of the Piscataqua River, the city seems like some profound old sage, locked in a bygone era yet quite vibrant and progressive at the same time.

Stone sidewalks and ivy-clad brick buildings, their walls holding two centuries of memories, gather stoically along the harbor. In central downtown, known as Market Street, immaculately restored 18th- and 19th-century enclaves mingle with sleek new highrises. Young artists and professionals continue to arrive from Boston, New York and Maine, polishing the cultural patina and dynamic night scenes of this port city.

There's so much to see here, and the best place to get organized is the **Greater Portsmouth Chamber of Commerce** (500 Market Street; 603-

436-1118). Pick up a *Portsmouth Trail*, a sort of treasure map leading to eight of New England's most well-preserved historic houses.

Built between 1716 and 1807, the houses vary architecturally and enjoy their own special museums and personalities. At the **John Paul Jones House** (43 Middle Street; 603-436-8420; admission), a 1758 Georgian design, you'll find a room arranged with marvelous wedding gowns worn in the 1800s as well as the oldest piano in the United States. There's also a collection of Civil War guns, a nifty wooden bathtub and oars and paddles from the South Seas.

George Washington dropped by a party at the **Governor John Langdon House** (143 Pleasant Street, Portsmouth; 603-436-3205) back in 1789. According to memos he later penned, George found the home quite warm and its proprietor, New Hampshire Governor John Langdon, very hospitable. Today, beautiful wood carvings and precious period furnishings adorn the interior.

One treat that goes with the Portsmouth Trail is the opportunity to meet the congenial docents (many are Portsmouth natives) who fill you with history and interesting anecdotes. Most of the trail homes close during winter and open only a few days each week the rest of the year, so call ahead.

To find out what makes Portsmouth tick, stroll southeast on Market Street down to **the docks**, where the Piscataqua River laps at the city's edge. Back in the 18th and 19th centuries, furniture makers, potters, coopers and shipbuilders gathered along the waterfront to ply their trades, while a flourishing sawmill industry provided Great Britain with thousands of ships' masts. Today, tugboats, fishing vessels and sailboats scoot across the dark waters that flow to nearby Kittery, Maine.

From here you can catch a harbor cruise or take a longer jaunt to the Isles of Shoals. Several outfits provide trips, including **Isles of Shoals Steamship Co.** (315 Market Street, Portsmouth; 603-431-5500) and **Portsmouth Harbor Cruises** (64 Ceres Street, Oar House Dock, Portsmouth; 603-436-8084).

Follow the water northwest to Marcy Street, where you'll discover Portsmouth's most prized gem, **Strawbery Banke** (entrance off Marcy Street south of Court Street; 603-433-1100; admission), site of the original settlement. Sheltered within ten acres of rambling gardens and colonial buildings is a wonderful lesson on New England architecture and the struggles and lifestyles of America's founders. The area gets its moniker from the profusion of berries found here in 1630 by the city's first English settlers.

Thanks to the foresight of local leaders, the banke's 38 buildings, dating from 1695 to 1945, were spared demolition in the 1950s. Every place offers some fascinating historical insight, and it takes a full day to see it all. There's the **Daniel Webster House**, where Webster and his wife, Grace, lived from

1814 to 1816, and the **First New Hampshire State House**, built in 1758 and the boyhood home of author Thomas Bailey Aldrich.

The 1766 **Pitt Tavern**, perhaps the banke's most historically significant building, was a meeting place for loyalists and then patriots. Revolutionary War strategies were devised within these walls, which now display ads from 1770s newspapers announcing those historic meetings.

Before you leave town, stop by the **North Cemetery** (Maplewood Avenue and Russell Street), purchased by the town for 50 pounds back in 1753. Buried on this unassuming grassy swell are John Langdon, former New Hampshire governor and signer of the Constitution, and General William Whipple, who signed the Declaration of Independence.

The coastline bustle takes on a gentler cadence as you head north of Portsmouth. **Dover,** a working class mill town with charm, was founded by fishermen during the early 1600s and remained independent until 1642, when it joined the Massachusetts Bay Colony. Route 9 trundles right through town, flanked by huge mansions sporting multiple chimneys, many built last century by wealthy mill owners.

You can mull over the town's beginnings at the **Woodman Institute** (182 Central Avenue, Dover; 603-742-1038), which houses an excellent display of New Hampshire memorabilia, wildlife and natural history.

Travel south on Route 108 to the college town of Durham, where the **University of New Hampshire** (Route 4; 603-862-1234) provides a restful haven for strolling. A third of the campus' 200 acres is a nature preserve, crisscrossed with walking trails and lakes perfect for winter ice skating.

West on Route 108, **Durham Landing** recalls the venue of a bloody battle in 1694, when more than 200 Indians attacked about 100 settlers, destroying their houses and garrisons along the Oyster River.

In nearby **Exeter,** you'll find a constant drum of traffic and human motion caused by the presence of exclusive **Phillips Exeter Academy** (Front and Water streets; 603-772-4311). One of the oldest and most renowned preparatory schools in the country, the academy has aged beautifully. Founded in 1783, the school boasts lovely brick buildings that lay masked in tangled ivy and are edged by green lawns and maple trees. Through the years, its hallowed halls have seen students like Daniel Webster, historian George Bancroft and Booth Tarkington.

MERRIMACK VALLEY

For the last two centuries, towns have grown alongside the Merrimack River, their inhabitants making use of its swift waters first for fishing, then for running textile mills. Today many of New Hampshire's 1.1 million residents call the Merrimack Valley home, making the area a seat of commerce and the state government.

This industrial region takes in a string of sizable cities, including Nashua, often called a "suburb" of nearby Boston, as well as the metropolis of Manchester and the capital, Concord. Spiraling out from these cities are bedroom communities and fragments of endearing rural areas.

Scenic Route 111 twists its way southwest from Exeter to one of the state's most peculiar phenomena. **America's Stonehenge** (Haverhill Road, off Route 111, North Salem; 603-893-8300; admission), also known as Mystery Hill, may seem to some like a big pile of rocks. To archaeologists and astronomers, who have pored over its contents for 50 years, it presents an unsolved puzzle. How old is it and where did it come from?

Spread across 30 acres, the erratic stone walls and bizarre rock formations are reputed to be an astronomical site of an ancient civilization— some claim it goes back 4000 years. England's Stonehenge it's not, but it's worth a look.

A short drive northward will land you in **Manchester**, New Hampshire's largest city with a population of over 100,000. Get a feel for this predominantly industrial city by strolling Elm Street, the main drag, lined with tired brick buildings and coffee shops and crowded with businesspeople. The **Greater Manchester Chamber of Commerce** (889 Elm Street; 603-666-6600) can point you to the best local sights.

It's enough just to stand outside and ogle the **Currier Gallery of Art** (192 Orange Street; 603-669-6144), its lustrous limestone facade and gorgeous mosaics resembling a Renaissance palace. But step inside and your eyes will feast on a series of archways and carved ceilings, then trail off to a substantial collection of artworks ranging from the Romanesque and Byzantine eras to modern times. There's also a fascinating collection of blown vases and mid-1800s photography. The Currier ranks as one of the finest small museums in the country, and the best news is, there's no admission.

The valley's other large city, **Concord**, is the state capital and probably best known for its Concord Coach. Drop by the **New Hampshire Historical Society Museum** (30 Park Street; 603-225-3381) for a peek at these painted wood carriages that helped connect America's East and West during the 19th century.

Pick up a copy of *The Coach and Eagle Trail* walking tour map, which will direct you to the city's choicest sites. They're available at the **Greater Concord Chamber of Commerce** (244 North Main Street, Carrigan Commons; 603-224-2508), which also supplies general information on Merrimack Valley.

Locals are fond of saying the carpets are rolled up at dusk in this very conservative city, and that holds some truth. The streets do clear out around dinner time, and except for a couple of watering holes, you'll be hardpressed to find much activity around here.

Of course, people who go to Concord looking for action will ultimately be sidetracked by the **State House** (107 North Main Street; 603-271-1110), a beautiful 1819 building coated in smooth granite and capped with a gold-plated dome. Inside this grand old edifice throbs the pulse of the city, setting the political, social and oftentimes cultural agenda for the entire state. It's the nation's oldest state house in which the legislature still occupies the original chambers.

After you've roamed the capital streets, head north for the wilds of **Canterbury Shaker Village** (Shaker Road off Route 106, Canterbury; 603-783-9511; admission). Stashed way out in an agrarian sanctuary, this insightful place will hold your attention for hours. Founded in the mid-1700s by one very progressive woman named Ann Lee, the religious sect lived in self-contained villages and aspired to create a utopia. Each of Canterbury's 22 buildings reflect principles of not wasting space: drawers are built into walls and wall pegs are used to eliminate floor clutter.

Exhibits display Shaker inventions, including the circular saw, clothespin, flat broom and metal pen point. There's also a Paul Revere bell, and a Shaker woman who has been living here since the late 1800s. Shakers believed in equal rights, shared work and celibacy, the last of which may have caused their virtual disappearance in the early 1900s.

MONADNOCK REGION

Curled along the southwest bend of New Hampshire, the Monadnock Region makes up a collage of all the virtues one associates with New England. White steepled churches and old covered bridges, itinerant country roads edged by miles of wild woods and lazy lakes, and lovable Currier and Ives towns all mesh to give this domain a warm Yankee flavor.

General stores, coffee shops and old-time pharmacies line the streets of **Peterborough**, founded in 1738 and believed to be the model for Thornton Wilder's *Our Town*. It's easy to see why Wilder may have taken to this mountain hamlet, which has spawned old saltbox homes and very congenial townsfolk.

A friendly caretaker at the **Peterborough Historical Society Museum** (19 Grove Street; 603-924-3235) will walk you through exhibits of the town's heritage and commercial interests, including thriving agriculture and manufacturing industries and, lately, electronics and publishing.

South on Route 202, **Jaffrey** purports to be the only Jaffrey in the world but more important is home to **Mount Monadnock**, which looms 3165 feet over the entire region like an astute sentinel. This imposing butte has become world famous as the most-climbed peak; myriads ascend its 30 miles of trails each year.

Henry David Thoreau and Ralph Waldo Emerson scaled Monadnock, now part of **Monadnock State Park** (off Route 124, Jaffrey; 603-532-8862; admission), where you'll also find an environmental center with historical and geological displays. (See the "Beaches and Parks" section in this chapter.)

Just east of the park on Route 124 you'll encounter Jaffrey's grandest manmade structure, the **Colonial Meeting House**. Its huge clock and bell tower, built in 1773, are framed by Mount Monadnock, an arousing sight for sure. Behind it rests a shaded cemetery and the graves of novelist Willa Cather and Amos Fortune, an African-born slave who purchased his freedom.

Some of Monadnock's choicest views can be had at **Cathedral of the Pines** (off Route 119, Rindge; 603-899-3300), a captivating wood and stone shrine built by local parents for a son who was slain in World War II. There are guided tours, offering views of the precious artifacts donated from countries around the world. A piece of the Rock of Gibraltar is there, along with a fragment from the Blarney Stone. You'll also see a holy ark that for several centuries resided in a Portuguese synagogue. When these church bells ring, they reverberate down the mountain and make melodies for miles.

Nature has surely blessed the Monadnock Region, and nowhere is it more evident than at **Rhododendron State Park** (Route 119, Fitzwilliam; 603-532-8862). Arrive in mid-July and be rewarded with 16 acres smothered in fields of wild rhododendrons. There's a one-mile trail through this riot of color. (See the "Beaches and Parks" section in this chapter.)

LAKE SUNAPEE–DARTMOUTH AREA

The area north of the Monadnocks—edged on the west by the Connecticut River—is a long, lazy union of cornfields and hills and big tufts of wildflowers tossed against Vermont's western border. Bustling mill towns, Ivy League schools and colonial hamlets bless this quiescent region. Inland, Lake Sunapee exists as a world unto itself, stretching ten glittering miles beaded with sylvan villages and a statuesque mountain crisscrossed with ski trails. Life here is lived slowly, a welcome pace for travelers seeking bona fide tranquility.

In the summer of 1777, General John Stark, commissioned by New Hampshire's legislature, organized a military force in **Charlestown**, the first town we visit in this area. That 1500-man troop marched westward across Vermont's border and defeated British-German forces in the famed Battle of Bennington. Now a **historical marker** (Route 12) pays homage to these local heroes.

Of course, Charlestown had its own share of skirmishes, as you'll see over at **The Fort at No. 4** (Route 11; 603-826-5700; admission), a re-creation of the great log stockade village built by pioneers in 1744. The fort suffered a three-day attack in 1747 by French and Indian forces, who were staved off by a 31-man garrison. Today, a medley of log cabins, barns, blacksmith shop and saw pit are displayed alongside original 18th-century tools. A nice trip back in time.

North of Charlestown, the industrial town of **Claremont** sustains a maze of centuries-old mills, weaving sheds and mansions. The folks in this blue-collar town are quite congenial. Stop by the **Claremont Chamber of Commerce** (Tremont Square, Main Street; 603-543-1296) for a walking tour map of the **Historic Mill District** (bounded generally by Main, Spring and Central streets).

From here, the **Lake Sunapee** area presents an obvious side trip and promises panoramas of small towns, rocky coastlines, rhythmic beaches and distinguished lighthouses. Tourism has certainly hit this outdoor playground, but it's not yet overwhelming. Start by rounding the lake on Routes 11 and 103, gazing across pristine waters at the windsurfers and small boats and gentle backdrop of forest-covered Mount Sunapee.

The **M.V. Mount Sunapee II** (Sunapee Harbor, off Route 11; 603-763-4030; admission) offers narrated tours of the lake from mid-May through mid-October. Go during fall foliage season to appreciate the area at its peak.

Head back east to Route 12A and the hushed town of **Cornish**, where you'll find the country's longest covered bridge. Just in sight of the cornfields, the **Windsor–Cornish Covered Bridge** arches 470 feet across the Connecticut River, linking Vermont and New Hampshire. Built in 1866, it was the third at the site, the first two falling victim to raging floodwaters. An ancient sign still warns today's travelers to "Walk your horse or pay a two-dollar fine."

Cornish became a cultural mecca during the late 1800s and early 1900s when a series of noted artists, writers, poets, musicians and sculptors arrived and formed the Cornish Colony. They included novelist Winston Churchill, poets Percy MacKaye and Witter Bynner, former *New Republic* editor Herbert Croly, landscape painter Willard Metcalfe and actress Ethyl Barrymore.

This mass migration was spurred by the 1885 arrival of Augustus Saint-Gaudens, one of America's foremost sculptors, whose works include the Admiral David Farragut statue in New York's Madison Square and the statue of Abraham Lincoln in Chicago's Lincoln Park.

Those artists and writers left Cornish long ago, but the **Saint-Gaudens National Historic Site** (Route 12A; 603-675-2175; admission) survives as a marvelous tribute to that great era. Saint-Gaudens' white brick house, his studios and beautiful formal gardens afford an endearing glimpse of a prolific life. High hedges of pine and hemlock and birch-lined paths are a testament to Saint-Gaudens affection for gardening, while originals and copies of his sculptures reveal his gift of hand.

North of Cornish throbs the valley's pulse, *the* reason why thousands pour into the region, and *the* place to go at night. Ivy League **Dartmouth College** (corner Main and Wheelock streets; 603-646-1110) exists in the archetypical New England college town of **Hanover**, although many would argue it *is* the town.

(Text continued on page 454.)

The Roads Less Traveled

They crisscross the state like a tangle of veins, concealing treasures that can be unlocked only by foraging through unfamiliar terrain. The **roads less traveled** (★) may not be the shortest way to get there from here, but you can bet they're the most scenic.

New Hampshire's byroads exist everywhere, yet they are chosen by very few. They link towns and lakes, clamber up mountains, trundle through isolated villages and navigate miles of wild forest. They sometimes lead to nowhere, but they always harbor a special prize: an 18th-century cemetery, a glistening pond or beach, a wildlife hollow or perhaps a vista to ignite your spirit.

To natives, these tireless country routes are known as "shunpikes," used to "shun" crowded main roads and highways. During fall-foliage time, shunpikes are ripe with brilliant splashes of red and gold and purple leaves that form one incredible spectacle. They undoubtedly provide the best leaf-peeping seats in the house.

You'll discover glorious back roads in all of New Hampshire's six regions:

When you get tired of battling traffic on Route 1A along the seacoast, take a jog on **Willow Avenue**, which starts just north of Little Boars Head, and relish a peaceful ride that explores grand 19th-century mansions and manicured lawns and gardens.

Few think of the seacoast in terms of fruit farms and old barns, but they're here, right along **Routes 88** and **84**. These roads twist through 1700s farmhouses and lonely stretches of pastureland, apple orchards and raspberry farms (where you can pick your own). Both begin in Hampton Falls. Take Route 88 from Route 1 to Route 101C; Route 84 starts at Route 1 and Wild Pasture Road.

New Hampshire's most populated region, the Merrimack Valley, manages to have some fine less-traveled roads. One of the best, **North Pembroke Road**, snakes through five miles of rural scenes between Route 28 near Allenstown and Route 106. It winds past a cornfield, wildflower farm, several log cabins, an old cemetery and a sap house where you can buy maple syrup.

The Monadnock Region shelters dozens of shunpikes, but perhaps the most beautiful is **Route 119**, which hovers near the Massachusetts border between Routes 202 and 10. Wend your way through the bucolic town of Rindge, then along remote Pearly Pond, where lakefront homes peek out from evergreen

forests and reflect against the water. At sunset, bright orange light bands ignite the pond and make it appear to be on fire.

For unmatched views of Mount Monadnock, veer off Route 124 onto **Webb Depot Road** in Marlborough. Here you'll spy an old stone bridge and wonderfully clear vistas across open fields toward the vast summit.

Way out in the boondocks of the Lake Sunapee-Dartmouth area, **Stage Road** is one shunpike worth finding. It scouts out the soul of this fertile region, fording three brooks and a covered bridge and miles of hardwoods and idle hills. You'll find this gem between Route 120 in Meriden and Route 12A.

In the Lakes Region, seek out **West Shore Road** along the west side of Newfound Lake. A series of hairpin curves through patched tar and forest, the road frequently squeezes between the mountains and lake and dispenses unobstructed water vistas.

Scenic Drive is like a secret pass along the west brink of Lake Winnipesaukee. Prized by local residents for its peaceful, uncongested feeling, this shady bypass affords breathtaking panoramas of one of New England's most prominent lakes. It picks up just south of Weirs Beach.

In the White Mountains, **Bear Notch Road** is a cool, misty tryst with nature, a natural high of rock grottos, evergreen spires and tiny patches of blue sky. Keep your eye out for the pretty sandy cove along the Swift River, a solitary respite for those lucky enough to uncover it. The road runs from the Kancamagus Highway at Passaconaway to Route 302.

Route 116 from Jefferson to Franconia is the archetype of New England tranquility. Cows graze on grassy knolls, windmills twirl across hayfields and old farmhouses repose against the mountains. During fall foliage season, maple and elm trees flail their yellow and orange canopies across the road, truly a sight to behold.

Before you take the roads less traveled, get a good map, and when in doubt, ask for directions at a local general store. Shunpiking is primarily a summer and fall sport, since many byroads are jammed with snow the rest of the year. Don't be afraid to venture upon these foreign passages. It's virtually impossible to get lost, and if you do, there's always someone to set your straight again.

There's no other way to say it: this campus is absolutely beautiful. It at once impresses with masterful old buildings that seem to go on forever. Stately red brick Federal styles stand next to softer Georgian architecture, erected in the late 1700s and so unaffected by age or wars or government strife.

Dartmouth was actually started in Lebanon, Connecticut in 1755 as a school for Native Americans, called Moor's Indian Charity School. A donation of 3300 Hanover acres—plus a generous sum of money from England's second Earl of Dartmouth—put the school on its current site in 1769. Its charter, dated that year, can still be found in the hallowed halls of **Baker Library** (603-646-2560), as can celebrated murals by Mexican painter José Clemente Orozco.

Two must sees while you're here: **The Hopkins Center for the Performing Arts** (Wheelock Street; 603-646-2422) and the **Hood Museum of Art** (Wheelock Street; 603-646-2808). The exterior of Hopkins resembles the Lincoln Center in Washington, while inside, barrelled ceilings, dramatic plant sculptures and abstract art combine to make this a work of great beauty.

Next door at the Hood, you'll encounter a splendid small museum fashioned after a 19th-century mill. Its diverse permanent collection features works by American and European masters such as Whistler, Eakins, Paul Revere, Picasso and Dürer. There are also excellent examples of African, Native American and Oceanic art, Assyrian reliefs and Chinese bronzes and ceramics.

Dartmouth's distinguished life, combined with nearly 5000 students, spills over nicely into the town of Hanover. Gracious tree-lined streets, underground pubs and polished shops make the town a great place for strolling but awful for parking. For more information, stop by the **Hanover Chamber of Commerce** (37 South Main Street; 603-643-3115).

LAKES REGION

Strewn across New Hampshire's heart like a strand of aquamarine beads, some 273 lakes range from sealike to pondlike. Skirted by olive hills and sheltered coves, the lakes weave about 39 towns and three cities and engender a slew of outdoor pursuits. Many of the lakes bear Indian names, including Kanasatka, Ossipee, Squam and Winnipesaukee, queen of them all.

One of the westernmost—and least visited—lakes is **Newfound,** whose fine sandy shores are covered by spiraling evergreens, sand and chimney-topped cabins. It lies along Route 3A.

The town of Hebron, on the northwest corner, harbors an unexpected treasure known as **Sculptured Rocks** (★) (unmarked gravel road off North Shore Road, just southwest of town center). This geological treat comprises dozens of undulating rocks, carved into designs by thousands of years of swift water. There's a frowning face, a seal, a camel and other interesting sculptures.

Tucked away in North Groton you'll find a darling clapboard cottage that was the **Mary Baker Eddy Home** (★) (Hall's Brook Road; 603-786-9943; admission). Eddy, an astute woman who founded the Christian Science religion and *Christian Science Monitor*, lived here from 1855 through 1860. The house has been nicely maintained and features her old iron pot-bellied stove and bed strung with ropes.

Eddy left North Groton in 1860 and moved to nearby Rumney, where her **colonial frame house** (★) (Stinson Lake Road; 603-786-9943; admission) rests behind a white picket fence. Here she penned the poem "Major Anderson and Our Country" in response to the Civil War and waged her own war against slavery. The late-1700s house is adorned with relics like a banjo clock, melodian piano and unusual wall drawers used to store ammunition.

From here, head east though the mountains and cut over to **Squam Lake**, speckled with fishing skiffs, sailboats and flocks of loons. Antique shops, decoy stores, rustic cabins and miles of tall trees give this area a peaceful milieu, a setting that no doubt attracted makers of the movie *On Golden Pond*, parts of which were filmed here.

Get close to those crazy loons at the **Science Center of New Hampshire** (Route 113, Holderness; 603-968-7194; admission), a 200-acre wildlife preserve near Squam Lake. From the trails here you can spot whitetail deer, black bears and bald eagles, visit ponds and a turtle island and view otter and raptor (bird of prey) exhibits. Kids love the hands-on nature exhibits, games and puzzles.

South on Route 25, **Meredith** is a very lucky place. Resting on a finger of Lake Winnipesaukee, it also touches Lakes Wicwas, Waukewan, Pemigewasset and Winnisquam. The town bears a charming demeanor with cosmopolitan touches like small shopping malls, art galleries and numerous restaurants and motels.

The **Meredith Chamber of Commerce** (south of Routes 3 and 25, across from the town docks; 603-279-6121) can provide area sightseeing information.

Drawing more people than any shopping mall, **Annalee's Doll Museum** (Reservoir Road and Hemlock Drive, Meredith; 603-279-6542; admission) stocks every doll imaginable (and even those you can't imagine). Displays are colorful and creative, featuring animals, presidents, Indians, spiders and witches, a Christmas section that would impress Santa himself, and much more.

But more fascinating is the story of Annalee, a housewife who began making dolls at her kitchen table in the 1950s. Turned down for a loan because banks considered her business impractical, Annalee worked at home

New Hampshire*

without electricity or running water and delivered dolls door-to-door from her VW Bug. Today, she's the area's largest employer.

Lake Winnipesaukee (pronounced Win-a-peh-SAW-kee), which translates as either "the smile of the great spirit" or "smiling water in a high place," is by far the state's largest and most impressive lake, spanning 72 square miles with 283 miles of shoreline and 274 habitable islands. If you care to explore the big lake by train, show up at **Winnipesaukee Railroad** (Route 3, Meredith; 603-528-2330; admission) and catch the next choo-choo south to Weirs Beach. Of course, you can hop on at the Weirs Beach station (Lakeside Avenue) for the return trip.

At **Weirs Beach**, New Hampshire's own little Coney Island, a well-roamed boardwalk extends several blocks along Lake Winnipesaukee, sprinkled with arcades and bumper cars, pizzerias and souvenir shops. There's also a dock where you board the **M.S. Mount Washington** (603-366-5531), a 230-foot passenger ship that glides across the lake on sightseeing excursions.

Winnipesaukee's southeastern joints shelter miles of wooded estuaries and broad water vistas, and you can wind your way around on Routes 11 and 28. You'll soon land in **Wolfeboro**, a busy little town wedged between Lakes Winnipesaukee and Wentworth. The village harkens back to 1763, when Governor John Wentworth built the country's first known summer resort here.

A fine source of local and regional information is **The Lakes Region Association** (1 Varney Road; 603-569-1117).

Scattered under some maple and elm trees, the **Clark House Historical Exhibit and Museum** (South Main Street; 603-569-4997) is a trio of buildings that recall the town's earlier years. There's a one-room clapboard schoolhouse built in 1805, a 1778 Cape Cod-style house with painted plank floors and marvelous antiques, and a late-1800s fire station with a shiny red fire engine.

One local resident nicely catalogued Wolfeboro goings-on, and the results can be seen at the **Libby Museum** (Route 109, Wolfeboro; 603-569-1035; admission), a natural history collection with a refreshing funky flavor. Here you'll find rows of stuffed birds, fish, animals and other native wildlife, relics from the long-destroyed Governor Wentworth mansion, an early American living collection, and great Indian artifacts.

Tucked in a forest off the road, **Abenaki Tower** (★) (Route 109 about five miles north of Wolfeboro in Melvin Village) is one place you can have all to yourself. The post-and-beam tower, erected by local townsfolk, will seduce you with stirring vistas of surrounding lakes and random wooded islands.

Castle in the Clouds (off Route 171, Moultonboro; 603-476-2352; admission) is an incredible place, cloaked in secrets and almost magical in design. Fashioned as a medieval castle and tangled in vines that droop from its awnings, it sits high on a mountain and gives the illusion that it's floating. The castle's maker, shoe magnate Thomas Gustave Plant, bought 6300 acres —including seven mountains—and paid $7 million to have his dream built between 1911 and 1914.

The 16 rooms and 8 bathrooms add to the mystique with their five- and eight-sided designs, doors of English lead, an enormous skylight, fluted windows and the curious absence of any nails. Plant had 12 closets and a secret reading room seen by others only after his death. At one time, he was worth $21 million. But on the advice of friend Teddy Roosevelt, Plant invested heavily in Russian bonds during the 1930s. In 1946, he died a penniless man.

WHITE MOUNTAINS REGION

A bold sweep of compelling peaks hover against New Hampshire's northern horizon. The White Mountains, which cover more than 760,000 acres, were named by 19th-century sailors for their brilliant crowns of snow framed by blue sky. Their drama—for centuries painted on landscape canvases—lies amid swift waterfalls, rocky gorges, rugged passes, granite silhouettes and one of the most stirring foliage displays in all of New England.

Towering above the region, broad Mount Washington is etched with jagged ravines and topped with rock-strewn grassy lawns. At 6288 feet, it's the highest peak east of the Mississippi and north of the Carolinas.

For the sightseer, the White Mountains insure exploration at its height. Roads are scenic, usually remote and almost always dotted with hidden treasure. Even short distances can take a while to cover on mountain roads, so always allow extra travel time.

Franconia Notch (off Route 93, Franconia) must be one of New England's seven wonders. At first glance, it is entirely overwhelming, offering dozens of natural phenomena and activities that could fill several days. A dramatic mountain gap caused by eons of glacial and river erosion, the notch lies within **Franconia Notch State Park's** 6500 acres and draws more than two million visitors annually.

Most sights can be accessed by scenic **Franconia Notch Parkway**, which *is* Route 93 for the eight-mile length of the park. The best place to start is the **Park Headquarters** (north end of Franconia Notch Parkway; 603-823-5563), which will help organize the numerous activities.

From the park headquarters, board the **Cannon Mountain Aerial Tramway** (603-823-5563; admission) for a five-minute cable car ride with panoramic views into Canada, Vermont, Maine and New York. The mountain, whose rocky profile resembles the barrels of a cannon, has the first engineered ski slopes in the United States.

Here also is the trail leading to pretty **Profile Lake**, headwaters of the Pemigewasset River. Pemigewasset, Indian for "swift waters," provides a reflecting basin for the granite profile of **Old Man of the Mountains**, his gnarled eyebrows and prominent chin looming 1200 feet up and keeping watch over the notch.

South on the Parkway, turn off for a look at **The Basin**. Formed 25,000 years ago, this large pothole of whirling azure waters and smooth rock is bored 15 feet into the Pemigewasset River. It has long intrigued spectators, including Henry David Thoreau in 1839 and Samuel Eastman in 1858, the latter calling it "a luxurious and delicious bath fit for the ablutions of a goddess."

The next stop south, **Flume Visitor Center** (Franconia Notch Parkway; 603-745-8391), is a state-of-the-art complex with historic films and photographs of the park. It's also the entrance to The Flume (admission), a dramatic chasm that plummets 800 feet to the base of Mount Liberty. Carved before the Ice Age by the rushing waters of the Pemigewasset River, The Flume is banked in rare flowers and mosses and takes two hours to visit fully.

After you leave the park, head northward to the town of **Franconia**, a lovely mountain burg where you'll find **The Frost Place** (off Route 116; 603-823-5510; admission). An old mailbox with the inscription "Frost" rests against a shady dirt lane, adjacent to the modest frame home where Robert Frost spent several years. Here he penned "Evening in a Sugar Orchard," "The Tuft of Flowers," "Mending Wall" and many other poems, gleaning inspiration from a backyard filled with sugar maples and wildflowers. A Poetry Trail winds through the area, right by the Mending Wall.

Sugar Hill, Franconia's sister town, is just as charming and bucolic. The Abenaki Indians once hunted in this area, which today is sprinkled with whitewashed colonial buildings and country stores. The **Sugar Hill Historical Museum** (Route 117; 603-823-8142) traces local ancestry to the 1600s and has two barns filled with farm tools, old photographs and other juicy relics.

Work your way eastward to Route 302, a picturesque mountain trail that crawls to Crawford Notch. A nice side trip from here, **Santa's Village** (Route 2, Jefferson; 603-586-4445; admission) is a tot's fairy-tale world. The place is laid out like a fantasyland, with gingerbread houses and miniature trains, sleigh rides, a "Rudolph-Go-Round" and "Frosty's Freezer."

Then on to **Crawford Notch**. Moose hunter Timothy Nash discovered the pass in 1771, reporting his find to Governor John Wentworth. Nash could have a large piece of land, Wentworth said, if he took his horse through the treacherous notch. Nash and a friend got the horse through, sometimes hoisting him over ledges with ropes. In 1775, the first notch road opened.

The geographical pinnacle here is the big guy himself, **Mount Washington**. Sighted from the ocean back in 1605, the mountain soars 6288 snow-capped feet across the skyline. It's reputed to be the most dangerous small mountain in the world, with wind-chill temperatures tantamount to those in Antarctica. The highest wind velocity ever recorded at a surface weather station (231 mph) was logged at Mount Washington.

Perhaps this fierce reputation only heightens the mountain's intrigue, as several hundred thousand people scale its slopes each year. One of the most popular ascents is on **The Mount Washington Cog Railway** (Route 302, Bretton Woods; 603-846-5404; admission), a three-hour round-trip with great vistas.

The other easy climb is via **Mount Washington Auto Road** (Route 16, Pinkham Notch in Gorham; 603-466-2222; toll), a considerable drive east then north from the railway. The road takes a relaxed zigzag up the northeast ridge named for Benjamin Chandler, who died of exposure on the mountain in 1856.

About 20 miles south, **North Conway** and **Conway** are the White Mountains' tokens of modern development. Actually it's the stretch of Route 16 *between* the two towns—jammed with outlet stores, fast-food joints, tacky tourist centers and condominiums—that seems so out of place in this earthy setting.

North Conway, which stays very crowded year-round, features quaint shops, restaurants and century-old buildings ringed with mountains. The **Mount Washington Valley Chamber of Commerce** (Main Street; 603-356-3171) is there to assist with your travels.

Smaller Conway is the gateway for the **Kancamagus Highway**, one of the most inspiring treks in the White Mountains. Officially it's pronounced Kan-ka-MAW-gus, but don't worry if you get it wrong—locals are quite used to abuse of this Indian word for "the fearless one." Cool and evergreen, the road is rimmed with shaded glens, scenic overlooks, ponds, rocky gorges and lovely waterfalls.

The top half of the White Mountains region, for the most part, still belongs to nature. This is wild country, an unremitting stretch of land peppered with jagged hills, lucid ponds and very green, very tall trees. There's only a handful of people up here, including some old-timers so firmly rooted they seem part of the very earth.

Between civilization and Canada, several geographic points do stand out. **Dixville** is known for two things: its extremely remote location and as the first town in the nation to vote in presidential elections. The town lies within **Dixville Notch**, a stunning, narrow mountain pass formed by glaciers. Mention you've been to Dixville Notch and the likely response is: "You went all the way up *there*?"

Indeed, this area truly is "at the end of the world"—New Hampshire's world, that is.

Shopping

This land of contrast sports shops ranging from glitzy to down-home to avant-garde. Surf emporiums and art galleries dot the seacoast, decoy and bait centers saturate the Lakes Region, and ski outlets and old-time general stores skirt the White Mountains. Don't forget, there's no sales tax in New Hampshire—a nice added touch to any shopping spree.

SEACOAST SHOPPING

For shopping in Hampton Beach, you can slum it on the boardwalk, bartering with vendors for jewelry, T-shirts and endless assorted souvenirs. The main action is along **Ocean Boulevard** from Nudd Avenue to Haverhill Avenue, where you can snag everything from leather jackets and tattoos to fake photo IDs and suntans (in tanning salons, of course).

North Hampton Factory Outlet Center (Route 1, North Hampton; 603-964-9050) is your place for discounted designer effects. There's a nice variety of items, from linens, shoes and coats to lingerie, toys, leather and ingenious kitchenware.

Bona fide mallaholics should head straight for **Newington Mall** (off Spaulding Turnpike, Newington; 603-431-4104), where some 70 stores and eateries provide quality browsing amid fashionable surroundings.

It's so much fun to stroll Portsmouth's colorful, funky shops that you'll likely forget you're spending money.

Spacious and entertaining, **G. Willikers!** (13 Market Street; 603-436-7746) has enough toys, stuffed animals, tiny clothes and other kiddie paraphernalia to make a tot go crazy.

Handmade paper sneakers, techno-romantic jewelry and "butt heads"—cigarettes painted with faces—are among the wonderfully crazy artwork at **Gallery 33** (111 Market Street; 603-431-7403).

Another great art stop, **N. W. Barrett Gallery** (53 Market Street; 603-431-4262) proffers wood, handblown glass and other crafts by local and nationally acclaimed artists. On the second floor, there's a fine art gallery with, among other gems, museum quality ship models.

It's Raining Cats and Dogs (13 Commercial Alley; 603-430-9566) is an animal lover's delight. Fake fire hydrants, doggie raincoats and cat-to-cat greeting cards are but a few of the crazy critter antics.

The avant-garde woman shops at **Le Club Boutique** (★) (25 Market Street; 603-433-4455), an underground emporium of offbeat postcards, nouveau attire and bangle earrings displayed in a pinball machine.

MERRIMACK VALLEY SHOPPING

For a good variety of locally produced art, check out **The Art Group, Inc.** (28 Hanover Street, Manchester; 603-669-6081). Acrylics and oils, photography and graphic abstracts, and white line block prints are featured here.

Remember *Archie*, *Superman* and *The Avengers*? You'll find them over at **Comics, Etc.** (796 Elm Street, Manchester; 603-647-4035), right next to all your other favorite classics.

Pompanoosuc Mills (3 Eagle Square, Concord; 603-225-7975) proffers contemporary and Shaker-style furnishings such as plush couches and silk arrangements and oak and pine dressers.

It's well worth a trip into the countryside to peruse **Shaker Gifts** (★) (at Canterbury Shaker Village, Shaker Road, Canterbury; 603-783-9511), an 1825 carriage house stocked with cookbooks, potpourri, handmade sweaters and crafts.

MONADNOCK REGION SHOPPING

Wanna feel better? **Maggie's Marketplace** (14 Main Street, Peterborough; 603-924-7671) supplies natural foods like organic corn chips and no-cholesterol ice cream, plus nifty kitchen gadgets and cookbooks.

Your literary layover is **The Toadstool Bookstop** (3 Main Street, Peterborough; 603-924-3543), a small-town shop jammed with everything from warship catalogues and world radio handbooks to New England journals.

It's mall shopping 19th-century style at **Colony Mill Marketplace** (West Street, Keene; 603-357-1240). Located in a recycled 1838 mill, the aesthetic trading center houses a medley of stores offering clothes, gifts, cards, home decor items and books.

LAKE SUNAPEE–DARTMOUTH AREA SHOPPING

Powerhouse Mill Arcade (Glen Road off Route 12A, West Lebanon; 603-643-1992) is like a fairyland, adorned with barreled ceilings and colored strands of light. The stores are imaginative and often feature a single theme. **Artifactory** (603-298-6010), for instance, leans toward the unusual with Egyptian art T-shirts, colorful fabric plants and tie-dyed socks. **Home-Scapes** (603-298-6038) has furniture, glassware, rugs and other accessories for home styles ranging from colonial to contemporary to high-tech. The **Music Gallery** (603-298-5210) is a record/art store where you'll find compact discs, tapes and an extensive collection of music books as well as T-shirts, posters and picture frames.

Hanover, home of Dartmouth College, presents numerous shopping possibilities, particularly along Main Street, where upscale shops are plentiful. **Dupré**, in the Galleria (80 South Main Street; 603-643-9474) has a collection of nouveau women's wear, from polka-dot jackets to provocative swimwear and shiny shorts. In the same plaza, **Trillum** (603-643-9484) sells jewelry and natural body products.

If cooking is your passion, stop in **Board & Basket** (45 South Park Street, Hanover; 603-643-6920) for the latest kitchen gadgets, cookbooks and gourmet foods.

LAKES REGION SHOPPING

You'll snore better after a visit to **Rainy Nights Futons** (Main Street, Ashland; 603-968-3146), which stocks all types of Oriental bedding and big, fluffy pillows.

Tucked in a 1700s roadside barn, **William F. Dembiec Antiques (★)** (Routes 3 and 25, Holderness; 603-968-3178) is a gem of a place with old brass mirrors, porcelain, '50s and '60s baseball cards and other fun collectibles.

A friendly craftsman owns **The Decoy Shop (★)** (Route 3, Holderness; 603-968-3950), where you can pick up ornamental ducks, loons, swans, geese and other carved replicas of lake inhabitants.

Mill Falls Marketplace (Route 3, Meredith) is a pretty lakeside complex where Christmas and bath shops mingle with sports stores, candy kitchens and art galleries. One of the largest stores here is **Country Carriage** (603-279-6790), a purveyor of American folk art, Yankee candles and other fine New England gifts.

WHITE MOUNTAINS REGION SHOPPING

Don't miss a visit to **The League of New Hampshire Craftsmen** (Route 112, Lincoln; 603-745-2166), which has several shops across the state. The league turns out quite an array of attractive works including pottery, woodwork, paintings, silver, porcelain and sweaters.

If it's nippy out, drop by **Jack Frost** (Route 16, Jackson; 603-383-4391) for earmuffs, colorful sweaters, leather goods and skiwear.

Conway and North Conway extend endless shopping opportunities. Quaint, eclectic marts line Main Street in North Conway, while Route 16 between the two towns is shoulder-to-shoulder with factory outlets and novelty stores.

North County Angler (Route 16, North Conway; 603-356-6000) combines a wildlife art gallery with loads of fly-fishing paraphernalia. This is also your spot for expert local fishing advice.

Nightlife

Despite its stringent liquor laws—which mandate that bars must be part of restaurants, ski lodges or similar businesses—New Hampshire manages an ample share of lively establishments. Even more alive are top-quality performing arts, which extend into even the most remote burroughs.

SEACOAST NIGHTLIFE

The 1600-seat **Casino Ballroom** (169 Ocean Boulevard; 603-929-4100), one of those great old big-band clubs built in the 1920s, headlines top-name rock-and-roll, jazz, country-and-western and comedy.

An under-25, high-beach-fashion crowd shows up at the **Electric Wave** (85 Brown Avenue, Hampton Beach; 603-926-8666), a cavernous bilevel disco with a giant dancefloor and occasional comedians and live bands. Cover.

Nautical decor and contemporary tunes set the scene at **The Pelican Club** (at the Galley Hatch Restaurant, Route 1, Hampton; 603-926-6152). Live music plays Fridays and Saturdays at this popular, upscale oasis.

You can dance your heart out at **Rosa's** (80 State Street, Portsmouth; 603-436-9715), a swanky speakeasy that jams with Dixieland, rock-and-roll and rhythm-and-blues. Cover.

Have a home-brewed beer (and watch it being brewed) at **Portsmouth Brewery** (56 Market Street; 603-431-1115). On weekends, you can also hear local rock-and-roll bands in the downstairs lounge.

Nautical in style, **Dolphin Striker** (15 Bow Street, Portsmouth; 603-431-5222) resides in an underground tavern built curiously around a spring-fed well. Feed the exotic fish that swarm the well, or relax to piped-in reggae or occasional live piano music.

Set in a 19th-century brick brewery, the beautiful **Bow Street Theatre** (125 Bow Street, Portsmouth; 603-433-4472) stages Shakespearean plays and other drama, major musicals and comedy in an intimate 260-seat pit theater.

MERRIMACK VALLEY NIGHTLIFE

The best place to catch top-quality international and national plays is the **Palace Theatre** (80 Hanover Street, Manchester; 603-668-5588), an ornate, 883-seat downtown arena that also hosts ballet, concerts and magic shows.

There's high-energy dancing at **High 5** (555 Canal Street, Manchester; 603-626-0555), which hosts nightly acts ranging from local comedy to karaoke sing-alongs.

Thumbs (Thursday's Restaurant, 6 Pleasant Street, Concord; 603-224-2626) is a dim, underground gathering spot for politicians and a crowd of folks in their 20s. Live blues, rock or folk is featured most nights. Cover.

MONADNOCK REGION NIGHTLIFE

One of the most respected theater troupes in New England, the Peterborough Players perform at the **Sterns Farm** (Middle Hancock Road, Peterborough; 603-924-7585) in a marvelous converted barn.

A solid local hangout, the **Coppertop Lounge** (Boiler House Restaurant, Route 202 South, Peterborough; 603-924-9486) is a chic place to bend an elbow. Depending on the bartender's mood, you'll hear taped jazz, blues or contemporary.

Romantic interludes await at **Jake Copley's** (Route 202 in Northgate Plaza, Peterborough; 603-924-3344), where a brass and glass decor provides the atmosphere for acoustic and contemporary music.

LAKE SUNAPEE–DARTMOUTH AREA NIGHTLIFE

The historic **Claremont Opera House** (Main Street in Tremont Square, Claremont; 603-542-4433), with its arched stained glass and scrolled columns, is a superb place to see regional and national opera, orchestra, ballet and musicals.

There's a folk and rock-and-roll lineup at the **Tower Lounge** (Main Street in Tremont Square, Claremont; 603-542-6515), a second-floor restaurant bar with worn formica tables and a small dancefloor.

Dartmouth College nightlife sizzles on the underground circuit. Among the best below-ground pubs, **Five Olde Nugget Alley** (Olde Nugget Alley, off Wheelock Street, Hanover; 603-643-5081) features a long, battered pine bar, a round of pine tables and piped-in contemporary music.

Step down a flight of stairs to **Peter Christians Tavern** (39 South Main Street, Hanover; 603-643-2345), a cozy establishment with high-back wood booths and a perpetual crowd of lively students.

Dartmouth College's dazzling **Hopkins Center for Performing Arts** (Wheelock Street, Hanover; 603-646-2422) hosts major drama, musicals, concerts and films in two auditoriums.

LAKES REGION NIGHTLIFE

Don't miss the one-man, six-piece band at **The Common Man** (The Common Man restaurant, Main Street, Ashland; 603-968-7030), a lively place featuring '50s-style couches, shag lamps and dart boards.

Occupying an old train car, **Red Rib Smokehouse** (Route 3, Meredith; 603-279-7777) sizzles nightly with a mix of recorded Top-40s, oldies, blues and reggae. Occasionally, a live band plays. Wooden booths cozy under a solarium overlooking Meredith Lake and a stunning mountain range—not a shabby venue. Cover.

The Barnstormers (off Route 113, Tamworth Village; 603-323-8500), New Hampshire's oldest professional theater group, perform a variety of summer comedy, mystery and drama in an old barn.

Farm tools, wagon wheels and an American flag set a rustic tone at **Chequers Villa** (Route 113, Tamworth; 603-323-8686), a friendly, crowded nook with saucy tunes and excellent pub grub.

WHITE MOUNTAINS REGION NIGHTLIFE

If you're under 30, the place to hang is **The Down Under** (Main Street, Plymouth; 603-536-3983), a college bar with minimal decor but outstanding rock-and-roll bands and a dancefloor that cooks. Cover.

The **North Country Center for the Performing Arts** (Route 112, Lincoln; 603-745-2141), located in a partially rehabbed 1800s machine shop, presents musicals, concerts and stellar drama.

Arrive before 9 p.m. at **The Red Parka Pub** (Route 302, Glen; 603-383-4344) or you'll probably stand in line. The wildly popular après ski bar hosts rock-and-roll bands that keep things cranking.

Wear a kilt and a drink is on the house at **Scottish Lion Pub** (Scottish Lion Restaurant, Route 16, North Conway; 603-356-6381), a mellow joint with brick walls, candlelit tables and piped-in classical music.

Horsefeathers (Main Street, North Conway; 603-356-2687) wins hands-down as the hippest mountain pub, a genuine rooting place with sports decor, crazy bartenders and a rough pine bar where patrons stand three-deep.

Looking like a low-slung barn, **Up Country Saloon** (Route 16, North Conway; 603-356-3336) jams with loud rock-and-roll and mixes Tiffany lamps and greenery with pinball machines and a rambling oak bar.

CHAPTER NINE

Maine

Mention you're going to Maine and you get all sorts of envious looks. People automatically envision the Andrew Wyeth landscapes, the pine-scented woods, the candy-striped lighthouses, the huge platters of lobster and baskets of steamers. Over the years, its name has practically become synonymous with the word "vacation." License plates even read "Vacationland." Indeed, visitors can find many opportunities to vacate cluttered lives in this spectacularly scenic New England state.

Maine has the Ice Age to thank for its smashingly good looks. Massive glaciers left over 6000 lakes and ponds and 32,000 miles of rivers and streams in their wake as well as the towering peaks of Cadillac Mountain and Mt. Katahdin (the latter stretches about a mile high). The coast is made of a series of deeply cut indentations and narrow peninsulas and has more offshore islands than you can count. Measure the seaboard in a straight line and you come up with about 230 miles. Count every inch of shoreline and it's an amazing 3478 miles.

The state's name supposedly came from sailors' use of the term "main" for the mainland apart from the offshore islands. In later years, Maine was given the nickname "Pine Tree State" because nearly 90 percent of its land is covered with fragrant evergreens.

Maine's beauty, however, is not skin deep. It's home to some 1.23 million year-round residents, a startlingly small number when you consider it's as big as all of the other New England states put together. The people who live here are really what make this state so special. Real Mainers—or State-of-Mainers as the most patriotic refer to themselves—are full of pride. They're also very individualistic and don't put on any airs. They are who they are, whether you like it or not. And they're tough. While carloads of tourists and summer residents pack up and head south at the end of the summer, they prepare for the long, cold winters ahead. Many Mainers also devotedly preserve the traditions of the past. You see crafts such as wooden boatbuilding, quilting and weaving still very much alive all over the state.

The biggest concentration of the population is clustered around the harbor-perched city of Portland, the state's commercial and cultural center. Established in 1624, Portland was destroyed four times, twice by Indians in the 1600s, once by the British in 1775 and again by the great fire of 1866. Today the phoenix—the mythical Egyptian bird that rises from the ashes of destruction—is the city symbol.

A very progressive city, Portland has attracted people from across America as well as immigrants from Greece, Cambodia, Jamaica, Finland and a host of other countries. Maine's statewide residents are a mix of nationalities as well. These include Abenaki Indians whose ancestors can be traced back 2000 years and Europeans whose forefathers settled along the coast in the beginning of the 1600s.

Most historians believe that Maine was sighted by Vikings as early as the year 1000, but since no real evidence can be found, the credit of discovering the area has been passed along to others. It is believed that John Cabot saw the Maine coast on his second voyage to the New World in 1498, thereby establishing all future British claims to the land. However, the first European colony was established at the mouth of the St. Croix River in 1604 by French explorers Sieur de Monts, Pierre du Guast and Samuel de Champlain. The colony didn't last very long, however. In 1605, England's King James I included the area in the land grant given the Plymouth Colony.

The years that followed were marked by territorial struggles between the English, French and Indians. In spite of its bitterly cold winters, Maine had an abundance of natural assets to fight over, including dozens of deep-water harbors, timber-filled forests, navigable inland rivers and waters teeming with fish. The fighting eventually led to the 18th-century French and Indian Wars. After the British were victorious, what would be the State of Maine became a part of the Commonwealth of Massachusetts. Not until 1820 was Maine admitted to the union as a free state.

About 50 years later, word got out that Mount Desert Island and its then-sleepy little fishing village of Bar Harbor was an exceptionally beautiful place. Indeed, with its rock-hewn shores and sky-poking mountains, it's certainly spectacular. Before long, the island became an exclusive retreat for wealthy and powerful American families who came by steamboat and train. Folks with names like Rockefeller and Vanderbilt built sprawling summer "cottages" on bluffs overlooking the sea. They hired locals to staff these homes and the well-appointed yachts on which they hosted glamorous cocktail parties. By the turn of the century, there were over 200 magnificent mansions on Mount Desert Island. Other areas along the coast south of Bar Harbor started to become popular summering spots as well, as trains brought in the moneyed people looking to build by the sea.

These golden years did pass, however, their demise brought by the Depression and World War II. But the final blow to Bar Harbor's days of grandeur came when a fire broke out in 1947 and burned over a third of Mount

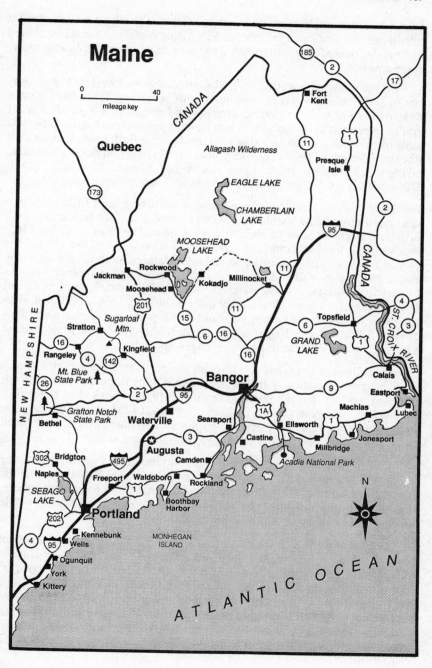

Maine

0   40

mileage key

CANADA

Quebec

Allagash Wilderness

Fort Kent

Presque Isle

EAGLE LAKE

CHAMBERLAIN LAKE

MOOSEHEAD LAKE

Rockwood

Jackman

Moosehead

Kokadjo

Millinocket

Topsfield

GRAND LAKE

CANADA

ST. CROIX RIVER

Calais

Eastport

Lubec

NEW HAMPSHIRE

Sugarloaf Mtn.

Stratton

Kingfield

Rangeley

Mt. Blue State Park

Grafton Notch State Park

Bethel

Bangor

Waterville

Searsport

Machias

Castine

Ellsworth

Jonesport

Millbridge

Acadia National Park

Bridgton

Naples

SEBAGO LAKE

Freeport

Waldoboro

Camden

Rockland

Augusta

Portland

Kennebunk

Wells

Ogunquit

York

Kittery

Boothbay Harbor

MONHEGAN ISLAND

N

ATLANTIC OCEAN

Desert Island, including nearly 70 of its estates. The island was eventually rebuilt but in a less-opulent fashion. Affordable motels and hotels sprouted like mushrooms after a rain, making the area much more accessible to average tourists.

Maine's coastal beauty is still what attracts most travelers today. Dozens of little fishing villages here burst with character. Some have gone a little overboard trying to attract tourists and are a bit too gussied up. If you're interested in seeing places that haven't sprung into tourist hubs, you have to be willing to go an extra yard. Follow the little roads that turn off like stray thoughts. They may take you to a tiny village on the sea. Consider taking a boat trip out to an island you've never heard of. And go north! The coast above Mount Desert Island is still largely undiscovered.

Bear in mind that Maine is enormous, so taking on a little piece at a time is all any visitor should do. We've broken it up into four areas, each of which might be seen in about a week's time. The coast is divided into two sections, the Southern Coast (between Kittery and Bucksport) and the Downeast Coast (from Castine to Calais). Maine's most visited area, the Southern Coast is well endowed with hotels, restaurants and other facilities geared for tourists. It's also home to some of the state's most beautiful beaches. The Downeast Coast is not quite as busy and less developed, with the exception of Bar Harbor, an enormously popular vacation hub. This chapter follows Route 1 right up the coast, taking you to the major tourist towns as well as the little-known villages and islands.

Our third section takes you through the northern woods, which Henry Thoreau praises endlessly in his book *The Maine Woods*. An area of unmatched wild beauty, it's home to the state's highest peak (Mt. Katahdin), the biggest state park (Baxter) and the largest lake (Moosehead). Its year-round residents include hearty-souled State of Mainers and a large black bear population, in addition to moose, bobcats and scores of birds.

Our final section—the western lakes and mountains—takes you to the White Mountains and the sprawling Indian-named lakes that are set in hills like precious gems. The woods that wrap around them teem with moose, deer and all sorts of songbirds. There are also several picture-perfect little villages crammed with antique and craft shops.

Like all the New England states, Maine has four distinctly different seasons. Summer—especially July and August—is the customary time to visit. That's when the bays swell with pleasure boats and towns open up like roses. Though the weather is predictably unpredictable (one day the harbor is bundled in mist, the next it's clear as a window), it's always lovely. Temperatures all over the state remain comfortable, hovering around 70° in the daytime. Nights, however, can get nippy, especially along the coast where the breezes off the sea can be chilling.

Some say autumn is the very best time to visit Maine. The summer-only residents have packed up and left. The partying vacationers are back at work and in school. The real full-time Mainers reappear. You're no longer one of many tourists but an appreciated guest. The weather is often phenomenally beautiful, with blue skies and sunshine. And, of course, you can see the fall colors. Spring, too, is appealing, as new life appears.

Winter brings on a whole array of snow-based activities, including great skiing, especially in the northern and western parts of the state. Maine's long and cold winters create a died-and-gone-to-heaven land for winter sports enthusiasts.

In this chapter, we introduce you to just some of Maine's attractions. In many ways, this is a very American state, but in others it feels almost like a foreign country. One visit and you'll inevitably feel compelled to return.

Easy Living

Transportation

ARRIVAL

The most common way to enter Maine is from the south, on **Route 95**, the interstate. It's the fastest way to reach Portland, Augusta and Bangor. It's also the quickest way to get to most of the coastal resort areas between the border of New Hampshire and Mount Desert Island, and to the edge of the northern woods.

An alternative to Route 95 is **Route 1**, which roughly runs along the coast from Kittery to Calais. At Calais, it turns north and follows the Canadian border all the way up to Fort Kent in the state's northern reaches. A word of caution: Route 1 is notoriously slow, especially in the south during the summer months, when tourists are traveling and stopping at the scores of factory outlets that line it. It's also hilly in parts (especially in the north), which makes passing quite dangerous.

You can easily reach towns throughout the southern half of the state on the well-maintained webwork of roads that cover it. The north is a bit more difficult, however. There are times when you may have to go north, south, north, south just to get from a western town to an eastern town. Fortunately, the scenery in these parts more than compensates. One more note about the north. Once you get north and west of Millinocket, you'll spend most of your time on dirt roads. Some are downright rough and rugged. And some are private and require permits.

BY AIR

There are two major airports in the state: the **Portland International Jetport** and the **Bangor International Airport**.

Portland is served by four major carriers—Continental Airlines, Delta Air Lines, United Airlines and USAir—plus several regional airlines. Flying into Bangor are Delta Air Lines and United Airlines, as well as regional air carriers.

At both, you'll find plenty of taxis to take you into town.

In Portland, you can bus in with the **Metro Bus Company** (207-774-0351). There are also small airports in Auburn/Lewiston, Augusta, Bar Harbor, Frenchville, Presque Isle, Rockland and Waterville—all serviced by either Continental Express or Valley Airlines.

BY BUS

Greyhound Bus Lines (207-772-6587) cruises up Route 1, stopping in Portland, Yarmouth, Freeport, Brunswick, Bath, Wiscasset, Rockland, Camden, Searsport, Lewiston, Augusta, Bangor and other points.

BY BOAT

From Nova Scotia, Canada, you can ferry to Portland on one of the **Prince of Fundy Cruises** (207-775-5616). Arrivals and departures are from Commercial Street near Million Dollar Bridge.

CAR RENTALS

Unless you're planning to stay put in one hotel or in one city for the duration of your trip, you'll most likely need a car in Maine.

At the Portland airport, you'll find **Avis Rent A Car** (207-874-7500), **Hertz Rent A Car** (207-774-4544), **Budget Rent A Car** (207-772-6789), **National Car Rental** (207-773-0286) and **Thrifty Car Rental** (207-772-4628).

At the Bangor airport, there are **Avis Rent A Car** (207-947-8383), **Budget Rent A Car** (207-945-9429), **Hertz Rent A Car** (207-374-5519), **National Car Rental** (207-773-0286) and **Thrifty Car Rental** (207-942-6400).

PUBLIC TRANSPORTATION

For getting around Portland on your own, there's a very good bus system called the **Metro** (207-774-0351). It has regularly scheduled routes throughout the greater Portland area. There's also the **Portland Trolley** (207-772-6829), which circles through the downtown area.

TAXIS

Several taxi companies serve the Portland International Jetport, including **Town Taxi Co.** (207-773-1711). In Bangor, try **Barons** (207-945-5671) or **Checker** (207-942-5581).

BOAT TOURS

Hundreds of boat companies along the Maine coast offer excursions that range from one-hour cocktail cruises to day-long whale-watching expeditions to week-long cruises on historic windjammers. You'll find the biggest concentrations of such companies in Kennebunkport, Boothbay Harbor, Rockland and Rockport, and on Mount Desert Island. Keep in mind that these are generally offered only in the summer months. Here are a few to try:

In Kennebunkport, you can go whale-watching aboard the 65-foot **Nautilus** (207-967-5595) or glide by the presidential complex and other lovely oceanfront homes on the **Elizabeth II** (207-967-5595), a narrated sightseeing cruise. Both leave from the Arundel Shipyard.

Cap'n Fish Boat Trips (Pier 1, Boothbay Harbor; 207-633-3244) is just one of many excursion companies competing for your attention on the Boothbay Harbor wharf. They offer cocktail cruises, sunset cruises and nature-viewing trips that spot seals, exotic birds and whatever else decides to fly or swim by.

Penobscot Bay is where you'll find Maine's tall-masted windjammers. You can spend three days or a week sailing on one, staying in comfortable cabins and eating like royalty. Contact the **Maine Windjammer Association** (P.O. Box 317, Rockport, ME 04856; 207-374-5400) for a complete listing of all the possibilities.

For a scenic cruise to the legendary artist colony of Monhegan Island, head south from Thomaston to Port Clyde and board the **Laura B.** (207-372-8848). The cruise leads past seabird rookeries to idyllic Monhegan Island. Here you'll learn the fascinating story of renaissance man Rockwell Kent and see the summer home of artist Jamie Wyeth.

From Stonington, the **Miss Lizzie,** Isle au Haut's mail boat, doubles as a sightseeing cruise boat. Ninety-minute cruises depart from the Atlantic Avenue Dock (207-367-5193). **Palmer Day IV** also departs from Stonington and offers cruises around the waters of Penobscot Bay.

On Mount Desert Island, there are a number of boating possibilities, including lobster fishing with **Acadia Boat Tours & Charters, Inc.** (60 West Street, Bar Harbor; 207-288-9505), whale-watching with **Acadian Whale Watcher** (Bar Harbor; 207-288-9776) and nature-viewing with **Sea Princess Naturalist Cruises** (Northeast Harbor; 207-276-5352).

Hotels

Maine accommodations come in all sizes and shapes, from conventional sea-viewing motels to European-style inns. Most are concentrated along the coast, predominantly in the southern and midcoast regions. Many places are seasonal, open only during the warm-weather months, so you should call ahead if you're traveling during the late fall or winter.

SOUTHERN COAST HOTELS

You have two options at **Dockside Guest Quarters** (Harris Island Road, York; 207-363-2868). You can stay either in the main house (a stately 19th-century building with five guest rooms) or in one of the 17 modern shore-hugging units. If it's charm you're after, go for the main house, where rooms are individually decorated with antiques and floral fabrics. Two rooms share a bath while the other three have private baths. Choose one of the so-called "units" for extra privacy. Though not exactly oozing with charm, they're very separate. Budget to moderate.

In a state rife with bed and breakfasts, **The Wild Rose of York** (Long Sands Road, York; 207-363-2532) is a real standout. The house itself is an eye-catcher, an 1814 sea captain's house surrounded by fragrant gardens. Inside, there are three guest rooms filled with antiques and New England folk art. The innkeepers, Fran and Frank Sulliver, really make the place special by offering nature walks and afternoon teas. Moderate.

Though right on Route 1, **Cape Neddick House** (Route 1, Cape Neddick; 207-363-2500) provides the kind of hospitality and homeyness you'd expect to find in the deep woods of Maine. There are six antique-furnished bedrooms in this 110-year-old farmhouse, each named after one of the New England states. You can't help but feel as if you're living back in the 1800s when you stay here. Moderate.

Walking into the **Wooden Goose Inn** (Route 1, Cape Neddick; 207-363-5673), you almost feel as if you've been thrown a life preserver, rescuing you from the tourist clutter that has colonized this part of the Maine coast. The Wooden Goose, indeed, is an island of elegance in a sea of souvenir merchants. All six rooms are exquisitely furnished with antiques and Early American pieces but have some modern comforts as well, such as air conditioning and wall-to-wall carpeting. The food competes for your attention, however, starting with huge breakfasts and ending with afternoon teas that blow the British teas right out of the water. Deluxe.

It would be great if everyone were lucky enough to spend a night or two at the **Morning Dove** (30 Bourne Lane, Ogunquit; 207-646-3891), a restored 1860s farmhouse. There are six guest rooms, all handsomely decorated with country antiques. Breakfast is always a treat to look forward to, set out on the porch. The beaches, the galleries and everything else that makes Ogunquit special are all within walking distance. Moderate to deluxe.

A former Catholic church, **The Haven** (Church Street, Wells; 207-646-4194, 617-965-2845 in winter) is now a delightful bed and breakfast lovingly operated by the La Rose family. Two of the eight rooms share a bath, while the common areas include a lobby with a three-story cathedral ceiling. You'll find a direct view of the ocean and a beach only 200 steps away. Moderate.

One of the most wonderful things about the **Captain Lord Mansion** (Pleasant and Green streets, Kennebunkport; 207-967-3141) is that it successfully combines impeccably good taste with true comfort. Designed by Captain Lord, a wealthy merchant and shipbuilder, it's a stunning three-story Federal-style building that dates back to 1812. Inside, it has all the hallmarks of a ship carpenter's craft, including a suspended elliptical staircase, blown-glass windows and mahogany doors with brass locks. Each of its 16 rooms has been thoughtfully decorated with period-reproduction wallpaper, exquisite antiques and four-poster beds. Many have working fireplaces; all have private baths. Deluxe to ultra-deluxe.

For Bush-watchers, **Cape Arundel Inn** (Ocean Avenue, Kennebunkport; 207-967-2125) is the place to be—it overlooks the presidential compound. But even if you couldn't care less about the Summer White House, it's a good choice. Propped up on cliff-hanging Ocean Avenue, it's just one of several eye-poppingly beautiful shingle-style buildings that line the road. From the front porch and some of the 13 rooms, you have a wide-angle view of Walker's Point (the presidential compound) and the Atlantic all around. Deluxe.

During the month of August, when George Bush is in town, the **Shawmut Inn** (Turbot's Creek Road, Kennebunkport; 207-967-3931) turns into a buzzing hive of reporters, all stepping over one another trying to get an angle on the president's summer vacation. It makes sense that the Bushes would choose this property. It's set apart from the rest of the village on its own 22 oceanfront acres. Its 98 unimaginatively decorated rooms are spread out in the eight buildings on the property. Deluxe to ultra-deluxe.

Back in the late 1800s when wealthy out-of-staters were flocking to Maine to build their summer houses, the **Black Point Inn** (Prouts Neck; 207-883-4126) came into being. Like many of its neighbors, it's a massive shingled building complete with a front porch and far-reaching ocean views. The main house has 60 guest rooms, and there are another 20 in cottages on the grounds. Rooms are decorated very simply with white crewel bedspreads, crisp white curtains and rock maple beds. The ultra-deluxe price tag includes three meals.

The **Inn at Park Spring** (135 Spring Street, Portland; 207-774-1059) is the type of place that doesn't have to advertise. Its seven rooms are usually filled with found-it-by-word-of-mouthers. Owned by the proprietors of the well-known Horsefeathers Restaurant, it's a three-story townhouse very elegantly furnished. Some rooms have ornamental fireplaces with decks or terraces. Deluxe.

The **Inn on Carleton** (46 Carleton Street, Portland; 207-775-1910) not only sounds like a place you'd find in London but looks like it, too. This townhouse in the Western Promenade part of town offers seven rooms lavishly decorated with Victorian antiques. Moderate for shared bath, deluxe for private.

If you want the big-city hotel experience, try the **Sonesta Portland Hotel** (157 High Street, Portland; 207-775-5411). It's certainly big (203 rooms) and offers all the typical metropolitan-hotel services and amenities, including a health club, ballrooms and a choice of restaurants and cocktail lounges. Rooms are conventionally furnished with wall-to-wall carpeting and soft earth tones. Many have delicious harbor views. The building itself is a landmark, originally built in 1927 as the Eastland Hotel. Deluxe.

If being near L. L. Bean and the profusion of factory outlets that have taken over the once very New England (now almost mall-like) town of Freeport, consider booking a room at the **Harraseeket Inn** (162 Main Street; 207-865-9377). It's a lovely bed and breakfast in an 1850 Greek Revival home within walking distance of all the shops and outlets. There are 54 guest rooms, with jacuzzis or steambaths and canopied beds. Ultra-deluxe.

Serenely situated on Westport Island, the **Squire Tarbox Inn** (Wiscasset; 207-882-7693) offers 11 guest rooms. Four of them are located in the main Federal-style house, the others, well, er . . . they're in the barn. But don't panic—it's a lovely barn dating back to 1763. And it's spanking clean. Meals in the colonial dining room are a big part of any stay at the Squire Tarbox Inn. They usually are accompanied by goat cheese, fresh from the resident goats. Ultra-deluxe (includes breakfast and dinner).

Though the **Boothbay Harbor Inn** (37 Atlantic Avenue, Boothbay Harbor; 207-633-6302) is clearly a motel (and not an inn as the name leads one to believe), it does have some personality. For one thing, it's smack-dab on the water. You walk into your room, roll open the glass doors and *voilà!* The bobbing buoys, the wooden fishing boats, the screaming gulls—you feel as if you've just walked into the postcard you bought down at the desk. Besides the view, though, don't get your hopes about the rooms. They're about as generic as motel rooms get. Moderate to deluxe.

One look at the cluttered little streets of Boothbay Harbor and you'll be happy you're staying at the **Spruce Point Inn** (Spruce Point; 207-633-4152). It's set apart from the ongoing carnival of town, on a 100-acre peninsula at the eastern end of the harbor. There's a main inn as well as a handful of cottages and lodges scattered around the grounds. Sports are big here, with a pool, tennis courts, a putting green and some lawn games. Deluxe.

You can walk to the center of the village in minutes from the **Old Broad Bay Inn & Gallery** (1014 Main Street, Waldoboro; 207-832-6668), a lovely colonial house offering bed and breakfast. Rooms are *very* New England with canopy beds and brightly polished antiques. Take time to stroll around the art gallery, which is run by innkeeper Libby Hopkins and her husband, Jim. Budget to moderate.

Many of the most beautiful houses in the state of Maine were once sea captain's homes. Such is the case with **Cap'n Am's** (Flood's Cove, Friendship; 207-832-5144), a bed and breakfast right on the water. The large, rambling Cape-style abode, originally built in the late 1700s, has a lovely wraparound porch. There are three guest rooms, two with far-reaching ocean views and all with shared baths. Moderate.

For years, **The Trailing Yew** (★) (Monhegan Island; 207-596-0440) has been a favorite among artists visiting Monhegan. It's a friendly place where returning guests are welcomed as if family. Its 40 rooms—in a main house and some neighboring cottages—are very basic, with kerosene lamps and shared baths. Meals are hearty, home-cooked and served family-style around big tables. Moderate.

A former sea captain's house, the 26-room **East Wind Inn** (Tenants Harbor; 207-372-6366) looks like something right out of Sarah Orne Jewett's *Country of the Pointed Firs*. Indeed, the author wrote the book in nearby Martinville. All of the rooms are beautifully furnished with antiques and gaze out over the harbor. This view brings you the Maine coast just as you've pictured it—lobster traps piled high and wooden boats gently undulating with the tide. Moderate.

For budget-to-moderate bed and breakfast lodgings try the **Captain's Rest** (25 Gleason Street, Thomaston; 207-354-2000). This seven-room, century-old sea captain's home offers queen-sized and brass beds. Take your breakfast on the handsome porch and relax in the big garden. A short walk from the harbor, this turreted inn is a best buy.

Choosing just one inn in Camden is like picking one chocolate out of a whole box. There are many you'll want to try. Be that as it may, you definitely won't be sorry if you stay at the **Edgecombe-Coles House** (64 High Street; 207-236-2336). Set back behind a tall private hedge, it's a beautifully maintained 19th-century house with half a dozen rooms. Three of them are especially blessed with views of Penobscot Bay, which sparkles like mica off in the distance. All the rooms are attractively decorated with Early American furniture, antique knickknacks and the innkeepers' collection of turn-of-the-century art. Deluxe to ultra-deluxe.

An 1873 music store, the restored **Phenix Inn** (20 Westmarket Square, Bangor; 207-947-3850) has four floors of guest rooms decorated with reproduction antiques such as canopied beds. Located near the town's business district, the inn includes most modern amenities. Moderate.

DOWNEAST COAST HOTELS

If you're looking for the perfect New England inn in the perfect New England village, consider detouring off Route 1 to Castine and the **Castine Inn** (Main Street; 207-326-4365). The 1898 inn is ideally situated in town minutes from the water's edge. Its 20 antique-furnished rooms are bright, big and lovingly maintained by innkeepers Mark and Margaret Hodesh. Most have views of the sea. Moderate to deluxe.

Poised on Castine's stately Main Street is the main building of the **Pentagoet Inn** (207-326-8616), a large old Victorian. Guests can stay either in that house or at neighboring Ten Perkins Street, a 200-year-old building where all guest rooms have country antiques. Between the two, there are 16 rooms, all with private baths. Breakfast and dinner are included in rates. Ultra-deluxe.

Snugly set on 48 acres, **Blue Hill Farm** (Blue Hill; 207-374-5126) seems to attract a healthy, life-loving crowd, including the occasional troop of Vermont Country Cyclers who come pedaling in on their inn-hopping tours. There are just seven guest rooms in the farmhouse, all looking as though they might have been photographed for *Country Living* magazine. The highlight every morning is breakfast: fresh-out-of-the-oven breads, homemade granola, juicy fresh fruits and an assortment of cheeses. Moderate.

The **Pilgrim's Inn** (Deer Isle; 207-348-6615) has found its way into travel and gourmet publications all over the United States and Canada. It's not surprising. Perched on a shiny millpond directly opposite Northwest Harbor, this 1793 house is impeccably maintained and run by experienced innkeepers Jean and Dud Hendrick. Rooms—a total of 13, plus a neighboring guest cottage—are simply decorated with antiques, Laura Ashley fabrics and artwork and crafts by local artists, who are numerous in these parts. Tourists and Mainers from as far as Bar Harbor come for the dinners here, which are among the best in the midcoast area. Ultra-deluxe rates include breakfast and dinner.

As one totally satiated guest said while stretching his legs in a lounge chair and peering out at the fog-bundled sea with its hooting vessels, "This may not be luxurious, but you can't beat the setting." The **Captain's Quarters Inn and Motel** (Stonington, Deer Isle; 207-367-2420) is not for everybody, with its motelish decor and somewhat cramped, close quarters. However, stepping out on the deck that hangs over the harbor is like walking right into a painting. There are 15 suites and housekeeping units all set smack-dab on the water. Another plus here, the coffee—a selection of freshly ground roasts—is a real find in a state where the brew is often served as transparent as tea. Budget.

Though many visitors take the mail boat out just to spend the day on Isle au Haut, you can overnight there. **The Keeper's House (★)** (Robinson's Point; 207-367-2261) is a stone lighthouse-keeper's-cottage-turned-inn that still uses kerosene and candles for its lighting. There are four large, airy and simply decorated bedrooms along with a dining room in the main cottage, a separate accommodation in the tiny Oil House with its own outdoor shower and another unit in the Wood Shed. Three meals provided; ultra-deluxe.

You can spend hours—no, days—roaming around the rooms of **Clefstone Manor** (92 Eden Street, Bar Harbor; 207-288-4951), which are filled with European bric-a-brac that's been collected over the years. The house is a huge, 30-room mansion built in 1894 as a summer home for James Blair, secretary of the Navy under President Lincoln. Its 16 ornately decorated guest rooms are all named for British nobility and writers. The grandly proportioned Romeo and Juliet room, with its shiny brass canopy bed, beamed ceilings, Oriental rugs and fireplace, is worth taking a peek at if you happen to be staying in one of the others. However, all are jaw-droppingly impressive. Ultra-deluxe.

If you want to glimpse what life was like in turn-of-the-century Bar Harbor summer cottages, consider staying at the **Ledgelawn Inn** (66 Mount Desert Street; 207-288-4596). You can have your pick of rooms in either the main house, the Carriage House or the Balanced Rock Inn on the water. There are 39 rooms, some with working fireplaces and verandas and, for a modern touch, whirlpool baths and saunas. All are handsomely decorated with beautiful antiques. Guests enjoy access to a heated oceanfront pool. Deluxe to ultra-deluxe.

You have to book well in advance to get a room at **The Tides** (119 West Street, Bar Harbor; 207-288-4968). This marvelous Greek Revival manse is propped on a carpet of lawn with a stunning view of the bay and its own beach. Classical music streams through the living room, a grand but cozy affair adorned with plush champagne carpets and a fireplace. There are just three guest rooms, each elegantly furnished with Victorian and Empire pieces. The master suite with its canopy bed and fireplace is the most coveted, but the other two rooms—with private balconies—are worth calling ahead for as well. The innkeepers are extra-friendly and hospitable, preparing breakfasts that look like they might grace the cover of a gourmet magazine. Ultra-deluxe.

Listed in the National Register of Historic Places, the **Manor House Inn** (106 West Street, Bar Harbor; 207-288-3759) is yet another summer cottage that has been restored and preserved. This lovely 22-room Victorian mansion, built in the late 1800s, has 14 guest quarters, all with private baths, working fireplaces and Victorian furnishings. Moderate to ultra-deluxe.

Fortunately, some things never change. Such is the case with the **Claremont** (Claremont Road, Southwest Harbor; 207-244-5036), Mount Desert Island's oldest summer hotel (it dates to 1885). Of course, this grande dame (listed in the National Register of Historic Places) has been renovated—heavily. But it still manages to preserve the old Maine vacation traditions such as dressing for dinner (that means jacket and tie) and socializing with fellow guests. The large, rambling, shingled building has a wide veranda lined with wicker rocking chairs. The view—of Cadillac Mountain across Somes Sound—is nonpareil. The food—lots of lobster and seafood dishes— is unfailingly good. The rooms (a grand total of 39, nine of them cottages) are homey and comfortable. On top of all that, guests can sample the many on-site sporting facilities, including clay tennis courts, badminton, water sports equipment, rowboats and croquet courts. The ultra-deluxe rates include breakfast and dinner.

Many guests intending to spend one or two nights at the **Weston House** (★) (26 Boynton Street, Eastport; 207-853-2907) end up extending their stay. From what we could tell, it was the combination of the bed and breakfast itself (it feels very European) and the enormously interesting town of Eastport. There are five guest rooms and two baths on the upper level of the house, a stately old Federal built in 1810. All the rooms are thoughtfully furnished with comfortable beds covered by handmade quilts, along with tasteful antique pieces and little touches like fresh flowers in season. The house is right in town, within walking distance of everything. The breakfasts are unmatchable, featuring all sorts of inspired recipes. Moderate.

The Inn at Eastport (13 Washington Street; 207-853-4307), a former sea captain's house, has five very attractive guest rooms furnished with antiques. It's a good in-town base. The piece de resistance is an outdoor hot tub with an ocean view. Also, a real rarity in these parts, the inn provides evening turndown service. Shared bath, budget; private bath, moderate.

NORTHERN WOODS HOTELS

Before setting out into the wilderness of Baxter State Park, you can fuel up for a night by staying at **Pamola Motor Lodge** (973 Central Street, Millinocket; 207-723-9746). It's just as it sounds, a basic motor lodge with 30 generic motel rooms and efficiencies. Budget to moderate.

Like a little nest hidden up in the trees, **Pray's Cottages & General Store** (Ripogenus Dam; 207-723-8880) is a homey spot tucked away in the thick woods. It's the takeoff point for many bear-hunting groups and whitewater rafters, as well as a civilization-stopover for rugged campers desiring some hot water and electricity for a change. There are four one-bedroom efficiency units in a ranch-style building and three separate cottages. All are practically furnished with the kind of things you might have used to decorate your first apartment, but they're comfortable nonetheless. They also have all the modern kitchen conveniences. The general store is the hub of activity here, which is at its best around 6 a.m. during bear-hunting season, when the hunters congregate to swap eyebrow-raising stories before heading out again. Budget.

Anglers are the biggest fans of **Frost Pond Camps** (three miles beyond Ripogenus Dam near Baxter State Park; write: 36-H Minuteman Drive, Millinocket, ME 04462; 207-723-6622). It's a group of ten campsites and eight rustically furnished housekeeping cabins set on Frost Pond, which is loaded with trout. But it's also a great place for canoe groups, families and hunters (in the fall). Budget.

The scenery around **Katahdin Lake Wilderness Camps** (★) (three and a half miles off Roaring Brook Road, Baxter State Park; write: Box 398, Millinocket, ME 04462) is gaspingly beautiful. There are ten log cabins (two to seven people can stay in each one) and a main lodge propped up on a bluff overlooking a lake. Each cabin is rustically furnished with the basic essentials (including kerosene lamps and a supply of firewood); some have gas stoves. There's no auto access to the camps, so you must arrange to be met by the owner with pack horses, or fly in from Millinocket Lake. Moderate.

Remotely situated within the Allagash Wilderness Waterway (50 miles north of Millinocket), **Nugent's Chamberlain Lake Camps** (write: Box 632, Greenville, ME 04441) is a collection of eight rustic log cabins. The best way to reach them is to fly in (contact Folsom's Air Service, 207-695-2821). Otherwise, it's a five-mile boat (or snowmobile) trip up Chamberlain Lake. This is a year-round sporting camp offering fishing, canoeing, cross-country skiing and snowmobiling. Budget to moderate.

Located at the base of the ski lifts on Moosehead Lake, **Squaw Mountain at Moosehead** (Greenville; 207-695-2272) is a big, family-focused hotel. You'll find everything under its one roof, including a dining room, bar (there's dancing on weekends), indoor pool, sauna and game room. Outdoors, there's a full range of sporting activities, including water sports, tennis, riding and lawn games. Come winter, there's skiing and snowmobiling. The 60 guest rooms are traditional hotel accommodations. Moderate.

Try to get one of the two rooms that has a fireplace at the **Greenville Inn** (Norris Street, Greenville; 207-695-2206). But if you can't, don't worry. All ten guest rooms at this former lumber baron's home are wonderful. There are antiques throughout, and in the common rooms cherrywood and mahogany panels warm up all the corners. Best of all are the views of Moosehead Lake and the encircling mountains from the porch and the dining room. Moderate to deluxe.

You can stay right in Chesuncook, a 19th-century lumberman's village that's on the National Register of Historic Places, at the **Chesuncook Lake House** (★) (Route 76, Greenville: 207-745-5330). It's a beautifully maintained 1864 farmhouse with six gas-lit rooms (also equipped with electricity) and three separate cabins. To reach it, you can be picked up by boat at Cushing's Landing or fly in. Three meals a day are included; moderate.

If images of a palace and castles run through your head when you hear about **Chalet Moosehead** (on Moosehead Lake, just off Routes 6 and 15, Greenville; 207-695-2950), forget them. It's just a motel with a fancy name. It is ideally situated, however, overlooking Moosehead Lake. The "chalet" is also a very inexpensive way to settle into the area, with nine efficiency units, a standard room and one cabin as well as a slew of diversions to keep you happily occupied (including a private beach and free use of canoes). Moderate.

Poised on the shores of Moosehead Lake, **The Birches** (two miles from Rockwood Village; 207-534-7305) is a string of 17 log cabins privately spaced out in a grove of birch trees. All of them have porches and wood-burning stoves or fireplaces; some have kitchens. There's a main lodge complete with an open-timbered dining room where the fare is wholesome and good. Major pastimes include hiking, fishing, swimming, canoeing and boating. There's also tennis and golf nearby. In winter, visitors can glide over 25 miles of cross-country trails. Moderate.

Gazing over at Mt. Kineo on Moosehead Lake are the **Rockwood Cottages** (Rockwood; 207-534-7725). Eight cottages come with fully equipped kitchens, baths with showers, and screened porches. There's a long list of activities to enjoy, including fishing, hunting, white-water rafting, seaplane rides, tennis and hiking. Come winter, there's ice fishing, snowmobiling and both alpine and cross-country skiing. Moderate.

Maynards in Maine (Rockwood; 207-534-7703) is one of Moosehead Lake's oldest established sporting camps. The centerpiece of it all is a grand old lodge filled with memorabilia from earlier hunting trips (such as stuffed fish and moose heads) and comfortable sofas and chairs that date back to the early 1900s. The dining room is always abuzz with outdoor lovers who congregate for two hearty meals a day. The camp has 12 cabins, with one to three bedrooms and full baths. Moderate.

There are just six units at **Sundown Cabins** (Route 15, Rockwood; 207-534-7357), so be sure to reserve yours early. Located on Moosehead Lake, these one-to-three bedroom kitchenette units are moderate to deluxe in price. Ideally located for water sports and fishing.

WESTERN LAKES AND MOUNTAINS HOTELS

There are over 300 condominium units available through **Sugarloaf Mountain Corporation** (Sugarloaf Mountain; 207-237-2200). Each has its advantages. Some are close to the lifts, others to the restaurants and shops. They range from very modern accommodations with all sorts of new conveniences to ones that are older but more affordable. Some are bare-bones hotel rooms, others full-fledged homes. Nearby is the **Sugarloaf Mountain Hotel** (207-237-2222), a seven-story building with one- to three-bedroom suites. Ultra-deluxe.

You can stay near the Sugarloaf area at the **Widow's Walk** (★) (Route 27, Stratton; 207-246-6901), an exceptionally friendly inn that attracts lots of skiers in winter and nature lovers in summer. Listed on the National Register of Historic Places, it's a beautiful Victorian house that was built in the late 1890s. There are six guest rooms, all with basic New England furnishings. Budget.

Fanatical skiers on a budget have a choice of bare-bones motels to choose from in this area, including **Cathy's Place** (Stratton; 207-246-2922), which actually is quite homey in spite of its generic looks. Rooms are ultra-basic but can accommodate between two and five guests. It's great for a pack of friends. Budget.

About 17 miles south of Sugarloaf Mountain stands **The Herbert** (Kingfield; 207-265-2000), an alternative to the mountain condominiums. It's a grand old hotel with 33 tastefully decorated guest rooms—all with combo jacuzzi/steambaths in the bathrooms. The main lobby area offers a warm reprieve, and it's often filled with rosy-cheeked skiers who don't feel guilty about taking an afternoon off from the slopes to sit in front of the fireplace and listen to piano music. Moderate.

Named after Amos Winter, the founder of the Sugarloaf ski area, the **Inn on Winter's Hill** (Kingfield; 207-265-5421) is a Georgian revival mansion with 18 charming antique-filled rooms in the main house and connecting barn. Registered as a National Historic Property, the Inn's lavishly decorated common rooms look as if they should be roped off like a museum, but actually they're very comfortable. Additional amenities include a pool, hot tub and tennis court. Moderate to ultra-deluxe.

The **Sugarloafer's Ski Dorm** (Kingfield; 207-265-2041) is just as it sounds: a basic dorm. It was designed especially for ski groups and has six separate dormitories (each accommodating up to 40 people). Moderate.

Right on the water in Rangeley, the **Rangeley Inn and Motor Lodge** (Main Street; 207-864-3341) is a town landmark. The older building—erected back in the railway and lake steamer days—is a three-story shingled structure with 36 remodeled guest rooms. There's also a newer motel wing with 15 guest rooms, some offering fireplaces or wood-burning stoves, waterbeds and whirlpool baths. Moderate to deluxe.

Magnificently situated on a hill overlooking Rangeley Lake and surrounded by an 18-hole golf course, the **Country Club Inn** (Country Club Road, Rangeley; 207-864-3831) is a grand old summer resort built by a wealthy sportsman back in the 1920s. The living room is lavishly endowed with two immense fireplaces that face each other. The 20 guest rooms are nothing to get excited about though. They're rather ordinary for this extraordinary setting. Ultra-deluxe.

Sunset Point Cottages (★) (on Mooselookmeguntic Lake, outside of Rangeley; 207-864-5387) could be in Sweden. As the name implies, Sunset Point is a sprig of land jutting into spectacularly scenic Mooselookmeguntic Lake. It's colonized by a quintet of housekeeping cottages (with one, two or three bedrooms), all inches from the water's edge. Though satisfyingly rugged (wood burning stoves, gas lights), the place provides real plumbing and hot showers (!) in one common bathhouse. Moderate.

Bald Mountain Camps (Oquossoc; 207-864-3671) are the woods of Maine just as you pictured them. They're right on Mooselookmeguntic Lake, surrounded by hundreds of miles of dense wilderness. Guests stay in small cabins (there are 15, all with fireplaces) that are warm and homey. No fancy furnishings here—you never have to worry about the kids spilling things. Meals are taken in the log dining room, which is always alive with vacationers who come back to their same cabin year after year. Ultra-deluxe.

If you've never experienced a real Maine lodge, consider staying at the **Kawanhee Inn** (Weld; 207-585-2243). It has the works: exposed timber beams, an immense stone fireplace, woodsy smelling rooms. Guests can stay in one of ten rooms with basic furnishings in the main lodge or settle into a cabin (each of the 12 accommodates two to seven people). All of the cabins have their own fireplaces and screened-in porches. The setting is lovely—on a hill overlooking Lake Webb—and guests can use the small beach and boats. Deluxe.

A lovely old Victorian house surrounded by five piney acres, **The Douglass Place** (Bethel; 207-824-2229) is beautifully situated in the small mountain town of Bethel. There are four guest rooms, all with twin beds and attractively furnished with antiques. Guests are welcome to use the common rooms as well, including the game room (with a piano, pool table and ping-pong table), living rooms, den and screened-in gazebo. Moderate.

The **Bethel Inn and Country Club** (On the Common, Bethel; 207-824-2175) is a large resort-type place that has everything. By everything, we mean 137 rooms (all with their own telephones and bathrooms), a well-respected dining room and an array of sporting options including golf, tennis, fishing, swimming, exercise rooms, sauna and cross-country skiing in winter. A huge, sprawling yellow building right on the town's common, it's impossible to miss. The individual rooms are decorated in a ho-hum style with all the modern comforts. The common rooms are very formally attired in antiques. Ultra-deluxe.

Within walking distance of the town's shops and restaurants, **L'Auberge** (Mill Hill Road, Bethel; 207-824-2774) is the kind of place you fall in love with and then hesitate to tell even your best friends about. Formerly a barn, it has seven guest rooms simply but elegantly furnished with country antiques. Guests are free to roam about the common rooms, which include a living room with a hearth, grand piano and the kind of chairs and couches you sink into. During the winter months, you can cross-country ski right from the door. Moderate to deluxe.

Gazing out onto the village green of North Waterford is the **Old Rowley Inn** (Route 35; 207-583-4143), a beautifully maintained place that dates back to 1790. The seven guest rooms are all warmly furnished with floral prints and country antiques. There are also three dining rooms, a game room and a network of cross-country ski trails. Moderate.

The Noble House (37 Highland Road, Bridgton; 207-647-3733) offers nine moderate to deluxe rooms in a turn-of-the-century Queen Anne. Set on a hill, this bed and breakfast is comfortably furnished with antiques. Some of the rooms and suites come with whirlpool baths and porches. You're welcome to play the baby grand piano or the pump organ. Explore the inn's private lake frontage with a canoe or foot-pedal boat, or just watch the sunset from the comfort of your own hammock.

Surrounded by 34 lakeside acres, the **Tarry-A-While Resort** (Highland Ridge Road, on Highland Lake, Bridgton; 207-647-2522) looks like something you'd find in Switzerland. It's a grand old summer hotel with ten main-house rooms and another 16 in a quartet of cottages that punctuate the grounds. The innkeepers—Hans and Barbara Jenni—pride themselves on their unending hospitality. You almost feel as if you're guests in a private home. There's an array of active diversions nearby, including water sports (three beaches plus canoes, rowboats, motorboats, sailboats and windsurfers), tennis and golf. Deluxe.

Restaurants

SOUTHERN COAST RESTAURANTS

The **Cape Neddick Inn and Gallery** (Route 1; 207-363-2899) is a local legend of sorts, having been remarkably rebuilt after a fire damaged the original landmark building. The new dining room is very tastefully accoutred with artworks on loan from the nearby Walt Kuhn Gallery. And though you are actually sitting in a gallery, there is a wonderful warmth to the place. The art changes every six weeks, as does the menu, which generally features lots of fish, lamb and duckling dishes accompanied by celestial sauces. Moderate to deluxe.

The **Cape Neddick Lobster Pound** (Route 1A and Shore Road, Cape Neddick; 207-363-5471) is not just lobster and clams. It boasts an array of other dishes such as bouillabaisse and baked sole. Its setting is fairly predictable in these parts—a shingled building right on the water. Moderate.

Follow your noses into **Pie in the Sky Bakery** (Route 1 and River Road, Cape Neddick; 207-363-2656) if you're looking for a snack. Baker/owners John and Nancy Stern seem to be on a never-ending roll of creating one yummy treat after another, including breads in all sizes and shapes, muffins and, of course, pies. Budget.

For a quiet, elegant dinner in Ogunquit, try **Tavern at Clay Hill Farm** (Agamenticus Road; 207-646-2272). It's a lovely New England restaurant located in an old farmhouse just west of the village. The menu is rather refined, with items like broiled salmon marinated in cajun spices and roasted lamb noisettes. A dreamy pianist provides the background music throughout dinner, and there's dancing later. Moderate to deluxe.

Look for crowds outside **Barnacle Billy's** (Perkins Cove, Ogunquit; 207-646-5575). It's your basic Maine lobster joint where you pull a number, wait to be called and then settle in for a feast. You can sit in the dining room, which has the air of a bustling fish house, or on the deck, where you can gaze out at boats while you eat. Moderate.

The menu is what drew us into the **White Barn Inn** (Kennebunk Beach; 207-967-2321), a barn-turned-restaurant. The cuisine is somewhat of a departure from the norm in these parts, offering irresistible dishes such as bacon-wrapped sea scallops with maple mustard cream and char-grilled veal chops with a diced shallot comfit and blanched bacon. You can, however, order the reliable standbys such as lobster (baked, stuffed, steamed, shelled or sautéed in butter). All this in a lovely candlelit barn. Deluxe to ultra-deluxe.

The **Old Grist Mill** (Mill Lane, Kennebunkport; 207-967-4781) has President Bush's seal of approval. When you walk in, the first thing you see is a photo of him with a note thanking the owner for a great meal. The dining room is very attractive, with pink tablecloths, fresh flowers and lots of windows offering views of the coastal inlet. The menu features a good choice of seafood dishes and New England specialties. Desserts are dull, so don't bother. Moderate to deluxe.

Expect perfection at the **Kennebunkport Inn** (Dock Square, Kennebunkport; 207-967-2621). This ultra-elegant restaurant prides itself on making sure everything is just right. The hushed colonial dining room is a fitting background for flawlessly grilled native swordfish and a mustard and ginger rack of lamb. Deluxe.

Windows on the Water (Chase Hill Road, Kennebunkport; 207-967-3313) has a major-league claim to fame. Its chef—John—was one of 52 who prepared food for President Bush's inauguration. Admittedly, the food is right up there with the best, including dishes like baked sea scallops au gratin and *gravlax* (marinated salmon). The *spécialité de la maison* is the lobster-stuffed potato, a duney little concoction of fresh lobster, cream and Jarlsberg cheese fitted into one half of a hot baked potato. Scrumptious! The view almost one-ups the meal, however. Diners look out at the busy little port through the arched windows or from the terrace during warm-weather months. Moderate to deluxe.

Everything in Bush Country (remember, Kennebunkport is home to the Summer White House) tends to be a bit pricey these days, so don't think you're going to save much by seemingly slumming it at the low-slung shed called **Nunan's Lobster Hut** (Route 9, Cape Porpoise; 207-967-4362). But do go, especially if you want some ultrafresh lobster or a heaping platter of steamers. Moderate.

To say **Green Mountain Coffee Roasters** (15 Temple Street, Portland; 207-773-4475) has the best coffee in town would be an understatement of classic magnificence. The selection of coffees here is nonpareil. As you walk in the door of this red brick building the aroma engulfs you—much of it coming from the enormous roaster that churns beans from around the world, producing all sorts of we'll-never-give-you-the-recipe blends. The place resembles a Parisian café, with high ceilings, black-and-white-tiled floors and a throw-the-diet-out-the-window selection of pastries. Budget.

The raw bar at **The Oyster Club** (164 Middle Street, Portland; 207-773-3760) draws a crowd of fanatical regulars—many of them young urban professionals grabbing a bite after work. Downstairs is a whole different story. There you can settle in for a very hushed seafood dinner amid very clubby furnishings. Moderate to deluxe.

If you want to combine dining with a bit of partying, find your way to the **Great Lost Bear** (540 Forest Avenue; 207-772-0300). This is one of Portland's most popular bar-cum-restaurants where you can count on getting the old standbys like chili, burgers, steaks and salads. It's located in the former Cameo Theater in Portland's tiny SoFo District (Southside Forest Avenue). Moderate.

The *New England Monthly* chose **Alberta's Café** (21 Pleasant Street, Portland; 207-774-0016) as one of 16 New England restaurants to earn their seal of approval. It's easy to see why. They serve a wide variety of cuisines, including Italian, Tex-Mex, Cajun and California—all prepared by four or five very innovative chefs who take turns in the kitchen. It's a stylish little spot with pink walls. Moderate to deluxe.

For Northern Italian, choose **Raphael's** (36 Market Street, Portland; 207-773-4500). They prepare a heavenly rack of lamb marinated in Madeira, whole grain mustard and tarragon. The atmosphere is very Northern Italian as well with dimly lit lights and crisp white tablecloths. Moderate to deluxe.

The owners of **Le Garage** (Water Street, Wiscasset; 207-882-5409) have a good sense of humor. After all, this really is a 1920s-era garage-turned-restaurant. You'd hardly know it though, since they've gussied the place up and added on a glassed-in porch. Well, okay, the floors are concrete, but the food is very good (predominately seafood, but lamb and steaks, too) and the value unmatchable. Moderate to deluxe.

A two-story restaurant right in the pulsating heart of things, the **Black Orchid Restaurant** (5 By-Way, Boothbay Harbor; 207-633-6659) serves by-the-book Italian. In its dimly lit and somewhat cramped rooms, you can stuff yourselves on all the standard Mediterranean favorites such as fettucine Alfredo and spaghetti smothered in a tomato sauce as well as a selection of local fish dishes. Save room for the cheesecake or spumoni. Moderate to deluxe.

McSeagull's (on the wharf, Boothbay Harbor; 207-633-4041) is a real sociable place where the party set congregates all afternoon and well into the evening. Your best bet is to stake out a table outside, order a platter of steamed clams and a chilled beer and just sit, sip and take in the whole scene. The more serious entrées—veal français, charbroiled teriyaki chicken —can be iffy. Moderate to deluxe.

Smack-dab on the wharf and snazzily appointed with polished teak and brass, **J. H. Hawk Restaurant and Pub** (on the wharf, Boothbay Harbor; 207-633-5589) has a fun-loving collegiate feel to it. The waiters are lively and tan, often humming along to the tunes that blast out of the speakers.

The food runs the gamut from fat burgers with all the trimmings to Cajun swordfish. Moderate.

One look at the tiny yellow house called **No Anchovies** (4 Todd Avenue, Boothbay Harbor; 207-633-2130) and you can't resist going in. It's super casual inside, with vinyl booths. Though pizza is the main attraction here, consider ordering a big bowl of linguine laced with pesto. Budget to moderate.

In spite of its magnet-for-tourists location, **Andrew's Harborside Restaurant** (at the western end of the footbridge, Boothbay Harbor; 207-633-4074) attracts quite a few locals for all three meals. Lines form outside for the breakfasts, which are prefaced by large cinnamon rolls fresh out of the oven and dripping with a glassy icing. Lunch and dinner dishes are largely of the seafood variety, though you can get meat and poultry dishes as well. The restaurant is unimaginatively decorated, but the setting—inches from the water's edge—makes it enormously appealing. Moderate.

Tired of understated decor? Then make a beeline for the **Harbor View** (1 Water Street, Thomaston; 207-354-8173) where you'll find carriages hanging from the ceiling, airplanes built out of tin cans, nautical mementos, violins, trombones and enough mirrors to make a Caesar's Palace executive feel right at home. Graze on appetizers like fried mozzarella, mussels in cream or the smoked seafood sampler. Then move in on scallops au gratin, filet mignon or a shrimp boat. There's prime rib on weekends. Ask for a seat on the enclosed deck and you'll enjoy a great view.

Any trip to Maine would not be complete without one meal at a diner. That's where you see the real characters, the perennial Mainers. One of our favorites is **Moody's Diner** (Route 1, Waldoboro; 207-832-7468). It's been passed down through the Moody family for generations. The decor is authentic dineresque. The menu is mainstream but good enough to make you want to go back several times—especially for breakfast! Budget.

Even the most definitive, self-assured diners can't make up their mind what to order at **The Waterfront** (Bayview Street, Camden: 207-236-3747). The dinner menu lists an inviting selection of specialties including broiled scallops. And, of course, there are lobsters and steamers to further throw you into a tizzy. The setting—right on the harbor—is unmatchable. Moderate.

Scooping up spoonfuls of clam chowder at **Cappy's Chowder House** (Main Street, Camden; 207-236-2254) is close to having a spiritual experience. But that's just the chowder. Cappy's is also famed for its seafood dishes, pasta, burgers—you name it. It's a pubby kind of place with nautical decor, always abuzz with both out-of-towners and salty locals. There's a raw bar upstairs for quick meals. Upstairs it's more laid-back, with booths and tables. Moderate.

One of the oldest family-operated restaurants in Maine (opened in 1940), **Pilot's Grill** (1528 Hammond Street, Bangor; 207-942-6325) serves up home-style American food, with an accent on local seafood as well as steaks, roast beef and lamb chops. The neat brick eatery has tables covered with linen and fresh flowers. Moderate to deluxe.

DOWNEAST COAST RESTAURANTS

In a little town as amphibious as Castine, it's surprising to find just one restaurant on the water. Fortunately, the food at **Dennett's Wharf** (Sea Street; 207-326-9045), a net-hung, bustling fish house, is just as appealing as the view of the sailboat-dotted harbor. A lunch of freshly cracked oysters followed by a grilled crab salad and a chilled glass mug of beer is deliriously good. Dennett's is ultracasual, with college-break waitresses sporting jeans and miniskirts and giggling when you tell them you need a fork. Moderate.

The **Castine Inn** (Main Street, Castine; 207-326-4365) is elegantly accoutred with wall murals depicting harbor scenes and pretty table settings. The changing menu features innovative entrées including roast pork loin with peach chutney, salmon ravioli with a tomato-saffron sauce and chicken and leek pot pie. Be sure to try the crabcakes served with a mustard sauce or any of the delicious desserts such as baked Indian pudding, crème brulée and pumpkin gingerbread. Moderate to deluxe.

The town of Blue Hill has a very sophisticated summer crowd who spend their evenings dining well and attending chamber concerts. However, there are still only a handful of truly commendable restaurants, including **Jonathan's** (Main Street; 207-374-5226), with its two lovely dining rooms. The front room is very colonial, with antique blue-and-beige walls and lots of woodwork throughout. The rear room has a more rustic feel, with exposed beams and oak tables. On the ever-changing menu, you'll find lots of seafood dishes with imaginative sauces you'll beg to have the recipe for. Jonathan's also boasts one of the coast's best wine lists. Moderate to deluxe.

The **Left Bank Café** (on Route 172, northern edge of Blue Hill; 207-374-2201) is a little too trendy for its own good, with its Greenwich Village coffeehouse and in-house art gallery, but it's fast becoming an institution for the local crowd. It offers lots of just-hits-the-spot dishes such as pad Thai noodles, Caribbean stew and Cajun chicken. Best of all are the bakery desserts, especially the strudel. Moderate.

If you can't stay at **Pilgrim's Inn** (Deer Isle Village, Deer Isle; 207-348-6615), by all means do have dinner there. Your five-course meal—prepared by a chef trained at the Culinary Institute of America and served in a converted timber-beamed barn—could be a butter-soft poached salmon with beurre blanc, tenderloin with cabernet, mushroom and leek sauce or perhaps glazed roasted duck. Among the other courses, you'll find wonderful bisques or chowders, salads (largely from the garden out back), home-baked breads and write-home-about desserts. The prix-fixe dinner is priced ultra-deluxe.

The light of wallet but discriminating seafood eater won't find a better value than **Fisherman's Friend Restaurant** (★) (School Street, Stonington, Deer Isle; 207-367-2442). Go when you're starving—the place prides itself on its generous servings of spanking fresh fish and seafood. The diner decor could use some gussying up, but with a platter piled high with clams, who cares? Budget to moderate.

We sat for hours at our window seat in the **Reading Room Restaurant** at the Bar Harbor Inn (Newport Drive, Bar Harbor; 207-288-3351), mesmerized by the view. In addition to the expansive dining room with a circular view of the bay, there's an outdoor waterfront terrace. The food is lovely, too, with specialties like fresh lobster pie and roast duckling with a raspberry sauce. Deluxe.

When driving the Park Loop Road in Acadia National Park, you couldn't ask for a better place to stop for lunch, tea or dinner than **Jordan Pond House** (Park Loop Road, Bar Harbor; 207-276-3316). Along with a mountain view, it offers Maine specialties such as lobster pie and broiled halibut —all backgrounded by classical music and a fire in the hearth. Moderate to deluxe.

Children are in their glory in the delightfully decorated **Brick Oven Restaurant** (21 Cottage Street, Bar Harbor; 207-288-3708). The owners— Fred Pooler and Susan Jackson—are antique toy collectors. Everywhere you spot old toys, tools and other gadgets, each having a story of its own. The food is good old Americana, with standard favorites like grilled steaks and boiled lobster. And there are more innovative dishes as well, including shrimp fettucine and chicken cordon bleu. Moderate.

For a casual lunch with a bit of people-watching, plant yourselves on the patio of **The Mary Jane Restaurant** (Main Street, Bar Harbor; 207-288-3410). It has the standard Maine lunch specialties, including lobster rolls and grilled fish dishes, as well as simple burgers and salads. Moderate.

Certain restaurants tend to get everyone's recommendation, and such is the case with **Porcupine Grill** (123 Cottage Street, Bar Harbor; 207-288-3884). This jewel of a place, tucked down a residential street, offers New American dishes with a Maine twist. The chef, a former instructor at New England Culinary Institute, turns out inspiring creations such as caesar salad crowned with fried clams, grilled duck with cheese polenta and a famous porcupine stew chocked full of local seafood. Flickering oil lamps, art deco accents and big oak tables—spread far apart—make this one venue not to miss. Deluxe.

Beal's Lobster Pier (Clark Point Road, Southwest Harbor; 207-244-7178) is another outstanding place to stuff yourselves on clams or lobster. It's super casual, with picnic tables set outside in nice weather. They'll pack lobsters in ice to go and arrange air freight as well. Moderate.

If hunger strikes while you're driving north on Route 1, stop in Milbridge at **The Red Barn** (Main Street; 207-546-7721), a very casual, knotty-pine-paneled spot with some counter seats, booths and a separate dining room. It has a mainstream menu (pastas, burgers, steak, seafood) as well as some house specialties like the seafood stew, a delicious concoction of shrimp, scallops, haddock and crabmeat. Budget to moderate.

Lubec may be the easternmost point of land in the continental United States, but you'd never know it while sitting in the **Hillside Restaurant** (Route 189; 207-733-4323). In a town where everyone takes views for granted, this little plainly decorated eatery has none (by plain we mean plastic tablecloths). It does have some hearty Downeast cooking, however, with fish just minutes out of the water. Budget.

Located in an old sea captain's home, **Rolando's Harbor View Restaurant** (118 Water Street, Eastport; 207-853-2334) offers candlelit Italian dining. Bentwood furniture and linens on the table add to the charm of this moderately priced establishment. Try the alfredo dishes, veal or spaghetti with garlic, olive oil and black olives. Homemade desserts include chocolate walnut pie and carrot cake. Moderate.

The **Waco Diner** (Water Street; 207-853-4046) solves the pesky problem of wanting a shot of local color. Here you'll see all the local Eastport characters, including salty seafaring types and former sardine cannery workers. The food—standard diner fare—is nothing to get excited about, but that's not the point. You're here for the Eastport atmosphere. Budget.

The **Flag Officer's Mess** (71 Water Street, Eastport; 207-853-6043) is the first yuppie establishment to appear in town. It has all the ingredients: the fashionable menu, the teak and brass decor, the large glass windows, the carefully chosen stereo music. You can take your pick of entrées such as Eastport salmon, baked stuffed haddock, lobster Newburg, shrimp scampi and veal scallopini marsala. Moderate.

Man does not live by seafood alone. Try the salsa, enchiladas, burritos or Mexican pizzas at **La Sardina Loca** (28 Water Street, Eastport; 207-853-2739) the easternmost Mexican restaurant in the United States. And on those cold Maine winter nights there just can't be a better place to sip a margarita than the skylight bar. The eatery is decorated with balloons, grandfather clocks and antiques. Budget to moderate.

Before taking off for the northern woods, do yourselves a favor and have a meal at **Chandler House** (20 Chandler Street, Calais; 207-454-7922). This warm and popular restaurant is well known in these parts for its prime rib and seafood dishes. All the baking is done right there. Moderate.

NORTHERN WOODS RESTAURANTS

In this neck of the woods, you'll find most meals are included in the price at camps and lodges. They're often served family-style and consist of good solid home cooking. But there are a handful of restaurants you might want to try.

We were a little turned off when we saw the waitress/chef/cashier/store manager spray the grill with some aerosol and squeeze cheese out of a tube to make our grilled cheese at **Pray's General Store** (Ripogenus Dam; 207-723-8880). But hey, what can you say about a meal for under five bucks? And good luck finding another place to eat out in these woods. Budget.

One of the most elegant meals you can have in the northern woods is at the **Greenville Inn** (★) (Norris Street, Greenville: 207-695-2206). In its graciously decorated dining room, there's a good selection of continental dishes, all enhanced by festive sauces created by an adept kitchen. Deluxe.

The barn-shaped **Cabbage Patch** (Routes 6 and 15, Greenville Junction; 207-695-2252) is known for its lobster and sirloin tip dinner. This establishment also boasts a big salad bar, homemade bread, steaks and, for those larger than average appetites, gingerbread and brownie sundaes. The interior features enough antique farm equipment to turn the back 40 into a moneymaker. Moderate.

If you in the mood for a burger or a big bowl of chili, make your way to **Flatlander's Pub** (Pritham Avenue, Greenville; 207-695-3373). They serve heaping platters of Americana. It's a casual spot, attracting plain folks and backpacker types. Budget.

Kelley's Kitchen (Greenville Junction; 207-695-4438) is a great diner-style spot for breakfast. It opens at 6 a.m. and has a traditional American menu. Budget to moderate.

WESTERN LAKES AND MOUNTAINS RESTAURANTS

For a quick but satiating meal between ski runs, try **Gepetto's** (Village West at Sugarloaf; 207-237-2192). You can warm up with a bowl of seafood chowder or a thick slice of pizza or settle in for fresh chicken and seafood dishes. From its windowed walls (it's the greenhouse style) you can sit and watch skiers schussing down the mountain. Moderate.

The **Stratton Diner** (Stratton; 207-246-9485) is a good spot to mingle with the locals. It's a family business that's been going strong for about 20 years. The Stratton has a mainstream menu along with a lot of characters. Budget.

The ornate dining room at **The Winter's Inn** (School Street, Kingfield; 207-265-5421) is as romantic and handsomely decorated as the rest of the historic building it occupies. The restaurant offers fine French-American cuisine along with breathtaking mountain views. Lunch, dinner and brunch; ultra-deluxe.

The area's most highly regarded restaurant is **One Stanley Avenue** (1 Stanley Avenue, Kingfield; 207-265-5541). It's housed in a Queen Anne-style Victorian building and offers classic regional cuisine (maple cider chicken, saged rabbit with raspberry sauce). Desserts can be counted on to elicit oohs and aahs. Moderate to deluxe.

The peach-colored, antique-filled dining room is so pretty you'll want to linger for hours at **The Herbert** (Main Street, Kingfield; 207-265-2000). A lovely spot for dinner, the changing menu offers a host of American dishes. Moderate.

The food at the **Country Club Inn** (Routes 4 and 16, Rangeley; 207-864-3831) is almost upstaged by the view. From your table you can look out over Rangeley Lake, often as smooth as glass and interrupted only by a lone canoe. All around loom mountains that seem to change colors as often as you change courses. Fortunately, the food holds its own, with a selection of traditional American dishes along with some French recipes. Moderate to deluxe.

When locals want to celebrate birthdays or anniversaries, they usually go to the **Rangeley Inn** (Main Street, Rangeley; 207-864-3341). It has a formal, turn-of-the-century dining room where you can feast on French or American specialties. Moderate to deluxe.

If you just don't feel like cooking in your housekeeping cottage yet you're not in the mood to dress up for dinner out, pull up to the **Red Onion** (Main Street, Rangeley; 207-864-5022). It's your basic pizza and subs kind of place that's crammed with locals and tourists alike. Don't be surprised if you have to wait a few minutes for a table to free up. Deck dining during summer months. Budget to moderate.

If you're not staying at the **Bethel Inn** (On the Common, Bethel; 207-824-2175), at least treat yourselves to dinner there. The fare at this lovely country resort is traditional New England served in the formal dining room (with views of the golf course and hills), in the Mill Brook Tavern downstairs or on the screened-in veranda during the warm-weather months. Moderate to deluxe.

You can't help but fall in love with **Mother's** (Upper Main Street, Bethel; 207-824-2589). It's a gingerbread house with wood stoves, crammed bookshelves and all sorts of eclectic adornments filling three dining areas. Lunches are simple and light (soups, salads, sandwiches), while dinners include a selection of seafood, pasta and chicken dishes. Budget to moderate.

It's tempting to fill up on the homemade breads that start off every meal at the **Olde Rowley Inn** (Route 35, North Waterford; 207-583-4143). But do save room for the delicious salmon or chicken dishes and the scrumptious desserts. The dining room is absolutely beautiful, with exposed timber beams and stenciled walls. Moderate.

If you get a craving for wienerschnitzel while hiking around these alpine hills, you're in luck. The **Switzer Stubli Restaurant** (Bridgton; 207-647-2522) in the Tarry-A-While Resort serves Swiss cuisine! While you take turns dunking homemade bread in the rich fondue, you can peer out at Highland Lake. Moderate to deluxe.

True gourmands find their way to the **Oxford House Inn** (Main Street, Fryeburg; 207-935-3442), a 1913 house that faces the White Mountains. It has a lovely repertoire of dishes including salmon Pommery and grilled pork tenderloin. During the summer, cocktails are served on the piazza. Deluxe.

The Great Outdoors
The Sporting Life

CANOEING
In a state where the sea, lakes and rivers sparkle like diamonds, you couldn't ask for a better way to explore than in a canoe. Here's where you can rent canoes on the coast: **Valley Mountain Cabins** (Route 201, Jackson; 207-668-5621), **Maine Sport** (Route 1, Rockport; 207-236-8797), **Sea Touring Kayak Center** (6 John Street, Camden; 207-236-9569), **Acadia Bike & Canoe Inc.** (48 Cottage Street, Bar Harbor; 207-288-5483) and **Mansell Boat Rental** (Main Street, Southwest Harbor; 207-244-5625). Up in the north, in Millinocket, contact **Katahdin Outfitters** (207-723-5700) or **Allagash Wilderness Outfitters** (207-723-6622). On Moosehead Lake, contact the **Wilderness Expeditions** (Rockwood; 207-534-2242). In western Maine, try **Saco River Canoe & Kayak** (Fryeburg; 207-935-2369) or **Town & Lake Motel** (Main Street, Rangeley; 207-864-3755).

DEEP-SEA FISHING
Opportunities to get out on deep-sea fishing boats abound on Maine's coast. Here are some outfits to contact: **Seabury Charters** (York Harbor, York; 207-363-5675), the **Deepwater**, run by Captain Ben Emery (Arundel Shipyard, Kennebunkport; 207-967-5595), the **Anjin-San**, with Captain Greg Walts (Portland; 207-772-7168), the **Devil's Den**, with Captain Harry Adams (DiMillo's Marina, Portland; 207-761-4466), the **Anjin-San** (near town landing, South Freeport; 207-772-7168), **Bingo Cruises** (Tugboat Inn, Boothbay Harbor; 207-882-9309), **The Henrietta** (Rockland Harbor, Rockland; 207-594-5411), **Masako Queen** (Southwest Harbor; 207-288-5927) and **Frenchman Bay Boating Company** (West Street, Bar Harbor; 207-288-3322).

GOLFING
The central part of the coast is where you'll find Maine's largest concentration of golf courses, including **Kebo Valley Golf Club** (Eagle Lake Road, Bar Harbor; 207-288-3000), **Bar Harbor Golf Course** (Junction of Routes 3 and 204, Trenton; 207-667-7505), **Castine Golf Club** (Battle Av-

enue, Castine; 207-326-8844), **Island Country Club** (Route 15A, Sunset, Deer Isle; 207-348-2379, **White Birches Golf Course** (Thorsen Road, Ellsworth; 207-667-3621), **Causeway Club** (Fernald Road, Southwest Harbor; 207-244-3780), **Grindstone Neck Golf Course** (Grindstone Avenue, Winter Harbor; 207-963-7760), **Northeast Harbor Golf Club** (Northeast Harbor; 207-276-5335) and the **St. Croix Gold Club** (River Street, Calais; 207-454-8875).

SAILING

You'll find every kind of sailboat imaginable in Maine's waters, from simple Sunfish to tall-masted windjammers. Contact the following: **Maine Sail School** (Ocean Avenue, Kennebunkport; 207-967-5043), **Saco Bay Sailing** (Beach Avenue, Saco; 207-283-1624), **Friendship Sloops** (Linekin Bay, East Boothbay; 207-633-4780), **Holladay Marine** (West Boothbay Harbor; 207-633-4767), **John Ames Associates** (Pier 8, Boothbay Harbor; 207-633-4188), **Schooner Captains** (Rockland; 207-594-8007), **The Timberwind** (Rockport Harbor, Rockport; 207-236-3639), **Camden Yacht Club Sailing Program** (Bayview Street, Camden; 207-236-3014), **Chance Along Sailing Center** (Belfast; 207-338-1833), **Great Harbor Charters** (Northeast Harbor; 207-276-5352) and **Golden Anchor Sloop** (Golden Anchor Pier, Bar Harbor; 207-288-9505).

CROSS-COUNTRY SKIING

Gliding through Maine's miles and miles of pine-scented trails on skis is a beautiful way to experience the essence of the state's winters. Here are some touring centers that can help: **Squaw Mountain at Moosehead** (Moosehead; 207-695-2272), **Currier's Flying Service** (Greenville; 207-695-2778), which offers fly-in touring trips, **Birches Ski Touring Center** (Rockwood; 207-534-7305), **Carrabassett Valley Ski Touring Center** (Carrabassett Valley, Kingfield; 207-237-2205), **Ski Nordic Touring Center at Saddleback** (Rangeley; 207-864-5671), **Bethel Inn and Country Club** (Bethel; 207-824-2175) and **Sunday River Ski Touring Center** (Bethel; 207-824-2410).

DOWNHILL SKIING

Maine's downhill skiing revolves largely around **Sugarloaf/USA**, (Carrabassett Valley, Kingfield; 207-237-2000), which is the biggest ski mountain in New England. However, there are several other mountains to check out: **Moosehead Resort and Ski Area** (Greenville; 207-695-2272), **Moosehead Nordic Center** (Route 16 at Indian Hill; Greenville; 207-695-2870), **Saddleback Mountain** (Rangeley; 207-864-3380), **Sunday River Ski Area** (Bethel; 207-824-2187), **Shawnee Peak at Pleasant Mountain** (Bridgton; 207-647-8444) and **Camden Hills State Park** (Camden; 207-236-3438).

WHITEWATER RAFTING

The northern woods are laced with choppy-water rivers. Try these on for size: **Eastern River Expeditions** (Greenville; 207-695-2411), **Wilderness Rafting Expeditions** (Rockwood; 207-534-2242), **Northern Outdoors, Inc.** (The Forks; 207-663-4466), **Voyagers Whitewater** (The Forks; 207-663-4423) and **Crab Apple White Water** (The Forks; 207-663-2218).

BICYCLING

One of the best ways to see the Maine coast is by pedaling along it. You can basically pick a spot—any spot—and start riding. Just watch out for summer traffic.

A lovely 22-mile loop on **Cape Elizabeth**, just south of Portland, starts and finishes at the Scarborough Public Library on Route 207. It winds through Scarborough Marsh, by several beaches (including Scarborough Beach and Crescent Beach State Park) and through Lights State Park and Prouts Neck Bird Sanctuary.

The **Boothbay Harbor** area is a lot more manageable on two wheels than four. From Boothbay Harbor itself, try pedaling east to East Boothbay and then south to Ocean Point (about 14 miles round-trip). Or do the loop around Southport Island (about 16 miles starting and finishing in Boothbay Harbor).

On **Deer Isle,** there are several bicycling possibilities. From the center of the village, you can ride through silent woods out to the Haystack Mountain School of Crafts (seven miles one way) or to the little lobstering village of Stonington (six and a half miles one way). Or take your bikes over on the mail boat to **Isle au Haut** and ride along the sea for a couple of miles.

There are over 50 miles of carriage paths on **Mount Desert Island** to cycle on. One of the most exhilarating trips is the 28-mile **Acadia National Park Loop** (the car route with detours). The steep ascent of Cadillac Mountain is not for everyone though.

There are also some pleasant inland trips as well, though distances tend to be long and—if you're in the western region—hilly or mountainous. A stunningly beautiful trip for big-time bicyclers can be had up at **Baxter State Park.** It's about 46 miles, between Ripogenus Dam and Spencer Cove. You pass waterfalls, whitewater rivers and miles of majestically beautiful forest and you can see Mt. Katahdin looming on the horizon.

BIKE RENTALS   In Kennebunkport, bikes are for rent at **Cape-able Bike Shop** (Townhouse Corners; 207-967-4382). In Rockport, you can rent regular bikes or mountain bikes at **Maine Sport** (Route 1; 207-236-8797). To rent bikes in Bar Harbor, contact **Acadia Bike & Canoe** (48 Cottage Street; 207-288-5483). At Moosehead Lake in the Northern Woods bikes are available at **The Birches** (Rockwood Village; 207-534-7305).

Beaches and Parks

SOUTHERN COAST BEACHES AND PARKS

Rachel Carson National Wildlife Refuge—This 4,600-acre preserve offers coastal access in 11 towns along a 45-mile stretch from Kittery to Cape Elizabeth. Each of ten divisions protects estuarine rivers forming a salt marsh where they meet the Atlantic. Hiking trails make it easy to explore the coast and adjacent woodlands. The Wells headquarters offers a mile-long wheelchair accessible trail. This unit is also adjacent to Laudholm Farm, a public facility offering seven miles of trails.

Facilities: Picnic area and restrooms. *Fishing:* Saltwater and freshwater; information, 207-646-9226.

Getting There: Headquarters is located on Route 9, just north of Kennebunkport.

Ogunquit Beach—Driving along Route 1, you can't help but pull over and gasp at the beauty of this spacious beach. It's utterly magnificent. You see the wild ocean crashing in, waves breaking in a series of prismatic explosions. On a good day, the sky's a beautiful blue punctuated with perfect white clouds. Wide and smooth, the beach stretches for three miles and divides into three main areas. You'll find the most popular expanse at the foot of Beach Street. The Footbridge Street area, slightly less crowded, is off Ocean Street. Moody Beach, off Eldridge Street, is even less peopled.

Facilities: Changing rooms and toilets at the main beach area, restrooms only at the Footbridge Beach. *Swimming:* Since the water temperature rarely exceeds 60° even in July and August, not all people would say swimming is good here. However, for northern Mainers and Canadians, it's tepid.

Getting there: Located near Ogunquit, just off Route 1.

Wells Beach—Just north of the wave-slapped sands of Ogunquit Beach, this is similar in its natural beauty. The beach is wide and smooth and has great bodysurfing waves but, ooooooh, is the water chilly. It does, however, go a bit overboard with the tourist clutter. There are motels, clam shacks, even a boardwalk boasting all sorts of Atlantic-City-type diversions.

Facilities: Toilets, playgrounds, casino, clam shacks.

Getting there: Located on Route 1 in the village of Wells Beach.

Kennebunk Beach—One look at this beach and you'll understand why President Bush lives nearby and why everyone else bought summer cottages in this area. It's wildly spacious, long and wide (some fine sand areas, some shingle patches) and smashed by waves that drown out any conversation you might try to have. Add a couple of diving gulls and an invigorating breeze and what more could you possibly want?

Facilities: None.

Getting there: Located on Beach Avenue, one and a half miles southwest of Kennebunkport.

Arundel Beach—This small sandy pocket has a marvelous air of exclusivity in spite of its Bush Country location. It's backed by huge rocks that are fun for climbing on. It's also right down the coast from Walker's Point, where the Summer White House is located.

Facilities: None.

Getting there: Located right off Ocean Avenue in Kennebunkport.

Ferry Beach State Park—Hugging the coastline, this 117-acre preserve is densely scenic. Along with patches of pines and other northern trees, there's a surprising stand of tupelo trees, which are rare at this latitude. The whole park is threaded with self-guiding trails. The beach—a sweep of white smashed by Atlantic waves—is perhaps its biggest attraction.

Facilities: Picnic tables, toilets, changing rooms; information, 207-283-0067. *Swimming:* Good.

Getting there: Located off Route 9 on Bayview Road, between Camp Ellis and Old Orchard Beach.

Scarborough Beach State Park (★)—Just before following Route 207 out to Prouts Neck (a funny shaped little peninsula), you can turn off and find yourselves face to face with a drop-dead gorgeous sandy beach that's backed by dunes and marshes. It's not big, and it's not heavily populated, thanks to limited parking.

Facilities: Changing rooms, drinking water, lifeguards; information, 207-883-2416. *Swimming:* Good, almost no undertow. Good bodysurfing waves.

Getting there: Take Route 207, three miles south of Route 1, from the town of Scarborough.

Crescent Beach State Park—Located in Cape Elizabeth, this park is known for its sandy beach that sprawls on for a mile. It attracts lots of Portlanders, especially during summer weekends. They come to swim in the sudsy surf and to soak up rays. The beach is situated so that you're protected from the real cool Atlantic and northern breezes. Elsewhere in the park, you'll find a rocky headland, tidal pools, a freshwater marsh, a spruce and oak forest and abundant wildlife and birds.

Facilities: Picnic tables, changing rooms with showers, playground, snack bar; information, 207-767-3625. *Swimming:* Good.

Getting there: Located along Route 77, eight miles south of Portland.

Wolf's Neck Woods State Park—You don't have to go very far from L. L. Bean's to try out your new hiking boots or cross-country skis. This 250-acre park is in Freeport, about five miles away. It's woven with well-maintained trails that offer achingly beautiful views of Casco Bay, its spruce and fir-covered islands and the coast's rocky shoreline. The park is largely covered with woods colonized by birds that belt out arias as if they were opera singers.

Facilities: Picnic tables, restrooms, nature programs; information, 207-865-4465.

Getting there: Located on Wolf Neck Road, south of Freeport.

Popham Beach State Park—Seemingly at the end of the world, this park offers an array of beachy pleasures. Along with a spacious sandy beach, there are tidal pools, smooth rocks to climb around on and a sand bar to explore when the tide goes out. It's right at the mouth of the Kennebec River.

Facilities: Bathhouses, freshwater showers, charcoal grills; information, 207-389-1335. *Swimming:* Good.

Getting there: Located off Route 209 south of Phippsburg.

Reid State Park—The centerpiece here is a great expanse of sand beach that stretches nearly a mile and a half and is backed by dunes and marshes. In addition to ocean swimming, there's a saltwater pond that is especially great for young children. Fortunately, the area never seems to get too crowded.

Facilities: Bathhouses with freshwater showers, fireplaces, snack bar; information, 207-371-2303. *Swimming:* Good.

Getting there: Located off Route 127, 14 miles south of Woolwich.

Rachel Carson Salt Pond Preserve—Named for the author of *Silent Spring*, this lovely Pemaquid Peninsula refuge offers a wide range of habitats to explore. Located a few peninsulas north of Boothbay Harbor, the one-acre salt pond is encircled by rocks and home to a multitude of marine species, ducks and other waterfowl.

Facilities: None.

Getting there: From New Harbor, follow Route 32 for about a mile and look for the entrance sign.

Camden Hills State Park—A huddle of gentle hills, this state park is always lovely whether bundled in mist or reflective as mica. It's laced with wooded trails that wrap around the hills like vines, offering beautiful views of Penobscot Bay, the wind-swept mountain scenery and the piney forests.

Facilities: Picnic area; information, 207-236-3109. *Camping:* Permitted.

Getting there: The entrance is about two miles north of Camden on Route 1.

DOWNEAST COAST BEACHES AND PARKS

Acadia National Park—One of Maine's most scenic areas, Acadia National Park encompasses a large portion of Mount Desert Island, the Schoodic Peninsula on the mainland and teeny Isle au Haut. For exploring on Mount Desert, consider driving the Park Loop Road. It hits the major highlights, including Frenchman Bay Overlook, a spectacular lookout point complete with interpretive signs pointing out the islands before you; the Wild Gardens of Acadia, a colorful wildflower garden; Champlain Mountain Overlook, another jaw-dropping view of the island-dotted Frenchman Bay area; Sand Beach, made up of the crushed shells of marine animals; and the summit of Cadillac Mountain, an above-the-clouds view of it all. The Schoodic Peninsula provides a good day-long side trip. A one-way road wraps around the peninsula, offering sweeping views of Frenchman Bay, the Atlantic Ocean and the Mount Desert Mountains, while another climbs to the top of Schoodic Mountain. It takes a bit of planning to reach Isle au Haut, but once there, you can go hiking, birding and camping.

Facilities: Information center, picnic areas, restrooms, souvenir shops; information, 207-288-3338. *Camping:* Permitted at designated sites only. The two campgrounds are Blackwoods and Seawall. For information, write: Superintendent, Acadia National Park, Box 177, Bar Harbor, ME 04609. *Fishing:* Try Jordan Pond for salmon and lake trout; Long Pond for landlocked salmon; Eagle Lake for brook trout, salmon and lake trout; Echo Lake for brook trout and salmon; Upper and Lower Hadlock Pond for brook trout. *Swimming:* At Sand Beach. The sand is the biggest attraction here, made up of shell fragments.

Getting there: The best way to approach Mount Desert Island is via Route 3 from Route 1 at Ellsworth. Isle au Haut is reached by a mail boat (207-367-5193) that makes regular trips from Stonington. The Schoodic Point peninsula is farther up the coast, off Route 186.

Lamoine State Park—Located on Frenchman Bay, Lamoine State Park offers spectacular views of the dramatic peaks of Mount Desert Island. Its own 55 acres of woods and waterfront are popular for camping and picnicking.

Facilities: Picnic tables, restrooms, dock and boat launch. *Camping:* Permitted; for information call 207-667-4778. *Fishing:* Good. *Swimming:* There's no lifeguard, and swimming is cold.

Getting there: Follow Route 184 from Ellsworth to Lamoine.

Roque Bluffs State Park—Carved out of Englishman Bay, Roque Bluffs is a 300-acre park with both a saltwater and freshwater beach, plus lots of wooded trails. Unfortunately, it's frequently too windy to use the pebble beach on the ocean. The other beach is sandy and skirts the edge of a sheltered freshwater pond.

Facilities: Picnic areas, changing areas, toilets, playground; information, 207-255-3475. *Swimming:* Good but very cold! *Fishing:* Very good.

Getting there: Located about six miles off Route 1; turn off Route 1 just beyond Jonesboro.

Cobscook Bay State Park—An extremely scenic park, Cobscook (an Indian word that means "boiling tide") sits on the shores of Cobscook Bay, where tides can reach 24 feet. Its 888 acres are covered with spruce and fir trees and snaked by hiking and cross-country ski trails. It's also a good place to spot bald eagles.

Facilities: Picnic area, restrooms. *Camping:* Permitted; information, 207-726-4412. *Fishing:* Permitted in the bay. Also, you can try your hand at clamming. *Swimming:* Good.

Getting there: Located on Route 1 in Dennysville.

Quoddy Head State Park—Dramatically situated at the easternmost point of land in the continental United States, Quoddy Head State Park offers some magnificent views of the Atlantic Ocean and Grand Manan Island. The biggest attraction here is the red-and-white-striped lighthouse that surveys the Bay of Fundy, known for its extreme tides. Hiking trails ribbon through spruce groves; one skirts a high ledge along steep cliffs that drop into the sea.

Facilities: Picnic tables, fireplaces; information, 207-764-2040.

Getting there: From Route 1, take Route 189 to the town of Lubec and follow the signs.

Reversing Falls Park—You're not alone if you're wondering what reversing falls are. This is definitely one of those go-see-for-yourselves sit-

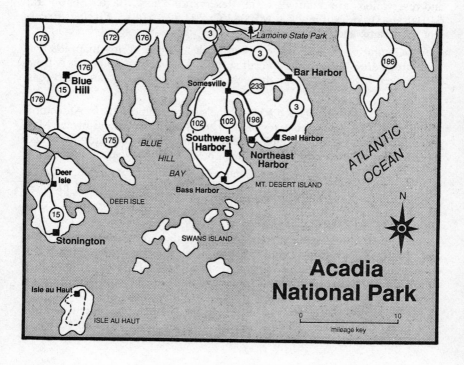

uations. The falls are actually a field of rapids dramatically galloping in the middle of the waterway. The Baltic scenery around it is part of a 140-acre park with hiking trails and picnic sites.

Facilities: Picnic tables and grills, outhouses.

Getting there: Traveling north on Route 1, you'll pass the turn-off for Cobscook Bay State Park. Continue on for nine and a half miles and turn right at Antone's Triangle Store. Almost immediately, you'll turn right again at the red building. Follow that for three and a half miles, then turn right again. Follow for almost three miles, bearing left at the water. It's easier than it sounds, but none of these dirt roads have names.

NORTHERN WOODS BEACHES AND PARKS

Baxter State Park—Maine's grande dame of parks, this 200,000-acre wilderness preserve is magnificent. There are over 75 miles of hiking trails that take you through pine forests, by rivers of rapids, alongside blue lakes and up mountains—including Mt. Katahdin (5267 feet), the highest in Maine. Katahdin is the northern terminus for the Appalachian Trail. Wildlife and birds are abundant here, as are a phenomenal variety of trees and plants.

Facilities: Once you're in the park, there's no food, fuel or supplies. Stock up in Millinocket. *Camping:* Permitted in ten campgrounds; permit and reservations are required; write: Reservation Clerk, Baxter State Park, 64 Balsam Drive, Millinocket, ME 04462; 207-723-5140. *Fishing:* Excellent in streams and lakes. *Swimming:* Yes, if you can stand the cold.

Getting there: You can't miss this place. Look at any map, it's that huge green area in the central north section. Your easiest approach is from Millinocket. If you arrive from the west, expect a couple of hours of dirt-road travel.

Aroostook State Park (★)—Maine's northernmost park, Aroostook covers 577 thickly wooded acres on the shores of Echo Lake. Between May 15 and October 15, it's an outdoor lover's paradise, with hiking trails and secluded glassy coves for swimming. The rest of the year, it's closed.

Facilities: Picnic sites, boat and canoe rentals, boat launch. *Camping:* Permitted; information, 207-768-8341. *Swimming:* Good. *Fishing:* Good, especially trout fishing on Echo Lake.

Getting there: Located off Route 1, just south of Presque Isle.

Allagash Wilderness Waterway—Stretching for 92 miles from Telos Lake (north of Ripogenus Dam) to the far north near Fort Kent, this famous corridor of lakes and rivers is most well known for its flatwater/white-water canoe trips. It's quite beautiful and known as "God's Country." The strip also boasts good fishing waters and snowmobiling in winter. If you plan to canoe, it's necessary to register. Write the Maine Department of Conservation, Bureau of Parks and Recreation, State House Station #22, Augusta, ME 04333.

Facilities: None; information, 207-289-3821, May through October; 207-723-8518, November through April. *Camping:* Permitted. *Swimming:* Very good in clear lakes.

Getting there: Most of the Allagash Wilderness outfitters are in Millinocket or at Ripogenus Dam. If you're on your own, a good put-in point is Chamberlain Thoroughfare at the junction of Chamberlain and Telos lakes. You'll find rangers at Allagash Lake, Chamberlain Thoroughfare, Eagle Lake, Churchill Dam, Long Lake Thoroughfare and the Michaud Farm.

Lily Bay State Park—This is a beautiful wilderness area on the shores of 40-mile-long Moosehead Lake. The lake really does sparkle and is framed by evergreen forests and mountains that look like waves plastered against the sky. There is a hiking trail, but most of the activity revolves around the water—swimming, fishing or boating. In winter, snowmobiling and skiing takes over.

Facilities: Two boat launches with berths. *Camping:* Permitted; information, 207-695-2700. *Fishing:* Moosehead Lake is well known for its brook trout, salmon and lake trout (togue). *Swimming:* Good.

Getting there: Located about eight miles north of Greenville on the eastern shore of Moosehead Lake.

WESTERN LAKES AND MOUNTAINS BEACHES AND PARKS

Rangeley Lake State Park—This is unadulterated wilderness. Pine trees point to the sky, while white birch are perfectly reflected in the glassy lake. Moose are seen here frequently. The park covers 100 acres, taking in lots of forest and the southern rim of Rangeley Lake. People that know about the Rangeley Lake State Park usually keep it to themselves.

Facilities: Picnic sites, children's play area, boat launch. *Camping:* Permitted; information, 207-864-3858. *Fishing:* Famous for trout and landlocked salmon. *Swimming:* A small lake beach.

Getting there: Located on Route 17 south of Oquossoc.

Mount Blue State Park—An enormous 3500-acre park that encompasses Mount Blue and Lake Webb, Mount Blue offers one jaw-droppingly beautiful vista (mountains, lakes, more mountains) after another. There are plenty of trails to hike along, as well as boating opportunities on Lake Webb. The park offers guided nature walks.

Facilities: Picnic area, bathhouse, boat launch, amphitheater and recreation hall, canoes for rent. *Camping:* Permitted; information, 207-585-2347. *Fishing:* Good for bass, perch, trout and salmon in Lake Webb. *Swimming:* A small sandy beach.

Getting there: Located off Route 156 in Weld.

Grafton Notch State Park—Over on the Maine/New Hampshire border, between Upton and Newry, you'll find Grafton Notch. The 2000-mile Appalachian Trail passes through it on the way to its northern terminus,

Mt. Katahdin. Throughout the park, you'll see waterfalls, caves and beautiful mountain scenery (it's at the end of the Mahoosuc Range).

Facilities: Picnic tables, grills, toilets, water pump.

Getting there: Located on Route 26, about 16 miles north of Bethel.

Sebago Lake State Park—Some days, this gigantic lake shines like one huge sheet of aluminum foil. You'll find the water deliciously clear (it's Portland's main water supply). Many people come just for the day to swim and play on and off the sandy beaches. Some stay at the campsites that are spread out along the shores and in the woods on the northern end.

Facilities: Picnic sites with tables and grills, bathhouses, lifeguards, boat ramp. *Camping:* Permitted; information, 207-693-6613. *Fishing:* Good, especially for salmon and togue. *Swimming:* Extensive sand beaches.

Getting there: Off Route 302, between Naples and South Casco.

Hiking

SOUTHERN COAST TRAILS

The **Fore River Trail** (1 mile) goes through the heart of Portland's Fore River Sanctuary. It's an easy walk weaving through woods and marshes to a 30-foot-high waterfall. Several other trails veer off the main loop.

The whole of Monhegan Island is prime hiking territory, but if time is limited, at least try to follow **Cliff Trail** (about 2 miles). It takes you through the most densely scenic part of the island, over the dramatic headlands and coves that make up the eastern shore. You'll probably spend about half the day following it, but the views (plunging cliffs, deeply indented coves, open sea) are worth it.

The hike to the top of **Bald Rock Mountain** (1 mile round-trip) in Camden Hills State Park rewards trekkers with glorious views of Penobscot Bay, Blue Hill, the rugged peaks of Mount Desert Island and the islands anchored offshore. It's a fairly easy climb that passes through forests ablaze with wildflowers. To reach the trailhead take Route 1 north of Camden to Lincolnville Beach. Turn left on Route 173 and take another left when you reach Young Town Road. The trailhead is near a fire road (Bald Rock Road).

DOWNEAST COAST

Duck Harbor Mountain (★) (1 mile) is a delightful short hike on Isle au Haut. From its peak, you can see much of the island itself, which is covered largely with dense stands of spruce and fir, marshlands, streams and ponds and some spectacular cliffs.

From atop **Blue Hill** (2 miles round-trip) you won't be able to take your eyes off the view. Like a painting, the peaks of Mount Desert Island and the sailboat-dotted waters of the Blue Hill Bay spread out before you. On a clear day, you can see the villages of Penobscot and Castine and the

Camden Hills. The trail itself passes through thick spruce and fir forests. To reach it, turn west on the Mountain Road opposite the entrance to the Blue Hill Fairgrounds and you'll see the trailhead about a mile down on the right.

Acadia National Park has an enormous network of hiking trails that attract hikers and rock-climbers from around the world. The Visitors Center has an information sheet, profiling many of the trails, which range in difficulty from very easy paths to strenuous hikes.

The **North Ridge of Cadillac Mountain** (3.8 miles) in Acadia Park is a moderate trail with some steep grades and level stretches. By and large, though, it's a gradual ascent with exhilarating views of the island-dotted bays, coastline and clouds—below you.

If you feel up to it, consider climbing **Acadia Mountain** (2.5 miles), also in Acadia National Park. It's fairly strenuous but offers achingly beautiful views of the mountains, the offshore islands (from the top they look like croutons floating in soup) and Somes Sounds, the only fjord of the eastern U.S. seaboard.

Another good, though strenuous hike inside Acadia National Park is **Beachcroft Trail** (2 miles), whose trailhead is along Route 3 at the northern end of the Tarn. The trail takes you up—steeply—the side of an ice-carved valley where you can read the glacial record.

Beech Mountain (1.3 miles) over in Southwest Harbor is our personal favorite. As you ascend, the land seems to fall off all around you, revealing increasingly magnificent views of the sea and islands. There's a fire tower at the summit if you really want to stuff yourselves on gorgeous scenery.

NORTHERN WOODS TRAILS

Baxter State Park's **Owl Trail** (3 miles) begins gradually, passing through woods and by streams. However, it does get steep in patches, taking you through bouldery cliff areas. If you've got the physical fortitude, it's worth it. From the wind-slapped summit, you can see the lakes and streams that wash through this startlingly beautiful chunk of Maine. To reach the Owl Trail, start off on the Hunt Trail at the Katahdin Stream Campground. You'll see blue markers indicating where the Owl Trail turns off.

One of the most spectacular routes to Baxter Peak is the **Cathedral Trail** (1.8 miles). It is very steep and rocky, though, so be forewarned. Its name comes from the cathedrals you'll see—huge outcroppings of vertical rock slabs. To return, pick up either the **Dudley Trail** or **Knife Edge Trail**, which are not as treacherously steep and easier to descend. All three trails begin and end at the Chimney Pond Campground in Baxter State Park.

Along the Allagash Waterway at Umsaskis Lake begins the trail up **Priestly Mountain** (7 miles round-trip). From the fire tower that crowns its peak (about 1900 feet), you'll have far-reaching views of the whole water-webbed Allagash area. To reach the trail, leave your canoes at the park ranger's camp about halfway down the western shore. You'll see a sign.

Two trails lead to the summit of **Mount Kineo**, which rises dramatically from the middle of Moosehead Lake. **The Indian Trail** (1 mile) is the tougher of the two, taking you along steep cliffs. The **Bridle Trail** (1 mile) is easier but not half as beautiful. Either way you choose, the views from the bald summit make your heart throb. To reach the mountain, you have to boat in. There are motorboats for rent along the Moose River and in Rockwood, on the western shore of Moosehead Lake as well as hourly shuttle boats from Oak Lodge.

If you take just one hike while in New England, let it be at **Gulf Hagas** (10 miles round-trip), otherwise known as "Maine's Grand Canyon." This area is perhaps the most scenic in the state, taking in the three-mile canyon, five major waterfalls and 40-foot-high vertical walls. The only catch is finding this place. It's east of Greenville and west of Katahdin Iron Works. Your best bet is to consult *The Maine Atlas*, where it's clearly indicated.

The **Sally Trail** (6 miles round-trip) winds its way up Sally Mountain through forests of birch hardwoods and fir trees. From the summit, you can see island-dotted Attean Pond and other mountains that loom up all around. To reach the trail, drive two miles south from Jackman on Route 201 to Attean Road. Turn right and follow the road for about two miles to the Attean Lake Resort. The trail starts near the lake landing, by the railroad tracks.

WESTERN LAKES AND MOUNTAINS TRAILS

A good "starter" mountain in the Rangeley Lakes Area is **Bald Mountain** (2 miles round-trip), where the trail gradually ascends through hardwood forests. From the top you can see portions of Mooselookmeguntic Lake and other nearby lakes. You'll also see the Kennebago Mountains to the north, the Aziscohos and Deer Mountains to the west and Saddleback Mountain to the east. To reach the trailhead, follow Route 4 from the Oquossoc Post Office for one mile and take a sharp left onto Bald Mountain Road.

The **Cascades** in the Rangeley Lakes area are a lovely sight and an easy walk (2.7 miles). It's a series of waterfalls and clear pools formed by a stream that has cut a gorge on its route to Rangeley Lake. The trail can be picked up near the one-room Greenvale School, about four miles south of Rangeley.

The somewhat tricky trail up **Little Jackson Mountain** (6.5 miles) climbs above the timberline through pretty woods and patches of blueberry and cranberry bushes. The view of the Weld area from the summit is worth the hike. To get there, follow the unmarked road that heads west out of Weld Corner. Stay on it until you see a cemetery. Just beyond that, turn right onto the bumpy dirt road.

Step Falls (1 mile) is a long, dramatic string of cascades and icy pools. During summer months (even late August), take along your bathing suits for a dip in the thrilling nature water slide. The falls are located off Route 26, about 15 miles northwest of Bethel. There's no sign, but you'll see cars parked at the trailhead.

A simple walk recommended for young families is the trail to the summit of **Sabattus Mountain** (1.5 miles round-trip), which passes through silent woods on gentle inclines. From the top, there are wide-angle views of the mountains all around. To reach the trail, follow Route 5 to just north of Center Lovell, then turn right on the dirt road. When you come to a fork, stay right. Continue on past a white house to the parking area.

Travelers' Tracks

Sightseeing

SOUTHERN COAST

Many people cross the New Hampshire border into the state of Maine expecting to find what they've always pictured: postcard fishing villages with salty characters, sprawling farms, pine forests. Well, dear readers, you have to look a little to find these pictures in southern Maine. What you're most likely to notice first along the Southern Coast—besides scores of factory outlets that line Route 1—is a profusion of hotels, motels, inns and every other kind of tourist accommodation conceivable, along with clam shacks and lobster joints broadcasting their low, low prices.

This is the gateway to the Vacation State. Just about everybody passes through the narrow southern tip on their way to the big tourist hubs like Boothbay Harbor and Mount Desert Island as well as the never-heard-of-before villages and hamlets that line the coast and lie scattered around the northern and western parts of the state. Interstate 95 can get you up north much faster, but we're going to take it slow, meandering up Route 1.

Southern Maine does have an abundance of something the rest of the state can envy—sandy beaches. In fact, even though Maine boasts nearly 3500 miles of coastline, sandy beaches skirt fewer than 100 of those miles, and the majority lie below Portland. They start almost immediately around Kittery, Maine's southernmost town. As you drive along Route 1, don't hesitate to detour along shore roads and Route 1A, which lead right by the beaches.

You can pull over at any time (why not, everybody else does—the traffic problem is part of the fun) to gaze out at the fury of the sea and the beach crowd. Beachgoers in this part of the world dress the gamut from string bikinis to down parkas and wool socks in August (the winds can really send chills racing through your body). If you want to take a swim, you can have your pick of beaches in Kittery, York, Cape Neddick, Ogunquit, Wells and other spots (see the "Beaches and Parks" section in this chapter).

These southern towns are also rife with worthwhile attractions. In **Kittery,** you might want to take a look around the **Kittery Historical and Naval Museum** (Route 1, just north of the Route 236 Rotary; 207-439-3080; admission). It's filled with naval relics from the Portsmouth Naval Yard and exhibits explaining the history of the Southern Coast.

In **York,** several historic structures have been beautifully restored. Costumed guides take you through buildings including the **Old Schoolhouse,** the **Emerson-Wilcox House** (a tavern/family dwelling-turned-general-store-turned-tailor-shop) and the 18th-century **John Hancock Warehouse and Wharf.** Orientation and tours start at **Jefferds Tavern** (Route 1A, York Village).

One of the more intriguing of York's historic sights, the **Old Gaol** (Route 1A, York Street) first opened its doors and dungeons in 1720. Today a museum, the goal gives visitors a look at its gruesome relics—cramped cells, the disciplinary pit and jailer's quarters. You'll also find displays of Indian and pioneer artifacts.

Ogunquit, named for an Algonquin word meaning "beautiful place by the sea," is a well-known art colony. You can see some of the area's most cherished works at the **Museum of Art of Ogunquit** (Shore Road; 207-646-4909) and **The Barn Gallery** (Shore Road and Bourne Lane; 207-646-5370).

If you can drag yourselves away from the beaches in **Wells,** there are some good attractions for children, including the **Wells Auto Museum** (Route 1; 207-646-9064), where over 70 antique cars are displayed. Birdwatchers can log in some remarkable sightings at Wells' public preserves, such as the **Rachel Carson National Wildlife Refuge** (off Route 9; see the "Beaches and Parks" section in this chapter) and **Wells Research Reserve** (Laudholm Farm Road, off Route 1; 207-646-1555).

Just north of Wells, you'll come to the Kennebunks—the commercial center of **Kennebunk** and the port town, **Kennebunkport.** Both towns were early shipbuilding and fishing settlements. The latter is now referred to as **Bush Country,** since it's home to the Summer White House. The little town itself is a bit too gussied up for tourists (with prices to match), but it's a worthwhile stop, nonetheless. Consider putting the car in a lot for a good part of the day and picking up a copy of the *Kennebunkport Walking Guide* (available at the **Kennebunk–Kennebunkport Chamber of Commerce,** 105 Main Street, Kennebunk; 207-967-0857, and at various lodgings and restaurants around town). In summer months, there are walking tours of Kennebunkport's historical area on Tuesday and Friday mornings. They start at **Nott House** (Maine Street, Kennebunkport; 207-967-2513), a stately Greek Revival building that dates back to 1853.

If you want to join the scores of Bush-watchers (especially in August, when the president is vacationing) or just get a glimpse of the presidential compound, take a drive along mansion-dotted **Ocean Avenue**. If the president is in town, you may have to park along the cliffs and walk. It's quite a scene, with a battery of Secret Service agents, the Maine State Police accompanied by ferocious-looking German shepherds and the media all trying to find an angle on Bush's summer vacation. **Walker's Point** is the name of the Bush compound. It's a beautiful promontory surrounded by the horizonless waters of the Atlantic. The brown-shingled house (heavily damaged in the 1991 hurricane) is the centerpiece.

While you're in the neighborhood, you might want to stop at the **Seashore Trolley Museum** (Log Cabin Road, Kennebunkport; 207-967-2712; admission). Its comprehensive collection of antique electric trolley cars includes samples from around the world—Japan, Germany, Canada and Boston. And visitors can hop aboard one train for a two-and-a-half-mile journey.

Back inland, you can take an architectural walking tour of Kennebunk's **National Register District**. It includes **The Brick Store Museum** (117 Main Street; 207-985-4802), a block of restored early-19th-century commercial buildings. One of the most well-known attractions in southern Maine is the **Wedding Cake House** (Summer Street). As the name implies, it's a white house with intricate latticework that looks like lace. The story goes that a local sea captain was forced to return to sea before a wedding cake could be baked, so he more than made it up to his bride later by building the house. The public is not welcome inside, however.

As you continue north from the Kennebunks, you can either pick up Route 1 (at Kennebunk) or opt for the more scenic Route 9 from Kennebunkport. The latter takes you past several sun-soaked beaches. When you reach the town of Scarborough, turn right onto Route 207, which leads to **Prouts Neck**. This oddly shaped peninsula juts into Saco Bay about eight miles south of Portland. Much of its coastal scenery—steep cliffs, swirling surf and dwarfish rock-clinging trees—can be seen on the canvases of American painter Winslow Homer, who lived and worked here. His studio, a converted stable overlooking the ocean, is open to the public for touring. There's also the **Prouts Neck Bird Sanctuary** at the tip, where all sorts of exotic birds have been spotted.

Portland, Maine's largest city, is the next stop. Often called "The Little San Francisco of the East," it's a lovely city of hills surrounded by water. Many of Portland's streets are lined with beautifully preserved Victorian buildings. Very progressive, the city boasts a horde of museums, galleries, shops and restaurants.

Since so many people come to Maine to get away from the urban life, they often steer clear of Portland. The very pleasant result is that you get to enjoy a city without having to skirt around all the tourist clutter. You can also see most of it on foot. Tops on our list of priorities is the **Portland**

Museum of Art (7 Congress Square; 207-775-6148). Housed in a striking postmodern building designed by Henry N. Cobb of I. M. Pei's firm, it has extensive collections of Maine-based artists such as Andrew Wyeth, Edward Hopper and Winslow Homer, among other exhibits. Just down the street is the **Wadsworth Longfellow House** (485 Congress Street; 207-772-1807; admission), where the poet spent his childhood.

One of the most interesting districts in the city is the **Old Port Exchange**, between Exchange and Pearl streets, on the waterfront. Here you'll see old brick and granite buildings that were erected during the early 19th century, when Portland was a major rail center and shipping port. Many now house restaurants, taverns and shops.

For exploring Portland's historic districts, consider stopping by the **Maine Office of Tourism** (142 Free Street; 207-772-5800), where you can pick up self-guided walking tours of the Old Port Exchange, **Congress Street** (Portland's most important commercial street since the early 1800s), **State Street** (a wealthy residential district with large Federal-style mansions) and the **Western Promenade** (a fascinating selection of architectural styles, including high Victorian Gothic, shingle-style and Italianate mansions).

For a wonderful view of the city and island-dotted Casco Bay, climb the 102 steps up the **Portland Observatory** (138 Congress Street; 207-774-5561). For a seal's-eye view, you can take a guided boat tour from Commercial Street. Contact **Casco Bay Lines** (Casco Bay Ferry Terminal, Commercial and Franklin streets; 207-774-7871) or **Bay View Cruises** (Fisherman's Wharf; 207-761-0496).

About 20 miles north of Portland along Route 1 is the world-famous town of **Freeport**, home of the legendary **L. L. Bean** (Route 1; 207-865-4761). The mall-like shop looks just like the catalogs: it's wall-to-wall camping gear, outdoor wear and sporting equipment. Aside from Bean's, the whole town has sprouted into a factory-outlet hub. You'll find all the big-name designers (Polo–Ralph Lauren, Calvin Klein, Laura Ashley) have set up shop here. This is definitely the place to come with your Christmas lists.

A few miles down the road, Brunswick is home to **Bowdoin College** (College Street; 207-725-3000), founded in 1794. Such luminaries as Nathaniel Hawthorne and Henry Wadsworth Longfellow have walked the halls of this venerable school. On campus, the **Bowdoin College Museum of Art** (Walker Art Building; 207-725-3275) showcases colonial and federal portraits, including Gilbert Stuart's *Thomas Jefferson*, as well as Winslow Homer paintings and a few works by Andrew Wyeth. Brunswick's also the spot where Harriet Beecher Stowe wrote *Uncle Tom's Cabin*, reportedly after seeing a vision.

The next town along the coast is **Bath**, which holds in its borders a wealth of shipbuilding history. In the days of wooden ships, nearly half the world's seacraft came from Bath's shipyards. For a journey back to that era, stop by the **Maine Maritime Museum** (243 Washington Street; 207-443-1316; admission). From June to October, visiting vessels are docked here and open to visitors. The museum's four venues also showcase marine artifacts, a working shipyard, a lobstering exhibit and a shop where apprentices learn the shipbuilding craft.

To glimpse a retail business that's dramatically different than the Freeport scene down the coast, pull off in Woolwich (just beyond Bath) at the **Montsweagg Flea Market** (Route 1). One of the state's biggest flea markets, Montsweagg features hundreds of dealers peddling everything from old postcards to used trailers. Even if you're not in the market for anything, it's worth stopping just for the shot of local color.

Wiscasset is a very worthwhile stop as you travel north on Route 1. This lovely little village of sea captain's houses and beautifully maintained old brick buildings was a very prosperous shipping port between the years of the American Revolution and the War of 1812.

Museum of Musical Wonders (★) (18 High Street, Wiscasset; 207-882-7163; admission) has a vintage collection of antique music boxes, musical automata, victrolas, talking machines and advertising icons such as the RCA Victor dog. Owner Danilo Konvalinka plays the rare Steinway player grand piano, the classic boxes and other instruments during the tour. The museum, located a 30-room sea captain's house, is one of the authentic treasures of the Maine Coast. Don't miss it.

There's something incredibly lovable about the seaport of **Boothbay Harbor**, down a peninsula south of Wiscasset. Admittedly, it's about as overripe as a tourist town can be—and it's hit by around 500,000 visitors each summer. But Boothbay (which started life as a tiny lobstering and fishing town) definitely has a personality of its own.

If you've come to Maine for the serenity of the sea, you're best off totally skipping Boothbay. Though there are the customary seaside elements (soaring seagulls, lobster traps, bobbing buoys), this village leans more to manmade amusements. Just pause on the footbridge that stretches across the harbor and you'll hear bowling balls trundling down alleys, the ringing and dinging of pinball machines and the smack of a cue stick hitting a pool ball. The beauty of Boothbay, however, extends far beyond the footbridge. Walk into any restaurant, and you're sure to be served by a genuinely cheery college waiter or waitress whom—by the end of the meal—you'll know absolutely everything about.

Besides popping in and out of the dozens of shops and galleries that crowd around the hilly little streets, there are several ways to amuse yourselves in Boothbay. One of the very best is by taking a boat trip. Several booths down on the wharf sell tickets for anything from a one-hour sunset cruise to an all-day outing to nearby Monhegan (see the "Beaches and Parks" section in this chapter). If time is limited, at least go out on a short trip. You'll glide by tiny islands covered with spruce and fir trees, colonies of seals lounging around with their bellies up and the kinds of birds you've seen on the pages of *National Geographic*. If you're lucky, you'll spot a great blue heron standing in the water like a caryatid.

The sweet little village of **Waldoboro** is one of the next towns you'll come to as you continue up Route 1. It has several old homes and a Lutheran church that dates back to 1771. Farther out on that peninsula (following Route 220) is **Friendship**, a picturesque lobstering port. You have to go around the inlet and then out to the tip of St. George Peninsula to get to **Port Clyde**, launching site for the mail boat to Monhegan Island. You can head out to the island from here or take a boat from Boothbay Harbor. **Monhegan Island**, a mere smidgen on the map (less than two miles long and one mile wide), has been known as a popular artists and writers retreat for years. Its scenery is striking: steep cliffs thrashed by Atlantic surf and graced with pine forests and golden meadows. The lighthouse was built in 1824. The island's many hiking trails give the visitor on foot a chance to scout out its lovely terrain.

On your way back to Route 1, take time out to visit the picture-perfect waterfront towns of **Tenants Harbor** and **Sprucehead**. Around this point of the coast—at **Penobscot Bay**—you start to see the Maine coastline everyone has always raved about. There are startlingly beautiful islands rising abruptly out of the choppy waters with sparkling sailboats gracefully skimming the waves.

Most beautiful, though, are the tall-masted **windjammers** that are famous in this area. You can spend three to six days on one eating hearty home-cooked meals and flitting about from one drop-dead gorgeous island to another. The main departure points are in the Rockland and Camden areas. (For more details, contact the **Maine Windjammer Association**, P.O. Box 317, Rockport 04856; 800-624-6380.) These towns are fishing villages that have been discovered by tourists. They are "cute" and can be counted on for restaurants, shops and inns. Some say they're too cute and have given into the pressures of pleasing tourists, therefore losing their original charms.

Worthwhile attractions in this area include the **William A. Farnsworth Library and Art Museum** (19 Elm Street, Rockland; 207-596-6457), where Andrew Wyeth's *Christina's World* and *Her Room* are displayed; the **Owls Head Transportation Museum** (just south of Rockland on Route 73; 207-594-4418), which houses one of the country's most impressive collections of antique planes and cars; and the **Maine Coast Artists Gallery** (Russell Avenue, Rockport; 207-236-2875), which showcases contemporary Maine.

As you continue up the coast, you'll come to **Searsport**, an old shipping port with stately old sea captains homes and a multitude of antique shops. Bucksport is next. That's home to the **Fort Knox State Park** (west of Bucksport on Route 1; 207-469-7719), a very impressively constructed fort that was manned during the Civil and Spanish-American wars.

From there, you can take Route 15 right into **Bangor**, Maine's third-largest city and a commercial and lumbering center. Take time to stroll around the **West Market Square Historic District** (a mid-19th-century block of shops) and the **Broadway Area**, where you'll see one lumber baron's mansion after another lined up as if contestants in a beauty contest. Then, jumping from the sublime to the unusual, you can spot the huge— 31-foot-tall, 3000-pound—statue of **Paul Bunyan** (Main Street), which commemorates the town's great logging past.

DOWNEAST COAST

Maine's Downeast Coast extends roughly from the east side of Penobscot Bay up to Calais on the Canadian border. Except in patches, it's not quite as built up as the Southern Coast. The farther north you go, the more apt you are to find hidden places and Mainers (who, up here, are called Downeasterners) who are still genuinely curious about travelers. Don't expect to find lots of restaurants, nightlife and that sort of thing. The Downeast Coast—especially in the northern parts—is worlds away from big-city life. We continue up Route 1, veering off to several villages. Our first stop is Castine, poised on the tip of a peninsula about half an hour's drive from Bucksport.

If the state of Maine were to have a Tidy Village Award (like the Cotswolds in England), it would probably go to the village of **Castine** (★). The attraction here is the town itself: a community of 18th- and 19th-century Georgian and federalist houses standing in impeccable condition. Most of these were originally erected in the mid-19th century when Castine was a prosperous shipbuilding town. Many have since been restored by people "from away" (in other words, big city folks with money to invest). Much to the objection of some natives, the town is beginning to look and feel like an open-air museum. Like most of these small coastal villages, Castine is best seen *à pied*. Stop by the **Town Office** (Court Street; 207-326-4502) for a free copy of *Welcome to Castine*, a walking tour and map that gives a capsulated history of each building.

From Castine, it's a short, steadily scenic drive over to the village of **Blue Hill**. You'll pass storybook farmhouses, ponies with tangled manes, shiny blue coves surrounded by firs and golden meadows rippling off in every direction. Blue Hill is not for everyone. In fact, many neighboring towns consider it snobby and pretentious. Indeed, it does have a big summer-home-owning community, and you're likely to see BMWs, Mercedes Benzes and turbo-engined Saabs with New York or Massachusetts plates.

The name Blue Hill comes from the hill that looms up behind, supposedly covered with blueberry bushes. The town itself is home to 75 buildings listed on the National Historic Register. Take time out to walk around

(Text continued on page 516.)

State of the Artists

Like all beautiful places, Maine draws artists like a magnet. Along the shore, you'll spot painters studying the colors of the sea before easels firmly rooted in the sand. Shops often display watercolors, sculpture and jewelry by local artisans. Even in rural villages, you'll find artwork as impressive as that of sophisticated urban areas and European capitals. In fact, many resident Maine artists hold national or international reputations. Some of their studios and workshops are open to the public. Here's a sampling of what you'll find.

In Portland's Old Port District lies the **Maine Potter's Market** (376 Fore Street; 207-774-1633), a cooperative gallery featuring the work of a number of local potters.

A striking postmodern building designed by Henry N. Cobb of I. M. Pei's studio, the prominent **Portland Museum of Art** (7 Congress Square; 207-773-2787) houses extensive collections of Maine-based artists such as Andrew Wyeth, Edward Hopper and Winslow Homer.

It may be just a barn, but that building behind the **Broad Bay Inn and Gallery** (Main Street, Waldoboro Village; 207-832-6668) features a complete gallery of paintings and crafts. It's open from late June until mid-October.

You'll find metal sculptures at **The Open Air Gallery** (Route 131; St. George; 207-372-8057). This studio specializes in maritime themes.

The art of building wooden boats is still very much alive in the state of Maine. This is certainly evidenced at the **Rockport Apprenticeshop** (Sea Street, Rockport; 207-236-6071), where visitors can tour workshops and exhibits and browse around the store.

Maine Coast Artists (Russell Avenue, Rockport; 207-236-2875), located in a historic firehouse, is a nonprofit gallery dedicated to promoting contemporary Maine art.

A self-taught artist, Jud Hartman has created a series of bronze sculptures depicting the Amerindians of the Northeast. You can view them at the **Jud Hartman Gallery and Sculpture Studio** (Main Street, Blue Hill; 207-374-9917), along with changing exhibits of watercolor paintings.

Works by over 30 contemporary Maine artists are on view at the well-known **Leighton Gallery** (Parker Point Road, Blue Hill; 207-374-5001). The exhibit changes monthly, and the grounds also feature a sculpture garden.

A large number of artists and craftspeople live and work on Deer Isle. For starts, you'll find **Ronald Hayes Pearson's Studio/Gallery** (Old Ferry Road; 207-348-2535). This is definitely a high-risk zone if you're trying not to spend money; his sterling silver jewelry pieces are stunning. The **Turtle Gallery** (Main Street; 207-348-9977) features works by regional artists, photographers and craftspeople.

In the tiny fishing village of Stonington on Deer Isle, the **Eastern Bay Cooperative Gallery** (Main Street; 207-367-5006) showcases the work of over 50 Maine craftspeople and artists.

On that same serene little island, at the end of a bumpy dirt road, you'll find the **Haystack Mountain School of Crafts** (Route 15; 207-348-2306). Here artists from around the world gather to produce works in metal, textiles, wood, glass, pottery and paper. The school is housed in a series of studios designed by noted architect Edward Larrabee Barnes. Works created here are not for sale at the school, but you can purchase them at various studios and galleries around the island, including the Blue Heron Gallery and Studio in Deer Isle Village. A free tour of the school is conducted daily.

Kennedy's Studio (4 Cottage Street, Bar Harbor; 207-288-9411) offers watercolors featuring maritime and village landscapes.

As one Eastport artist put it, "All great places are discovered—or rediscovered—by artists." Such is the case with this former sardine canning town on the northernmost coast of Maine. Here, the painters and potters are the prominent citizens, and their works are on display at the **Eastport Gallery** (51–53 Dana Street; 207-853-4166), a converted warehouse building.

With this list in hand, visitors will surely have a great deal of Maine art to choose from or simply to browse through. But travelers in these parts will undoubtedly find worthwhile art throughout the state, sometimes where they least expect it—in a hole-in-the-wall café, perhaps. Or you might discover the next Andrew Wyeth standing right next to you on a scenic stretch of beach, touching up his canvas.

and poke in the pottery and crafts shops for which Blue Hill is well-known (see the "Shopping" section in this chapter).

If you head southwest of Blue Hill, you'll eventually cut through a corner of Little Deer Isle and then climb an arching suspension bridge that takes you over to **Deer Isle** (★), a wonderful little island almost too beautiful to promote. Thanks to its seemingly end-of-the-world location, it gets only the serious Maine visitors. For a small island, it's well endowed with attractions—both manmade and natural.

Tops on our list of worthwhile stops on Deer Isle is the sweet little town of **Stonington** (★) at the southern tip. In a state where once-quaint fishing villages turn into Disneyesque attractions seemingly overnight, this town is a welcome relief. It has everything you've been expecting in Maine —shingled houses, lobster traps piled high, seagulls screeching above, a harbor bundled in mist—but hasn't been completely colonized by the "Kennebushport" crowd. Ask one of the locals to point you in the direction of **Ames Pond**, about a two-minute drive east from the center of town. During the summer months, the rare pink lilies in the pond bloom, turning it into a meadow of pink blossoms.

From the Atlantic Avenue Hardware dock in Stonington, you can catch the mail boat, *Miss Lizzie* (207-367-5193), for a day trip over to elf-sized **Isle au Haut** (★). Since you've come this far, you might as well not miss it. Part of Acadia National Park, it has some mapped out trails to explore and picnic areas. It's also home to a one-room school house and a general store.

Back on Deer Isle, plan on arriving for the tour that starts at 1 p.m. at the **Haystack Mountain School of Crafts** (south of Deer Isle Village, turn left off Route 15, and follow signs for about seven miles; 207-348-2306). Dramatically situated amidst deep piney woods right on the water, the shingled buildings house artists studios where you can observe devoted artisans skillfully manipulating clay, blowing glass or working in other media.

As you drive back in the direction of the mainland, go slow where you probably missed the turnoff on the way out to **Nervous Nellies** (Sunshine Road, Deer Isle; 207-348-6182), a jam and jelly kitchen surrounded by landscape sculptures by one of the owners. You're welcome to sample the jams and jellies. We took home a bottle of hot sauce and instantly became hooked. Thank goodness they do mail order.

One of the nicest ways to enjoy Deer Isle is on foot or by kayak (see the "Sporting Life" and "Hiking" sections in this chapter). Think twice about riding bikes, though. With the narrow, shoulderless roads, it's not only dangerous, but apparently the locals abhor bikers slowing down traffic.

Ever since the mid-19th century, **Mount Desert Island** has been one of Maine's most popular destinations. Once you cross the bridge connecting it to the mainland, it's easy to see why. The island (New England's second-largest) is home to **Cadillac Mountain**, at 1530 feet the highest point on the Atlantic coast of the United States. Looming all around are 16 other mountains that drop right down into the sea. Fortunately, most of the island (35,000 acres) is under the protection of **Acadia National Park**, which is threaded with miles of hiking, driving and biking trails.

Wherever your peregrinations take you, there's plenty to keep you enormously busy for at least a couple of days on Mount Desert Island. By the way, Mount Desert Island is pronounced like "dessert," the sweet course that follows a meal. It was given the name by French explorer Samuel de Champlain, who discovered the island in 1604. He named it *L'Isle des Monts Déserts* because of its bare, desertlike mountaintops.

Start by heading to **Acadia National Park's visitors center** (207-288-4932) off Route 3 and pick up a copy of the *Official Map and Guide to Acadia*. There's also a 15-minute introductory film and several racks of nature books. Ask for a copy of *Acadia's Beaver Log*, a park newspaper, if you're interested in finding out that week's naturalist activities.

The **Park Loop Road** takes in the major sights of the park, including Frenchman Bay Overlook, a scenic lookout that faces Schoodic Peninsula; Sieur de Monts Spring, with its nature center; the Wild Gardens of Acadia, a lovely patch featuring local flowers, trees and shrubs; Sand Beach, made partially of the crushed shells of marine animals; the Abbe Museum of Stone Age Antiquities, showcasing prehistoric artifacts of the area's original Indian tribes; and the summit of Cadillac Mountain. The road traverses approximately 27 miles up mountains, by the sea, through forests and past ponds and lakes, taking in the park's highlights (see the "Beaches and Parks" section in this chapter). For a closer look at the park's multitude of attractions, consider hiking along the many foot trails or signing up for a naturalist program. There are also boat trips, fishing opportunities and places to swim. In winter, there's cross-country skiing, snowmobiling, ice fishing and winter hiking. For more information, write: Superintendent, Acadia National Park, P.O. Box 177, Bar Harbor, ME 04609.

The island's main town is **Bar Harbor**, which back in the late 1800s was a thriving resort community for very wealthy and powerful American families. They built over 200 enormous summer homes along the sea that were just as opulent as the Newport mansions. The Depression years and two world wars really took a toll on the community, however. And finally, the Great Fire of 1947 all but wiped it out. Many of the grand old hotels and about 70 mansions were destroyed.

Bar Harbor did recover, but it emerged as a more middle-class resort. Today, during summer months, it's crawling with tourists. The main street is a tangle of T-shirt shops, motels and restaurants busy with teeny-boppers and young families. We recommend visiting the **Bar Harbor Historical Society** (Jesup Memorial Library, Route 3; 207-288-4245), which features a collection of early photographs of the town before the big fire, and the

Natural History Museum (College of the Atlantic, Route 3; 207-288-5015), a small museum that showcases stuffed birds and animals from the area.

A quartet of other towns on the island—Northeast Harbor, Southwest Harbor, Seal Harbor and Somesville—are likely to appeal more to the traveler in search of hidden attractions. They're quintessential Maine fishing villages. Two especially worthwhile stops to make are the **Asticou Azalea Gardens** (Route 3, near the junction of Route 198, Northeast Harbor), a lovely spot devoted to azalea and Japanese gardens, and the **Wendell Gilley Museum** (Route 102, Southwest Harbor; 207-244-7555; admission), if you're interested in seeing bird carvings. Families with children will want to stop at the **Mount Desert Oceanarium** (Clark Point Road, Southwest Harbor; 207-244-7330; admission), where you'll find plenty of hands-on exhibits, live sea animals and a touch-tank with sea snails, starfish and horseshoe crabs.

Back on the mainland, in busy Ellsworth, try not to miss the **Colonel Black Mansion** (West Main Street; 207-667-8671; admission), a startlingly beautiful Georgian mansion built as a wedding present in 1862 by one smitten John Black. Also worth visiting in Ellsworth is the **Stanwood Museum and Birdsacre Sanctuary** (Route 3; 207-667-8460; admission), a 130-acre nature preserve centerpieced by an old homestead that dates back to 1850.

As you work your way up the coast, you'll see less traffic, fewer commercial buildings and increasingly beautiful scenery (rolling farmlands, pine forests, glimpses of the sea). You'll also notice fewer tourists—here they're chiefly RV families and rugged outdoor sports enthusiasts en route to the dense wilderness of Baxter State Park. Your chances of meeting real, hard-working, homespun locals are much greater here than along the Southern Coast, where everyone grows up learning how to treat "people from away" properly so they'll come back. You'll find Downeasterners love to strike up a conversation with a "foreigner" and have a wonderful sense of humor.

Continue to follow Route 1, veering off whenever a road looks appealing. There are several interesting detours to watch for, including **Jonesport** and **Beals Island** (★), which you have to squint to find on most maps. Ask any Maine aficionado which are their favorite coastal villages and they're sure to mention this little duet of lobstering and fishing towns at the end of Route 187. The two are connected by a bridge and in people's minds— rarely do you hear someone mention one without the other. Your best bet is to park in Jonesport and wander around aimlessly. You'll find a handful of restaurants, antique stores and other salty little shops.

Back on Route 1, don't miss the **Ruggles House** (Columbia Falls; 207-483-4637). Built by a wealthy lumber dealer named Thomas Ruggles, it's a very extravagant Federal-style building with a flying staircase and meticulously carved woodwork throughout.

Machias is one of the next towns you'll come to. It's worth pulling over and getting out to take a stroll around. An old commercial center, it now has a handful of shops and restaurants and is home to the **Maine Wild Blueberry Company** (Elm Street; 207-255-8364), which you can tour. Machias is supposedly an Indian word that means "bad little falls," named because of the falls that run through the middle of town, where you'll also find a nice picnicking spot. Less than 15 minutes away is **Machiasport**, another photogenic village.

At East Machias, you can either continue on Route 1 or sidetrack to Route 191, taking in the little fishing village called **Cutler**. Consider taking one of Captain Norton's excursions (207-497-5933) out to see puffins on **Machias Seal Island** (May through August).

Next stop is **Lubec**, a once-very-active sardine-canning town. Today, it has sort of a lonely, end-of-the-world feel to it, but it's lovable nonetheless. For some background on its past, stop in at **The Old Sardine Village Museum** (Route 189, on the approach to Lubec; 207-733-2822; admission).

Lubec is a stepping-stone to **Campobello Island** (506-752-2922), noted as the summer home of Franklin Roosevelt's family, which is actually in New Brunswick, Canada. You don't need passports or any special papers or even toll change to cross over the bridge and spend the afternoon visiting FDR's house. At **Roosevelt Campobello International Park** (506-752-2997), visitors can tour the 34-room "cottage" where Roosevelt spent his boyhood summers from 1905 to 1921. Start by watching the excellent 15-minute movie. Then explore the house, which has been maintained exactly as the family left it. The grounds are decorously landscaped with flower beds and woven with over eight miles of trails through piney woods and along the shore. Elsewhere on the island are 15 miles of park drives and the perfect-snapshot **East Quoddy Head Lighthouse**, at the end of a long bumpy dirt road. Signs warn visitors not to venture out when the tide is coming in. It rises five feet per hour and could leave you stranded for eight hours.

Back in Lubec, follow South Lubec Road to the end to get to the **West Quoddy Light State Park**. You've undoubtably seen this lighthouse before: the candy-striped, red-and-white tower is practically an emblem for the state of Maine. Its big claim to fame is that it's at the easternmost point of the land in the continental United States. There are some hiking trails to wander along as well as benches if you feel like sitting and waiting for the sun to come up.

Route 189 will take you back out to Route 1 and up through West Pembroke, where you can detour off to see **Reversing Falls** (see the "Beaches and Parks" section in this chapter).

You might also consider taking another detour along Route 214 to **Meddybemps**. The road stretches out like a canvas over one waterslide of a hill after another, edged by wheaty fields right out of an Andrew Wyeth painting. One little hill-clinging farm has a stand of vegetables with a self-service sign. Meddybemps itself is an adorable little village with a white church, white houses and a general store. There's also a pier on Meddybemps Lake and a small beach where you can swim.

It's worth arranging to spend a few days in **Eastport** (★), an intriguing port city set on Moose Island in Passamaquoddy Bay. For years, it's had a statewide reputation of being somewhat down and out, but actually it's quite charming and those who have discovered—or rediscovered—the spot keep it to themselves. At one time, Eastport was a bustling town with 18 sardine canneries. The population had reached 5300 by the turn of the century. But between 1937 and 1943, it went bust. Canneries closed, and people moved out, leaving houses standing empty. Today, grand old Federal and Victorian houses remain as testimony to its better days. The skeletal population (maybe 2000) is a combination of old-timers remaining from the town's heyday, a thriving artist population and a small infusion of investment-seeking out-of-towners.

The best way to get acquainted with Eastport and the Eastporters is to wander along its streets. Water Street is the hub, with more empty commercial space than filled. The town has been slowly upgrading and has completed a revival of the 19th-century storefronts on the waterfront. Unfortunately, few tenants have moved in. However, many say Eastport is the next frontier. The next Bar Harbor. We hope not. The star attraction is the **Eastport Gallery** (Dana Street; 207-853-4166), a highly respected and lovingly cared for showcase of local art. In addition to a changing ground-floor exhibit, upstairs you'll find an ongoing display featuring the works of 20 regional artists.

Try to get your hands on the Eastport edition of the Maine magazine called *Salt* (sold in various shops in town). It has beautiful essays about the town's wonderful characters. Another publication to pick up is the *Quoddy Tides*, a bimonthly newspaper highlighting all the area's goings-on, including the new titles the Lubec Library has added. Don't laugh. Some people love this little tabloid so much, they end up getting a subscription sent to their Park Avenue apartment.

One way to take in a big bite of this part of the coast is to drive the **Quoddy Loop**. Also known as "The Loop," it's a network of car-ferry services linking the New Brunswick mainland with Campobello Island, Deer Island (not to be confused with Deer Isle, farther down the coast) and Eastport. The route—which easily fills up a full day—is mapped out in a free pamphlet you'll find in shops and restaurants around town. You can also call 207-255-4402 for more information.

Calais (pronounced CAL-lus) is the last real stop along this stretch of coast, and actually it's set on the St. Croix River a little inland. It's a jumping-off spot for many outdoors sportspeople, since it lies near **Grand Lake**, one of Maine's most beautiful and salmon-rich lakes. While in the area, stop at the **St. Croix Island Overlook** at Red Beach. It's a view of the island on which French explorers established the first European settlement in North America north of Florida (in 1604).

Another worthwhile stop in this area is the **Moosehorn National Wildlife Refuge** (Calais; 207-454-3521). Managed by the U.S. Fish and Wildlife Service, it's the northeast end of a chain of migratory bird refuges that extend all the way up the East Coast. Two areas make up the park, the largest (16,000 acres) in Baring, north of Calais, and the other about 20 miles south near Edmunds. This is a wilderness area crisscrossed by hiking trails.

NORTHERN WOODS

Dense wilderness is what you'll find in this part of Maine. Thick woods that seem to go on forever. Mountains holding shiny blue lakes as if they were precious gems. Rivers roaring through canyons. The air here is invigoratingly fresh. Hiking, fishing, camping and other outdoor pastimes abound. For serious nature lovers, the northern woods provide the ultimate nirvana.

Not until you actually go to northern Maine can you understand how big the state really is. You can go for hours passing only an occasional farmhouse or two. You can't take anything for granted (such as service stations and restaurants). Once you decide to travel up there, be sure to take a good map (you'll really need one, since there's often nobody to bail you out of jams). Your best bet is to pick a destination for the day and take your time getting there.

Continuing on from Calais, you can stay on Route 1, which turns from a coastal road into an inland route and can be taken to **Aroostook County**, where lakes and forests reign. **Presque Isle** is the hub up here and also the commercial center of Maine's potato country.

We will, however, head for the Baxter State Park and the northern lakes area in the central northern part of the state. It'll take several hours to get to **Millinocket** (pronounced the proper Maine way, it's Mill-a-NORK-it), and there's not much in between. You can finally leave Route 1 at Topsfield, turning onto Route 6 East and following the network of roads that eventually get you into the heart of Millinocket, where even one of the main streets is dirt. This town's biggest claim to fame is very big indeed. Being the home of Bowater Inc., it is one of the largest producers of newsprint in the United States.

Don't get your hopes up for anything more, though. Look at it as a good place to stock up on supplies and gas before heading off to the wilderness areas. In fact, do yourselves a favor and stop by the **Baxter State Park Headquarters** (64 Balsam Drive; 207-723-5140) for some detailed maps. Millinocket is also a popular takeoff point for canoe trips to the **Allagash Wilderness Waterway**. This 95-mile passage comprises 200,000 acres of interconnected lakes and rivers than run from Telos Lake to the

Canadian border. Before attempting to canoe the waterway, one should have some experience (see the "Beaches and Parks" section in this chapter).

You'll find the main entrance to **Baxter State Park** about 20 miles north of Millinocket. Sprawling majestically over 200,000 acres, this largest of Maine's parks is awe-inspiring. It was a gift to the state in 1931 by Percival Baxter, who, while serving as a legislator and as governor of Maine, urged creation of a park around Mt. Katahdin. Rebuffed, the governor bought the land with his own capital and deeded to the state of Maine the land "to be forever left in its natural, wild state."

The centerpiece is, indisputably, **Mt. Katahdin**. At 5267 feet, it's the highest peak in Maine. It's also the northern terminus for the **Appalachian Trail**. Open mid-May to mid-October, the park has 45 other peaks and over 175 miles of well-marked trails. You can drive around the perimeter in less than three hours. (See the "Beaches and Parks" section in this chapter.)

As you continue west of the park, you'll come to **Ripogenus Dam**, where the mighty waters of several interconnected lakes are halted and washed out the other side in a narrow river that races triumphantly through a deep gorge. This is the departure point for several white-water rafting trips. It's also the turnoff for those driving into the Allagash Wilderness Waterway.

A dirt road takes you south of Ripogenus Dam to **Kokadjo**, an adorable little complex of camps and a general store that was built as the headquarters for a lumber company in the early 1900s.

Continue south, stopping at **Lily Bay** (see the "Beaches and Parks" section in this chapter) and **Greenville**, a major New England seaplane base. You can stuff yourselves on local steamboat history at the latter's **Moosehead Marine Museum** (Greenville; 207-695-2716), which displays local memorabilia as well as the restored steamship Katahdin, now a floating museum.

From there, drive up the western coast of **Moosehead Lake** to the waterfront towns of Moosehead (a lumberman's depot and departure point for wilderness excursions) and Rockwood. The whole area is mesmerizingly beautiful, with mountains looming all around and evergreens perfectly reflected in the lake. It's very common to see moose in these parts.

Moosehead Lake is the biggest of Maine's countless lakes (it's 40 miles long and 20 miles wide). It's also the center for the state's wilderness sports and the source of the Kennebec River. For more information, contact the **Moosehead Lake Chamber of Commerce** (P.O. Box 581, Greenville, ME 04441; 207-695-2702).

WESTERN LAKES AND MOUNTAINS

Maine's coast may come alive in warm-weather months, but its inland regions—especially the western mountains—hit a tourism peak in winter. The star attraction is **Sugarloaf/USA**, the state's second highest mountain and its biggest ski mountain (see the "Sporting Life" section in this chapter).

At the top, you'll find New England's largest self-contained ski village, complete with hotels, restaurants, shops and a church. Below is **Carrabassett Valley**, home to the Carrabassett Valley Ski Touring Center, an enormous network of cross-country trails. The town of **Kingfield**, at the southern entrance to the Carrabassett Valley, was founded in 1816. It has a fine collection of shops, restaurants and inns.

Year-round, however, inland Maine is becoming more and more popular, especially the **Rangeley Lakes** region. Like the northern woods, this whole western area is almost solid wilderness punctuated with an occasional town (by town, we often mean a post office, a church and a general store). Moose, bear, wildflowers that look as strange as their Latin names, and birds who know a good thing when they spot one, are the most abundant residents. Some of the biggest lakes have names that are almost impossible to pronounce, but go ahead, try. They're Mooselookmeguntic, Kennebago, Aziscohos, Cupsuptic and Umbagog. Okay, we'll throw in a few easy ones: Rangeley and Richardson. They're all busy with boaters and anglers in summer months. And scattered along the shores are small camps with rustic log cabins hidden behind thick pine trees or in birch groves.

The town of **Rangeley** is evolving fast. Too fast, according to some old-timers. Seemingly overnight, it has gone from a sleepy backwoods town to an up-and-coming tourist center. Besides the little town of Oquossoc down the road, it's really the only place where you'll find restaurants, a handful of shops, gas stations and, of course, ice cream parlors. The truth is, however, that Rangeley can't hold a candle to the real tourist towns on the coast. It's still a little town in the middle of the woods, no matter how many out-of-state license plates you count.

Rangeley does have some wonderful attributes on top of being one of the only signs of civilization for miles. It's *right* on the water. The silky ripples of Rangeley Lake practically slosh up onto the main street. It also has a landmark **library** (in the middle of town) that according to one resident, "still smells the way it used to in the '40s." The library shares an 1820 house with the **Phillips Historical Society** (207-639-2088), which has an interesting collection of pictures from the area's early days when a narrow-gauge railroad connected nearby lumbering communities.

As you move south of the Rangeley Lakes region, you come to the **Bethel** area, which is in the Oxford Hills, not far from the **White Mountain National Forest** on the New Hampshire border. Bethel itself is a lovely 19th-century village with a meticulously maintained green and stately old houses. The town's highlights include the **Moses Mason Museum** (15 Broad Street; 207-824-2908), a restored Federal-style house displaying period furnishings and local historic exhibits; the **Gould Academy** (207-824-2161), a very widely respected prep school; and the **Broad Street Historic District**, which is lined with historic homes. Come winter, Bethel is a thriving cross-country skiing area.

The area south of Bethel (including Waterford, Bridgton and the towns near Sebago Lake) is loved mostly for its profusion of lakes and rivers (see the "Beaches and Parks" section in this chapter). In fact, from the summit of **Pleasant Mountain**, you can see about 50 lakes. These include crystal-clear **Sebago Lake**, Maine's second largest, popular with fishers and city folk from nearby Portland.

In addition to water sports galore, the area is rife with *terra firma* attractions, including the **Sabbathday Lake Shaker Community and Museum** (Route 26, New Gloucester; 207-926-4596), a complete Shaker settlement and one of the oldest in the United States; **Nathaniel Hawthorne's Boyhood Home** (Hawthorne Road, South Casco); and the **Jones Gallery of Glass and Ceramics** (Douglas Hill; 207-787-3370), which displays over 3000 works in glass and china.

Shopping

SOUTHERN COAST SHOPPING

The most southern part of Maine, along Route 1, seems to be suffering —actually, prospering would be a more accurate term—from factory-outlet- and mall-"itis." Discount stores are everywhere. Unless you've come specifically to scout out bargains, you might be better off sniffing out the small shops, especially those that specialize in Maine arts and crafts. (See "State of the Artists" in this chapter.)

In York, stop by **The Old York Historical Society Museum and Gift Shop** (Route 1A and Lindsay Road; 207-363-4974). It offers a delightful array of traditional Maine crafts along with a large collection of Maineana books.

Cape Neddick is home to **Cape Neddick Woolens** (off Route 1, near the post office; 207-363-4294), where you'll inevitably walk out with a new sweater. There's a stunning selection of quilted-front sweaters by Michelle Moody.

R. Jorgensen Antiques (Route 1, Wells; 207-646-9444) is definitely worth stopping at, unlike some of the *faux*-antiques shops that have staked out prime tourist territory on the coast. There's a little bit of everything here including genuine Americana and 18th- and 19th-century antiques.

If you're in the market for some pottery, stop by **The Good Earth** (Dock Square, Kennebunkport; 207-967-4635). It's filled with decorative stoneware and cooking pieces in a fascinating array of designs—all produced by local potters.

Some very attractive wood carvings and functional wooden wares can be found at **Gerard Craft Woodproducts** (510 Mitchell Road, Cape Elizabeth; 207-799-3526). They're all skillfully handcrafted by Gerry and Linda Laberge.

For American crafts, make your way to **Abacus** (44 Exchange Street, Portland; 207-772-4880). Over 200 of the country's craftspeople are represented here. (There's also a gallery in Boothbay Harbor.)

The Maine Potters' Market (376 Fore Street, Portland; 207-774-1633) is just as it sounds: a place to shop for clay works created by local potters. There's a wonderful selection of traditional pieces as well as some avant-garde finds.

It's been called the preppy mecca, among other things. But love it or not, don't deny yourselves the privilege of seeing **L. L. Bean** (Route 1, Freeport; 207-865-4761). This American institution was started by an avid outdoorsman who built up a mail-order business for his Maine hunting shoe. Today, the quality of the rugged outdoor clothes and equipment is legendary, and the store—a huge mall-like building—is open 24 hours a day. L. L. Bean's success comes largely from marketing the image of Maine (outdoors, fresh-air, healthy) and the Maine people (hard-working, rugged, independent).

Right in the heart of the factory outlet town of Freeport stands the **Harrington House Gallery Store** (45 Main Street; 207-865-0477), a lovely Greek Revival house. It holds fine examples of the state's craftmanship, from handwoven baskets and wooden toys to 18th-century pieces.

Pop into the Boothbay Harbor branch of **Abacus** (8 McKown Street; 207-633-2166) just to take a quick look around and an hour later, you realize you're still there. It has a captivating selection of crafts by a variety of American artisans. Check out the hardwood kaleidoscopes by David Collier.

It may never have occurred to you that you needed a chowder mug. But one look at the selection of Edgecomb potters' mugs at **Hand in Hand** (McKown Street, Boothbay Harbor; 207-633-4199) and you can't live without one. But that's not all. The potters' high-gloss, berry-colored pieces come in all sizes and shapes, from very attractive creamer and sugar sets to huge bowls.

A silver-mirrored disco ball hangs from the ceiling of **Enchantments** (16 McKown Street, Boothbay Harbor; 207-633-4992), casting confetti-like shadows as it twirls around. The floor is littered with colored metallic stars. This is the place to go for crystals and healing gemstones. It also has a book section broken into categories such as Findhorn, New Age, Astrology, Kabbalah, Runes and Fairies and Lore.

A delicious array of mohair, silk and cotton handwoven scarves, stoles and throws are the results of **Nancy Lubin Designs'** (13 Trim Street, Camden; 207-236-4069) hard work. A very worthwhile stop.

Étienne and Company (20 Main Street, Camden; 207-236-9696) specializes in fine designer jewelry. Though somewhat pricey, they're cherishable works of art.

Crafts, crafts and more crafts can be found at the **Maine Gathering** (4 Commercial Street, Camden; 207-236-9004). Over 80 of the state's craftspeople and artisans are shown here.

DOWNEAST COAST SHOPPING

Though you probably won't find any bargains in the little shops and art galleries of Castine, you can find yourselves happily occupied looking at all the truly original fashions, the nautical gifts and the New England crafts and artwork. Here are some to find your way to: the **Compass Rose** (Main Street; 207-326-9366), a bookstore-cum-art gallery (it has the best postcards in town); **McGrath Dunham Gallery** (Main Street; 207-326-9797), a showcase for New England artists; **Oakhum Bay Ltd.** (Main Street; 207-326-9690) for antiques, quilts, jewelry, pottery, decoys, and other country items; and the **Water Witch** (Main Street; 207-326-4884), where the fashions look like works of art.

The village of Blue Hill is well known in the area for its profusion of potters and artisans. You'll find some of their works at **Rowantrees Pottery** (Union Street; 207-374-5535), **Rackliffe Pottery** (Route 172; 207-374-2297), **Cole House Quilts** (10 Union Street; 207-374-2175) and **Handworks Gallery** (Main Street; 207-374-5613).

William Mor Stoneware (Reach Road, Deer Isle; 207-348-2822) is a good source for some good-looking—and functional—stoneware and porcelain kitchen pieces.

Any visitor to Maine really ought to stop at **Nervous Nellie's Jams and Jellies** (Sunshine Road, Deer Isle; 207-348-6182). Though it's actually a mail-order company, walk-in customers get to sample the goods—Hot Tomato Jelly, Strawberry Rhubarb Conserve, Spicy Apple Cider Jelly just to name a few—before deciding what to buy.

One good reason to take the mail boat over to Isle au Haut is to check out the handknit traditional Guernsey sweaters sold at **Island Creations Paula Runge** (available at the Innkeepers House, Robinson's Point, Isle au Haut; 207-367-2261). They're custom-designed, using all Maine island wool yarns.

Bar Harbor is chockablock with shops, many of them purveying the standard tourist goods—T-shirts that say "Baa-Haa-Bah" (the way Mainers pronounce it), multicolored wind socks (a craze here) and Maineana books, calendars and cards. However, there are some worthwhile galleries and shops to make a point of finding.

Look for **MDI Workshop** (Route 3; 207-288-5252), a showcase for arts and crafts created by disabled Mainers; **Birdnest Gallery** (12 Mount Desert Street; 207-288-4054) for oils, watercolors and graphics by contemporary New England artists; **Island Artisans** (99 Main Street; 207-288-4214), a cooperative with works by local artists, and **The Lone Moose** (78 West Street; 207-288-4229), a good source for made-in-Maine baskets, woodwork, furniture, jewelry, crafts and clothes. Another interesting shop in Bar Harbor is **The Woodshop Cupolas, Inc.** (Route 102, Town Hill; 207-288-5530), where you can buy handcrafted cupolas and weather vanes.

The number of shops and galleries dramatically drops off as you go north of Ellsworth on Route 1. We managed to find a few, though, including **Hands On** (Main Street, Milbridge; 207-546-2682). It's filled with pottery, quilts, sculpture and woodworks by a consortium of local craftspeople. **The Sow's Ear** (7 Water Street, Machias; 207-255-4066) has a sweet selection of toys, some made-in-Maine clothes and a good collection of books about Maine.

If you're interested in pottery, be sure to get to **Connie's Clay of Fundy** (Route 1, East Machias; 207-255-4574) where you'll find museum-quality contemporary earthenware. If you're lucky, you may see the artist at work in her adjoining studio.

Eastport is the salmon aquaculture capital of America. To sample this local specialty, stop by **Jim's Smoked Salmon** (37 Washington Street; 207-853-4831).

For a selection of regional titles visit **Fountain Books** (58 Water Street, Eastport; 207-853-4519), housed in a former drugstore. A reminder of that bygone era—when Eleanor Roosevelt frequented the store—is the old-fashioned marble soda fountain which brings in large summer crowds.

You may not find anything to buy at **Border Crafts** (Water Street, Eastport), but it's worth browsing around. There are a lot of hand-sewn and knitted garments made by the "local ladies" who have lived there for decades, as well as so-called "antiques" that probably fall more aptly into the "second-hand" or "thrift" category. Like Eastport itself, this little shop is bursting with local charm.

NORTHERN WOODS SHOPPING

There's not much in the way of shopping in the northern woods, unless you're into hunting gear and camouflage hats. Here are just two places you might want to pull up to.

The Indian Store (Greenville; 207-695-3348) is filled with baskets, pottery and other Indian-inspired items.

You'll find an array of wood items at **Bowl & Bowl** (Greenville; 207-695-2247). Among the numerous products are birdhouses, puzzles, utensils and pegs.

WESTERN LAKES AND MOUNTAINS SHOPPING

If you lose your ski hat or mittens, head straight for **Keenan Auction Company** (Kingfield; 207-265-2011), where you can find all sorts of great bargains.

Lively patterned ski sweaters are the forte of **Patricia Buck's** (Main Street, Kingfield; 207-265-2101; also in the Alpine Village at Sugarloaf).

But she also sells hats, mittens, leg warmers and an array of items like books and cards.

We first became acquainted with **The Chamomile Shop** (Stephens Road, Rangeley: 207-864-5261) when we found a copy of their catalog in our cottage. It's the kind of shop you could easily spend hours in, buying all sorts of pine-stuffed pillows and dried-herb arrangements.

The **Yarn Barn Crafts School** (Route 4, on Rangeley Lake, Oquossoc; 207-864-5917) sells everything from supplies for spinners, weavers, knitters and basket makers to beautiful final products such as rugs, place mats, sweaters and pottery.

Bonnema Potters (Main Street, Bethel; 207-824-2821) specialize in lamps, but they also have a beautiful assortment of functional stoneware pieces and porcelain pottery. Ask about seconds.

Ironworks, baskets, hand-painted T-shirts and stained-glass items are just some of the gems you can expect at the **Wood and Glass Gallery** (Main Street, Bethel; 207-824-2591) where many Maine artists are represented.

In Bridgton, over 30 Maine craftspeople have also joined together to form the **Society of Southern Maine Craftsmen, Stone Soup Artisans** (72 Main Street), where their works are sold.

The **United Society of Shakers** (Route 26, New Gloucester; 207-926-4597) sells Shaker furniture, herbs, tea and handcrafted items.

There's a beautiful selection of contemporary quilts, duvet covers and other fabric items at **B. Smith Quilts** (Raymond, 207-655-3107). Call ahead for an appointment.

Nightlife

SOUTHERN COAST NIGHTLIFE

The **Ogunquit Theater** (Route 1, Ogunquit; 207-646-2402) draws theater-goers from all over southern Maine. It has a ten-week season every summer, usually with three musicals and two dramatic plays. They're performed in a converted garage that had its first season in 1933.

Portland is where you'll find the most to do après-dark in southern Maine. It's rife with cultural diversions, including the **Portland Stage Company** (Portland Performing Arts Center, 25-A Forest Avenue; 207-774-0465), which puts on about half a dozen plays per season. The **Mad House Theatre Company** (955 Forest Avenue; 207-797-3338) also presents a selection of plays every year. The **American Renaissance Theater** (Portland; 207-871-9325) is an itinerant theater company which produces classical plays utilizing local actors. You can also get tickets for performances by the **Portland Symphony Orchestra** (30 Myrtle Street; 207-773-6128), the **Portland Concert Association** (262 Cumberland Avenue; 207-772-8630), the **Portland Performing Arts** (Portland Performing Arts Center, 25-A Forest Avenue; 207-774-0465) and the **Ram Island Dance Company** (25-A Forest Avenue; 207-773-2562).

Portland also has quite a few thriving night spots, such as **Gritty McDuff's Brew Pub** (396 Fore Street; 207-772-2739), where you can chomp on fish and chips and down some beers brewed right on the premises. It's a rowdy spot, especially on Saturday nights, when you may have to scream your order across the copper-topped bar.

Another good pub is **Three Dollar Dewey's** (446 Fore Street, Portland; 207-772-3310), an English-style tavern that prides itself on its wide selection of draught beers and three-alarm chili. A large following of fanatical regulars really whoops it up here, knocking 'em down at long tavern tables.

For rock, reggae or folk music groups on the weekends try **Father O'Hara's** (45 Danforth Street, Portland; 207-871-1579). This two-story black, white and teal establishment features a balcony where you can watch the dancefloor action. Located in a brick commercial building, O'Hara's has three bars, and offers an Irish night every Sunday. Cover.

Head to **Café No** (20 Danforth Street, Portland; 207-772-8114) for live jazz Thursday, Friday and Saturday. There's an open jam session Sunday. The 60-seat club, located in an old warehouse, is considered Maine's premiere jazz club. Cover.

Alternative rock, world beat, reggae and African music are all performed at **Zootz** (31 Forest Avenue, Portland; 207-773-8187). Adorned with works from local artists, this dance club features two dancefloors and a full bar. Cover for live shows and on weekends.

Raoul's Roadside Attraction (865 Forest Avenue, Portland; 207-775-2494) is a hot spot for rock-and-roll.

If you're timing is right, someone famous—like Bonnie Raitt—will be putting on a show at the **Cumberland County Civic Center** (1 Civic Center Square, Portland; 207-775-3458).

For additional entertainment suggestions in the Portland area pick up a copy of the **Casco Bay Weekly** (207-775-6601).

If you're in the Freeport area after dark, you can get in on some of **L. L. Bean's** evening workshops and clinics at the Casco Street Conference Center (Casco Street; 207-865-4761, extension 7800). They offer a vast variety of programs including an introduction to maps and compasses and instruction in outdoor photography, wilderness survival, canoeing and kayaking. Call ahead for details and reservations.

The **Broad Arrow Tavern** (126 Main Street, Freeport; 207-865-9377) presents a folk guitarist Saturday nights. Mahogany furniture, a dinner menu and a cozy fireplace setting overseen by a mounted moose head add to the enjoyment.

Forget about getting to bed early on a Saturday night if you're staying in the heart of Boothbay Harbor. The live music that pours out of **McSeagull's** (on the wharf; 207-633-4041) dominates the village. This is where the young congregate for drinks and partying. No dancing, though.

If you're interested in something more sedate, consider making reservations at the **Carousel Music Theatre** (Route 27, on the approach to Boothbay Harbor; 207-633-5297), a dinner theater offering lively cabarets.

Gilbert's Public House (Bayview Street, Camden; 207-236-4320) offers live bands playing rhythm-and-blues, jazz, pop and rock-and-roll as well as dancing in a maritime bar setting. Cover.

DOWNEAST COAST NIGHTLIFE

One look at Castine and it's clear: no neon-zapped discos here. Not even a sleazy bar. Most visitors plan their nights around a big, satiating seafood dinner. You can also catch a performance by **Cold Comfort Productions, Inc.** (P.O. Box 259, Castine, ME 04421). It's a summer theater group that puts on plays such as *The Glass Menagerie, South Pacific* and *Agnes of God.*

The big night out in Blue Hill is attending concerts at the **Kneisel Hall Chamber Music Festival** (for information, write: P.O. Box 648, Blue Hill, ME 04614; 207-374-2811). From early July to mid-August, string and ensemble performances are held on Friday evenings and Sunday afternoons at the old summer school. You can also see a performance by the **Surry Opera Company** (Blue Hill; 207-667-9551), a young but internationally respected group.

Lights go off early on Deer Isle and Isle au Haut, as well. In Bar Harbor, we managed to scrounge up a couple of things to do after dark. The hottest pub spot is **Geddy's** (11 Main Street; 207-288-5077), a magnet for the young, hip and trendy. Everyone congregates to hear folk and dance music, pop or rock—whatever happens to be on that night's playbill.

Another way to spend the evening is to take a **Sunset Cruise** (Bar Harbor; 207-288-9794). Cruises leave Golden Anchor Pier a couple hours before sunset, every day between June and October.

Acadia National Park (207-288-3338) offers all sorts of nocturnal diversions, including ranger-led walks that focus on "Stargazing over Sand Beach" or learning about the nightlife of a beaver. There are also slide presentations in the amphitheaters at Seawall and Blackwoods Campgrounds. Programs are listed in the daily Ranger Activity Schedule.

Like many parts of the Maine coast, Mount Desert Island has a flourishing cultural life. Check the local papers to find out what performances are on while you're on the island. The **Acadia Repertory Theatre** (Route 102, Somesville; 207-244-7260) puts on nearly half a dozen plays a season in the Somesville Masonic Hall. The **Deck House Cabaret Theatre** (Swan's Island Ferry Road, Bass Harbor; 207-244-5044) features outstanding cabaret shows by its waiters and waitresses. Between mid-July and mid-August, the **Bar Harbor Music Festival** (Rodick Building, 59 Cottage Street, Bar Harbor; 207-288-5744) is in full swing. Concerts by well respected pianists, violinists, jazz and chamber music groups are given at various sites around town. Also from mid-July to mid-August, there's the **Mount Desert Festival of Chamber Music** (Neighborhood House, Main Street, Northeast Harbor; 207-276-5039), a series of chamber concerts. **The Arcady Music Festival** (207-288-3151) draws a big crowd with performances that range from small ensembles to baroque orchestras in various locations on the island.

Once you get north of Ellsworth, you'll find even less to do after dark. This is real Maine country, where going to the movies constitutes the big night out.

In July and August, there are a series of chamber music concerts hosted by the **Machias Bay Chamber Concerts** (Center Street Congregational Church, Machias; 207-255-3889).

In Eastport, check to see if there's anything going on at the **Eastport Gallery** (Dana Street; 207-853-4166). In the summer they have a Friday night series of concerts and films that is a magnet for the intellectuals, artists and literati that have discovered the area.

NORTHERN WOODS NIGHTLIFE

Moosehead Resort at Big Squaw Mountain (Route 6 and 15, Greenville; 207-695-2272) offers weekend bands in the summer and après ski lounge entertainment in the winter. Enjoy light rock, rock-and-roll, contemporary or country music.

WESTERN LAKES AND MOUNTAINS NIGHTLIFE

Nightlife in this area is also limited. In many towns, you're lucky if there's even a movie theater.

However, if you're in the Rangeley Lakes Region, you might be able to see a performance sponsored by **Rangeley Friends of the Performing Arts**. They're put on throughout July and August at local churches, lodges and the high school. Contact the chamber of commerce for this year's program (P.O. Box 317, Rangeley, ME 04970; 207-864-5364).

The **Sebago-Long Lake Region Chamber Music Festival** (Bridgton Academy Chapel, North Bridgton; 207-647-3322) is a series of concerts held in July and August. Call for information.

Index

Abbreviations used for chapter areas are: (B) Boston, (CT) Connecticut, (CWM) Central and Western Massachusetts, (MC) Massachusetts Coast, (ME) Maine, (NH) New Hampshire, (RI) Rhode Island and (VT) Vermont.

Abbreviations have been used for parks, beaches, sightseeing attractions, and some natural features, but generally not for towns or cities. Hotel and restaurant names have not been indexed, unless cited as a sightseeing or historical attraction. Generally, trail names also have been excluded.

HIDDEN MEXICO

Covers the entire 6000-mile Mexican coastline in the most comprehensive fashion ever. 444 pages. $13.95

CALIFORNIA
The Ultimate Guidebook

Definitive. From the Pacific to the desert to the Sierra Nevada, it captures the best of the Golden State. 504 pages. $13.95

HIDDEN COAST OF CALIFORNIA

Explores the fabled California coast from Mexico to Oregon, describing over 1000 miles of spectacular beaches. 468 pages. $13.95

HIDDEN SOUTHERN CALIFORNIA

The most complete guidebook to Los Angeles and Southern California in print. 516 pages. $13.95

HIDDEN SAN FRANCISCO
AND NORTHERN CALIFORNIA

A major resource for travelers exploring the San Francisco Bay area and beyond. 444 pages. $13.95

FOR FREE CATALOG OR TO ORDER DIRECT For each book send an additional $2 postage and handling (California residents include 8% sales tax) to Ulysses Press, 3286 Adeline Street, Suite 1, Berkeley, CA 94703

About the Authors and Illustrator

Stacy Ritz, the principal author of this second edition, is the author of *Disney World and Beyond: The Ultimate Family Guidebook* and co-author of *Hidden Florida* and *Florida's Gold Coast: The Ultimate Guidebook*. A regular contributor to the *Fort Lauderdale/Sun Sentinel*, she has also written for the *Washington Post* and *Miami Herald*.

Patricia Mandell, author of the introductory and Boston chapters, has lived on Boston's South Shore for ten years. She belongs to the American Society of Journalists and Authors and has published in the *Christian Science Monitor*, *New England Monthly*, *Caribbean Travel and Life*, *Dallas Morning News*, *Miami Herald* and *Denver Post*.

Ryan Vollmer, who penned the Massachusetts Coast chapter, is a freelance writer based in New York. She is the author of *Affordable Spas and Fitness Resorts* (Ventana Press) and has written for the *New York Times*, *Rolling Stone*, *New York Daily News*, *San Francisco Chronicle*, *Self*, *Psychology Today* and *Woman's Day*.

Alberta Eiseman, author of the Connecticut chapter, is a long time resident of the state and a native of Italy. She is a regular contributor to the Travel and Connecticut sections of the *New York Times* and has written for the *International Herald Tribune*. She is the author of numerous books for children and young adults.

Susan Farewell, a graduate of Boston University, contributed the chapter on Maine. She has written about New England for newlyweds (*Bride's* magazine), young parents (*Child* magazine) and Japanese travelers (*Gulliver* magazine). Farewell is the author of the *Mobil Road Atlas* and *Trip Planning Guide* and has published in *Travel & Leisure* and the *New York Post*.

B. J. Roche, author of the chapter on Central and Western Massachusetts, has lived in the region for over a decade. A graduate of the University of Massachusetts at Amherst, she is a regular contributor to the *Boston Globe* and has written for the *Washington Post*, *Los Angeles Times*, *USA Today* and the *Chicago Tribune*.

Brenda Fine, who wrote the Rhode Island chapter, has contributed to Birnbaum's U.S.A. and Europe guides. A member of the Society of American Travel Writers, she is the author of *The Women's Travel Guide*. Her articles have appeared in the *New York Daily News*, *Frequent Flyer*, *Diversion*, *Chicago Sun-Times* and the *New York Post*.

Tim Carroll, the illustrator for *Hidden New England*, has worked as a graphic designer for almost a decade. He has illustrated several other Ulysses Press guidebooks, including *Hidden Florida* and *Hidden Southern California*. His artwork has also appeared in *Esquire*, *GQ*, the *Boston Globe*, *San Francisco Focus*, *Premiere* magazine and the *Washington Post*.